Third Edition

THE *new*

HARBRACE GUIDE

Genres for Composing

CHERYL GLENN
The Pennsylvania State University

CENGAGE
Learning·

Australia • Brazil • Mexico • Singapore • United Kingdom • United States

CENGAGE
Learning·

The New Harbrace Guide: Genres for Composing, **Third Edition**
Cheryl Glenn

Product Director: Monica Eckman

Product Manager: Laura Ross

Content Developers: Lisa Moore and Phoebe Mathews

Senior Content Developer: Leslie Taggart

Product Assistant: Claire Branman

Marketing Manager: Kina Lara

Content Project Manager: Rebecca Donahue

Senior Art Director: Marissa Falco

Manufacturing Planner: Betsy Donaghey

IP Analyst: Ann Hoffman

IP Project Manager: Erika Mugavin

Production Service: Thistle Hill Publisher Services

Compositor: Cenveo® Publisher Services

Text Designer: Alisha Webber, Cenveo® Publisher Services

Cover Designer: Chrissy Kurpeski

Cover Image: © iStockPhoto.com/ mgkaya

For product information and technology assistance, contact us at **Cengage Learning Customer & Sales Support, 1-800-354-9706**

For permission to use material from this text or product, submit all requests online at **www. cengage.com/permissions**. Further permissions questions can be emailed to **permissionrequest@cengage.com**.

Library of Congress Control Number: 2016945333

Student Edition:
ISBN: 978-1-305-95678-0

Loose-leaf Edition:
ISBN: 978-1-305-95919-4

Cengage Learning
20 Channel Center Street
Boston, MA 02210
USA

Cengage Learning is a leading provider of customized learning solutions with employees residing in nearly 40 different countries and sales in more than 125 countries around the world. Find your local representative at **www.cengage.com**.

Cengage Learning products are represented in Canada by Nelson Education, Ltd.

To learn more about Cengage Learning Solutions, visit **www.cengage.com**.

Purchase any of our products at your local college store or at our preferred online store **www.cengagebrain.com**.

Printed in the United States of America
Print Number: 02   Print Year: 2017

Contents

The Writer as Reader 35

Rhetorical Success in a Digital World 51

MindTap®
Additional
readings online.

MindTap®
Additional
readings online.

Investigative Reports 112

MindTap®
Additional
readings online.

Position Arguments 132

Proposals 156

Evaluations 174

MindTap®
Additional readings online.

MindTap®
Additional readings online.

MindTap®
Additional
readings online.

Critical Analyses 194

MindTap®
Additional
readings online.

Literary Analyses 215

Synthesizing Sources: Summary, Paraphrase, and Quotation 322

Acknowledging Sources in MLA Style 338

Acknowledging Sources in APA Style 376

PART FIVE Real Situations for Real Writing: A Thematic Reader 403

Food and the (Cultural) Experience of Taste 403

Preface

Composing in a Digital Age

"Digital Natives." That's the term frequently used to refer to your generation of college students, you who have always read and written—communicated—using digital media. Accompanying the technological developments that have led to ubiquitous cell phones, satellite television, and the Internet are developments in the ways in which people actually create and circulate information. With the growing accessibility of the Internet, increasing numbers of people communicate their ideas and information about their lives through blogs, Facebook, Twitter, podcasts, Reddit, and YouTube. Somehow, the flurry of their online activities enhances their influence compared to that of people with little or no access to technologies such as computers, Internet connections, and digital and audio production equipment.

Given the demands and expectations of your digital generation, *The New Harbrace Guide: Genres for Composing*, Third Edition, helps by guiding your composing in today's college, workplace, and community environments. *The New Harbrace Guide* will introduce you to or expand your knowledge of online courses, web content, podcasts, video links, course-management systems, PowerPoint presentations, and other kinds of electronic aids. Composing with all these various media (multimedia composing) is here to stay. For example, *The New Harbrace Guide* will help you understand the principles behind collaborating effectively with community-service agencies or businesses in order to fulfill their expectations for research and writing; it will also help you conduct scholarly collaborative projects via social-networking sites and compose in any one of a variety of other, largely digital or multimodal situations. Understanding these principles and practices will help you productively employ *rhetoric*—the strategy of communicating persuasively—as you address and resolve problems, whether those problems are social, academic, or work-related.

Key Features

The New Harbrace Guide distinguishes itself from other writing guides on the market by its sustained focus on a rhetorical situation, one that establishes an opportunity for using language to make change. Guidance on specific rhetorical techniques is provided to help you shape your ideas into language that is best suited for your audience and purpose, as well as most appropriate for the media that are now routine for composing different kinds of writing. Thus this guide to composing is theoretically sophisticated yet easily practical: you will come to see the ways that using language purposefully (whether you're writing or speaking) is an integral part of your daily life, in and out of school. In addition, this comprehensive and richly flexible writing guide includes a rhetoric, a research manual, and a reader. Its key features include

- **A Rhetorical Approach.** By emphasizing rhetorical techniques that will help you understand how to evaluate a rhetorical situation, identify and respond to an opportunity for change, and address a problem rhetorically, this introduction to rhetoric teaches principles that have empowered readers, speakers, and writers for millennia—techniques that are transferable to your other writing tasks, whether in school, the workplace, or the community. Part 1 introduces you to the rhetorical principles that underlie all writing situations and provides you with a basic method for using those principles in the digital, print, and multimodal spheres of composing.
- **A Guide to Genres and Persuasion.** The principles outlined in Part 1 are also reinforced for each genre (memoir, profile, investigative report, position argument, proposal, evaluation, critical analysis), with a featured **Writing Guide** for composing persuasively. By following a demystified step-by-step process, each Writing Guide breaks down composing into manageable tasks that build toward a larger writing project. These Writing Guides for each genre use simple, direct, and incremental advice to help you create forceful, persuasive compositions.
- **Integrated Multimodal/Multimedia Coverage.** Your writing today needs to take into consideration the most effective medium (print, digital, verbal, visual, multimodal) for delivering your message. *The New Harbrace Guide* supports effective twenty-first-century composing practices in Part 1 with a chapter on rhetorical success in a digital age that builds on the rhetorical knowledge of media you bring to the classroom—from text messages to Facebook profiles to Internet searches and more—with multimodal examples and guidance for each genre to help you choose when and how to use digital, verbal, visual, and print media for various audiences, purposes, and situations. **Identifying an Opportunity for Change, Writing in Three Media,** and **Additional Assignments: Knowledge Transfer** present a number of multimodal possibilities for each genre.

In short, then, *The New Harbrace Guide* guides you through various composition processes and genres that will enhance your education as well as your success in the workplace and your community.

How Does the Book Work?

In this new streamlined edition, you'll find many innovations (large and small) that have helped to create a more user-friendly, portable, and easy-to-access guide (both in print and through an online MindTap version).

- **Colorful Tabs** help you to locate quickly the information you need in the book. Each chapter has a tab, color-coded by the part of the book where the chapter is located. These tabs can be seen at the top of the page and when you flip through the book.
- **Color-Coded Writing Guidance** uses purple for advice on creating effective introductions, green for advice on creating coherent bodies of text for your writing projects, and blue for advice on conclusions. You'll find this in the annotated essay example in each chapter in Part 2 and in the corresponding Writing Guides in each chapter.
- **Writing Guides** in each chapter in Part 2 provide step-by-step guidance for creating effective compositions. To locate this information more easily, a new tab runs down the entire page so you can easily locate the Writing Guides in each chapter.
- **Marginal Glossary Definitions** for rhetorical terms are placed next to the term for easy reference.
- **Marginal Cross-References** to other parts of the book are provided where a refresher—or additional information—on particular topics might come in useful.

What Will You Find Online?

MindTap® English helps you stay engaged with real-world writing assignments and motivated by information that shows where you stand at all times—both individually and compared to the highest performers in class. MindTap® English eliminates the guesswork, focusing on what's most important to your instructor with a learning path designed specifically by your instructor and for your English course. Improve your college writing and research skills with built-in tools, such as a professional tutoring service, a database of scholarly sources and interactive videos to support your research papers, a dictionary, and tools to keep you organized and on track.

- **Additional Online Readings** are available if you would like to explore topics further, see additional examples, or use vetted and trustworthy sources for your research.
- **Grammar and Usage Resources** appear in an online handbook and a glossary of usage.

What Is a Rhetorical Approach?

The book has been carefully designed with many practical, specific tips as well as step-by-step guidance so that you can respond strategically and effectively to your writing assignments in your first-year composition course. That said, *The New Harbrace Guide* has also been designed to help you develop skills you can transfer to other rhetorical situations, whether you find yourself writing for another class, for a social or civic setting, or for the workplace.

As you get started with *The New Harbrace Guide*, you'll notice that **Part 1, Entering the Conversation,** introduces you to the rhetorical principles that underlie all writing situations and provides you with a basic method for using those principles. You'll also notice that many of the examples in Part 1 are by students, to reinforce that none of these skills is beyond your reach as a first-year student.

- **Chapter 1, Understanding the Rhetorical Situation,** focuses on understanding writing as an opportunity to create change. This is the most powerful part of answering the age-old question: Why write? Through analyzing strategically your rhetorical context you will understand better when and how your writing can create a change of heart, mind, or action. **Analyzing the Rhetorical Situation** prompts also occur throughout the book to guide you.

- **Chapter 2, Responding to the Rhetorical Situation,** focuses on persuasive writing. When you understand how writing can change you and your audience, you will be better able to recognize when purposeful writing delivered in any of its forms is the best, most persuasive response to a rhetorical situation. Examples of persuasive writing in a variety of media help make concrete the principles of persuasion (commonly referred to as *ethos, logos,* and *pathos*). These principles are part of the guidance in each of the assignments in this book.

- **Chapter 3, The Writer as Reader**—new to this edition—provides a foundation for reading both critically and rhetorically and for using the skills of synthesis and analysis that are required in college writing and beyond. This new chapter shows how analyzing what you read rhetorically is helpful both in understanding what you read and in providing an opportunity for writing and for creating those broader thinking skills that are embedded in persuasive writing practices. Rhetorical reading also assists you in conducting research in college and in life on those occasions when you bring sources together that must be weighed, reflected on, explained, and often challenged. Tips for **Researching** for each genre (Researching a Memoir, Evaluation, Profile, Position Argument, and so forth) and for **Using Synthesis and Analysis** are also included in each of the assignments in this book.

- **Chapter 4, Rhetorical Success in a Digital World,** gets us back to where we started at the beginning of this Preface, the idea that as "digital natives" you are part of a brave, new world of writing. Chapter 4 helps you identify and analyze the rhetorical elements of multimedia compositions and recognize when multimedia is part of a fitting response. Today, choosing a medium that effectively reaches the audience you hope to change is part and parcel of being a successful citizen of the world, and this emphasis is reflected in all the assignments included in this book.

Why Focus on Genres and Media?

Examples, examples, examples. We all learn best when the desire to create a change is married to an example of how to do it. A genre is a type of writing with identifiable characteristics that have emerged over time. The assignments in Part 2, Writing Projects: Rhetorical Situations for Composing, provide eight writing projects anchored in the fluid concept of a genre (such as memoir, position argument, critical analysis, etc.), each chosen because it exercises specific skills that should be helpful as part of your toolkit for responding to a broad range of writing situations. The strategies you use to create a memoir (storytelling or the use of poignant personal examples) might find their way into a position argument and vice versa. To say you are writing one genre or another is to identify the primary purpose and social context for your writing and your audience—especially since no single genre limits the rhetorical strategies you can employ in response to a rhetorical opportunity for change.

These chapters have been restructured and streamlined, breaking down the writing process into incremental steps that are straightforward and manageable. Each chapter includes

- **Identifying an Opportunity for Change** at the beginning of the chapter with advice on a consideration of the visual, audio, digital, and print options for each genre.
- **Plentiful Examples** beginning with a "micro" example of a subtype of the genre (such as a food memoir, a public service announcement, or a film review) in the new **Genre in Focus** section and an annotated example—often by a student—in the new sections on **Reading Rhetorically**. These examples help you identify the **Key Characteristics** of that genre and provide guidance on **Using Synthesis and Analysis**. Additional examples can be found in MindTap, the Thematic Reader, and the **Writing in Three Media** examples in each chapter.
- **Step-by-Step Writing Support** for each of these eight chapters provides tips for research in that genre, helps you develop a topic, and guides you in

identifying your rhetorical audience and purpose. The Writing Guide breaks down into manageable tasks specific guidance on writing persuasively and walks you through writing a strong introduction, a well-supported body, and a meaningful conclusion.

- **Revision and Editing Support** takes you from your first draft to what will become your final paper or media project. Each **Writing Guide** includes guidance for revision, your own as well as your peers'. You may find yourself required to evaluate the writing of a fellow student ("peer"), or you might want your peers to advise you on your own work. To that end, you will find a section titled **Revision and Peer Review**. You will also find a **Grammar in Context** feature to help you and your peers revise and edit your drafts. A full handbook and glossary of usage are available through MindTap.
- **Knowledge-Transfer Assignments** will also help you recognize the specific ways your academic assignments prepare you for composing in other contexts (work and community) as well as in different print, visual, audio, and digital media.

Finding Your Writing Process

Your writing process is as individual as you are. You may be a writer who especially likes composing the first draft—by hand or keyboard. Maybe you enjoy the tactile sensation of writing with a gel pen on a yellow legal pad or the friction of moving a felt-tipped pen across pulpy paper. Maybe you draft at your computer, entertaining yourself by connecting particular fonts with particular ideas in your draft.

Or maybe you're one of those writers who is relieved when she finishes a draft so that she can use her energy to work with and against that draft. You may like to print out your piece, sit back in a comfortable chair, and read it line by line, penciling in new sentences, crossing out entire sections, fiddling with your word choice, and drawing arrows to reorganize your paragraphs. However you write and revise, you'll want to find a way to enjoy polishing your writing until you're proud to submit it. As internationally known writer Susan Sontag put it:

> **You write in order to read what you've written and see if it's OK and, since of course it never is, to rewrite it—once, twice, as many times as it takes to get it to be something you can bear to reread.**
>
> **—Susan Sontag, "Directions: Write, Read, Rewrite. Repeat Steps 2 and 3 as Needed."**

For writers like Sontag, the enjoyment they get from rereading their revised work is the best part, whether or not they send it on to someone else to read.

Whatever your process, Part 3, Processes and Strategies for Composing, provides a number of tips that could save you time and strengthen your writing practice. Chapter 13, From Tentative Idea to Finished Project, includes examples for getting started if you've hit a writing block as well as for writing a thesis statement, creating a structure for your writing, drafting, revising, and editing. In Chapter 14, Rhetorical Methods of Development, you'll find examples of additional strategies for developing skills in narrative, description, definition, exemplification, comparison-contrast, classification and division, process analysis, cause-and-effect analysis, and argument. You'll also find these methods cross-referenced in the margins of the text when one of these rhetorical strategies is particularly useful for a particular assignment in Part 2. Taken together, these two chapters provide additional support for successful composing to be used as needed as you develop your writing process.

A Value Proposition

Of course, textbooks are expensive. What is the "value proposition" that makes *The New Harbrace Guide* worth it? In addition to the specific writing advice, *The New Harbrace Guide* includes a **Guide to Research**, a **Thematic Reader**, and unparalleled digital support in **MindTap**. The added value of MindTap includes the text itself online—with enhanced media support for your learning and writing—as well as additional online readings and an online handbook. For research, you'll find EasyBib and Questia in MindTap—premier tools for researching sources and formatting your research papers.

Part 4, A Guide to Research, presents research as an effective way of responding to certain rhetorical opportunities, rather than as a set of rules and requirements. Guidance is provided on developing a research question, and because different research questions require different research methods, *The New Harbrace Guide* includes coverage of library, online, and field research. In addition, you'll find help reading sources critically as well as summarizing, paraphrasing, and quoting sources. *The New Harbrace Guide* also includes two separate chapters—with sample papers—on formatting papers in styles for MLA (Modern Language Association) according to the eighth edition of the *MLA Handbook* (2016) and APA (American Psychology Association). Research can be daunting, so *The New Harbrace Guide* continues to focus on the ways students experience the research process by including **Tricks of the Trade** tips from fellow students throughout these chapters.

Part 5, A Thematic Reader, includes readings and themes, contemporary and thought-provoking clusters, that will appeal to your interest in analyzing yourself and the world around you. We have returned to popular themes such as **Food and the (Cultural) Experience of Taste (Chapter 21)**, **The Millennial Generation (Chapter 22)**, and **Taking Up (Public) Space (Chapter 23)**, while introducing new ones that reviewers have embraced, addressing issues such as race in **Whose Lives Matter? (Chapter 24)** and science in **STEM vs. STEAM (Chapter 25)**. The readings can be used as additional examples for each genre or as topics for your research. Assignments are included so that you can use these readings as the basis for writing in a particular genre or to connect writing to making a change in your community. More readings on each topic are available online on MindTap.

What Does This Mean for You?

So far, I've been telling you about all the ways that this *Guide* will support your academic writing, the kind of writing that too often intimidates new college students. But you shouldn't feel intimidated; after all, you've been writing almost all your life. When you were a small child, you grabbed crayons, felt-tip markers, or chalk and wrote on whatever surfaces you could find: paper, coloring books, sidewalks, chalk boards, table tops, walls, lampshades. As you think back on your earliest memories of composing, keep in mind the process of composing that you practiced then. You gathered up your materials and set to work. The entire process—from start to finish—was simple, often fun. Like the human animal you are, you were marking your territory—leaving messages for the people who entered your world. Award-winning author Joyce Carol Oates cannot recall a time when she wasn't writing:

> **Before I could write what might be called human words in the English language, I eagerly emulated grown-ups' handwriting in pencil scribbles. My first "novels" . . . were tablets of inspired scribbles illustrated by line drawings of chickens, horses and upright cats.**
>
> **—Joyce Carol Oates, "To Invigorate Literary Mind, Start Moving Literary Feet"**

Like the writing you did as a child, let college composing be satisfying, even when it isn't *always* fun, let alone easy. The process might at times seem demanding, but the results are often exhilarating, something you're proud of. If that weren't the case, you wouldn't worry about writing well or care what your teacher thought of your writing. Perhaps the best way to make composing a pleasurable activity is to build on what you already do well and enjoy as you write. Use this book as your guide as you fulfill your assignments for this class—it is designed to do that—but also use the book to discover the skills you already have and use them as you prepare to write outside of class.

For writers like you, the enjoyment you get from writing may be learning to develop your thinking into clear words and images, submitting your essays to instructors who respond with proof that they've actually read your words, or transforming your ideas into a multimedia message for your friends. Writing doesn't require any one specific satisfaction but often calls up many overlapping ones. Here's hoping that your college writing launches your thinking, creativity, and intellectual curiosity as you write your way through college and on into the workplace and community.

For Instructors: A Note about Online Course Materials

MindTap® English for Glenn's *The New Harbrace Guide: Genres for Composing,* **Third Edition,** engages your students to become better thinkers, communicators, and writers by blending your course materials with content that supports every feature of the writing process.

- Interactive activities on grammar and mechanics promote application to student writing.
- An easy-to-use paper management system helps prevent plagiarism and allows for electronic submission, grading, and peer review.
- A vast database of scholarly sources with video tutorials and examples supports every step of the research process.
- Professional tutoring guides students from rough drafts to polished writing.
- Visual analytics track student progress and engagement.
- Seamless integration into your campus learning management system keeps all your course materials in one place.

MindTap lets you compose your course, your way.

The Instructor's Manual for Glenn's *The New Harbrace Guide: Genres for Composing,* **Third Edition,** includes detailed sample syllabi and chapter-by-chapter suggestions for using the guide in your classroom. The detailed syllabi comprise three annotated course plans that can be followed or consulted when teaching with this text in programs that focus on academic writing, writing in the disciplines, or service learning. Activities, exercises, and journal-writing prompts are provided for each class meeting, along with suggested goals and materials for instructors to review.

Acknowledgments

All books demand time, talent, and plenty of hard work. For that reason, I could not have produced this textbook without the help and support of a number of colleagues, friends, and students. I found myself calling on their expertise at various times throughout the creation of this book. Sarah Adams provided me examples of successful student essays, for which I'm grateful. She also contributed a paper that can be found on MindTap, along with papers from fellow students Cole Harding, Ryan Insley, Bailey Young, Marianna Williamson, Greg Coles, and Emily Grandinette. In addition to the paper on MindTap, Greg Coles gave generously of his time and wisdom as a teacher, scholar, and writer. He helped me conduct research into multimedia sources and locate new readings as well as contributors for various parts of the book, and provided an essay he wrote as a first-year student for the MLA chapter. Mohammed Samy allowed us to reprint an infographic on how a genre comes to be (which he had originally composed for Professor Pavel Zemliansky's composition course at the University of Central Florida). Undergraduate intern Marianna Williamson helped with various research and proofreading duties, all demonstrating a professionalism beyond her years. I remain grateful to them all, as well as to those whose work as students comes to us from previous editions: Caledonia Adams, Grace Randolph, and the Viz-a-GoGo web creators from Texas A&M University, whose work appears in Part 1; Anna Seitz, Alicia Williams, and Alexis Walker, who contributed papers to Part 2; Anastasia Simkanin, who allowed us to see her process as well as her paper in Part 3; and for Part 4, Cristian Nuñez and Keith Evans, for tips in "Tricks of the Trade," Jacob Thomas, for his summary of "DoubleSpeak," and Catherine L. Davis, whose paper appears in the APA chapter. I know of several students whose essays are featured in the Thematic Reader for this book, too: David Fallarme, Karen Hernandez, and Malcolm Aime-Musoni. Likely there are others I've missed, but suffice it to say this book would not have been possible without the contribution of students to the book and to my teaching and learning.

At Cengage, Senior Content Developer Leslie Taggart oversaw the progress of the project, relying (as we all have) on the good sense and keen insights of Product Director Monica Eckman, Content Project Manager Rebecca Donahue, and English Product Manager Laura Ross. New to our team in this edition, Kina Lara has already demonstrated her marketing prowess. Editorial assistant Claire Branman helped launch the substantive improvements to this edition. For their painstaking production of this book, I thank Rosemary Winfield, who, upon retiring, handed it off to Corinna Dibble and Rebecca Donahue, Cengage production editors; Angela Williams Urquhart and Kathy Smith, Editorial Director and copy editor at Thistle Hill Publishing Services; Ann Hoffman, tireless intellectual property analyst; Erika Mugavin, tireless intellectual property project manager; and Marissa Falco, this *new* book's designer. But my biggest thanks goes to my new editor extraordinaire, Lisa Colleen Moore, whose intellect and publishing sense have far exceeded my greatest expectations. For many months now, she's been my constant intellectual companion and my out-of-this-world partner in developing this new guide.

Finally, I have learned from a phenomenal group of reviewers, including the following instructors who offered their guidance on the second edition:

Jared Abraham, *Weatherford College*
Jeff Andelora, *Mesa Community College*
Amy Azul, *Chaffey College*
Andrea Bewick, *Napa Valley College*
Lee Brewer-Jones, *Georgia Perimeter College*
Sue Briggs, *Salt Lake Community College*
Mark Browning, *Johnson County Community College*
Mary Burkhart, *University of Scranton*
Mary Carden, *Edinboro University of Pennsylvania*
Jo Cavins, *North Dakota State University*
Ron Christiansen, *Salt Lake Community College*
Stephanie Dowdle, *Salt Lake Community College*
Rosalyn Eves, *Southern Utah University*
Eugene Flinn, *New Jersey City University*
Patricia Flinn, *New Jersey City University*
Rebecca Fournier, *Triton College*
Powell Franklin, *Jackson State Community College*
James Green, *Northern Kentucky University*
Kevin Griffith, *Capital University*
Anna Harrington, *Jackson State Community College*
Martha Holder, *Wytheville Community College*
Dawn Hubbell-Staeble, *Bowling Green State University*
James Mayo, *Jackson State Community College*
Kate Mohler, *Mesa Community College*
Sheryl Mylan, *College of DuPage*
Randy Nelson, *Davidson College*
Dana Nkana, *Illinois Central College*
Eden Pearson, *Des Moines Area Community College*
Jason Pickavance, *Salt Lake Community College*
Jeff Pruchnic, *Wayne State University*
Amy Ratto Parks, *University of Montana*
Marsha Rutter, *Southwestern College*
Adrianne Schott, *Weatherford College*
Wendy Sharer, *East Carolina University*

Noel Sloboda, *Pennsylvania State University–York*
David Swain, *Southern New Hampshire University*
Sharon Tash, *Saddleback College*
Michael Trovato, *Ohio State University–Newark*
Cynthia VanSickle, *McHenry County College*

And for this third edition, I'm grateful for the thoughtfulness of the comments by so many who reviewed this book. Their good suggestions helped make this book better, especially when hard decisions needed to be made about how to shorten the book while retaining and enhancing the most useful content.

Emory Abbott, *Georgia Perimeter College*
Camila Alvarez, *Indian River State College*
Krysten Anderson, *Roane State Community College*
Joe Antinarella, *Tidewater Community College*
Rebecca Babcock, *University of Texas of the Permian Basin*
Edith Baker, *Bradley University*
Jessica Bannon, *University of Indianapolis*
Craig Bartholomaus, *Metropolitan Community College*
Crystal Bickford, *Southern New Hampshire University*
Melinda Borchers, *University of Tennessee*
Anthony Cavaluzzi, *SUNY Adirondack*
Christie Diep, *Cypress College*
Amber Dinquel, *Richmond Community College*
Michael Doolin, *Monroe Community College*
Margaret Dwyer, *Milwaukee School of Engineering*
Jeremiah Dyehouse, *University of Rhode Island*
Karen Engels, *Waukesha County Technical College*
Tyler Farrell, *Marquette University*
Audrey Forrest-Carter, *Winston-Salem State University*
Kelley Fuemmeler, *Missouri Valley College*
Lynee Gaillet, *Georgia State University*
Barbara Goldstein, *Hillsborough Community College*
Jason Graves, *Kilgore College*
Kevin Griffith, *Capital University*
Kim Haimes-Korn, *Kennesaw State University*
Ismail Hakim, *Richard J. Daley College*
Stephen Hancock, *Brigham Young University–Hawaii*
Beth Heim de Bera, *Rochester Community and Technical College*
Jeffrey Hornburg, *Keiser University*
Geraldine Jacobs, *Jackson College*
Joanne Jacobs, *Shenandoah University*

Cecilia Kennedy, *Clark State Community College*
Debra Knutson, *Shawnee State University*
Laura La Flair, *Belmont Abbey College*
Dawn Lattin, *Idaho State University*
Nancy Lee-Jones, *Endicott College*
Lindsay Lewan, *Arapahoe Community College*
Carol Lewis, *Three Rivers College*
Anna Maheshwari, *Schoolcraft College*
Bonnie Markowski, *University of Scranton*
Michael Martin, *Stephen F. Austin State University*
Michael McClure, *Virginia State University*
Nancy McGee, *Macomb Community College*
James McKeown, *McLennan Community College*
Trista Merrill, *Finger Lakes Community College*
Deborah Miller-Zournas, *Stark State College*
Dr. Jan Modisette, *Jacksonville College*
David Norman, *Savannah Technical College*
Lara Nosser, *Richmond Community College*
Lonetta Oliver, *St. Louis Community College*
James Ortego, *Troy University*
Jarrod Patterson, *Alabama A&M University*
Jerry Petersen, *Utah Valley University*
John Pleimann, *Jefferson College*
Dan Portincaso, *Waubonsee Community College*
Brad Prestwood, *Caldwell Community College and Technical Institute*
Amy Ratto Parks, *University of Montana*
Laura Rotunno, *Penn State Altoona*
Debra Ryals, *Pensacola State College*
Jamie Sadler, *Richmond Community College*
Beth Sherman, *San Diego State University*
Dr. Brenda Tuberville, *Rogers State University*
Matthew Turner, *Lone Star College-CyFair*
Janice Walker, *Georgia Southern University*
Jeana West, *Murray State College*
Katy Whittingham, *Bridgewater State University*
Mary Williams, *Midland College*
Nancy Young, *Curry College*
Janet Zepernick, *Pittsburg State University*

Cheryl Glenn
June 2016

Praise for *The New Harbrace Guide: Genres for Composing*

It's the best treatment of rhetoric I've seen in any text in 8 years of teaching.
— Justin Jory, Salt Lake Community College

The 'knowledge transfer' sections highlight re-purposing possibilities for projects to be delivered to different audiences with multimodal opportunities. This is an attractive feature.
— Jerry Peterson, Utah Valley University

Quite honestly, the best outline/guide structure I have seen yet in a text.
— Jamie Sadler, Richmond College

I like the student friendly language and step-by-step guidance.
— Tyler Farrell, Marquette University

I really like the reorganization and condensing in this new version.
— Beth Sherman, San Diego State University

User friendly. Current. I like the structure!
— Anna Maheshwari, Schoolcraft College

I really liked the focus on rhetorical situations as opportunities for change. I think that is a great emphasis for helping students understand the importance of writing well for different audiences and purposes.
— Craig Bartholomaus, Metropolitan Community College

The book takes a rhetorical stance to writing, offering students clear advice for how several different genres can be rhetorically persuasive.
— Jeremiah Dyehouse, University of Rhode Island

This book makes critical thinking relevant to students.
— Krysten Anderson, Roane State Community College

THE *new*

HARBRACE GUIDE

GUIDE TO IDENTIFYING THE ELEMENTS OF ANY RHETORICAL SITUATION

As you enter any rhetorical conversation—from friendly text-ing to college papers to business presentations—consider the elements of the rhetorical situation to help you shape a persuasive message.

Maartje van Caspel/Getty Images

- **Opportunity** Identify the opportunity for change that encourages you to enter the rhetorical situation. Ask yourself: What is it that tugs at me? Why do I feel the need to speak, write, take a photo, share an image? What attitude, action, or opinion do I want to change?

- **Purpose** Connect the opportunity for change with your purpose (and then your audi-ence). Ask yourself: What can I accomplish with rhetoric? How do words or visuals allow me to respond to this opportunity?

- **Audience** Knowing that your purpose is to stimulate change in a specific audience, carefully consider the character of that audience: Who are its members? What opinions and values do they hold? And, most important, how might they help you address or resolve the problem?

- **Stance** The success of your message often depends on the attitude you project toward your topic and your intended audience. A respectful tone toward your topic and audience is often the most effective.

- **Genre** Each genre is distinguished by well-established yet flexible features and format-ting, so determine what form will best convey your message—an academic essay or evaluation; a memoir, report, proposal, profile, résumé, letter, or review. The genre you choose should not only fulfill your purpose but also be familiar to your audience.

- **Medium** Your choice of materials and medium—spoken or written (perhaps with addi-tional visual elements)—depends on the elements of the specific rhetorical situation, especially the ability of your audience to access that medium.

Understanding the Rhetorical Situation

The prime characteristic of the rhetorical situation is identifying an opportunity for change.

> MindTap®   Understand the goals of the chapter and complete a warm-up activity online.

RHETORIC SURROUNDS US

Too often, the word *rhetoric* implies empty words, manipulation, deception, or persuasion at any cost. But rhetoric and rhetorical situations are frequently neutral, often positive. They are everywhere—as pervasive as the air we breathe—and play an essential role in our daily lives as we work to get things done efficiently and ethically.

    Rhetoric is the purposeful use of language and images. That definition covers a great deal of territory—practically every word and visual element you encounter every day. But it's the word *purposeful* that will guide you through the maze of words and images that saturate your life. When you use words or images to achieve a specific purpose—such as explaining to your instructor why you must miss class—you are speaking, writing, or conveying images rhetorically.

> **rhetoric** communication to achieve a specific purpose with a specific audience

IDENTIFYING AN OPPORTUNITY FOR CHANGE

rhetorical opportunity the issue, problem, or situation that motivates the use of language to stimulate change

Every time an issue, problem, or situation motivates you to write or speak, you have identified a **rhetorical opportunity**, an occasion to make change through language, whether visual, written, or spoken. For instance, by asking a question, your instructor creates an opportunity for change in the classroom (usually a change in everyone's understanding). Similarly, if your company wants to grow its online business, it will need to update its website and online marketing plan—through language. And if you and your friend have argued, you might not want to put your feelings into writing; you might want to phone to say, "I'm sorry." These rhetorical opportunities all call for the kinds of change that language can make possible.

Unless you perceive something as an opportunity, you cannot respond to it. In other words, *something* needs to stimulate or provoke your interest and call for your response. When you take an essay examination for an American history midterm, you might be given the choice of answering one of two questions:

1. The great increase in size and power of the federal government since the Civil War has long been a dominant theme of American history. Trace the growth of the federal government since 1865, paying particular attention to its evolving involvement in world affairs and the domestic economy. Be sure to support your analysis with relevant historical details.
2. Compare and contrast the attempts to create and safeguard African American civil rights in two historical periods: the first era of reconstruction (post–Civil War years to the early twentieth century) and the second era

of reconstruction (1950s to 1970s). Consider government policies, African American strategies, and the responses of white people to those strategies.

If you are lucky, one of these questions will spark your response and engage your intellectual energy. Think of every college writing situation as a rhetorical opportunity for you to use language in order to resolve or address a problem.

ACTIVITY
What Is an Opportunity for Change?

Decide whether each problem listed below is also a rhetorical opportunity for change. Be prepared to share the reasoning behind your responses with the rest of the class.

- The Internal Revenue Service is charging you $2,000 in back taxes, asserting that you neglected to declare the income from your summer job.
- Your college library has just sent you an e-mail informing you that you're being fined for several overdue books, all of which you returned a month ago.
- After Thanksgiving dinner is served, your brothers and mother resume their ongoing argument about U.S. politics: health care, the wars, and the economy.
- In the student section at the football stadium, some fans throw empty soda cans, toss beach balls, boo the opposing team, and stand during most of the game. You're quickly losing interest in attending the games.

DECIDING TO ENGAGE

The most important feature of any rhetorical opportunity is the **writer** or speaker, who believes that language (spoken, written, visual) can bring about change. If you witness a car accident, for example, you are an observer; you may decide to volunteer to testify about it and thus engage in the opportunity as a speaker. If you identify an old friend from a newspaper photograph, you may decide to e-mail him. You might hear a song and decide to perform it and post a video of your performance on YouTube. Or you might decide to begin introducing yourself to people participating in an online video game. Whatever

writer someone who uses language to bring about change in an audience

the opportunities are and however they are delivered (whether spoken, printed, online, or in some other way), you can decide how or whether you want to act on them.

Every day, you encounter dozens of rhetorical opportunities to make a change by engaging with language. If your good friend applies for and gets the job of her dreams, you have an opportunity to engage with a response. How will she know that you are happy for her unless you send her a congratulatory card, give her a phone call, invite her to a celebratory lunch—or all three? The death of your neighbor creates an opportunity to respond with a letter to the family or a bouquet of flowers and an accompanying condolence note. A friend's illness, an argument with a roommate, a tuition hike, an essay exam, a sales presentation, a job interview—these are all opportunities for change through spoken or written words or with visuals.

ACTIVITY

To Engage or Not to Engage

1. Describe a time when you identified an opportunity to address a problem but either did not respond at all or did not respond well. If you could do it over, how might you respond? How would you take into consideration each element of the rhetorical situation in order to come as close to persuasion as conditions allowed?

2. Describe a rhetorical opportunity to which you felt compelled to respond. Describe the features of the rhetorical situation and how you took them all into consideration in your response. Share your response with the rest of the class.

---

message the main point of information shaped to influence an audience

audience those who receive and interpret the message of a communication

As the writer or speaker, you engage the opportunity with a **message** that includes content you have shaped in a way that stimulates change (Figure 1.1). What information must you include to teach, please, and change your **audience**, those readers, viewers, or listeners you are trying to influence with your message? Consider the message in the release of posters for *Star Wars: The Force Awakens* (Figure 1.2, p. 8).

Figure 1.1 *The writer must design the message so that it reaches the intended audience, whether it is delivered verbally, orally, with images, in print, or digitally.*

MindTap® Interact with the Rhetorical Triangle online.

The Force Awakens // NOVEMBER 4, 2015

Figure 1.2 *Star Wars: The Force Awakens Character Posters Revealed.*

See stunning new images of Rey, Leia, Kylo Ren, Han Solo, and Finn!

Star Wars: The Force Awakens is almost here—and now you can get an up-close look at the film's classic and new characters.

The official character posters for Rey, Leia, Kylo Ren, Han Solo, and Finn were revealed today, featuring powerful portraits and a striking design motif. Rey holds her staff defiantly; Leia confidently peers through a data screen; Kylo Ren's lightsaber crackles; a grim Han Solo holds his blaster at the ready; and Finn looks stoic with a blue-bladed Jedi weapon.

Carrie Fisher, Daisy Ridley, and John Boyega each revealed their own posters via Twitter and Instagram. Take a look at their posts and check out the full posters below!

Stay tuned to StarWars.com for more on *Star Wars: The Force Awakens*, coming to theaters December 18, 2015!

StarWars.com. All Star Wars, all the time.

With museum exhibitions, television commercials, trailers, and spoilers, the creators of *Star Wars: The Force Awakens* are leveraging the features of the rhetorical situation for the explicit purpose of stimulating worldwide ticket sales. Online, the *Star Wars* website features the latest news (global and national) about the film, as well as updates on its progress, the characters, and the actors themselves. There is an online community, which features photographs of its members when they meet f2f (face to face), as well as background on the various characters and the history of the saga itself.

But to stay as wildly successful as it already is, the franchise needs to deliver its message in other media as well. Online, televised, and print news sources are featuring controversies surrounding the much-anticipated film: CNN asks, "Does the ethnically diverse cast mean the film is 'anti-white'?" Print newspapers and magazines carry stories on the film, with accompanying visuals; television features an animated *Star Wars* program and *Star Wars* advertising introducing young boys playing with light sabers. The franchise has also pushed its message into retail, with tie-ins of books, comics, toys, games, posters, apps, costumes, and even *Star Wars* themed events at the Disney parks. The creators are purposefully sending their message to a broad audience, composed of people of all ages, races, cultures, and nationalities, long-time and new fans alike. The message is that everyone and anyone should see *Star Wars: The Force Awakens*—because they will love it.

ANALYZING THE ELEMENTS OF THE RHETORICAL SITUATION

When you decide to engage a rhetorical opportunity, understanding the elements of the **rhetorical situation** helps you shape the content of your message to enhance your chances of changing your audience's attitude, action, or opinion. Creating change through language is not about overpowering your audience or winning an argument. Rather, creating change involves understanding the rhetorical situation you are entering. Before speaking or writing, taking the time to analyze the elements of your rhetorical situation is a first step in discovering what you might say or write.

rhetorical situation the context that influences effective communication

Opportunity What is the occasion? What has motivated you to engage in a rhetorical opportunity for change?

Purpose How might your message change your audience in some way? What do you want your language to accomplish? What action do you want to occur because of what you compose?

Audience To whom are you writing (or speaking)? What is your relationship to the person or group of people? After all, you will direct your writing, speaking, or visual display to a specific audience in an attempt to change some opinion, attitude, or action.

Stance How do you view your message and its recipients? Your attitude toward your audience and topic is revealed through your word choice and tone and can be positive, negative, neutral, reasonable, unreasonable, or something else.

Genre Which features and formatting should your message follow? The distinctive yet flexible characteristics of each genre—profile, memoir, analysis, biography, proposal, evaluation, and so on—help you frame your message, connect with your audience, and achieve your purpose.

Medium How will the medium of delivery (online, visual, print, oral) enhance or detract from your message? Are you sure that your audience can receive (access) your message through this medium?

ACTIVITY

Identify the Elements of the Rhetorical Situation

For each of the rhetorical situations below, try to identify the opportunity and the purpose, audience, message, medium of delivery, and stance that should be considered in order to help you craft an effective response.

- A friend of a friend, whom you have never met, has invited you to be his Facebook friend.
- You are applying for a scholarship and need three letters of recommendation. You do not know any of your instructors very well.
- As a member of a wedding party, you are expected to make a toast at the reception in front of two hundred guests.

MindTap® Interact with the Rhetorical Situation online.

THINKING RHETORICALLY ABOUT PURPOSE AND AUDIENCE

purpose in rhetoric, the reason for a communication

rhetorical purpose the specific change the writer wants to accomplish through the use of language

rhetorical audience the specific audience most capable of being changed by a message or of bringing about change

Many writers equate **purpose** with their reason for writing: they are fulfilling an assignment, or meeting a deadline; they want a good grade or want to make money. When you are writing with a **rhetorical purpose**, however, you move beyond goals like those to consider how you might influence a specific **rhetorical audience**, those people you hope to influence in some way.

As we have just seen, the studio that launched *Star Wars: The Force Awakens* used posters to reach a broad audience before the movie opened in theaters. Barnes & Noble, on the other hand, targeted a more *specific* audience when it released the last novel in the Harry Potter series, *Harry Potter and the Deathly Hallows* (Figure 1.3). Barnes & Noble e-mailed only those people who had in the past purchased Harry Potter books or calendars, notebooks, or other items, and who would be familiar with the tradition of arriving at a store hours ahead of the book's release ("Join us . . . as you count down the final moments to Harry's arrival!"). Like the audience for the new *Star Wars* movie, the rhetorical audience for Barnes & Noble was closely related to its purpose (enticing these people to purchase Harry Potter items in the near future). Additionally, because Barnes & Noble was reaching these people through the medium of e-mail, the message included information about ordering the book online—just a click away for those already reading e-mail.

As you direct your message to your rhetorical audience, you will need to keep in mind the nature of your audience (their power, status, values, interests) and their character (sympathetic or unsympathetic, opposed to or in favor of your message). These people are capable of being influenced by your message and bringing about change, either by their own actions or their influence on others. How you approach your rhetorical audience affects the success of your message. Your writing conveys an attitude toward your topic and audience,

Figure 1.3 *Messages such as this one from Barnes & Noble are created with a rhetorical audience in mind.*

your **stance**. Try to shape your stance in terms of content, tone, examples, appropriateness, and timeliness to enhance its chances of influencing your audience. Consider whether you are talking to your instructor, one of your parents, your physician, or a friend—and how in each case you would respectfully and truthfully represent your beliefs and values if your audience held beliefs and values that differed from yours. Try to keep in mind the kind of information you would need to deliver—as well as how and when to deliver it.

THINKING RHETORICALLY ABOUT GENRE AND MEDIA

As you know by now, narrowing your purpose is important because each rhetorical opportunity for change requires its own audience, genre, and medium of delivery. Fortunately, genre and medium are fairly easy to identify.

stance the attitude your writing conveys toward your topic, purpose, and audience

Considering Genre

genre a category of writing that has a particular format and features, such as memoir or argument

A **genre** is a type of writing categorized by a well-established format with familiar features. Writers deliberately choose a single genre or a purposeful combination of genres in order to reach a specific audience. For instance, the genre of memoir usually follows a chronological narration (sometimes peppered with flash forwards or flashbacks), features distinctive characters who contribute to dialogue in unique ways, and presents a well-described setting—all of which are rich in sensory details. You would never mistake a memoir for a lab report. And you would not want to submit a memoir instead of a résumé to a potential employer. But, because the features of any genre are flexible and adaptable, you might employ many of the same features as those in a traditional memoir in a job application letter—such as describing the significant points in your life that led you to a particular career. Or you might include your personal experience as evidence in an argument. And you might find yourself considering a memoir as a historical document in your research. Some familiar genres include the position argument, profile, evaluation, and proposal. The more you learn about the qualities of each of these genres, the easier it will be to determine which genre is most effective for your message and when it would be effective to blend genres to best address your rhetorical situation.

medium method of communication: oral, visual, verbal, digital, or print

media (plural of medium) *mass media* is a term used for media like radio, television, and various online forums that reach a broad audience

Considering Medium of Delivery

You choose a particular **medium** (method of communication)—or a combination of oral, visual, verbal, digital, or print **media**—for delivering your message because it most effectively reaches your rhetorical audience. How you deliver your message can be just as important as the content of that message, whether you are speaking, building a website, or text messaging. A person without a powerful computer may prefer print documents; a techno-wizard may abhor paper and prefer to receive everything digitally.

Because we enjoy so many ways of communicating—visually, verbally, digitally—we rarely stop to consider why we have chosen a particular medium for delivery. Thinking rhetorically, however, you will consider which medium you should use to deliver your purposeful message in order to reach your rhetorical audience: a letter, an e-mail, a phone message, a greeting card, an oral presentation with PowerPoint, a YouTube video. Naming the medium is not as important as analyzing the reasons for the writer's decision, however. What are the advantages to this choice of medium? Are there disadvantages? Should you deliver your message orally (face to face or over the phone), in writing (using a letter or note, an e-mail or instant message, or a web page), or via film, video, still images, or other visuals? Where might you most successfully deliver that message: in class, at church, at the coffee shop, at a town meeting? For instance, if you are interviewing for a job, would you prefer to present yourself on paper, in person, over Skype, or in a phone call?

In the last few years, students have begun to use multimedia to address rhetorical opportunities in a number of inventive ways. *TXTmob*, *coup de texte*, *going mobile*, *text brigades*, and *swarms* are some of the terms used all over the world for the ways political mobilizations are conducted, allowing group leaders to control, minute by minute, the appearance and movements of demonstrators. The demonstrators themselves—the TXTmobbers and text brigaders—analyze the multimedia messages in order to read the situation, decide what to do, and stay synchronized. Thanks to such untraditional media outlets as Twitter and YouTube, the rest of the world became aware of the protests over the apparently rigged reelection of President Mahmoud Ahmadinejad in 2009 (Figure 1.4).

Figure 1.4 *A young woman whistles as she films the scene around her at a 2009 election rally in Tehran, Iran.*

Jacobs by Marc Jacobs . . . tote bag

Figure 1.5 *"Jacobs by Marc Jacobs . . ."
tote bag, Marc Jacobs, 2008.*

Not all situations that call for multimedia responses or analysis involve wide-scale political movements. Not everyone will be able to stream videos or download podcasts. While some people might be browsing from a smartphone or a powerful notebook, others might be using a computer lacking the capacity to handle large video or audio downloads. Still others may not always have access to wireless connections. Knowing that people could be easily reached with the use of everyday items, designers Marc Jacobs and Anya Hindmarch sent their messages on tote bags, expressions of their creative vision as well as their political message (Figure 1.5).

In other words, accessibility is always a rhetorical issue for you and your audience: the medium of delivery you select affects how much of and what parts of your message an audience ultimately sees, hears, and appreciates. Thus, your delivery choices determine not only who constitutes your audience but also how your audience experiences your message.

 ASSIGNMENT: RHETORICAL OPPORTUNITIES

> MindTap® Read, highlight, and take notes online. Request help and feedback from a tutor. If required, participate in peer review, submit your paper for a grade, and view instructor comments online.

Whether you are reading an essay, listening to a speech, or looking at a visual, you will understand the message better if you begin by determining the rhetorical opportunity that calls for specific words or visuals. Very often, the responses you are reading or viewing call for even further responses. Whether your response is spoken, written, or composed visually, its power lies in your understanding of the rhetorical opportunity. Reading for rhetorical opportunity helps you develop your skills in analyzing the way the elements of the rhetorical situation work together to influence change.

Life as We Know It

MICHAEL BÉRUBÉ

English professor Michael Bérubé writes widely about academic matters: curriculum, teaching loads, classroom management, tenure, and cultural studies. But with the birth of his second son, James (Jamie), Bérubé ventured into another kind of writing aimed at a wider audience. The following piece is from the introduction to Life as We Know It: A Father, a Family, and an Exceptional Child, *a chronicle of his family's experiences with Jamie, who has Down syndrome.*

My little Jamie loves lists: foods, colors, animals, numbers, letters, states, classmates, parts of the body, days of the week, modes of transportation, characters who live on Sesame Street, and the names of the people who love him. Early last summer, I hoped his love of lists—and his ability to catalogue things *into* lists—would stand him in good stead during what would undoubtedly be a difficult "vacation" for anyone, let alone a three-year-old child with Down syndrome: a three-hour drive to Chicago, a rush-hour flight to LaGuardia, a cab to Grand Central, a train to Connecticut—and *then* smaller trips to New York, Boston, and Old Orchard Beach, Maine. Even accomplishing the first of these mission objectives—arriving safely at O'Hare—required a precision and teamwork I do not always associate with my family. I dropped off Janet and nine-year-old Nick at the terminal with the baggage, then took Jamie to long-term parking with me while they checked in, and then entertained Jamie all the way back to the terminal, via bus and shuttle train. We sang about the driver on the bus, and we counted all the escalator steps and train stops, and when we finally got to our plane, I told Jamie, *Look, there's Mommy and Nick at the gate! They're yelling that we're going to lose our seats! They want to know why it took us forty-five minutes to park the car!*

All went well from that point on, though, and in the end, I suppose you could say Jamie got as much out of his vacation as might any toddler being whisked up and down New England. He's a seasoned traveler, and he thrives on shorelines, family gatherings, and New Haven pizza. And he's good with faces and names.

Then again, as we learned toward the end of our brief stay in Maine, he doesn't care much for amusement parks. Not that Nick did either, at three. But apparently one of the attractions of Old Orchard Beach, for my wife and her siblings, was the small beachfront arcade and amusement park in town, which they associated with their own childhoods. It was an endearing strip, with a roller coaster just the right size for Nick—exciting, mildly scary, but with no loop-the-loops, rings of fire, or oppressive G forces. We strolled among bumper cars, cotton candy, games of chance and skill, and a striking number of French-Canadian tourists: perhaps the first time

Rhetorical Situation

our two little boys had ever seen more than one Bérubé family in one place. James, however, wanted nothing to do with any of the rides, and though he loves to pretend-drive and has been on bumper cars before, he squalled so industriously before the ride began as to induce the bumper cars operator to let him out of the car and refund his two tickets.

Jamie finally settled in next to a train ride designed for children five and under or thereabouts, which, for two tickets, took its passengers around an oval layout and over a bridge four times. I found out quickly enough that Jamie didn't want to *ride* the ride; he merely wanted to stand at its perimeter, grasping the partition with both hands and counting the cars—one, two, three, four, five, six—as they went by. Sometimes, when the train traversed the bridge, James would punctuate it with tiny jumps, saying, "Up! Up! Up!" But for the most part, he was content to hang onto the metal bars of the partition, grinning and counting—and, when the train came to a stop, pulling my sleeve and saying, "More, again."

This went on for about half an hour, well past the point at which I could con-vincingly share Jamie's enthusiasm for tracking the train's progress. As it went on my spirits began to sink in a way I do not recall having felt before. Occasionally it will occur to Janet or to me that Jamie will always be "disabled," that his adult and ado-lescent years will undoubtedly be more difficult emotionally—for him and for us—than his early childhood, that we will never *not* worry about his future, his quality of life, whether we're doing enough for him. But usually these moments occur in the relative comfort of abstraction, when Janet and I are lying in bed at night and won-dering what will become of us all. When I'm *with* Jamie, by contrast, I'm almost always fully occupied by taking care of his present needs rather than by worrying about his future. When he asks to hear the Beatles because he loves their cover of Little Richard's "Long Tall Sally," I just play the song, sing along, and watch him dance with delight; I do not concern myself with extraneous questions such as whether he'll ever distinguish early Beatles from late Beatles, Paul's songs from John's, originals from covers. These questions are now central to Nick's enjoyment of the Beatles, but that's Nick for you. Jamie is entirely *sui generis*, and as long as I'm with him I can't think of him as anything but Jamie.

I have tried. Almost as a form of emotional exercise, I have tried, on occasion, to step back and see him as others might see him, as an instance of a category, one item on the long list of human subgroups. *This is a child with Down syndrome,* I say to myself. *This is a child with a developmental disability.* It never works: Jamie remains Jamie to me. I have even tried to imagine him as he would have been seen in other eras, other places: *This is a retarded child.* And even: *This is a Mongoloid child.* This makes for unbearable cognitive dissonance. I can imagine that people might think such things, but I cannot imagine how they might think them in a way that prevents them from seeing Jamie *as* Jamie. I try to recall how I saw such children when I was a child, but here I guiltily draw a blank: I don't remember seeing them at all, which very likely means that I never quite saw them *as* children. Instead I remember a famous passage from Ludwig Wittgenstein's *Philosophical Investigations:* "'Seeing-as' is not part of perception. And for this reason it is *like* seeing, and then again *not* like." Reading Wittgenstein, I often think, is something like listening to a brilliant and cantankerous uncle with an annoying fondness for koans [riddles]. But on this one, I know exactly what he means.

ACTIVITY: Analyzing the Rhetorical Situation
"Life as We Know It"

1. What rhetorical opportunity called for the writing of this essay? State that opportunity in one sentence.
2. Who composed this message? What information does the writer supply about his identity?
3. What does this essay say? Compile the details that describe the writer's feelings about his son; then write one sentence that conveys Bérubé's main message.
4. Why does the essay say that? Drawing on your previous answer, identify three or four passages from the text where Bérubé supports his main message.
5. How does the essay respond to that opportunity? What change in attitude, opinion, or action does the author wish to influence?

MindTap® Reflect on your writing process, practice skills that you have learned in this chapter, and receive automatic feedback.

Responding to the Rhetorical Situation

Rhetoric is the art of observing in any given situation the available means of persuasion.

MindTap® Understand the goals of the chapter and complete a warm-up activity online.

THINKING RHETORICALLY ABOUT PERSUASION

The Greek philosopher Aristotle, who coined an authoritative definition of *rhetoric* over 2,500 years ago, tells us, "Rhetoric is the art of observing in any given situation the available means of persuasion." Let us take this definition apart and examine its constituent elements. "Rhetoric is the art [or mental ability] of observing. . . ." Notice that Aristotle does not call for you to overpower your audience (your readers or listeners) with words or images, nor does he push you to win an argument. Instead, he encourages you to observe what kind of rhetorical situation you are entering. Chapter 1 stressed the importance of identifying the elements of a rhetorical situation (opportunity, purpose, audience, stance, genre, and medium of delivery): Who is your audience? What is your relationship to that person or group of people? What is the occasion? What do you want your language to accomplish (that is, what is your purpose)? By answering these questions, you are establishing the elements of the "given situation."

Now that you can identify these elements, you can evaluate the wide range of possible responses you can offer. Of course, each rhetorical situation is different, and you will need to consider that you can come only as close to persuasion as the rhetorical situation allows. Still, with experience and knowledge, you will take note of the tools that comprise "the available means of persuasion" to make more informed, strategic decisions. Rhetorical consciousness (and success) comes with recognizing the vast array of options at your disposal, including those already in existence and those you can create, and leveraging all the "available means" to achieve your purpose.

A PROBLEM-SOLVING APPROACH

The opportunity for change arises from a **problem** that can be addressed or even resolved by you and your audience. The writer (or speaker) enters the rhetorical situation in order to shape a message that can address a problem. It is up to you to observe what measure of change is possible in each case and to choose a response that will be most persuasive in achieving that change—be it an attitude, action, or opinion—in your intended audience. The writer identifies that problem as an opportunity to make change through the use of language, whether visual, written, or spoken. The response is dictated by the situation, by the specific opportunity for change.

problem in rhetoric, a question for discussion, exploration, and possible solution

Some responses to a problem will address the problem better than others. To be persuasive you need to choose a response that suits the problem. In other words, a **problem-solving approach** invites a response that *fits* the rhetorical situation. For instance, if you were bothered by your friend's weekend alcohol consumption, you would probably want to find an appropriate time and place to talk with her about it in a calm, respectful manner. You may want to focus on the dangers to her own well-being and physical safety, or you might discuss the pros and cons of drinking for college students. This situation invites such a **fitting response**—not a subpoena, lawsuit, call to her parents, or visit from a physician—at least not yet.

problem-solving approach in rhetoric, an examination of a question on an issue or situation directed at a specific audience

When you successfully use language to address a problem, you deliver a fitting response using the available means of persuasion, the medium you use to send your message, and the rhetorical appeals to your audience. Depending on the problem, responses in different media may reach and satisfy the rhetorical audience. Dictated by the situation, a fitting response to a problem

fitting response a communication whose tone, content, and delivery are carefully constructed to connect to the interests of a specific audience

- addresses the opportunity for change;
- is appropriate in content, tone, and timing;
- is delivered in an appropriate medium; and thus
- reaches, satisfies, and maybe even changes the actions, opinions, or attitudes of the intended audience.

((◉)) MAKING CLAIMS

Once you have identified a problem (from your friend's weekend alcohol consumption to bad food at a restaurant to something larger like poor-quality public schooling or homelessness in your town), it is up to you to determine which measure of change can be accomplished at this point given the interests and values of your audience. Your purpose may be to convince your audience that a situation needs a solution, or to call your audience to action to resolve the problem. You may want to help your audience make a decision. Or you may want your audience to explore an issue further. Your proposed change becomes your purpose, which you will shape into a **claim** (or assertion) that identifies the problem and proposes your solution. Your claim—usually expressed as a single, clearly focused, specifically worded **thesis statement**—invites the audience to understand your position and anchors your response. (For more on thesis statements, see CHAPTER 13, CRAFTING A WORKING THESIS STATEMENT.)

The kind of claim you make will also be guided by your rhetorical situation, however. If you are composing a memoir, for example, the change you are proposing is likely one of self-realization. Your claim in a proposal will be a call to action. A literary analysis will include the main point of your interpretation of the work of a particular author. A position argument is likely to focus on new evidence that the audience has not yet considered on a particular issue. Whether you are writing an evaluation or a profile, your thesis statement should include enough of the unexpected to arouse interest in the main point you are making about the problem you have

claim an assertion that identifies a problem and proposes a solution

thesis statement a clearly worded statement of your claim that guides the structure of a paper, presentation, or multimedia text

pages 246–247

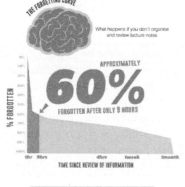

Produced by urbanest student.

Through a combination of words, images, and statistics, this infographic on note taking uses the web to deliver its message that note taking will solve the problem of forgetting important information in class lectures.

identified. You may not have a clear thesis statement in mind when you begin writing. What you think about an issue is likely to evolve while you are writing and researching your topic. This is as it should be. Just as your audience will learn something from your response, so you will likely discover new ways of looking at a topic as you translate your purpose into a compelling message.

 USING THE AVAILABLE MEANS OF PERSUASION

Earlier in this chapter, you learned that Aristotle defined *rhetoric* as "the art of observing in any given situation the available means of persuasion." Given that the prime characteristic of any rhetorical situation is its opportunity for change, the most significant part of any claim is that you can make a case for the change you have proposed using the available means of persuasion. The **available means of persuasion** include the place where you create a message (via your laptop or other electronic device, in person, over the telephone, by postal service), the physical means you use to deliver your message (in person, digitally, visually, in print), and the rhetorical elements you use in your presentation to appeal to your audience. Basically, you will want to establish your authority (or credibility) on the issue at hand, provide evidence that supports your claim, and make an authentic emotional connection with your audience. Altogether, authority, evidence, and connection are the available means of persuasion in any message, whether it is delivered verbally, visually, in print, or digitally.

available means of persuasion include the methods of communication (visual, verbal, digital, print) as well as rhetorical appeals of ethos, logos, and pathos (see pp. 23–24)

The Available Means Are Anchored to the Writer's Place

Every time a writer sends a message, he or she does so from a particular place. Whether that person is writing at a desk, talking on a cell phone, preaching from a pulpit, speaking from a podium, typing on a laptop, or skywriting in a plane, both the message itself and its means of delivery are influenced by that specific place.

The 2014 Nobel Peace Prize awardee Malala Yousafzai began life in rural Pakistan, where she studied at a school run by her father. She loved school—the learning, the friendships, the sports. But when the Taliban government took over, life in the Swat Valley changed drastically and for the worse. By 2007, education and shopping were banned for girls and women, while television watching and music were banned for everyone. Suddenly, women and girls were expected to wear burqas (long, loose garments that cover the entire body and feet).

Despite the bans and the physical danger to her and her family, Malala recognized a rhetorical opportunity, one that invited her words on the problem of repression. She began speaking about education rights as early as 2008, accompanying her father to local civic groups. Soon, she was "discovered" by the BBC. A representative of BBC Urdu (the official language of Pakistan) asked if she would be willing to blog anonymously about her life—about violence and politics—under the Taliban. With her parents' permission, she agreed, writing out her thoughts by hand and passing them off to a BBC reporter who scanned and e-mailed them to the BBC offices. Malala was eleven years old when she began writing a diary for BBC Urdu.

> MindTap® Read, highlight, and take notes online.

BBC Blog Entries

I AM AFRAID—3 JANUARY 2009

"I had a terrible dream yesterday with military helicopters and the Taliban. I have had such dreams since the launch of the military operation in Swat. I was afraid going to school because the Taliban had issued an edict banning all girls from attending schools. Only 11 students attended the class out of 27. The number decreased because of Taliban's edict.

On my way from school to home I heard a man saying 'I will kill you'. I hastened my pace . . . to my utter relief he was talking on his mobile and must have been threatening someone else over the phone."

INTERRUPTED SLEEP—15 JANUARY 2009

"The night was filled with the noise of artillery fire and I woke up three times. But since there was no school I got up later at 10 a.m. Afterwards, my friend came over and we discussed our homework. Today is the last day before the Taliban's edict comes into effect, and my friend was discussing homework as if nothing out of the ordinary had happened.

"Today, I also read my diary written for the BBC in Urdu. My mother liked my pen name Gul Makai. I also like the name because my real name means 'grief stricken'."

ACTIVITY: Analyzing the Rhetorical Situation

Malala's Blog

1. If the purpose is to raise awareness for girls' education, what, exactly, is the rhetorical opportunity?
2. Who is the rhetorical audience? Who can actually help bring about this change? Who will be affected by such a change?
3. What means were available to Malala from her place in rural Pakistan to get her message to reach her rhetorical audience?
4. How did Malala use her physical place to her advantage in making her case for girls' education in rural Pakistan?

The Available Means Include the Rhetorical Elements of the Message Itself

When writers and speakers purposefully compose messages for their intended audience, they consider how best to appeal to the interests and values of that audience. To do so, writers and speakers turn to three persuasive strategies, which are referred to as the **rhetorical appeals** of ethos, logos, and pathos. The use of these appeals is balanced in most successful messages, for to exaggerate any one of the three is to risk losing the audience and thereby fail to achieve the rhetorical purpose.

rhetorical appeals the strategies established by ancient Greeks as the foundation for persuasion: ethos (the writer's credibility), logos (the good reasons of the argument), and pathos (the emotional connection with the audience)

Ethos

Writers and speakers can leverage the available means in different ways. First of all, when you compose your own message for a specific audience, you will also need to keep in mind exactly how you will come across to your audience, how you can assure them that you have their best interests in mind. Often this includes establishing common ground with the interests of your audience in order to get that audience to listen. **Ethos** is the ethical appeal of the writer's credibility, goodwill, and trustworthiness. Will the audience find the writer believable? Does the speaker or writer establish **common ground**, a belief or value that provides the basis of agreement? By calibrating the tone of your response, you can also control the attitude you project to your intended audience.

ethos the ethical appeal of the writer's credibility, goodwill, and trustworthiness

common ground a belief or value shared by the writer and audience that provides the basis for agreement

Logos

Logos is an appeal to reason or logic. When you shape your message, you will need to provide good reasons that are supported by evidence that connect coherently to your claim. In other words, does the evidence support the claim you are making about a problem or issue? **Evidence** includes testimonials and anecdotes, statistics, facts, and expert opinions. The rhetorical situation guides you in determining what structure and evidence will be most effective. As you shape your response, what stories do you tell, what examples do you use, and what facts and figures do you use to establish logos? Statistics and facts might be used more extensively in a position argument than in a profile, where testimonials and anecdotes prove the point. You are likely to use examples to make your point in an evaluation, and possibly relate an extended anecdote (or story) about a particular person or situation in a memoir. A cause-and-consequence structure might be used to support the logic of your position argument. (See

pages 270–272 CHAPTER 14, CAUSE-AND-EFFECT ANALYSIS, FOR MORE ON USING THIS RHETORICAL METHOD OF DEVELOPMENT.) You will want the logos of your response to support

logos an appeal to the audience's reason through the logical construction of the argument

your ethos by making a positive impression with the evidence you deliver and demonstrating that you are both well informed and fair-minded.

evidence support for your claim that includes testimonials and anecdotes, statistics, facts, and expert opinions

Pathos

Evidence alone is not always enough, however. Human beings are not always persuaded to believe or act in a certain way based exclusively on facts or only on what can be proved. Using the available means of persuasion also means making an authentic emotional connection with your audience. **Pathos** is the emotional appeal of language and examples that stir the audience's feelings (within a reasonable limit). When you appeal to emotion, you are appealing to your audience's sympathy and empathy, which means you will need a clear understanding of the beliefs and values of your intended audience.

pathos an authentic emotional connection with the audience

MindTap® Read, highlight, and take notes online.

Ain't I a Woman?

SOJOURNER TRUTH

As you think through the available means of persuasion, consider the following passage from a speech that former slave Sojourner Truth (born Isabella Baumfree, 1787–1883) delivered at the 1851 Women's Rights Convention in Akron, Ohio. Truth's speech provides a useful textual

context for examining the available means of persuasion. Truth used the example of her own hardworking life to establish her authority as a woman just as suited for voting rights as any man. And for evidence to support her argument, Truth wisely went straight to the Bible, which served not only as the ultimate authority but also as the highest form of evidence for all her listeners, whether they were Northern or Southern, black or white, male or female, educated or uneducated. Although Truth's 1851 speech circulated in at least four versions, all of them recorded by white people, no version of her speech has appeared in **Standardized English**, the style of writing and speaking expected in most academic and business settings.

Library of Congress

Sojourner Truth, whose 1851 speech survives as an example of the available means of persuasion skillfully used.

Well, children, where there is so much racket there must be something out of kilter. I think that 'twixt the Negroes of the South and the women of the North, all talking about rights, the white men will be in a fix pretty soon. But what's all this here talking about?

Standardized English a uniform style of grammar, spelling, vocabulary, and pronunciation that is well established as acceptable for educated and professional language

That man over there says that women need to be helped into carriages and lifted over ditches, and to have the best place everywhere. Nobody ever helps me into carriages, or over mud puddles, or gives me any best place! And ain't I a woman? Look at me! Look at my arm! I could have ploughed and planted, and gathered into barns, and no man could head me! And ain't I a woman? I could work as much and eat as much as a man—when I could get it—and bear the lash as well! And ain't I a woman? I have borne thirteen children, and seen them most all sold off to slavery, and when I cried out with my mother's grief, none but Jesus heard me! And ain't I a woman?

Then they talk about this thing in the head; what's this they call it? ["Intellect," somebody whispers.] That's it, honey. What's that got to do with women's rights or Negros' rights? If my cup won't hold but a pint, and yours holds a quart, wouldn't you be mean not to let me have my little half measure-full?

Then that little man in black back there, he says women can't have as much rights as men, 'cause Christ wasn't a woman! Where did your Christ come from? Where did your Christ come from? From God and a woman! Man had nothing to do with Him.

If the first woman God ever made was strong enough to turn the world upside down all alone, these women together ought to be able to turn it back, and get it right side up again! And now they is asking to do it, the men better let them.

Obliged to you for hearing me, and now old Sojourner ain't got nothing more to say.

ACTIVITY: Analyzing the Rhetorical Situation
Rhetorical Appeals

Ethos, logos, and pathos are often distributed among three sections of any piece of powerful writing, with ethos emphasized in the introduction, logos throughout the body, and pathos in the conclusion—appearing separately and in richly overlapping forms. Reread "Ain't I a Woman?" to identify Truth's use of the rhetorical appeals as available means of persuasion.

1. A speaker in Truth's position (black, female, uneducated) had to devote most of her words to establishing her ethos; after all, she needed to be heard and believed as the black woman she was. In her opening paragraphs, Truth describes the struggle for women's rights as she sees it. How does this description help establish her ethos?

2. How does her first paragraph establish common ground with the white women in her audience? What is their basis of agreement?

3. What is her purpose in demonstrating her goodwill toward her audience, her good sense and knowledge of the subject at hand, and her good character?

4. Like many successful speakers, Truth spends the body of her speech emphasizing logos, the shape of her reasoning, particularly her response to arguments against women's rights. Paraphrase in one sentence the logic of her argument.

5. In the closing sentence of her speech, how does her expression of gratitude for being allowed to speak emphasize pathos?

The Available Means Deliver a Message in a Genre and Medium That Reach the Audience

The genres and media of delivery people choose for their message—video, audio, petition, concert, debate, speech, lecture, phone call, e-mail, and so on—reflect the specific ways they take advantage of the available means.

For example, Malala Yousafzai took advantage of the available means of blogging to reach an audience beyond her place in rural Pakistan. Sojourner Truth, knowing that she wanted to appear at the Women's Rights Convention, used the available means of an oral genre, a speech, to reach her rhetorical audience of educated white Northerners, mostly women. Only these women could help Truth bring about the change that was women's rights. It was important that they realize the importance of women's rights for black women as well as for white women like themselves. To enhance the oral medium of delivery, Truth emphasized her able body, pulling up her sleeve to show her bare arm and her developed muscle, a daring embodiment of rhetorical prowess for anyone, especially for a woman.

The following efforts of the Amethyst Initiative exemplify a similarly fitting response to a serious problem.

Figure 2.1 *This MADD35 web page emphasizes the little-known statistics about the dangers of underage drinking.*

Given the nationwide concern about underage drinking, especially binge drinking, college and university administrators have joined Mothers Against Drunk Driving (MADD), the Center on Alcohol Marketing and Youth (CAMY), and other concerned groups in an effort to combat this national health concern. Statistics such as those on the MADD35 website (Figure 2.1) underscore the dangers that the administrators want to address. In addressing the problem, those administrators have come to rely on yet another genre and medium to reach a broad audience: the petition. Representing the Amethyst Initiative (from the ancient Greek *a methustos*, or "not intoxicated"), these administrators hope their petition will spark a sustained, national conversation on underage drinking. With its long and rich history, the petition, a written request (or demand), usually signed by many people, can work almost like a pledge on the part of the signees. Its key characteristics include

- an explicit statement of the problem,
- essential background information,
- a statement of what should be done to resolve the problem,
- a named audience who can initiate change (that is, a rhetorical audience),
- a request for signatures or support, and
- strategic delivery of the message, often accompanied by some kind of publicity.

Every petition is a response to a rhetorical opportunity for change that calls for spreading the effort more widely. Those who read and sign the petition will likely understand the public nature of the petition because they have encountered that genre before. In other words, the genre has created expectations in readers.

In addition to comprising a fitting response to the problem at hand, the Amethyst Initiative's statement has been delivered through an easily accessed medium that immediately reaches a wide audience: the World Wide Web. College administrators and faculty, parents and organizations, students and citizens alike can read the online document, or they can download and print a PDF version of the statement. But not all who read the statement are invited to sign it. At the bottom of the petition, the writers clearly indicate their rhetorical audience: *Currently, membership in the Amethyst Initiative is limited to college and university presidents and chancellors. If you are not a president or chancellor, but would like to become part of this larger effort, please sign up here.* The sentence ends with a link to the website of a broader organization called Choose Responsibility. A rhetorical audience is not only capable of being influenced by the message but also capable of acting on it or influencing others to do so. The writers of the Amethyst Initiative's statement realize that college and university presidents and chancellors are those most capable of starting campuswide conversations about policies that can encourage responsible alcohol use, and so they chose this group as their rhetorical audience.

MindTap® Read, highlight, and take notes online.

Persuasion

It's Time to Rethink the Drinking Age

THE AMETHYST INITIATIVE

In 1984 Congress passed the National Minimum Drinking Age Act, which imposed a penalty of 10% of a state's federal highway appropriation on any state setting its drinking age lower than 21.

Twenty-four years later, our experience as college and university presidents convinces us that . . .

Twenty-one is not working

A culture of dangerous, clandestine "binge-drinking"—often conducted off-campus—has developed.

Alcohol education that mandates abstinence as the only legal option has not resulted in significant constructive behavioral change among our students.

Adults under 21 are deemed capable of voting, signing contracts, serving on juries and enlisting in the military, but are told they are not mature enough to have a beer.

By choosing to use fake IDs, students make ethical compromises that erode respect for the law.

One means available to the Amethyst Initiative for creating a fitting response is this website.

How many times must we relearn the lessons of Prohibition?

We call upon our elected officials:

> To support an informed and dispassionate public debate over the effects of the 21-year-old drinking age.
>
> To consider whether the 10% highway fund "incentive" encourages or inhibits that debate.
>
> To invite new ideas about the best ways to prepare young adults to make responsible decisions about alcohol.

We pledge ourselves and our institutions to playing a vigorous, constructive role as these critical discussions unfold.

Please add my signature to this statement:

Name _____

Signature _____

Institution _____

ACTIVITY: Analyzing the Rhetorical Situation
A Fitting Response

For each of the following problems, decide whether you could shape a response that fulfills the three requirements for being fitting: language that suits the problem, is delivered in an appropriate medium, and reaches the intended audience. Be prepared to share your answers with the rest of the class.

1. Consider a problem that you are currently experiencing. Consider, too, who could resolve or help you resolve that problem.
2. Your English instructor has announced that she must use the entire range of grades. Less than 50 percent of your class can receive an A.
3. The person you are dating wants to get engaged. But you do not.
4. Your history instructor has assigned a research paper that is due on the same day as your biology midterm.
5. After taking your LSATs, you receive mailings from more than twenty law schools.
6. In order to obtain a green card (indicating U.S. permanent resident status), your Romanian friend wants to arrange a fraudulent American marriage.

◎ RESOURCES AND CONSTRAINTS

Persuasive writers know that no two situations are ever exactly the same. In each situation, you will need to evaluate what **resources (advantages)** you have to effect change and what **constraints (limitations)** you might have to overcome to achieve your purpose. The advantages you have—as well as the limitations you face—are part of any rhetorical situation and affect the rhetorical choices you are able to make to achieve your purpose.

As a writer in an academic setting, you are no doubt aware that many of your rhetorical situations share various constraints. For instance, an academic research assignment usually involves some specifications from an instructor. Following are some common constraints for such writing assignments:

- *Expertise*. As a student, you rely to some degree on documenting what others have said in order to build credibility.
- *Geography*. Although the Internet gives researchers unprecedented access to materials not available locally, most students are still somewhat constrained by what is close at hand.
- *Time*. In most cases, your research will be subject to a time limit. Your readers—whether they are instructors, colleagues, or other decision makers—need to see your research before it goes out of date and before the deadline to make a decision (about what action to take or what grade to assign) has passed.

Just as in the case of Malala Yousafzai and Sojourner Truth, constraints such as these can, however, suggest resources. What primary documents might you have access to in your geographical location? What unique opportunities do you have for reaching your audience that a recognized expert might not have? Given that you are just learning about the topic, might you be more respectful of and engaged with the research of others? Might working within an assigned time frame provide motivation? In every rhetorical situation, there will be advantages (given your resources) and limitations (given your constraints).

Consider the limitations faced by Malala Yousafzai, Sojourner Truth, and the Amethyst Initiative and how they turned these into advantages through the rhetorical choices they made. For example, Sojourner Truth was the only black person in attendance at the 1851 conference. Truth had been listening carefully to the speeches, many of which denounced the rights of women. She delivered her speech at a time when white women were rarely permitted to speak in public, especially to a "promiscuous assembly," one that included both

resources (advantages) in rhetoric, the means needed to effect change in an audience

constraints (limitations) the obstacles a writer has to overcome to reach and perhaps persuade an audience men and women. Truth was constrained by being illiterate, black, and a woman, and she knew her spoken ideas would be met with resistance if not outright objection. Some of her constraints, however, proved to be her richest resources. Truth's use of dialect, for example, authenticated her as an uneducated former slave. Her not being an educated white "lady" permitted her to ascend the platform and address the audience.

✈ ASSIGNMENT: WRITING A RHETORICAL ANALYSIS

MindTap® Request help and feedback from a tutor. If required, participate in peer review, submit your paper for a grade, and view instructor comments online.

Choose a selection for rhetorical analysis that meets the following criteria.

- Is the text responding to an opportunity to make a change through verbal (spoken or written) or visual language?
- What is the rhetorical opportunity for change?
- How is it identified?
- Is the response verbal or visual?

After you have selected a text, read it carefully, keeping in mind that *the ultimate goal of a rhetorical analysis is twofold: (1) to analyze how well the rhetorical elements work together to create a fitting response, and (2) to assess the overall effectiveness of that response.* Then, write answers to the following questions, citing material from the text or visual itself to support each answer:

Are the available means anchored to the writer's place?

1. Who created the text? What credentials or expertise does that person or group have? Why is the creator of the text engaged with this opportunity? Is this an opportunity that can be modified through language? What opinions or biases did the person or group bring to the text?
2. What is the place (physical, social, academic, economic, and so on) from which the creator of the text forms and sends the response? What are the resources of that place? What are its constraints (or limitations)?
3. Who is the audience for the message? What relationship is the creator of the text trying to establish with the audience? What opinions or biases might the audience hold? How might the audience feel about this rhetorical opportunity? And, most

important, can this audience modify or help bring about a modification of the rhetorical opportunity? How?

Do the available means include the rhetorical elements of the message itself?

1. Identify the rhetorical elements of the message itself. In other words, where and how does the person or group employ the rhetorical appeals of ethos, pathos, and logos? How are credentials, goodwill, or good sense evoked to establish ethos? How is evidence (examples, statistics, data, and so forth) used to establish logos? And how is an emotional connection created to establish pathos? Keep in mind that the rhetorical appeals can sometimes overlap.
2. What kind of language does the creator of the text use? Is it plain or specialized, slang or formal? How does the choice of language reveal how the person or group views the intended audience?

Do the available means deliver a message in a genre and medium that reaches the audience?

1. Is the intended audience for the text a rhetorical audience? Draw on evidence from the text to support your answer.
2. If the audience is a rhetorical one, what can it do to resolve the problem?
3. Does the response address and fit the rhetorical opportunity? How exactly? If not, how might the response be reshaped so that it does fit?
4. Is the response delivered in an appropriate medium that reaches its intended audience? Why is that medium appropriate? Or how could it be adjusted to be appropriate?
5. Can you think of other responses to similar rhetorical situations? What genre is commonly used? Does the creator of this text use that genre? If not, what is the effect of going against an audience's expectations?

Now that you have carefully read the text and answered all of the questions, you are ready to write your rhetorical analysis. How does your analysis of the use of the available means reveal

1. *How well the rhetorical elements work together to create a fitting response to an opportunity for change?*
2. *How effective the response is?*

As you begin, search your answers for an idea that can serve as your claim or thesis. For example, you might focus on the declared goal—if there is one—of the creator of the text and whether it has been achieved. You might assess how successfully that creator has identified the rhetorical audience, shaped a fitting response, or employed

(continued)

the best available means. Or you might focus on the use of the rhetorical appeals and the overall success of their use. Whether or not you agree with the text is beside the point. Your job is to analyze in an essay how and how well the text's creator has accomplished the purpose for that text.

MindTap® Reflect on your writing process, practice skills that you have learned in this chapter, and receive automatic feedback.

The Writer as Reader

Many people consider writing an *active* intellectual activity and reading a *passive* one. But that is not the case. As you know well, reading in college can be, well, hard work. College-level reading demands that you up your game in terms of expanding your vocabulary, building background information, and becoming more familiar with various genres and situations. For instance, when you enter the field of psychology, you may feel pounded by all the new vocabulary (often technical terms) you need to learn: *anxiety, attachment disorder, cohort, disregulation, egocentric, stimming, threshold.* Of course, turning to a dictionary always helps, but so does figuring out how those terms are used in context, as does checking for a glossary of specific terms you need to know.

College-level reading also demands that you familiarize yourself with different genres, from textbooks, online supplements, and trade (or popular) books to scientific reports, literature reviews (a summary of scholarly articles on a particular topic), and editorials (opinion pieces). Each of these academic genres—and many others that you will encounter—requires different reading strategies. For instance, you will read essay exam questions much more strategically (knowing how best to respond efficiently and effectively) than you might read a literature review (understanding what various experts are contributing to the scholarly conversation).

Just as various genres ask you to take a different role as reader, different rhetorical situations ask you to do the same thing, whether you are reading

© Michaeljung/Shutterstock.com

When you read rhetorically, you read purposefully, actively analyzing the writer's purpose and choice of genre, the key parts of the text itself, and your own preparation and purpose for reading.

for information or reading critically. You will be asked to read opinions with which you readily agree (on abortion, free speech, right-to-carry laws, climate change, ISIS, or the president) and those with which you do not. Thus, you will often be expected to read with Democrats and Republicans, with liberals and conservatives, with internationals and Americans, with feminists, neuro-diverse and sexually diverse people, with atheists and with religious fundamentalists. In short, college-level reading asks that you be rhetorically nimble, willing and able to participate in the complex multitude of reading situations.

READING STRATEGIES

When you read actively, you are using your rhetorical skills, taking into consideration who composed the message, the purpose of the message, and your role as reader (as audience). The best of critical readers follow a **reading process**, a series of steps much like the ones you employ when you write.

reading process
series of steps, including previewing, skimming, reading, and annotating

1. **Preview** You begin by previewing the entire text to gauge the time and expertise necessary to read it. You might examine the title, the table of contents (or headings), and any follow-up questions. Your goal at this

point is to estimate your familiarity with the vocabulary, content, and genre of the reading itself—in other words, what the reading demands of you.

2. **Skim** While you skim, stay alert for the author's major points, pausing to read over any information about the author and examine any visuals that accompany the text. Your goal is to learn what you can about the author of the text (what the author's relationship is to the subject matter), its audience and purpose (where the text originally appeared—and for whom), and the rhetorical context in which it was written (what rhetorical opportunity the author was addressing).

3. **Read** Next, you will read quickly for comprehension, to glean content information while you follow the author's line of reasoning. At this point, your goal is to consider the line of reasoning, the logic (logos) of the message, the major claim, and supporting information. At the same time, you will look up vocabulary, mark places you do not understand, and highlight major points.

4. **Annotate** Finally, after skimming and reading, you will pass through the text once again, this time reading deliberately and critically for analysis. You will annotate the margins with questions and mark contradictory information, unsupported reasoning, unacknowledged assumptions,

Using different methods of annotation, we all try to mark important passages and indicate our questions and responses.

omitted information, and emotional connection or manipulation. You may find yourself wanting to respond to or question the author's important points, as though you were carrying on a conversation. To do so, you can use a pen, sticky notes, or an online annotation tool.

The Believing and Doubting Game

One strategy to help you think about what you read is to play the **Believing and Doubting Game**, which Peter Elbow proposes in *Writing Without Teachers*. When you withhold any kind of judgment as you read, you are playing the "Believing Game." By wanting to believe what the author is saying, you are better able to understand the author's message, ideas, and reasoning. Playing the "Doubting Game," on the other hand, demands that you read critically, asking questions and challenging the author as you read. Elbow advocates a balanced approach—one that uses "believing" as well as "doubting"—in college reading.

Believing and Doubting Game strategy that includes both reading while believing the writer (and in so doing understanding the writer's message better) and reading while doubting the writer (and in so doing finding the gaps and questions that emerge from the selection)

Reading Rhetorically

As you annotate the text, you will ask questions that help you locate and respond to the specific features of the rhetorical situation: the writer's opportunity to propose change, the purpose of and audience of the message, the genre shaping the message. As you consider the context of the message, you will also think about the writer's place (where the writer is "coming from") and how that place influences the writer's stance toward the topic and you, the audience. Your challenge is to identify the rhetorical elements used to persuade you to believe the message and perhaps act on it, and evaluate the effectiveness of the delivery of the text in terms of genre and medium.

Reading for the writer's place

Questions about the writer's place provide information about the author that enriches your understanding of the message. You want to know as much as possible about the author so you can consider how social, educational, historical, or cultural influences affected the author's message. What rhetorical opportunity called for the author's use of specific words or visuals? Who is the author writing to? If not readily available, you can usually find out about the author's educational background, personal experiences, and stance (position or attitude) toward the topic by conducting some quick online research.

Reading for rhetorical elements

To understand the author's argument, you will need to identify the author's thesis. What claim is the author making about the topic? Follow your annotations to map your agreements, disagreements, and questions with the author's line of reasoning. Focus on those specific points as you develop your response. You will also attend to the author's use of the available means of persuasion: how the rhetorical appeals of ethos, logos, and pathos have been established (or not), especially how well the author makes an authentic connection with the audience and whether the evidence adequately supports the reasons the author employs to support and develop that claim.

Reading for genre and medium

Because we enjoy so many ways of communicating—visually, verbally, digitally, in print, and vocally—we rarely stop to consider why we are choosing a particular medium. We just use it. As you annotate the text, however, you need to ask questions about the author's success in using the key characteristics of the chosen genre to make a particular point, or the decision to use a particular medium to deliver his or her message. What are the advantages to these choices? Are there disadvantages?

Hone your skills as an active, informed reader and use these reading strategies—one at a time—to read the following essay rhetorically, considering the elements of the rhetorical situation.

1. First, preview the essay quickly. For example, what does the title tell you about the topic? What knowledge of autism did you bring to the essay? In one sentence, what do you expect to learn from this article?
2. Then, skim the essay. Who is the author, and what is his relationship to the subject matter? Why did the author write the article, and for whom? Write down five key words that indicate the author's major points in the article.
3. Now, read the essay, marking places you do not understand. Write out the major claim and some supporting information.
4. Finally, annotate the essay as if you were having a conversation with the text, asking questions, checking for contradictory information or unsupported points, and confirming assertions. You can write in the margins or on sticky notes, or if you are reading online, use the "comment" feature.

MindTap® Read, highlight, and take notes online.

Uniquely Human: A Different Way of Seeing Autism [Animated Movies and Social Development]

BARRY M. PRIZANT

© Barry Prizant

Professor, scholar, consultant, and researcher, Barry M. Prizant has, for forty years, supported children and adults with Autistic Spectrum Disorder (ASD) and others who have related developmental disabilities. He also works closely with their families, teachers, therapists, and caretakers. An internationally known and widely published scholar-researcher, Prizant recently ventured into another kind of writing, writing aimed at a wider audience. The following essay is taken from Uniquely Human: A Different Way of Seeing Autism, *in which he argues that people with autism use all their human traits but in ways different from their neurotypical counterparts (*neurotypical *is preferred over the word* normal *by Prizant and others to describe those whose neurological development and behavior are more typical). Echolalia, the repetition of speech by a child learning to talk, is one such human trait often intensified in children with autism. Rather than focusing on the perceived deficits of people with ASD, however, Prizant stresses the value of recognizing their uniqueness, potential, and humanness.*

My simple advice: Listen, observe, and ask "Why?"

When parents, teachers, and caring professionals do that—when they pay close attention to words and gestures and context—they often understand intuitively that **echolalia** is part of the process of learning to communicate. I watched that happen in Namir, a little boy I first met when he was two and a half and captivated by Disney videos.

echolalia repeating what has just been said as if an "echo"

That's a common theme in the children with whom I have worked. Animated movies of all kinds hold a particular fascination for children on the autism spectrum. . . . Why? Many children find the predictability and consistency of animated characters (as well as the music) comforting, a welcome contrast to the unpredictable nature of real people in everyday situations. . . . And repetitive viewings engender a reassuring sense of familiarity and mastery.

Many parents express concern that their children are spending too much time focusing on *The Lion King* or *Shrek,* worried that this is harmful to their development . . . only serving to provide more fodder . . . for more useless phrases for children to echo.

I learned from Namir and his parents to take a longer perspective, a more nuanced view. As a three-year-old, Namir seemed lost in Disney films. Much of what came out of his mouth consisted of snippets from *Peter Pan*, his favorite. Instead of using language to interact with other people, he would repeat lines from the movie to himself, sometimes seeming oblivious to the real human beings surrounding him.

Others might have tried to dissuade him by reacting with demands to stop using such speech, convinced that this "meaningless parroting" was hindering his progress. Instead Namir's parents listened to him—and joined him. They bought *Peter Pan* action figures and interacted with him as he acted out imaginary scenes with the toys. They honored his interest and supported his engagement, so that Namir felt listened to and respected.

In time his play progressed. He showed increasing understanding of what he was saying. He was still using the phrases he had picked up from *Peter Pan*, but he found ways to use the Disney dialogues in their appropriate social context.

. . .

By encouraging his unique efforts to communicate, Namir's parents dramatically aided his development. Between preschool and elementary school, he transformed from a boy who seemed lost in a world of random scripting and playing alone to an interactive and social little boy.

Prizant, Barry M. *Uniquely Human: A Different Way of Seeing Autism.* New York: Simon & Schuster, 2015. 50–52. © Childhood Communication Services, Inc.

ACTIVITY: Analyzing the Rhetorical Situation
"Uniquely Human"

1. To what opportunity is the author responding?
2. Who is the audience for his response? In other words, what was the work's original purpose? What is his main point? What does the author want you to do with the information?
3. Do you find the author a trustworthy authority on this topic? How does he establish his credibility (ethos)? What does the author know about these issues?
4. How does the author employ logic and reason (logos) to structure his essay? What evidence does the author use to support his point? Do you find his reasons convincing? Does he provide sufficient evidence to persuade you? What are the overall strengths and weaknesses of the essay Prizant presents?
5. Does the author make an authentic emotional connection (pathos) with his audience?
6. How effective is his choice of a mix of genres—profile, argument, evaluation—and the use of print to deliver his message? How might he use other media to effectively deliver his message?

⦿ SUMMARY

summary a type of writing that condenses a selection to its main points

abstract brief objective summary of an article, especially used in writing papers for the social sciences

Now that you have carefully read the text and answered all of the questions, try to summarize the essay. A **summary** condenses the main points of a piece to represent its message objectively. Summary writing forces you to engage with the text closely, enhances your memory of it, and helps you understand it. When writing a summary, it is crucial that you understand the hierarchy of information in the original text, identifying the thesis statement, the major points, the supporting evidence and details, and the concluding thoughts. When you are reading for information, you are playing the Believing Game. Whether or not you actually agree with the text is beside the point. In your summary, you will show that you have understood the main point of Prizant's essay. Summaries are short—but they are powerful. In college, you will find summaries (sometimes referred to as **abstracts**) at the beginning of research articles, in conference programs, and on book jackets. You will also be required to write them. The following summary is one example of how to condense the Prizant essay into one paragraph, taking care to include information from the introduction, the body, and the conclusion to identify his thesis and supporting evidence to show a full understanding of Prizant's argument.

Thesis statement.

A story about Namir illustrates the thesis.

The author uses description to emphasize his point.

Prizant uses cause-and-consequence analysis, based on his expert knowledge, to support the thesis.

More support for the value of echolalia as a natural consequence of watching animated videos.

1

Echolalia, so common in the lives of people with autism, is part of the process of learning to communicate. When young children are supported in this practice, the results of their echolalia can be gratifying. The example of Namir, whom Prizant met as a little boy, serves as a case in point. Namir was captivated by Disney videos. Like many people with autism, Namir took comfort in the predictability, consistency, and unmistakable good or evil of animated characters (unlike the unpredictable nature of real people). Repetitive viewings of these videos provided sentences and phrases for him to echo, a phenomenon called echolalia. •Namir's parents joined him in his •····The use of process analysis and narration to illustrate a point.

echolalia, buying *Peter Pan* action figures to interact with their son as

they all played out scenes. Such encouragement—and faith in

Namir—aided his development. •He showed increasing understanding •····The author uses evidence to support the claim in his thesis statement.

of what he was saying, finding ways to use the Disney dialogues in

their appropriate social and educational contexts and connecting with

others until he became an interactive and social boy who could speak,

research, and write.

Now condense the essay into one sentence. The following is a sample of a one-sentence summary of Prizant's essay.

The practice of echolalia can contribute to the language and social

skills of children with autism.

CRITICAL RESPONSE

When you read critically, you show that you know how to play the Doubting Game, questioning, agreeing, and talking back to the text. You may be in full agreement with the author, but you are, nevertheless, nudging and prodding the text in order to reveal the rhetorical situation from which it was composed, sent, and received:

- when, where, and how the rhetorical exchange takes place;
- the writer's credibility;

- the appropriateness of the message in terms of both content and delivery; and
- the connection the writer makes with the audience.

critical response a reaction in writing to a text that explains why you agree or disagree with the text

Whether you are reading or writing, your task in a **critical response** is to summarize the main point of the work and then explain your reaction to it. *Critical* does not mean negative. It does mean prioritizing your comments, establishing patterns in the text, and remaining civil if not positive. In a critical response you need to react to the text—explaining why you agree or disagree (wholly or partly) with a particular point the text is making—but it is more important to support your reaction with strong reasons based on the evidence from the text itself than it is to agree or disagree. Include the title of the work, anchor your response in a thesis statement that shows how or why you think the author got it right—or wrong—and then support that thesis with evidence from the original text itself. A sample thesis for a critical response to the Prizant essay follows.

Example of critical response thesis that disagrees with Prizant

> Barry Prizant's unrealistic view on autism grows out of his experience as a consultant who sees these children only on a part-time—not a full-time—basis.

Example of critical response thesis that agrees with Prizant

> Barry Prizant's essay "Uniquely Human: A Different Way of Seeing Autism" is overdue. Looking at individuals on the Autism Spectrum as "sick" undermines their treatment and dehumanizes those who have autism.

ANALYSIS AND SYNTHESIS

Your role as a college-level reader (and writer) includes understanding, interpreting, contextualizing, questioning, and analyzing the material you read, some of it complex, challenging, even contradictory. Two of the most valuable intellectual skills you can develop are analysis and synthesis, which will sustain you throughout college—and beyond. You conduct **analysis** when you break something down into its constituent parts or elements, critically examining each part so that you understand it, just as you did when you annotated the Prizant essay. You use analytical skills when you determine the main point in a summary and as you respond to a text, both by analyzing the rhetorical situation and by determining how well the writer has used the available means of persuasion. Your analysis will provide a reliable basis of discussion or interpretation. **Synthesis,** you will be happy to know, is a natural outgrowth of analysis. With synthesis, you combine those separate, already analyzed parts or ideas into a coherent whole, creatively producing a new thesis, theory, or understanding. Both of these skills are valuable, with analysis preparing you to conduct synthesis, and synthesis preparing you to research, discuss, converse, and interpret both responsibly and knowledgeably.

analysis a breaking down of a text into its constituent parts accompanied by a critical examination of the ways the text responds to the rhetorical situation

synthesis an examination of how the individual parts of a text or different points of view from different texts fit together and diverge to bring a new perspective to the whole work

Managing the Complexities of Reading

No longer are you learning by rote or by memorization. In the process of reading deeply and widely you very often encounter conflicting information, wildly different viewpoints about an issue. Very often, your reading for class or for a research project requires that you encounter conflicting information. Perhaps two authors disagree, perhaps one study contradicts another, or perhaps your own experience provides evidence counter to another author's thesis. You may also have found flaws in the reasoning or gaps in the evidence. Look closely at these areas of complex tension, because they indicate your growing ability to read critically and to analyze an issue from many dimensions—historically, contextually, socially, politically, personally. Recognizing such complexity as you read also signals your ability to imagine alternative solutions, approaches, and opinions. You have moved beyond the simplistic "right-or-wrong" thinking and are moving into the complex world of more adult problem solving. Such complex tension can provide a rhetorical opportunity and a purpose for your reading and your writing. It may also find its way into your thesis statement, surely into the body of your argument. One thing is for certain: when your own audience realizes that you have considered multiple viewpoints, including theirs, they are more likely to consider your argument.

Reading to Synthesize Ideas

Twentieth-century rhetorician Kenneth Burke calls our need to engage with others the "unending conversation," urging each of us to "put in our oar":

> **Imagine that you enter a parlor. You come late. When you arrive, others have long preceded you, and they are engaged in a heated discussion, a discussion too heated for them to pause and tell you exactly what it is about. . . . You listen for a while, until you decide that you have caught the tenor of the argument; then you put in your oar.**
>
> —*The Philosophy of Literary Form*, pp. 110–11

Writers are "putting in their oars" when they enter an ongoing "conversation" on a topic. Sometimes you may know a fair amount about the topic that you have been asked to examine, but, chances are, you will encounter new topics in college that you do not know much about yet. In those instances when you are asked to read just one author's contribution to a conversation, it helps to familiarize yourself with what others have said.

The synthesis question

The best synthesis essays often grow out of an author's discomfort with the current positions on the topic. Such discomfort serves as a rhetorical opportunity, a problem for the author to address or resolve. Often, that discomfort is translated into a **synthesis (or critical) question,** one question that directs, focuses, and launches your research. Prizant, for instance, asks how people with autism might best be treated.

synthesis (or critical) question the question that directs, focuses, and launches your research

> **Here is my central message: The behavior of people with autism isn't random, deviant, or bizarre, as many professionals have called it for decades. These children don't come from Mars. The things they say aren't—as many professionals still maintain—meaningless or "nonfunctional."**
>
> **Autism isn't an illness. It's a different way of being human. Children with autism aren't sick; they are progressing through developmental stages as we all do. To help them, we don't need to change them or fix them. We need to work to understand them, and then change what *we* do.**
>
> —**Barry Prizant,** *Uniquely Human*

The synthesis process

Critical analysis and synthesis—as reading and writing strategies as well as intellectual skills—are crucial when you consult various sources. You will

Reading

need to analyze them (their agreements, disagreements, and contradictions), synthesize their research, and then establish your own stance toward the topic. (See also CHAPTER 18: SYNTHESIZING SOURCES: SUMMARY, PARAPHRASE, AND QUOTATION.) Sometimes, your instructor will provide you with a topic. More often, however, you will be expected to come up with a topic of your own, a topic that interests you enough to spend time researching, thinking, and writing about it. The following representative studies offer a set of complex tensions around the vast research on autism. Successful synthesis writing relies on several steps.

pages 322–337

1. Identify a problem to address or resolve.
2. Review the articles and books you have read (the scholarly conversation) pertaining to the problem. Critically analyze and summarize the strongest voices in the conversation.
3. Prepare to enter that conversation with your own view.
4. Offer a synthesis question that quickly turns into a thesis statement as a way to contribute to what has already been said about the topic.
5. Combine ideas from the research you have read and your experiences at the same time you forward your thesis.

Read through the following selections on autism to get a general idea of who the author is, what the author's relation to the topic is, and what the author's main point is. In the first selection, actress Jenny McCarthy describes her response to her son's diagnosis of autism:

> I read everything on that Web site ["Generation Rescue"] and took a leap of faith and said: "I'm going to follow the path of hope, because the medical community is offering none. . . . And I decided to try the first thing that they recommended . . . , which is the gluten-free, casein-free diet. I thought to myself, you know what? It's just wheat, and it's just dairy. I'd called my pediatrician at the time, and he said: "It's a load of garbage. It's not real. It hasn't been studied. It's a waste of time. Why would you do that? It could have nutritional deficiency issues." And I still said to myself: "Well, that sounds like no hope. I think I'll try this way."
>
> And I removed wheat and dairy, and within two weeks, Evan had better eye contact, and he doubled his language. He was saying about two words per sentence, like "Juice, Mama," and he went to "I want juice, Mama," which is huge in our community. It's like we count the words they say in a sentence. So within two weeks I saw a jump. And I went, "Oh, this is the path I'm supposed to be on."
>
> —Jenny McCarthy, *The Path to Hope*

In his memoir about Mary, his long-institutionalized twin, composer Allen Shawn shares his ongoing struggle with her label of autism:

> I am still struggling. . . to grasp the meaning of the terms used in her diagnosis. . . . I also struggle to determine in my own mind where I, as her twin, fit into the picture. . . . Dr. Trombly tries to allay my lifelong guilt about Mary's "brain damage," suggesting that the evidence now conclusively shows that most forms of autism are genetic in origin and not the result of birth trauma or of events occurring after birth. He tells me that Mary's nature was not suddenly impaired by her violent entrance into the world—a violence in which I was an infant participant—but was most probably formed from within, as she herself was forming. . . . "I view autism as a broad heterogeneous category," he says, "with all the colors of the spectrum. I think that people are misled by the idea, commonly presented in the press, that autism is a single disorder whose cause must urgently be discovered. Autism consists of many disorders with many different causes. It is one of two major developmental disorders of childhood."
>
> —Allen Shawn, *Twin*

Working at the scholarly intersection of rhetoric and science studies, Jordynn Jack argues that the way we describe autism plays a significant role in how we see the individuals who have autism:

> [H]ow we speak and write about autism matters in important ways to all concerned. Representations of autism also matter because they tend to support problematic narratives that position it as something to be overcome or beaten, rather than a neurological difference that can be recognized and even celebrated. The autistic individuals who are most often featured in popular rhetoric are those who have "overcome" autism to become successful artists, professors, or performers (such as Temple Grandin, the well-known animal science professor and author) or as autistic savants, characters who are portrayed as "profoundly autistic" but who possess unusual talents, such as the artist Steven Wiltshire or Kim Peek, the man who inspired the character Raymond Babbitt in the film *Rain Man*. In this way, portrayals of autism in popular media echo tendencies in portrayals of people with disabilities more generally. . . . Popular media tend to favor portrayals of individuals who have overcome their disabilities through tremendous force of will, such as the sprinter Oscar Pistorius, who used two prosthetic legs but recorded times rivaling those of top nondisabled sprinters, or geniuses like Stephen Hawking, who has motor neurone disease and uses a wheelchair but has made major scientific discoveries. Disability studies scholars and advocates call such individuals

"super-crips"—people who are celebrated for surmounting disabilities but who do so by creating an impossibly high standard for other people with disabilities.

—**Jordynn Jack,** *Autism and Gender: From Refrigerator Mothers to Computer Geeks*

Read through the preceding perspectives on ASD once again. What, for instance, is McCarthy asking of her audience? What about Shawn and Jack? Reading critically means analyzing the text in order to understand the context in which the author is composing a message. Crucial to that understanding is knowing about the ongoing conversation that the message is entering. After all, few of us can work alone—we converse with others to learn information and to get things done. Either annotate the selections or take notes, answering the following questions.

- What do all the authors have in common?
- What question (or problem) are they each trying to address?
- How is each author's point of view distinctive?
- How do they differ? How do their differences align?
- What resources, expertise, experience, and/or knowledge are these authors leveraging? Or is the lack of any of those features the author's biggest constraint?
- Using your answers from the preceding questions, briefly describe (or synthesize) the various views—and stances—that people have toward autism (or ASD). Share your answer with the rest of the class.
- Now describe the (tentative) position you might take in the scholarly conversation about autism or ASD. Write it out—and share it.

Example of synthesis

Depending on your own experience with autism—as a friend or family member, a physician, a therapist, or a consultant—you may think of it as a curable "disorder," one of the many ways to be human, a tragedy. What everyone agrees on is that people with autism are not neurotypical, yet they can be wonderfully so.

**ASSIGNMENT**

The Synthesis (or Research) Essay

Whether you are reading for a class or for a research project—in literature, history, psychology, or anthropology—you will want to familiarize yourself with what others have said about a topic (the scholarly conversation). (For more on research projects, see PART 4, A GUIDE TO RESEARCH.)

page 279

- Choose two sources on a topic that interests you. What do each of these sources have to say about the topic? Where do they agree—or not?
- Blend (or synthesize) their ideas in order to create a synthesis question, one that responds to the rhetorical opportunity or problem these sources present.
- Create a thesis that shows how these sources are different, what their areas of tension are, and what your position is toward the information in these sources.
- Analyze the rhetorical situation and use of available means of persuasion in these sources.
- Conclude with points of similarity.

MindTap® Reflect on your writing process, practice skills that you have learned in this chapter, and receive automatic feedback.

Rhetorical Success in a Digital World

MindTap® Understand the goals of the chapter and complete a warm-up activity online.

You are called "digital natives," the generation who has always had access to at least a hundred television stations and turned to the World Wide Web for your academic, social, and work needs. Yet, it is just this immersion in an increasingly digital and visual culture that calls for us to pay careful attention to the information we might otherwise simply take for granted. In CHAPTER 2, we discussed the principles of persuasion. Those same principles can be applied to how we read visual representations of information and also how we use **multimedia** (images or visuals, text, audio, and video) in our compositions. In this chapter, then, you will learn to consider how the constituent elements of a multimedia (also referred to as *multimodal*) composition work separately and together to convey a persuasive message.

pages 18–34

multimedia images or visuals, text, audio, and video used in combinations in a composition

 ## THINKING RHETORICALLY ABOUT MULTIMEDIA TEXTS

Multimedia compositions can be as simple as using a flip chart with your speech, and adding tables and graphs to your essay, or as digitally complex as creating websites and PowerPoint presentations that include a range of embedded media. Whether you choose an audio recording, a video, still images, or a written text, your medium or combination of media affects your message and your audience. As you know well, when composing is done in digital environments, the boundaries among the different media begin to blur. For example, a website usually consists at least of images and text working together to create meaning. Many include audio and video as well. Knowing how and when to mix and blur the lines among media is an important rhetorical skill.

All these digital and print technologies offer opportunities for you to enhance your message as well as adapt it for an audience who might not otherwise have access to it. To organize multimedia elements, such as images or sounds, multimedia designers pay attention to the elements of the rhetorical situation—opportunity, audience, purpose—and apply the same rhetorical principles you use when writing an essay or drafting a speech: principles of design, style, persuasion, and delivery. The best composers, whether working with multimedia or a single form, take their rhetorical situation into consideration as they shape a message:

- Who is the source?
- What is the opportunity for change?
- What is the purpose?
- Who is the intended audience, and what is the composer's relationship to the audience?
- Why has the composer chosen this genre or medium?
- How effective is the medium of delivery in reaching the rhetorical audience?

ACTIVITY: Analyzing the Rhetorical Situation
Reading a Visual Text for Rhetorical Opportunity

Whether you are reading an essay, listening to a speech, or looking at a visual, you'll understand the message better if you begin by determining the rhetorical opportunity that calls for specific words or visuals. Very often, the responses you are reading or viewing call for even further responses. Whether your response is spoken, written, or composed visually, its power lies in your understanding of the rhetorical opportunity. Consider the Callout Card here and the ways it addresses the problem of electronic harassment (Figure 4.1). This card may well be an effective response to a rhetorical opportunity for change. Obviously, the sender of "David, wrapped in a towel" does not want to receive visuals that are "naughty," maybe even pornographic. Studying this image and text as a rhetorical response helps you analyze it rhetorically and "read" it more thoroughly than you might have otherwise.

1. *Who composed this message?* Consider what you know or can find out about the groups responsible for the message: the Family Violence Prevention Fund,

Figure 4.1 *This Callout Card, available at Thatsnotcool.com, is a visual response to a rhetorical opportunity.*

Sponsored and co-created by the Family Violence Prevention Fund, the Office on Violence Against Women, and the Ad council.

the Office on Violence Against Women, and the Ad Council for the website Thatsnotcool.com.

2. *What is the rhetorical opportunity that called for the creation of this visual?* Using the information you have compiled in response to the previous questions, identify the opportunity that calls for this visual response.

3. *How does the visual respond to the opportunity?* What message does this visual send to viewers? How might this visual work to address the problem of electronic harassment? It might help to keep in mind that Callout Cards can also be shared through e-mail or Facebook.

DESIGNING MULTIMEDIA TEXTS TO PERSUADE

Writers organize words into sentences and paragraphs that establish coherence, develop ideas, and achieve their purpose, just as multimedia designers structure the visual, verbal, and sound elements of their texts to do the same. In addition, multimedia compositions provide resources (images, videos, music, web links, and audio) to strengthen their message. In so doing, multimedia texts use the same rhetorical appeals of ethos, logos, and pathos that were discussed in CHAPTER 2.

- **Ethos** How you establish your credibility in a multimedia composition includes creating images that have not been "doctored" to create a false impression and using design elements, such as fonts (see the box on Font Styles), that are appropriate for your message. As you know, a polished composition—whether written, spoken, or recorded—is always important in establishing your ethos.
- **Logos** Logos, the logical appeal of your response to a rhetorical situation, lies in the (literal) shape—or arrangement—of the argument of your multimedia text. The arrangement and layout should logically highlight the most important elements. Infographics, such as tables and charts, also condense information visually to support an argument.
- **Pathos** Advertisements are often pathos-driven, but any image or design element that is used to make an emotional connection appeals to pathos, as do colors that draw on your emotion and graphic images (see, for example, the image on page 71 of a young boy in the arms of his father).

Multimedia texts purposefully (and often persuasively) design words in a particular font style and size and use color, layout and arrangement, images, and often sound as a means of capturing a particular mood, delivering a specific message, or provoking a specific action. Review the elements of design that follow, and see how these elements work together in the Pink Ribbon website on page 57.

FONT STYLES

Fonts (styles of print type) can enhance or detract from the effectiveness of your message. For example, many advertisements and nearly all websites use clean, professional-looking, and audience-friendly fonts like **Verdana**, Arial, or **Helvetica**. Informal and light-hearted documents, on the other hand, might use *Comic Sans*. Among the serif fonts, mostly used for professional communications, **Bookman Old Style** is considered the "most trustworthy" of fonts.

Curlz
Papyrus
Courier
Arial
Typewriter Futura
Baskerville Gill Sans
Garamond Helvetica
Mrs. Eaves Avenir
Walbaum Neutraface
Archer Gothem

© 2018 Cengage Learning

- **Fonts** Styles of print type, called **fonts**, are composition's most basic visual element. *Serif* fonts (with those little foot-like tips, called *serifs*, on the ends of some letter strokes), such as **Times New Roman**, make reading printed documents easier. *Sans serif* fonts such as Verdana (with no serifs on the ends of the strokes) have become the standard for websites, making online reading easier.

© MariyaF/Shutterstock.com

Figure 4.2 *Bright, noticeable colors, such as yellow and red, can be used to emphasize a point or idea, even danger or emergency.*

- **Color** Color should be used for both emphasis and visual balance. Most designers recommend using no more than three main colors in your multimedia document design, although you may use varying intensities or shades of the same color to connect related materials (see Figure 4.2).
- **Arrangement** The organizational pattern of visual, verbal, and sound (if used) elements of your composition creates a *hierarchy* of information that makes obvious which information is most important and which is less so.
- **Layout** The **layout** helps readers scan and yet absorb large amounts of information quickly, using position, size, and **white space** (blank areas around blocks of text or around graphics or images) to identify the most important information.
- **Images** Whether still or moving, images tell a "story." Images can bring in characters, dialogue, plot, setting, and theme. Culturally significant images draw on visual symbols (for example, the eagle as a symbol for freedom).
- **Sound** Sonic elements, too, enhance your message (see Figure 4.3). Consider the solemn, stately soundtrack that complements *Titanic*, the fascinatingly new-yet-familiar score of *Star Wars: The Force Awakens*, the lively musical score that brings to life the upbeat plot of *Frozen*, and the pathos-drenched musical displays throughout *Mockingjay, Part 2*, which concludes *The Hunger Games*.

fonts styles of print type

serif fonts with foot-like tips on the ends of letters

sans serif fonts with no serifs on the ends of the letters

layout the way words and images are positioned in relation to each other on a page

white space blank areas around text, graphics, or images

Cleveland Museum of Art

Figure 4.3 *The Cleveland Museum of Art created a Storybooth that uses video and sound technology so that visitors can record their stories about the museum. These stories are then posted on the CMA Storybooth YouTube Channel.*

When organizations like Pink Ribbon International decide to use online multimedia, their web designers and content suppliers choose purposefully from a seemingly infinite assortment of images, texts, and layouts. Pink Ribbon International's home page (see Figure 4.4) balances text and images to help its audience absorb information quickly, using a layout that helps readers immediately identify the most important information. Visual headings aid readers as they quickly scroll through the site. (Remember that most people do not linger over a web page the way they might over a book page.) The organization also takes care to use inviting, easy-to-read sans serif fonts that have proved to be visually effective and taken seriously on web pages, again demonstrating an awareness of the best way to engage and reach its rhetorical audience. The simplicity of the font allows the sincere message to take precedence. As a fundraising organization, Pink Ribbon International needs to solicit donations—a focus made prominent on its website. A visitor to the site is likely to notice immediately the large banner urging readers to "Donate Now."

Because we read from left to right and from top to bottom, the top left corner is often the first place we look. The PinkRibbon.org website uses that space for a logo; as a result, the organization's promotional materials are always prominent on the website.

The PinkRibbon.org website uses a subtle gray as a secondary color to balance the thematic pink menu and highlights. Shades of pink and gray project femininity and calmness in the home page.

Not only does the website allow easy access to information about breast cancer but it does so using links to a forum, a blog, a calendar, and educational videos.

Most websites use images to break up large blocks of text, just as Pink Ribbon does with the image-heavy attention to the thesis: "Let's live together."

Visual headings highlight major ideas ("Forum," "Blog," "Calendar," and "Shop"), helping the audience scan the web page.

The image of a perfectly manicured hand, a live flower, and freshly cut grass communicates vitality and connects perfectly with the headline, "Let's live together."

The hierarchy of information is clear in the layout with a prominent focus on the large banner urging readers to "Donate Now."

Although "Donate Now" and "Support Us" appear just under this image and headline, the emphasis on what readers can do for Pink Ribbon quickly balances with what Pink Ribbon can do for readers: "Pink Ribbon is very interested in your opinion" and "Welcome." The "Quick Poll" and "Welcome" sections invite the audience into the site and emphasize the major claim of living together.

Shorter chunks of text, in conjunction with that main image, help the audience focus on the important elements of the site. The additional text is kept in small, contained blocks to make it easy for the audience to scan and absorb large amounts of information quickly.

Figure 4.4 Pink Ribbon International home page.

ACTIVITY: Analyzing the Rhetorical Situation
Using Design to Create Emotional Connection

As mentioned above, the pinks and grays of the PinkRibbon.org website home page echo the name of the site itself, connect with the feminine, and soften the horrors of cancer. The Santa Fe, New Mexico, website (Figure 4.5) uses brown and blue, no doubt intending to conjure up images of the browns of the surrounding mountains and adobe architecture and the blues of turquoise jewelry and the stunning northern New Mexico skies. Browns convey comfort and dependability, while blues express honesty and loyalty. Such colors connect easily with potential visitors to Santa Fe.

Source: Santa Fe

Figure 4.5 *Santa Fe travel website.*

Analyze the Santa Fe travel website. As an in-class writing exercise or a formal assignment, produce a composition that responds to the following questions:

1. To what opportunity for change is the writer/designer responding?
2. How is the situation or phenomenon described?
3. How does this situation or phenomenon affect the audience? Who is the audience?
4. What is the writer's purpose?
5. Identify the thesis statement or major claim.
6. How does the author establish ethos? Where in the presentation is logos confirmed? How does the author make an authentic emotional connection with the audience (pathos)?
7. How do images support or advance the thesis? What about the colors? And sonic elements?
8. Is there any kind of conclusion? In other words, what does the author want you to take away from the multimodal document in terms of information, attitude, or action?

🔊 HOW IMAGES TELL A STORY

Ours is a visually intense environment of photographs, magazines, graphic novels, Facebook (and other social media sites), Pinterest, Etsy, television, movies, YouTube, and other media. Whether consciously or unconsciously, we respond to visual culture in the same ways we respond to print: we sense the rhetorical appeals of ethos (trustworthiness), logos (logic), and pathos (emotional connection) conveyed by the key features of visual representation: point of view, focal point, characters, setting, color and alignment, and visual references that are culturally significant. Images make use of these key features to tell a story and create a dominant impression. As you analyze images, look at how these key features work together to create an immediate overall effect and ask yourself: What story does the image tell? What am I supposed to take away from it?

- **Point of View** Point of view is the **angle of vision** used to create an image. The image might be seen from eye level, from above (bird's eye view) or below (worm's eye view). It might be a close-up or a panoramic view from a distance. The point of view creates drama, frames the image, and leads your eye to the central focus of the image.

  angle of vision the position of the camera in relation to the image

- **Focal Point** The focus is the center of activity or attention in the image. **Cropping**—where parts of an image are edited out of the overall image—might be used to help draw the viewer's attention to what is central and create more visual drama. For any image, ask yourself these questions: What holds the central image? What might it signify?

  cropping the process of editing an image to draw the viewer's attention to the focal point

- **Characters** The objects that are represented in an image work together in the same way that characters work together in a novel. The main "character" is the focal point. Other objects around the focal point bring in harmony or discord. When determining the story, ask yourself these questions: What are the specific parts (background, objects, and people) of the visual? How are they arranged? How are these parts pieced together?

- **Setting** The way objects and people are arranged, the lighting, and a contrast in color or sizes work together to create the setting in the image. The setting can identify the time and place for the image and contribute to the mood created by the image. When analyzing an image, ask yourself these questions: What might be the significance of the background, especially in relationship to any text? What about colors? What mood or feeling do the colors convey? How do the visual elements contrast in terms of color, size, or lighting?

- **Cultural Signs** Cultural signs include symbols and significant cultural references, such as costumes or historical references. Some are obvious, such as the traditional skull-and-crossbone symbol for danger seen earlier in this chapter. Others are implied, such as a smiling face to indicate that buying a particular product will make you happy.

© Lynn Wohlers

Photographer Lynn Wohlers describes point of view as the "creative stance you take when you shoot." This close-up creates drama through an unusual angle on plants emerging from the soil.

ACTIVITY: Analyzing the Rhetorical Situation
Visuals

We respond to visuals by making judgments about the overall quality, strengths and weaknesses, characters, setting, as well as any measure of dialogue, plot, or theme. Examine the photograph of Ieshia Evans and Baton Rouge police during a protest over the death of Alton Sterling (see Figure 4.6). Evaluate its effectiveness in telling a story, the power of the visual representation itself, and how well the design elements work together to create a dominant impression. What story is the photograph trying to tell?

1. Who or what holds the central position in the photograph? To what significance?
2. What is the significance of the setting?
3. What are the cultural symbols or references?
4. What might the "plot" of the visual be?
5. How credible is the visual in terms of plot, characters, setting? In what ways are any of these features "doctored"?
6. How well does the photographer establish ethos, logos, and pathos?
7. What is the overall effect of this photograph? What action, attitude, or belief are you being asked to consider, maybe even to change?

Figure 4.6 *A study in contrasts, police in full riot gear confront a serene protester in Baton Rouge, Louisiana. The protester, Ieshia Evans, was peacefully arrested, along with over 100 others who came together on July 9, 2016, over the death of Alton Sterling. The 37-year-old Alton Sterling had died a few days earlier in a conflict with police outside a convenience store in Baton Rouge. The photograph by Jonathan Bachman for Reuters News Agency spread quickly through social media.*

INFOGRAPHICS

Whether yours is a print-only text with a thesis and well-supported and purposefully ordered assertions or a multimodal composition that includes words, images, and sounds that advance and support a claim, the arrangement of information in your composition affects how reasonable your argument appears to your audience (logos). Many documents—print and multimodal—include **infographics**—images, tables, charts, pie charts, and figures that condense statistics, facts, and other information into a persuasive visual representation that helps support your argument. Infographics such as those included here, the 2016 Federal Budget (Figure 4.7) and "Protecting Our Planet" from the National Oceanic and Atmospheric Administration (Figure 4.8), are densely packed with information about a single topic yet clearly arranged, with words and visuals that are large enough to comprehend. Easy to read and easy to understand, infographics present detailed information quickly and clearly.

infographics
images, tables, charts, pie charts, and figures that condense information into a visual presentation

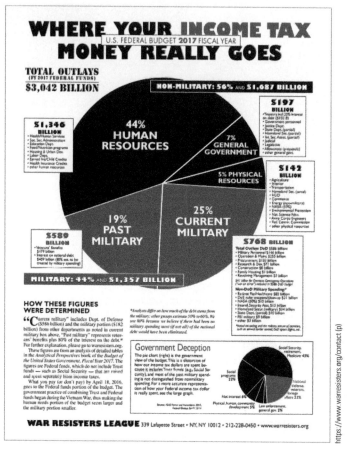

Figure 4.7 *The U.S. Federal Budget in 2016 is explained in an infographic that includes two simple pie charts.*

(◉) CONSIDERING AUDIENCE, PURPOSE, AND ACCESSIBILITY IN MULTIMEDIA COMPOSITIONS

Your design decisions as well as your choice of media (your means of communicating orally, visually, verbally, digitally, or in print) usually depend on the rhetorical situation itself: What media do you know how to use? What media can your audience easily access? What media will most effectively deliver your purposeful message to your audience? If your purpose is to address or resolve

PROTECTING OUR PLANET STARTS WITH YOU

BIKE MORE DRIVE LESS

reduce REUSE recycle
Cut down on what you throw away. Follow the three "R's" to conserve natural resources and landfill space.

choose sustainable
Learn how to make smart seafood choices at www.FishWatch.gov.

Trees provide food and oxygen. They help save energy, clean the air, and help combat climate change. **PLANT A TREE**

EDUCATE
When you further your own education, you can help others understand the importance and value of our natural resources.

CONSERVE WATER
The less water you use, the less runoff and wastewater that eventually end up in the ocean.

-SHOP- WISELY
Buy less plastic and bring a reusable shopping bag.

Don't send chemicals into our waterways.
Choose nontoxic chemicals in the home and office.

Volunteer!
Volunteer for cleanups in your community. You can get involved in protecting your watershed too!

Long-lasting light bulbs **- ARE A - BRIGHT IDEA**

Energy efficient light bulbs reduce greenhouse gas emissions. Also flip the light switch off when you leave the room!

oceanservice.noaa.gov

Multimedia

Figure 4.8 *This infographic from the National Oceanic and Atmospheric Administration quickly provides ten things you can do to protect the earth, all of which support the thesis, "Protecting Our Planet Starts with You."*

the opportunity for change, then you must find ways to ensure that your purposeful message reaches its destination.

When thinking about issues of audience, especially on sites like Facebook, consider the complicated nature of who your audience is in a forum as public as those found online. Even though the primary audience for your Facebook profile might be your friends, anyone with a Facebook account can become part of your audience unless you have carefully adjusted your privacy settings. Having such a large potential audience is not necessarily bad—unless you are unaware of it. After all, social networking sites can be effective tools for announcing information, stimulating collaborations, and celebrating achievements you think are important.

Accessibility is also a rhetorical issue: the medium of delivery influences what parts of your message an audience ultimately sees and hears. Not everyone will be able to stream videos or download podcasts. Some people might be browsing from a smartphone or a netbook; others might be using an older computer that lacks the memory capacity to deal with large video or audio downloads. Still others (grandparents, perhaps) may have no interest in learning how to do so. People with physical disabilities will face their own challenges with regard to seeing, hearing, or manipulating the keyboards necessary for full access to various media. Therefore, when you begin designing a multimedia composition such as a website, you should consider what information is accessible to which people in

accessibility in rhetoric, the extent to which a message is designed to be easy to read by those with disabilities that affect seeing, hearing, and manipulating a particular medium

what ways. Your delivery choices determine not only who constitutes your audience but also how your audience experiences your composition.

A Rhetorical Approach to Social Networks as a Medium of Delivery

Although you probably do not think of the rhetorical principles of design, style, persuasion, and delivery each time you tweet or update your Facebook status, these principles are always at work—otherwise, you would not use the "edit" button when you wanted to make improvements. As you examine the following example of a group's Facebook page, consider the ways the writers combined various media to form fitting responses.

The Brazos Gumbo Facebook page (Figure 4.9) constitutes a purposeful response to a specific problem: the poetry community in the Brazos Valley of East Texas was badly organized. Poetry readings were advertised only by word of mouth, and the poets did not know about one another or have access to others' poetry. Identifying this problem as a rhetorical opportunity, a small group of student poets realized that a Facebook page would allow poets whose work had been published in a local journal, *Brazos Gumbo*, to discuss their work, organize readings, and share news that was important to the community. The group eventually grew to encompass local poets and writers from a variety of backgrounds and a range of ages.

Some rhetorical advantages of using Facebook for such a project included the potential for wide distribution, the familiar and standardized interface, and

Figure 4.9 *The Brazos Gumbo Facebook page provides an online space where local poets can discuss their work, plan upcoming events, and share photos of local poetry readings.*

the interactivity of the platform. Notice that the "Info" page for Brazos Gumbo has the same familiar layout as other group pages and profiles on Facebook—it provides a basic, easily accessible description and contact information for the group. Such accessibility proved to be important for a group determined to increase its visibility. A secondary rhetorical purpose for the Facebook page was to build community among local poets, which the group's formal discussion pages and informal wall of communication helped to develop. For the poets of the Brazos Valley, a high-traffic online space like a Facebook page was ideal for building a network of local poets.

A Rhetorical Approach to a Web Page as a Medium of Delivery

For nearly twenty years now, students in visualization sciences classes at Texas A&M (the Aggies) have held Viz-a-GoGo, a visual art show that introduces multimedia student work to the student body and the larger college town community (Figure 4.10). By giving individual artists and other interested students

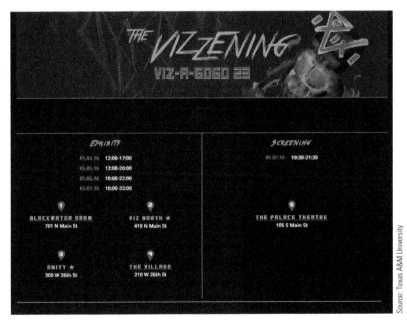

Figure 4.10 *Courtesy of Texas A&M, Visualization Laboratory, www.viz.tamu.edu. Visitors to the site can preview the artists' work in the gallery.*

something to link to (via Twitter, Facebook, LinkedIn, Instagram, Tumblr, Vimeo, or an e-mail message), the website helps target a broader rhetorical audience for the show than just the program alumni, the "Aggie Vizzers" who had long been the sole audience. In fact, once the organizers opened the sophisticated website, news of the visual art show quickly began to reach a wide audience of students, instructors, and community members. This wider audience joined the "Aggie Vizzers," many of whom have careers at Industrial Light & Magic (ILM), DreamWorks, Walt Disney Animation Studios, Pixar, Blue Sky, Electronic Arts, Rhythm & Hues Studios, Reel FX, Sony Pictures Imageworks, and Microsoft. In turn, the program alumni shared the site with their coworkers, who then became part of the even wider audience.

A Rhetorical Approach to YouTube as a Medium of Delivery

Video provides yet another medium for composing and delivering multimedia compositions.

Actress and activist Calpernia Addams uses YouTube videos to discuss transsexual issues that are often ignored by the mainstream media (Figure 4.11).

Figure 4.11 *A scene from one of Calpernia Addams's YouTube videos.*

She has posted a video entitled "Bad Questions to Ask a Transsexual" in order to achieve two goals: (1) to lampoon offensive questions people often ask her, and (2) to promote resources for transsexuals and education programs about transsexualism. Addams's video also provides links to websites such as Genderlife.com and to a response by one of her critics. A critical analysis of what Addams says (and what she leaves unspoken), how she chooses to deliver her message, who comprises her audience (and who does not), and the purpose of her message is the best means of assessing the overall success of her multimedia composition.

Good delivery in a video follows many of the principles that apply to effective audio compositions—you should speak clearly into the microphone, pace yourself when delivering a monologue, and practice your performance ahead of time. However, you must also consider the visual dimensions of video, including what you and other performers wear and what material and visual elements you include in each scene. For instance, in the *Beyond the Trailer* segment in which she reviews director Peter Landesman's *Concussion* (which is available on YouTube), Grace Randolph wears a simple black T-shirt and stands alongside giant digital slides, all the while delivering her monologue-review (Figure 4.12). The slide show features video clips from the movie itself, including stars Will Smith, Alec Baldwin, and Luke Wilson, as well as clips from NFL

Figure 4.12 *American entertainment personality, comic book writer, and creator of YouTube channels* Beyond the Trailer, Movie Math, *and* Think About the Ink *Grace Randolph hosts a review of* Concussion *on YouTube.*

games; infographics on football-related injuries; and photographs of the real Dr. Bennet Omalu and his family. Even though Randolph is casually dressed, she has chosen her attire and props purposefully, establishing her ethos and logos as an objective, well-informed viewer of NFL politics and this movie. Establishing pathos is harder, she admits, because *Concussion* itself is "all brain and no heart," making it easy for viewers to refuse the science and defend football in the same way they defend gun rights. The combination of the visual elements, her fact-filled monologue, and her richly detailed and contextualized review confirms her status as an expert reviewer.

Delivery does not just apply to your performance on film, however. You also need to consider how you will distribute (or deliver) the video to your audience. YouTube and other sites that host streaming video have made distribution easier. However, because of the public nature of such sites, you may want to choose a different distribution method, such as e-mail, in order to more carefully control who is in your audience.

A Rhetorical Approach to Oral Presentations as a Medium of Delivery

When Demosthenes, the greatest of ancient Greek orators, was asked to name the three most important features of rhetoric, his response was "Delivery, delivery, delivery." His concerns included the properties of the speaker's voice, diction, and gestures as well as the style of his sentences and the quality of his argument. Like all ancients, Demosthenes was also concerned with the speaker's appearance. His were multimodal concerns even then.

Location

Ultimately, the success of an oral presentation depends on your strategic employment of the available means. You will want to establish the rhetorical appeals of credibility, reasonableness, and connection (ethos, logos, and pathos) in the content of your presentation, but your oral presentation will also be affected by the resources and constraints (limitations) of the physical location itself. If you are speaking in front of a classroom, you will reach all of your classmates if you speak clearly and look up from your notes as often as possible. If you are speaking in a lecture hall, however, you may find yourself dependent on a microphone, and you may want to practice with it beforehand. A lecture hall offers a few other challenges as well, not the least of which is the need to ensure that audience members who have hearing or visual impairments can follow your presentation. You may want to make printed handouts available so that individuals with hearing impairments can follow along more easily. And you will want to concentrate on facing your audience so that they can see your facial expressions and even read your lips, all the better to "hear" your words.

Presentation Software

When you must make a decision about whether to deliver your information as spoken words only or as spoken words along with other media (visuals, videos, other sonic elements), consider that your oral presentation states your claim, while the visual and sound elements expand and energize that claim. You can decide whether to bring items such as a handout, a flip chart, a transparency, a poster, a film clip, a podcast or an audio stream, or a PowerPoint, Prezi, or other type of digital presentation. Nothing can be more aggravating than a speaker reading a series of bulleted points to the audience while the audience is reading along. Your goal is to get the attention of your audience and impress them. Text-heavy slides will do just the opposite, so concentrate on using big bold images and sound elements to emphasize your words. Even as you use big bold images, you can still maintain a consistent design throughout all your slides as well as consistent background color. In fact, some experts go so far as to say that the background colors you use in your slides should complement the colors of the room in which you are presenting! Thus, as you consider the use of visuals and audio, keep in mind that they should complement your words—not mirror them. Some of the most effective digital presentations are cascades of visuals that accompany—and enhance—a speaker's words.

The Rhetorical Arrangement of Presentation Elements

As with any other multimodal composition, the text, images, and sound you decide to include need to reflect your rhetorical situation as well as the topic of your presentation. For instance, you may have identified a problem that you can address by way of research, a public controversy that you want to investigate, or a personal problem that you want to resolve. Perhaps your church has asked you to do a presentation for its drive to help Syrian refugees.

- If your purpose is to provide background to the events occurring in Syria, then you could provide a range of images such as statistical tables that show the change in population, economic productivity, or casualties over the course of the civil war, or maps that show the changing territorial

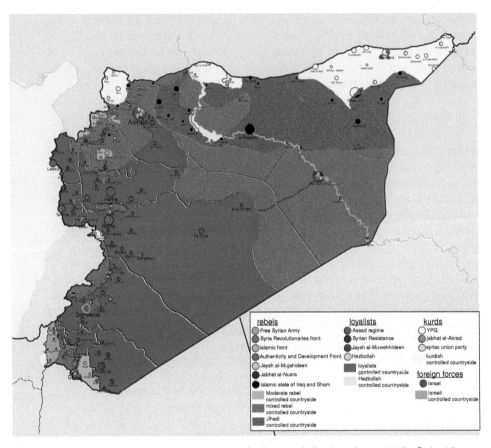

Figure 4.13 *This map uses color to represent areas under the control of various elements in the Syria civil war.*

dominance of the various political and sectarian factions that are in play (Figure 4.13).

- On the other hand, if your presentation is persuasive rather than informative, your choice of images can greatly influence the overall effectiveness of your work. Photographs showing bombed-out structures of an urban landscape, refugees fleeing to neighboring countries, or the faces of those who have remained behind, for instance, could heighten the appeal of pathos if your thesis involves finding a solution to resolve the plight of civilians in that conflict (see Figure 4.14).

The elements you choose to include—and at what point you include them— will need to reflect and support the key points you are trying to make in

Reuters/Yousef Albostany

Figure 4.14 *A Syrian man carries his injured son after his neighborhood was destroyed.*

your presentation. In developing his strategies for effective presentations, professional coach Carmine Gallo (an Emmy award–winning television anchor and media consultant for many major companies) draws his advice directly from what he noticed about the presentations of the late Apple CEO Steve Jobs.

Here are the five basic elements found in every Jobs presentation:

1. **A headline.** Steve Jobs positions every product with a headline that fits well within a 140-character Twitter post. . . . In his 2007 iPhone launch, he wrote, "Apple reinvents the phone" (Figure 4.15).
2. **A villain.** In every classic story, the hero fights the villain. . . . This idea of conquering a shared enemy is a powerful motivator and turns customers into evangelists. For Jobs, all other cell phones were villains, in that they were not smart and were hard to use. Apple's iPhone would prove to be smart and simple.
3. **A simple slide.** Apple products are easy to use because of the elimination of clutter. The same approach applies to the slides in a Steve Jobs presentation. In this presentation, he showed one picture of the iPhone—nothing else on the slide—and called it "gorgeous."
4. **A demo.** Neuroscientists have discovered that the brain gets bored easily. Steve Jobs doesn't give you time to lose interest. [In most of his presentations] he's . . . demonstrating a new product or feature and having fun

Figure 4.15 *Indeed, Apple reinvented the phone, as Jobs demonstrated in this simple slide backdrop for his 2007 launch of the product.*

doing it. . . . So, he pulls out his iPhone and starts playing around with it, demonstrating its functions as an iPod, a computer, and a phone.

5. **A holy smokes moment.** Every Steve Jobs presentation has one moment that neuroscientists call an "emotionally charged event." Jobs was so excited about the iPhone that he admitted to his huge audience, "I didn't sleep a wink last night." The emotionally charged moment is the equivalent of a mental sticky note that tells the brain, Remember this! . . . (© 2009. Reprinted by permission.)

ACTIVITY: Analyzing the Rhetorical Situation

Planning an Oral Presentation

Not every presentation has a villain in the way Steve Jobs's presentation would. Use these same basic elements to plan a presentation that builds consensus. In your presentation, recast the "Villain" as a rhetorical opportunity to achieve a goal.

1. If you decided to make one key change to your presentation, how would that influence the other elements of your presentation? For instance, what if you were to use an audio clip in place of a key image, or what if your thesis were primarily informative rather than persuasive?

2. What rhetorical opportunities or challenges are best resolved by the strategies described? How did the strategies described help you to address engaging your audience and structuring your approach to the topic?

3. In academic presentations, using the idea of a "Villain" may seem counterintuitive. But if the purpose is to find something that most everyone in the room can agree on (e.g., Steve Jobs's contention that cell phones could do more but still be easy to use), how might such a strategy help you to build consensus around issues instead of enflaming differences? What kinds of topics or rhetorical situations might suggest dropping the "Villain" altogether?

4. If you liked the ideas you came up with in your outline, think about ways in which you might address this topic in a different assignment. How would you do this as an essay?

 ASSIGNMENT: ANALYZING IMAGES

Nike's market dominance in the United States does not look like it will fade anytime soon. What with clothing, shoes, and accessory lines for every single sport as well as for men, women, and children, the Nike brand is flourishing, thanks, in no small part, to its legendary logo, the "swoosh." "Just Do It," Nike's long-time challenge, has been translated into languages all around the globe, exerting a significant force on consumers. In the twenty-first century, Nike has swooshed its way beyond that simple challenge as fitness itself has become one of America's most noble goals, to some almost a religion.

ACTIVITY: Analyzing the Rhetorical Situation

Imagine, if you can, the amount of purposeful planning that went into the Nike advertisement in Figure 4.16 (p. 74) and analyze it accordingly, considering the overall rhetorical power of the ad itself. After answering all of the following questions, compose a short essay in which you analyze and synthesize your findings to determine the effectiveness of the Nike advertisement. Consider all the rhetorical elements: opportunity, purpose, audience, and medium of delivery as well as the advantages and limitations of that medium. Consider, too, how this ad employs the rhetorical appeals of ethos, logos, and pathos to persuade viewers to buy Nike products.

1. What holds the central position in this poster? What might it signify?
2. What other features—culturally significant, familiar, and fresh—are in the poster? What might be missing?
3. What might be the significance of the background (especially in relationship with the text itself)?

Advertising Archives

Figure 4.16 *Nike advertisement.*

4. What role does the text play? What might be the significance of the different sizes of text?
5. How do the colors in this advertisement vary? What mood do the colors create?
6. How does the positioning of the runner affect your perception of the ad?

MindTap®   Reflect on your writing process, practice skills that you have learned in this chapter, and receive automatic feedback.

Memoirs

Canopy/Corbis

MindTap® Understand the goals of the chapter and complete a warm-up activity online.

Human beings have always been storytellers, whether telling stories about a successful hunt, a dangerous journey, a harrowing childhood, the intervention of a god, even a good meal. We humans have always made connections in the world by telling stories, and now we regularly do so over pizza, in the car, and through e-mail, Facebook, blogs, and Twitter. Even a 140-character tweet can carry a punch:

(((Dan Hodges))) ✓ @DPJHodges

In retrospect Sandy Hook marked the end of the US gun control debate. Once America decided killing children was bearable, it was over.

Jun 19, 2015, 1:07 PM

In his tweet, Dan Hodges speaks to the turning point in the gun-control debate that was Sandy Hook and recognizes the current gun-control laws as an opportunity for change—one that can be accomplished through words.

Throughout this chapter, you, too, will identify an opportunity for change that can be addressed or resolved with words. As you determine what you want to share in your memoir, consider which medium of delivery will give you the best chance for reaching and engaging your rhetorical audience.

Print Memoir
written for a
community or
campus newspaper
or a local zine or church

Audio Memoir
recorded for a local
radio station, for a
podcast, or for your
family back home

Online (Multimodal or Multimedia) Memoir
written as a blog entry,
a series of tweets,
a contribution to a website, or a
YouTube video

Memoirs

GENRE IN F☉CUS The Food Memoir

memoir a narrative that reflects on a personal experience or series of experiences

Memoirs can focus on traumatic events, of course, like the Sandy Hook killings. But they can also focus on everyday subjects like family, travel, spirituality, and food. Food triggers vivid memories for all of us—some joyous or satisfying, others painful or awkward. For example, Diana Abu-Jaber's memoir of her childhood in upstate New York and Jordan, *The Language of Baklava*, centers on food but is also a reflection on living between two cultures. Food-related memoirs, like other memoirs, present past experiences that resonate with a larger historical, psychological, or social meaning. In her blog *Chocolate & Zucchini*, Clotilde Dusoulier's description of high-quality chocolate suggests that Parisians connect food more with pleasure and fun than with nourishment and sustenance.

On a Sunday afternoon, after a copious lunch, wait for your next-door neighbor Patricia to knock on your window with a wooden spoon. Agree to come over to their place for coffee. From the special chocolate cabinet in your kitchen (surely you must have one) grab what's left of the excellent dark chocolate with fragments of roasted cocoa beans that your friend Marie-Laure brought you last time she came for dinner. Walk next door in your socks. Leave Maxence and Stéphan to chat about Mac OS-X and guitar tuners in the living room, while you watch Patricia brew coffee on their espresso machine. When asked, opt for the designer coffee cups. Bring the four cups to the table on a metal tray. Take a cup, break a square of the chocolate, sit down, relax. Have a bite of chocolate, then a sip of coffee.

—Clotilde Dusoulier, "Happiness
(A Recipe)"

The rhetorical response of a food memoir can serve to explore our relationships, just as one about music, art, travel, sports, or small children might do.

To determine if a memoir is the most fitting response to your rhetorical opportunity, keep in mind your opportunity for composing, your audience, and your purpose. If, as you are composing, you realize that your message includes characters, dialogue, an event (or two), and a specific setting, you can rely on the memoir for all or part of your message (see more on the rhetorical strategies FOR NARRATION, DESCRIPTION, AND CAUSE-AND-EFFECT ANALYSIS pages 262–264 and 270–272 IN CHAPTER 14). As you reflect on your own experience, you may find yourself writing to entertain, explain, evaluate, or connect with your audience—all elements of the memoir.

 ASSIGNMENT

Think back to a meaningful moment in your life, maybe a pivotal event (or sequence of sensory, physical, or emotional events) from your childhood or one from the more recent past. Then, relying on the narrative techniques of fiction, draft a memoir in which you include vivid, sensory-rich descriptions, characters, dialogue, setting(s), and plot (a cause-and-effect narrative structure). Since your memoir is not fiction, you will want to take special care to establish yourself as a trustworthy observer of your own life by including a reasonable analysis and establishing the significance of your experience for you as well as your readers. As you write, vary your descriptions by emphasizing different descriptive and sensory features of the situation: pleasant or unpleasant memories, people, feelings, and other senses that this experience stimulated.

READING RHETORICALLY

You can read an entertaining, inspirational, or instructional memoir with pleasure and profit if you read rhetorically. You might read chronologically (in order of occurrence) or recursively (moving forward and looping back), a process that includes (1) previewing the text itself (to determine what the text demands in terms of time, effort, and previous knowledge); (2) reading for content (to note the author's major points, key terms, and phrases); and (3) rereading for understanding (to determine the author's specific purpose, the overall organization, and the specific development of ideas). When reading a memoir, pay special attention to the feelings the memory has stimulated in the writer, both during the experience itself and now, upon reflection. You will also want to determine how the writer's memoir works to connect with readers.

Key Features of a Memoir

Memoirs focus on an experience or series of experiences in the writer's life and their significance in shaping the writer's perspective. Sensory details help readers visualize, hear, smell, feel, and even taste key events in a writer's life. Dialogue reveals the characters, with specific words or phrases helping the reader "hear" the relationship of the characters with the writer and the connections among the characters. Transitions are crucial to keeping the narrative moving forward with clarity and grace. Memoirs share the following characteristics:

- Memoirs focus on a significant or then-insignificant experience or series of experiences in the writer's life. Rather than narrating from birth to adulthood, the way an autobiography does, a memoir focuses on those experiences or events that have proved to be meaningful in shaping who the writer is and his or her perspective on the world.
- Memoirs contain ample sensory details to help readers visualize, hear, smell, taste, or feel key events, characters, experiences, and objects.
- Memoirs include dialogue or quoted speech that reveals something unique about or central to a character or the character's relationship with other people, events, or objects in the story.
- page 248 Memoirs include clear transitional phrases to show how events relate to one another in time and how the action of the narrative unfolds. (See CHAPTER 13, COMMON TRANSITIONAL WORDS AND PHRASES.)
- Memoirs provide reflection on or analysis of the key narrative events to help readers understand their significance for the writer's development and his or her perspective on everyday life.

The student example that follows is annotated to show the characteristics found in most memoirs. As you read the following essay, ask yourself

- Who is the author? What does the memoir tell you about her?
- What is her relationship to the subject of this essay? Is she angry, happy, remorseful about this experience? Why is it important to her? What is her purpose in writing the essay?
- Which of Seitz's major points and key terms did you notice?
- What specific details, key terms, and dialogue did Seitz use to sustain her purpose?
- What storytelling techniques does she use to try to make her memoir come to life? How successful is she?

MindTap® Read, highlight, and take notes online.

Herb's Chicken

ANNA SEITZ

The following memoir centers on a turning point in the writer's life. Seitz and her husband dreamed of being sustenance farmers until she witnessed the reality of such sustenance: killing a chicken. Why is the memoir a good choice for Seitz's rhetorical situation?

Last year, my husband Bill and I, fueled by farmers' market fantasies, decided we wanted to keep some backyard chickens. Since we had to wait until spring to order birds, we spent the winter getting our coop, and ourselves, ready. We read stacks of books and magazines on raising chickens, and we decided to ask our friend Herb to teach us to "process" them.

> Seitz's memoir uses the narrative form, which includes a setting, characters, dialogue, and a sequence of events.

When we pulled into Herb's driveway on the big day, he was already hanging out the back door, gesturing to the cane at the bottom of the steps. He's 87 years old and has been a poultry farmer since he got back from the war. He shuffles slowly, hunched over. He can't hear much of what we say. When he can hear, he usually just rolls his eyes. Bill handed him the cane, and Herb led us to the last of his coops that still has chickens. His farm of 6,000 birds is down to 75. "Well, how many you want?" Herb asks.

> The significant experience related in this memoir arose from Seitz's "farmers' market fantasy" of raising chickens. [Seitz provides the context for the memoir as well as her opportunity for writing.]

> Seitz includes many sensory details to help her readers visualize the setting and Herb's character.

"I don't know," said my husband. "Got one that's not layin'?"

"Get that one there," said Herb. He pointed his finger in the direction of a group of three birds, and my husband, appearing to know which one Herb meant, took a couple of steps toward them. They immediately dispersed.

> The husband offers a detail important to the memoir. The dialogue reveals the characters' relationships to one another as well as to the raising of chickens.

Herb grabbed a long handle with a hook at the end, resembling the sort of wand I've used to roast weenies over a campfire, and handed it to Bill. He pointed again. "There," he said. Bill grabbed the tool and managed to at least tangle up the bird's feet. Herb snapped up the bird with the efficient movement of someone who has snapped up tens of thousands of birds, and handed the bird, upside-down, to me.

I held it carefully by the ankles and got a little shiver. It flapped its wings a few times, but it didn't really try to fight me. It actually looked pretty pitiful hanging there. Herb was already walking back to the house.

"Pull up that bird feeder, Billy," barked Herb, in his thin voice.

My husband had worked digging graves with Herb since he was fifteen, and he was used to taking orders. "Yup," he said. He walked up to a bird feeder on a stake and pulled it up from the ground.

> This paragraph works as a transition between the present series of events and the past relationship of the characters.

Herb unhooked a metal cone which he'd been using on the stake as a squirrel deterrent and slid it off the bottom. "For the chicken," he told me as I caught up to them. "I'll open the cellar."

Bill and I waited outside the bulkhead for Herb. He opened it up, still holding the metal cone in his hand. "Come on," he instructed. We made our way down into the dark. The chicken tried to arch its head up, to peck me. I handed it over to Bill.

In the cellar, Herb hooked the cone to a beam. "Give me that," he said to me, gesturing at a dusty bucket on the floor next to me. I pushed it with my foot until it was under the cone.

Seitz describes the chicken-killing process in detail

"All right!" said my husband brightly. I stiffened. He pushed the chicken head-first into the cone, until her head poked through the opening at the bottom and her feet stuck out the top. The chicken got one wing free, but my husband put a rubber band around her feet and hooked it on the nail that held the cone. She was stuck.

Herb fished through his pocket for his knife, and my eyelids started to wrinkle. I held my lips tightly closed. "You just need to go through the roof of the mouth and get them right in the brain," said Herb. "It's better than chopping the head off because they don't tense up. Makes it easier to get the feathers off."

Seitz's dialogue is vivid and purposeful, moving the narrative forward. This series of five short paragraphs includes graphic details and purposeful dialogue.

"Won't it bite you?" I asked.

"So what if it does?" answered Herb. "Last thing it'll ever do." Herb easily pried the mouth open with his left hand, and with his right, he pushed the knife into its brain and turned it. It was over. I furrowed my brow.

"Then you gotta bleed it," he said. Herb pulled the knife down, and in one quick motion, cut the chicken's throat from the inside. Blood spilled from its open beak into the bucket. My husband watched with interest, offering the same occasional "Yup" or "Uh-huh" that he uses when listening to any good story. I watched with my eyes squinted and my face half turned away.

Herb rinsed the knife in the washbasin and announced, "Gotta get the water. Anna, it's on the stove. Hot but not boiling." I went up to the kitchen and fiddled with the temperature under a big soup pot. It looked about right, I guessed.

By the time I got the water down to the cellar, Herb and Bill had already pulled the chicken out of the cone and tossed the head into the bloody bucket. It looked more like food when I couldn't see the eyes. Herb told my husband to dip the bird in the hot water a few times, and he did, holding it by the rubber-banded legs. When he pulled it out, some of the feathers on its chest started to drop off.

From under the stairs, Herb pulled out a large plastic drum, the sides dotted with rubber fingers. He put the chicken inside and switched it on. After a few minutes, he pulled out a mostly featherless chicken. The feathers stuck to the sides of the drum. "Get that," he said to Bill. While Bill pulled feathers out of the plucker, Herb held the chicken by the feet and pulled off the remaining feathers—mostly large wing and tail feathers, and a few small pin feathers. By now there really wasn't any blood left, and the chicken looked pretty close to what you might get in the store, except skinnier.

"From under the stairs" begins a strong transitional sentence.

Seitz uses specific vocabulary like "plucker" to bring life to her memoir.

Bill brought the chicken and the bucket up to the kitchen, and Herb and I followed. Herb took the bird and dropped it down into the sink with a smack. "Now, you cut out the crop," Herb said. He pointed to something I couldn't see, then cut into the throat and showed us a little sack full of stones and grain. "It's how they chew, I guess," he added. He tugged on it, and it brought with it a large section of the windpipe. "To get the rest of the guts out, you gotta cut in the back."

Herb made an incision and stuck in his hand, making a squishy sound. He pulled out a handful of guts and dropped most of it into the bucket. He cut off one section and held it toward Bill. "You got the wrong bird," he said. The slimy tube was sort of transparent, and through it we could see a string of about eight little eggs of increasing size, beginning with a tiny yolk, and ending with an almost full-sized egg.

"Can you eat 'em?" I asked.

"Guess you could," said Herb, throwing the whole mess into the bucket, "but I got eggs." He turned the chicken, lopped off the feet, and tossed them into the bucket. They landed toes up, like a grotesque garnish. "Well, want a plastic bag?"

I accepted the grocery bag and some plastic wrap and wrapped the carcass up while Herb and Bill took the bucket outside. They talked for a while, and then Herb directed Bill up onto a ladder to check a gutter. I stood with my back to the carcass, examining Herb's wife's display of whimsical salt and pepper shakers.

When my husband and I got back in the car, I put the carcass at my feet. "That was great!" said my husband. "Think we can do it on our own?"

I thought through the steps in my mind. "I think I can," I chirped. I thought of the bucket and the toe garnish. "But I'm not eating it."

Seitz reflects on the narrative events, helping her readers understand their significance to her changing perspective.

Using Synthesis and Analysis

When composing a memoir, you will be translating lived events into a narrative, one that triggers your reflection on or analysis of those events in a way that helps your readers understand the significance of those events to your development. In these ways, reflection and analysis underpin the body of a memoir. You will want to synthesize the people and events as the whole of one experience and then analyze that experience for its significance and its consequence. Whether you are reading or composing a memoir, pay attention to the ways specific details relate to the significance of a particular experience for your own or a character's self-development.

MindTap® Find additional examples of memoirs online.

See also CHAPTER 1, MICHAEL BÉRUBÉ, *Life as We Know It*

See also CHAPTER 2, MALALA YOUSAFZAI [I Am Afraid] [Interrupted Sleep] (blog entries)

See also CHAPTER 3, JENNY MCCARTHY, *The Path to Hope*

See also CHAPTER 3, ALLEN SHAWN, *Twin*

See also CHAPTER 24, MALCOLM-AIME MUSONI, *Being an 18-Year-Old Black Man a Year after Mike Brown*

 RESPONDING TO THE RHETORICAL SITUATION

Memoirs provide an opportunity to explore or explain a turning point in your life. The need to introduce yourself, explain your old (or new) self, analyze your change of plans or heart, or describe a transformative experience calls for the memoir. But who will read, watch, or listen to your memoir and perhaps be influenced by what you have to say? A fiancé, parent, teacher, hiring committee, friend, or classmate might be a suitable rhetorical audience, one needing your introduction, explanation, analysis, or description. A personal letter, face-to-face meeting, letter of application, YouTube video, podcast, and personal essay are all possible media for delivering a fitting response in the genre of memoir.

Opportunity   Audience and Purpose   Genre/Memoir   (Medium of) Delivery

Understanding the Rhetorical Situation

Memoirs are used to narrate and analyze significant—even sometimes seemingly insignificant—life experiences (sharing chocolate, killing a chicken) that have shaped the writer's perspective. Memoir writing helps us investigate, contemplate on, and understand more deeply the impact of incidents, events, and people in our lives. Each of the following questions provides an opportunity to think about your life experiences in a way that could launch a memoir.

- What is one food-related moment in your life that changed how you thought, acted, or felt? For instance, were you treated surprisingly well in a restaurant you thought was snobbish? Or, identify a key moment when you were first introduced to an unfamiliar kind of food. How did that event affect you?
- Have you ever given in to peer pressure with good—or unfortunate—results?
- When you witnessed (or participated in) racism or sexism, did you intervene—or not?
- Was there a first impression you or someone else made that changed later?

✶ RESEARCHING THE MEMOIR

Memoir writing seems to be rooted in memory or recall. But the best memoirs often incorporate research, which can include conducting interviews with family and friends; researching contemporary newspaper accounts of weather, current events, dates, addresses; or examining photographs and documents that are stored at home or in an institution of some kind. (Think of rummaging through family photos, looking over childhood keepsakes in the attic, or examining legal documents that are stored in a shoebox.) Research findings like these are analyzed and then synthesized into the interesting details, facts, and anecdotes that help you compose a personalized, and, thereby, effective memoir.

Identifying an opportunity for change

What you are searching for is an experience, event, or relationship that has played a vital role—and has helped you understand something about life that you want other people to know. How did this experience change you, your attitude, your actions? How would writing about this experience help you learn more about yourself? How would relating this experience to others change those who read about it or help them understand you better?

1. Make a list of your three most memorable or most meaningful experiences. Put a plus or minus in front of each experience, listing detailed reasons for its being positive or negative. Then, sketch out the contributing factors (including people, occasion, setting) that led up to each experience and the possible transformative results of each experience.
2. Choose one of the experiences in your list and make sketches or take photos of the location where your experience, event, or relationship occurred, paying particular attention to the sensory details, characters, and dialogue that you still remember as being most intriguing about the experience. Write out two or three different ways that you and others might perceive that same experience.

Relating rhetorically to your audience

The following questions will help you identify your rhetorical audience as well as their relationship to the experience you have decided to write about. Knowing your audience helps you decide whether your purpose is to be informative, entertaining, explanatory, analytical, or argumentative. Once you have connected your audience with your purpose, you are in a good position to select effective descriptive details and decide on the most fitting way to deliver your message to that audience.

1. List the names of the persons or groups who might be most receptive—or most resistant—to your story and need to hear about it.
2. Next to the name of each potential audience list the personal, professional, social, or spiritual reasons they would have for acknowledging the significance of your experience.
3. Think about the kinds of responses to your memoir you might reasonably expect from each of these audiences. Consider similar experiences that the audience might have had, their openness to new opinions, or their desire for familiar, confirming experiences.
4. Keeping the interests, experiences, and perspectives of your audience in mind, review your visual and verbal descriptions and the significance of that experience (#2 in the preceding section on "Identifying an

Opportunity for Change"). Determine which of those descriptions will most likely engage your audience, maybe connecting your experience with their own. Now is the time to revise those descriptions accordingly, tailoring them to your rhetorical audience.

Planning an effective rhetorical response for your purpose

Once you identify your opportunity and audience, use the following questions to help you narrow your purpose and shape your response:

1. What purpose do you have in conveying your memoir to this audience?
2. Might your memoir change a specific perception, attitude, opinion, or action of your rhetorical audience? Might they rethink their own experience in terms of yours? Or might they reassess you and your experience?
3. What would be the most effective medium for delivering your memoir to your audience? What medium or media do they have easy access to? As you consider the various options for delivering your memoir (print, electronic, verbal, visual, multimodal), focus in on the one that will best convey the purpose of your message and reach your audience.

LINKS TO MEMOIRS IN THREE MEDIA — MindTap®

Links may change due to availability.

© Anton Novik/Shutterstock.com

Pacific Press/Getty Images

© B. and E. Dudzinscy/Shutterstock.com

Print Memoir
The memoir at the beginning of this chapter was written as a student paper, and in it Anna Seitz remembers her first experience "processing" a chicken.

Audio Memoir
This audio memoir about an Italian American family restaurant was recorded for StoryCorps.

Online Memoir
This blog entry by Ree Drummond, also known as "Pioneer Woman," presents an illustrated memoir about her first encounter with Nova salmon.

WRITING A PERSUASIVE MEMOIR: A Guide

*T*o be persuasive, a memoir should rely on the narrative techniques of fiction (novels and short stories): vivid descriptions, characters, dialogue, and setting as well as a cause-and-consequence structure. Like fiction, memoirs are structured as a chronological sequence of events, sometimes using flashbacks and flash forwards to emphasize specific moments. But memoirs are not fiction, so you will need to establish your personal credibility as an insightful observer of your life experiences (your ethos) as well as the reasonableness (logos) of your feelings so that your story makes an authentic emotional connection (pathos) with the lives and experiences of your readers. (See *CHAPTER 2, THE AVAILABLE MEANS INCLUDE THE RHETORICAL ELEMENTS OF THE MESSAGE ITSELF.*)

pages 23–26

ADVANTAGES AND LIMITATIONS

Advantages

- **Writer:** You have considerable latitude to explore a more personal voice to engage readers, taking a casual, even intimate, tone.

- **Message:** The memoir allows you to build ethos and pathos through personalized anecdotes and vivid experiences, all of which shape the body, the supporting material, of your memoir.

- **Media and Design:** Memoirs can be presented in numerous ways: through audio, video, print, electronic series of print images, or images and text.

Limitations

- **Writer:** Be sure that you are comfortable with a personal voice—and that it is appropriate for your intended audience. Resist breaching your boundaries of personal privacy for the sake of a memoir.

- **Message:** Memoirs rely on personal experiences, knowledge, and observations for logos, the logical appeal. Facts and figures work best when they are rooted in the writer's own experience or in related research.

- **Media and Design:** Reaching and engaging your rhetorical audience are the determining factors for your choice of medium.

Introduction

- **Engage your audience.**
- **Establish your trustworthiness as a narrator (ethos).**

Announce your focus As you have learned in this chapter, a memoir focuses on a specific event or series of meaningful events. The introduction hooks readers by dropping them right in the middle of an interesting situation or an especially vivid description of your specific event, experience, or personality. For instance, Anna Seitz writes, "We read stacks of books and magazines on raising chickens, and we decided to ask our friend Herb to teach us to 'process' them."

Ask yourself . . .
- How does my opening situation or compelling language engage my reader(s)?
- How have I stated or alluded to the main point(s) my memoir will address?
- Will approaching my main topic directly or indirectly be more effective?
- How have I begun to establish my ethos as a writer or character to my audience?

- **Present the main narrative in a distinctive setting.**
- **Provide specific sensory details of sight, sound, taste, feeling, and smell.**
- **Develop characters and dialogue.**
- **Begin to reflect on and analyze what has happened.**

Structure your memoir as a story The body of a memoir presents the narrative, which focuses on a specific sequence of events. Use transitional phrases that help readers see how the events relate to one another in time. These events allow you to illustrate a point or convey the message you want to send by means of vivid language, memorable characters, and dialogue. Seitz's second paragraph fulfills all of these criteria of using transitions ("When we pulled into Herb's driveway on the big day, he was already hanging out the door") and memorable characters ("He shuffles slowly, hunched over. He can't hear much of what we say. When he can hear, he usually just rolls his eyes").

Add vivid description Vivid descriptions and sensory details invite readers to imagine, connect with, and invest themselves in the lives and activities of the major characters, including you. Seitz's description of the processing itself includes "Herb made an incision and stuck in his hand, making a squishy sound. He pulled out a handful of guts and dropped most of it into the bucket."

Create dialogue Equally important, you will want to create dialogue among the characters to reveal their personalities and relationships. Dialogue or quoted speech gives readers deeper insight into the thoughts and emotions of your characters. Herb and Bill discuss the chicken to be processed with "How many do you want?" and "Got one that's not layin'?"

Reflect on your experience You can achieve rhetorical success as you narrate the events in your memoir by stopping the action to provide a few sentences of reflection and analysis. Midway through the chicken processing, Seitz reflects that the bird "looked more like food when I couldn't see the eyes."

(continued)

Ask yourself . . .

- How do I know that I am relating all the pertinent details of the event?
- As I reconsider my narrative, which details have I purposefully excluded? Which ones might I want to include now?
- Which of my details are especially vivid, especially sensory?
- How have I described the characters in my memoir so that they seem realistic? How do they present contrasting viewpoints that enhance the complexity of the events?
- How exactly do the events and characters I am describing connect to the main point I want to make?

Conclusion

- **Satisfy your audience with an understanding of the significance of the events for you as well as for them.**
- **Reinforce your message.**

Relate the significance of the event to your readers' interests You might conclude your memoir with a scene that captures precisely the mood you want readers to experience or the image you want them to remember. Or you might decide to conclude your memoir with a more traditional paragraph that, like your reflective components, speaks fairly explicitly about the point of the events that you have described. Either way, your readers will respond favorably to your conclusion if it helps them see how the events have significance both for you as the writer and for them as your readers. Seitz's comparative descriptions of Herb's, Bill's, and her own response to the processing make for a humorous, though realistic, account that turns serious when she announces that she will not eat it. Many readers will identify with her response.

Check your message in your conclusion The conclusion of a memoir reinforces the message or the point of your story. The important consideration here is to be sure the events you have narrated, the details you have provided, and the reflection you have composed all work together to deliver a clear, coherent message. Seitz's final sentence, "But I'm not eating it," makes for a perfect conclusion.

Ask yourself . . .

- How explicit do I want my language to be?
- How "conclusive" do I want my conclusion to be? Am I really certain about how I feel?
- Might it be more effective to leave some questions unanswered, so that readers can arrive at their own conclusions?

MindTap® Request help and feedback from a tutor. If required, participate in peer review, submit your paper for a grade, and view instructor comments online.

Revision and Peer Review

After you have drafted your memoir, ask one of your classmates to read it, providing advice on revising and strengthening it. Ask your peer to help you address your rhetorical audience, fulfill your purpose, and deliver it in an appropriate medium.

Questions for a peer reviewer

1. What change does the writer hope to make? How do you know?
2. What do you think the writer's thesis or main point is? Where, exactly, did you get your information?
3. Who might be the writer's rhetorical audience?
4. What might be the writer's purpose? How do audience and purpose connect?
5. What suggestions do you have for the writer for enhancing the effectiveness of the introduction?
6. Underline descriptive details that are especially vivid. Which ones describe characters, the setting, emotions?
7. How and where, exactly, do transitions help the reader keep track of the narrative? Identify places that could use transitional words or phrases.
8. Which passage did you most enjoy? Why?
9. What did you learn from the conclusion that you did not already know after reading the introduction and the body? What information does the writer want you to take away from the memoir? Does the writer attempt to change your attitude, action, or opinion? In other words, how does the writer address the opportunity for change?
10. What changes would you make if this were your memoir?

MindTap® Reflect on your writing process.

✈ ADDITIONAL ASSIGNMENTS

Knowledge Transfer

Too often we classify the memoir as personal writing, almost private. But memoir writing can be used in contexts other than English courses. Your field notes, application letters, letters to the editor (op-eds), and even lab reports employ many of the same features as

(continued)

the memoir: a sequence of events, characters (from baboons to chemical elements), a setting, synthesis, and analysis.

 COLLEGE Literacy Narrative Typically, the academic memoir has focused on learning to read and write in academic English. Compose a two- to three-page memoir in which you chart your literacy development, failures, breakthroughs, and successes. As you include features of narrative, characters, dialogue, and setting, be sure to synthesize and analyze the sequence of events so that your literacy memoir makes a significant point.

 COMMUNITY Eulogy Your best friend's father has passed away, and the family is asking that close friends—like you—speak at the funeral. Tapping the genre of the memoir, compose a narrative that captures a significant sequence of events that you shared with this man, making sure to include characters, dialogue, and setting. You will want to include rich descriptive details that capture how this good man lived his life.

 WORKPLACE Application Letter Compose a one- to two-page letter of application for a job, scholarship, or academic program. After you establish your credibility as a candidate (ethos), provide a narrative of events, your experience (including other characters), and your accomplishments that strongly position you for the job. Correct formatting helps build credibility in a business letter. Business letters are double-spaced. The most common format includes your address at the top of the letter, flush left, then the date, then the name and address of the person who is responsible for the position. Address your letter formally (Dear Ms. Jones) and follow the salutation with a colon. Paragraphs are flush left with a space between them in most business letters. Include the position you are seeking in the first sentence of your letter.

MULTIMODAL PowerPoint Presentation: Technology Literacy Narrative By now, you are no doubt computer, smartphone, and iPad literate. You can keyboard without thinking, access podcasts, upload YouTube videos, and sustain your active Twitter account. In an essay of two to three pages, compose a technology literacy narrative, one that focuses on your experiences as you have learned to process, produce, maybe even build technologies that allow you to engage with others, take pleasure, and experience deep frustrations. You might explore the positives of mastering technologies, or you might consider what you might be missing by not reading a physical book, sending or receiving letters through the mail, or being off-line, unhooked. Incorporate the features of a traditional memoir as you compose your narrative, but do not limit yourself to a print delivery. Try PowerPoint or PechaKucha.

GRAMMAR IN C⊙NTEXT Thinking Rhetorically about Verb Tense

A fiction (or memoir) writer may use the present tense to tell a story because it makes the events seem more immediate. To get a sense of the difference between the uses of the present and past tenses, imagine the following passage with all the underlined verbs in the past tense.

> We <u>drive</u> past Half Moon Bay and Pacifica and Seaside, the condos on the left and the surfers on the right, the ocean exploding pink. We <u>pass</u> through cheering eucalyptus and waving pines, cars <u>reflect</u> wildly as they come at us, they <u>seem</u> to come right for us, and I <u>look</u> through their windshields for the faces of those coming at us, for a sigh, for their understanding, for their trust, and I <u>find</u> their trust and they <u>go</u> by. Our car <u>thrums</u> loudly, and I <u>turn</u> up the radio because I <u>can</u>. I <u>drum</u> the steering wheel with open palms, then fists, because I <u>can</u>. Toph <u>looks</u> at me. I <u>nod</u> gravely.
>
> —**Dave Eggers,** *A Heartbreaking Work of Staggering Genius*

MindTap® Find additional handbook coverage of grammar, punctuation, and style online.

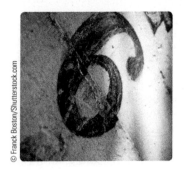

© Franck Boston/Shutterstock.com

Profiles

W e all like to compose profiles, whether we are preparing our parents to meet our romantic partner, describing Paris or the Burning Man festival to our neighbor, or writing a letter of application. Whether it analyzes, informs, entertains, or even provokes, a **profile** characterizes people, places, or events by emphasizing their unique features: your partner's musical abilities, Paris's fantastic street food, art at Burning Man, or the perfect alignment of your background with the job description. Profiles of local people, celebrities, vacation destinations, rock concerts, racehorses, and former presidents regularly appear in newspapers and magazines, sometimes in the form of interviews. In this chapter, we will focus on profiles of people.

profile a portrait in words of a person, place, or event

Profiles are not always wildly positive—or negative. As you work to discover what person most interests you, consider the medium, or the most fitting means of delivery for your profile.

IDENTIFYING AN OPPORTUNITY FOR CHANGE

 Print Profile written for a community, campus, or corporate newspaper or magazine; a flyer, or a performance program

 Audio Profile recorded for a local radio station or as a podcast, perhaps in concert with your subject

 Online Profile composed as a blog entry, class bulletin board, multimedia presentation, or YouTube video (using SlideShare, PechaKucha, or iMovie)

GENRE IN F⊙CUS The Bio

Nearly sixty years ago, on August 28, 1963, the Reverend Dr. Martin Luther King, Jr., spoke at the March on Washington for Jobs and Freedom.* King's legacy in U.S. history centers on his great victories in the civil rights movement. This legacy was shaped, in part, by his enviable ability to put his message into words:

> **So even though we face the difficulties of today and tomorrow, I still have a dream. I have a dream that one day this nation will rise up and live out the true meaning of its creed . . . that all men are created equal. I have a dream that one day even the state of Mississippi, a state sweltering with the heat of oppression, will be transformed into an oasis of freedom and justice. I have a dream that my four little chil dren will one day live in a nation where they will not be judged by the color of their skin but by the content of their character. I have a dream today. And if America is to be a great nation, this must become true.**
>
> **—Martin Luther King, Jr., "I Have a Dream"**

Nearly every profile of King emphasizes his brilliant oratory, with some also highlighting his extraordinary abilities as a strategist and leader. We are naturally curious, so even if we recognize the results of King's efforts, we may want to learn more about what motivated King (or the subject of our own profile) to

*Reprinted by arrangement with The Heirs to the Estate of Martin Luther King Jr., c/o Writers House as agent for the proprietor New York, NY. Copyright © 1963 Dr. Martin Luther King Jr., © renewed 1991 Coretta Scott King.

say or do the things he did. We may want to learn more about when, where, and how the person we are profiling became effective, accomplished, or influential—or just the opposite. We may pursue answers to these questions because we have been inspired, angered, or even moved to tears or action by this person's example.

Taylor Branch examined the King era in his award-winning trilogy on the civil rights movement. On his website (www.taylorbranch.com), Branch creates a vivid portrait of King in this excerpt from the final volume, *At Canaan's Edge: America in the King Years 1965–68*.

> **The triumphs of the Montgomery bus boycott and the March on Washington with its stirring "I Have a Dream" speech, the passage of the Civil Rights and Voting Rights acts and the winning of the Nobel Peace Prize were all behind Martin Luther King Jr. when he began the last and perhaps loneliest year of his life in January 1968. Now black-power militants and even some of his closest advisers were rejecting King's philosophy of nonviolence. Many white supporters of the civil rights movement had redirected their enthusiasm—and their dollars—to opposing the war in Vietnam. Other whites chastised King for speaking out against the war. Constant travel to rally support for his Southern Christian Leadership Conference (SCLC), along with his frequent affairs on the road, strained King's marriage. Premonitions of death stalked him. Meanwhile, the FBI stepped up its harassment with wiretaps and dirty tricks. Determined to revitalize his mission and himself, King hoped he could achieve both by leading a multiracial crusade against poverty. He called it the Poor People's Campaign, and although his staff had deep reservations about the idea, he spent what would be his last months planning a new march on Washington.**
>
> **—Taylor Branch, *At Canaan's Edge***

Writers create profiles to help readers (including themselves) gain a deeper understanding of another person, whether that person is well known or not. Sometimes writers create profiles to analyze the individuals who have shaped history, influenced other people, set a good example, or caused great harm. The rhetorical response of a profile can serve to provide insight into a person through several rhetorical strategies of development, from narration and pages 262–265 and 275–278 description to exemplification and argument (see CHAPTER 14, NARRATION, DESCRIPTION, EXEMPLIFICATION, AND ARGUMENT). Profiles explain, describe, analyze pages 270–275 causes and effects or processes, inspire, or entertain (see CHAPTER 14, CAUSE-AND-EFFECT ANALYSIS AND PROCESS ANALYSIS).

ASSIGNMENT

Among the people you know, whom do you find fascinating? What intrigues you about them—their approach to life, their accomplishments, their unusual interests or hobbies? As you consider which individual to profile, think about each person in more detail: What is your dominant impression of him or her? What do you already know about this person that supports your impression? What seems to contradict or temper that impression?

In your profile, you will select details that together add up to the dominant impression of your subject that you have developed and refined through further investigation, including, possibly, interviews with the subject and about the subject, as well as online and library research. Gather anecdotes about your subject from diverse sources, facts that may interest your readers, and any other kinds of information that will allow your readers to become as fascinated by your subject as you are.

READING RHETORICALLY

Profiles demonstrate to readers the dominant impression the subject makes. In these relatively brief pieces, you want to be able to identify the subject and examine that person's personality, words, actions, maybe body language, and influence on others. You should also get a sense of the opportunity to which the writer may be responding as well as the writer's purpose.

Key Features of a Profile

In a biographical profile, for instance, writers paint a portrait with words to describe a person in detail and to show how the descriptive pieces fit together to form the whole person. If you want to share your understanding (or judgment) with a specific audience, consider writing a profiles. Biographical profiles commonly have the following features:

- Profiles have as their subject someone readers will find compelling, interesting, maybe even puzzling.
- Profiles provide descriptive, sensory details to help readers imagine how the subject looks, sounds, acts, maybe even smells!

- Profiles include several direct quotations from the subject or others that help readers understand the person's opinions and perspectives.
- Profiles draw on evidence and insights from a variety of sources, such as personal observations, interviews, and library and online research.
- Profiles present several anecdotes about the subject that show readers the background and experiences that have shaped the subject.
- Profiles lead readers to a particular emotional response to, fresh take on, or logical conclusion about the subject.

In the following profile, *People* contributors offer a profile of the three American men who defused a deadly situation when they disarmed a gunman on a Paris-bound train in August 2015. "Dude, let's go" were the words that launched their heroic acts.

As you read through the following essay, consider

- What makes these three men worthy of a profile?
- What makes them likable people you want to know more about?
- How are they ordinary guys? Extraordinary men?

MindTap® Read, highlight, and take notes online.

Heroes on the Train: "It Was Either Do Something or Die"

SANDRA SOBIERAJ WESTFALL WITH PETER MIKELBANK, NINA BIDDLE, ANDREA DAMEWOOD, SUSAN KEATING, ROSE MINUTAGLIO, AND SUSAN YOUNG

We seem to be fascinated by people who demonstrate courage, especially under extreme pressure. In this piece, the People *writers use a profile to help readers understand the motivations, backgrounds, and split-second decisions these three childhood friends were able to put into service for the public good.*

MCMULLAN CO/SIPA/ AP Images

As rowdy 7-year-olds, Spencer Stone and Alek Skarlatos chased in and out of each other's neighboring houses in Carmichael, Calif., with toy guns. By middle school Anthony Sadler made it a carefree trio and playing pretend war gave way to playing football.

Typical boys, "they wanted to be policemen, firemen," Skarlatos's mom, Heidi Hansen, tells *People.* Stone bagged groceries in high school then joined the Air Force. Skarlatos and Sadler each worked at Costco—Skarlatos before deploying with his Army National Guard unit to Afghanistan; Sadler to help pay for classes at Cal State Sacramento. Says his dad, Anthony Sadler, Sr.: "They're good boys. They could get into their share of mischief but nothing too dramatic."

The writers make clear that they have conducted interviews that provide opinions and perspectives.

Until now.

On Aug. 21 the childhood buddies, now in their 20s, shot to international acclaim after they charged and tackled a heavily-armed man aboard a Paris-bound Thalys train packed with 554 people. President Obama telephoned to say he was impressed by their bravery. French President François Hollande welcomed the threesome into the Élysée Palace to present each with the red-ribboned medal of France's highest award, the Legion d'honneur. "You averted what could have been a true carnage," Hollande said. Fellow passenger Jean-Hugues Anglade, a French actor, put it this way: "We were in the wrong place but with the right people."

The writers provide descriptive details that breathe life into their subjects.

"Our parents like to say that whenever we get together, there's always something that happens," Sadler, 23, says. . . . But that *something*, this time, was supposed to be simple: three buddies ambling across Europe to celebrate Skarlatos's safe return this summer from Afghanistan and to take advantage of both Sadler's summer break from school and Stone's leave from Lajes Field air base in Azores, Portugal, where he serves as an emergency medical technician.

The writers use quotations and background information to show that the three have long been great friends—and good guys. These quotations provide different points of view.

Instead it was just three days into their adventure when they scrapped thoughts of an extra night in Amsterdam . . . and boarded the Friday afternoon train to Paris. . . . The narrative of what happened next is drawn from accounts by the three men and other witnesses.

The writers provide descriptive background details that have shaped their subjects.

As Stone was "in a deep sleep" in his assigned First-Class seat, a passenger in the next car, 51-year-old American professor Mark Moogalian was telling his wife, Isabelle, there was "something strange" about the man—later identified by French authorities as Ayoub El-Khazzani, 26, of Moroccan origin—who took his bag into the bathroom. When the man emerged, he was shirtless and brandishing an AK-47. . . . Moogalian told [Isabelle] to get down, she said, then "threw himself" at the gunman, who fired.

In the following section, the writers depend on narrative techniques to tell the story. The breadth of their research shows readers why a team of writers was necessary to get this story out in such a short time.

"The gunshot was the first noise I heard," says Skarlatos. He hit Stone on the shoulder and said, "Dude. Let's go!" Stone charged at El-Khazzani, followed by Skarlatos and Sadler. "We saw him cocking the AK-47. So it was either do something or die," says Sadler. The gunman put up a fight. "Tackled him.

We hit the ground," Stone explains. "Alek came up and grabbed the gun while I put the guy in a choke hold. It seemed like he just kept pulling out more weapons, left and right." El-Khazzani, who also carried a handgun and a box cutter, slashed at Stone, nearly severing his thumb before the bulky airman "choked him unconscious" at the same time Skarlatos beat El-Khazzani in the head with the muzzle of one gun and Sadler secured the other gun. . . . While Skarlatos and [another passenger] hog-tied El-Khazzani with passenger's neckties and scarves, Sadler searched for a first-aid kit, and Stone, though badly injured, aided Moogalian. . . . "We just kind of acted," Skarlatos says. "There wasn't much thinking going on."

. . . .

While those who know Stone, Skarlatos and Sadler best await their homecoming . . . , none of them seem surprised by the trio's heroics—or that they were in it together. Sadler's father says he made the men promise before their trip "that they wouldn't go anywhere by themselves and that they would have each other's backs." As Skarlatos later joked of their togetherness, "We're probably going to be buried in the same casket!" Fortunately, just no time soon.

Source: Sandra Sobieraj Westfall et al., "Heroes on the Train: 'It Was Either Do Something or Die'." Published in *People;* 9/7/2015, Vol. 84 Issue 10, pp. 54–58.

Marginal notes:

This paragraph gives readers a sense of how the events unfolded and how the three friends worked together to subdue the shooter.

Despite a harrowing narrative, the writers keep the focus on the three men, developing their character, sense of humor, strength, and deep friendship.

The writers help readers understand the backgrounds and experiences of three Americans on a European train who risked their own lives to save those of others.

Using Synthesis and Analysis

With purpose linked to audience, you will want to determine who the writer's intended audience might be: who might care about this subject? As you read, the overall impression you are making of the subject depends, in great part, on the writer's stance toward the subject (positive, negative, puzzled, or neutral?). And that stance is often revealed by the kinds of research findings the writer includes: interviews, observations, firsthand experience, and library and online research. As you read through the profile, analyze the opening, the way the writer works to hook you into the story. Pay careful attention to the organization of the profile (chronological, emphatic, or rhythmic, with the give-and-take of an interview). And then observe carefully the closing. What words, what impression does the writer leave you with?

MindTap® Find additional examples of profiles online.

See also CHAPTER 22, DAVID FALLARME, "A Look at How Gen Y Communicates"

See also CHAPTER 22, JOEL STEIN, "Millennials: The Me, Me, Me Generation"

See also CHAPTER 22, THE BELOIT COLLEGE MINDSET, "List for the Class of 2019"

See also CHAPTER 23, PIERRE CHRISTIN AND OLIVIER BALEZ, *Robert Moses: The Master Builder of New York City* [The Battle with Jane Jacobs] (graphic novel)

See also CHAPTER 25, MELISSA DAVEY, *Neil deGrasse Tyson Calls Scientific Illiteracy a Tragedy of Our Times*

RESPONDING TO THE RHETORICAL SITUATION

Profiles are often the best response to a rhetorical opportunity that calls for specific information about a person, place, or event. Although profiles can be used to describe, judge, or reevaluate, most profiles are descriptive and informative. Academic departments, for instance, often feature profiles (also known as personal web pages) of the faculty and staff, course offerings, scholarships, majors, and minors. Businesses, hospitals, and organizations purposefully design electronic web pages, printed brochures, and portfolios, using descriptive words, specific details, and images to deliver relevant information about their personnel or their services to students, clients, and patients. When an opportunity calls for you to describe someone or something to an interested audience, a profile may be the best genre for you to develop.

Opportunity   Audience and Purpose   Genre/Profile   (Medium of) Delivery

Understanding the Rhetorical Situation

Whatever opportunity you take to write a profile, you will be shaping it purposefully for a specific audience. In the process, you will be conducting research, summarizing your findings, synthesizing your research into a dominant impression, and then assembling supporting details, examples, facts, figures, and anecdotes. In a profile, you describe the dominant impression your subject makes. What are the traits that convey this impression? What words, behaviors, and appearances bring this impression to life? You may need to conduct informal and formal research—at the library, in person, or on the screen. You also may need to conduct some interviews. (For more on observation and interviews, see FIELDWORK IN CHAPTER 16.) Drawing on your research findings, your observations, and your insights, compose a profile that is rich in revealing details of appearance, speech, experience, education, beliefs, or actions. Your glimpse into a person's private life and personal experience might even explain the very visible work or actions that person performs.

pages 304–305

RESEARCHING THE PROFILE

Rare is the profile written without the benefit of research. Even if you are intrigued by your subject, chances are you do not know enough to write about it to compose a compelling profile of interest to other readers. Most writers of profiles need to conduct research on their subjects, using interviews, library and online research, observations, scrapbooks and other pertinent materials. Writers working on biographical profiles may want to interview the subject or their family members, observe that person in action (face to face or on the screen), or look through scrapbooks, diaries, recipe books, or stored memorabilia.

Identifying an opportunity for change

To identify a rhetorical opportunity, consider the people who work, study, or perform in your community. Whose voices are shaping the dialogue about pressing campus, community, church, or even national concerns? Whose voices are influencing the attitudes and actions of others? Preachers, for instance, often craft their messages with deft rhetorical style, as do teachers, coaches, civic leaders, and certain family members. These individuals create opportunities for others to develop talents, activism, and abilities, or they work behind the scenes unnoticed. Maybe you want to learn more about these people. Maybe others need to know about them as well. (Many of the following ideas can be translated into a profile of a place, event, or memorial as well.)

1. List three people who have recently impressed you. Have any of your fellow students motivated others to action through their words? Any teachers encouraged students to develop their talents and join conversations or activities on campus? What about entertainers, or writers, or local leaders

in your community (maybe an elected official who initiated rent control or someone who started a soup kitchen)? For each person on your list, write a few sentences describing your initial impressions. Explain those impressions by writing down as many details as you can about these people and what drew you to them. Who else might find these individuals impressive?

2. For one or two of the people you listed in response to question #1, locate images—or, if the opportunity presents itself, take photos—that capture the individuals' qualities or actions. Then spend several minutes writing about what the visuals convey about the ability of these individuals to inject life, energy, and direction into their words or actions. Who might want to know about these people?

3. Select one person for your profile and compose four or five sentences describing instances and ways that this person has succeeded or failed. Spend several minutes freewriting about the contexts in which this person has influenced and inspired people. Describe what you know about the person's background and analyze how this background might have shaped her or his drive, purpose, or success.

Relating rhetorically to your audience

The following questions will help you identify your rhetorical audience for your profile. Your answers will also help you describe and analyze your subject's effective way with words, action, or even silence.

1. List the names of the persons or groups (students, faculty, administrators, community members, or alumni) likely to be engaged—positively or negatively—by your subject.

2. Next to the name of each potential audience, write reasons that audience could have for appreciating the subject. In other words, what would persuade these audiences that they need to learn about this person's experiences, perspectives, and motivations in greater detail?

3. How could each of these audiences be influenced by a profile of this individual? What emotional responses or logical conclusions could you expect your profile to lead to? Consider the implications of these emotional responses or logical conclusions for each audience and the motivations each audience might have for learning more about the personal experiences, values, and worldview that have affected your subject.

4. With these different audiences' interests and motivations in mind, consider what descriptive details, images, and compelling quotes or audio snippets (if you conduct and record interviews) will enable your

readers to feel invested in exploring the life of this person who has helped shape the campus or the local or broader community. A compelling description will help your audience more clearly visualize the person in action, appreciate how he or she has moved people, and understand how this individual has affected you or the local or broader community. Tailor your best description to connect closely to your audience's needs and interests.

Planning an effective rhetorical response for your purpose

Once you have identified a reason to compose a profile, you will want to focus on your audience, the people who want to learn more about your subject, whether that subject is you, another person, an event, or a place. Different audiences require different kinds of texts—delivered through different media. For example, if you are writing a profile about yourself, say in a résumé and cover letter, you will want to deliver those informative materials according to a potential employer's preference: electronically through an online portal or in print via the postal service. If you are writing a profile about an unsung student researcher on campus, you could compose an inspiring feature article for the alumni magazine or create a YouTube video for the Office of Student Life website. Your celebratory profile of a family member—even one capturing family lore—could be the PowerPoint centerpiece of a family reunion. Once you identify your opportunity, locate your audience, and find your purpose, you will determine what kind of text will best respond to the rhetorical situation.

Use the following questions to help you narrow your purpose and shape your response:

1. What facts, details, and images are necessary for creating a vivid picture of your subject and your subject's influence? What research will produce that information?
2. What experiences, activities, actions, and personal qualities make your subject compelling to your audience?
3. What specific information does your audience need to understand your subject's motivation and appreciate that person's significance for the family, school, or community? What research is necessary?
4. What is your ultimate goal? Will your audience adopt a new perspective on your subject, take a specific action, or something else?
5. What is the best way to reach this audience? That is, to what kind of text—print, electronic, verbal, visual, video—will this audience most likely respond?

Links may change due to availability.

Print Profile
In the example at the beginning of this chapter, *People* magazine writers wrote a profile on three men who stopped a terrorist attack.

Audio Profile
The audio profile of Bill McKibben was written and recorded by Alena Martin and produced at WBYX at the University of Oregon.

Online Profile
The online profile of Beverly Wright of the Deep South Center for Environmental Justice was composed by Faiza Elmasry.

Profiles

🧭 WRITING A PERSUASIVE PROFILE: A Guide

*W*riting a persuasive profile involves evidence. Profiles persuade by using vivid details, snippets of conversation, short anecdotes, and maybe even images that reveal the subject's character. Most profiles are organized around the rhetorical appeals of ethos, logos, and pathos. The writer must establish the credibility of the subject (ethos), shape the argument with evidence and good reasons (logos), and make an emotional connection (pathos) with the reader. (See *CHAPTER 2, THE AVAILABLE MEANS INCLUDE THE RHETORICAL ELEMENTS OF THE MESSAGE ITSELF*.) After capturing your readers' attention in the introduction with a brief image of the subject, you will want to shape the body of your profile with assertions that point to the fuller description of the subject and influence to come.

pages 23–26

ADVANTAGES AND LIMITATIONS

Advantages

- **Writer:** Profiles offer the opportunity for you to find out more about someone who (or something that) already impresses you, a subject that does not have to be globally known or significant. Your subject can be close by, even familiar. Researching and composing a profile helps satisfy your curiosity about your subject and often reveals new, refreshing details.

- **Message:** Profiles provide insight into a person, place, or event, using rhetorical strategies of narration, description, exemplification, and argument. You can deliver your profile in an energetic, friendly way, if you choose.

- **Media and Design:** Profiles offer you the pleasure of sharing your impression with others, through conversation, a print essay, or a visual presentation.

Limitations

- **Writer:** Unfortunately, you cannot always meet your subject in person. Most profiles require research, at the library, online, through interviews, and by observation.

- **Message:** Commissioned profiles are often much more formal in tone and frequently demand clear images.

- **Media and Design:** Unless you have been asked by an organization to produce a specific profile, you must make an effort to locate a rhetorical audience, one that could be changed in some way by learning more about your subject.

Introduction

- **Show readers that the subject is someone they need to know more about.**
- **Present the dominant impression made by the subject and highlight key features of the subject's personality, character, or values.**

Highlight features your readers will want to know more about Supply your readers with a compelling incident about, a powerful description of, or convincing results produced by your subject to persuade them to keep reading. The *People* writers, for example, open with a brief story of a wholesome childhood threesome that ends with a father's quote: "They're good boys. They could get into their share of mischief but nothing too dramatic." This is followed by the transition "Until now." "Uh oh," readers think. "What now?" And they read on to discover a dominant impression of "nice-guy heroes."

Create goodwill for your subject To entice readers to continue, a profile writer must quickly establish the rhetorical appeal of credible *ethos*. The *People* writers introduce the future heroes as children, "rowdy," "carefree," and "typical," creating a sense of goodwill and good sense, while alluding to the heroism to come. Thus, these writers supply a believable, trustworthy account of Spencer Stone, Alek Skarlatos, and Anthony Sadler.

Connect your subject to your readers' interests and values By establishing a positive ethos, the *People* writers connect a story of bravery and daring with the admiration, even aspiration, of their readers. "Would I be so brave in the same situation? I hope so." And they establish common ground with their readers as well, the shared concern of "safety from terrorism."

Ask yourself . . .
- How can I connect my concerns about my subject with the interests of my audience?
- What incident, descriptive details, and examples might most successfully engage my readers' interest at the same time they reveal my dominant impression of my subject?
- How can I best establish my credibility and my subject's significance?

- **Present a fuller description of the subject, emphasizing the key features of that overall impression.**
- **Include specific details, descriptions, conversations, and anecdotes that help readers visualize the subject in body, words, and actions.**
- **Provide logical appeals in the form of good reasons, backed up with detailed examples that demonstrate the effect of that subject on the lives of people like the readers themselves.**

Establish good reasons for your dominant impression of the subject Writers use the body of a profile to establish logos, the logical appeals of good reasons. These reasons often appeal in the form of multiple supporting examples and details. The assertions and supporting examples make obvious the work, influence, personal qualities, and actions of the subject.

Show how your subject has made a difference In the story of the heroic threesome, the *People* writers tell how, in order to overcome the gunman, the three collaborated with one another as well as with other passengers, who helped them tie up the gunman with their neckties and scarves. Most readers would like to think that they, too, would pitch in and help the heroes, if they were not the heroes themselves.

Provide quotations that give the profile credibility The *People* writers conducted a great deal of research in order to provide quotations from the heroes' parents, the heroes themselves, people on the train, and government officials. All the quotations support the dominant impression of heroism, bravery, and wholesomeness—as well as the heroes' significance to the greater community. These quotations enhance the writers' ethos, one of responsible reporting, while supporting the logos of the essay. Yes, these heroes are daring, brave, and strong—but just as much evidence speaks to their status as "good guys," an inspiration to us all.

(continued)

Create a story through vivid description Incorporate narrative to draw readers closer to the subject. Readers of the *People* magazine article, for example, can vicariously experience what happened at the most crucial moment: "'The gunshot was the first noise I heard,' says Skarlatos. He hit Stone on the shoulder and said, 'Dude. Let's go.' . . . 'We saw him cocking the AK-47. So it was either do something or die,' says Sadler. The gunman put up a fight. 'Tackled him. We hit the ground,' Stone explains. 'Alek came up and grabbed the gun while I put the guy in a choke hold. It seemed like he just kept pulling out more weapons, left and right.' . . . at the same time Skarlatos beat El-Khazzani in the head with the muzzle of one gun and Sadler secured the other gun."

Ask yourself . . .
- What assertions am I making about my subject that bring the dominant impression to life?
- What specific examples, details, anecdotes, and results can I supply for each assertion?
- How believable or relatable do these examples seem to be?

- **Capture with one final quote or anecdote the dominant impression of the subject.**
- **Trace the influence of the subject and perhaps predict that person's future influence.**
- **Work to connect the treatment of the subject with the readers' sensibility or emotions.**
- **Bring readers into the present day, if the profile has had a historical scope.**

Capture the essence of your subject in a final quotation The conclusion of a profile often contains one final quote or anecdote that nicely captures the essence of the individual. The *People* writers, for example, use a quote from Sadler's father as their setup: he made the men promise before their trip "that they wouldn't go anywhere by themselves and that they would have each other's backs."

Reinforce the connection to your readers The writers follow that quote with one of the heroes' own, joking back on their togetherness, "We're probably going to be buried in the same casket!" The essay ends with, "Fortunately, just no time soon." Thus, this conclusion reinforces the dominant impression of lifelong friends who stick together through thick and extra thin, an impression that readily connects with the emotions of readers who yearn to be brave, stay safe, and protect others.

Ask yourself . . .
- What impression do I most want to leave with my readers?
- How can I stimulate the readers to consider the lasting effects of my subject(s)?

Revision and Peer Review

After you have drafted a strong version of your profile, ask one or two of your classmates to read through it. You will want your classmate to respond to your work in a way that helps you revise it into the strongest profile it can be, one that addresses your intended audience, helps you fulfill your purpose, and is delivered in the most appropriate means available to you. In other words, if your profile were your peer's, how would that classmate revise it?

Questions for a peer reviewer

1. What is the dominant impression the profile expresses?
2. Who might constitute an interested audience for this profile?
3. What is the writer's purpose in composing for this audience?
4. Why might the writer feel a need to compose this profile?
5. Where in the profile do you find the answers to the first four questions?
6. How and where did the writer "hook" you into the story? How might that hook be strengthened?
7. How and where did the writer establish credibility or ethos? (This might be in several places.)
8. Underline the supporting details and examples the writer provides that bring the subject and subject's influence to life, that shape the logos of the profile.
9. Put a squiggly line under the experiences and actions that make the subject interesting to you. In what way could the writer help you better understand what influences this subject has or what the effects of this subject might be? Be specific.
10. Where and how does the writer make an emotional connection (establish pathos) with the reader? How might the writer strengthen this rhetorical appeal?
11. What did you learn from the conclusion that you did not already know after reading the introduction and body? What information does the writer want you to take away from the profile? Does the writer attempt to change your attitude, action, or opinion?
12. Which section of the profile did you most enjoy? Why?
13. Which section of the profile was the most difficult for you to follow? Why?

MindTap® Reflect on your writing process.

✈ ADDITIONAL ASSIGNMENTS

Knowledge Transfer

The profile need not be limited to people. Places, organizations, and events also merit profiles. When you visit the Smithsonian Institution museums, national parks, or famous landmarks, you can usually obtain a profile in the form of a brochure, which relays the dominant impression you should take away from the place and supplies a multitude of facts and details that breathe life into that place. Businesses and organizations, too, post profiles, often online, as do events, like Burning Man, the Macy's Thanksgiving Day Parade, even your first-year writing course.

COLLEGE Ethnography An ethnography is a profile of individual peoples and cultural customs using personal observation and experience. It is often used in anthropology courses. After or instead of conducting an interview, you might arrange to observe the person you interviewed at work, shadowing that person throughout the day and interviewing coworkers. Again, you will want to glean ample background information (education, experience) in order to connect the person's present to the past—and then to the future. You might ask coworkers what impresses them most about the person, what challenges that person has overcome, or what problems continue to vex that person.

COMMUNITY Introduction Compose a profile of your hometown, delivering it in print, in visuals, or electronically (with visuals and audio), and introduce yourself by way of advertising your hometown. You can rely on your own observations and experiences, interviews, and some local research in order to collect enough detailed information that you can create a dominant impression. Be sure also to reveal the places and events that distinguish your hometown.

WORKPLACE Interview If you know someone whose occupation interests you, arrange to conduct an interview with that person, taking with you a list of generative questions that will help you arrive at a dominant impression. Be sure to ask about background, education, experience, daily life on the job, goals, and, if appropriate, domestic life. Come up with a question that might reveal something about the individual's personality: What role has disappointment played in your life? Or, what place would you most like to visit?

MULTIMODAL Video Résumé Although the use of video job applications is not yet widespread, chances are it soon will be, given that Skype interviews have already replaced many face-to-face ones. Compose a profile of yourself, showing how your experience, education, and goals align with specific job criteria. Before recording yourself and your voice, write out a script you want to follow, deciding whether the job calls for you to present yourself as business-like, formal, casual, or creative. The same goes for your dress. Whether you use iMovie, your smartphone, or a camera to film yourself, you can easily revise what you see and hear.

GRAMMAR IN C⊚NTEXT Thinking Rhetorically about Inclusive Language

Language used to identify people in terms of their religion, race, education, politics, or other characteristics presents a distinctive challenge. Most people feel that their individuality transcends their membership in any one group. If you must mention others as belonging to a group, the best way to show them respect is to use the name they have chosen for themselves (whether that is *American Indians, Native Americans, Indigenous People, First Americans,* or *Indians; Latino/Latina* or *Chicano/Chicana;* or some other name). Although there are countless groups, only a few frequently found in print are discussed here.

Referring to gender Sentences that needlessly single out a person as being male or female can be revised fairly easily.

- Make a pronoun or determiner and its antecedent plural.

  Reporters   *they describe*
  A reporter should be sure that he describes events accurately.

Some authors choose to use *they* or *she* as an alternative to the generic *he.* However, sentences such as *A reporter should be sure that they describe events accurately* and *A reporter should be sure that she describes events accurately* are not considered standard.

- Rephrase to avoid using a pronoun.

  A reporter should be sure to describe events accurately.

- Use a noun phrase instead of a pronoun.

  that person
  If someone questions the procedures, he should consult the supervisor.

- Use both *he* and *she.*

  or she
  If an individual questions the procedures, he should consult the supervisor.

This option should be avoided when possible because of its awkwardness.

- Use an article instead of a possessive determiner.

  a

  Every employee has ~~his own~~ locker.

- Drop the possessive determiner.

  A student should submit ~~his~~ papers on time.

- Choose gender-neutral terms.

  working people

  Labor unions benefit ~~the working man.~~

Other gender-neutral terms include the following:

~~anchorman, anchorwoman~~	anchor, news anchor
~~businessman~~	business executive, businessperson
~~chairman, chairwoman~~	chair, chairperson
~~clergyman~~	member of the clergy
~~congressman~~	member of Congress, representative, senator
~~man, mankind~~	human, human beings, humanity, humankind
~~repairman~~	technician, repair technician
~~salesman~~	salesperson, sales representative, salesclerk
~~workman~~	worker

Referring to race and ethnicity Determining which terms a particular group prefers can be difficult because preferences sometimes vary within a group and change over time. One conventional way to refer to Americans of a specific descent is to include an adjective before the term *American: African American, Asian American, European American, Latin American, Mexican American, Native American.* These terms are widely used, especially by people who are not members of a given group. However, members of a particular group may identify themselves in more than one way. In addition to *African American* and *European American, black* and *white* have long been used. People of Spanish-speaking descent may prefer *Chicano/Chicana, Hispanic, Latino/Latina, Puerto Rican, Mexican,* or another term. Descendants of peoples who were indigenous to North America before European settlers arrived may prefer a specific name such as *Diné* or *Haida,* though some also accept *American Indian.* An up-to-date dictionary that includes notes on usage can help you choose appropriate terms.

Referring to age Although some people object to the term *senior citizen*, a better alternative has not yet been suggested. When used respectfully, the term refers to a person who has reached the age of retirement (but may not have decided to retire) and is eligible for certain privileges granted by society. However, if you know your audience would object to this term, find out what is preferred.

Referring to disability or illness A current recommendation for referring to disabilities and illnesses is "to put the person first"; in this way, it is believed, the focus will be on the individual rather than on the limitation. Thus, *persons with disabilities* is preferred over *disabled persons*. When you are writing, you can find out whether such person-first expressions are preferred by noting whether they are used in the articles and books (or by the people) you consult. Be aware, though, that some writers and readers find this type of expression unnatural sounding, and others think that it does not serve its purpose because the last word in a phrase can carry the greater weight, especially at the end of a sentence.

Referring to sexual orientation Terms for sexual orientation such as *gay, lesbian,* and *bisexual* are used most often as adjectives rather than as nouns. In fact, using a noun to refer to specific people may be considered offensive. Noting professions or participation is thought to be more respectful: two gay lawyers, three lesbian participants. But again, note sexual orientation only when it is relevant to the discourse.

Referring to geographical areas Certain geographical terms should be used with special care. Though most frequently used to refer to people from the United States, the term *American* may also refer to people from Canada, Mexico, and Central or South America. If your audience may be offended by this term, use *people from the United States* or *U.S. citizens* instead.

The term *Arab* refers to people of Arabic-speaking descent. Use this term only when you cannot use more specific terms, such as *Iraqi* or *Saudi Arabian,* and only when you are sure that a country's people speak Arabic and not another language. Iranians, for example, are not Arabs because they speak Farsi.

It is often helpful to distinguish between the terms *British* and *English*. *British* is the preferred term for referring to people from the island of Great Britain or from the United Kingdom. *English* refers to people from England (a part of the United Kingdom).

MindTap® Find additional handbook coverage of grammar, punctuation, and style online.

© Roman Sigaev/Shutterstock.com

Investigative Reports

MindTap® Understand the goals of the chapter and complete a warm-up activity online.

If you think investigative reports appear only on *Law & Order* or *CSI* (*Crime Scene Investigation*), then you may want to reconsider. Print, online, and televised news provide investigative reports; textbooks report subject-specific information, just as organizations (museums, clubs, initiatives, and government agencies) give you factual information that has been objectively investigated—or researched. The result of fact-finding or data-driven research, a **report** serves to highlight the author's expertise with the purpose of informing or educating an audience.

report a presentation of objective information on a topic

Throughout this chapter, you will work to identify an opportunity to investigate and then report your findings to a specific audience. As you determine what you want to investigate and who could be educated by your report, consider, too, the most fitting means of delivery.

IDENTIFYING AN OPPORTUNITY FOR CHANGE

 Print Report written for a community or campus newspaper or as a lab report for your chemistry professor

 Video Report filmed for your cultural anthropology course or filmed and uploaded to YouTube for your friends and family

 Online Report composed for your online campus newspaper or your personal blog

In only 0.42 second, Google provides 153,000 hits for the phrase "bad student writing." The American public has long complained about the quality and character of student writing, blaming the influences of television, rock 'n roll, teen apathy, self-absorption, and now digital communication. (See CHAPTER 14, CAUSE-AND-EFFECT ANALYSIS.) When researchers at Carnegie Mellon University investigated the issue, they outlined several contributing factors: pages 270–272

> During their high school careers, most of our students were not writing with the frequency we might expect, nor were they doing the types of writing that we will require of them in their college years. In a study at George Washington University (2007), first-year undergraduates reported that the most frequently assigned high school writing tasks required them to offer and support opinions, with a secondary emphasis on summarizing and synthesizing information. Students were rarely required to criticize an argument, define a problem and propose a solution, shape their writing to meet their readers' needs, or revise based on feedback. Furthermore, according to a survey conducted by *The Chronicle of Higher Education* (2006), 61% of high school teachers said their students have never written a paper that was more than five pages. As a result, students have not had enough practice to develop a set of sophisticated writing skills. When students lack skills in these areas, their writing may be unsatisfactory in multiple ways—from poor grammar and syntax to unclear organization to weak reasoning and arguments.
>
> —"Why Are Students Coming into College Poorly Prepared to Write?"

In "Bad Student Writing? Not So Fast!" Laurie Fendrich takes issue with the Carnegie Mellon explanation. In her article, Fendrich compares complaints about the most recent generation of students to those made by ancient Greeks. (See CHAPTER 14, COMPARISON AND CONTRAST.) pages 268–270

> It would be good for the blood pressure of everyone involved in criticizing education—state legislators, education policy professionals, professors, school administrators, parents—to take a deep breath. Put aside the statistics, the studies, the anecdotes, and take a look at the big picture.
>
> Here's what Edith Hamilton had to say about education, in *The Echo of Greece* (1957), one of her many trenchant books on the subject of the ancient Greeks:
>
>> If people feel that things are going from bad to worse and look at the new generation to see if they can be trusted to take charge among such

Investigative Reports

dangers, they invariably conclude that they cannot and that these irresponsible young people have not been trained properly. Then the cry goes up, "What is wrong with our education?" and many answers are always forthcoming.

Note the droll and ironic, "and many answers are always forthcoming." Perhaps studying people who lived so long ago—people who invented the very idea of education as a route to genuine freedom, and understood freedom to be worthwhile only when coupled with self-control—gave Hamilton one of those calm, stoical uber-minds that comprehends competing pronouncements about education never to be more than opinion.

—Laurie Fendrich, "Bad Student Writing? Not So Fast!"

investigative report an analysis of the "who, what, where, and why" of a topic

pages 266–268
pages 272–275
page 24

An **investigative report** provides information on the "who, what, where, and why" of a situation or topic. It is a rhetorical response often triggered by a desire to correct misinformation. A report will first need to define the issue being investigated. (See CHAPTER 14, DEFINITION.) After establishing the "what," an investigative report might focus on an explanation for the situation or process (see CHAPTER 14, PROCESS ANALYSIS) or an analysis of the causes behind particular consequences, as in the Carnegie Mellon report. Even an objective and fair-minded report of information will have to present evidence that supports your conclusion. (For more on types of evidence, see CHAPTER 2, LOGOS.) If you are interested in an issue about which there is a need for more information, especially a problem that is controversial or one where you have come across information with which you do not agree— such as students are not writing well because they are not well prepared for college writing—an investigative report helps you get information to interested readers.

Pacific Press/Getty Images

Elmira Ismayilova speaks to the press after the politically motivated arrest of her daughter, award-winning investigative journalist Khadija Ismayilova. After her later release on probation, Khadija Ismayilova pledged to continue reporting on financial corruption in Azerbaijan.

ASSIGNMENT

When you want to find out more about why a particular issue is the way it is, you will want to compose an investigative report in order to present the results of research you have conducted about that problem or one with which you have personal experience. In other words, what topic bothers you to the point that you would like to investigate and report on it? What misinformation would you like to correct? What audience is affected by this topic and would be interested in your report?

If you live in a college community, you may be wondering how underage drinking, littering, physical assault—or even homelessness—affects your community in some way. On or away from campus, you might either have firsthand knowledge of or want to research consequences of such issues as divorce, eating disorders, chemical waste, or genetic testing. For your investigative report, gather trustworthy and factual information that enables you to confidently report your findings in a manner that establishes your fair-mindedness, the reasonableness of your argument, and an authentic connection to the concerns of your audience.

MindTap® Request help and feedback from a tutor. If required, participate in peer review, submit your paper for a grade, and view instructor comments online.

READING RHETORICALLY

When you read an investigative report, your charge is to read what is there—and identify what has been left out. Because investigative reports are presented as factual and objective, it can be difficult to measure the amount of research the writer undertook. It is up to you to imagine what sources or points of view are not represented. You also want to determine the audience for the report: who are likely affected by the information? How are they affected? How might they use the information?

Key Features of a Report

An investigative report commonly has the following features:

- Defines an issue, problem, or phenomenon in precise terms.
- Makes clear why the topic under consideration needs to be investigated.
- Provides trustworthy facts and details that help readers understand the effects of this topic and determine who has a stake in the situation.

- Uses direct quotations to convey the perspectives of various groups with a stake in the issue.
- Relies on appropriate organization and design.
- Identifies the conclusion readers should reach.

In the report that follows, Christine Rosen responds directly to students' complaints (reported in "The Beloit College Mindset List for the Class of 2019," see Chapter 22) that "e-mail is just too slow," taking the opportunity to explain the common perceptions—and misperceptions—about multitasking. As you read through Rosen's report, keep notes on what is really happening in our brains when we try to pay attention to many things at once.

- What experts does Rosen consult? What are their viewpoints on multitasking (its causes, consequences, and complications)?
- How does Rosen establish her credibility?
- Who is her intended audience?
- How is her report a fitting response to the problem, particularly in terms of reaching her rhetorical audience?

MindTap®   Read, highlight, and take notes online.

The Myth of Multitasking

CHRISTINE ROSEN

Christine Rosen is a senior editor for The New Atlantis: A Journal of Technology & Society, *where she frequently writes about ethics and the cultural impact of technology.*

Kris Connor/Getty Images Entertainment/Getty Images

Rosen opens with age-old advice about the wisdom of doing one thing at a time. She has identified a rhetorical opportunity for addressing the modern-day practice of multitasking.

In one of the many letters he wrote to his son in the 1740s, Lord Chesterfield offered the following advice: "There is time enough for everything in the course of the day, if you do but one thing at once, but there is not time enough in the year, if you will do two things at a time." •To Chesterfield, singular focus was not merely a practical way to structure one's time; it was a mark of intelligence. "This steady and undissipated attention to one object, is a sure mark of a superior genius; as hurry, bustle, and agitation are the never-failing symptoms of a weak and frivolous mind."

In modern times, hurry, bustle, and agitation have become a regular way of life for many people—so much so that we have embraced a word to describe our efforts to respond to the many pressing demands on our time: *multitasking.* Used for decades to describe the parallel processing abilities of computers, multitasking is now shorthand for the human attempt to do simultaneously as many things as possible, as quickly as possible, preferably marshalling the power of as many technologies as possible.

In the late 1990s and early 2000s, one sensed a kind of exuberance about the possibilities of multitasking. Advertisements for new electronic gadgets— particularly the first generation of handheld digital devices—celebrated the notion of using technology to accomplish several things at once. The word *multitasking* began appearing in the "skills" sections of résumés, as office workers restyled themselves as high-tech, high-performing team players. "We have always multitasked—inability to walk and chew gum is a time-honored cause for derision—but never so intensely or self-consciously as now," James Gleick wrote in his 1999 book *Faster.* "We are multitasking connoisseurs—experts in crowding, pressing, packing, and overlapping distinct activities in our all-too-finite moments." An article in the *New York Times Magazine* in 2001 asked, "Who can remember life before multitasking? These days we all do it." The article offered advice on "How to Multitask" with suggestions about giving your brain's "multitasking hot spot" an appropriate workout.

But more recently, challenges to the ethos of multitasking have begun to emerge. Numerous studies have shown the sometimes-fatal danger of using cell phones and other electronic devices while driving, for example, and several states have now made that particular form of multitasking illegal. In the business world, where concerns about time-management are perennial, warnings about workplace distractions spawned by a multitasking culture are on the rise. In 2005, the BBC reported on a research study, funded by Hewlett-Packard and conducted by the Institute of Psychiatry at the University of London, that found, "Workers distracted by e-mail and phone calls suffer a fall in IQ more than twice that found in marijuana smokers." The psychologist who led the study called this new "infomania" a serious threat to workplace productivity. One of the *Harvard Business Review*'s "Breakthrough Ideas" for 2007 was Linda Stone's notion of "continuous partial attention," which might be understood as a subspecies of multitasking: using mobile computing power and the Internet, we are "constantly scanning for opportunities and staying on top of contacts, events, and activities in an effort to miss nothing."

Dr. Edward Hallowell, a Massachusetts-based psychiatrist who specializes in the treatment of attention deficit/hyperactivity disorder and has written

Rosen defines her topic in precise terms: multitasking has become a way of life, or at least an expectation.

Because we cannot remember life before multitasking, Rosen determines that the practice should be investigated.

Rosen provides facts and details that complicate the once-easy notion of multitasking. She enumerates the negative effects of multitasking on specific people and provides compelling facts and details.

a book with the self-explanatory title *CrazyBusy*, has been offering therapies to combat extreme multitasking for years; in his book he calls multitasking a "mythical activity in which people believe they can perform two or more tasks simultaneously." In a 2005 article, he described a new condition, "Attention Deficit Trait," which he claims is rampant in the business world. ADT is "purely a response to the hyperkinetic environment in which we live," writes Hallowell, and its hallmark symptoms mimic those of ADD. "Never in history has the human brain been asked to track so many data points," Hallowell argues, and this challenge "can be controlled only by creatively engineering one's environment and one's emotional and physical health." Limiting multi-tasking is essential. Best-selling business advice author Timothy Ferriss also extols the virtues of "single-tasking" in his book, *The 4-Hour Workweek*. . . .

Throughout her report, Rosen uses direct quotations to convey various perspectives, both positive and negative.

Changing Our Brains

To better understand the multitasking phenomenon, neurologists and psychologists have studied the workings of the brain. In 1999, Jordan Grafman, chief of cognitive neuroscience at the National Institute of Neurological Disorders and Stroke (part of the National Institutes of Health), used functional magnetic resonance imaging (fMRI) scans to determine that when people engage in "task-switching"—that is, multitasking behavior—the flow of blood increases to a region of the frontal cortex called Brodmann area 10. (The flow of blood to particular regions of the brain is taken as a proxy indication of activity in those regions.) "This is presumably the last part of the brain to evolve, the most mysterious and exciting part," Grafman told the *New York Times* in 2001—adding, with a touch of hyperbole, "It's what makes us most human."

Evidence from careful research helps Rosen establish her ethos and enhances the logos of her overall argument as well as its trustworthiness.

It is also what makes multitasking a poor long-term strategy for learning. . . . In one recent study, Russell Poldrack, a psychology professor at the University of California, Los Angeles, found that "multitasking adversely affects how you learn. Even if you learn while multitasking, that learning is less flexible and more specialized, so you cannot retrieve the information as easily." His research demonstrates that people use different areas of the brain for learning and storing new information when they are distracted: brain scans of people who are distracted or multitasking show activity in the striatum, a region of the brain involved in learning new skills; brain scans of people who are not distracted show activity in the hippocampus, a region involved in storing and recalling information. Discussing his research on National Public Radio recently, Poldrack warned, "We have to be aware that there is a cost to the way that our society is changing, that humans are not built to work this way. We're really built to focus. And when we sort of force ourselves to multitask, we're driving ourselves to perhaps be less efficient in the long run even though it sometimes feels like we're being more efficient."

If, as Poldrack concluded, "multitasking changes the way people learn," what might this mean for today's children and teens, raised with an excess of new entertainment and educational technology, and avidly multitasking at a young age? Poldrack calls this the "million-dollar question." Media multitasking—that is, the simultaneous use of several different media, such as television, the Internet, video games, text messages, telephones, and e-mail—is clearly on the rise, as a 2006 report from the Kaiser Family Foundation showed: in 1999, only 16 percent of the time people spent using any of those media was spent on multiple media at once; by 2005, 26 percent of media time was spent multitasking. "I multitask every single second I am online," confessed one study participant. "At this very moment I am watching TV, checking my e-mail every two minutes, reading a newsgroup about who shot JFK, burning some music to a CD, and writing this message."

The Kaiser report noted several factors that increase the likelihood of media multitasking, including "having a computer and being able to see a television from it." Also, "sensation-seeking" personality types are more likely to multitask, as are those living in "a highly TV-oriented household." The picture that emerges of these pubescent multitasking mavens is of a generation of great technical facility and intelligence but of extreme impatience, unsatisfied with slowness and uncomfortable with silence: "I get bored if it's not all going at once, because everything has gaps—waiting for a website to come up, commercials on TV, etc." one participant said. The report concludes on a very peculiar note, perhaps intended to be optimistic: "In this media-heavy world, it is likely that brains that are more adept at media multitasking will be passed along and these changes will be naturally selected," the report states. "After all, information is power, and if one can process more information all at once, perhaps one can be more powerful." This is techno-social Darwinism, nature red in pixel and claw.

Other experts aren't so sure. As neurologist Jordan Grafman told *Time* magazine: "Kids that are instant messaging while doing homework, playing games online and watching TV, I predict, aren't going to do well in the long run." "I think this generation of kids is guinea pigs," educational psychologist Jane Healy told the *San Francisco Chronicle*; she worries that they might become adults who engage in "very quick but very shallow thinking." Or, as the novelist Walter Kirn suggests in a deft essay in *The Atlantic*, we might be headed for an "Attention-Deficit Recession."

Noting potential negative effects on children is a good way for Rosen to establish pathos, to make a strong emotional connection with her readers.

Paying Attention

When we talk about multitasking, we are really talking about attention: the art of paying attention, the ability to shift our attention, and, more broadly, to exercise judgment about what objects are worthy of our attention. People who have achieved great things often credit for their success a finely honed skill for paying attention. When asked about his particular genius, Isaac Newton responded that if he had made any discoveries, it was "owing more to patient attention than to any other talent."

Rosen moves toward a conclusion by quoting Newton and James, historical figures whose contributions to culture have been monumental. Each of them, like Lord Chesterfield, recommends paying attention to one thing at a time.

William James, the great psychologist, wrote at length about the varieties of human attention. In *The Principles of Psychology* (1890), he outlined the differences among "sensorial attention," "intellectual attention," "passive attention," and the like, and noted the "gray chaotic indiscriminateness" of the minds of people who were incapable of paying attention. James compared our stream of thought to a river, and his observations presaged the cognitive "bottlenecks" described later by neurologists: "On the whole easy simple flowing predominates in it, the drift of things is with the pull of gravity, and effortless attention is the rule," he wrote. "But at intervals an obstruction, a set-back, a log-jam occurs, stops the current, creates an eddy, and makes things temporarily move the other way."

Rosen organizes her report appropriately, opening with a problem to be investigated, objectively reporting various viewpoints, providing factual evidence, quoting the experts, and building toward a sensible conclusion.

To James, steady attention was thus the default condition of a mature mind, an ordinary state undone only by perturbation. To readers a century later, that placid portrayal may seem alien—as though depicting a bygone world. Instead, today's multitasking adult may find something more familiar in James's description of the youthful mind: an "extreme mobility of the attention" that "makes the child seem to belong less to himself than to every object which happens to catch his notice." For some people, James noted, this challenge is never overcome; such people only get their work done "in the interstices of their mind-wandering." Like Chesterfield, James believed that the transition from youthful distraction to mature attention was in large part the result of personal mastery and discipline—and so was illustrative of character. "The faculty of voluntarily bringing back a wandering attention, over and over again," he wrote, "is the very root of judgment, character, and will."

Rosen reaches the conclusion that "our collective will to pay attention seems fairly weak," and she has provided factual, objective evidence to support that conclusion.

Today, our collective will to pay attention seems fairly weak. We require advice books to teach us how to avoid distraction. In the not-too-distant future we may even employ new devices to help us overcome the unintended attention deficits created by today's gadgets. As one *New York Times* article recently suggested, "Further research could help create clever technology, like sensors or smart software that workers could instruct with their preferences and priorities to serve as a high tech 'time nanny' to ease the modern multi-tasker's plight." Perhaps we will all accept as a matter of course a computer governor—like the devices placed on engines so that people can't drive cars beyond a certain speed. Our technological governors might prompt us with reminders to set mental limits when we try to do too much, too quickly, all at once.

Then again, perhaps we will simply adjust and come to accept what James called "acquired inattention." E-mails pouring in, cell phones ringing, televisions blaring, podcasts streaming—all this may become background noise, like the "din of a foundry or factory" that James observed workers could scarcely avoid at first, but which eventually became just another part of their daily routine. For the younger generation of multitaskers, the great electronic din is an expected part of everyday life. And given what neuroscience and anecdotal evidence have shown us, this state of constant intentional self-distraction could well be of profound detriment to individual and cultural well-being. When people do their work only in the "interstices of their mind-wandering," with crumbs of attention rationed out among many competing tasks, their culture may gain in information, but it will surely weaken in wisdom.

Rosen admits that perhaps it's too late to turn back the clock on multitasking and that modern society may need to resign itself to a tradeoff between information and wisdom.

Source: Christine Rosen, "The Myth of Multitasking," *The New Atlantis*, Number 20, Spring 2008, pp. 105–110.

Using Synthesis and Analysis

Take a minute to review Rosen's report. Cluster all the positive statements about multitasking, keeping track of the differences among the responses. Then do the same with all the negative statements. What is the overall opinion of each side of the argument? How do the opinions on each side vary? What opinions may be missing from her report?

Although Rosen offers positive and negative opinions rooted in facts, she concludes with a negative report about multitasking. Can you determine what her opinion might have been as she entered her investigation? Why the topic captured her interest in the first place? What textual evidence supports your belief?

MindTap® Find additional examples of investigative reports online.

See also CHAPTER 21, MICHAEL POLLAN, "Out of the Kitchen, Onto the Couch"

See also CHAPTER 22, PEW RESEARCH CENTER, "Most Millennials Resist the 'Millennial' Label—Generations in a Mirror: How They See Themselves"

See also CHAPTER 23, ANTHONY FLINT, *Who Really Owns Public Space?*

See also CHAPTER 23, ABBY PHILLIP, *Oklahoma's Ten Commandments Statue Must Be Removed, State Supreme Court Says*

See also CHAPTER 23, EMILY BADGER, "How Smart Phones Are Turning Our Public Places into Private Ones"

See also CHAPTER 24, TODD S. PURDUM, *Whose Lives Matter?*

See also CHAPTER 25, TERENCE MONMANEY, *How Much Do Americans Know about Science?*

See also CHAPTER 25, NORA CAPLAN-BRICKER, *New Evidence: There Is No Science-Education Crisis*

RESPONDING TO THE RHETORICAL SITUATION

In every case, reports are responses to rhetorical opportunities, problems, or questions that might be addressed or resolved by research findings. "What can be done about 'bad student writing'?" "How much 'underage drinking' is there on my campus?" "What are the disadvantages and advantages of multitasking?" These are the kinds of issues that often launch the research necessary for composing a knowledgeable, credible report for an audience who wants to know.

Opportunity ⟩ Audience and Purpose ⟩ Genre/Report ⟩ (Medium of) Delivery

Understanding the Rhetorical Situation

pages 304–305 Whatever topic you choose, your investigation might take the form of personal experience as well as observations, interviews, surveys (see FIELDWORK IN CHAPTER 16), or traditional research in the library or online. The quality of

RESEARCHING THE INVESTIGATIVE REPORT

As you research your topic, you will want to be clear about your own stance. Why does the topic interest you in the first place? What specific belief, attitude, or action do you want to investigate—maybe even challenge? Once you have established your attitude toward your topic, you will want to measure the gap between what you already know (or think you know) and do not know about the topic. And you will want to use your library and online research to fill that gap. As you discover how experts (published authors and scholars) weigh in on the topic, you might compare their views with your own as well as with those of people in your circle whom you have interviewed. If you are lucky, you can apply some of your own personal experience to the topic. During your research process, you may discover that your topic is too narrow or too broad and that you need to adjust it accordingly so that it meets the criteria for your assignment. Your goal is to compose an investigative report that interests both you and your audience.

your research findings (factual, data-driven, observed, and experienced) will enhance your ethos, help you strengthen the logos of your message, and perhaps bolster your pathos, the emotional connection you make with your audience. (See CHAPTER 2, THE AVAILABLE MEANS INCLUDE THE RHETORICAL ELEMENTS OF pages 23–26 THE MESSAGE ITSELF.)

Identifying an opportunity for change

Identify an issue that affects your community or you personally. How does it affect the people on your campus or in the surrounding community? Maybe the gym closes too early on weekends, the cafeteria serves only brunch and supper on Sundays, or the library has no writing center. Freewrite for five minutes on such an issue. (For exploration strategies in addition to freewriting, see CHAPTER 13, EXPLORATION.) In your investigative report, clearly describe the pages 239–244 problem and explain its significance to the lives of certain individuals or groups.

- Describe the problem or issue with as much objective detail as possible.
- What individuals or groups are affected by this issue?
- Who might be interested in or disagree with your determinations?
- What are the consequences of the particular issue you are exploring? Where might you begin researching for information to answer your question?
- What groups or individuals might have a stake in the findings of an investigative report on this topic?

Thinking rhetorically about audience

The following questions will help you identify the rhetorical audience for your report. Once you identify an audience who will be interested in or affected by your analysis, you will be able to choose the best way to deliver your report.

1. List the names of the persons or groups who are affected by or have an interest in your topic. (This step may require some research.)
2. Write out the reasons that your investigative report might be important to each of them.

3. Explore what might motivate each potential audience to learn more about the topic. Emotionally, how might each audience respond to your report? What logical conclusions might the potential audiences reach? What actions or attitudes might they change in response?

4. Keeping in mind the interests and values of your audience, tailor your description so that your audience feels invested in your topic and in the ways it affects them.

Planning an effective rhetorical response for your purpose

Once you identify your rhetorical opportunity, audience, and purpose, you need to determine what kind of text will best respond to the rhetorical situation. Use the following questions to help you narrow your purpose and shape your response:

1. What facts and details do you need to provide in order to get your audience to recognize the significance of the topic you are investigating?

2. What are the various (perhaps conflicting) perspectives that you must acknowledge?

3. What is your purpose in reporting this information? Are you asking the audience to adopt a new perspective, or do you want the audience to take a specific action?

What is the best way to reach this audience—and get their response? If it is in print, you can insert pictures, figures, and tables. You can also quote from and cite sources. But if you deliver your report online, you can insert videos and direct links to supporting sources.

LINKS TO REPORTS IN THREE MEDIA   MindTap®

Links may change due to availability.

Print Report
In the report at the beginning of this chapter, Christine Rosen uses print journalism to report on multitasking.

Video Report
PBS News Hour filmed a report on the Pew Research Center's study of the Millennials.

Online Report
NASA's online report investigates the topic of "Global Climate Change: Vital Signs of the Planet." [climate.nasa.gov]

WRITING A PERSUASIVE INVESTIGATIVE REPORT: A Guide

*T*o be persuasive, an investigative report should present different perspectives in a fair, even-handed way, balancing the ethical appeal of good sense with the logical appeal of trustworthy support and concluding with an emotional connection with the audience (their interests and values) that invites them to change their attitude or actions.

ADVANTAGES AND LIMITATIONS

Advantages

- **Writer:** Investigative reports offer you an opportunity to research a topic that interests you and that affects you and others. Because you already care about the topic, chances are others will as well.

- **Message:** As you clarify your own informed stance with regard to the topic, you can better visualize your audience, modifying your purpose to that specific audience whose attitudes or actions you hope to change.

- **Media and Design:** Because investigative reports appear in nearly every medium (print, sound, visuals, digital), you can choose the medium that your audience can most easily receive and appreciate.

Limitations

- **Writer:** Your stance toward your subject should appear objective and fair-minded, so discover a problem you would like to address and be careful to use neutral language in discussing it.

- **Message:** If you are investigating a topic you care about, chances are you will end up with more factual information and data than you will be able to use. Your task is to select the information that best supports your thesis, purposefully organizing that information.

- **Media and Design:** When the expectations of your rhetorical audience limit you to print or digital delivery, call on the strengths of print (words and visuals) or of digital media (videos, audios, print, and multimedia). Most colleges now have multimedia labs where you can go for assistance—and ideas.

Introduction

- **Establish the topic as interesting by hooking the reader.**
- **Establish your expertise (ethos).**
- **Describe or define the issue.**
- **State the thesis.**

Describe the issue in your introduction The introduction of a report provides readers with a specific description of the topic. In "The Myth of Multitasking," Rosen defines multitasking as

(continued)

"the human attempt to do simultaneously as many things as possible, as quickly as possible, preferably marshalling the power of as many technologies as possible." After setting up the problem, Rosen moves to her thesis: "[M]ore recently, challenges to the ethos of multitasking have begun to emerge."

Ask Yourself . . .

- What specific incident, startling statistic, or personal narrative can I use to hook my readers into my topic?
- Why does my topic matter to me? Why might it matter to others?
- How have I established my credibility, my ethos?

Body

- **Establish the objectivity of your report with evidence (logos).**
- **Provide facts, details, and direct quotations.**
- **Organize the information purposefully.**
- **Trace the effects of the issue on various groups.**

Provide facts, details, and direct quotations to clarify the issue Rosen cites research that challenges the efficiency of multitasking: "Numerous studies have shown the sometimes-fatal danger of using cell phones and other electronic devices while driving." "Workers distracted by e-mail and phone calls suffer a fall in IQ more than twice that found in marijuana smokers." Rosen's use of quotations clarifies the issue, shapes the logic, and enhances the persuasiveness of her report. Graphics or other visuals would augment the credibility of her sources.

Attribute your evidence to credible sources to establish trust Every use of examples, facts, statistics, and other data is an opportunity to build trust between you and your audience. For that reason, Rosen quotes the research of physicists, investigative reporters, professors, psychiatrists, psychologists, and neuroscientists, using attributive tags to show where each piece of credible evidence comes from.

Describe groups affected by the issue The body of a report fairly and factually characterizes the positions and motivations of the different groups affected by the issue. Rosen describes the negative effects of multitasking on drivers, office workers, school children, teens, and adults.

Arrange information purposefully, either spatially, chronologically, or emphatically Rosen arranges her information emphatically, starting with the power of single-tasking and moving through the various categories of humans who experience the negative effects of multitasking. She closes with a prediction that our overstimulated children will face a future "that may gain in information but . . . will surely weaken in wisdom."

Body

Ask yourself . . .
- How am I presenting a balance of factual evidence?
- Which of my sources is the most—and least—trustworthy?
- How have I identified the individuals and groups most affected by this topic?
- Which of my supports is the most powerful? Where should I place it for the greatest impact?

Conclusion

- **Bring together various perspectives, making an emotional connection.**
- **Make a final attempt to connect with the audience, establishing pathos.**
- **Include a (reasonable) appeal to the audience to adopt a particular attitude or undertake a specific action.**

Bring together various perspectives In her conclusion, Rosen softens her stance to "our collective will to pay attention seems fairly weak," followed by "then again, perhaps we will simply adjust and come to accept what James called 'acquired inattention.'" Nevertheless, she comes down on the negative side of the issue with her last line about gains in information but losses in wisdom.

Connect the issue with the interests of your readers A report often concludes with a final appeal for readers to adopt a specific attitude or take a specific action. Rosen strongly suggests that we dial back "this state of constant intentional self-distraction," using an emotional appeal (pathos) to connect her own concerns about the future with those of her audience.

Ask yourself . . .
- How can I best connect my concerns with the values and interests of my rhetorical audience? What part of my findings will be most convincing to them?
- Have I suggested a plan of action based on my investigation?

MindTap® Request help and feedback from a tutor. If required, participate in peer review, submit your paper for a grade, and view instructor comments online.

Revision and Peer Review

After you have drafted a strong version of your report, ask one of your class-mates to respond to it, helping you revise it into the strongest report it can be. Be sure to identify a rhetorical opportunity, purposefully address your intended audience, consciously arrange your research findings, and deliver it in the most appropriate medium available to you and your audience.

Questions for a peer reviewer

1. What reasons does the writer give for investigating this topic?
2. What information does the writer provide that makes you want to continue reading?
3. How does the writer describe the issue, problem, or phenomenon? What suggestions do you have for the writer regarding the introduction?
4. Who is the intended rhetorical audience? Why do they care about this topic?
5. What is the writer's purpose? Is it obvious from the thesis statement? How can that specific audience help the writer fulfill this purpose?
6. What kinds of factual evidence does the writer provide for support? What are the sources? Who is quoted? How do you know these sources are credible? Whose perspectives are represented? Whose are not? Why? Mark any place where the writer needs stronger evidence or more detail to support a point.
7. What facts and details explain how the issue affects different individuals or groups?
8. Follow the line of argument the writer uses. How is it organized, spatially, chronologically, or emphatically? How does that order enhance the report's overall effectiveness? Which of the assertions might you reorder? Why?
9. How does the writer establish ethos? How could the writer strengthen this appeal?
10. How does the writer make use of pathos? How exactly does the writer connect his or her cause with the interests of the rhetorical audience?
11. What specific conclusion do you reach about the issue or phenomenon as a result of reading the report?
12. What one thing did the writer do especially well? Look back through your feedback and list the three things that you think are most important for the writer to focus on while revising. What one thing will most improve the report?

MindTap® Reflect on your writing process.

✈ ADDITIONAL ASSIGNMENTS

Knowledge Transfer

As you take on more responsibilities, you will find that you are conducting investigative reports—large and small reports that deliver information. Which school to attend, which neighborhood to live in, which car to buy—these kinds of decisions are all made in response to investigative reporting, whether the reporting is done through conversation or delivered in print. Your investigative report is always the result of your fact-finding or data-gathering investigation.

 COLLEGE Hospitality Report on Campus Eateries When your Hospitality Management professor asks you to investigate the problem of food waste in the dorms, you can conduct an investigative report, gathering, preserving, and evaluating evidence of food waste. You may want to focus on the practices of just one dorm cafeteria, gathering evidence by conducting library and online research focusing on the amount of food that is wasted each year at your school, interviewing the head of Food Services, observing several meal lines—and trash lines—in that cafeteria, and interviewing cafeteria workers as well as students. After researching the amount of food waste in this dorm, you might compare your findings with the official, campus-wide findings, and even with national results. Various types of research will all contribute to your results.

COMMUNITY Report on Neighborhood Safety Your Neighborhood Watch Organization has asked you to investigate one facet of neighborhood safety: thefts and break-ins. You will conduct an investigative report, gathering, preserving, and evaluating evidence of those particular crime statistics (from the police department) as well as those unreported crimes that you learn about when you are conducting interviews with your neighbors. Using either a flip chart or a sequence of PowerPoint slides, you will present your findings orally at the next neighborhood gathering, where the group will decide if it wants to invest in hiring a security guard.

WORKPLACE Worker Satisfaction Report You have just been selected as a representative to the committee for improving worker satisfaction at your job. Your charge is to interview fellow employees, research similar companies, and help devise a set of desired recommendations, in collaboration with the other committee members.

MULTIMODAL YouTube Video on a National Controversy For your Contemporary American Politics course, you have decided to analyze a current widely televised national controversy (on immigration, health care,

(continued)

minimum wage, etc.), a controversy on which you have not yet developed an opinion, only curiosity. You want to study the quality and character of the assertions and responses of various spokespeople, the credibility of their sources, the trustworthiness of their answers, and their onscreen deliveries. You plan to do some fact-checking as well. In order to provide pivotal scenes from the controversy as well as links to informational sites, you will submit your investigative report as a YouTube video, one that allows you to deliver your script, insert debate footage, and include your fact-checking findings.

GRAMMAR IN C⊚NTEXT Thinking Rhetorically about Attributive Tags

attributive tags phrases that identify the source of your information

The words you use to indicate who the author is and what he or she is doing are called **attributive tags** because they attribute information to a source. Attributive tags help you assign credit where credit is due. Most tags consist of the author's name and a verb. These verbs are often used in attributive tags:

acknowledge	criticize	insist
advise	declare	list
agree	deny	maintain
analyze	describe	note
argue	disagree	object
assert	discuss	offer
believe	emphasize	oppose
claim	endorse	reject
compare	explain	report
concede	find	state
conclude	illustrate	suggest
consider	imply	think

Other attributive tags are phrases, such as *according to the researcher, from the author's perspective,* and *in the author's mind.*

After introductory attributive tags A comma always follows an attributive tag. Although these tags may appear in the middle or at the end of a sentence, they often appear at the beginning in order to introduce the material.

> **She replied, "Yeah, right."**
>
> **As Bill would say, "Where there's no hope, there's no hurry."**
>
> **According to Azar Nafisi, "What we search for in fiction is not so much reality but the epiphany of truth."**

With attributive tags Commas separate the words in a quotation or dialogue from an attributive tag.

> **"Being a hippie," explains DiFilippo, "means approaching life's obstacles in a way that promotes freedom, peace, love, and respect for our earth and all of humankind."**
>
> **No one was injured, according to the sheriff's report.**

MindTap® Find additional handbook coverage of grammar, punctuation, and style online.

© Rebekah McBride/Shutterstock.com

Position Arguments

Throughout this chapter, you will work to identify an opportunity to compose a position argument. As you determine the position you want to take, consider that composing a position argument will help you understand a controversy and clarify what you actually believe. You will also need to understand the values and beliefs of your rhetorical audience—the audience that might be changed by your argument—as you choose the most fitting means of delivery for reaching that audience.

We take positions and argue them every day: "I must drop this course"; "Our Congress members must find a way to work together"; "Everyone should exercise." A **position argument**, like the antismoking ad that follows, takes a point of view and uses ethical, logical, and emotional appeals to help an audience understand, maybe even accept, that claim. In "Smokers Never Win," the former smoker in the bottom right-hand corner establishes the credibility or ethos of

position argument
the assertion of a point of view about an issue supported by reasons and evidence

IDENTIFYING AN OPPORTUNITY FOR CHANGE

Print Argument
written in essay form (with or without visuals for illustration) for a community or academic publication

Visual Argument
composed as a cartoon or an advertisement for a print or online publication

Online Argument
written as a blog entry, a contribution to a website, even a tweet

Source: NeilMan Communications

A position argument, like this antismoking ad, delivers a point of view and helps an audience understand, and maybe even accept, that position.

the argument by kicking cigarettes; the game of Hang Man indicates the logos of the argument by indicating the steps to losing; and the filth of the cigarettes themselves, along with the dirty chalkboard, makes an emotional connection with the audience. Such pathos might even inspire some members of the audience to kick the habit themselves. (See also CHAPTER 2, THE AVAILABLE MEANS INCLUDE THE RHETORICAL ELEMENTS OF THE MESSAGE ITSELF and CHAPTER 14, ARGUMENT.) pages 23–26 and 275–278

GENRE IN F⊙CUS The Commentary

Position arguments, which assert their claim in the thesis statement (see CHAPTER 2, MAKING CLAIMS), often serve as an individual's or a group's means for participating in debates on a range of issues. In the following commentary, for instance, linguist Geoffrey Nunberg, a researcher at Stanford University's Center for the Study of Language and Information and radio commentator for National Public Radio, joins the debate on the political, economic, social, and cultural consequences of language diversity in the United States. In this article, Nunberg examines the reasoning process behind English-only advocates who concern themselves with the symbolic importance of the English language, which Nunberg claims signals for them a commitment to American ideals and values. page 20

David McNew/Staff/Getty Images News/Getty Images

Advertisers try to brand themselves as part of the local community with Spanish-language billboards in Hispanic neighborhoods, especially in America's biggest cities.

Linguistic diversity is more conspicuous than it was a century ago. To be aware of the large numbers of non-English speakers in 1990, it was necessary to live in or near one of their communities, whereas today it is only necessary to flip through a cable television dial, drive past a Spanish-language billboard, or (in many states) apply for a driver's license. As a best guess, there are fewer speakers of foreign languages in America now than there were then, in both absolute and relative numbers. But what matters symbolically [are] the widespread impressions of linguistic diversity, particularly among people who have no actual contact with speakers of languages other than English. . . .

The debate is no longer concerned with the content or effect of particular programs, but the symbolic importance that people have come to attach to these matters. Official English advocates admit as much when they emphasize that their real goal is to "send a message" about the role of English in American life. From this point of view, it is immaterial whether the provision of interpreters for workers' compensation hearings or of foreign-language nutrition information actually constitute a "disincentive" to learning English, or whether their discontinuation would work a hardship on recent immigrants. Programs like these merely happen to

Native American students at the Carlisle Indian School in Pennsylvania, where students were not allowed to wear their traditional clothing or use Native American languages. In Impressions of an Indian Childhood *(1921), Zitkala-Ša argues that English-only practices at the Carlisle Indian School led to "ridiculous" and "unjustifiable frights and punishments" from a "cold race whose hearts were frozen hard with prejudice." Thousands of Native American children went to off-reservation English-only boarding schools at the turn of the twentieth century.*

be high-visibility examples of government's apparent willingness to allow the public use of languages other than English for any purpose whatsoever. In fact, one suspects that most Official English advocates are not especially concerned about specific programs per se, since they will be able to achieve their symbolic goals even if bilingual services are protected by judicial intervention or legislative inaction (as has generally been the case where Official English measures have passed). The real objective of the campaign is the "message" that it intends to send.

What actually is the message? . . . . Proponents of Official English claim that they seek merely to recognize a state of affairs that has existed since the founding of the nation. After two hundred years of common-law cohabitation with English, we have simply decided to make an honest woman of her, for the sake of the children. To make the English language "official," however, is not merely to acknowledge it as the language commonly used in commerce, mass communications, and public affairs. Rather, it is to invest English with a symbolic role in national life and to endorse a cultural conception of American identity as the basis for political unity.

—Geoffrey Nunberg, *The Official English Movement: Reimagining America*

Issues surrounding language diversity have been part of the country's history since at least the early 1800s, when French-speaking Louisiana was admitted to the Union. Nunberg presents his reasons for opposing Official English not only as a practical matter affecting bilingual education and social services but also as a culturally significant issue. Nunberg also shows his understanding of the issue when he includes the position of those who favor the legislation of a common language as a cultural glue to help unify the country.

 ASSIGNMENT

Compose a position argument on a significant problem (or issue) and direct your argument to a specific audience. Whether you are taking a stand on a personal experience, a newsworthy situation, or a lifestyle, educational, or religious belief, provide a vivid description of the issue so that your audience can appreciate the significance of the problem and understand your position (or claim). Your description should reveal the importance of the issue to you as well as its effect on your audience. Your clear position on the issue should appear in your thesis statement. Support your thesis with reasons that are themselves supported by specific details, examples, and anecdotes. As you draft your position argument, be sure to acknowledge and address any concerns or beliefs that oppose your own.

READING RHETORICALLY

When reading a position argument, your first challenge is to locate the writer's position. What opportunity is the writer taking to deliver a point of view or position? As you move from there, you will want to trace out the reasons the writer supplies for that position, marking or underlining those reasons as you go. Do the reasons provide the overall organization for the position argument? Are the reasons believable, logical, and feasible? After you have mapped out the reasons the writer provides, circle back and locate the support the writer supplies for each reason. Many writers tap examples, details, personal anecdotes, statistics, tables, and research findings to support their claim. Are these reasons and their support credible and persuasive? Finally, read the conclusion to see what the writer is asking you to do or think. These steps help you analyze the credibility, logic, and emotional connection of the argument (or the lack thereof).

Key Features of a Position Argument

A position argument offers a focused, well-presented claim that is organized by credible, well-supported reasons. Position arguments commonly have the following features:

- Arguments vividly describe a problem or issue.
- Arguments are directed toward an audience with a clear connection to or an investment in the problem being addressed as well as a clear understanding of the audience's beliefs and values.
- Arguments include a concise statement of the writer's claim, or position, which appears in a thesis statement.
- Arguments provide background information about the issue and why it matters.
- Arguments provide good reasons in support of the writer's position, and each supporting reason takes into account the audience's beliefs, attitudes, and values.
- Arguments contain specific, convincing evidence—details, examples, direct quotations, statistics, anecdotes, research findings, and testimony—that support each reason.
- Arguments acknowledge counterarguments, positions different from, maybe even in opposition to, the writer's claim. Writers consider, accommodate, even accept, if possible, some or parts of the counterarguments.
- Arguments appeal to readers' values by describing the benefits that will be achieved by responding to the writer's position in the intended way or explaining the negative situation that will result from ignoring it.

The key features of a position argument are illustrated in the following paper written by Alicia Williams on American Sign Language (ASL). She points out that deaf people have been pressured to lip-read and speak English—not sign it—for years. Williams takes the position that ASL should be considered yet another language in our already language-diverse nation. As you read rhetorically, look for answers to the following questions:

- What is Williams's position on the topic? What is her claim?
- What did you learn about the author? How did she establish herself as trustworthy?
- What is Williams's purpose for including the images that she took herself?
- What good reasons does Williams supply for her position? How are those reasons organized? How effective is her organizational pattern?

- What kinds of evidence does she supply (personal anecdotes, research findings, statistics, examples, and so on)?
- How does she connect her position to the interests and sympathies of her readers? How successful is she?

The Ethos of American Sign Language

ALICIA WILLIAMS

Williams is no stranger to the Deaf community. She has a hearing impairment, and her sister is an interpreter. Educated in "bilingual" schools that approached ASL as a language just like Tagalog, Spanish, or Mandarin Chinese, she has personal experiences that have influenced her strong feelings on this subject. She is a graduate of Penn State University.

Williams identifies a problem and establishes herself as an informed, engaged, and reasonable writer. At the end of this paragraph, she directs her readers to her thesis, a concise statement of her point of view regarding the problem.

Williams provides a historical overview of the problem as well as reasons for her point of view. She includes specific details and a direct quotation as evidence (logos).

Williams's superscript indicates that she will supply additional information in an endnote at the conclusion of her essay.

The termination of the Bilingual Education Act was followed by the No Child Left Behind Act (2001), thus removing a bilingual approach from the education tracks of non-English native speakers. The loss of bilingual education has caused the political group English First to lobby hard for an English-only education that purports to produce truly American citizens. This, in turn, produces more momentum for the group's side project: making English the official language of the United States of America. Not only does this negate the melting pot of languages in America, but it diminishes the impact of a truly unique language—American Sign Language (ASL). The drive for English-only education treats the manifestations of language through a purely verbal platform, thereby perpetuating long-held prejudices and the common mistaken assumption that ASL is not, in fact, a language.

Only fifty years ago did ASL receive its long overdue recognition as a distinct language, rather than being perceived as a "hindrance to English," a "bastardization of English," or even a "communication disorder." By the end of the nineteenth century, during the rise of formal educational instruction in ASL for the Deaf, an oppositional camp known as Oralists had fervently portrayed signing by the Deaf community as a pathological version of spoken language.[1] A few even preposterously correlated deafness with low intelligence. Ironically, the husband of a Deaf woman, Alexander Graham Bell, who was the inventor of the telephone and hearing aids, was a supporter of the Oralists' philosophy. He endorsed "genetic counseling for the deaf, outlawing intermarriages between deaf persons, suppression of sign language, elimination of residential schools for the deaf, and the prohibition of deaf teachers of the deaf " (Stewart and Akamatsu 242).

Oralism faced counteractions by the numerous, though less famous, people who were working for the needs of the Deaf community as its educators. They understood that ASL is requisite for a deaf person's social, cultural, and lingual needs. The Deaf community managed to keep its educational programs intact without losing ASL, though not without struggle. It was not until a half-century later, in the 1960s, that William Stokoe's linguistic analysis of ASL produced the much-needed equilibrium between the Deaf and hearing communities concerning the legitimacy of ASL. Even so, when most people talk about language, their thinking assumes communication through speaking: most classify as unconventional forms of language outside of a verbal modality. Native signers such as myself understand that our minority language must coexist with a dominant majority language, but the practice of reducing ASL to a type of communication disorder or, worse, obliterating it for the spoken English-only movement, ignores the historical presence of Deaf culture in America, as well as the key characteristics ASL shares with the evolution of languages.

ASL was derived from French Sign Language (FSL) in the early nineteenth century. Harlan Lane and François Grosjean, prominent ASL linguists, found supporting evidence for this date from "the establishment of the first American school for the deaf in 1817 at Hartford, Connecticut. . . . Its founders, Thomas Gallaudet and Laurent Clerc, were both educated in the use of FSL prior to 1817" (Stewart and Akamatsu 237). Historically speaking, David Stewart and C. Tane Akamatsu have determined that "approximately 60% of the signs in present-day ASL had their origin in FSL" (237). The modification of a parent language, such as FSL for the birth of ASL, is part of the process spoken language has undergone in its evolution throughout history, producing our contemporary languages. For instance, the English spoken in England during Shakespeare's lifetime is not the same English spoken in America today; nonetheless, they are both of English tradition.

Another characteristic that ASL has in common with other languages is that it changes from one generation to another. Undoubtedly, spoken languages continue to change. For instance, slang words used now may not be the same when the toddlers of today are in college. ASL also experiences these changes,

Williams is quoting from page 242 in Stewart and Akamatsu, an essay listed in her Works Cited.

Williams makes an assertion related to her thesis, which is followed by specific narrative details, arranged in chronological order (logos). She ends this paragraph with an emotional connection with her audience (pathos).

Williams continues to shape her argument with additional specific details and facts (logos).

Williams opens this paragraph with another assertion that supports her thesis (logos), using process analysis with information arranged chronologically for support.

which is contrary to a common misconception that the signs in ASL are concrete in nature, meaning there are no changes. For example, an obsolete sign for "will/future" is conveyed by holding your right arm bent in a ninety-degree angle with your fingertips parallel to the ground. Then you move your entire forearm upward to a forty-five-degree angle in one swift movement. The modern sign starts with an open palm touching the right jawline, underneath the ear; then the forearm moves forward until the arm is in a ninety-degree position, equivalent to the starting position of the arm in the old form. The evolution of signs is comparable to the changing connotations of various words found in the history of languages.

In the process of its shift to physical hand gestures and appropriate facial expressions, ASL does not discard the traditional syntax of language, maintaining its legitimacy as a distinct language. The rich complexity of ASL's syntax conveys itself through designated facial expressions and specific sign constructions, demonstrating that "ASL is governed by the same organizational principles as spoken languages . . . [despite] essential differences based on the fact that ASL is produced in three-dimensional space" (Neidle et al. 30). As every language has a syntactical structure, so does ASL.

Despite its similarities to languages such as English, it is a mistake to think of ASL as a pathology of spoken English. Perpetuating this myth is the misconception that ASL signs are direct translations of English. ASL has rules of its own, which are not identical to those of English syntax. In English, for instance, one says, "Who hates Smitty?" but in ASL, it is signed "Hate Smitty who?" The photos in Fig. 1 show another example of how signs in ASL are not a direct

Another assertion is supported with a detailed comparison-and-contrast analysis and direct quotations (logos).

An assertion is supported with specific examples, including the use of visuals (logos).

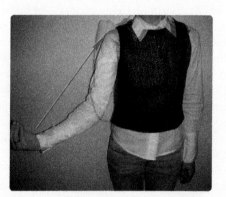

Fig. 1. The photograph on the left shows the signing of "Me give to him or her," and the photograph on the right shows that of "Me give to you." (Photographs by the author.)

translation of English, but also show how differing hand placements denote different pronouns used with the verb *give*.

Stokoe's work establishing the legitimacy of ASL spurred a movement for a bilingual approach in educating the deaf. The teaching of ASL was a top priority because of the hardship of expecting the Deaf community to acquire English as our native language, which carries a disadvantage by working on a modality inaccessible to us—hearing. In the bilingual approach, after the deaf child has attained a solid working background in ASL, some parents elect to have oral English taught as a second language. The success of English as a second language is largely subject to the individual's capabilities, which are dependent on numerous factors. My parents chose the bilingual approach in my education track at Rufus Putnam Elementary School (for the Deaf). While I maintained my fluency in ASL, I developed an efficacy at speech reading (informally known as lip reading). For instance, when I speak, I am able to convince hearing persons that I am not deaf. In my Deaf community, I always resort to my first language—ASL. All this would not be possible if Oralism or English First were successful in a push for *spoken* English only.

More historical background leads into Williams's personal experience as a deaf person, thereby establishing logos, ethos, and pathos.

My bilingual background has been met with fierce opposition from hearing people who believe ASL is a crutch language and that it is an antiquated solution for the Deaf community. In other words, they believe the advances of medical technology will enable researchers to develop revolutionary digital hearing aids, while aggressively diagnosing deaf children at younger ages should cause a decreasing need for ASL, which they assume is a diminished form of English. But if ASL meets all other criteria of what linguists consider a language—with the exception of the use of a vocal apparatus—how can it be called a "crutch language"? And hearing aids only amplify whatever remaining hearing a deaf person has, if any at all; they do not compensate for hearing loss. Even if a doctor diagnoses a deaf child at birth, the child's sensorineural hearing loss may be so severe that spoken language will be impractical to acquire, whereas ASL will be a better approach for the child.[2] In rare cases, adults who become deaf later in their lives find comfort in ASL, rather than English. The naturalization associated with the visual-spatial lingual framework of ASL is uniquely characteristic of the Deaf community because it operates to their advantage, bypassing the confines of oral-aural languages. The use of a verbal apparatus in spoken languages is a natural reaction from the body possessing a functional audio-physiological system. Often this is not the case within the Deaf community; hence that is why ASL is deeply embedded in its culture and will remain the staple of its community, regardless of technology's novelty or the hearing community's desire to push for English-only education.

Williams addresses the opposing point of view and refutes it with specific support for her stance, reasonable questions, and good examples. In this paragraph, she augments her ethos, logos, and pathos.

The final paragraph establishes a strong emotional connection with the audience (pathos).

The most primeval function of language is to create a medium for people's desire to outwardly express themselves to others. Whatever form language may take—visual or verbal—it lays the foundation for humanity's collective identity as great storytellers. Through language we have been able to pass on stories of past heroes and enemies, warn future generations of failed philosophies, create new ideals for better living, share our aspirations and fears, even express our wonder at all that remains unknown to us. Language binds us as humans, and its diverse forms are reflected in the embodiments of its heterogeneous natives. ASL is but another paintbrush of language, and yet proof of humanity's palette of mutability.

Williams supplies both Notes and a Works Cited list at the end of her essay, enhancing her ethos and her logos.

Notes

1. I realize the use of the term *Deaf* might seem archaic, but for the purpose of this paper, it is representative of all members who psychologically or linguistically identify themselves as members of the Deaf community through ASL as their common language, regardless of their physiological hearing capacity.
2. There are three basic types of hearing loss: conductive hearing loss, sensorineural hearing loss, and mixed hearing loss, which is any combination of the first two. All three types can make speech hard to acquire.

Works Cited

Neidle, Carol, et al. *The Syntax of American Sign Language: Functional Categories and Hierarchical Structures.* MIT P, 2000.

Stewart, David A., and C. Tane Akamatsu. "The Coming of Age of American Sign Language." *Anthropology & Education Quarterly,* vol. 19, no. 3, Sept. 1988, pp. 235–52. *JSTOR,* www.jstor.org/stable/3195832.

Using Synthesis and Analysis

When we readily agree with a position or claim, we rarely analyze the argument for its careful reasoning. But when we do not agree or begin to get suspicious, we begin to notice problems of sloppy reasoning, snap judgments, quickly drawn conclusions, missing data, or one-sided opinions. Even the most experienced writers inadvertently make these errors in arguments. Start your analysis by rereading the argument to detect flaws in reasoning. (See the box on Logical Fallacies on the next page.) Rereading the article with an eye toward detecting fallacies can also be helpful when analyzing an argument with which you readily agree, perhaps one in this chapter (Nunberg's or Williams's). As you read, note that in most cases, readers are persuaded to change by the writer's or speaker's trustworthiness and by a well-reasoned argument.

LOGICAL FALLACIES

Non sequitur Latin for "it does not follow," the *non sequitor* presents a faulty conclusion about consequences, such as "Helen loves the stars; she will major in astronomy."

Ad hominem Latin for "toward the man himself," an *ad hominem* attack draws attention away from the actual issue under consideration by attacking the character of the person rather than the opinion that person holds.

Appeal to tradition Many people resist change—it unsettles their routines and makes them uncomfortable. Such people often invoke an appeal to tradition; in other words, "That is how it has always been done, so it should continue." This appeal is often used in political campaigns ("Four more years"), by social groups ("We have never invited X or Y to our events; why start?"), and in many other situations ("My family always fills the gas tank before getting on the highway, so you should fill up now.").

Bandwagon The bandwagon argument is "Everyone is doing it, so you should, too." For example, highway patrol officers often hear "Everyone else was speeding, so I was merely keeping up with the traffic."

Begging the question Often referred to as a "circular argument," begging the question involves simply restating the initial claim as though it were already a conclusion or a good reason. "We must test students more in order to improve their test scores." The initial claim needs to be established and argued in order to establish whether low test scores can be blamed on too little testing.

False analogy Effective writers often use analogies to equate two unlike things, explaining one in terms of the other—for example, comparing a generous grandma with an ATM machine or a diamond ring with eternal love. False analogies, however, stretch beyond the valid resemblance to create an invalid comparison. "Vietnam War veterans were greeted by the animosity of an antiwar U.S. populace; Iraqi war veterans will surely return to the same antipathy."

False authority False authority fallacies assume that an expert in one field is credible in another field. Just think of all the professional athletes and celebrities who argue that a particular brand of car, coffee, undershorts, or soft drink is the best one.

False cause Also referred to by the Latin phrase *post hoc, ergo propter hoc*, the fallacy of false cause is the assumption that because A occurs before B, A is therefore the *cause* of B. We all know that events that follow each other do not necessarily have a direct causal relationship—although they may have some relationship: "Jim got fired from his job, and his wife divorced him; therefore, his job loss caused his divorce." Jim's job loss might have been the last of several job losses he suffered in the past three years, and his wife, tired of depending on him to hold a job, filed for divorce.

(continued)

False dilemma Also referred to as the "either/or fallacy," the false dilemma fallacy sets up only two choices in a complex situation, when in fact there are more than two choices. The false dilemma offers the writer's choice as the only good choice, presenting the only other choice as unthinkable. "If we do not spank our children, they will run wild." "If you do not get straight A's, you will not be able to get a job."

Guilt by association An unfair attempt to make someone responsible for the beliefs or actions of others, guilt by association links that person with untrustworthy people or suspicious actions. Social tensions in the United States often stem from this fallacy and are passed on for the same reason: "those people" are bad—whether they are members of a racial, ethnic, or religious group, a particular profession, or a certain family.

Hasty generalization A conclusion based on too little, exceptional, or biased evidence, the hasty generalization results in statements such as "Fred will never get into law school when he did not even pass his poli sci exam." The otherwise very intelligent Fred may have a good reason for failing one exam.

Oversimplification Closely related to hasty generalization, oversimplification occurs when a speaker or writer jumps to conclusions by omitting relevant considerations. "Just say 'No'" was the antidrug battle cry of the 1980s, but avoiding drug use can be much more complicated than just saying no. The "virginity pledge" is an oversimplified solution to the problem of unwanted teenage pregnancy, as it ignores the fact that many teenagers need to become educated about human sexuality, safe sex practices, sexually transmitted disease, and aspects of teen social and sexual behavior.

Red herring A false clue or an assertion aimed at diverting attention from the real issue, the red herring is intended to mislead, whether it appears in a mystery novel or in an argument. "We cannot defeat the piracy in Somalia when we are involved in the Israeli-Palestinian conflict." The real issue in the preceding statement (defeating piracy) is blurred by other issues that, while important, are not the primary ones under consideration.

Slippery slope In order to show that an initial claim is unacceptable, increasingly unacceptable events are said to be sure to follow from that initial claim: "Confidential letters of recommendation allow for damning comments." We hear slippery slope arguments every day, in contexts from weight loss ("You are losing too much weight; you will end up anorexic") to taste in music ("Once you start listening to gansta rap, you will become violent").

MindTap® Find additional examples of position arguments online.

See also CHAPTER 2, SOJOURNER TRUTH, "Ain't I a Woman?"
See also CHAPTER 3, BARRY PRIZANT, *Uniquely Human*

See also CHAPTER 21, MARGARET MEAD, "The Changing Significance of Food [Overnourished and Undernourished in America]"

See also CHAPTER 21, KAREN HERNANDEZ, "Why We Should Ditch the Slow Food Movement"

See also CHAPTER 25, MARGUERITE DEL GIUDICE, "Why It's Crucial to Get More Women in Science"

RESPONDING TO THE RHETORICAL SITUATION

Every day, you find yourself witnessing the positions others have taken, whether you are discussing films and television with your friends, posting tweets, or watching sports news. Bullying, gun control, marriage rights, standardized testing, and immigration are just a few of the many issues you are likely to encounter. Once you have established your position, or claim, determine the most appropriate audience for considering your position. Your goal is to reach that rhetorical audience, the audience that is capable of helping you resolve the issue.

Opportunity   Audience and Purpose   Genre/Argument   (Medium of) Delivery

Understanding the Rhetorical Situation

Many times you will be asked to take a stand—take a position on an issue. A position argument can serve to explore both the stated and underlying reasons why we take positions. Is your opinion one you have inherited from your family or your friends? Have you witnessed firsthand the consequences of your position—or that of people who take a position different from yours? What opportunity does your position respond to? Often, you must conduct research to supply evidence and examples for your reasons. By demonstrating your own

┌─ **RESEARCHING A POSITION ARGUMENT** ────────────────────

A position argument is not just your opinion. It is a carefully constructed point of view based on reasons and evidence. Bring your supporting reasons to life with research through detailed, credible evidence and examples, whether personal anecdotes, statistics, or other details.

Because you want your audience to consider seriously your position, conduct research to see what evidence your opposition uses. Acknowledging the values and beliefs of your audience helps you establish common ground. In doing so, you make clear that you respect and understand you audience—and hope they will try to understand you as you work to persuade them to change their attitudes or actions.

good reasons at the same time you acknowledge the values, concerns, and interests of your audience, you establish your ethos, logos, and pathos.

Identifying an opportunity for change

Consider the communities you are part of—academic, activist, artistic, athletic, professional, civic, ethnic, national, political, or religious. What practices or attitudes have shaped your experiences within each group? You might, for example, think about what it means for you that you have a new kind of close relationship with your soccer team members (or other sport), one not shared by family members or friends on the sidelines. Or perhaps you are bilingual and want to explore why your ability to communicate in more than one language has been seen as a positive thing in many of your communities but not, strangely, in others. Maybe you are a member of an online community and have witnessed cyberbullying, shaming, and name-calling and want to speak out about it. The point is to reflect on an issue where your unique role within a particular group helps you identify a rhetorical opportunity for change.

1. Make a list of the communities with which you identify most strongly. For each group, list several experiences that have marked your participation in that group. If the experiences were positive, explain why, providing as many details as possible. If the experiences were negative, describe the factors that made them difficult or unpleasant. Also, write down any rules—whether written or unwritten—that influence the ways you or other group members participate in the community.

2. Choose one or two of your communities, and take photos or sketch pictures of group members interacting. Or download a screenshot illustrating a relevant example of the group's interactions, possibly a text or an update posted to Facebook or Twitter. Whatever visual you choose should illustrate details or features that make the community compelling to examine.

3. Choose the community you want to write about and compose four or five descriptions of a problem related to that community. Vary the ways you describe the problem. For example, one description might emphasize how some people are marginalized by that community, and another might emphasize the ways in which others in the community respond to the unwritten rules of participation in that community. Another description

might focus on the process by which new group members are subtly initiated into the group, and yet another might describe what ideal seems to guide that particular community.

4. You can also move through steps 1–3 by focusing on a community to which you do not belong, for whom you are an outsider.

Relating rhetorically to your audience

The following questions can help you locate your rhetorical audience as well as identify the audience's relationship to the problem you are addressing. Once you have established the audience's values as well as the positions other people may hold about the problem, you will be in a better position to describe that problem responsibly and knowledgeably.

1. List the names of the persons or groups who are affected directly or indirectly by the problem you are addressing.
2. Next to the name of each potential audience, write reasons that audience could have for acknowledging the existence of your problem. In other words, what evidence or personal connection would persuade these audiences that something needs to change or that they need to view the situation in a new way?
3. What actions could these audiences reasonably be persuaded to perform? What new perspectives could they be expected to adopt? In other words, consider what each audience would be able to do to resolve this problem.
4. With your audience's interests and capabilities in mind, look again at the descriptions of the problem that you composed in the preceding section. Decide which description will best help your audience feel connected to the situation as you have described it. Be open to revising your best description in order to tailor it to the audience's attitudes, beliefs, experiences, and values.
5. Consider what others have already said and done about the problem, especially if their ideas are counterarguments, ideas markedly different from or maybe even opposed to yours.

Planning an effective rhetorical response for your purpose

Different purposes and different audiences require different kinds of texts. For example, a lack of local resources for people who speak languages other than English might prompt you to create a church newsletter that draws attention to the daily challenges these people face and argues for a greater church commitment to alleviating this problem. Parent association debates over an open-carry policy or teachers-with-guns program might lead you to write an Op-Ed to the local newspaper or a letter to the school board to highlight an important feature of the ongoing gun-control debate that they—and their teachers—may be overlooking. As these two examples suggest, once you identify your problem, position (or claim), audience (and their values), and purpose, you need to determine what kind of text will best respond to the rhetorical situation.

Use the following questions to help you narrow your purpose and shape your response:

1. What is the issue that prompts your taking a position, making a claim?
2. What is your explicit claim?
3. What reasons support the argument you want to make? What evidence or examples can you provide to persuade readers that each supporting reason is valid? What else has been said or done about this issue?
4. Which supporting reasons are most likely to resonate with your audience? How might you adapt a reason or two to accommodate the interests of your audience? What beliefs, attitudes, experiences, and capabilities on the part of the audience help guide you as you shape your argument? What are the counterarguments that you need to address?
5. What exactly do you want your audience to do? Feel more confident in its current position? Listen to and consider an overlooked position? Or make a change in attitude or take a specific action to address the problem you are trying to resolve?
6. How best can you reach your audience? That is, what kind of text is this audience most likely to respond to?

LINKS TO ARGUMENTS IN THREE MEDIA · MindTap®

Links may change due to availability.

Courtesy of Adair Rispoli

Universal Uclick

Gary Conner/Getty Images

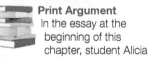 **Print Argument**
In the essay at the beginning of this chapter, student Alicia Williams uses a position argument on ASL to help her develop and present her thoughts for others—especially policy makers.

Visual Argument
This visual argument is in the form of an editorial cartoon by Gary Trudeau.

 Online Argument
The National Rifle Association's NRABlog Staff posted "Does Your Child Know What to Do If He or She Finds a Gun?"

*Y*ou are likely familiar with the form and arrangements of position arguments because you come across examples of this genre in your daily life. The author's introduction grabs your attention because it relates a problem to your own values; the body of the position argument outlines the reasoning behind the author's point of view; and the conclusion reinforces the issue's significance at the same time that it connects with you emotionally.

ADVANTAGES AND LIMITATIONS

Advantages

- **Writer:** Position arguments allow you to showcase your credibility and research skills. You can be friendly, open, and knowledgeable.

- **Message:** Position arguments invite you to investigate a troublesome issue, clarify your own understanding, and take a reasonable position that might help alleviate the problem for you and your audience.

- **Media and Design:** Position arguments can be delivered in print, digitally, verbally, and with art and images—or any combination.

Limitations

- **Writer:** Your challenge is to discover the values, interests, and concerns of your audience so that you can work to accommodate them at the same time as you advance your argument.

- **Message:** What you consider to be a problem may not be perceived as one by others—or they may take a position markedly different from your own. The challenge is to establish common ground where you can come together to discuss your differences.

- **Media and Design:** Deciding on which medium and design will reach your rhetorical audience—maybe even please them—can be daunting, until you take the time to analyze your audience.

Introduction

- **Establish your credibility (ethos).**
- **Describe the problem.**
- **Make clear how the problem concerns the audience.**
- **Emphasize why the time to address the problem is now.**
- **State an explicit claim in a thesis statement.**

Establish your credibility One way to establish the reasonableness of your argument is by taking a fair-minded tone and respectful stance toward the issue. It is easy to feel like those who disagree with you are "the enemy," but note how Williams creates common ground with references to the American "melting pot" and draws on the emotions of her audience to

(continued)

sympathize with her position by invoking a fresh surprise in the English First debate—"the impact of a truly unique language—American Sign Language (ASL)."

Identify an immediate problem The introduction of an argumentative essay grabs an audience's attention as it describes the problem in a way that helps readers see how it concerns them as well as explains why the situation needs their attention right now. When you look back over Williams's essay on ASL, you will see that the elimination of bilingual education removed opportunities for deaf students to be mainstreamed in classes. The introduction leads up to the thesis statement.

Make your claim, or position, in your thesis statement The thesis presents the writer's argument in a single sentence or short string of sentences; supporting reasons might also be presented in the introduction in a cluster of concise sentences following the thesis statement. Williams's thesis statement is concise and explicit: "The drive for English-only education treats the manifestations of language through a purely verbal platform, thereby perpetuating long-held prejudices and the common mistaken assumption that ASL is not, in fact, a language."

Ask yourself . . .

- How is the issue I am exploring actually a problem for others?
- Who are the others who might share my concern?
- What is my position on the issue?
- Have I translated my position into an explicit thesis? Library and online research—as well as interviews, observations, and lab experiments—all help you finalize and support your position (your thesis statement).

- **Outline the major reasons supporting the position.**
- **Connect the reasons to the thesis statement.**
- **Present evidence and examples in the form of facts and figures, direct quotations, brief narratives, statistics, testimony, and so on.**
- **In other words, establish logos by supplying a well-reasoned, well-supported, and well-organized argument.**

Organize your reasons The body of an argumentative essay provides the major reasons supporting the argument. You must decide whether to organize the major reasons chronologically, spatially, or emphatically. Many writers choose the emphatic arrangement, either starting or ending with the most significant reason.

Support your claim with reasons that connect to your readers' values Here you not only present your supporting reasons in a purposeful order but also explain how each reason strengthens your position. The stronger supporting reasons are those that connect to readers' beliefs, values, and attitudes.

Present evidence for your reasons In addition, you use the body of an argumentative essay to present evidence and examples. Writers present facts and figures, direct quotations, and brief narratives to persuade readers that each supporting reason strengthens the larger argument. Any of these supports may be presented through words (written or spoken) or images.

Acknowledge counterarguments The body of an argumentative essay also acknowledges and responds to counterarguments and opposing viewpoints. This helps you address possible gaps in opposing arguments while you strengthen the logic of your own argument. By acknowledging other points of view, you project a more convincing ethical appeal to readers to consider, even accept, alternative perspectives on the issue. Williams acknowledges and refutes the viewpoints that ASL is a "crutch language" and an "antiquated solution."

Ask yourself . . .
- Which of my reasons is the most compelling? Have I organized my reasons in a way that leads to or ends with that compelling reason?
- Which of my reasons is the weakest? How might I strengthen it?
- What is the most compelling evidence I have provided for my reasons?
- How have I acknowledged viewpoints different from my own position?
- Have I assimilated any of those other positions into my own position?

- **Reinforce for an audience the benefits of responding to the writer's argument in the intended way.**
- **Illustrate the negative situation that will result if the writer's argument is ignored.**
- **Work to connect the writer's claim with the interests and values of the audience, establishing pathos.**

Conclude with the benefits of your position for your readers Finally, the conclusion of an argumentative essay reinforces the benefits that will be realized if the audience responds to the writer's argument in the intended way. Or, conversely, the conclusion may illustrate the negative situation that will result if the writer's argument is ignored. The conclusion is your last opportunity to connect with your audience. In her conclusion, Williams uses pathos to appeal to her readers by citing humanity's common desire for self-expression.

Ask yourself . . .
- How have I made clear that this topic matters to more people than just myself?
- How have I asked my audience to do something within their capabilities?
- How have I asked them to do something that will benefit them—as well as others?
- Where do I indicate that my position aligns with their interests?

MindTap® Request help and feedback from a tutor. If required, participate in peer review, submit your paper for a grade, and view instructor comments online.

Revision and Peer Review

After you have drafted your argument, ask one of your classmates to read it. You will want your classmate to respond to your work in a way that helps you revise it into the strongest argument it can be, one that addresses your intended audience, helps you fulfill your purpose, and is delivered in the most appropriate means available to you.

Questions for a peer reviewer

1. To what opportunity for change is the writer responding?
2. Who might be the rhetorical audience?
3. What might be the writer's purpose?
4. How does the writer establish the importance of the topic? What suggestions do you have for improving the introduction?
5. Note the writer's thesis statement. If you cannot locate a thesis statement, what explicit thesis statement might work for this position argument, or claim?
6. Note the assertions the writer makes to support the thesis. Are they presented in chronological, spatial, or emphatic order? How might you reorder some of the assertions for overall effectiveness?
7. If you cannot locate a series of assertions, what assertions could be made to support the thesis statement?
8. Note the supporting reasons that the writer uses to reinforce his or her assertions. What specific evidence and examples (anecdotes, statistics, research findings, details, etc.) does the writer use for support?
9. How does the writer establish ethos? Logos? Pathos? How could the writer strengthen these appeals? (See questions #6–8.)
10. Where does the writer acknowledge other points of view? Where does the writer accept the validity of another point? Might doing so strengthen the writer's credibility?
11. What did you learn from the conclusion that you did not already know after reading the introduction and the body? What information does the writer want you to take away from the argument? Does the writer attempt to change your attitude, action, or opinion?
12. Which section of the argument did you most enjoy? Why?

MindTap®   Reflect on your writing process.

ADDITIONAL ASSIGNMENTS

Knowledge Transfer

We use position arguments every time we want to persuade an audience to modify their attitude, action, or belief on issues as large as whom to vote for in a presidential election and as small as where we should call to order pizza.

 COLLEGE Social Organization Your college social organization is considering becoming an alcohol-free zone. You have been elected to take a position against (or for) the ban, and your job is to interview your friends; conduct research on the feasibility, advantages, and disadvantages of such a ban; and use personal experience as well as observations to support your position. You and one other person will present your positions at the next organizational meeting.

 COMMUNITY Op-Ed People submit opinion pieces to their local newspapers when they feel strongly about a community issue—and want local citizens to join them in supporting or protesting that issue. For instance, if your schools are in bad repair and yet the tax levies are voted down year after year, you may want to gather research and shape it into a position argument in favor of a tax levy. Stay alert to local issues so that you can join the discussion, obtain important information, understand the issue, and take a clear position. Then compose an opinion piece for your local newspaper or community magazine.

 WORKPLACE Cover Letter Every time you apply for a job, you take a position, arguing that you are the best person for the job. Referring to the job position and your résumé, compose a letter of application arguing that your experience and education align perfectly with the criteria for the position.

MULTIMODAL Short Film on Controversial Topic If a topic such as your school's attendance policy, the price of tuition, charges of college students' binge drinking, or some other social issue bothers you, create a short film on the topic. First, you will want to compose a script and then consider the features of background music, images, video clips, and text that will enhance your script. As you create your film (with a camera, your smartphone, or your computer), practice reading the script while the film is progressing, editing as you go. Be sure to bring in a peer to help you make editing decisions.

GRAMMAR IN C⊙NTEXT Thinking Rhetorically about Coherence—Word Choice, Repetition, and Sentence Structure

It is especially important in an argument that your language not appear biased. Use the following information to help you choose words that will build a trustworthy tone.

Words with associated meanings By choosing specific nouns, determiners, and pronouns, you can tightly connect one sentence to the next. Here is a brief overview of strategies for making your writing coherent through word choice:

- Use nouns with related meanings.

  We found most of the <u>directions</u> easy to follow, especially those in the first three chapters. Several of us, though, had difficulty understanding the <u>instructions</u> in Chapter 4.

- Use determiners to indicate old information.

  The students had to write a paper comparing American and Japanese management styles. <u>The assignment</u> was due Thursday.

- Use pronouns to refer to old information.

  Susan started playing the piano at the age of six. <u>She</u> was eighteen when she began strumming the guitar.

Repetition of words and phrases Repeating words or phrases will provide coherence in a paragraph, especially when your focus is a specific item or concept. In the following paragraph, the author focuses on taboos and thus, of course, repeats this word.

<u>Taboos</u> come in all sizes. Big <u>taboos</u>: when I was a kid in the Italian neighborhoods of Brooklyn, to insult someone's mother meant a brutal fight— the kind of fight no one interferes with until one of the combatants goes down and stays down. Little <u>taboos</u>: until the sixties, it was an insult to use someone's first name without asking or being offered permission. Personal <u>taboos</u>: Cyrano de Bergerac would not tolerate the mention of his enormous nose. <u>Taboos</u> peculiar to one city: in Brooklyn (again), when the Dodgers were still at Ebbets Field, if you rooted for the Yankees you kept it to yourself unless you wanted a brawl. <u>Taboos</u>, big or small, are always about having to respect somebody's (often irrational) boundary—or else.

—Michael Ventura, "Taboo: Don't Even Think about It!"

Be careful, though, not to overdo repetition. Repetition in the following sentences is ineffective because the word being repeated is not significant:

spend endless time browsing without buying anything.

Some shoppers ~~shop around but do not buy anything. They have time to shop, so they spend it looking through all the shops in the mall.~~

Parallelism—linking through structure **Parallelism** refers to the repetition of a grammatical structure. Like repeated words and phrases, this type of repetition makes your writing more cohesive, but it is also considered aesthetically pleasing, just like the repeated patterns in waves, leaves, or textiles. In the following excerpt from John F. Kennedy's inauguration speech,* you will find examples of parallel words, phrases, and clauses. Note that some of these elements are embedded within others.

> **We dare not forget today that we are the heirs of that first revolution. Let the word go forth from this <u>time</u> and <u>place</u>, to <u>friend</u> and <u>foe</u> alike, that the torch has been passed to a new generation of Americans, <u>born in this century</u>, <u>tempered by war</u>, <u>disciplined by a hard and bitter peace</u>, <u>proud of our ancient heritage</u>, and <u>unwilling to witness or permit the slow undoing of these human rights</u> <u>to which this nation has always been committed</u>, and <u>to which we are committed today</u> <u>at home</u> and <u>around the world</u>.**

parallelism the repetition of a grammatical structure

You can use correlative conjunctions to link parallel elements, and in doing so, emphasize the connection between them.

He won gold medals in the 100-meter dash and the 400-meter relay.

He won gold medals in <u>both</u> the 100-meter dash <u>and</u> the 400-meter relay.

As you revise, make sure that elements joined by *both . . . and, either . . . or, neither . . . nor,* and *not only . . . but also* are parallel in structure.

either

They will ~~either~~ **meet with the supervisor** ‸ **today or tomorrow.**

They not only give money to charities but they also do charitable work.

MindTap® Find additional handbook coverage of grammar, punctuation, and style online.

---

*John F. Kennedy, inaugural address, Washington, DC, January 1961.

Proposals

MindTap® Understand the goals of the chapter and complete a warm-up activity online.

Every day, we seek to solve problems. Sometimes, all we need is expert advice and friendly suggestions: "New tires will reduce your gas mileage"; "Take a baby aspirin every morning to prevent a heart attack"; "Why not take your draft to the Writing Center?" Any one of these homely suggestions serves as a **proposal**, a message that calls for improvement, calling an audience to action, using a rhetorical "ought." Of course, proposals are just as often more formal and aimed at a larger audience. Public service announcements (PSAs) addressing social problems—such as bullying, gun violence, global warming, littering, water shortages, and the like—work to convince a large group of people to take action (or feel guilty if they do not!).

proposal message that calls for improvement through action

This chapter gives you the opportunity to consider problems that you might like to address, even resolve. As you consider a topic that engages your passion, also consider the most fitting means of delivery for your proposal.

IDENTIFYING AN OPPORTUNITY FOR CHANGE

 Print Proposal written for a community or campus newspaper or sent directly to the rhetorical audience

 Oral Proposal or Short Film recorded as a short film or video podcast

 Online Proposal posted to an appropriate site and featuring images illustrating the problem and/or solution

GENRE IN F⊕CUS The Public Service Announcement

In 2010, Philadelphia launched an UnLitter Us campaign through a series of public service announcements. Their purpose was to inspire the cleanup of a big city that had long suffered from a reputation as "filthy, dirty." Once civic leaders identified the opportunity for action, they created purposeful proposal arguments aimed directly at their city's residents, the only people who could resolve the problem. The poetry that overlays the man's head below identifies the problem itself: "The city has a heartbeat/with broken glass/plastic wrappers/clogging its arteries."

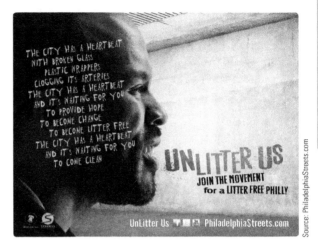

This call to "Unlitter Us" uses poetry as part of the public service campaign. Just as the poetry appears to be in the man's head, "UNLITTER US" seems to be coming out of his mouth.

It also targets a specific audience: "The city has a heartbeat/and it's waiting for you/to provide hope/to become change/to become litter free." But the bold blue letters of "UNLITTER US" are what we see first; they serve as the thesis statement, the "ought" of the proposal.

Imagining that Philadelphia's youth would be drawn to the message itself by the delivery of poetry, the civic leaders were disappointed when their poetry-based PSAs did not work, so they took another tack: they used profiles of "real Philadelphians" who were committed to unlittering the city (see p. 158).

The focus on specific neighborhoods and neighborhood leaders who wanted to clean, improve, and, therefore, strengthen their communities was a much more successful proposal: it used the rhetorical appeals of ethos, logos, and pathos much more effectively than the previous PSA, especially the pathos that connected the audience emotionally with people in other neighborhoods who had already taken the pledge to unlitter. (For more on ethos, logos, and pathos, see CHAPTER 2, THE AVAILABLE MEANS INCLUDE THE RHETORICAL ELEMENTS pages 23–26 OF THE MESSAGE ITSELF.) Both PSAs are proposals, and both end with a call for action in line with their thesis: "UNLITTER US."

As you, no doubt, realize, a proposal is arranged much like an argument. (See CHAPTER 14, ARGUMENT.) Audiences are more likely to be persuaded by pages 275–278

Source: PhiladelphiaStreets.com

This proposal focuses on specific profiles of "real Philadelphians" who were committed to unlittering the city.

solutions that make responsible use of resources and that benefit a group of people rather than just a few. Once you have identified and defined the problem for an audience who can help resolve that problem, either by showing support, giving permission, or working toward the solution itself, you can begin to consider the acceptability, cost, and feasibility of your proposal. Proposals like Philadelphia's are a common response to this question: How can something be feasibly and acceptably improved? In the case of this PSA campaign, the writers make clear that it costs little to unlitter—all it takes is community involvement.

ASSIGNMENT

When you have identified a social, university, or community problem or practice that you would like to address or resolve, you will want to compose a proposal argument. Your job is to describe the problem that you feel should and can be changed in such a way that your audience understands what is at stake, especially for them. You will want to chart out your proposed plan of action, a proposal that should be possible, desirable (by your audience), and financially responsible, keeping in mind that some proposals will cost nothing at all. Your goal is to convince your audience that your proposed solution is the most effective option available to them.

READING RHETORICALLY

Reading a proposal rhetorically means working through the following steps:

1. Identify the problem itself, assessing whether a significant problem actually exists and why it has not been resolved before. Who, exactly, does this problem affect—and to what extent?

2. Evaluate the proposed solution, taking into consideration the amount and quality of research the author has undertaken before advising readers what ought to be done. How feasible and acceptable is the proposal in terms of cost, time, and effectiveness?
3. Weigh the pros and cons of enacting the proposal; after all, the benefits ought to outweigh the costs, with this proposal proving to be better than the alternatives. Assess the reasons the author provides for justifying this proposal.

Key Features of a Proposal

When you want to argue for the best way to improve on a situation, consider composing a proposal. Proposals commonly have the following features:

- There is a clear, identifiable problem that the proposal seeks to resolve.
- This problem is of concern to a significant number of people.
- The proposed solution will resolve the problem in a way these people will find acceptable (without harming or greatly inconveniencing others).
- The proposal contains specific details about the costs, feasibility, acceptability, and benefits of the solution.
- The proposal is directed to an appropriate audience and demonstrates a good understanding of that audience's needs and interests.
- The proposal clearly explains the steps or processes required to enact the solution.

In the following proposal, small-business owner Simon Arias proposes a reconsideration of Pennsylvania's minimum wage, which has not risen since 2009. As you read through Arias's proposal, pay careful attention to the features of a proposal.

- What serves as his opportunity to respond?
- What problem does he identify?
- What is his purpose for writing to this rhetorical audience? How are purpose and audience connected in this proposal?
- How feasible, costly, and acceptable might his proposal actually be?

MindTap® Read, highlight, and take notes online.

Raise Pennsylvania's Minimum Wage: Everyone Benefits When All Workers Make a Decent Living

SIMON ARIAS

Simon Arias

Very often, proposals appear in print—and they can be lengthy, much lengthier, of course, than a PSA. Simon Arias published his proposal in the Pittsburgh Post-Gazette *(October 29, 2015) as a letter to the editor during a period when states had begun to take into their own hands the issue of raising the federal minimum wage and when a number of minimum wage proposals had come before the Pennsylvania state senate. Arias, who owns an insurance agency, wanted his voice to be heard during these legislative negotiations. He could have rented a billboard, taken out radio or television spots, or submitted his proposal to the print or online version of his local newspaper. He believed his local newspaper was the best medium to reach his rhetorical audience: legislators, voters, and other small-business owners.*

The author identifies a clear problem: Pennsylvania's minimum wage has not increased since 2009.

Pennsylvania's minimum wage has been stuck at $7.25 an hour since 2009, which is bad for business as well as workers. We lag behind 29 states that have higher minimum wages, including all six of our neighboring states.

We might as well have highway signs saying, "Welcome to Pennsylvania—Where the Minimum Wage Is Less than Maryland, New Jersey, New York, Ohio, Delaware and West Virginia."

Arias argues that Pennsylvania's comparatively low minimum wage affects many people, more than a million workers as well as business owners themselves.

Policy makers need to remember that workers are also customers. Today's minimum wage has less buying power than the minimum wage had in the 1960s. That's bad for business.

He proposes that the minimum wage be raised to $10.10, which will help resolve the problem in ways people will find acceptable. And doing so will not harm anyone else; in fact, doing so will improve the lives of others as well.

As a business owner with offices in Pittsburgh, Erie, Wilkes-Barre, State College and Canonsburg, I know that the proposal to raise the state minimum wage to $10.10 makes good business sense. It will increase the wages of more than a million workers, boosting sales at Main Street businesses across our state.

Arias establishes his ethos as a successful, credible business owner. The following paragraphs illustrate the ways the daily lives of workers will be improved, the material benefits of raising the minimum wage.

I started my life insurance agency in 2008 and by 2012 it was named Pittsburgh's Top Workplace among small businesses by the *Pittsburgh Post-Gazette* and maintains its A rating.

The minimum wage is a kind of insurance. Set at a decent level, the minimum wage helps ensure that people who work full-time make enough to put food on the table and keep a roof overhead.

Raising the minimum wage will help provide basic, daily needs.

Unfortunately, the current minimum wage is not decent. It keeps even full-time workers in poverty and undermines our economy.

My life insurance agents visit more than 1,200 working families in Pennsylvania a week. Every day we hear from hard-working Pennsylvanians who want to provide for their families but are struggling to make ends meet.

Many families who want to purchase life insurance to protect their financial futures simply cannot afford to do so. Working for $7.25 an hour, 40 hours a week, comes to just $15,080 a year. It's not a livable wage. It's not the solid wage floor we need to assure the healthy consumer demand that sustains strong job growth.

I pride myself on offering a fair wage and treating my employees as the best investment in my agency's long-term growth. My starting wage is $15 an hour—more than double the current minimum wage. We also offer health insurance, vacation time and paid sick leave.

Businesses claiming Pennsylvania can't phase in a $10.10 minimum wage should look to the problems in their business model.

Paying a higher wage has not hurt my business—it has been a sustaining factor in our growth. My employees are focused on their work and not distracted by continual financial stress.

Our employee turnover is very low, which saves me from the costly cycle of hiring, training and losing employees that plagues many low-wage businesses. My employees know they can grow along with my business and that good customer service benefits everyone.

Most business owners support at least a $10.10 minimum wage. In a nationally representative 2014 poll, 61 percent of small-business owners with employees favored a $10.10 minimum wage, plus cost of living adjustments in future years.

Business owners like me are signing the Pennsylvania Business for a Fair Minimum Wage statement supporting an increase because we know that raising the minimum wage will be good for business, customers and our economy.

We know that decent wages bring lower employee turnover, increased productivity, better employee performance and a higher level of customer satisfaction.

We know we cannot revitalize the American Dream when a growing number of full-time workers are turning to food stamps, food banks and other assistance to survive.

In the words of Roger Smith, the CEO of American Income Life, "Raising the minimum wage makes good economic sense, but it's much more than that. You cannot have a strong economy or fulfill the promise of the American Dream when most Americans are running in place or falling behind while the richest Americans pull further away from the rest."

It's time to stop holding Pennsylvania back with a woefully inadequate minimum wage. It's time to move forward.

He establishes logos by providing researched details about the economic lives of minimum-wage workers.

In addition to helping them meet daily needs, raising the minimum wage will also allow workers to insure their futures.

Arias enhances his ethos by declaring that he pays his workers more than twice the current minimum wage.

And to further increase the logos of his opinion, he provides specific examples of the ways his better-paid workers add value to his business.

He has conducted more research that supports his argument: the majority of business owners favor an increase in the minimum wage.

Arias outlines broadly the steps that need to be taken: groups need to band together in support of a higher minimum wage so that the issue can be put to a vote.

Arias closes by invoking an emotional connection with his readers; after all, all Americans yearn to fulfill the "American Dream."

Using Synthesis and Analysis

Arias's proposal gives you much to consider: the history and purpose of the minimum wage, the current value of the minimum wage, and what a difference a livable wage would make to those who earn the minimum wage. As you break down his argument, consider the elements of the rhetorical situation: Who is Arias? What is the context for his letter to the editor? What does he hope to accomplish? How does knowing who the author is and the context for his proposal affect your interpretation of his argument?

When you analyze to understand, interpret, and contextualize a text, you will also question the material you read. Break down Arias's arguments for an increase in the minimum wage. What is his main point? What evidence does he present for why the minimum wage is a problem in the first place? What does he present as the most troubling effects of the current minimum wage? How does he demonstrate the feasibility, acceptability, and benefits of his proposed solution? How does he address the arguments against raising the minimum wage? What perspectives might be included that are currently missing? Explain the logic of his reasons and whether you agree with this logic.

Given Arias's arguments and the context for making them, how do you see rhetoric—either written or spoken—helping to resolve the problem? Who will be positively (and negatively) affected by this solution? Who has the capability to resolve or affect the resolution of that problem? Are you persuaded that his proposal presents a viable solution and a reliable basis for discussion, interpretation, or action? Why or why not?

> MindTap® Find additional examples of proposals online.

See also CHAPTER 2, THE AMETHYST INITIATIVE, *Underage Drinking Statistics*

See also CHAPTER 22, CORBY KUMMER, *Good-bye, Cryovac* [Local Food, College Food Service, and Scraping Your Own Plate]

See also, CHAPTER 25, ANNE JOLLY, *STEM vs. STEAM: Do the Arts Belong?*

 RESPONDING TO THE RHETORICAL SITUATION

To understand the full complexity of the situation, you will first want to identify the problem and consider whom it affects. Then, you will want to consider who of those people could serve as your rhetorical audience, the people who could actually help you work toward a solution. Your purpose is to invite them to join you in resolving or addressing the problem. Your genre, then, is "proposal." How you deliver your proposal depends on how best you can reach your intended audience: e-mail, letter, PSA, talk, and so on.

| Problem | Audience and Purpose | Genre/Proposal | (Medium of) Delivery |

Understanding the Rhetorical Situation

When you identify a problem, you often think about possible solutions. Proposals offer an analysis of the problem and the best of solutions, best in terms of feasibility, cost, and benefits. Your task as a proposal writer is to give the problem a presence in the lives of your audience. Because not everyone will readily accept your proposal, it is important that you recognize other possibilities and weigh their pros and cons as well. You may even want to include some of the best ideas in your own proposal. In the end, you will need to justify why your proposal is the best one, the one most beneficial to your audience and yet not harmful to others.

RESEARCHING A PROPOSAL

Successful proposals (whether informal advice or formal proposals) rely on research, knowledge, and personal experience. As you advocate for your plan, take into consideration similar as well as competing proposals, researched facts and data, and the interests and values of your audience. Library, online, field, and naturalistic research (interviews, observations) and experiential knowledge will provide you with the specific facts, figures, and research studies you need to persuade your audience to act on what you propose. But you will also need to research your rhetorical audience in order to make your case that what you propose is in their best interest. After all, you want to be especially careful to introduce ideas that can be proved to be feasible, acceptable, and financially responsible, rather than reintroducing parts of a proposal they have already rejected. Without the necessary research, your proposal is merely your opinion.

Identifying an opportunity for change

You want to identify a problem that merits a solution that you can propose. How does this problem affect you? How does it affect others? How present is it in your life? How would writing about this problem help you begin to conceptualize a solution? How might a solution affect you and others?

1. Identify three problems that you encounter on a daily or weekly basis. How do they make themselves present in your life? Which of them could easily

be resolved—if only someone would make a change? If it were resolved, how would you be affected? How would others be affected?

2. In terms of the problem that offered the richest details for development, how might it be resolved? What other possible resolutions can you think of? What is the feasibility of each of the proposed resolutions? What is the cost? What are the benefits?

3. Freewrite for ten minutes, identifying one problem, describing how it manifests itself in your life and how it affects your life and the lives of others. (For more on freewriting and other ways to jump-start your writing, see CHAPTER 13, EXPLORATION.)

4. Then write for another ten minutes, outlining a proposed solution to that problem. Be sure to include the steps necessary for making your proposal a reality. Who else needs to be involved? What ought they do? How, exactly, will you and they benefit? What are the pros and cons of your proposal?

5. In order to vary your emphasis, describe other proposals that may be in circulation. What are the pros and cons of those proposals? Whom will they benefit? Whom might they harm?

pages 239–244

Relating rhetorically to your audience

The following questions can help you locate your rhetorical audience as well as identify its relationship to the problem you have identified. Then, you will be able to choose the best way to describe that problem.

1. List the names of the persons or groups who are in the best position to help you make your proposal a reality. This step may require some research and legwork.

2. Next to the name of each potential audience, write reasons that audience could have for acknowledging the very real presence of your problem. In other words, what would persuade these audiences that something needs to change?

3. What actions could these audiences reasonably be persuaded to perform? Consider what each audience would be able to do to address the problem—and what each audience ought to do.

4. With your audience's interests and capabilities in mind, look again at the descriptions of the problem that you composed in the preceding section. Decide which description will best help your audience feel connected to the features of the problem you outlined and invested in improving them. At this point, it may be necessary to revise your best description to tailor it to your audience. Remember to consider whether the most fitting description will include print, images, video, and/or audio.

Planning an effective rhetorical response for your purpose

Identifying a problem and getting others to recognize it as a problem are only the first steps in responding to a rhetorical situation. You also need to identify and support a suitable solution to the problem. Your solution should consider the information you gathered about your audience, such as their interests and capabilities, as well as detailed information about the problem itself (its history and its presence) and your proposed solution (its actual benefits, costs, and feasibility). In terms of feasibility, your proposal ought to be an efficient, cost-effective, and widely beneficial way to go about making a positive change.

Use the following questions to help you narrow your purpose and shape your response:

1. How would you efficiently and effectively solve the problem you have identified?
2. What does your proposed solution require of your audience?
3. Are you asking your audience simply to support your solution or to perform a particular action?
4. What is the best way to reach this audience? You might draft a petition, compose a video, or speak to student and community groups. The point is that once you have identified your problem, audience, and purpose, you need to determine how best to deliver your proposal.

LINKS TO PROPOSALS IN THREE MEDIA MindTap°

Links may change due to availability.

Print Proposal In the letter to the editor by small-business owner Simon Arias presented earlier in this chapter, Arias chooses his local newspaper to reach readers most interested in the issue of minimum wage.

Oral Proposal or Short Film The National Football League sponsors PSAs on Domestic Violence (see the short film on www.youtube.com/watch?v=5Z_zWlVRlWk, which aired during Super Bowl XLIX).

Online Proposal Many proposals feature images illustrating the problem and/or solution and are posted to an appropriate online site, like this water conservation PSA.

⊘ WRITING A PERSUASIVE PROPOSAL: A Guide

*T*o write persuasively, you will need to establish your credibility, or ethos, as you demonstrate your understanding of the situation and the ways it affects your audience. Next, you will establish logos (the logic of your proposal) by creating an information-based argument: the background of the problem, the immediate effects of the problem itself, and the feasibility and acceptability (monetary, practical, and aesthetic) of the solution you are proposing. Finally, you will create pathos when you connect with your audience, showing them how the implementation of your proposal will benefit them—and not at great expense or inconvenience to others.

ADVANTAGES AND LIMITATIONS

Advantages

- **Writer:** You have insight into a troublesome situation, and you have some good ideas about addressing or resolving that problem.

- **Message:** Proposals invite you and others to improve the world you live in, on both a broad, public scale and a smaller, private one.

- **Media and Design:** The possibilities are many, from print and visual to online and multimodal. You can select the medium of delivery that will reach, maybe even please, your audience.

Limitations

- **Writer:** Because you may not be the first person to identify and try to resolve the problem, your audience may not be (immediately) receptive to your proposal (or any proposal, for that matter).

- **Message:** Not everyone will agree that improvements are needed, especially if they are expected to take action. Or they may not agree on your proposed solution.

- **Media and Design:** Like the UnLitter Us campaign at the beginning of this chapter, your first attempt to reach your audience may need to be revised. Often, writers find themselves having to revise and resubmit their proposals.

Introduction

- **Frame the problem by offering necessary background and by emphasizing the presence of the problem.**
- **Establish the problem as one both the writer and audience share and will want to resolve (establishing credibility as a writer or speaker).**
- **State your thesis by defining the problem and outlining a sensible solution.**

Define the problem The introduction emphasizes the presence of the problem and offers credible information on the history of that problem, maybe even its causes or consequences. For example, in his proposal, Arias explains that Pennsylvania's minimum wage has been "stuck" since 2009, charging that the situation is bad not only for workers but for businesses as well.

Present a sensible solution The introduction states a thesis, which conveys the essence of the proposed sensible solution. Arias proposes that the state minimum wage be increased to $10.10/hour, which he claims will increase the wages of more than one million Pennsylvania workers and boost sales in all their home towns. For him, the solution is ethical, feasible, and practical.

Ask yourself . . .
- Have I described the context of the problem with enough detail so that my audience understands its urgency?
- Have I demonstrated the ways that the problem not only affects me but them as well?
- Have I proposed a solution that is sensible, feasible, and acceptable—as well as ethical?

- **Support the proposed solution with researched evidence, establishing logos.**
- **Review previous attempts to resolve the problem. You may also be able to establish how this solution has worked elsewhere, but do not overpromise benefits.**
- **Discuss the feasibility of the solution: the time, money, and effort required.**
- **Address the acceptability of the solution, including possible objections.**

Use evidence to support the logic of your solution The body of a proposal provides supporting evidence for the suggested solution, particularly in terms of its consequences or results. The researched content of the overall argument helps establish logos. Arias, for instance, supplies specific details about the lives of those on minimum wage, hard workers who, he knows for sure, can barely afford to put food on the table and keep a roof overhead, let alone buy life insurance.

Show how the solution is acceptable and feasible in terms of time, money, and human effort Take your readers through the steps necessary to bring the proposal into reality. Careful research is crucial to the success of this section. Arias argues that 61 percent of small-business owners already favor a higher minimum wage that includes cost-of-living adjustments because they know that "decent wages bring lower employee turnover, increased productivity, better employee performance, and a higher level of customer satisfaction."

Provide examples of success Provide examples of other instances in which your proposed solution (or a similar one) has had positive results, not just for a few, but for many. Benefits may include saved time, saved money, happiness, less suffering, and so on. In his own business, Arias starts his employees at $15/hour, more than double the current minimum wage in Pennsylvania, stating that doing so has been the best investment in the long-term growth of his business because his "employees are focused on their work and not distracted by continual financial distress."

(continued)

List the logistical challenges Concede the challenges to your proposal and supply detailed responses to each of the challenges, demonstrating how all or most of them can be overcome. Weigh the benefits with the costs. The biggest challenge Arias faces is that he and his colleagues have not been able to convince the Pennsylvania State legislature to raise the minimum wage. People who already have a living wage (legislators, for instance) do not seem to understand the situation.

Acknowledge objections and tradeoffs Not everybody will approve of your proposal. Acknowledge those objections and discuss tradeoffs. Arias admonishes that "businesses claiming Pennsylvania cannot phase in a $10.10 minimum wage should look to the problems in their business model." In the end, he invokes the "American Dream," which is being unfulfilled so long as "a growing number of full-time workers are turning to food stamps, food banks, and other assistance to survive."

Ask yourself . . .
- Have I researched the background of this problem?
- Am I informed about previous proposals for resolving this problem?
- How, exactly, can my audience benefit from my proposal?
- Will anyone be harmed by it?
- Have I researched and addressed the possible objections to my proposal?
- Do I have the necessary information to address each of those objections?
- What further research must I conduct in order to present a well-rounded argument for my proposal?

- **Predict positive outcomes of the solution.**
- **Establish an authentic emotional connection with the audience by linking the solution to their benefit.**

Predict the positive results of your solution Finally, the conclusion of a proposal predicts the positive consequences or improvements that will result from the proposed solution, results that far outweigh any negatives. Arias makes clear that raising Pennsylvania's minimum wage will help move the state's economy forward.

Identify the solution with the interests of your readers Also, the conclusion should make clear just how the audience will profit from this proposal, which will benefit many, not just a few. Using pathos, you will connect your proposed solution with the needs and interests of your audience. In this case, Arias explains the many ways that raising the minimum wage will improve not only the lives of full-time workers but also Pennsylvania's economy. He claims everyone will profit from such an investment in Pennsylvania's workforce.

Ask yourself . . .

- How can I demonstrate that my proposal is the most beneficial to the most people?
- What additional research should I conduct?
- What else do I need to know about the needs and interests of my audience?
- Have I listened carefully to all of their concerns?

MindTap® Request help and feedback from a tutor. If required, participate in peer review, submit your paper for a grade, and view instructor comments online.

Revision and Peer Review

After you have drafted your proposal, ask one of your classmates to read it. You will want your classmate to respond to your work in a way that helps you revise it into the strongest proposal it can be, one that addresses your intended audience, helps you fulfill your purpose, and is delivered in the most appropriate means available to you.

Questions for a peer reviewer

1. What problem has the writer identified? How does the writer frame that problem? How does the problem offer an opportunity to respond?
2. Who is the writer's rhetorical audience? Why might this audience care about the problem?
3. Where does the writer indicate how the problem will affect the audience? What does the writer think the audience ought to do? How does the writer establish ethos?
4. Identify the writer's thesis statement, which clearly states the proposed solution, perhaps repeating the problem as well. If you cannot locate a thesis statement, what thesis statement might work for this document?
5. What kinds of research has the writer conducted in order to provide support for the proposed solution, in terms of its feasibility, cost, and acceptability?
6. What steps are necessary for realizing this solution?
7. Identify the supporting ideas (presented through narration, cause-and-effect analysis, description, exemplification, process analysis, or definition) that the writer uses to support his or her assertions.

8. What additional evidence might the writer provide to better support the solution's feasibility? How has the writer established logos?
9. Where does the writer address potential objections to the solution?
10. How does the writer make use of images? Is there any place where a graph or chart could be included, to display costs or otherwise provide readers with a sense of what will be expected of them or the community?
11. What does the solution ask of the audience? Is the requested action explicit or merely implied?
12. How does the writer connect with the audience in terms of aligning the proposed resolution with their needs or expectations (establishing pathos)?
13. What did you learn from the conclusion that you did not already know after reading the introduction and the body? What information does the writer want the audience to know? Does the writer attempt to change readers' attitudes, actions, or opinions?
14. Which section of the proposal did you most enjoy? Why?

 MindTap® Reflect on your writing process.

 ADDITIONAL ASSIGNMENTS

Knowledge Transfer

Often, students collaborate with community-service agencies or businesses to fulfill their research or writing assignments, conduct scholarly collaborative projects via social networking sites, and spend their summers as interns, earning professional experience rather than money for next semester's expenses. Proposal writing is useful beyond English classes for all these venues.

COLLEGE Letter to the School Administration You are required to take an upper-division writing course in your major, but you—and many of your classmates—cannot register for that writing course until the last semester of your senior year. You and some of your closest friends compose a joint letter to the dean of your college, asking her to help you resolve this problem: after all, you all need to have that course much earlier in your college careers. You propose a solution that you think she can implement, perhaps by working with the dean of the College of the Liberal Arts (where writing courses are housed). You might consider asking for more sections of this course, hybrid courses, or even priority for majors.

COMMUNITY Letter to the Editor As you consider your entry into college, make a list of the resources (advantages)—and constraints (limitations)—associated with your experiences so far. Describe factors that make them positive or negative. Finally, choose one feature of your *experience* that has been problematic. Write a letter to your campus newspaper (see one example that follows, which appeared in the *Centre Daily Times* [State College, PA]).

There is a recurring problem in . . . State College to be exact.

Local drivers continue to pass stopped mass-transit buses in neighborhoods clearly marked with solid double yellow lines.

These lines have one purpose: Do not pass in these areas!

You . . . are inviting a collision with an oncoming car in the other lane. You are at fault should you kill another driver.

Stop it. . . . Obey the traffic laws, or buy a bike.

**Dan Stoicheff
State College
12 Sept. 2015**

WORKPLACE Memorandum for Reallocation of Resources You have noticed that many people in your office have hotpots and small microwaves in their offices or cubicles, leaving the entire office area messy and sometimes smelly. Many people complain about the situation but cannot think of how best to resolve it. You and a couple of close colleagues have noticed that a janitor's closet is no longer being used as such. Since it already has a sink and electrical outlets, you propose that it be transformed into a kitchenette of sorts, with an electric teakettle, microwave, and small refrigerator. In fact, the three of you will be happy to make the transformation during work hours or with overtime. You agree to write the proposal memo to your supervisor, outlining the problem; the effects of the problem; the feasibility, cost, and acceptability of your proposed solution; and the benefits for all.

MULTIMODAL Public Service Announcement As you review the UNLITTER US campaign used by the city of Philadelphia presented earlier in this chapter, consider ways that your community (campus, city, church, or hometown) could be improved. What is an abiding problem in that community? What have been the attempts to address that problem? Who has tried? What insights can you offer into the problem? How do you propose it be addressed? Who could help you? How would they benefit? Using a multimodal approach (any combination of words, images, video, audio), compose a Public Service Announcement aimed at and easily available to your rhetorical audience.

Just as successful proposal writers forge strong links between a problem and a solution, good writers forge strong links between their sentences.

Linking through old-new sentence patterns

One way good writers do this is by presenting old, or given, information at the beginning of a sentence, saving the new information for the end of the sentence. The given information is familiar and expected; the new information is unknown or unanticipated until the sentence has been read. Think of it this way: if you are at an awards ceremony, you expect the announcer to say, "The winner is Carlos Rico," not "Carlos Rico is the winner." *The winner* is old information (you are at an awards ceremony and so you assume a winner will be chosen); the name of the winner is the new, highly anticipated information.

By ordering information in this way, you create a chain: old new old new old new. What was new becomes old. After declaring the winner at the awards ceremony, the announcer may continue by describing the person's accomplishments: "Mr. Rico has starred in five Broadway plays in just eight years." Notice that in this sentence the winner's name is now old information placed at the beginning of the sentence, with the new information following it. Although there are other ways to ensure text coherence, if you want to provide this type of linking, alter the order of some of your sentences so that new and old information are tightly connected.

On top of one of the snow banks sat three teenagers.

The snow plow left ample evidence of its work.~~Three teenagers sat on top of one of the snow banks.~~

Her first poem was published when she was only sixteen.

She wrote most of her poems between 1936 and 1954.~~She was only sixteen when her first poem was published.~~

Linking through verb-noun pairs

Look at the following pairs of words:

discuss/discussion	*occur/occurrence*	*apply/application*
describe/description	*depend/dependence*	*recommend/recommendation*
allude/allusion	*prescribe/prescription*	*present/presentation*

The first word in each pair is a verb; the second word, derived from the verb, is a noun. You can use this feature of English, called **nominalizing**, to link sentences together (the root of *nominalize* means "noun" or "name"). After using the verb in the first sentence, you can use the noun in the second. The noun becomes the old information that is linked to the new information of the previous sentence. Here is an example:

> The grammar of the written language <u>differs</u> profoundly from that of the spoken language. This <u>difference</u> is attributable to the constant innovations of spoken language.

Most verbs take endings when they are nominalized, but some do not—for example, *request, address,* and *excerpt.*

Adjectives can also be nominalized (*sad/sadness, scarce/scarcity*). Note, though, that nominalizations, whether derived from verbs or adjectives, are abstractions. A sentence with too many nominalizations seems static, because verbs showing movement have crystallized and forms of *be* have replaced them as the main verbs. A sentence with too many nominalizations may also frustrate readers because it demands that they mentally record a number of nominalized actions or states. In the following sentence, the reader has to determine how four nominalized actions are related.

nominalizing
creating a noun
from a verb or
adjective

> The firm is now engaged in an <u>assessment</u> of its <u>procedures</u> for the <u>development</u> of new <u>products.</u>

To revise a sentence like this one, locate the most important action and recast the sentence with this action as the main verb. The revised sentence is more concise—and quite likely clearer to your readers.

> The firm is now <u>assessing</u> its procedures for <u>developing</u> new products.

You may also decide that some actions or ideas are less important and thus can be discarded. For the preceding example sentence, the action of engaging was not important enough to be included.

MindTap®   Find additional handbook coverage of grammar, punctuation, and style online.

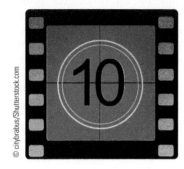

Evaluations

MindTap® Understand the goals of the chapter and complete a warm-up activity online.

Your familiarity with evaluations has developed over a lifetime of reading them and making your own. You have seen examples of this genre in the form of movie reviews that regularly appear in newspapers, magazines, and conversations; you have also seen product reviews that appear in print and online publications such as *Consumer Reports* and *PC Magazine*. Both kinds of evaluations work to persuade you that particular films, appliances, and electronics are the best, average, or not so hot. By now, you also intuitively know that an **evaluation** (or a review) has two basic components: (1) a judgment meant to persuade, and (2) the criteria used to arrive at that judgment.

evaluation
a judgment based on relevant criteria and meant to persuade

As you determine the specific situation, problem, phenomenon, or cultural element (movie, art object, political event, or everyday detail of life) that merits your evaluation and relevant criteria, consider, too, the most effective means of delivering that evaluation to your audience: print, online, orally, visually, or multimodally.

IDENTIFYING AN OPPORTUNITY FOR CHANGE

Print Evaluation
written for a campus newspaper or zine

Oral Evaluation
presented live to your rhetorical audience using a video, digital slide show, or presentation software

Online Evaluation
posted on a film review site, a video game site, an educational site, or other website

GENRE IN F⚙CUS The Film Review

Consider one of the most common forms of an evaluation: the movie review. A reasonable and insightful movie evaluation establishes the criteria and includes judgments on those criteria, such as the overall quality, strengths and weaknesses, cast, setting, and technical features in the film. In addition, a movie review might include a consideration of the significant cultural references in the film, such as costumes or historical references in the movie's plot line—or, as in the following review of *The Force Awakens*, references to previous films in the franchise.

In an early positive review of the most recent iteration in the *Star Wars* franchise of films, *Star Wars: The Force Awakens*, *New York Times* film critic Manohla Dargis announces, "It's good!" Like many of the first reviewers, Dargis praises the film primarily for its balance of what she calls "cozy favorites" (in other words, Harrison Ford), "new kinetic wows," and "a scale and sensibility that are rooted in the human." Dargis clearly lays out all the criteria she uses to evaluate a true blockbuster film: rather than privileging "special effects," it needs to promote "story, character, directorial vision, or just a little creative intelligence." To prove that her assessment is the right one, Dargis provides vivid descriptions of characters and specific scenes to explain how she sees the film stacking up on these criteria. Familiar (white) characters (Luke, Leia, and Han) carry out the plot with newcomers (Latino Poe, African American Finn, and the scene-stealing white female Rey) in event after rich event. For instance, resistant fighter pilot Poe maneuvers his ship much the way Han always has; Imperial Stormtrooper Finn leaves the Dark Side and comes over to the good; and desert scrap-metal-scavenger Rey proves herself to be every bit as resourceful and nimble as Luke Skywalker ever was as she saves Finn, directs Han, and overcomes the evil that is Kylo Ren. Though she seems to be crazy about this chapter of the *Star Wars* franchise, Dargis acknowledges that *The Force Awakens* falls short, in that "it won't save the world, not even Hollywood." But she leaves her readers with a strong sense that, overall, the movie's combination of compelling story, charismatic characters, and innovative visual techniques makes it worth seeing. In closing, Dargis writes,

> Over the decades, as "Star Wars" grew into an entertainment machine, it took on the aspect of a cult. That, at any rate, is how it could feel to those of us looking at it from the outside in, especially as one mediocre movie after another with noxious creations like Jar Jar Binks crushed the box office. Mr. Abrams [J.J. Abrams, the director] may be as worshipful as any "Star Wars" obsessive, but in "The Force Awakens" he's made a movie that goes for old-fashioned escapism even as it presents a futuristic vision of a pluralistic world that his audience already lives in. He hasn't made a film only for

true believers; he has made a film for everyone (well, almost). So, will Rey, Finn and Poe save the day? Will they battle Kylo Ren and Oedipus, too? Stay tuned for the next potentially thrilling, or at least pretty good, adventure.

—Manohla Dargis, *"Star Wars: The Force Awakens" Delivers the Thrills, with a Touch of Humanity*

Taking a different position, *LA Times* film reviewer Michael Hiltzik offers a negative evaluation of *The Force Awakens* as he weighs various criteria (plot, connection to prequels and a sequel, technical effects, characters, and acting). In fact, in his headline, he says it "stinks."

Haven't we seen this movie before? . . .

On Christmas Day, I fulfilled my duty as an American consumer and took the family to see the new "Star Wars" movie. The excursion solved a mystery: Why do so many of the reviews, even the enthusiastic ones, carry an undertone of disappointment?

The simple answer is that "Star Wars: The Force Awakens" is not very good. It's professionally made in the sense that it displays an industrial level of [Disney] Quality Control. But it's depressingly unimaginative and dull in long stretches, and—crucially—reproduces George Lucas' original 1977 movie slavishly almost to the point of plagiarism.
. . .

Whether out of his own instincts or via directives from the suits at Disney, J.J. Abrams, the co-writer and director of "The Force Awakens," plainly labored under a mandate to not get the thing wrong. . . . Abrams seems to follow the precept that the surest way to keep from putting a foot wrong is to walk only within the footprints of one's predecessors. As has been noted by a few reviewers . . . , the new movie obsequiously replicates the formula of the original—its set pieces, rhythm, pacing, even dialogue— even without advancing the story at all. . . .

Abrams' big advance is said to be supplanting the whiter-than-white protagonists of the original "Star Wars" with a young woman and a black male. This hardly is a cinematic breakthrough, as other moviemakers who understand the demands of a gender- and culturally diverse audience have been doing it for years. But as a "rebooting," the term ubiquitously applied to "The Force Awakens," it feels entirely market-oriented, the way the Tide logo gets periodically redesigned to look fresh or the trademark figures of Betty Crocker and the Gerber Foods baby are redrawn to stay "modern." But redesigning logos and brand icons is a technique drawn from Madison Avenue, not traditional moviemaking. . . .

"The Force Awakens" will reinforce even more strongly a block-buster, sequel-oriented style of moviemaking and marketing that has

**sapped Hollywood of its creative energies. Why be creative when . . .
recycling is more dependably profitable.**

—**Michael Hiltzik,** *Admit it: "Star Wars: The Force Awakens"
Stinks—and Here's Why*

A film review is essentially an argument that often begins with a thesis statement and is intended to persuade others that your evaluation is accurate. (See CHAPTER 14, ARGUMENT.) Thus, even though Hiltzik presents a set of evaluation criteria similar to those of Dargis, Hiltzik arrives at a different conclusion, pages 275–278 a negative evaluation that he supports with specific evidence and compelling examples. Ultimately, both Dargis and Hiltzik are trying to persuade their readers that the criteria they use to evaluate the film (and the examples from the film to which they apply the criteria) are the most important ones to consider. Whatever the reviewer argues, it is paramount that he or she supplies specific—and relevant—evidence to support that claim (for example, that a movie is ground-breaking or derivative, suspenseful or confusing). (For more on thesis statements, claims, and evidence, see CHAPTER 2, MAKING CLAIMS.) page 20

 ASSIGNMENT

Whether conscious or unconscious, evaluations are value judgments about whether an object, event, individual, or document meets, exceeds, or does not satisfy the criteria. Every day we evaluate movies, political candidates, academic programs, partners, green designs for new cars or architecture, or issues and objects that affect our daily life. Often you will determine the relevant criteria for your evaluation; other times, the criteria are already in place (symptoms for a specific illness, for example).

As you consider your evaluation, focus on an object, phenomenon, event, or person that merits your attention as well as the attention of your audience. You may want your audience to understand your topic differently from how they currently understand it. Describe your topic and list detailed criteria (either traditional or fresh) for your evaluation, synthesizing your overall evaluation into a thesis statement. Your goal is to help your readers appreciate the significance of your evaluation by aligning the criteria you have developed with the object of your evaluation and the interests of your audience.

READING RHETORICALLY

You regularly make judgments or choices determined by criteria. When you read rhetorically, you examine an evaluation through the criteria used to make that judgment. You may be examining the evaluation of an event or phenomenon that affected you, an object you needed to buy, or a choice you needed to make. As you read, place your object—and the criteria—within a social, cultural, and/or financial context, explaining how the object coincides with or diverges from the criteria used as the basis of your evaluation. Read actively and critically for the key features of a strong evaluation. In fact, the better you can analyze someone else's evaluation, the stronger your own evaluations will be.

Key Features of an Evaluation

Evaluations help us make decisions and are particularly useful for understanding the logical and emotional responses that are being shaped in ourselves and others. Whether spoken, visual, or written, evaluations argue either whether something *meets* a specific set of criteria or whether the set criteria *determine* the status of that object under consideration. In addition, to be persuasive, evaluations often draw on a particular emotional response with the use of descriptive, relevant details. Such details help the audience visualize the criteria and match them with the features of the object being evaluated. In short, evaluations commonly share most of the following features:

- Evaluations make clear why a particular object or phenomenon needs to be evaluated.
- Evaluations describe the particular object or phenomenon in a way that the rhetorical audience will understand and value.
- Evaluations ultimately identify the precise category into which the object or phenomenon fits: successful movie, effective detergent, dependable computer, easy-to-use smartphone. Just consider the ways your doctor evaluates your symptoms before determining your illness.
- The criteria on which the object or phenomenon is to be evaluated are presented clearly, persuasively, authoritatively, and often in an order indicating importance. Criteria can be categorized into three groups: *necessary* (crucial but not enough to meet your overall assessment), *sufficient* (meeting all of your minimum standards, including the necessary ones), and *accidental* (unnecessary but an added bonus to the necessary and sufficient criteria).
- Concrete evidence and relevant examples from your personal experience and research illustrate the ways (usually in the form of assertions) the object or phenomenon does or does not meet each evaluative criterion. These fair and balanced assertions support the thesis statement.
- Evaluations articulate a clear argument (usually in the form of a thesis statement) about whether or not the object or phenomenon meets the criteria on which it is being evaluated.
- The evaluator has demonstrated an ethical approach to the process.

You can see how these key features work in the following essay by Penn State-Fayette student Alexis Walker. In it Walker evaluates the effect of a new Dunkin' Donuts on the aesthetics of the downtown area where she lives. As you read, consider the rhetorical situation and the key criteria Walker presents.

- Determine Walker's motive for writing. What does she want to accomplish?
- Identify the criteria used to evaluate Dunkin' Donuts at Easton's Center Circle.
- Examine the language Walker uses to frame her evaluation as fair and balanced. Does her evaluation seem fair to you?
- Decide whether you agree with Walker's evaluation. Why or why not?

Evaluations

MindTap® Read, highlight, and take notes online.

Donuts at Easton's Center Circle: Slam Dunk or Cycle of Deterioration?

ALEXIS WALKER

Faced with the problem of a big ugly welcome sign in the shape of a Peace Candle, Alexis Walker was determined to write. She could have devised a PowerPoint presentation for the city council, e-mailed photos of the architectural defacement to the local historical preservation association, or composed a purposeful verbal evaluation of the situation. She chose to do the latter, arguing for a downtown renewal initiative based on bringing in major businesses and sponsoring local events as a way to attract the townsfolk to the city center. She distributed her evaluation to her friends and neighbors.

The way any city looks—its skyline, the buildings, the streets, even the greenery—affects how we experience that city and perceive what that city has to offer us. Whether from the hectic, crowded environment of New York to the calming, empty quality of a farming town, our feelings are influenced by what surrounds us. Therefore, the center of any city or town should, ideally, portray the very best the city has to offer (or, at least, what it hopes to offer).

Walker defines and describes a typical city center.

The most obvious are the visual clues, the businesses and events that popu-
late the downtown area and indicate the values and interests of the town and
bring people together, even a town as small as our own Easton.

A quick scan around the downtown of my hometown, Easton, on a
winter weekday afternoon makes disappointingly clear that this eastern
Pennsylvania town leaves much to be desired. Prominently placed at the
center of the traffic circle sits a huge Peace Candle. No matter from which
direction one enters the circle, the Peace Candle is straight ahead, failing to
actualize its intended purpose from any and every direction. Grungy,
neglected off-white concrete representing the melted wax drips down the
sides of the candle, with light blue cascades of faded color encrusting each
corner of the so-called candle holder. An unassuming dull, stiff flame of
orange and red metal sits atop the structure, unable to project any vibrancy.
And the entire creation is supported by a series of highly visible black cables
emphasizing the candle's behemoth existence. It would be a menacing sight
were it not so pitiful. This sad display of candlelight is supposed to signify
the fire, energy, and soul of Easton, as though it's a bustling hub of city
commerce rather than the old, dull, and mostly rundown commercial space
it actually is. Encircling the mammoth centerpiece are darkened window-
panes and boarded up entrances.

The bright white, freshly painted outside of the new Dunkin' Donuts contrasts sharply with the lifeless grey buildings that surround it. The signature
orange and pink lettering adorns both sides of this corner edifice, and its large
windows showcase the kinds of satisfied patrons the establishment wants
to attract. All of these attributes (freshness, cleanliness, paying customers),
dissimilar to the dreary
display downtown Easton
usually offers, might suggest that the area is on the
rise. Indeed, the revamped
Dunkin' Donuts building
and the business it brings
are nice—but they are not
nearly enough.

Dunkin' Donuts is
one of a small number of
notable exceptions to the
lifeless environment of
downtown Easton, inter-
mittent exceptions among

Figure 1. *Historic downtown's Dunkin' Donuts
(photograph courtesy of James Kirkhuff).*

the otherwise rundown and abandoned properties. Despite its neon green sign, Pearly Baker's restaurant sits inconspicuously in one corner. And Crayola crayons, an Easton institution, makes its colorful (if not gaudy) presence known. A relatively new and clean building complex dominates the city center, advertising all things Crayola and its McDonald's. And a giant crayon box serves as a sign to the Crayola gift shop entrance.

Considering the already successful Crayola complex, what with its built-in McDonald's, it is clear that bigger corporations are present and welcome in our downtown. •And with the addition of a new Dunkin' Donuts, a precedent has been set for what types of companies can succeed within the city circle: any big name company. Crayola, Dunkin' Donuts, and McDonald's all have major name recognition, which is a primary reason they are the most prominent attractions to Easton's center. The chance the center circle once had to become a thriving, eclectic, small-town neighborhood is now impossible. Even if small businesses remain for a while, it is a Dunkin' Donuts or a McDonald's that will draw business from Crayola's downtown existence, not insurance companies, bakeries, boutiques, five-and-dimes, or hair salons. The patronage these major businesses will bring to downtown might create some spillover business for the other establishments, but these primary attractions seem to complement one another the most.

In this passage, Walker explains the only kind of business that can succeed in Easton's center circle.

And so the problem remains: the fewer the small businesses, the fewer downtown attractions for Eastonians. There will never be tantalizing postcards of a charming, bustling Easton to sell, only that of an easily imaginable but much less compelling image of a humdrum town with a mediocre strip mall.

•There are bright spots within this dismal image, though. During the summertime, providing good weather, Easton's center circle plays host to a weekly farmers' market. Farmers with stands of products, ranging from fresh farm produce and honey to freshly milled soaps and flowers, can draw a local crowd. This alternative business-offering, transient as it may be, brings people to the downtown city center. And those crowds are outside, socializing, and enacting a lively image of our downtown, livelier than it's been for decades.

Next, she points out a concrete reason why the circle won't succeed: most businesses don't meet the criteria for success. In mentioning the farmers' market, Walker offers one concrete example of how the center circle might meet the second criterion of drawing patrons to the downtown.

Should one take a picture of these two different downtown environments, position them next to each other, and then draw conclusions about what type of place Easton is to live in, the results would obviously be quite different. Whether one picture is more accurate, or whether the real Easton experience is somewhere in between, ultimately is irrelevant. The fact remains that a city projects a certain experience through its surroundings. Is it welcoming, impressive, expansive, busy, or a combination? •Usually a trip to Easton's center circle would not yield a particularly promising impression of what Easton has to offer. Maybe the recent addition of a Dunkin' Donuts will improve downtown's condition. On the other hand, maybe it will cement its deterioration.

Finally, Walker articulates a clear argument that Easton is not meeting the criteria required for a thriving center circle.

Using Analysis and Synthesis

Usually, the alignment (or matching) of each criterion with the problem (an object, phenomenon, event, or person—in this case, the new Dunkin' Donuts downtown) becomes an assertion that supports the thesis statement. Using analysis, determine the criteria used in the evaluation and consider such questions as the following: What is the immediate overall effect of the event, object, or phenomenon? What are its specific parts? How are these parts pieced together? What is the overall effectiveness of these parts? These types of questions lead to detailed evaluations as well as thoughtful analyses of issues or objects that we experience, use, or need every day and that often shape our society. Synthesize the results by determining the author's main point and whether she has delivered a carefully reasoned, ethically derived evaluation.

> MindTap® Find additional examples of evaluations online.

See also CHAPTER 21, ALBERTO MINGARDI, "Embrace the Food Tech That Makes Us Healthier—'Locavores' and other sustainability advocates oppose the innovations that extend and improve life."

See also CHAPTER 22, JOEL LANDAU, "VIDEO: Filmmaker apologizes on behalf of entire Millennial generation: 'We Suck and We're Sorry'"

 RESPONDING TO THE RHETORICAL SITUATION

Situations that call for clarity, a decision, a plan, or a change are situations that call for an evaluation. Whether you are evaluating the quality of potential living quarters, a set of physical symptoms, a college course, a specific airline, or a movie, an effective evaluation is based on a set of carefully researched criteria that is then delivered to a specific audience (possibly yourself).

In addition to the wide range of opportunities for evaluation are the means of delivering those evaluations: visually, verbally, orally, or by some combination of these media. Your challenge is to choose the medium of delivery that will most easily reach and please your rhetorical audience, the people who could be affected by your evaluation. A personal letter, newspaper opinion piece, PowerPoint presentation, recommendation letter, or YouTube video are all possible media for delivering a fitting response in the genre of evaluation.

Opportunity ⟩ Audience and Purpose ⟩ Genre/Evaluation ⟩ (Medium of) Delivery

Understanding the Rhetorical Situation

Evaluations are used to review, analyze, and synthesize the features of a problem, object, phenomenon, or other cultural element, whether it is the latest film sensation, the city center, brides' dresses, or a required course. To succeed with any rhetorical exchange, you must start by evaluating the rhetorical situation itself, the context. Your evaluations are rooted in context. In other words, where you are, the specific audience you want to reach, and your purpose are features of the context that help you develop specific criteria for the evaluation as well as assess where the most reliable and expert information comes from.

Evaluations—whether others' or our own—persuade us as we answer questions, resolve problems, and make decisions within specific contexts. For instance, you see your doctor for a professional evaluation (she diagnoses your symptoms of fever, cough, and weakness as pneumonia). You turn to your well-read, movie-going friends for an evaluation of the best movie to see on Friday night. And when you decide to apply to graduate school, you work with a respected faculty member to evaluate, using the criteria that you develop together, which programs are best for you. You seek or make evaluations within a specific context, using specific, often context-specific, criteria.

┌─ **RESEARCHING AN EVALUATION** ──────────────

Evaluation writing is rooted in judgment—not the kind of judgments we make on a daily basis, but rather on *informed* judgment. For your judgment to be informed, it must be based on research, whether online searches, traditional library research (professional books and articles), interviews with experts in the field, or conversations. The results of

(continued)

your research will guide you as you establish criteria for your evaluation and match those criteria with specific features your topic has to offer. Furthermore, the results of your research will also enrich your ability to evaluate within a specific context. Those research findings will also assist you in establishing a thoughtful hierarchy of criteria: necessary, sufficient, and accidental. Thus, researching will improve your ability to establish criteria, deepen your understanding of your topic, and enhance your rich descriptive details and facts that comprise an effective evaluation.

Identifying an opportunity for change

Rhetorical situations that call for a judgment are those calling for an evaluation. The opportunity for change is the opportunity to replace uncertainty with clarity—for yourself and others. As simple as a weekend outing might be, it calls for a cascade of evaluations: whom to invite, which movie to see, how good the movie was, where to eat afterwards, how good the pizza was. All of these evaluations were initiated by you and your friends, calling for you to establish criteria; match the criteria to your topic (potential invitees, movie, pizza); decide which criteria are necessary, sufficient, and accidental; and direct your persuasive evaluation to one another as well as to other friends who are interested in the movie or the pizza joint.

To identify an opportunity for change, freewrite for five minutes in response to the following everyday opportunities. (For more on freewriting and pages 239–244 other ways to jump-start your writing, see CHAPTER 13, EXPLORATION.)

1. What big purchase did you make before coming to college? A smartphone, computer, car, bicycle? What process did you go through before making the purchase? What criteria did you develop for this purchase? Where did you turn (a person, an organization, a professional reviewer) for advice? What did you learn through the process of researching, developing criteria, and purchasing? When have you evaluated something or someone without developing and following through with specific criteria? What were the results? What did you learn about yourself and/or the evaluation process?

2. As you contemplate your major, make a list of criteria that are important to you, keeping in mind that your criteria for a major may or may not align with your criteria for a career. Be prepared to share your reasoning with the rest of the class.

3. Make a list of five problems you have encountered over the past week that affect the work or play of people on your campus. For example, are there any computer labs that make you feel mentally and physically exhausted—or all

revved up? Are there any couches or chairs in the common area that seem to be particularly inviting—or just the opposite? Write a few sentences describing the problem and your overall impressions when you first noticed it. Provide as many details as you can to help readers visualize and emotionally respond to the problem (in either a positive or negative way).

Relating rhetorically to your audience

The following questions can help you locate your rhetorical audience as well as identify the relationship they have to what you are writing about. Answering them can help you determine the best medium (or media) for delivering your evaluation.

1. List the names of the persons or groups most likely to be affected by what you have chosen to write about. These are potential audiences for your evaluation.
2. Next to the name of each audience member, list reasons that person might have for considering your topic in more detail. In other words, what would persuade these audiences that what you are writing about needs to be evaluated?
3. Explore how each of these people could reasonably be influenced or persuaded by an evaluation. In other words, what emotional responses or changes in attitudes, behavior, or beliefs might they have after reading, hearing, or seeing your evaluation? What motivations might they have for analyzing this subject?
4. With your audience's interests and motivations in mind, look again at the descriptions that you composed in the preceding section. Which description(s) will enable your readers to feel engaged in your evaluation and invested in exploring your topic in greater depth? A richer, detailed description not only allows readers to create a vivid mental picture but also helps them understand why and how your subject affects them. At this point, it may be necessary to revise your best description to tailor it to your audience's needs and interests.

Planning an effective rhetorical response for your purpose

As you know, focusing your purpose is important, because different purposes require different kinds of texts, delivered through different media. For example, if you are evaluating an image such as a photograph or a painting, you might compose an essay that would appear as part of a museum display or in an exhibition catalog. Your evaluation of a visually uninspiring university web page could be crafted as a letter to the staff in the admissions or alumni relations office. Your evaluation of the dysfunctional design of a computer lab could take the form of a widely distributed e-visual of a redesigned lab or an e-mail message aimed at gaining student support for the proposed changes. Once you have identified your opportunity, audience, and purpose, you will want to determine what kind of text will best respond to your rhetorical situation.

Use the following questions to help you narrow your purpose and shape your response:

1. What kinds of researched facts or details and personal experience define the context in which your topic influences or affects people on a daily basis?
2. What kinds of facts or details make your topic particularly compelling? What specific audience do these details attract?
3. Are you asking the audience to adopt a new perspective, or do you want the audience to perform a particular action in response to your persuasive evaluation?
4. What is the best way to reach this audience? That is, what kind of text is this audience most likely to respond to?

LINKS TO EVALUATIONS IN THREE MEDIA MindTap®

Links may change due to availability.

Courtesy of James Kirkhuff

Nick DeNardis

© Sarunyu L/Shutterstock.com

Print Evaluation In the essay at the beginning of this chapter, student Alexis Walker locates a rhetorical opportunity in the changing landscape of her city's downtown.

Oral Evaluation *EDU Checkup* is a video blog (vlog) that reviews college and university websites. To view the evaluation of Southwest Minnesota State University's website, go to the MindTap.

Online Evaluation Corrine Heller posted a roundup of evaluations of *Star Wars: The Force Awakens* (2015) on E-Online, http://www.eonline.com/news/724456/star-wars-the-force-awakens-review-roundup-spoiler-free.

WRITING A PERSUASIVE EVALUATION: A Guide

*P*ersuasive evaluations are researched, well reasoned, ethically derived, and connected to the values and interests of a specific audience. In addition, every evaluation should have a thesis statement that is richly supported with specific evidence. In these ways, an effective evaluation establishes your ethos (or credibility), validates the logos (or good reasons) of the overall argument, and authenticates pathos (an authentic emotional connection with your audience). (For more on ethos, logos, and pathos, see *CHAPTER 2, THE AVAILABLE MEANS INCLUDE THE RHETORICAL ELEMENTS OF THE MESSAGE ITSELF.*)

pages 23–26

ADVANTAGES AND LIMITATIONS

Advantages	Limitations
• **Writer:** You have considerable latitude in the topic you select (from laundry detergent or pizza to a film or artwork) and the way you place that topic in context.	• **Writer:** We evaluate so regularly throughout our day that we often skip over the important step of establishing criteria, let alone researching those criteria.
• **Message:** An evaluation can be casual, negotiated among friends, and rooted in personal experience (emphasizing ethos and pathos) or more research-based and formal (emphasizing ethos and logos).	• **Message:** Given the frequency of our casual evaluations, we must take time to consider the interests and values of our intended audience—and our purpose for reaching and engaging them.
• **Media and Design:** Evaluations are presented in many ways: as conversation, video, print, or multimodally (as most evaluative advertising is done).	• **Media and Design:** Given the many visual, verbal, and multimodal possibilities for delivering an evaluation, the primary consideration must be the audience's access to and interest in the medium of delivery.

Introduction

- **Define the subject to be evaluated.**
- **Establish the author's ethos.**
- **Explain why the subject should be evaluated.**
- **Identify the ways in which the subject is to be evaluated.**
- **Explain why readers should care about the evaluation.**
- **Offer a persuasive thesis statement.**

Define what you are evaluating Writers of evaluations use the introduction to define and describe the topic, explain its cultural significance, enumerate the evaluation criteria, and persuade readers that the evaluation has significance for them. These concepts come together

(continued)

in a persuasive thesis statement, such as Walker's claim that "the center of any city or town should, ideally, portray the very best the city has to offer."

Establish your expertise By providing researched details, cultural understanding, and often personal experience, the writer establishes her expertise and knowledge, qualifying her as an ethical evaluator. Walker establishes her credibility when she calls Easton "my hometown." By recognizing the ways the evaluation meets the values and interests of her audience, she confirms her positive ethos.

Ask yourself . . .
- Why do I care about this topic?
- Who else will care about it?
- Does my detailed description connect with the interests and values of my audience?
- How do the criteria I offer reflect on my ethos?
- How does my thesis statement present a reasonable evaluation?

- **Provide evaluative criteria.**
- **Match those criteria to features of the topic.**
- **Explain the context that gives the topic particular significance.**
- **Establish logos through good reasons and persuasive matches of criteria to detailed examples from the topic.**

Establish your criteria The body of an evaluation provides the criteria for the topic, object, or phenomenon to be evaluated. Following the concepts of sufficient, necessary, and accidental, the criteria will be presented as assertions that support the thesis as Walker does with her assertion that a decline in small businesses downtown will result in less downtown traffic. These criteria make—and shape—the argument at the same time that they establish the logos (the good reasons) of the evaluation.

Use facts, details, even quotations To accompany each criterion, the writer offers researched facts, details from cultural observation or social experience, and even direct quotations in her analysis of how features of the topic being evaluated match (or do not match) the specific evaluative criteria. Such specific facts and details enhance the description of the topic, explain its cultural significance, and strengthen the connection of the topic with the audience. Walker explains the cultural significance of the decline by describing the central position and "sad display" of the peace candle in downtown Easton.

Use sensory details as evidence Details grab and maintain the readers' interest. Sensory details (such as Walker's "neon green sign" and "giant crayon box") help the writer to persuade her readers that the evaluation is based on a careful, complete analysis of all the elements that make up the object or phenomenon.

Body

Explain the context for your evaluation The body of an evaluation often attempts to explain the political, economic, social, or cultural context that gives this object or phenomenon particular significance. For Walker, the addition of a new Dunkin' Donuts as a generic chain store thwarts "the chance the center circle once had to become a thriving, eclectic, small-town neighborhood." This contextual evaluation helps deepen readers' understanding of how the object or phenomenon influences their daily lives.

Ask yourself . . .
- How do I know that my criteria for evaluation are ethical, logical, and informed?
- Which of them are necessary, sufficient, or accidental? Are they important in that same order?
- How do I connect my criteria with the interests and values of my audience?
- Which persuasive details come from my research? Which from my observation and experience?
- What are the contextual details that demonstrate the significance of this topic, this evaluation, to me and to my audience?

Conclusion

- **Synthesize criteria and collected evidence.**
- **Make one final appeal for readers to adopt a specific attitude or opinion.**
- **Confirm pathos.**

Connect the criteria and supporting evidence in your conclusion The conclusion of an evaluation synthesizes the evidence of matches between various criteria and the features of the topic itself in order to make one final appeal for readers to adopt a specific attitude or opinion (for Walker, for example, that the new Dunkin' Donuts contributes to the "deterioration" of downtown Easton).

Confirm pathos Throughout the evaluation, you have worked to connect your persuasive thesis (for Walker, that the city center reflects the "best the city has to offer") in an ethically responsible manner to the interests and values of your audience (which Walker does when she asks if downtown Easton is "welcoming"). The conclusion offers you one last chance to confirm that you have made an authentic emotional connection.

Ask yourself . . .
- How can I reaffirm my thesis statement without repeating it? How might I close with the implications of my argument if it is accepted or rejected?
- How can I make a final appeal to my audience without seeming to be manipulative or desperate?

MindTap® Request help and feedback from a tutor. If required, participate in peer review, submit your paper for a grade, and view instructor comments online.

Revision and Peer Review

After you have drafted your evaluation, ask one of your classmates to read it. You will want your classmate to respond to your work in a way that helps you revise it into the strongest evaluation it can be, one that addresses your intended audience, helps you fulfill your purpose, and is delivered in the most appropriate means available to your audience.

Questions for a peer reviewer

1. Why is this evaluation necessary, even important?
2. Why is the topic important to the writer?
3. How might it be important to the writer's intended audience as well?
4. What might be the writer's purpose? How do audience and purpose come together in this evaluation?
5. What information did you receive from the introduction? How does the writer introduce the particular object or phenomenon she is exploring? How does the writer suggest why it needs to be evaluated? What suggestions do you have for the writer regarding the introduction?
6. Note the writer's thesis statement. If you cannot locate a thesis statement, what thesis statement might work for this evaluation?
7. Note the assertions the writer makes to support the thesis. (These may be in the form of criteria the writer establishes.) Are they presented in chronological or emphatic order? Does the writer use the order that seems most effective? How could the writer improve the order of these assertions?
8. If you cannot locate a series of assertions, what assertions could be made to support the thesis statement?
9. Note the concrete evidence and examples that the writer uses to show how the subject meets or does not meet the criteria established.
10. How does the writer establish ethos? How could the writer strengthen this appeal?
11. What material does the writer use to establish logos? How might the writer strengthen this appeal (see questions #6–8)?
12. How does the writer make use of pathos?
13. What did you learn from the conclusion that you did not already know after reading the introduction and body? What information does the writer want you to take away from the evaluation? Does the writer attempt to change your attitude, action, or opinion?
14. Which section of the evaluation did you most enjoy? Why?

MindTap® Reflect on your writing process.

ADDITIONAL ASSIGNMENTS

Knowledge Transfer

 COLLEGE Literature Review *Literature* in this context refers to scholarship on a particular topic. When your instructor asks for your evaluation of a book, research study, or scholarly article, your job is to take a position and argue it. In response to such an assignment, compose a review in which you make a claim (advance a thesis) and argue a position about the quality of the work. You will use textual evidence from the work itself, information you have researched, and your own experience to support your assertions.

 COMMUNITY Low-Income Housing Evaluation You are a member of the township council, and you have all been charged with evaluating bids for the low-income housing project. As you consider the bids, you will need to review the criteria for the low-income housing that you produced a year ago and match those criteria with the information in each bid. The bids may prompt your council to rethink the criteria themselves or the hierarchy of criteria. In evaluating your final selection, be sure to offer a thesis statement, provide assertions of how each criterion is met (or exceeded) by the successful bid, and supply concrete examples and evidence that support each of the assertions.

WORKPLACE Professional Recommendation When you supervise or collaborate with others, they may ask you to serve as a reference for them. In response to a request for a recommendation, your task is to evaluate your colleague according to the criteria constituting the new position, promotion, fellowship, internship, or graduate school. Compose a recommendation for a colleague in which you match (or do not match) the criteria of the new position with the personal and professional qualities of your colleague.

MULTIMODAL Presentation with Visual Evidence You have been asked to evaluate the effectiveness of the additional traffic lights (traffic signals) that were installed in your downtown a year ago. In order to define "effectiveness," you will need to conduct research on the status of traffic accidents, speeding, and other traffic violations over the past year as well as on the degree of driver and pedestrian satisfaction with the new lights. Then, you'll need to compare these results with those of preceding years. In order to present the information effectively and efficiently, your evaluation must include charts and graphs. You may even want to include online links to the reports of citizens you have interviewed and videos of current traffic flow improvements or impediments.

Descriptive details are at the heart of any evaluation. Look to adjectives and adverbs to help harness the descriptive power of nouns and verbs.

adjectives words that modify nouns

Adjectives modify nouns. *Modify* means to "qualify or limit the meaning of." You should choose precise adjectives to help convey sensation or intensity. Like adjectives, **adverbs** are modifiers. Adverbs modify verbs, providing information about time, manner, place, and frequency.

adverbs words that modify verbs

Adjectives

If you use the noun *car* but want to limit the many different cars that may come to mind for your readers, you can add a modifier such as *black, rusty,* or *used.* **Attributive adjectives** modify nouns and pronouns directly, preceding or immediately following nouns or pronouns, as in *something special* or *time enough.* **Predicate adjectives**, on the other hand, also modify nouns or pronouns but always follow linking verbs such as *be, seem,* and *look* (when its meaning is "seem or appear"):

attributive adjectives words that modify nouns or pronouns directly

Predicate adjectives words that modify nouns or pronouns and always appear after linking verbs

> **My schedule is <u>full</u>.**   **She seems <u>nervous</u>.**   **His face looks <u>familiar</u>.**

So instead of describing a movie you did not like with the overused adjective *bad* or *boring,* you could call it *tedious* or *predictable.* When you sense that you might be using a lackluster adjective, search for an alternative in a thesaurus. If you come across unfamiliar words, be sure to look them up in a dictionary so that you do not misuse them.

- Find a movie review in a newspaper or online. Identify the adjectives used to describe the film and its actors, and note whether they are as precise as they can be.

Adverbs

Instead of modifying nouns, adverbs modify verbs, adjectives, and other adverbs. As modifiers of verbs, they provide information about time, manner, place, and frequency.

> *Time:*   **The festival begins <u>today</u>.**

> *Manner:*   **She stated her position <u>forcefully</u>.**

Place: **We will meet you there after lunch.**

Frequency: **They usually close at five.**

Depending on which words in a sentence you want to stress, you can move an adverb modifying a verb to other positions within the sentence:

Today the festival begins.

She forcefully stated her position.

Adverbs that modify adjectives or other adverbs intensify or otherwise qualify the meanings of these words.

Adverb modifying adjective: **The child was mysteriously clever.**

Adverb modifying another adverb: **He ran astonishingly fast.**

Adverbs of manner can help you create a sharp portrayal of an action.

After he entered the end zone, the fullback delicately set the ball down beneath the goalposts.

Adverbs can add detail to a description.

He was curiously intelligent.

Adverb-adjective combinations

Adverb-adjective combinations are common in book, movie, and theater reviews. Here are a few from *The New Yorker: blazingly apt, fastidiously elegant, enchantingly quaint, fascinatingly indecipherable, cautiously hopeful, mesmerizingly persuasive.*

- Write a short paragraph in which you describe a movie or someone performing a task. Include at least three adverbs.

MindTap® Find additional handbook coverage of grammar, punctuation, and style online.

© Takra/Shutterstock.com

Critical Analyses

MindTap® Understand the goals of the chapter and complete a warm-up activity online.

Y ou analyze critically every day—every time you examine something carefully and closely in order to identify patterns and relationships in your subject. Often times, you hone in on a scholarly article, a legal decision, or a design; other times you establish the causes or consequences of a feature of the world you live in (see CHAPTER 14, CAUSE-AND-EFFECT ANALYSIS). Based on careful examination, insights, and understanding (and including library, field, or experiential research), a **critical analysis** breaks something into parts, analyzes each part separately and studies the ways the parts work together, and then synthesizes those findings into a claim or thesis statement. (See CHAPTER 3, ANALYSIS AND SYNTHESIS and CHAPTER 2, MAKING CLAIMS.) Throughout this chapter, you'll work to identify an opportunity to conduct a critical analysis on a topic (or phenomenon) that interests you. You'll also consider the most fitting means of delivering your analysis to your rhetorical audience, using precise language.

pages 270–272

critical analysis a careful examination of the causes or consequences of a situation or phenomenon

pages 45–50 and 20

IDENTIFYING AN OPPORTUNITY FOR CHANGE

Print Analysis written for a community or campus newspaper

Oral/Multimedia Analysis presented live to your rhetorical audience

Online Analysis posted on a blog

GENRE IN F☉CUS Cultural Analysis

News once spread from person to person and from home to home, but now news spreads via cable and satellite to distant places. With technological developments allowing messages to be sent instantaneously around the world, many more people know about the affairs of communities and countries that may have once seemed distant from them—not only physically but intellectually as well. Understanding how media change the nature of communication is a topic that fascinated Marshall McLuhan, a mid-twentieth-century media analyst at the University of Toronto, who prophesied a far-reaching revolution spurred by changes in "electronic technology." In his first book, *Gutenberg Galaxy: The Making of Typographic Man* (1962), McLuhan imagines a world connected through technology: "The new electronic independence re-creates the world in the image of a global village."

While McLuhan's was an age of television, film, mass media, and consumer culture, he saw how media was already changing the fabric of society, and he did so long before the Internet, Facebook, blogs, Twitter, Instagram, cell phones, and YouTube. In his 1967 book, *The Medium Is the Massage* (a play on one of his famous quotations, "The medium is the message"), he explains how electronic media so quickly become extensions of our personal self, thereby merging any distinction between our public and private spheres to the point that we are all interconnected.

© eldar nurkovic/Shutterstock.com

TV director at a vision mixing panel in a studio gallery.

The medium, or process, of our time—electronic technology is reshaping and restructuring patterns of social interdependence and every aspect of our personal life. It is forcing us to reconsider and re-evaluate practically every thought, every action, and every institution formerly taken for granted. Everything is changing: you, your family, your education, your neighborhood, your job, your government, your relation to "the others." And they're changing dramatically.

—Marshall McLuhan, *The Medium Is the Massage*
["Technology and Interdependence"]

Paul Seaman, the founder of the blog *21st Century PR Issues*, questions the "logical implications" of this social and technological revolution in his critical analysis, "Marshall McLuhan: A Media Guru Reconsidered."

There's a lot to be admired about the "prophet of the electronic age" who "holds out the promise of a technologically engendered state of universal understanding and unity, a state of absorption in the logos that could knit mankind into one family and create a perpetuity of collective harmony and peace." That language, in the form of "one world, people and planet," is endorsed by much . . . of the mainstream corporate and PR world today.

. . .

[However,] the logical implication of [McLuhan's] notion of the "global village," a useful expression if ever there was one, is that national divisions in a globalised world would dissolve (it was very much in tune with John Lennon's *Imagine*, except that McLuhan [a devout Catholic] believed in Heaven above and Hell below us). But, paradoxically, our increasingly globalised economy has more nations today than ever; certainly there's many more than when McLuhan was writing in the 1960s.

I'm not suggesting for one moment that Marshall McLuhan books should not be read. On the contrary, they remain classics worthy of exploration for the many insights they contain. But that's no reason to buy into his main technological determinist message.

—Paul Seaman, "Marshall McLuhan: A Media Guru Reconsidered"

As you consider both McLuhan's and Seaman's critical analyses of the consequences of various forms of media, consider, too, how much you agree with either of them so far as the influence of communication technologies on the creation of a global village, a truly representative village or otherwise. Reflect on the ways your own campus or community resembles a global village to some measure.

TAUSEEF MUSTAFA/Getty Images

Living in a global village, as we do, we immediately read about and see what is happening all over the world—an awareness that few of our grandparents experienced. In this photo, we see a Kashmiri man watching protesters during a strike called by Kashmiri separatists.

✈ ASSIGNMENT

When you ask the question "Why?" you are already engaged in critical analysis. You and people around you are probably questioning the causes or consequences of a situation, phenomenon, object, person, or text. For your critical analysis, identify a situation, phenomenon, object, person, or text you are interested in. Perhaps like McLuhan and Seaman you will focus on a feature of the world we live in that interests you. You will examine your topic closely and carefully until you can determine patterns, details, and relationships within the topic you are analyzing. Whether you are interested in the declining numbers of liberal arts majors, a monumental football loss, the possibility of a cancelled airline flight, the occurrence of Type 2 (adult-onset) diabetes, or the Kashmiri protest, your goal is to analyze the topic in order to establish the causes or consequences that your audience needs or wants to know about. Often, you will rely on research findings to help support the determinations you have made.

(◉) READING RHETORICALLY

Close examination is the key to any critical analysis—whether you are writing or reading one rhetorically. The twofold purpose of critical analysis is for the author to analyze closely a phenomenon in order to establish a clear understanding of the phenomenon and then to explain a synthesis of that phenomenon (often a cause or consequence) for the audience. As you read for the features of the rhetorical situation—who the writer is, what occasion prompted the composition, who the writer's intended audience is, and what the purpose of the composition is—you can also gauge how well the writer incorporates the key rhetorical features of the genre into the critical analysis. Look for the critical question that prompts the analysis and determine how clear and logical the explanation is of the relationship between the cause or consequences and the phenomenon under analysis.

Key Features of a Critical Analysis

You are probably familiar with the form and arrangement of critical analyses because you read many of them in your daily life: editorials and feature articles, for example, are often in this genre. Whether you are writing or reading, you will notice that critical analyses typically include the following features:

- A critical question prompts the analysis and focuses the thesis.
- Precise description of the phenomenon helps readers understand why it merits analysis and why they should be invested in the analysis.
- Researched evidence, data, and examples sufficiently support that logical connection between the situation or phenomenon and its causes or consequences.
- The causes and/or the consequences connect logically to the situation or phenomenon.
- Alternative perspectives on the situation or phenomenon are acknowledged, analyzed, synthesized, and responded to.
- The author conducts and synthesizes research (from the library, observations, personal experience, or calculation/experiment) in order to enhance the analysis.

These features are illustrated in the following student essay by Anna Seitz, who uses her own experience with online learning for her critical analysis. As you prepare to read Seitz's essay, consider the following questions:

- What does the title tell you?
- What do you imagine the consequences of pursuing and receiving an online degree might be?

- What might she mean by "real-time"?
- What audience will be interested in or affected by the topic of an online degree?

> MindTap®   Read, highlight, and take notes online.

The Real-Time Consequences of an Online Degree

ANNA SEITZ

As she explains in her introduction, wife and mother Anna Seitz wanted to pursue the coursework for her graduate degree from her home computer. She excelled in both her courses and her practicum—questioning the consistency of the teaching and her learning all along the way.

I'm a mother of three small children, and I'm much more interested in spending time with my kids than spending time in a classroom. When I decided to pursue an advanced degree, I opted for an online program. I didn't know exactly what it would be like, but I knew what I wanted out of it—flexibility to complete the program on my own schedule. And while I got that, I also found that my decision had other consequences.

Seitz sets up her thesis: that there are both expected and unexpected consequences of working toward a degree online.

The primary consequence of taking online classes was that I did, in fact, have even more flexibility than I'd imagined. That was good and bad. I had an impressive selection of electives each term, especially because my advisor gave me almost total freedom to select my courses. The secondary consequence of this freedom is that I won't be graduating with the exact same skills and experiences as everyone else in my class—we all have different specialties and will be competing for different jobs. Also, none of my classes had set meeting or chat times, and I was able to do my readings, write my papers, and participate in discussion forums in fits and spurts (and in pajamas!). I read at night and during nap times, in the car, and at the playground. I learned to do most of my research online, and when I had to use local libraries, I simply packed up my gang for the children's story hour. Some of my professors provided the entire term's contents on day one, which helped me plan my work.

She opens with a positive consequence, one familiar to the millions of students getting degrees online.

She provides detailed support for her assertion about the first consequence.

Seitz moves on to a second consequence, which isn't as positive. This paragraph is detailed with incidents from her life, a life familiar to many parents who are working toward a degree (online or off).

The flip side of this particular consequence was that planning my work was a bigger challenge than doing the work. Because my days with the children were always unpredictable, I lost a lot of sleep while learning how to pace myself in terms of taking care of my family and keeping up with my school work. There were times when my kids got stuck with a distracted mommy who cut corners on suppers and bedtime stories. I had to keep careful records of tasks and due dates, and I had to create my own deadlines as I learned how to divide big projects into manageable sections. After all, with online courses, the only regular reminders and announcements from the teachers are discussion board reminders (only useful if you log in and read them, of course). I'm nearly finished with the program, and I still haven't settled on an acceptable frequency for checking the class message board. Either I waste time checking constantly and finding nothing, or I go out for a day only to come home and find out that I've missed contributing to some major discussion or development.

Taking responsibility for my own learning at my own pace has always been comfortable for me. I've always been independent, and the idea of doing these classes "all by myself" was very appealing. Unfortunately, a secondary consequence of the online environment caught me by surprise. I was soon forced to admit that as much as I wanted to do things myself, my way, my professors and my classmates profoundly affected my learning, my grades, and my enjoyment of the classes. I had a few professors who spent as much or more time on my online classes as they would have on a face-to-face class, producing online PowerPoint lectures, enrichment activities, and discussion prompts, and making personal contact with each student. In those classes, I got to know my classmates, worked with others on projects, and learned things that I can still remember years later. The efforts of our professors inspired us to put in our own best efforts, and I would count those experiences to be on par with my best face-to-face classroom experiences.

I also had a few "teachers" who simply selected textbooks that came with lots of extras, such as a publisher's Web site with quizzes and assignments. In one of those classes, the publisher's Web site actually did the grading for the quizzes and calculated my class grade. I was really offended and kind of disgusted that my "teacher" would be so lazy. I felt that I wasn't getting what I'd paid for, and I felt neglected. Ultimately, I was embarrassed because I felt that it gave merit to all of the criticisms that I'd heard about online education. In one of those classes, I simply sat down with my textbook and did the entire term's quizzes in one night. I didn't learn a thing. I should have acted like a grown-up and made the best of it, but I just jumped through the hoops and collected my credits. I got an A in that class doing work which would have flunked me out of any face-to-face class, and that made me mad, too.

One of the secondary consequences is that I began to consider my teacher's performance, and to discuss it with my classmates. When I was in college

Seitz claims that independent learning feels natural and easy to her—but admits that her independent nature doesn't always lend itself to online learning.

As she provides logical support for her assertions, Seitz also gives readers authentic glimpses into herself, a rhetorical move that emphasizes her credibility.

Seitz carefully differentiates the immediate from the remote consequences of taking an online degree.

at 18, I was more focused on what I was putting into my classes than what I was getting out of them. I didn't notice what the teachers were or were not doing. In my current program, however, nearly all of the students are busy adults with careers and families who are paying their own way through school so that they can enhance their careers. My classmates and I are only there to improve our skills, and we want to get our money's worth. There are a lot of complaints when we don't. I can think of dozens of examples of students voicing their complaints about the teacher, materials, or assignments as part of the class discussion, and since the communication is public, the teachers nearly always have to make improvements.

Another secondary consequence is that there is surprisingly little privacy in an online class when compared to a face-to-face class, and that was very difficult to get used to. I can't just slink in, sit in the back of the class, keep my head down, and hope the teacher never learns my name. The comments I am required to post each week can be read, and in fact *must be read* by the entire class. Everyone knows what I've read, what I think about it, and how well I express myself. Everyone reads my papers, and I read theirs. For an independent person like me, this was tough to swallow. I didn't like comparing my work to others', even when it compared favorably. I dreaded the times when it compared unfavorably, and when I saw a classmate do particularly good work, I wanted to, too. It was a healthy and productive sort of peer pressure, and I did things I'd never tried to do before, and sometimes even did them well.●·········· Seitz's relationship with her fellow students helps her successfully establish a sympathetic connection to her readers.

Using Synthesis and Analysis

Whether you are reading or composing a critical analysis, pay careful attention to the ways specific details and evidence connect the constituent parts and promote causes or consequences. In her critical analysis, Seitz examines her own experience in a way that clarifies her conclusions for others.

- How has she broken down her experience?
- What does she say about how the elements of her experience work together?
- What insight and evidence does she use in her analysis?
- How do conflicting opinions illuminate her analysis?
- What conclusion does she draw and why?

When you work through your own analysis and synthesis of Seitz's essay, bring together all the information you have collected such that your analysis and synthesis can serve as the foundation of your critical analysis of the success of her essay, leading you toward a clear understanding of the causes or consequences of the phenomenon itself. Explain whether you have a clearer understanding of online education after reading Seitz's critical analysis.

> **MindTap®** Find additional examples of critical analyses online.

See also CHAPTER 3, BARRY M. PRIZANT, *Uniquely Human: A Different Way of Seeing Autism* [Animated Movies and Social Development]

See also CHAPTER 3, JORDYNN JACK, *Autism and Gender: From Refrigerator Mothers to Computer Geeks* ["Savants" and "Geniuses"]

See also CHAPTER 23, JAMIE UTT, "From ManSpreading to ManSplaining—6 Ways Men Dominate the Space Around Them"

See also CHAPTER 24, ROXANE GAY, "A Tale of Two Profiles"

See also CHAPTER 24, CARIMAH TOWNES, "Obama Explains the Problem with 'All Lives Matter'"

RESPONDING TO THE RHETORICAL SITUATION

What rhetorical opportunity invites your engagement? Once you identify an opportunity, establish a purpose for your writing as well as an audience. Then, you need to determine what kind of text (or message) you can deliver that will best respond to your rhetorical situation. A critical analysis might be useful for examining issues such as whether new technologies give the richest and most powerful people and nations a louder voice, leaving the poor and powerless to fend for themselves—or, conversely, whether those who traditionally have not had a political voice can now announce their interests by transmitting their messages publicly. The most successful critical analyses often include research—library, laboratory, data-driven, or experiential research that supports the analysis and the findings. In addition, a critical analysis is best for exploring the causes and/or consequences of a situation or phenomenon.

> Opportunity ▷ Audience and Purpose ▷ Genre/Report ▷ (Medium of) Delivery

Understanding the Rhetorical Situation

Writers use critical analysis to help readers understand specific cultural, economic, political, and social forces, as well as to explore the consequences that have occurred or might occur as a result of these forces. A critical analysis can help people become more aware of the "how" and "why" in their daily lives. In some cases, a critical analysis can change how people think or act to create the kinds of communities in which they want to live and work.

RESEARCHING A CRITICAL ANALYSIS

When Sandra Bullock, Jennifer Lawrence, and other stars asked if Hollywood values were gendered, they raised a critical question that prompted critical analysis of Hollywood hiring practices. Through research, interviews, and observations, these women could cite facts, figures, and other documented data (including salaries, number of leading roles, number of directing opportunities) as well as their personal experiences. As they analyzed their data and synthesized their findings, they realized that Hollywood hiring practices are, indeed, gendered, and to the financial and cultural advantage of Hollywood men. Often, your instincts will lead you toward a critical analysis. But you will want to conduct the kinds of research the Hollywood women conducted to compose an ethically derived, evidence-based conclusion, one based on careful analysis and skillful synthesis.

Identifying an opportunity for change

Consider your understanding of and participation in the world in terms of the people with whom you communicate. To begin, freewrite for five minutes in response to each of the following prompts (or use any of the invention techniques presented in CHAPTER 13, EXPLORATION): pages 239–244

1. Make a list of the communications technologies you use regularly. For each technology, list the kinds of content you create or consume. Providing as many details as possible, describe each type of content and explain whether you found your experiences with that type of content to be positive or negative.

2. Locate two consumer-oriented websites or magazines that analyze something you need to buy: an electronic, an appliance, an insurance plan, for example. Carefully analyze them for their critical question, precise description of the object, rationale for analyzing it, researched evidence, alternative perspectives, and ultimate finding, keeping a record of your analysis. Then

present the analysis you find more persuasive along with the reasons for your judgment.

3. Make two columns in which you list the positive and negative features of a course you are taking: difficulty and interest in subject matter; quality and variety of the instruction, assignments, and evaluations; and cultural or social connections or differences. Analyze each of these features, providing specific details and discussing the causes or consequences of each feature and the ways the features work (or do not work) together.

4. Critically analyze your own sleep patterns to determine the causes as well as the consequences of a good night's sleep. You will want to describe and define what a good night's sleep actually is, using examples from your own experience as well as information you have researched. You will analyze each feature of a good night's sleep separately as well as together, synthesizing your insights, experience, and research findings into a short essay.

5. Take five minutes to analyze the differences between your virtual and physical interactions with people who live a distance from you, maybe even across the globe. How and what do you learn through each type of interaction? Be prepared to share your analysis with the rest of the class.

Relating rhetorically to your audience

The following questions can help you locate your rhetorical audience as well as identify the relationship they have to the phenomenon you are analyzing, whether it is a situation, text, event, or something else. Then, you will be able to choose the best way to present your analysis.

1. List names of groups who directly contribute to or who are directly affected by the phenomenon you are analyzing. On another list, write the names of groups who indirectly contribute to or are indirectly affected by the situation or phenomenon. You may need to do some research to compose a list that accounts more fully for all the various groups with a stake in analyzing this situation or phenomenon.

2. Next to the name of each potential audience, write possible reasons that audience could have for wanting a better understanding of the causes or consequences of the phenomenon.

3. What responses could these audiences reasonably be expected to have to your analysis? In other words, what conclusions might they be persuaded to draw, what attitudes might they be likely to adopt, what actions might they be willing to take? After exploring these possible responses, decide

which audience you most want or need to reach with your critical analysis.

4. With your audience's interests and capabilities in mind, look again at the descriptions of the types of content that you composed in the preceding section on identifying a rhetorical opportunity. Decide which description might enable these readers to feel connected to the phenomenon you want to analyze—and might help them become invested in understanding its causes or consequences. At this point, you may need to revise, tailoring your best description to your intended audience.

Planning an effective rhetorical response for your purpose

As you know, different audiences and different purposes require different kinds of texts, delivered through different media. Your goal is to create a response that reaches and engages your intended audience, addresses your critical question, and follows through the features of an ethical, logical critical analysis.

After all, critical analysis can be used on many objects, events, and phenomena and be targeted to a wide range of audiences, just so long as you accommodate their technological expectations and demands. (See CHAPTER 4, pages 62–74 CONSIDERING AUDIENCE, PURPOSE, AND ACCESSIBILITY IN MULTIMEDIA COMPOSITIONS.) For instance, if you decide to analyze the consequences for international understanding that derive from virtual tourism websites or software such as Google Earth, you might create your own web page or post an extended comment on the message board of such a site. On the other hand, your analysis of the causes that lead to the emergence of online communities for the world's youth might lead you to create a pamphlet for distribution at local public libraries.

Still, you might be more interested in analyzing the consequences of good coaching and practice by studying an individual sport at your college—gymnastics or track, for example. You might observe and analyze the critical elements that comprise the process of coaching and practice. You may want to photograph key moments, videotape practice, or tape conversations between the coach and the athlete. Your analysis could develop into a newspaper article, conference presentation, inspirational essay, or slim handbook.

As you work to develop a topic for a critical analysis, use the following questions to narrow your purpose, identify an audience, and shape your response:

1. What critical question has led you to this topic?
2. What specific claim do you want to make about the causes or the consequences of the phenomenon you are analyzing? What reasons support this

particular claim? What evidence or examples can you provide to convince readers that each reason logically supports your analysis? What research do you need to do?

3. Which supporting reasons for your claim are most likely to resonate with or be convincing to your audience? What are the audience's beliefs, attitudes, or experiences that lead you to this conclusion?

4. What specific response are you hoping to draw from your audience? Do you want to affirm readers' existing beliefs about the phenomenon? Do you want to draw their attention to overlooked information or have them reconsider their views on a particular type of content? Do you want readers to perform different types of activities as a result of your analysis?

5. What might be the best way to present your analysis to your audience? That is, what kind of text is this audience most likely to respond to and easily receive?

LINKS TO CRITICAL ANALYSES IN THREE MEDIA | MindTap°

Links may change due to availability.

Corbis Premium RF/Alamy Stock Photo

© Bonita R. Cheshier/Shutterstock.com

William West/AFP/Getty Images

Print Analysis In the essay at the beginning of this chapter, student Anna Seitz examines communications technologies and politics.

Oral/Multimedia Analysis In this interview, a young Malawian man named William Kamkwamba explains the causes that led him to build a windmill to harness electricity at his rural home and traces the amazing consequences. A link is also available to "Moving Windmills," a short film.

Online Analysis This online article analyzes the consequences of the YouTube video "Star Wars Kid," which is in the *Guinness Book of World Records* for most video downloads.

⊕ WRITING A PERSUASIVE CRITICAL ANALYSIS: A Guide

*T*o write persuasively, you will need to use language that seems precise and careful to your audience, which means you must understand how familiar your audience already is with the phenomenon and how well they already understand its possible causes and consequences. You will need to use facts, data, and other specific information (perhaps gleaned from your close and careful observations) to establish your claim about the phenomenon and use that explicit factual information to expand and support your claim. You will undoubtedly start with a question of how or with what causes or consequence the phenomenon occurs. You might even use a startling fact in your introduction, to "hook" your readers. In the process of helping your audience understand as well as you do, you will want to clarify which causes and/or consequences are primary and which are secondary, articulating how each cause contributes to or each consequence follows from the phenomenon you are analyzing.

ADVANTAGES AND LIMITATIONS

Advantages

- **Writer:** Critical analyses offer you the opportunity to follow your instincts (or insights) as to the causes and consequences of any situation or phenomenon. You have the opportunity to understand clearly a phenomenon that interests you—and then to educate an audience who is affected by the topic.

- **Message:** Research, insights, close examination, together with breaking the phenomenon down into significant steps or features, all combine to form a message that connects emotionally with the interests of your audience.

- **Media and Design:** The flexibility of critical analyses and the diversity of interested audiences invite you to post your analysis online, compile a print report, or compose an oral delivery. You can use visuals (tables, graphs, photographs), videos (of the process itself), or audio (music, interviews, other sounds) to enhance the delivery and design of your message.

Limitations

- **Writer:** Upon conducting the necessary research, you may discover that your instincts were wrong and that you must pursue another line of inquiry, starting with another close examination of the phenomenon.

- **Message:** Although it is tempting to conduct a critical analysis on the basis of your insights alone, analyses rooted in researched facts and data or in authenticated experience and observation are always more persuasive, at the same time that they enhance the ethos and logos of the message itself.

- **Media and Design:** Because critical analyses can be designed and delivered in so many ways, you will want to consider the expectations of your audience (or your instructor). A critical analysis for an English course, for instance, may call for a different design and medium (print only, perhaps) than for a political science or business course, which may call for graphs, tables, statistics, and visuals.

- **Describe the situation or phenomenon.**
- **Establish the rhetorical opportunity for analysis.**
- **State the thesis, a claim about causes or consequences.**
- **Build the writer's credibility by providing explicit, researched support for the claim.**

Begin with an example that illustrates why you are analyzing this specific situation or phenomenon The introduction of a critical analysis hooks readers' attention, presenting a detailed example that helps them recognize the rhetorical opportunity and understand why this situation or phenomenon should be analyzed. In "The Real-Time Consequences of an Online Degree," Anna Seitz describes the opportunity for her analysis: "I'm a mother of three small children, and I'm much more interested in spending time with my kids than spending time in a classroom. When I decided to pursue an advanced degree, I opted for an online program."

Introduce your claim with support to explain the causes or consequences of the situation The introduction also presents the writer's thesis, a claim about the causes or the consequences of the situation or phenomenon, with some support so that the readers trust the writer on this topic. Seitz's claim was that an online degree would give her "flexibility to complete the program on my own schedule." And she soon discovered that her "decision had other consequences."

Ask Yourself . . .
- How does my introduction feature a question that merits analysis—and audience interest?
- How clearly have I stated my thesis?
- Will I focus on causes or consequences of this phenomenon?
- What expertise or experience am I offering that helps me establish my ethos?

- **Present and elaborate on causes and/or consequences of the situation or phenomenon.**
- **Articulate how each cause contributes to or each consequence follows from the situation.**
- **Present researched reasons supporting the claim about each cause or consequence.**
- **Acknowledge and respond to alternative viewpoints from experience or research.**

Connect causes to consequences The body of a critical analysis presents and elaborates on the primary (and, depending on the depth of the analysis, the secondary) causes and/or consequences of the situation or phenomenon being analyzed. Seitz writes of the primary consequence of flexibility, enriching that flexibility with the fact that she "had an impressive selection of electives each term, especially because [her] advisor gave [her] almost total freedom to select [her] courses." But she found that such flexibility led to another consequence: "I won't be graduating with the exact same skills and experiences as everyone else in my class—we all have different specialties and will be competing for different jobs."

Introduction

Body

Make consequences vivid through anecdotes, quotations, and statistics Writers also create strong appeals to logos as they present brief anecdotes, direct quotations, and data and statistics to strengthen each supporting reason and to help readers see more clearly how each cause or consequence is linked to the situation or phenomenon. For Seitz, another consequence of online learning was planning out her work. Seitz writes that "because [her] days with the children were always unpredictable, [she] lost a lot of sleep while learning how to pace [her]self . . . ." At the end of her program, she still has not "settled on an acceptable frequency for checking the class message board. Either [she] waste[s] time checking constantly and finding nothing, or [she goes] out for a day only to come home and [find] that that [she has] missed contributing to some major discussion or development."

Bring in alternative viewpoints The body paragraphs of a critical analysis also acknowledge and respond to alternative viewpoints, a rhetorical move that enhances the believability of the writer's analysis by establishing the writer as fair-minded. Although Seitz is mostly positive about the consequences of online learning, particularly in terms of the flexibility it provided her, she also discusses her "worst fears" about online classes. And given Seitz's own independent nature, she was struck by the secondary consequence of having to post her reading analyses, class comments, and written work publicly, as participating in an online public forum was a requirement of the course, a requirement that other students enjoyed.

Ask yourself . . .
- How does my analysis reveal my close, careful examination of the phenomenon?
- What are the sources of my explicit evidence? How do they enhance (or not) the logos of my message?
- What research evidence do I include for each of my supporting assertions?
- Where do I include alternative viewpoints (professional and popular) on the phenomenon?
- Which passages feature the most precise language?

- **Reinforce the positive benefits to readers from analyzing the situation or phenomenon or the negative situation that may result if such analysis is ignored.**
- **Create effective appeals to pathos, making an authentic emotional connection with the audience.**

Emphasize consequences, positive or negative, for the reader Finally, the conclusion of a critical analysis reinforces the positive benefits that readers can reap from analyzing this situation or phenomenon. Or, depending on the topic, the conclusion can illustrate the negative situation that may result if readers ignore the writer's critical analysis. As Seitz recounts the consequences of her online degree program, she admits that when she compared her work with the work of her peers, she was often inspired to do better—even though such

(continued)

comparisons had never been part of her educational experience. In fact, she writes, she found the online experience to result in a "healthy and productive sort of peer pressure" that led her to do things she had "never tried to do before, and sometimes even did them well."

Ask yourself . . .
- What exactly am I encouraging my audience to do?
- Where do I balance the positive and the negative causes or consequences—or does my message require such balance?
- How, exactly, do I make an authentic emotional connection with my audience?

MindTap®   Request help and feedback from a tutor. If required, participate in peer review, submit your paper for a grade, and view instructor comments online.

Revision and Peer Review

After you have drafted a strong version of your critical analysis, ask one of your classmates to read it. You will want your classmate to respond to your work in a way that helps you revise it into the strongest analysis it can be, one that addresses your intended audience, helps you fulfill your purpose, and is delivered in the most appropriate means available to you and your audience.

Questions for a peer reviewer

1. To what critical question is the writer responding?
2. What are the strengths and weaknesses of the description of the situation or phenomenon? How might the audience better visualize the situation?
3. How does the writer establish the need to analyze this particular situation or phenomenon? Where does the writer indicate how the situation or phenomenon concerns the audience?
4. Who might be the writer's intended audience? Why might they be interested?
5. Identify the thesis statement of the analysis, in which the writer clearly states a claim about the causes or the consequences of the phenomenon being analyzed. If you cannot locate a thesis statement, what thesis statement might work for this document?
6. Identify the researched facts, data, evidence, and examples the writer provides in support of the claim.
7. Where does the writer address varying perspectives on the causes or consequences of the situation or phenomenon being analyzed?

8. Where does the writer establish an authentic emotional connection (pathos) with the audience?
9. What did you learn from the conclusion that was not already in the document? What does the writer want you to take away from the document in terms of information, attitude, or action?
10. Which section of the document did you most enjoy? Which section was most persuasive? Why?

MindTap® Reflect on your writing process.

✈ ADDITIONAL ASSIGNMENTS

Knowledge Transfer

Business, history, sociology, and psychology courses all ask students to conduct critical analyses.

 COLLEGE Bilingualism Analysis for Applied Linguistics Your family has been bilingual for three generations now, a phenomenon you take for granted. So when your applied linguistics professor assigns a critical analysis of bilingualism, you decide to analyze the consequences (social, intellectual, political) of being bilingual for yourself and others. Your researched analysis will be about ten pages long.

 COMMUNITY Address to City Council As president of your housing association, you are expected to report to the city council with regard to the mailbox vandalism in your neighborhood. You have been allotted ten minutes (four, double-spaced pages of script) during which, using precise language, you will describe the vandalism itself, explain the extent and frequency of the vandalism (including facts and figures on the matter), and provide a logical explanation of what you understand to be the causes of and perhaps the solution to the vandalism.

WORKPLACE Ad Campaign Analysis As part of your advertising internship, you are working with a research team focusing on an ad campaign that will be delivered as a television commercial. Your assignment is to critique it for credibility, logic, and emotional connection with the target audience. In the process, you will gather the preliminary findings from a focus group, combine them with the careful notes you have been jotting down as the ad has been taking shape, and compose a five-page summary on the potential consequences of this ad for the

(continued)

ADDITIONAL ASSIGNMENTS (*Continued*)

target audience. Your audience is the producer, who is already proud of the almost-final product.

MULTIMODAL News Analysis and Presentation Every week, another tragedy occurs in the United States, if not a mass shooting, then a terrible natural disaster or plane crash. Focus on one event in order to analyze the causes or consequences of that event. Watch television reports to see how the coverage of the event differs, taking careful notes and taping important segments, after which you will read online and print commentary about the event. Your purpose is to make an oral presentation to your Communication class, analyzing the event, synthesizing the variables in the coverage, and describing your findings. You will enhance your presentation with video and audio clips.

GRAMMAR IN C⦶NTEXT Thinking Rhetorically about Precise Language

Accurate words

Accurate words convey precise meanings. Although you may use words such as *thing* and *nice* in a rough draft, you will want to choose words with denotations and connotations that help you accurately portray your ideas. **Denotations** refer to dictionary definitions; **connotations** refer to associated meanings. A good dictionary includes entries that help you understand how one word is related to words with similar meanings, explaining connotations as well as denotations. For example, the following entry from *Heinle's Newbury House Dictionary* could help you choose the best word for describing an event that was extremely loud. Listed first are the definitions, followed by some synonyms.

> **loud** /laud/ *adj.* **er, est 1** having an intense sound, noisy: *The sound of city traffic is loud.* **2** unpleasantly bright in color: *He wears bright reds and other loud colors. n.* **loudness.**

> **loud 1** deafening, earsplitting | shrill, strident *frml.* **2** flashy, garish, gaudy.

Also be sure to consider your choice of verb when revising for accuracy: writers too often depend on a form of the verb *to be* (*am, is, are, was, were*), the most generic of verbs.

denotation the meaning of a word as defined by a dictionary

connotation the associated meanings of a word

Fresh expressions

As you explain a concept, you may want to use an image to make your point. Fresh images can help your readers "see" what you mean, what you are talking about. For instance, literature professor Susan Gubar wanted to explain how her mind was working as she listened to various arguments:

> **While others, judging by their ardent notetaking, found enlightenment, or, at least, points for debate, I precariously moved along a spider web of speculation.**
>
> **—Susan Gubar,** *Rooms of Our Own*

Spider web of speculation is a fresh phrase that expresses the jumbled mental state the author experienced.

You will often find that what were once fresh expressions or examples of vivid language have become so common that they have lost their impact: *white as snow, sick as a dog,* and *strong as an ox* are just a few examples of the cobwebbed expressions called **clichés**. If you find yourself resorting to clichés in your writing, or if a peer reviewer identifies a phrase as a cliché, you will want to revise your prose in one of the following ways: you can use language that does not call forth an image or make a comparison, try to invent a new expression, or tweak the original expression to make it fresh.

clichés expressions that have lost their freshness and impact

Cliché: *at the drop of a hat*

Literal synonym: *immediately*

New expression: *at the click of the Send button*

Original expression with a slight change:

> **We know by now that whenever politics and art collide, art loses—at least, in these United States, where anything cultural can become politicized *at the drop of a grievance.***
>
> **—Peter Schjeldahl, "Those Nasty Brits"**

Clear definitions

When you use a specialized term, one specific to your topic, ask yourself whether your audience will know its definition. If there is any chance that readers could confuse a term's intended meaning with another of its meanings (for example, the word *reservoir* has both a general and a technical meaning) or that readers may be unfamiliar with the term, provide a definition to help them choose the meaning you have in mind.

A definition can be a formal definition, a dictionary definition, a synonym, a stipulative definition (a definition specific to a particular context), or a negative definition. A formal definition places the term in a class and then differentiates it from other members of the class.

> **A *reservoir* [term] is an artificial body of water [class] that is retained by a dam [differentiation].**

A definition from a general or specialized dictionary may also be used.

> **Reservoir can refer to an "underground accumulation of petroleum or natural gas" ("Reservoir," def. 3).**

If you choose to quote from a dictionary, be sure to cite the number of the definition you used and include an entry for it in your bibliography. (See CHAPTER 19, MLA GUIDELINES FOR DOCUMENTING WORKS CITED and CHAPTER 20, APA GUIDELINES FOR DOCUMENTING REFERENCES.) Another way to define a word is to use a synonymous word or phrase set off by commas or dashes.

pages 342–363 and 380–394

> **They searched for a reservoir, a rock formation that retains natural gas underground, in an uninhabited area.**

When you use a definition, especially a formal definition, be sure the term being defined is followed by a noun or a noun phrase, not an adverbial clause. In particular, avoid using any construction that includes *is when* or *is where*.

> *the designing of systems*
>
> **Resource development is ~~when systems are designed~~ for using natural resources.**

> *the contest between*   *vying*
>
> **Exploitative competition is ~~where~~ two or more organisms ~~vie~~ for a limited resource such as food.**

MindTap® Find additional handbook coverage of grammar, punctuation, and style online.

Literary Analyses

MindTap® Understand the goals of the chapter and complete a warm-up activity online.

You have been conducting literary analyses for years—ever since you first started talking about the movies your parents took you to and the books they read to you. Some you liked and wanted to experience again; others, not so much. You talked about plot, characters, and setting, taking that ability with you when you entered school and began reading texts more closely. In a **literary analysis**, you make an argument for why and how a text should be read a certain way—your way.

literary analysis an argument for reading a text in a certain way

In this chapter, your goal will be to identify rhetorical opportunities for analyzing literary works, fiction, drama, poetry, essays, creative nonfiction, and memoirs. Maybe you belong to a book group, or you have given a favorite novel to a friend with a note saying, "Drop everything and read this book." Or perhaps you have returned from a film adaptation of a favorite novel complaining that one of the characters was miscast. In each of these situations, you were

---

IDENTIFYING AN OPPORTUNITY FOR CHANGE

Print Literary Analysis written for an undergraduate journal or as a review for your campus paper	**Oral Literary Analysis** recorded as a podcast, to be played for your class	**Online Literary Analysis** posted on a website such as GoodReads.com or LibraryThing.com, where you are participating in a book club

responding to and analyzing a literary work. Such a situation provides a starting point for determining what most interests you. As you work, then, consider the most fitting means of delivery for your literary analysis.

GENRE IN F◇CUS The Poetry Slam

Local book clubs and other such community programs seek to encourage people to carve out time and space to read, discuss, and write about literature of all kinds. Many people regularly read their essays, stories, and poetry to audiences in clubs, bars, coffeehouses, libraries, student unions, and writing centers in communities and on campuses across the nation. A prominent part of the movement to make poetry and other literary forms more accessible has been the Poetry Slam initiative, which features competitive performance poetry. Randomly selected members of the audience judge the different poets on their lyrical skills as well as their stage presence.

Phoenix-based Myrlin Hepworth, a poet, rapper, hip-hop artist, social-justice activist, and educator, earned his way through college by performing slam poetry on the street. Hepworth still often delivers his work at slams, though he has recently turned to hip-hop, performing his poetry to music: "The job of the poet is to speak to the humanity of everyone. My job is to humanize and create avenues for people to reach inside and find out more about themselves. . . . That's what I want to do, absolutely!"

Myrlin Hepworth performs his poetry at Tucson Youth Poetry Slam.

Although some literary critics have attacked the Poetry Slam movement as, in the words of Harold Bloom, "the death of art," many others dispute such a claim, with Hepworth celebrating the connection between poet and listener: "What I care about is that feeling you get when you see an artist, when there's nowhere else you want to be. There's a vibration, and you're connected. Not because you're supposed to idolize [the artist], but because you trust and feel naturally." Susan B.A. Somers-Willett, an award-winning poet and member of three national poetry slam teams, researched the impact of public poetry projects and writes,

> **More and more poets are ferrying the divide between [the academy and slam]. Former and current slam competitors are now studying or teaching in MFA programs; likewise, winners of academic poetry's most prestigious honors—the Yale Younger Poets Series, the National Poetry Series, and the Pulitzer Prize to name a few—have performed on the slam stage to acclaim. Still other slam competitors have taken their poetry to larger mainstream audiences, namely through commercial ventures such as the HBO series *Russell Simmons Presents Def Poetry* or through spoken word albums.**
>
> **The growing history and influence of the poetry slam, especially on a younger generation of writers, suggests that the practice is not just a passing fad. The serious critic must cease treating the slam as a literary novelty or oddity and recognize it for what it is: a movement which combines (and at times exploits) the literary, the performative, and the social potential of verse, and which does so with the audience as its judge and guide.**
>
> **—Susan B.A. Somers-Willett, "Can Slam Poetry Matter?"**

Whether inspired by a poetry slam, a hip-hop or dramatic performance, or a college literature course, the rhetorical opportunity for a literary analysis enables you to make an argument through a **close reading** of the text—a reading that carefully examines a text's style and structure. In a close reading you will examine literary elements individually (see the box on THE ELEMENTS OF LITERATURE LATER IN THIS CHAPTER) and then look at the relationship of those elements in how the text works as a whole. (See CHAPTER 3, ANALYSIS AND SYNTHESIS.) Your literary analysis may focus on one element as key or locate several factors that taken together make a work significant. In the case of the poetry slam, for example, Somers-Willett looks at the way "the literary, the performative, and the social potential of verse" work together to affect an audience. Most often, you will take a position on a question about the meaning, structure, or significance of the text and support your position using text-based evidence, usually quotations. In this way, your literary analysis creates an argument that shows how other readers should interpret the elements of a text and make meaning from them.

close reading an examination of the key characteristics (including style and structure) of a text

pages 218–219

pages 45–50

✈ ASSIGNMENT

Every time you read a piece of literature, you work to establish how that text should be read, because stories do not easily reveal themselves. Whether you are concentrating on the significance of a character, a repeated image, a specific scene, or the underlying theme of the text, you are reading and rereading the text in order to analyze it, to answer interesting questions about it. As you follow your initial reading of the text, work to establish the position you want to take on it, locating textual evidence—gleaned from a close reading—to support your thesis statement as well as the supporting assertions you are making.

You may want to focus on a text you are reading for class now, one you have long enjoyed but puzzled over, or one you recently heard read aloud. List the literary elements of that text—plot, for example, or main character—and consider which of them intrigues you most. Write a short essay in which you analyze the significance of that element to the text, making sure to compose a thesis statement and use details, examples, and evidence to support your assertions.

◉ READING RHETORICALLY

Whether it is fiction or nonfiction, there is no one specific way to make sense of any literary work. But reading a text actively—recording your reactions in the margins, highlighting passages that confuse you, noting sections that seem to be central to the events or the characters—is a first step toward making an argument about that work and its significance. During the reading process, you will sharpen your ability to read closely, synthesize meaning from the various elements of a text, and, thus, come to a better understanding about each of these individual elements and the ways in which they interact with one another. Moreover, you will be able to use evidence from the text to demonstrate to other readers, including your classmates, why your particular reading of the text is an important one for them to consider. That is, you will be able to convince readers that your interpretation helps improve their understanding of the literary text.

ELEMENTS OF LITERATURE

In a literary analysis, you will likely discuss the work's structure (character, plot, setting) and the writer's style (such as word choice, tone, figurative language).

- **Characters** The characters in a literary work are the humans or humanlike personalities (aliens, creatures, robots, animals, and so on) who carry along the action. The main character is called the *protagonist*. In prose literature, you often find extensive descriptions of the characters' physical, mental, or social attributes and appearance. In a play, you learn what a character is thinking by the thoughts he or she shares either with another character in dialogue or as "dramatic soliloquy" (a speech delivered to the audience by an actor alone on the stage).

- **Point of view** Each literary work is told from a certain point of view by a narrator (the speaker who is telling the story in the text, not to be confused with the actual author): *first-person narration* uses the first-person pronoun *I*; *third person, omniscient,* tells readers about the thoughts, motivations, and attitudes of all characters, referring to them by name or third-person pronouns (*he, she,* etc.); *third person, limited,* follows one character around, revealing just that character's thoughts.
- **Plot** The plot encompasses what happens in the work: the *exposition* introduces the characters, setting, and background and soon moves to a *conflict* that sets a sequence of significant events in motion, which leads to the climax, the most intense *turning point*, and ends in the *dénouement* (or *falling action*), a resolution of the conflict.
- **Setting** There is a physical setting as well as a social setting (the morals, manners, and customs of the characters). Setting also involves time (historical time and also the length of time covered by the narrative) and includes atmosphere, or the character's and the reader's emotional response to the situation.
- **Theme** The theme refers to the message the text delivers about a character, a relationship, an event, or a place. Common themes include person versus person, person versus self, person versus nature or technology, and person versus society.
- **Figurative language** Writers often use figurative language such as *metaphors* and *similes* to communicate complex ideas and meanings to readers. Using a metaphor, the writer refers to one thing as something else ("Hope is the thing with feathers"). Using a simile, the writer says that an object, idea, or person is *like* something else ("My love is like a red, red rose").
- **Symbol** A symbol is usually a concrete object that stands for an abstract one. A vivid description of a kitchen table, for example, might be a symbol for the significance of everyday experiences that take place around the table.
- **Imagery** Imagery refers to words and phrases that appeal to readers' senses, helping them "see" a particular image in their mind's eye. (The poet Marianne Moore, for instance, called on poets to help readers visualize "real toads" in "imaginary gardens.")
- **Rhythm and rhyme** Poets, in particular, arrange syllables, words, and line breaks to have either a regular rhythm and rhyme, with each line containing a particular pattern of short and long syllables and of corresponding internal or terminal sounds, or a less structured, even patternless rhythm and rhyme.

Key Features of a Literary Analysis

A literary analysis explains and interprets your reactions to a text. Whether you are writing or reading such an analysis, you will find that it has the following features:

- A literary analysis introduces interpretations of the literary work under investigation, often explaining what these perspectives might be missing.
- A literary analysis presents a specific question about the literary work that the writer believes needs to be answered.
- A literary analysis presents a clear argument, or thesis, about the literary work and explains how this thesis addresses some concern that other readers of this work may have ignored or misrepresented.
- To provide evidence supporting its thesis, a literary analysis quotes specific passages from the text.
- A literary analysis explicates, or explains, all quoted passages, directing readers' attention to specific features of the literary work that support the thesis.

Ralph Rees's article on the poetry of Marianne Moore, which follows Moore's poem on the next page, is annotated to illustrate some of the characteristics of a literary analysis. In his introduction, Rees suggests that he writes about Moore's work because she offers a compelling perspective on how imagination and reality interact with each another, and throughout his analysis, he presents specific evidence from her poem "Poetry," which follows. As you read the following poem, analyze the rhetorical situation.

- Why might Marianne Moore have begun "Poetry" with the line "I, too, dislike it"? With whom might she be agreeing? What rhetorical opportunity does Moore want to address with her poem?
- What is poetry, according to Moore? How does Moore use comparison and contrast to clarify her definition? What purpose does she see in writing poetry?
- What purpose does Rees see in poetry? How does his judgment align with that of poet Myrlin Hepworth?

MindTap® Read, highlight, and take notes online.

Poetry

MARIANNE MOORE

Marianne Moore won both the Pulitzer Prize and the National Book Award for her Collected Poems *(1951). As she accepted the National Book Award, Moore suggested that critics called her work "poetry" because there simply were no other categories to put it in. All types of writing are important, Moore suggests, but poetry, with its precise descriptions of both the physical world and the ideas conjured up by the human imagination, helps us better understand ourselves and the world around us.*

I, too, dislike it: there are things that are important beyond all this fiddle.
    Reading it, however, with a perfect contempt for it, one discovers that there is in
      it after all, a place for the genuine.
        Hands that can grasp, eyes
        that can dilate, hair that can rise
           if it must, these things are important not because a
high-sounding interpretation can be put upon them but because they are
      useful. When they become so derivative as to become unintelligible,
      the same thing may be said for all of us, that we
        do not admire what
        we cannot understand: the bat
           holding on upside down or in quest of something to
eat, elephants pushing, a wild horse taking a roll, a tireless wolf under
      a tree, the immovable critic twitching his skin like a horse that feels a flea,
                                     the base
ball fan, the statistician—
        nor is it valid
           to discriminate against "business documents and
school-books"; all these phenomena are important. One must make a distinction
      however: when dragged into prominence by half poets, the result is not poetry,
      nor till the poets among us can be
        "literalists of
        "the imagination"—above
           insolence and triviality and can present
for inspection, "imaginary gardens with real toads in them," shall we have
      it. In the meantime, if you demand on the one hand,
      the raw material of poetry in

all its rawness and

    that which is on the other hand

        genuine, you are interested in poetry.

Reprinted by permission.

MindTap®   Read, highlight, and take notes online.

The Reality of Imagination in the Poetry of Marianne Moore

RALPH REES

Bucknell professor Ralph Rees has been described as a "gifted teacher who transmits the love of learning to his students." He has published widely on Marianne Moore (1887–1972), one of the leading poets of the Modernist movement in the United States.

Rees uses a conventional strategy to open his essay. After telling readers the general topic—different perspectives on reality—in his first sentence, he presents several examples of different perspectives. Then he explains which perspective is Marianne Moore's.

Reality means different things to different people. To most, fact and the stimuli of the senses define reality; to some, the products of the intellect may be added to the above; to a few, the offspring of the imagination must also be considered. Marianne Moore belongs to the last group, for she finds imagination as much a part of reality as fact. Many realists ignore the figments of the mind because they do not feel that such things have actuality; they deal only with the apparent, the sensed. Moore finds a more immediate reality in thoughts than in facts and the things that arouse the senses. The imagined, because it is more individual and more personal than the other phenomena, seems to her the very essence of reality. The way a thing *seems* is truth; its definitions and its composition are not realities but stimuli to the imagination, which creates actuality. The experience of the fact and the sensed is reality.

Although he doesn't signal it explicitly, Rees presents his thesis in the second half of this paragraph. He also begins to build his argument that his interpretation of Moore's ideas is the appropriate way to read her work.

In speaking of poetry, Moore says,

nor till the poets among us can be
"literalists of
   the imagination"—above
     insolence and triviality and can present
for inspection, "imaginary gardens with real toads in them," shall we have
   it. In the meantime, if you demand on the one hand,

> the raw material of poetry in
>   all its rawness and
>   that which is on the other hand
>   genuine, you are interested in poetry. *(Collected Poems* 41)

Rees presents a passage from Moore's "Poetry" as evidence to support his argument.

It can be seen that she wants poets to accept the products of their imaginations as realities that can be put down in their poems as actualities. She sees no need for the poet to separate his imaginings from that which is sensed or founded in fact. A truer actuality exists in mental experiences than in sensuality. "A single shawl—Imagination's—is wrapped tightly round us since we are poor" (*Predilections* 43). Morton Zabel says,

Rees follows the quoted passage with his own analysis because he wants readers to understand it in a specific way. He uses an attributive tag before the direct quotation so that readers know the source.

> In her poem on [poetry] Miss Moore improves [William Butler] Yeats' characterization of [William] Blake by insisting that poets must be "literalists of the imagination"; they must see the visible at that focus of intelligence where sight and concept coincide, and where it becomes transformed into the pure and total idealism of ideas. By this realism, the imagination permits ideas to claim energy from what is usually denied them—the vital nature that exists and suffers, and which alone can give poetic validity to the abstract or permit the abstract intelligence to enhance experience. (329-30)

In finding "the visible at that focus of intelligence where sight and concept coincide" Moore discovers the matter and the method of her poetry. With such an approach a poet can find material in everything; no limits restrict a poetic concept. "The idealism of ideas" accepts everything and rejects nothing in establishing material suitable to poetry. As R. P. Blackmur has said,

Rees quotes other literary scholars' interpretations of Moore's work as a means of supporting his own argument.

> The whole flux of experience and interpretation is appropriate subject matter to an imagination literal enough to see poetry in it; an imagination, that is, as intent on the dramatic texture (on what is involved, is tacit, is immanent) of the quotidian, as the imagination of the painter is intent, in Velasquez, on the visual texture of lace. (267)

Imagination, then, must be looked upon as the force which blends the other qualities together; through imagination the experienced, the observed, the studied are brought into a single heightened experience, which enhances the singularity of the idea of a thing while discarding much that has adhered to it through constant usage and casual observance.

Just as he did with the passage from "Poetry," Rees follows quotations from other scholars with his own analysis of their arguments.

. . . This emphasis on imagination gives the cohesive quality to many of her poems. At first, the reader may have difficulty in finding the connections between

(continued)

the various subjects brought into a single poem; the search for traditional logical development deludes him. When he is willing to accept the imaginative connections between the various matters of the poem, he will readily see that the common qualities are brought about by the ideal states of the many things mentioned. For this reason, most ideas can be compared with objects, with other ideas, with animals, and with man. Within the world of the imagination no barriers limit the poet or the reader to believe that only obvious likes may be compared with each other or that comparisons may be made only between members of a single class.

Moore has said that "the artist biased by imagination is a poet" (*Nation* 192). By this definition many of our so-called poets may be placed in the artist class, which she seems to place below that of poet. The true poet, the person with aesthetic possibilities, permits his imagination to be the guide to his artistic capabilities. Such a person does not draw close distinctions between that which is dreamed of and that which is sensed. He accepts as the world of poetry all things that he can experience, whether physically or mentally. Imagination not only allows the poet to invoke comparisons that are fresh, interesting and constructive but to achieve a level of thought that is all-encompassing. The poet is the artist without bias, barriers, or prejudices of any kind; he permits his imagination to have full control of his creative processes and, by so doing, creates a world which seems new and startling to the unimaginative reader although the poet would say that this is the world that has always had existence, that has always remained the same while the factual was constantly changing through new concepts and ideas.

The power of imagination in its stimulation and growth from the factual and the sensed has the utmost importance to the poet. It demonstrates the mind at its most original and refreshing. The rest of experience is important only as stimuli; experience that does not stimulate the imagination is of little value. It is for this reason that Moore says, "The power of the visible/is the invisible" (*Collected Poems* 104). The "visible" gains importance only as it affects the imagination. In other words, Moore finds that the factual and the sensed, those things which most people accept as the "all" of reality, are important only as the stimuli of the imagination. Such an idea turns the world of the realist upside down; actuality becomes that which is not concrete and which can never be "proved."

It has been shown that Marianne Moore is a realist, by her own definition and by her own actions. The standard conception of realist would exclude her and her poetic creations; but, by showing that only that which

Rees explains how Moore's concept of reality connects to questions that concern readers: who is and is not a poet, and how we can best evaluate a poet's creative work.

Topic sentences such as this one help readers anticipate what the writer will discuss in a paragraph—in this case, the importance of imagination to poets and its relationship to the factual and the sensed.

she herself has experienced has actuality for her, she has designated herself a realist of the imagination. In his essay "Jubal, Jabal and Moore," M. L. Rosenthal says,

Rees circles back to the opening lines of the essay, where he presented different perspectives on reality.

> Miss Moore's vivid emphasis on the details of subhuman organic life— she is the botanist's and the zoologist's poet, as well as the poet's poet— makes her poetry swarm with symbolic observation. The pretense is that all this occurs in a hothouse or a zoo, where one watches the flora or the curious beasts with amused and sympathetic detachment, making polite conversation all the while. But how intense the interest really is, how uncompromising the preciseness of detail, how persistent the drive toward universalizing ethical import; how irritated the poet is with soft-headedness of any kind! The ostrich "digesteth harde yron" and is there-fore superior to all the absurdities of his appearance and, more important, to his ridiculous common mortality. Sometimes her famous "imaginary gardens with real toads in them"—Miss Moore's image for genuine poetic creations—are really not so far from [William] Blake's tiger-haunted forests. (21)

Rosenthal is not the only critic to point out Moore's battle against soft thinking; others have commented on her constant struggle for thought that is as direct as it is stimulating. Wallace Stevens says that she has "the faculty of digesting the 'harde yron' of appearance" (149). It is important to emphasize Stevens' use of the word "digesting," because Moore accomplishes such a pro-cess through her imagination; she "digests" fact by using her imagination. Without such a function to act upon it, the fact itself would be of little or no importance to the individual. Imagination, then, has become the only criterion by which reality and actuality can be measured.

Rees continues this process of circling around to his introduction, as he uses this last sentence to present his final answer to the question he first suggested in that initial paragraph—what is the meaning of reality, and how do we assess and understand it?

Works Cited

Blackmur, R.P. "The Method of Marianne Moore." *Language as Gesture,* Harcourt Brace, 1952.

Moore, Marianne, "Poetry." *Collected Poems,* Macmillan, 1951, p. 41.

—. "He 'Digesteth Harde Yron.'" *Collected Poems,* Macmillan, 1951, p. 104.

—. "A Bold Virtuoso." *Predilections,* Viking, 1955, p. 43.

—. "Paul Rosenfeld." *The Nation,* vol. 163, 17 Aug. 1946, p. 192.

Rosenthal, M.L. "Jubal, Jabal and Moore." *New Republic,* vol. 126, 7 Apr. 1952, p. 21.

Stevens, Wallace. "About One of Marianne Moore's Poems." *Quarterly Review of Litera-ture,* vol. 4, 1948, p. 149.

Zabel, Morton. "A Literalist of the Imagination." *Poetry,* vol. 47, no. 6, Mar. 1936, pp. 329–30.

Using Synthesis and Analysis

When reading the selection, ask: Who might be the rhetorical audience for Rees? How does his purpose connect with that audience? For example, what is revealed about his purpose and audience by his use of the third-person singular masculine pronoun? In Rees's analysis, for example,

- What major points and key terms did you notice?
- What is Rees's basic thesis?
- Where and how does Rees make an emotional connection with his readers?

Synthesis, which is a crucial part of analyzing a text, begins by making connections among different elements and evaluating how they work together as a whole. Examine how Rees uses these connections to relate to the thesis and to the interests of his readers.

- How does he extend and support his thesis with specific details from the text?
- In what ways does he work to connect his thesis with the interests of his readers?
- Does he use outside sources to support his thesis?
- How does he combine the use of examples from the primary source with outside information to create a unique reading of the work?

There is no single way to accomplish the many goals of a literary analysis. Approach the work with an analytical frame of mind, and synthesize multiple views—your own, those of other sources, and examples from the work itself—to go deeper as you read the text.

MindTap® Find additional examples of literary analyses online.

 RESPONDING TO THE RHETORICAL SITUATION

People compose literary analyses after reading or experiencing a text or performance. Most often, they make arguments about how readers (including themselves) should interpret the elements of a text, what subtle elements should be noticed, and how to make meaning from those elements. Such situations are opportunities for writers to compose a literary analysis for a rhetorical audience who is ignoring, misreading, or failing to understand (or notice) significant features of a text. They also compose literary analyses in order to discover answers to interesting questions, questions about the text itself, its potential influence on people and their interactions, and the various historical receptions of the text. Their analyses can be delivered orally (in book club discussions), in print or online (in newspapers, zines, and discussion boards), verbally (in podcasts or on the radio), and as YouTube videos or other visual media.

Opportunity ▸ Audience and Purpose ▸ Genre/Report ▸ (Medium of) Delivery

Understanding the Rhetorical Situation

Although all imaginative literature can be characterized as fictional, the term **fiction** applies specifically to the prose narratives of novels and short stories. **Poetry**, on the other hand, is primarily characterized by its extensive use of concentrated language, or language that relies on imagery, allusions, figures of speech, symbols, sound and rhythm, and precise word choice, all of which allow poets to make a point in one or two words rather than spelling it out explicitly. However, poetry, like fiction, may have a narrator with a point of view, and some poems have a plot, a setting, and characters. **Drama** shares many of the same elements as fiction (setting, character, plot, and dialogue), but differs in that it is meant to be performed—whether on stage, on film, or on television—with the director and actors imprinting the lines with their own interpretations. And like fiction, nonfiction, and poetry, drama can be read; in this case, you bring your interpretative abilities to what is on the printed page rather than to a performance of the work.

fiction prose stories based on the imagination

poetry a concentrated language relying on sound and image

drama a performance where a director and actors interpret a script

- Which form of literary expression would you be most interested in learning more about or analyzing in more detail? What most interests you about this form? What about this kind of text or the context in which it would normally be encountered makes it particularly compelling to you?

RESEARCHING A LITERARY ANALYSIS

As you consider your literary analysis, be sure to start by consulting the notes you took in your close reading of the text. Consider your personal responses and insights into specific elements of the text as the first steps toward the best reading of that text.

(continued)

Evidence for your literary analysis begins with the text itself, so dissecting text-based quotations is important in building your case, but evidence can also include facts and statistics (for example, how often a writer uses the word *blue* or has references to a *mirror*). Formal research can help by providing expert opinions from literary scholars that you might use to support your position or to show the complexities surrounding a text or even as a rhetorical opportunity to address a misreading of the text. Whether or not you use them, you will have more information to consider. But you may find that discussing your ideas with your teacher and classmates provides you with even more fruitful research findings; after all, you may discover why a particular reading of the text is important to them. After conducting this formal and informal research, be sure to read and then reread the text itself. When you read it aloud, you will notice details and connections that you would have otherwise missed.

Identifying an opportunity for change

interpretive question a question about the meaning, structure, or significance of a text

reading journal a record of personal thoughts, ideas, and questions about a text

pages 239–244

To compose an analysis that provides readers with significant insight, choose a feature of the literary work that genuinely interests you. Then, formulate an **interpretive question** that you will answer as the subject of your analysis, with supporting evidence, throughout your essay. To help you craft your interpretive question, consider keeping a **reading journal** in which you can freewrite in response to the following series of prompts. (For more on freewriting and keeping a journal and other ways to jump-start your writing, see CHAPTER 13, EXPLORATION.) Reading these prompts *before* you read the literary text will help you focus your thinking as you read; you can draft responses to the prompts after you have read the text once or twice. Later, your journal freewrites will help you identify and clarify the interpretive question on which you will focus your analysis of the literary work.

1. Freewrite for ten minutes in response to these questions about the characters in the literary work: Who is the most important character in the piece? What actions or inactions does this character take that most affect the work as a whole? In what ways does the character change—or not—throughout the course of the work? To what effect? How do the other characters in the piece contribute to, react to, or prevent this change?
2. Freewrite for ten minutes on the importance of the setting in the literary work: When and where does this literary work take place? How does "place" help explain the motivations of the characters or the events in the plot? Do you notice anything significant about the setting that affects how you read the piece?

3. Freewrite for ten minutes about the point of view of the literary work: Who is telling the story? What does the narrator (or speaker) know and not know? Is the narrator reliable? Biased or unbiased? How do you know? How does the narrator's (or speaker's) knowledge about events and the other characters shape how you read and understand the piece?
4. Freewrite for ten minutes, recording the sequence of events, or plot, of the literary work: What is the single most important event or moment? Why do you think this moment is so important or crucial? For whom is it crucial?
5. Freewrite for ten minutes about the theme, what the author is trying to say through the literary work: What kind of conflict does the piece make you think about? What are the effects of that conflict on the people and events of the story?

Relating rhetorically to your audience

The following questions can help you establish a rhetorical audience and iden-tify the relationship it has to your overall purpose in composing. Once you have established the connection, you can choose the best way to present and support your answer.

1. List the persons or groups who are talking about the literary work you are analyzing or who have questions about its meaning or importance.
2. Next to each name, write reasons that audience might have for acknowl-edging, even appreciating, your analysis of the literary work. In other words, what would persuade these people or groups to read and interpret the literary piece in a different way?
3. What responses could these audiences reasonably be persuaded to have to your essay and to the text you are analyzing?
4. With your audience's interests and capabilities in mind, look again at the question and initial answer you composed in the preceding section on identifying an opportunity. Decide how you might engage your audience with your question and interpretation. At this point, you may find it neces-sary to revise your question so that it speaks more directly to the interests of your audience.

Planning an effective rhetorical response for your purpose

Identifying an audience, purpose, and interpretive question is the first step; getting your audience to engage in your work is the second. After these initial steps, you are ready to plan out your analytical essay, keeping in mind what your audience already thinks about the text as you help them expand their understanding of that text. To be a fitting response, your literary analysis must also address the context within which your audience is likely to consider it. For example, you might consider writing an essay for the "Arts & Entertainment" section of the local newspaper or posting a blog entry on a website devoted to the work you are analyzing. In other words, once you identify your opportunity, audience, and purpose, consider what kind of literary analysis will best respond to the rhetorical situation.

Use the following two questions to help you narrow your purpose and shape your response:

1. Are you asking the audience to simply reread the literary work in a new light or to perform some particular action in response to this new way of interpreting the text?
2. What is the best way to reach this audience? That is, with what kind of text is this audience most likely to engage?

LINKS TO LITERARY ANALYSES IN THREE MEDIA   MindTap®

Links may change due to availability.

© Katrina Outland/Shutterstock.com

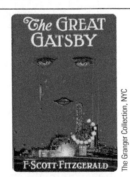

The Granger Collection, NYC

Courtesy of J. Keirn Swanson

Print Literary Analysis
In the literary analysis at the beginning of this chapter, Ralph Rees explores the nature of imagination through an analysis of Marianne Moore's poem, "Poetry."

Oral Literary Analysis
Slate's online Audio Book Club provides book reviews and discussions regularly. Among the archives is a podcast for *The Great Gatsby*, in which critics discuss what makes the novel endure, despite its flimsy plot.

Online Literary Analysis
J from Kent, Ohio, has posted more than eighty in-depth commentaries for his network of thirty-five friends on GoodReads.com. To view J's analysis of *The Historian*, by Elizabeth Kostova, go to GoodReads.com.

WRITING A PERSUASIVE LITERARY ANALYSIS: A Guide

*W*riting a literary analysis will give you an opportunity to sharpen your ability to read, interpret, and formulate ideas about the significance of literary texts. To make an effective argument for your interpretation, your primary focus will be on establishing the opportunity for and significance of your interpretive question, providing evidence from the text to support your interpretation, and explaining the larger implications of your answer for understanding the text. A careful, close reading enhances the writer's ethos, giving credibility to fresh interpretations. That interpretation (a series of assertions supported with textual evidence) provides the logos. Any emotional connection the writer makes with an already engaged audience can supply pathos. *(See CHAPTER 2, THE AVAILABLE MEANS INCLUDE THE RHETORICAL ELEMENTS OF THE MESSAGE ITSELF.)*

pages 23–26

ADVANTAGES AND LIMITATIONS

Advantages

- **Writer:** Literary analyses can serve as productive—even fun—discussions among people who are sharing the same literary experience. The writer can take advantage of other readers' desire for a deeper appreciation of the literature and its timelessness, as many literary texts connect to current events and trends.

- **Message:** A literary analysis provides an opportunity to advocate for an interpretation that has personal meaning and larger implications about the significance of a particular work.

- **Media and Design:** Literary analyses can be delivered in endless ways and variations: online, in print, through video or podcasting, or enhanced with music, audio, and images.

Limitations

- **Writer:** Compared to reviews, locating a rhetorical audience for the analysis outside of the traditional classroom may be difficult, especially if delivering the work in a purely print/text medium.

- **Message:** Missing details or connections (or simply getting them wrong) in the literary work distracts from the writer's credibility, the logos of the argument, and any positive emotional connection with the audience.

- **Media and Design:** Although an analysis of a purely written text can sometimes be hard to deliver in an alternate media or in multimedia, many people successfully do just that, thereby broadening their audience.

- **Identify the literary work being analyzed.**
- **Present an interpretive question and argue for its importance.**
- **Summarize other answers to the question.**
- **Present the thesis statement (the writer's answer to the interpretive question).**

Explain the work's significance Your introduction should explain which literary work you are going to analyze and why. Ralph Rees, for example, states that he will examine how Marianne Moore's poetry addresses the relationship between imagination and reality.

Present your interpretive question The introduction also presents your interpretive question about the literary work as well as your initial attempt to persuade readers that your question is an interesting and important one to answer. Rees's interpretative question asks how literary authors help us understand the relationship between imagination and reality.

Summarize possible answers to your question You can briefly summarize the different answers that other readers, including your classmates, have posed or might be likely to pose to this question. Rees, for example, reviews the three different perspectives that literary critics tend to have about reality.

Clarify your main point Keep in mind, too, that you might need to quickly summarize a main point or describe a main element of the text in order to help your readers understand the precise nature of the question that you are asking.

Include the answer you are prepared to support as your thesis The thesis statement advances a particular interpretation of the meaning of the text. Provide your thesis statement—which can be a one- or two-sentence answer to the interpretive question you have posed. You might present this answer in a statement that begins "In this essay, I argue that. . . ."

Ask yourself . . .
- How do I explain the reasons for my interpretation?
- How do I describe the significance of my interpretation?
- Have I shaped an opening that immediately engages my audience?
- Have I identified a rhetorical audience?

- **Present supporting reasons for the writer's answer to the interpretive question, usually one reason per paragraph.**
- **Strengthen the writer's appeal to logos by building toward the most interesting or persuasive reason.**
- **Include direct quotations from the literary work as evidence and support.**
- **Address others' interpretations of the text.**

Structure your analysis around the reasons for your answer Strengthen the logic of your argument (logos) by arranging your paragraphs in a pattern that moves readers progressively toward the most interesting or most persuasive of your supporting reasons.

Quote the literary work as evidence The body paragraphs provide readers with direct quotations and other supportive evidence from the literary work. Early in his analysis, Rees cites a long passage from the end of Moore's "Poetry." This quotation introduces several key terms, *literal, imagination, real,* and *genuine,* that Rees will explore as he presents his interpretation of Moore's work.

Bring in the experts Another way to support your thesis in the body paragraphs is to address other interpretations of the text. By citing other literary critics who share your perspective and those who do not, you have more credibility (ethos). Rees repeatedly cites Morton Zabel's reference to Moore's definition of the poet as a "literalist of the imagination." Conversely, you can also support your thesis by conceding or refuting alternative interpretations.

Ask yourself . . .

- How am I using assertions and textual evidence to establish my credibility, my ethos?
- How do those same features help to establish my logos?
- Which of my assertions is the most compelling? Why?
- Where have I addressed the possibility of other possible interpretations, especially those my audience may believe?
- In what ways have I established that my interpretation is the best one?

- **Explain how this analysis deepens readers' understanding.**
- **Point to related questions that could unlock additional meanings of the text.**

Situate your analysis as part of a critical conversation After providing sufficient textual evidence to support your major reasons, conclude your literary analysis by situating it within a larger conversation about the work you are analyzing. In other words, explain to readers how your answer to your interpretive question helps deepen their understanding of the entire work.

Ask yourself . . .

- How have I addressed the possibility of other interpretations?
- How have I tried to connect my interpretation with the interests of my audience?
- How assured do I want to be that mine is the best interpretation?
- What questions have I left with the audience?

MindTap® Request help and feedback from a tutor. If required, participate in peer review, submit your paper for a grade, and view instructor comments online.

Revision and Peer Review

After you have drafted a strong version of your literary analysis, ask one of your classmates to read it. You will want your classmate to respond to your work in a way that helps you revise it into the strongest analysis it can be, one that addresses your intended audience, helps you fulfill your purpose, and is delivered in the most appropriate means available to you and your audience.

Questions for a peer reviewer

1. How does the title of the analysis arouse your interest and guide your reading?
2. To what rhetorical opportunity is the writer responding? Why is it significant?
3. Where does the writer clearly state the interpretive question? How might he or she help the audience better understand—and care about—that question?
4. How does the writer establish ethos?
5. Who might comprise the writer's intended audience?
6. Identify the thesis statement, in which the writer clearly states his or her response to the interpretive question. If you cannot locate a thesis statement, what thesis statement might work for this analysis? What does the writer want the audience to do in response?
7. How is the analysis organized? Where does the writer use strong topic sentences? Which ones could be improved—and how?
8. Identify the evidence (in the form of direct quotations and other references to the text) the writer provides in support of and against the claim. In what other ways does the writer strengthen the logos of the writing?
9. How does the writer establish pathos?
10. Where do you agree and disagree with the writer's analysis?
11. What did you learn from the conclusion that you did not already know from reading the analysis? How did the writer give you a better understanding of the literary work overall?
12. Which idea or passage in the analysis is handled most successfully, and which least successfully?
13. What are two questions you have for this writer?

MindTap® Reflect on your writing process.

ADDITIONAL ASSIGNMENTS

Knowledge Transfer

Literary analyses are terrific preparation for other kinds of textual analyses, particularly those that demand understanding of the human condition.

COLLEGE History Research Paper on Nineteenth-Century America You have been assigned to research the working conditions of nineteenth-century America. To enhance your research, you read Rebecca Harding Davis's 1861 novella *Life in the Iron Mills,* which brings to life the bleak conditions of America's vulnerable workforce.

 COMMUNITY Book Club Discussion Your book club group is reading Wally Lamb's 2008 *The Hour I First Believed* to explore recent mass shootings. You have been asked to provide some background information for the book, so it is a good thing you have access to newspaper and online accounts of the Columbine massacre, the first school shooting to imprint our nation's consciousness. You and your fellow readers enhance your understanding of the motivations behind the shootings by comparing Lamb's assessment of the shootings with the nonfiction ones you are reading.

WORKPLACE Case Brief You have been charged with composing a legal brief on a current case. Your brief will consist of an analysis and synthesis of previous cases of the same kind, particularly where it comes to the precedents set by those previous cases. Your deep textual analysis of those previous cases will establish patterns of judicial action that are relevant to the current case.

 MULTIMODAL Genre Comparison You have been assigned a comparison between a book and its film adaptation. Your comparison includes links to excerpts from the film posted on YouTube either as part of a multimodal paper that is submitted digitally or as embedded video files in a PowerPoint for a class presentation.

GRAMMAR IN CONTEXT Thinking Rhetorically about Ellipses Points in Quotations

Quotations from the text you are analyzing comprise essential evidence for your interpretation. For more on formatting quotations, see Part 4 on Research (CHAPTER 18, QUOTING SOURCES). Here are some guidelines for using ellipses pages 335–337 points to indicate that material is missing from direct quotations.

. . . Ellipsis points

To indicate omitted words in a quotation Ellipsis points—three periods separated from each other as well as from adjacent words by spaces—indicate the omission of words from quoted sentences. An omission may occur within a quoted sentence or at the end of a quoted sentence. The examples of the use of ellipsis points that follow are based on this excerpt.

> **Within months of their 1st birthday, most kids start attaching names to things. And whether they're learning Swahili or Swedish, they go about it in much the same way. Instead of proceeding by trial and error—unsure whether "doggie" refers to a part of a dog, to one dog in particular, or to anything with four legs—children start with a set of innate biases. They assume that labels refer to wholes instead of parts (the creature, not the tail) and to classes instead of items (all dogs, not one dog). They also figure that one name is for any class of object (if it's a dog, it's not a cow). These assumptions are not always valid—there's only one Lassie, after all, and any dog qualifies as a mammal—but they enable kids to catalog new words with breathtaking efficiency. A typical child is socking away a dozen words a day by 18 months, and may command 2,000 of them by the age of 2.**
>
> **—Geoffrey Cowley, "For the Love of Language"**

Within a quoted sentence

> **According to Geoffrey Cowley, "Instead of proceeding by trial and error . . . children start with a set of innate biases."**

End of a quoted sentence Ellipsis points that replace words at the end of a sentence must be followed by an end punctuation mark (a period, a question mark, or an exclamation point).

> **According to Geoffrey Cowley, "A typical child is socking away a dozen words a day by 18 months . . . ."**

Beginning of a quoted sentence No ellipsis points are needed to indicate an omission at the beginning of a sentence.

> **According to Geoffrey Cowley, children learn "a dozen words a day by 18 months, and may command 2,000 of them by the age of 2."**

Omission of a sentence or more For an omission of a sentence or more, the ellipsis points should follow the end punctuation of the preceding sentence.

Geoffrey Cowley explains how young children learn language:

> **Within months of their 1st birthday, most kids start attaching names to things. . . . They assume that labels refer to wholes instead of parts (the creature, not the tail) and to classes instead of items (all dogs, not one dog). They also figure that one name is for any class of object (if it's a dog, it's not a cow). These assumptions are not always valid—there's only one Lassie, after all, and any dog qualifies as a mammal—but they enable kids to catalog new words with breathtaking efficiency. A typical child is socking away a dozen words a day by 18 months, and may command 2,000 of them by the age of 2.**

MindTap® Find additional handbook coverage of grammar, punctuation, and style online.

istockphoto.com/mattjeacock

From Tentative Idea to Finished Project

MindTap®   Understand the goals of the chapter and complete a warm-up activity online.

In this chapter, you will move through the three general steps of the writing process: planning, drafting, and revising. These steps are the same whether you are working online or off. As you read about each of these steps, you will learn when to consider the components of the rhetorical situation (components that include a problem, an opportunity for change (*exigence*), and a purpose, message, audience, genre, and medium of delivery) and when to set those components aside and just write. Eventually, all writers find a writing process that works for them, whether it is spending a lot of time up front on planning or drafting first and then going back to tease out the main points. The process can seem very private, but actually when we write we connect socially—as the following infographic shows—to a larger community of writers who have struggles and successes similar to our own.

PLANNING A RESPONSE

Experienced writers employ a variety of methods for exploring a topic or inventing things to say about it. The problem you have identified establishes your starting point; it is the opportunity for change that prompts you to use words to address an issue.

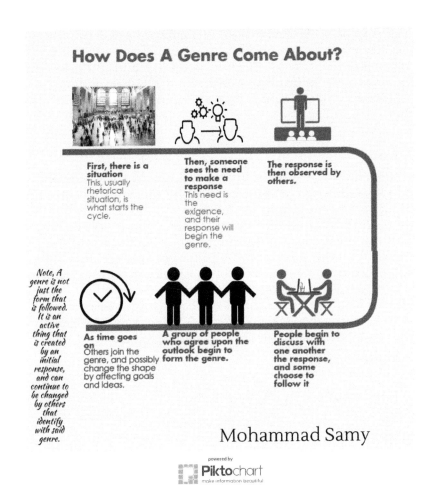

How Does A Genre Come About?

First, there is a situation
This, usually rhetorical situation, is what starts the cycle.

Then, someone sees the need to make a response
This need is the exigence, and their response will begin the genre.

The response is then observed by others.

Note, A genre is not just the form that is followed. It is an active thing that is created by an initial response, and can continue to be changed by others that identify with said genre.

As time goes on
Others join the genre, and possibly change the shape by affecting goals and ideas.

A group of people who agree upon the outlook begin to form the genre.

People begin to discuss with one another the response, and some choose to follow it

Mohammad Samy

powered by
Piktochart
make information beautiful

Mohammad Samy, a first-year student at the University of Central Florida, created this rhetorical infographic for his writing class. Exigence is another word for change.

Exploration

The most commonly used methods of exploration (also known as *invention strategies*) are listing, freewriting, questioning, and keeping a journal. But experienced writers also regularly use conversation, meditation, reading, and listening as ways to discover good ideas. They realize that good ideas come to them in all sorts of ways, so they keep a pen and a notebook with them all the time, even at night, because ideas often come just as they are falling asleep. They grab the notebook, scribble down their idea, and sleep soundly, no longer worried that they will forget the idea.

As you plan your college writing assignments, you will probably continue to rely on the methods that have worked for you in the past. When you are stuck, however, you may want to try out a new method, if only as a way to jump-start your writing.

Listing

As soon as you have some idea of what you are expected to write about, start a list of possibilities—and keep adding to it. These are the kinds of lists that can spark your thinking and writing.

On the first day of the semester, when her professor reviewed the syllabus for the course Writing and Technology, Stacy Simkanin learned about the requirements for her first essay. So, during the first week of classes, she started **listing**—jotting down some tentative ideas, knowing that, as time went by, she would keep adding possibilities for her formal essay. You can follow Simkanin's example and keep your list going for a few days. Or you can jot down all your ideas at one sitting, a kind of listing often referred to as **brainstorming**. What follows is the list Simkanin made and kept adding to.

computers	web searches	downloadable essays
chat rooms	Statistical Universe	forum discussions
visual culture class	plagiarism	electronic requests
photo essays	convenience	Internet
quality	online databases	time saver
constantly developing	online course notes	Google
full-length journal	classroom computers	
articles	social networking	

Freewriting

Freewriting means just what it says: it is the writing you do that costs you nothing. You do not have to worry about spelling or grammar; you do not even have to worry about writing complete sentences, because no one is going to grade it. In fact, no one (except you) may ever even read it. It is the kind of writing you do to loosen up your thinking and your fingers; it is the kind of no-pressure writing that can yield an explosion of ideas.

When Simkanin's teacher asked everyone in class to write for five minutes about the connection between technology and their college success, Simkanin wrote the following:

Spanish 3: used chat room discussion.

English 202: used chat room discussion to analyze Internet communication as it relates to literacy.

English 202 and Phil 197: used ANGEL's online forums.

Being an English major, I tend to see the biggest advantages of modern technology as those that have most helped my writing. My courses require hours of writing from me each week, and I know that, without access to all the online resources that have been available to me, the amount of time I have to spend working on a paper would probably double. For instance, technology helps me write a research paper before I've even typed the first word, because I can research my topic so much faster by first consulting the online catalogues, instead of going to the library and getting lost in the stacks. If there is material I need that this library doesn't have, I simply have it sent to me through interlibrary loan. Then, when I actually start writing, the process is made easier through referencing certain websites that I can't live without. And once I'm finished writing my paper, I can choose from plenty of web pages designed to show the proper way to cite any resources I've used. Of course, there are also some things that students get from the Internet that they'd be better to stay away from, such as downloadable essays and book notes that help you skip out of actually reading a text. With technology being so accessible, so fast, so convenient, so easy to use, so full of information, etc., it can be hard to make sure you don't rely on it too much. For instance, I don't think it's a good idea to always use information from the Internet as a replacement for going to the library, because sometimes I've found that the perfect resource for a paper I'm writing is sitting on a shelf in the university library. I think the best way for students to make use of modern advances is to draw on them to help build their own ideas and abilities, and not use them as a means of avoiding any real work.

Notice how Simkanin starts with a list of some courses that used technology. She does not seem to be heading in any one direction. Then suddenly she is off and running about how the use of technology affects her life as an English major.

Questioning

Sometimes when you are in a conversation, someone will ask you a question that takes you by surprise—and forces you to rethink your position or think

questioning
structured
speculation
used to
explore a
topic in a new
way

**journalists'
questions**
Who? What?
Where?
When? Why?
How?

about the topic in a new way. By using structured **questioning**, you can push yourself to explore your topic more deeply.

You are probably already familiar with the **journalists' questions**, which can readily serve your purpose: *Who? What? Where? When? Why? How?* As Simkanin answered these questions, she began to form an opinion about her topic.

Who is using technology? Teachers, students, librarians—everyone on campus, it seems. But I'm going to talk about how it affects me.

What technology is being used, and what is it being used for? All kinds of technology, from e-mail and web searches to PowerPoint presentations and voice mail, is being used, for instruction, homework, student-to-student communication, student-and-teacher communication, and research. I'm going to concentrate on my use of computer technology, mostly access to the Internet.

Where is technology being used? At the library, in the classroom, but most often in my bedroom, where my computer is.

When is technology being used? Usually at night, after I come home from classes and am doing my homework.

Why do students use or not use technology? I use it because it's more convenient than walking over to the library and searching. Not all students have Internet access in their apartments; others may not know all the online research techniques that I know.

How are students using it? Some students are using it to advance their education; others are using it to subvert it (like downloading essays and cheating schemes).

Keeping a journal

Some writing instructors expect you to keep a weekly journal, either in print or online. When you are writing in your journal, you do not need to be concerned with punctuation, grammar, spelling, and other mechanical features. If you write three pages a week for a journal or as part of your online class discussion, you may not be able to lift a ready-to-submit essay directly from your work, but you will have accumulated a pool of ideas from which to draw. Even more important, you will have been practicing getting thoughts into words.

journal a private
record of your
understandings and
reactions to reading,
assignments, class
discussion, and
lectures

In addition to using journal entries as a way to explore your topic, you might also use your **journal** to write out your understandings of and reactions to your reading and writing assignments and class discussions and lectures. As Simkanin considered her own upcoming assignment, she wrote in her ongoing electronic journal:

> I think I tend to take modern advances for granted, but when I look at how much more I use technology as a college student than I did, say, eight years ago as a junior high student, it's amazing to think of how much my studies have become dependent on it. I need computer access for almost everything anymore, from writing papers to updating my Facebook status, to doing research on the web. Not only that, but some of my favorite classes have been those that incorporated some form of technology into the course format. I think this is one of technology's major advantages—turning learning into something new and interactive, which gets students involved. I've had courses that used technology in basic ways, like my Biological Science class, in which the class lectures were recorded and saved online for students to listen to later. Some of my other courses, though, have used it in lots of interesting ways. In one of my English classes, for instance, we took a day to hold class in a chat room, and we all logged into the room from our computers at home. It was great as part of our discussions about literacy, because experimenting with computer literacy allowed us all to see how people communicate differently when they're not face to face. Of course, some people would argue that kids my age spend way too much time "chatting" and texting and that instant messaging is one of a student's biggest distracters. I guess, like any good thing, technology also carries with it some disadvantages.

The double-entry notebook

Whether you keep your notes in a notebook, on separate note cards or pieces of paper, or on your laptop, you can choose among various ways of recording what you observe and your responses. A **double-entry notebook** is a journal that has two distinct parts: observational details and personal response to those details. The double-entry notebook thus allows you to explore your observations separately from your responses (including biases and preferences) toward what you observe. In addition, it encourages you to push your observations further, with responses to and questions about what you see or think you see. Some writers draw a heavy line down the middle of each page of the notebook, putting "Observations" at the top of the left-hand side of the page and "Response" at the top of the right-hand side. Others lay the notebook flat and use the right-hand page for recording their observations and the left-hand page

double-entry notebook a journal with two distinct columns pairing observation and personal response

for responding to those observations. If you are using a computer, you can format your entries the way Simkanin did:

Observations	Response
My classmates and I rely on technology for our classes and our social lives—and for our personal lives as well. We rarely write anything. We type our to-do lists, our homework assignments, our communications to one another. We don't go anywhere without our phones, not even to the gym. I look at my e-mail messages while I'm walking on the treadmill, and my best friend does her e-mail while she works out on the stairmaster machine. We sleep with our phones nearby, and we always check our messages during meals and during class. We all take carry our computers in our backpacks so we can take class notes on our computers.	I just realized that my friends and I take technology for granted, to the point that it's almost invisible to us. We refer to things as "technology" or say that we're having "technological problems" only when we're still figuring out how to use them—not when we're already good at them, like with our cell phones. When I decided to pay closer attention to how we all take notes in class, I realized that many of us sneak away from our notes and answer e-mails, check Facebook, even shop. Yep, I've done most of my Christmas shopping online and during class. When I say that I use technology more now than I did as a junior high student, I have to admit that the notes I took in class back then were probably better than the ones I think I'm taking now.

After trying several methods of exploration (listing, freewriting, keeping a journal, and using a double-entry notebook), Simkanin found that she was starting to repeat herself. She did not yet have a point she wanted to make, let alone a controlling idea for her essay or a thesis. (See Crafting a Working Thesis Statement on page 246.) She needed to try a new tack.

Organization

Once you have explored your topic as thoroughly as you can, it is time to begin organizing your essay. Two simple methods can help you get started: clustering and outlining.

clustering a method using arrows, circles, lines, or other visual cues for connecting ideas

Clustering

Clustering is a visual method for connecting ideas that go together. You might start with words and phrases from a list you compiled or brainstormed and link

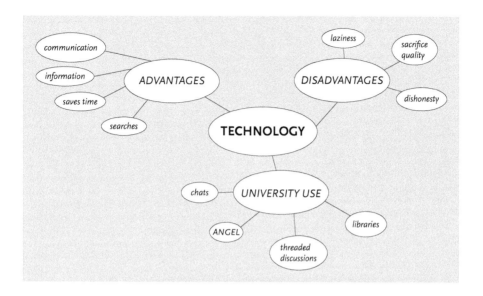

them with arrows, circles, or lines, the way Simkanin did. Notice how Simkanin used different sizes of type to accentuate the connections she wanted to make between technology and learning. (You might want to use color as well to help you make connections.) Interestingly, Simkanin has not yet put herself into her essay's plan.

Outlining

An **outline** establishes the limits of your topic at the same time as it lists the main parts. Outlining is a good way to plan, but only if you think of the result as a rough—not formal or final—outline. You will want to allow yourself to add and delete points and move things around so that outlining, like clustering, helps you visualize how things relate to one another. Simkanin's outline shows a close relationship to her clustering, but she has added details and a general title.

> **outline** a structure that lists the main parts and supporting points of an essay

Notice that Simkanin started out using Roman numerals for her main sections, but she switched to simply listing subpoints, thereby making her outline easier to put together and work with. As she was constructing her outline, Simkanin began thinking about methods of developing her paper that would be best suited to her purpose. (See CHAPTER 14, RHETORICAL METHODS OF DEVELOPMENT.) She also began thinking of what her thesis statement might be.

> pages 262–278

Technology and Learning

I. Advantages

    Information

        fast and convenient

        online catalogues

        eBay's First Edition or Rare Books page

        Google Books

        online concordances

        databases

    Communication

        ANGEL

        online forums

        new forms of interaction

        chat rooms

II. Disadvantages

    Academic laziness

        ignore traditional forms of research

        quality vs. convenience

        lose the value of a trip to the library

    Dishonesty

        free online book notes

        downloadable essays

        plagiarism

Crafting a Working Thesis Statement

The most important step to take as you begin to prepare your first draft is to write toward a thesis statement, an explicit declaration (usually in one sentence) of the main assertion or claim. (See CHAPTER 2, MAKING CLAIMS.) Your thesis statement will identify your topic and your stand on that topic. By forming a **working thesis**, you can test a possible framework for your response to an opportunity for change. Keep in mind that once you have drafted your thesis statement, you may need to adjust it. A working thesis lets you test your thesis

page 20

working thesis a statement that tests a possible framework and controlling idea for your paper as you try to support it in the body of your paper. Do not be concerned if you change your mind; writers often do. Writing a thesis is just a starting point in the drafting process.

Earlier in this chapter, a thesis was defined as a controlling idea. Chapter 2 stressed that your thesis anchored your response and helped the audience understand your position. More specifically, a thesis statement is a central idea stated in the form of an assertion, or claim, that indicates what you believe to be true, interesting, or valuable about your topic. The most important step to take as you begin to prepare your first draft is to write your thesis. Your thesis statement gives readers a clear idea of your purpose in writing, and it sometimes outlines the approach you will take. If you started the writing process with a question, now is the time to answer that question. Although it is often phrased as a single sentence, it does not need to be. Here is Simkanin's first attempt at a thesis statement:

> Technology provides many advantages for students and teachers alike, but it also brings with it some disadvantages. In this essay, I'm going to talk about my experiences with technology, the advantages I've experienced and the disadvantages I feel.

Simkanin identified her topic—use of technology by students and teachers—and forecast that she would be talking about both advantages and disadvantages.

DRAFTING A RESPONSE

After you have explored your topic, you will begin drafting. While some writers find the first draft the toughest part of the process, many others derive great pleasure from the two-step drafting process: drafting and evaluating. The joy of putting words together is exhilarating for many writers; in **drafting** they enjoy the freedom of combining an informal outline with a freewrite as they work to attend to all the elements of the rhetorical situation, including audience, purpose, genre, medium of delivery, and the opportunity for change that motivated you to write in the first place. A first draft is just that—words you will revisit again and again as you adjust your message to take into account all the elements in your rhetorical situation.

drafting a process that combines an informal structure with a freewrite

Some writers do not write the introduction and conclusion until they have drafted the body of the paper. Others use a loose introduction, body, conclusion structure to organize their draft. Most **introductions** will include your thesis. Simkanin also establishes her credentials for writing about this topic by

introduction the opening of your paper, often including your thesis and establishing your credibility on your topic

body an exploration of your topic that builds a logi-cal structure to support your thesis

conclusion a final appeal to your audi-ence by mak-ing clear how the issue you are exploring affects them

introducing her experience. In the first draft that follows, she goes on to draft the **body** of her paper, where she links ideas about her topic that explore the implications of her thesis. In a first draft it is most important to get your words onto the page (screen) and explore your topic with broad brushstrokes. Tran-sitional phrases and words can help to connect your ideas. In this part of your composition you point out the logic of the claim in your thesis and bring in supporting evidence, which can be fleshed out more fully when you revise. In your **conclusion**, a final appeal to your audience reveals or reinforces how the topic of your paper affects them or has larger implications.

COMMON TRANSITIONAL WORDS AND PHRASES

above all	for instance	in sum
also	however	on the contrary
as a result	in addition	on the one hand/other hand
at any rate	in contrast	then
at first	in fact	therefore
besides	in other words	thus
for example	instead	

When you are drafting, you will be considering your intended audience as well, particularly in terms of what you are hoping your audience can do to address (or help you address) the opportunity for change that sparked your writing in the first place. The following list may help you as you reconsider audience:

- Who can resolve the opportunity for change (or the problem) that you have identified?
- What exactly might that audience do to address, resolve, or help resolve it?
- What opportunities (if any) are there for you to receive feedback from that audience?

Answers to these questions will help you tie your purpose to your particular audience.

By thinking of her assignment as a rhetorical situation, Simkanin devel-oped a better idea of how to approach her draft. When an instructor does not write out an assignment, you should feel free to ask him or her to explain it in terms of the rhetorical situation—that is, ask your instructor specific questions about purpose, audience (or receiver), context, and constraints.

Here is Simkanin's first draft.

Technology for teaching and learning is especially strong here at State. It provides many advantages for students and teachers alike, but it also brings with it some disadvantages. In this essay, I'm going to talk about my experiences with technology, the advantages I've experienced and the disadvantages I feel. I'll draw upon my experiences in Spanish 3, English 202, Philosophy 197, Biological Sciences, Art History, and my internship.

Technology is rapidly becoming increasingly advanced, and much of it is used to enhance learning and writing. Not only does it increase the amount of information available, but it allows for stronger writing. I can search libraries around the world, use eBay to find rare manuscripts, use interlibrary loan, and file electronic requests for needed items.

Technology also makes the writing process faster, more convenient. I often access online concordances, view library books on my PC, e-mail librarians, and read full-text journal articles online. This technology is also allowing for more ways to develop ideas and new forms of written communication. For instance, I'm now experienced with chat room communication, forum discussions, and photo essays.

But at the same time that technology brings these advantages, it also inhibits learning and writing. I know that when I'm conducting online research I may be missing out on information or lowering the quality of information because I'm limiting my searching to electronic sources. Nowadays, students don't really have to learn to use the library, where often more information can be found than what appears in an online search. I fear that students are placing convenience over quality. I know I do sometimes. The information online isn't always reliable, either. Students don't often take the time to investigate sources.

For these reasons, campus technology may be promoting academic laziness in some students, and dishonesty as well. So much information is available that you can practically write a book report without ever reading the book. And online papers make plagiarism easy. In conclusion . . .

Simkanin's first draft has begun to address the components of the rhetorical situation: she understands that she needs to talk about her own experiences with technology and describe the technology that she uses. In getting her thoughts down, she is beginning to sketch out an organizational structure that starts with the advantages of this technology and ends with the disadvantages. She has made certain to add that some students take advantage of technology only in a way that cheapens their learning experience. Notice that she has not begun to shape a strong thesis yet, let alone a conclusion. Still, she is ready to begin revising.

REVISING A RESPONSE

revision a
process of
rethinking and
rewriting
parts of your
draft

Revision means evaluating and rethinking your writing in terms of the rhetorical situation. Writers use several techniques during revision. Some put the draft aside for twenty-four hours or more in order to return to it with fresh ideas and a more objective viewpoint. Others like to print out the draft and actually cut it into different sections so that they can experiment with organization.

TIPS FOR REVISION

- Identify the specific feature of your topic that best opens up a rhetorical opportunity—a problem your words might resolve or address.
- Finalize your claim about that specific feature so that your thesis statement includes the topic and your assertion about it.
- Mark the passages in your draft that best match your thesis.
- Adjust unmarked passages or your thesis accordingly.
- Establish how your introduction orients your readers to the purpose of your essay as well as engages them.
- Identify the topic sentence in each paragraph to determine how it supports or advances your thesis statement. Adjust accordingly.
- Relate each sentence in a paragraph to that topic sentence, eliminating or revising those that do not.
- If a paragraph conveys more than one idea, either revise the topic sentence to accommodate the ideas or split the single paragraph.
- Establish how your conclusion emphasizes significant points in your essay as well as wraps it up in a meaningful, thought-provoking way.

PEER EVALUATION

One of the most popular—and most effective—revision techniques is peer evaluation.

peer evaluation
a form of collaboration that provides
writing advice from
fellow students

   Peer evaluation is a form of collaboration that provides productive advice and a response from a fellow student writer. If the thought of letting a peer (a classmate or friend) read your first draft makes you uncomfortable, if you have tried peer evaluation before and it did not work, or if you are worried that you will not receive good advice, please reconsider. All effective writing is the result of some measure of collaboration, whether between colleagues, editors and writers, publishers and writers, actors and writers, students and teachers, or friends. Just consider for a moment all the writing you read, hear, and see

Processes

every day—newspapers, magazines, online chat, billboards, commercials, sit-coms, newscasts. A great majority of the words that you experience daily come to you as a result of collaboration and peer evaluation. Every day, experienced writers are showing their first drafts to someone else in order to get another point of view, piece of advice, or evaluation.

Peer evaluation is a valuable step in the writing process that you, too, will want to experience. No matter how good a writer you are, you will benefit from hearing what one or more real readers has to say about your message. They may ask you questions that prompt you to clarify points you want to make, nudge you to provide more examples so that your prose comes alive, or point out attention-getting passages. When you respond to a peer's first draft, you are not only helping that writer but also strengthening your own skills as a reader and writer. As you discover strengths and weaknesses in someone else's writing, you also improve your ability to find them in your own. Most important, the success-ful writing of a peer will energize your own writing in ways that the successful writing of a professional might not. A peer can show you how attainable good writing can be.

Although it is sometimes helpful to get pointers on things like grammar and word choice, you will usually want a peer reviewer to focus first on how well your draft responds to your rhetorical situation. The following set of ten questions can help guide a peer reviewer:

Peer evaluation questions

1. What opportunity for change (or problem) sparked this essay?
2. What is the topic of this essay? What is the main idea the writer wants to convey about this topic?
3. What can you tell about the writer of this essay? What is his or her relation-ship to this topic?
4. Who is the audience? What information in the essay reveals the audience to you? What do you imagine are the needs and concerns of this audience? What might this audience do to address, resolve, or help resolve this problem?
5. What seems to be the relationship between the writer and the audience? How is the writer meeting the needs and concerns of this audience? What specific passages demonstrate the writer's use of the rhetorical appeals (ethos, pathos, and logos)?
6. What is the purpose of the writer's message? What is the relationship among the writer, the audience, and the writer's purpose? Do you have any other comments about the purpose?
7. What means is the writer using to deliver this message? How is this means appropriate to the situation?

8. What constraints are on the writer and this message?
9. What idea or passage in the essay is handled most successfully? Least successfully?
10. What are two questions you have for this writer?

These questions can be answered fairly quickly. Although you might be tempted to have your peer reviewer go through them quickly and orally, you will be better served if you ask the peer reviewer to write his or her answers either on a separate piece of paper or directly on your draft. When it is your turn to evaluate a peer's draft, you may well come away from the experience surprised at how much you learned about your own writing. There is no better way to improve your own understanding than to explain something to someone else.

The peer reviewer of Simkanin's paper offered her a good deal of advice, most of which had to do with large-scale revising, as you can see from his responses to questions 6 and 9:

6. I cannot tell for sure what your purpose is in writing this essay. You describe technology, but I'm not sure why. Do you want to explain the opportunities, or do you want to show how bad it can be for students? And I cannot tell who you're writing to—maybe just any reader? Still, I think you have a good start on a strong essay because you know so much neat stuff about all the technology here at school. I didn't know half this stuff.

9. The beginning of your essay is the least successful part; I can't tell by reading it where you're headed with your topic, so I think you're going to want to revise with a stronger purpose in mind. But as I said earlier, the strongest part of your essay is all the specific information you already know about using technology. No wonder you get such good grades. You don't have any conclusion yet. I think if you get a better start on your introduction then you can pull together your overall argument in your conclusion. Maybe talk about how technology is always thought of as being better, an improvement, but that it's not always, not really.

The peer reviewer confirmed what Simkanin already thought: the introduction of the essay, especially the thesis statement, merited more of her attention. Her peer reviewer, though, was unclear about what Simkanin's purpose was. So, as she revised, Simkanin focused down on the connection between her purpose and audience as she created a thesis statement that narrowed her topic and made a comment on that topic.

Therefore, Simkanin drafted her initial general, ho-hum overview of the advantages and disadvantages of using technology at State (an introduction aimed at and engaging no one, in particular) into a vibrant introductory paragraph, opening with a provocative question, aimed at an audience interested in the educational advantages of technology, and featuring a specific thesis statement:

> Could today's college student survive without a microwave to heat Easy Mac in her dorm room, a smartphone to check in on Facebook friends, and a laptop streaming movies or music to escape the tedium of another evening spent doing coursework? The answer is debatable. What's not debatable, however, is that **even though technology of various forms has brought a certain ease to the lives of today's college students, it has also allowed them to embark on serious academic pursuits that would not be possible without technological innovation.**

EDITING AND PROOFREADING A RESPONSE

Although the peer reviewer focused on Simkanin's approach to the rhetorical situation, other evaluative responses had to do with smaller issues related to **editing**: improving word choice, adding specific details, and structuring sentences more effectively. Some writers revise, edit, and proofread simultaneously, while others focus their efforts on resolving the big issues (thesis statement, organization, and supporting information) before tackling editing and **proofreading**.

> **editing** improving word choice, adding details, and structuring sentences more effectively

> **proofreading** checking for spelling, typos, grammar, and punctuation errors

After the peer reviewer finished responding to Simkanin's essay (and she to his), Simkanin took his advice, wrote two more drafts, and edited and proofread her way to her final draft. Like most writers, Simkanin stopped revising because she had run out of time—not because she thought her essay was perfect in every way.

DESIGNING THE FINAL DRAFT

Document design within an academic context often means following the style guidelines of the disciplines, such as those published by the Modern Language Association for papers in the humanities or the American Psychological Association for papers in the social sciences. (See CHAPTER 19, ACKNOWLEDGING SOURCES IN MLA STYLE and CHAPTER 20, ACKNOWLEDGING SOURCES IN APA STYLE.)

> pages 338–375 and 376–402

When you submit your report, essay, or manuscript, then, you respect the formatting, style, and design of that academic discipline. In college, such design concerns usually include a title page or header, margins, line spacing, font style and size, works-cited page, and other formatting issues. Simkanin's final draft appears on the following pages. She formatted her paper according to Modern Language Association (MLA) guidelines.

Anastasia Simkanin

Professor Glenn

Writing and Technology, English 270

22 October 2015

Technology and the Learning Process: One Student's View

Could today's college student survive without a microwave to heat Easy Mac in her dorm room, a smartphone to check in on Facebook friends, and a laptop streaming movies or music to escape the tedium of another evening spent doing coursework? The answer is debatable. What's *not* debatable, however, is that even though technology of various forms has brought a certain ease to the lives of today's college students, it has also allowed them to embark on serious academic pursuits that would not be possible without technological innovation.

The thesis statement presents Simkanin's position on the topic.

The Internet, for instance, offers students a wealth of advanced search engines and online library databases. Many students find that such tools open up a world of information, allowing more expedient research and, in turn, stronger essays. But some people argue that the ease of computer searching and the availability of almost anything over the Internet expose students to the dangers of academic laziness and dishonesty. Which side is right? The incorporation of technology into the learning process is a complex matter and, like any powerful innovation, brings potential pitfalls as well as advantages. Perhaps the best way to approach both sides of the issue is to draw a clear picture of the pros and the cons, thereby assessing the different ways that technology has revolutionized learning in today's universities.

One major way that technological advances have facilitated the learning process is by supplying students with a wealth of information that could not be obtained without Internet resources. Online catalogues such as *WorldCat*, for instance, allow users to search libraries anywhere in the world for books, articles, and more in a single step. *Borrow Direct* allows students to simultaneously search all Ivy League university libraries, and the University Library (sponsored by the Committee on Institutional Cooperation) allows the same type of search within Big Ten schools. Alternatively, students can opt to go to a specific library website, such as the online catalogue of Oxford University libraries, and begin their search there. With such a vast array of resources available, only very rarely is a student unable to find pertinent information. Having located a needed item, a student can file an electronic request through interlibrary loan and have the item delivered to a convenient location or even made available as a PDF download. A student in the United States who needs a rare manuscript held at the University of Cambridge in England can view important pages online. Whereas once students' research was limited

Simkanin forecasts her approach, which involves looking at both pros and cons of the use of technology, and also clarifies her purpose: to assess technology's effect on learning.

This is one of the places where Simkanin responds to the peer reviewer's suggestion by including specific details about using resources.

Processes

to the resources in their own neighborhood, technology now allows them access to information in libraries across the Atlantic.

Not only does the Internet allow users to find information that is hard to obtain because it is held in distant locations, but it also allows them access to information that is hard to obtain for a variety of other reasons. On those rare occasions when students are unable to find a needed item by searching library catalogues, they can look on sites such as eBay's *First Edition* and *Rare Books* and possibly locate a volume that is to be found only in someone's living room.

Besides searching *for* books, searching *through* them has been aided by technology as well. Writing a paper on *Great Expectations* and want to find the exact passage where Pip admits that Biddy is "immeasurably better than Estella"? Web resources such as the *Concordance of Great Books* allow users to type in a word or phrase and instantly see all the occurrences of those words in a book, along with the surrounding text and chapter numbers. *Google Book Search* and *Hathi Trust Digital Library* let users search for keywords and phrases within millions of books without any more effort than it takes to Google their topic. The above quotation, by the way, is found in chapter 17 of the Penguin edition.

Even with all the time it can save a student, the average dot-com site is not necessarily the top rung of the ladder of searching expediency.

This transition sentence links this paragraph to the preceding one.

Processes

Today's students can easily write stronger, more persuasive papers by taking advantage of the information that online databases place at their fingertips. Compare, for instance, the effectiveness of saying "State University conferred many doctoral degrees in 2009" with the effectiveness of saying "State University conferred 513 doctoral degrees in 2009." Including statistics in their papers can make students' points sharper and more vivid, and databases such as *Historical Statistics of the United States* allow students to achieve this result. Other databases, such as *JSTOR* and *MUSE*, let students sort through full-length journal articles simply by moving their mouse. With libraries containing thousands of volumes of journals and periodicals, the amount of time saved through computer searches is immense. And, of course, consulting a database is a lot faster than surveying the 6,165 graduate students who were enrolled at State University in 2009.

Simkanin includes another specific detail that makes the essay more persuasive.

Not only is technology improving traditional methods of research and writing, it is also providing students with new ways to communicate and develop ideas. State University's *ANGEL* site is designed to give professors and students online space for managing their courses. By accessing *ANGEL*, students can click on the link for a course and view daily reminders, weekly assignments, selected lecture notes, and more. A favorite feature of *ANGEL* is its threaded discussion board. Online forums and live (online) office hours allow students and instructors to carry on the one-on-one discussion that is precluded by large class sizes and limited lecture time. In another step toward moving course discussion beyond the classroom setting, some instructors at State University—especially those who teach language classes—have experimented with "holding class" in a chat room. Online chats allow students to carry on multiple conversations at once, which gives them more opportunities to share and develop ideas. The fact that most students enjoy chat room discussion is an added bonus, as the appeal of something new and fun can go a long way in keeping students interested and eager to learn.

Given all the ways that technology is changing life for students, it is not surprising that some of the effects are less welcome than others. One possible pitfall of relying on technology is that, ironically, ignoring more traditional ways of research can sometimes reduce information—or at least information quality. Searching a library's database from home while a stereo plays in the background is more appealing to most students than taking a trip to the stacks, but what many students do not realize is that, though online catalogues are a great place to start, they are often not enough by themselves. Finding the approximate spot where a needed item is located and then looking through items on adjacent shelves or discussing resources with a reference librarian will almost always turn up more results than does an online catalogue search alone. When it comes to finding that approximate location, however, the catalogues are indeed the place to begin. The danger lies in placing convenience over quality. What many students find to be most convenient is conducting a simple online search using an engine like *Google*, but this method has its own set of problems. Anyone can create a page on the Internet: for example, my fourteen-year-old brother could post his middle school paper on how Jane Eyre's inheritance reveals Charlotte Brontë's secret obsession with the power of money. Would such a paper help a college student write a sophomore-level essay? Probably not. Being lured by the convenience of Web searches, students can sometimes forget to investigate the reliability of sources, thus compromising the quality of their work.

Perhaps the most serious dangers of depending too much on technology are the possibilities of academic laziness and dishonesty. There is *so* much information available online that a student can practically write a paper on a book without even opening it. Sites like *SparkNotes* are great when a student is running late for class and needs to quickly find out what happens in a particular chapter of a text or needs to refresh his or her memory of something read earlier, but a student will never get as much out of summary notes as out of reading the book. With free online literature notes replacing $5.99-a-copy *Cliffs Notes*, however, the temptation to skip out on one's assignments is becoming all the more pervasive.

More serious than simply consulting summary notes is another danger: plagiarism. Not only are notes on books available online, but so are entire essays on them. Whole sites are devoted to selling papers to students who are looking to avoid writing an essay themselves, and papers are sometimes available for free. Every college student knows the feeling of sitting at a computer screen late at night, trying to write a paper but having little success because of fatigue. Times like these are when the temptation to abuse technology arises, and a student might simply download someone else's essay, hand it in as her or his own, and get some sleep. While having an abundance of information available is usually a wonderful thing, today's college students need to be wary of letting technology do their work *for* them, rather than just helping them with it.

Because technology affects the learning process in so many ways, it cannot be judged as wholly positive or wholly negative. Perhaps it would not be fair to say either but to agree, instead, that though the value of Web content depends on how one uses it, the dramatic changes that have been brought on by recent advances are amazing. Technology is changing the way students learn and the way they write.

Visual Culture, a 400-level English course at State University,
encourages students to "write" essays in new ways, using images
instead of words. •Many students choose to obtain their images off the
Internet or to present their visual essay in the form of a PowerPoint
presentation or YouTube video. With "writing an essay" no longer
requiring actual *writing*, there's little—if any—room to doubt that
education today is being constantly shaped and molded as technology
continues to progress. It will be interesting to see what the future
brings.

············Closing the essay
with a focus
on a course at
her school
demonstrates
Simkanin's
awareness of her
audience—her
instructor.

Reflect upon the information in this chapter, particularly the passage on
Simkanin's writing process, and describe two specific ways in which you could
improve your own writing process. Be prepared to share your answer with the
rest of the class.

MindTap® Reflect on your writing process.

Rhetorical Methods of Development

MindTap® Understand the goals of the chapter and complete a warm-up activity online.

Narration, description, exemplification, definition, classification and division, comparison and contrast, cause-and-effect analysis, process analysis, argument—these rhetorical methods of development are strategies employed to explore, expand, and organize ideas. They are also the way we make sense of the world, no matter what media or genre we are using. Regardless of culture, nationality, gender, age, and ability, we all turn to these methods to find what we want to say and to situate it in a context. We also employ these methods as templates for interpreting what someone else is communicating to us. Each of these methods can stand alone, but more often they complement one another. When we use the method of *comparison*, for instance, we often need to *define* what exactly we are comparing.

narration a detailed account of events as in a story

characters people in the story

dialogue direct speech by the characters in a narration

setting the time and place of a narration

plot the sequence of events in a narration

 NARRATION

One of the rhetorical methods for development that you already know well is **narration**, which tells a story that has **characters** (people in the story), **dialogue** (direct speech by the characters), a **setting** (the time and place), description (selected sensory and sensibility details about the characters, dialogue, and setting—see also Description, discussed on page 264), and **plot** (the sequence of events). Narrations help us make sense of the world for ourselves and for others—whether we are retelling a fairy tale or family legend or recounting the final minutes of the Super Bowl or our canyon-bottom tour of Canyon de Chelly (pictured at right).

Narration can frame an entire story ("Robin Hood" or the first Thanksgiving), or it can provide an example (why you can depend on your brother) or support an

Strategies

argument (those final plays proved the Steelers to be the better team). Usually narrations are verbal—we want to tell "what happened." Verbal narration, which appears in newspapers, in movies, and in reports on television and radio, tells us, for example, about University of California students protesting tuition hikes, the latest child-abduction tragedy, the president's travels to the Middle East, a murder mystery or police procedural, a girl who has been sneezing for two weeks, obituaries, and the local school board meeting. Such verbal narrations might consist of one particular sequence of events or include a series of separate incidents that shape an overall narrative.

Were you to compose a narration about the photograph of the jeep and floodwater at Canyon de Chelly, what might it be? Would your narration account for your entire vacation, beginning when you left home, or might you concentrate only on the canyon-bottom tour? In addition to tapping all the elements of a narration (characters, dialogue, setting, description, and plot), would you also use an **anecdote** (a brief, illustrative story that propels the narrative)? From what **point of view** would you tell the story? (For more on point of view, see CHAPTER 12, BOX ON ELEMENTS OF LITERATURE.) Your own, that of the Navajo guide, your parents' perspective, or that of your sibling? And what might be the **climax** of your narration, the turning point toward a resolution? Would you recount your narration in chronological order, or might you use **flashback** to account for past events or **flash forward** to account for future events? Purposefully interruptive, these techniques add interest to a story, providing glimpses of other times that illuminate the present as it is being recounted in an otherwise straightforward, chronological organization.

Whether used to supply information, explain, provide an example, set a mood, or argue a point, narration easily reaches most audiences and often

anecdote brief story that illustrates a point

point of view the perspective of the narrator in telling a story

pages 218–219

climax turning point in a narration

flashback/ flash forward narrative technique that accounts for past or future events

serves as a fitting response to opportunities for change. Given its versatility, narration can serve as the basis for a good deal of your academic, personal, and work-related writing.

 # DESCRIPTION

Specific details converge in **description**, a verbal accounting of what we have experienced physically and mentally. Thus, our descriptions always carry with them **sensory details** having to do with our physical sensations (what we see, hear, smell, touch, or taste) or **sensibility details** having to do with our intellectual, emotional, or physical states (alertness, gullibility, grief, fear, loathing, exuberance, clumsiness, relaxation, agitation, and so on).

description a verbal accounting of physical and mental experiences

sensory details what we see, hear, smell, touch, or taste

sensibility details having to do with intellectual, emotional, or physical states

José Antonio Burciaga's description (and extended definition) of *tortilla* relies heavily on sensory details:

> **For Mexicans over the centuries, the *tortilla* has served as the spoon and fork, the plate and the napkin. . . . When I was growing up in El Paso, . . . I used to visit a *tortilla* factory in an ancient adobe building near the open *mercado* in Ciudad Juárez. As I approached, I could hear the rhythmic slapping of the *masa* as the skilled vendors outside the factory formed it into balls and patted them into perfectly round corn cakes between the palms of their hands. The wonderful aroma and the speed with which the women counted so many dozens of *tortillas* out of warm wicker baskets still linger in my mind. Watching them at work convinced me that the most handsome and *deliciosas tortillas* are handmade. Although machines are faster, they can never adequately replace generation-to-generation experience. There's no place in the factory assembly line for the tender slaps that give each *tortilla* character. The best thing that can be said about mass-producing *tortillas* is that it makes it possible for many people to enjoy them.**
>
> **—José Antonio Burciaga, "I Remember Masa"**

© Vulpix/Big Stock Photo

The sensory details that infuse Burciaga's description of *tortilla* make it entertaining and memorable. Because description relies on details, it defines what is being described in specific ways.

EXEMPLIFICATION

The rhetorical strategy of **exemplification** involves making a generalization and using an example or series of examples in support of that generalization. If you want to clarify why Veronica is the best salesclerk in your favorite sporting goods store, you can provide a series of examples that define *best salesclerk:* Veronica is herself a competitive athlete; she has positive energy and is knowledgeable about all the equipment, from running shoes and jackets to cycles and kayaks. She lets customers know when items will be going on sale, and, best of all, she never pushes a sale. She realizes by now that if customers really want it, they will come back for it when they have the money. Or if you want to add interest to a generalization about your terrific Santa Fe vacation, you might talk about the clear blue skies, warm days, and cool nights; you could include anecdotes about the bargain rate you found online for your hotel room, running into Jessica Simpson at the Folk Art Museum, attending the Santa Domingo Pueblo feast day, and joining a Friday night art gallery walk and meeting artists; you could describe shopping on the plaza, where you found turquoise jewelry, Acoma Pueblo pottery, and Hopi-made Christmas presents. You could also include tantalizing, sensory descriptions of the delicious regional food—Frito pie, chocolate-covered chile creams, *carne adovada*, and *natillas*. All these examples not only add interest to the generalization that you had a "terrific vacation" but also help define exactly what you mean by that phrase.

exemplification the use of examples

In the passage that follows, Pulitzer Prize winner William Styron defines *suicidal* through his examples of suicidal thoughts.

> **He asked me if I was suicidal, and I reluctantly told him yes. I did not particularize—since there seemed no need to—did not tell him that in truth many of the artifacts of my house had become potential devices for my own destruction: the attic rafters (and an outside maple or two) a means to hang myself, the garage a place to inhale carbon monoxide, the bathtub a vessel to receive the flow from my opened arteries. The kitchen knives in their drawers had but one purpose for me. Death by heart attack seemed particularly inviting, absolving me as it would of active responsibility, and I had toyed with the idea of self-induced pneumonia—a long, frigid, shirt-sleeved hike through the rainy woods. Nor had I overlooked an ostensible accident . . . by walking in front of a truck on the highway nearby. These thoughts may seem outlandishly macabre—a strained joke—but they are genuine.**
>
> **—William Styron, *Darkness Visible***

Styron admits to his physician that he is, indeed, depressed to the point of being suicidal, but he reserves the persuasive examples of his mental state for readers of his memoir.

© Noel Rowe, 2007

(◉) DEFINITION

If you were to define the animal in the photograph, you might classify it as a "mammal" and then distinguish this mammal from others similar to it, describing its features and perhaps coming up with a definitive name for it. Thus, **definition** makes use of other strategies such as classification and division, exemplification, and description.

Whenever we are introduced to something new—a new word, academic subject, sport, activity, or language—we need to develop a new vocabulary. Whether we are learning the vocabulary of cooking (*chop, slice, mince, stir, fold, whip, fry*), golf (*ace, birdie, bogey, chip, drive, duff*), or human evolution (*prosimians, hominoids, paleoanthropology, australopithecines*), we are expanding our world with new concepts and ideas. Definition is essential to our learning and our understanding.

definition a classification that distinguishes, describes, and names something

No matter what we are learning or learning about, we use definition. And whether or not we are conscious of it, we always employ the three steps of definition:

1. We name the specific concept, action, person, or thing; in other words, we provide a term for it.
2. Then, we classify that term, or place it in a more general category. (See Classification, page 268.)
3. Finally, we differentiate the specific term from all the other concepts, actions, persons, or things in that general category, often using examples. (See Exemplification, page 265.)

For instance, if you are studying human evolution, you will no doubt need to learn what distinguishes primates from other mammals.

Term	*Class*	*Differentiation*
Primates are	mammals	that have "a lack of strong specialization in structure; prehensile hands and feet, usually with opposable thumbs and great toes; flattened nails instead of claws on the digits; acute vision with some degree of binocular vision; relatively large brain exhibiting a degree of cortical folding; and prolonged postnatal dependency. No primate exhibits all these features, and indeed the diversity of primate forms has produced disagreement as to their proper classification" —(*Encyclopedia Britannica*)

The preceding is a **formal** (or **sentence**) **definition**, the kind you will find in a reference book. But it is not the only kind of definition. An **extended definition**, such as this one from primate.org, provides additional differentiating information:

> **Primates are the mammals that are humankind's closest biological relatives. We share 98.4% of [our] DNA with chimpanzees. Apes, monkeys, and prosimians such as lorises, bush babies, and lemurs make up the 234 species of the family tree. About 90% of the primates live in tropical forests. They play an integral role in the ecology of their habitat. They help the forest by being pollinators, seed predators, and seed dispersers.**

A **historical definition**, like this one from chimpanzoo.org/history of primates, provides a longitudinal (over a period of time) overview of what the term has described over time, offering additional concepts and terms:

> **65 mya** [million years ago]: Paleocene epoch begins. . . . The earliest primates evolve. These primates were small insectivores who were most likely terrestrial. During this epoch, primates began to include food items such as seeds, fruits, nuts and leaves in their diet.

> **53.5 mya:** Eocene epoch begins. Primates diversify and some become arboreal. Primates have developed prehensile hands and feet with opposable thumbs and toes and their claws have evolved into nails. Arboreal primates evolve relatively longer lower limbs for vertical clinging and leaping. Their eye sockets are oriented more frontally resulting in stereoscopic vision. Primates of this epoch belong to the prosimian family.

One of the best things about learning a new subject is that the initial vocabulary introduces more vocabulary, so the learning never ends.

Sometimes, you will need to write a **negative definition** to clarify for your readers not only what a term means but also what it does not mean. In conversation, you might say, "When I talk about success, I'm not talking about making money." For you, success might instead involve having personal integrity, experiencing fulfillment in interpersonal relationships, and taking on exciting professional challenges. Even primates can be defined negatively, as W. E. Le Gros Clark wrote in *The Antecedents of Man*: "The Primates as a whole have preserved rather a generalized anatomy and . . . are to be mainly distinguished . . . by a negative feature—their lack of specialization."

Finally, you may come across or come up with a **stipulative definition**, which limits—or stipulates—the range of a term's meaning or application, thereby announcing to the reader exactly how the writer is using the term in the specific rhetorical situation. For instance, if you find yourself writing about *success*, you might define your meaning for your readers like this: "In this paper,

Strategies

formal (or sentence) definition a dictionary or encyclopedia reference that classifies, describes, and names something

extended definition a classification that provides extended information to describe, distinguish, and name something

historical definition an overview over a period of time of how a concept or term has been used

negative definition a classification that distinguishes a concept or term by showing what it is not

stipulative definition a classification that is specific to a particular context

success will be defined in terms of how quickly college graduates obtain employment in their chosen fields." Or if you are writing about *primates,* you might stipulate that you are concentrating on a twenty-first-century conception of them. As you can see, definition provides the foundation for learning, understanding, and communicating. As you will see throughout this chapter, classification and division, exemplification, and description all work in service of definition.

CLASSIFICATION AND DIVISION

classification and division the act of creating categories that distinguish information, objects, or other concepts

Like definition, **classification and division** first places something in a general category and then distinguishes it from other things within that category. Department stores, hospitals, telephone books, libraries, grocery stores, and bookstores are all classified and divided in order to enhance accessibility to their information or contents. When you go into a hospital, for instance, you look at the directory by the entrance to find out how the areas in the building are classified (reception area, visitor information center, emergency room, outpatient clinic, waiting room, obstetrics, patient rooms, gift shop, and cafeteria). Then, when you make your way to one of those areas (patient rooms, for instance), you look to see how that general area has been divided up (into floors and individual rooms on those floors). In important ways, the classification of hospital areas and the further division and distinction of those same areas define those locations. The hospital room you want to find is defined by belonging to the category of *patient rooms* and then differentiated from (or divided from) other patient rooms by being on the fifth floor, at the end of the hallway, to the left. Just as with definition, then, when you use classification and division, you provide a term and then place that term in its general category of origin.

COMPARISON AND CONTRAST

comparison and contrast a description of similarities and differences

We use **comparison and contrast**, a two-part method of rhetorical development, from the moment we wake up (often comparing the advantages of getting up without enough rest with those of staying in bed) until we go to bed at night (comparing the option of getting rest with that of staying up and working). We use comparison to consider how two or more things are alike, and we use contrast to show how related things are different. This rhetorical strategy, which helps us clarify issues, can be used to explain, make a decision, shape an argument, open a discussion, or craft an entertaining narrative.

© Steven Lunetta Photography, 2007

Strategies

When you do decide to get up, you might want to choose a cereal to have for breakfast, knowing that you have Lucky Charms and Cheerios on your shelf. Because both of these share the characteristics of cold breakfast cereals, you have a **basis for comparison**. In order to decide which you want to eat, you will intuitively set up **points of comparison** to clarify the ways in which the two are the same (both are cereals, served cold, eaten for breakfast) as well as the ways in which they are different (in terms of taste, nutrition, ingredients). You may already know the answers to the questions of which cereal tastes better, which one is better for you, and which one will sustain you until lunch. But you may not be familiar with the information that supports those answers, information that appears on the cereal boxes themselves.

basis for comparison shared characteristics that are used to understand objects, people, and ideas

points of comparison areas that show how two things are the same and how they are different

The nutritional information panels on the boxes indicate that both cold cereals have been approved by the American Heart Association because both are low in saturated fats and cholesterol, with 0 grams of saturated fat and 0 milligrams of cholesterol. Both are also pretty low in sodium (200 milligrams and 210 milligrams), carbohydrates (25 grams and 22 grams), and protein (2 grams and 3 grams). But neither of the cereals comes close to fulfilling recommended daily allowances (RDAs) of carbohydrates and protein, as the charts on the boxes show. What about the recommended daily requirements (RDRs)

CHAPTER 14   RHETORICAL METHODS OF DEVELOPMENT | **269** for vitamins and minerals? The nutrition charts show that these cereals provide the same amounts of vitamins A, C, D, B_6, and B_{12}. In terms of other nutrients—calcium, thiamin, riboflavin, niacin, folic acid, and zinc—they are also the same. Cheerios, however, offers more iron (nearly half the RDR), phosphorus, magnesium, and copper. But will those differences affect your choice?

What distinctive contrast will be the deciding factor? The amount of sugar? Lucky Charms has 13 grams, whereas Cheerios has only 1 gram. The extra sugar might make Lucky Charms taste better, which may tip the scale. If you want enough energy to sustain you until lunch, however, you might choose Cheerios, so that you do not start your day with a sugar high and then crash midmorning.

The information you can glean from the side of a cereal box helps you understand the ingredients of the cereal and make an informed choice. If you wanted to discuss the choice of cereal with children and argue for the "right" choice, you could use much of that information. Whether you could ultimately persuade them to choose Cheerios over Lucky Charms is, of course, another story. You would, however, be informing them through the method of comparison and contrast.

CAUSE-AND-EFFECT ANALYSIS

cause-and-effect analysis an explanation for how some things have occurred or a prediction that certain events will lead to specific effects

Whenever you find yourself concentrating on either causes or effects, explaining why certain events have occurred or predicting that particular events or situations will lead to specific effects, you are conducting a **cause-and-effect analysis** (sometimes referred to as a *cause-and-consequence analysis*). The opportunity for change in these situations comes with your ability to use words to address your questions, to explore why some things happen, or to predict the effects of an event or situation. Cause-and-effect analysis can be used to explain (your opinion on why Ohio State is going to the Rose Bowl), to entertain (your description of what happens when the family gathers for Thanksgiving), to speculate (your thoughts on the causes of autism), or to argue a point (your stance on the effects of pollution).

We spend a good deal of time considering the causes of situations. For instance, when one of your bookshelves collapses, you check to see if the shelf braces are screwed into studs, if the books are too heavy, or if you need additional supporting braces. If you have a fender bender on the way to school, you think about what led to the accident. Some of the reasons may be outside your control: low visibility, an icy road, a poorly marked road, missing taillights on the car in front of you. Other causes may reside in you: your tailgating, speeding, or inattention (due to eating, putting a CD in, or talking or texting on your cell phone).

We spend just as much time—maybe even more—evaluating the effects of situations and events. You are enrolled in college and already considering the effects of having a college degree, most of them positive (you will have to pay for your coursework and work hard, but you are likely to be well employed when you are finished). If you are considering marriage, you are analyzing the positive and not-so-positive effects of that decision (you will live with the love of your life, but you will have to relocate to Sacramento, where you may not be able to transfer all your credits). If you follow current events, you know that the effects of the controversial wars in Iraq and Afghanistan include the deaths of nearly seven thousand Americans, well over one hundred thousand Iraqis, approximately twenty thousand Afghanis (estimates vary widely), and a good deal of public discontent.

Image courtesy of NOAA

Before-and-after photographs, such as the dramatic ones above and on the next page, often lead us to wonder what happened and what caused the change. The first of this pair of photographs shows a beautiful old church surrounded by big trees. It is Trinity Episcopal Church in Pass Christian, Mississippi, which was built in 1849. Set among live oaks and lush lawns, Trinity served as a landmark for over a century. In the second photo, some—but not all—of the big trees are still standing, but there is no church, just the stairs and pathway leading up to the church. This second photograph was taken on August 18, 1969, the day after Hurricane Camille smashed into the Mississippi Gulf Coast, with wind speeds in excess of two hundred miles per hour and

water levels twenty-four feet above normal high tide, making it the strongest storm in U.S. history. The effects of Camille, by the time it had dissipated on August 22, included 256 deaths and $1.4 billion in damages, the equivalent of nearly $693 billion in 2016. Even though chances are slim that anyone in your class will have heard of, let alone remember, Hurricane Camille, you understand its effects. Developing your ability to examine situations or events for their causes or effects, and teasing out a relevant analysis, will help you better understand your world.

PROCESS ANALYSIS

process analysis
breaking down into
a series of steps
how something
occurs

Whenever you develop your ideas in order to explain how something is done, you are engaging in **process analysis**. Process analysis involves dividing up an entire process into a series of ordered steps so that your audience can understand the relationship among those steps and maybe even replicate them. To that end, process analysis always includes a series of separate, chronological steps that provide details about a process and often reads like a narration. Many process analyses take the form of a list, with distinct and often numbered steps, as in recipes, instruction manuals (for tasks from using a small appliance to assembling a toy), and installation guides (for everything from showerheads and garbage disposals to computer software). Whether the purpose of the process analysis is to inform (how volcanoes erupt, how leukemia is treated), entertain (how to gain weight on vacation, how a ten-year-old boy makes hot chocolate), or argue a point (the best way to quit a job, learn to write, develop as a reader), the analysis itself responds to a problem: someone needs to know how to do something or wants to learn how something is done.

Television programs and YouTube videos present processes we can duplicate or appreciate: we can watch the Food Network to learn about Paula Deen's plan for an easy-to-prepare Thanksgiving dinner (one that includes deep-fried turkey and double-chocolate gooey cake) or be entertained by *Say Yes to the Dress*, a not-always-flattering analysis of the process brides-to-be move through in their search for the perfect wedding dress. We can view YouTube videos to learn how to compose an iron-clad will or *How to Draw Comics the Marvel Way*, although these analyses might not provide enough training for us to duplicate the processes they describe. Whether processes are conveyed orally, in writing, or visually, whether we are taking directions from our mom, reading a car-repair manual, or watching *30 Minute Meals*, we are using process analysis.

directive process analysis a series of steps used to teach an audience how to duplicate the occurrence of something

informative process analysis a series of steps used to explain how something occurs or has occurred

Process analyses come in two basic forms. **Directive process analysis** is used to teach the audience how to do something, how to duplicate the process. **Informative process analysis**, on the other hand, is used to explain a process so that the audience can understand, enjoy, or be persuaded. Either kind of process analysis can constitute an entire message or be one part of a larger message (within a novel, proposal, report, or essay, for example).

If you have ever taken an airplane trip, you are familiar with directive process analyses. Both the passenger safety card in the pocket of the seat in front of you (as shown to the right) and the oral instructions from the flight attendant serve as perfect examples. As you follow along with the card, the attendant recites and enacts the step-by-step directions for various safety procedures during takeoffs, landings, and emergencies: how to buckle and unbuckle your seat belt, how to put an oxygen mask on yourself and help a child do so, how to locate and inflate the life preserver, and so on.

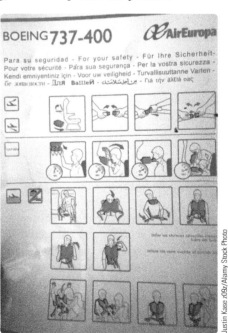

BOEING 737-400 &AirEuropa

Para su seguridad - For your safety - Für Ihre Sicherheit - Pour votre sécurité - Pára sua segurança - Per la vostra sicurezza - Kendi emniyentiniz için - Voor uw veiligheid - Turvallisuuttanne Varten - бе зопасности - Для Вашей - Για την άλεlά σας

Justin Kase z09z/Alamy Stock Photo

Strategies

Many passengers can understand the language in which the flight attendant is giving the instructions, but, for those who cannot, the visuals on the card provide the details necessary for full understanding. Whether the passengers take in the information aurally, visually, or both aurally and visually, the directive process analysis allows them to duplicate the steps described.

The following example of the second type of process analysis, informative process analysis, comes from a suspense novel. The author uses process analysis to address the problem emerging in the opening paragraph.

Detective Matt Chacon knew that unlike the TV cop shows—where actors sit in front of a computer monitor and instantaneously pull up a digital fingerprint record that matches a perp or a victim—trying to ID someone using prints in the real world can be mind-numbing work. There are thousands of prints that have never been entered into the computer data banks, and thousands more on file that, because of poor quality, are virtually unusable for comparison purposes. On top of that, figure in the small cop shops who haven't got the money, manpower, and equipment to transfer print records to computers, and the unknown number of print records that were left in closed felony cases and sit forgotten in basement archives at police departments all over the country, and you've got a data-bank system that is woefully inadequate and incomplete. Finally, while each fingerprint is unique, the difference between prints can be so slight that a very careful analysis must be made to confirm a perfect match. Even then, different experts can debate the results endlessly, since it isn't an exact science.

Chacon had started his career in law enforcement as a crime scene technician with a specialty in fingerprint and tool-mark identification, so of course Lieutenant Molina had sent him off to the state police headquarters to work the state and federal data banks to see if he could get a match.

He'd been at it all night long and his coffee was starting to taste like sludge, his eyes were itchy, and his butt was numb. Using an automated identification system, Chacon had digitally stored the victim's prints in the computer and then started scanning for a match against those already on file.

The computer system could identify possible matches quickly, but then it became a process of carefully analyzing each one and scoring them according to a detailed classification system. So far, Chacon had examined six dozen sets of prints that looked like possible equivalents and had struck out. But there was another baker's dozen to review.

He clicked on the next record, adjusted the monitor to enhance the resolution of the smudged prints, and began scoring them in sequence. Whoever had printed the subject had done a piss-poor job. He glanced at the agency identifier. It was a Department of Corrections submission.

> Chacon finished the sequence and used a split screen to compare his scoring to the victim's print. It showed a match. He rechecked the scoring and verified his findings.
>
> —**Michael McGarrity,** *Everyone Dies*

As it informs and entertains, this process analysis argues a point—that fingerprint matching is a complicated and often time-consuming procedure, not the quick fix depicted by popular media. Process analysis provides the overall structure of the passage—a thesis statement, chronological organization, and purposeful point of view. In addition, the passage uses several other rhetorical strategies for development: comparison and contrast, narration, description, exemplification, and cause-and-effect analysis.

In our culture, directions are no longer given and received only through print or face-to-face interaction. Instead of reading a cookbook, we might turn on the Food Network; instead of hiring a plumber, we might visit homedepot.com. So whether you decide to convey a process analysis in English or another language, over the telephone or by e-mail, in laborious detail or in shorthand, or with or without an accompanying visual depends on your audience's native language, access to various means of communication, and understanding of the subject matter. With process analysis, as with other rhetorical methods, it is important to consider the physical means of delivering and receiving information.

ARGUMENT

The words *argument* and *persuasion* are often used interchangeably, despite the technical distinctions between the two terms. **Argument** refers to the verbal or visual delivery of a point of view and the use of logical reasoning to help an audience understand that point of view as true or valid. **Persuasion,** on the other hand, refers to the use of emotions as well as logical reasoning to move the audience a step or two beyond the understanding that accompanies successful argument. The goal of persuasion is to change the mind, point of view, or actions of the audience. Because any visual or verbal argument can easily include emotional appeals as well as logical reasoning and because any argument holds the potential for changing the collective mind or actions of an audience, the broader term *argument* will be used throughout this chapter and this book. (For more on logical reasoning, including logical fallacies, see CHAPTER 8, POSITION ARGUMENTS.)

argument the presentation of a point of view in an effort to persuade an audience that something is true or valid

persuasion the use of emotions as well as logic to move an audience to change their minds or take action

pages 132–155

We employ and respond to arguments all day long, as we work to understand and explain to others the world around or within us. Sometimes, our arguments focus on defending our opinions or questioning the opinions of others—opinions about whether Charlie Sheen should have returned to *Two and a Half Men*, where to get the best pizza, which music venue offers the best nightlife, or whether a vegan diet is truly healthful. Sometimes, argument involves exploring and clarifying our own opinions, so we weigh all sides of an issue and various possible consequences of our final opinion. Often, we employ that kind of analytical argument when we are considering some of life's big issues: surgery, divorce, marriage, a new job, racism, sexism, and so on.

Other times, argument is invitational, in that it invites the audience to understand your position (even if they are not convinced to change their minds or action) and to explain their position to you (even if you are not convinced to change your mind or action). Invitational argument works especially well when the speaker and the audience need to work together to solve a problem (what to do about school violence, the spread of the AIDS virus, or unemployment), construct a position that represents diverse interests (for or against universal health coverage, the professionalization of college athletics, or affirmative action), or implement a policy that requires broad support (on establishing a draft system or allowing gay marriage).

When we analyze an argument—our own or one someone else is presenting to us—we can consider several elements: an identifiable issue, a claim, common ground, and rhetorical appeals. (For more on making claims, establishing common ground, and using the rhetorical appeals of ethos, logos, and pathos,

pages 18–34 see CHAPTER 2, RESPONDING TO A RHETORICAL SITUATION.)

identifiable issue
specific issue
related to a problem
that can be argued
for or against

An **identifiable issue** is the topic under discussion, one that we choose from a multitude of issues we confront daily, from limited service at the university health center to poverty, homelessness, poor-quality schooling, and so on. We do not always take the time to address any one of those problems in any productive way, perhaps because we cannot pinpoint the specific issue within that problem that we want to argue for or against. In other words, we cannot identify an opportunity for change that can be addressed with words.

Suppose you were experiencing both bad service and bad food at a restaurant. That experience might not be a very big deal unless you became violently ill and you thought it was from the salmon, which did not taste quite right. Now you have identified a specific issue you can argue as you express your opinion that either the storage of the fresh seafood or the sanitary conditions of that restaurant are in need of improvement. Or suppose you have identified one specific issue that contributes to the poor test scores of your neighborhood school: most children do not eat breakfast before they come to school.

Once you have identified an issue (that hungry school children test poorly), you can make a claim about it, an arguable position you take regarding that issue. Your claim could be that the school should launch a free breakfast program for students. The need for free school breakfasts would be the position you would take in your argument to parents, teachers, administrators, and the school board. As you think through the various claims that could be made about the issue (parents should feed their children themselves; parents should provide better after-school

Strategies

support; children need to work harder; teachers need to concentrate on the basics, and so on), you will want to make sure that your claim is one that can be argued and responded to. Citing research can be one of the most persuasive kinds of support, as the U.S. Department of Agriculture demonstrates in a flyer it produced:

> **There are many benefits of breakfast for children. Breakfast provides children with the energy and essential nutrients they need to concentrate on school work and learn. Studies show that breakfast provides as much as 25 percent of the recommended daily allowance for key nutrients, such as calcium, protein, vitamins A and B6, magnesium, iron and zinc.**
>
> **Research shows that children who eat breakfast have higher achievement scores, lower rates of absence and tardiness, and increased concentration in the classroom. . . .**
>
> **Another important benefit of breakfast for children is that establishing the healthy habit of eating breakfast early in life could stave off many adulthood health problems associated with poor diet, such as diabetes and obesity.**

Among all the possible views of school breakfast programs, yours—that school breakfast programs contribute to academic performance—will ground your thesis statement. (See also CHAPTER 13, CRAFTING A WORKING THESIS STATEMENT.) pages 246–247

In addition to supplying support for your claim, you will also need to establish common ground: the goal, belief, value, or assumption that you share with your audience. In this case, you might say that "academic performance needs to improve," and you could be reasonably certain that your audience would agree. Once you have established common ground, you have assured your audience that, despite any misunderstandings or disagreements, you both actually share a good deal, which provides a starting point for you to speak or write.

You will also employ the rhetorical appeals of ethos, logos, and pathos to make connections with your audience. By establishing common ground and speaking to a nationwide problem involving children and their school performance, you have emphasized *ethos*. By citing research to support your assertion that eating breakfast improves students' health, behavior, and academic performance, you are employing *logos*. And by listing ten reasons children should eat breakfast, starting with the obvious one that no child should go hungry, you are employing *pathos*.

Argument is a common part of everyday life, whether we are negotiating to change an airline ticket, discussing why Ohio State fired football coach Jim Tressel, or explaining why we do not want our roommate borrowing our clothes. In some ways, then, everything is an argument. Every time you transfer meaning or understanding from yourself to another person, you have made a successful argument. And every time you have understood what someone else is saying to you, you have responded to a successful argument. No matter what kind they are—visual or verbal, angry or informative, personal or bureaucratic—arguments work to fulfill one of three rhetorical purposes: to express or defend a position, to question or argue against an established belief or course of action, or to invite or persuade an audience to change an opinion or action.

MindTap® Reflect on your writing process, practice skills that you have learned in this chapter, and receive automatic feedback.

Thinking Rhetorically about Research

istockphoto.com/trenchcoates

MindTap®   Understand the goals of the chapter and complete a warm-up activity online.

Clues to Compulsive Collecting

Separating Useless Junk from Objects of Value

An intriguing new study may help researchers understand why some people are compelled to hoard useless objects. Steven W. Anderson, a neurologist, and his colleagues at the University of Iowa examined 63 people with brain damage from stroke, surgery or encephalitis. Before their brains were damaged, none had problems with hoarding, but afterward, nine began filling their houses with such things as old newspapers, broken appliances or boxes of junk mail, despite the intervention of family members.

> Why do some people collect useless objects like old newspapers, broken appliances and junk mail?

WR Publishing/Alamy Stock Photo

(continued)

These compulsive collectors had all suffered damage to the prefrontal cortex, a brain region involved in decision making, information processing and behavioral organization. The people whose collecting behavior remained normal also had brain damage, but it was instead distributed throughout the right and left hemispheres of the brain.

Anderson posits that the urge to collect derives from the need to store supplies such as food—a drive so basic it originates in the subcortical and limbic portions of the brain. Humans need the prefrontal cortex, he says, to determine what "supplies" are worth hoarding. His study was presented at the annual conference of the Society for Neuroscience.

—Richard A. Lovett

1. In "Clues to Compulsive Collecting," Richard Lovett describes research first presented by Steven Anderson and his colleagues at a neuroscience conference. After reading this article, write a paragraph or two in which you discuss the article in terms of Lovett's and the original researchers' rhetorical situations. How are they similar? How are they different?

2. In answering question 1, you likely noted significant differences in the rhetorical situations of the article writer and the original researchers, even though their subject matter was the same. In order to prepare for the research you may have to do for college classes, describe a rhetorical situation you might encounter in one of your classes. Explain how research would help you prepare a fitting response.

CONSIDERING THE RHETORICAL SITUATION

Like any other kind of writing you do, your research report needs to address the rhetorical situation. There are many different kinds of research, just as there are many different ways to present research findings. Shaping a fitting response means considering the following kinds of questions:

- *Is your researched response appropriate to the problem?* The focus, and thus the kind of research called for (library, Internet, naturalistic, laboratory, or some combination of these), depends on the nature of the problem. Engineers studying the question of how to prevent future natural disasters from causing the kind of damage wrought in New Orleans by Hurricane Katrina in 2005 would need to be sure their research focused on environmental and geographical conditions specific to that area. Research on the success of levees built along the Danube in Europe might not be applicable. The researchers would also likely need to combine many different kinds of research in order to determine the best method of prevention.

- *Is your researched response delivered in a medium that will reach its intended audience?* Writers presenting research findings want to be sure their work finds its way into the right hands. Engineers researching the issue of how best to rebuild the levees in New Orleans could certainly summarize their findings in a letter to the editor of the New Orleans *Times Picayune*. However, if they wanted approval from a government agency for future work, they would likely need to present the research in a document addressed directly to that agency, such as a written application for funding or a proposal in the form of a multimedia presentation.
- *Will your researched response successfully satisfy the intended audience?* Research papers in different academic disciplines have different types of content and formats. In consideration of your audience, it is important that you take care to notice the research methods used in the discipline and deliver writing that is presented and documented according to the accepted style of the discipline. (For information on the documentation style recommended by the Modern Language Association (MLA), see CHAPTER 19, ACKNOWLEDGING pages 338–375 SOURCES IN MLA STYLE. For information on the documentation style recommended by the American Psychological Association (APA), see CHAPTER 20, pages 376–402 ACKNOWLEDGING SOURCES IN APA STYLE.)

Of course, each rhetorical situation is different. In Chapter 2, you learned how the means available to you for responding are shaped by both the *constraints* (limitations) and the *resources* (advantages) of the rhetorical situation. Every time you begin research, you will face a new set of *constraints* and *resources*. To participate effectively in an ongoing conversation, you will need to identify specific resources to help you manage your particular set of constraints.

In reviewing the brief *Psychology Today* article that opened this chapter, you saw how one writer, Richard Lovett, worked with specific constraints and resources. You may have identified the primary elements of the rhetorical situation, such as the need to deliver complex and specialized information from the field of neurology to readers of a popular magazine. To address this constraint, Lovett made allowances for his readers' perhaps limited knowledge of how the brain works by defining unfamiliar terms (*prefrontal cortex*, for example). You may also have noted some of the resources available to Lovett in writing for this kind of publication. The image that accompanies his text allows readers to absorb the topic at a glance, while the pull-quote (the quotation in large type in the middle of the article) makes the scientists' research question explicit.

IDENTIFYING THE RESEARCH QUESTION

As you know from reading Chapter 1, the starting point for any writing project is determining your rhetorical opportunity for change. For research assignments, that opportunity for change also includes what has prompted you to look for more information. Once you are sure of your opportunity, you can craft a question to guide your research.

To make the most of your time, choose a specific question early in your research process. Having such a question helps you avoid collecting more sources than you can possibly use or finding sources that are only tangentially related. Choosing a general topic—say, the separation of church and state—will waste time if you neglect to narrow the topic into a question, such as one of the following: What did the framers of the Constitution have in mind when they discussed the separation of church and state? How should the separation of church and state be interpreted in law? Should the Ten Commandments be posted in government buildings? Should the phrase *under God* be removed from the Pledge of Allegiance?

Good questions often arise when you try to relate what you are studying in a course to your own experience. For instance, you may start wondering about the separation of church and state when, after reading about this topic in a history class, you notice the number of times politicians refer to God in their speeches, you remember reciting the phrase *under God* in the Pledge of Allegiance, or you read in the newspaper that a plaque inscribed with the Ten Commandments must be removed from public space in Oklahoma. pages 439–440 (See CHAPTER 23, ABBY PHILLIP, "OKLAHOMA'S TEN COMMANDMENTS STATUE MUST BE REMOVED, STATE SUPREME COURT SAYS.") These observations may prompt you to look for more information on the topic. Each observation, however, may give rise to a different question. You will choose the question that interests you the most and that will best help you fulfill the assignment.

To generate research questions, you may find it helpful to return to Chapter 13, where you read about journalists' questions (Who? What? Where? When? Why? How?). pages 241–242 (See CHAPTER 13, QUESTIONING.) Here are some more specific kinds of questions that commonly require research:

QUESTIONS ABOUT CAUSES

Why doesn't my college offer athletic scholarships?

What causes power outages in large areas of the country?

QUESTIONS ABOUT CONSEQUENCES

What are the consequences of taking antidepressants for a long period of time?

How might the atmosphere in a school change if a dress code were established?

QUESTIONS ABOUT PROCESSES

How can music lovers prevent corporations from controlling the development of music?

How does my hometown draw boundaries for school districts?

QUESTIONS ABOUT DEFINITIONS OR CATEGORIES

How do you know if you are addicted to something?

What kind of test is "the test of time"?

QUESTIONS ABOUT VALUES

Should the Makah tribe be allowed to hunt gray whales?

Would the construction of wind farms be detrimental to the environment?

✱ TRICKS OF THE TRADE

If the assignment does not specify a topic and you are not sure what you want to write about, you may need some prompting. Consider these questions.

- Can you remember an experience that you did not understand fully or that made you feel uncertain? What was it that you did not understand? What were you unsure of?
- What have you observed lately (on television, in the newspaper, on your way to school, or in the student union) that piqued your curiosity? What were you curious about?
- What local or national problem that you have recently heard or read about would you like to help solve?
- Is there anything you find unusual that you would like to explore? Lifestyles? Political views? Religious views?

As you consider which question will most appropriately guide your research, you may find it helpful to discuss your ideas with other people. Research and writing both require a great deal of time and effort, and you will find the tasks more pleasant—and maybe even easier—if you are sincerely interested in your question. Moreover, enthusiasm about your work will motivate you to do the best you can. Indifference breeds mediocrity. By talking with other people, you may find out that the question you have chosen is a good one. Or, you may discover that you need to narrow the question or change it in some other way. You may even realize that the question you initially chose really does not interest you very much. To get a conversation about your ideas started, have someone you know ask you some of the following questions.

- Why is it important for you to answer the question? What is the answer's significance for you? How will answering the question help you? How is the question related to your rhetorical opportunity?
- Will the answer to your question require serious research? (A genuine research question does not have a simple or obvious answer.)
- What types of research might help you answer your question? (You may already have some ideas; for more on library, online, and field research, see CHAPTER 16, IDENTIFYING SOURCES.) Will you be able to carry out these types of research in the amount of time you have been given?

pages 292–310

TRICKS OF THE TRADE

Save yourself time and frustration by asking your instructor to help you develop your vague idea into a strong research question. After all, yours is the kind of issue best resolved during office hours.

 LOCATING AN AUDIENCE

Knowing that your purpose is to stimulate change in a specific audience, your response to the opportunity for change needs to reach and satisfy the rhetorical audience. In order to meet the expectations of your readers, you must know something about them. First, you must find out who your audience is. If you are writing in response to a course assignment, your instructor may define your audience for you (usually, it is the instructor and your classmates). However, sometimes your instructor may ask you to imagine a different audience so that you have experience writing for a wider range of people. For example, your instructor might ask you to write a letter to the editor of your local paper. In this case, your audience still comprises your instructor and classmates, but it also includes the editor of the newspaper as well as all the newspaper's readers.

As your writing career progresses, the number of audiences you write for will increase. You may be able to easily name your audience—college students, science teachers, mechanical engineers, pediatricians, or the general public—but to make sure that you satisfy any audience you choose to address, you need to go beyond labels. When you do research, you must take into account what types of sources your audience will expect you to use and which sources they will find engaging, convincing, or entertaining.

Keep in mind that when you write for an audience, you are joining an ongoing conversation. To enter that conversation, you need to pay attention to what is being said and who the participants are. You can begin by reading the sources the participants in the conversation use. By reading what they read, you will learn what information is familiar to them and what information may need to be explained in detail.

The web page for the Pucker Gallery, seen below, as well as the following brief article from *Bostonia*, Boston University's alumni magazine, contains information about the artist Joseph Ablow. The audience for each is different, however. In the *Bostonia* article, the abbreviation *CFA* is not explained, because the intended audience, alumni of Boston University, will know that it refers to the College of Fine Arts. If you were writing an article for an alumni

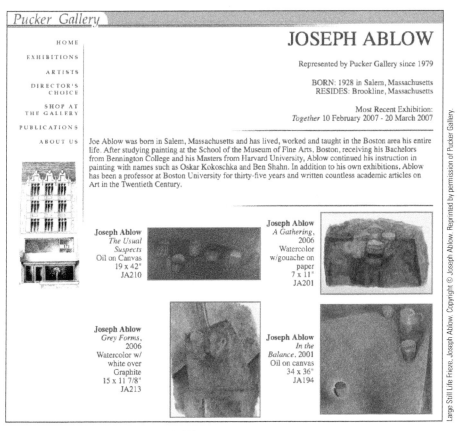

The Pucker Gallery Web page for Joseph Ablow

magazine, you too would be able to use abbreviations and acronyms familiar to those who attended that college or university. However, if your audience were broader, such abbreviations and acronyms would have to be explained the first time you used them. The same criterion can be used to make decisions about content. If you were researching one of Joseph Ablow's still life paintings, you would find that sources on Ablow's work do not define what a still life painting is; the authors of these sources assume that their readers are familiar with the term. However, if you were writing for readers who knew next to nothing about painting, you would provide a definition for the term.

Ablow's Objets d'Art

© puckergallery.com

Large Still Life Frieze, oil on canvas, 32" × 66", 1986.

In a lecture this fall at Amherst College, Joseph Ablow described a major change in his artistic direction in the late 1950s. He had been working on large, classically inspired themes for a decade and "something did not feel right."

"My subjects no longer held much meaning for me," said Ablow, a CFA professor emeritus of art, "and I began to realize that painting and inventing from memory had left me visually parched. It was obvious to me that I had to start over."

The reevaluation pulled him back to the studio, where, he says, "simply as exercises,

I returned to the subject of still life," something he had avoided since art school. "But it was not long before the motley collection of objects I had assembled began quietly to organize themselves into configurations that suggested unexpected pictorial possibilities to me.

"I soon discovered that these objects may be quiet, but that did not mean that they remained still. What was to have been a subject that suggested ways of studying the look of things within a manageable and concentrated situation became an increasingly involved world that could be surprisingly disquieting and provocative. I may have been the one responsible for arranging my cups and bowls on the tabletops, but that did not ensure that I was in control of them.

"The ginger jars and the compote dishes were real, particular, and palpable and yet had no inherent significance. Their interest or importance would be revealed only in the context of a painting."

Born in 1928, Ablow studied with Oskar Kokoschka, Ben Shahn, and Karl Zerbe. He earned degrees from Bennington and Harvard and taught at Boston University from 1963 until 1995. He is currently a visiting artist at Amherst College, which hosted the exhibition of his paintings that is coming to BU.

Still lifes painted over some thirty-five years highlight Joseph Ablow: A Retrospective, *from January 13 through March 5 at the Sherman Gallery, 775 Commonwealth Avenue.*

Readers of an academic research paper expect the author to be knowledgeable. You can demonstrate your knowledge through the types of sources you use and the ways you handle them. Because you are not likely to have established credibility as an expert on the topic you are researching, you will need to establish a thoughtful tone in your exploration of your topic and depend on the credibility of the sources you use. Once you have done enough research to understand your audience, you will be better able to select sources that will give you credibility. For example, to persuade your readers of the value of a vegetarian diet, you could choose among sources written by nutritionists, ethicists, religious leaders, and animal rights proponents. Your decision would be based on which kinds of sources your audience would find most credible.

TRICKS OF THE TRADE

To determine which sources your audience will find authoritative, study any bibliographies that you encounter in your research. If a source is mentioned on several bibliographic lists, the source is likely considered authoritative.

Readers of an academic research paper also expect the author to be critical. They want to be assured that an author can tell whether the source information is accurate or deceptive, whether its logic is strong or weak, and whether its conclusions are justifiable. Your readers may accept your use of a questionable source as long as you show why it is problematic. (See CHAPTER 17, EVALUATING SOURCES.) pages 311–321

ESTABLISHING YOUR PURPOSE

In Chapter 1, you saw how your rhetorical audience and your rhetorical purpose are interconnected. They cannot be separated. In general, your rhetorical purpose is motivated by an opportunity for change—an opportunity to have an impact on your audience; more specifically, your aim may be to entertain them, to inform them, to explain something to them, or to influence them to do something. Research can help you achieve any of these purposes. For example, if you are writing a research paper on the roots of humor for a psychology class, your primary purpose is to inform. You may want to analyze a few jokes in order to show how their construction can incite laughter, but you will need research to support your claim. Your audience will be more inclined to believe you if you show them, say, experimental results indicating that people routinely find certain incidents funny.

Writers of research papers commonly define their rhetorical purposes in the following ways:

- *To inform an audience.* The researcher reports current thinking on a specific topic, including opposing views but not siding with any particular one.

  Example: To inform the audience of current guidelines for developing a city park

- *To analyze and synthesize information and then offer tentative solutions to a problem.* The researcher analyzes and synthesizes information on a topic (for example, an argument, a text, an event, a technique, or a statistic), looking for points of agreement and disagreement and for gaps in coverage. Part of the research process consists of finding out what other researchers have already written about the subject. After presenting the analysis and synthesis, the researcher offers possible ways to address the problem.

  Example: To analyze and synthesize various national health-care proposals

- *To persuade an audience or to issue an invitation to an audience.* The researcher states a position and backs it up with data, statistics, texts illustrating a point, or supporting arguments found through research. The researcher's purpose is to persuade or invite readers to take the same position.

  Example: To persuade (or invite) people to vote for a congressional candidate

Often, these purposes coexist in the same piece of writing. A researcher presenting results from an original experiment or study, for instance, must often achieve all of these purposes. In the introduction to a lab report, the researcher might describe previous work done in the area and identify a research niche—an area needing research. The researcher then explains how his or her current study will help fill the gap in existing research. The body of the text is informative, describing the materials used, explaining the procedures followed, and presenting the results. In the conclusion, the researcher may choose, given the results of the experiment or study, to persuade the audience to take some action (for example, give up smoking, eat fewer carbohydrates, or fund future research).

The sources you find through research can help you achieve your purpose. If your purpose is to inform, you can use the work of established scholars to enhance your credibility. If your purpose is to analyze and synthesize information, sources you find can provide not only data for you to work with but also a backdrop against which to highlight your own originality or your special research niche. If your purpose is to persuade, you can use sources to support your claims and to counter opposing arguments.

USING A RESEARCH LOG

Without a clear plan and a method for monitoring your progress, it is easy to lose track of your ideas and goals. Research logs come in different forms, but whatever their form—electronic or printed, detailed or brief—they help researchers stay focused. Researchers make decisions about what to include in their logs by anticipating the kind of information that will be most important in helping them answer their research question and document their results. Rereading your initial entry every so often may help you stay focused.

1. In the introductory entry in your research log, identify your research question and your reasons for choosing it. You might include some preliminary, tentative answers to your question if you have any, given what you already know.

2. In your research log, create an entry that describes your prospective readers and explains what you need to keep in mind to ensure that you are addressing them. Let

A bike commuter.

PhotoAlto Agency RF Collections/Getty Images

Researching Rhetorically

us say you are interested in finding out about the possibilities of commuting by bicycle in your town. If you are aware that your audience knows nothing about bike commuting, you may want to provide an explanation (or process analysis) of how bike commuters get to and from work safely and comfortably. (See CHAPTER 14, PROCESS ANALYSIS.) You might even include a photograph of the kind of bike made for commuting—one with fenders to keep work clothes clean and panniers to hold cargo. However, if you are writing for an audience that has already been introduced to this type of transportation, a detailed description is unnecessary.

pages 272–275

3. Your introductory entry should also establish how you hope your research will stimulate change in your audience. What is your purpose in presenting your research to others: to inform, to analyze, or to persuade? Discuss why you are asking the question in the first place, what the benefits of answering the question will be, and what types of research are likely to be helpful.

RESEARCHING CALENDAR TOOLS

Strategies for planning a research paper are not that different from the general strategies you learned in Chapter 13: listing, keeping a journal, freewriting, questioning, clustering, and outlining. To keep your research moving ahead, take advantage of tools such as calendars. Use the features and tasks on Google Calendar to relate to the ways you work.

For the results of research to be valuable, the process must be taken seriously. Researchers who chase down facts to attach to opinions they already have are doing only superficial research. These researchers are not interested in finding information that may cause them to question their beliefs or that may make their thinking more complicated. Genuine research, on the other hand, involves crafting a good research question and pursuing an answer to it, both of which require patience and care.

MindTap® Reflect on your writing process, practice skills that you have learned in this chapter, and receive automatic feedback.

16

Identifying Sources

iStock/Getty Images

MindTap® Understand the goals of the chapter and complete a warm-up activity online.

Pop Cultures

Refrescos in Spanish, mashroob ghazi in Arabic, kele in Chinese: the world has many words, and an unslakable thirst, for carbonated soft drinks. Since 1997 per capita consumption has nearly doubled in eastern Europe. In 2008 Coca-Cola tallied soda sales in some 200 countries. Even the global recession, says industry monitor Zenith International, has merely caused manufacturers to lean on promotional offers and try cheap social-networking ads.

But some are sour on all this sweetness. U.S. obesity expert David Ludwig calls aggressive marketing in emerging nations—where people tend to eat more and move less as they prosper—"deeply irresponsible. That's the time of greatest risk for heart disease, diabetes, and obesity."

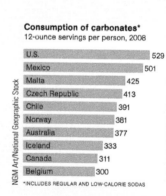

Consumption of carbonates*
12-ounce servings per person, 2008

U.S.	529
Mexico	501
Malta	425
Czech Republic	413
Chile	391
Norway	381
Australia	377
Iceland	333
Canada	311
Belgium	300

*INCLUDES REGULAR AND LOW-CALORIE SODAS

NGM Art/National Geographic Stock

Rebecca Hale/National Geographic Creative

As that thinking catches on, places—including New York and Romania—are mulling levies on sugared drinks. Others argue that taxing a single product isn't the fix: promoting healthy lifestyles and zero-calorie drinks is. Fizz for thought?

—Jeremy Berlin

292

1. Why do you think Jeremy Berlin (and the editors at *National Geographic*) decided to use a photograph and a list of statistics within the article "Pop Cultures"? What kind of research do you think he and his editors did to prepare this article and the accompanying graphics? In other words, what might they have read or observed, whom might they have questioned, and so on? If you wanted to check their facts, what would you do?

2. Think about a research paper you might write. What kind of research will you conduct for your project? Where will you go to find your sources? Given more time and more resources, what additional kinds of research might you do?

Although the library will probably play an important role in your research, it often will not be the only location in which you conduct research. During the research process, you might find yourself at home using the Internet, in your instructor's office getting suggestions for new sources, or even at the student union taking notes on what you observe about some aspect of student behavior. All along the process, you will want to use a research log. (See CHAPTER 15, USING A RESEARCH LOG.) pages 289–290

Your research log helps you stay focused on your research question, audience, and purpose during the process of identifying potentially productive sources and keeping notes. Here are some questions to ask yourself as you identify usable sources for your research project:

- What purpose might this source serve in my paper?
- What do I agree and disagree with?
- What do I not understand fully?
- What do I want to know more about?
- How does what this source says relate to (agree or disagree with) what other sources have said?
- How credible will my audience find this source?
- What other research should I conduct?
- What other sources will my audience find credible and why?

SOURCES FOR RESEARCH

primary sources firsthand accounts or original data

secondary sources sources that interpret or collect firsthand accounts or original data

In order to make effective decisions, you need to know what kinds of research you will be able to do at the library, on the Internet, and in the field. **Primary sources** are firsthand accounts or original data, which are used as the basis for **secondary sources** (sources that interpret, analyze, or collect those accounts or data). Primary sources include literary works, performances, experiments, historical documents, field research (interviews, for instance), discovered artifacts, and eyewitness accounts—things or events the researcher examines firsthand. An analysis of that eyewitness account that brings in evidence that counters, supports, or reinterprets the original account is a secondary source. Some research questions can only be answered by fieldwork, research carried out in a real-world or naturalistic environment. Most research, however, will target three main categories of information: books and periodicals, online sources, and audiovisual sources.

Books

The easiest way to find books on a particular topic is to consult your library's online catalog. Once you are logged on, navigate your way to the web page with search boxes similar to the one that is on this page. An author search or title search is useful when you already have a particular author or title in mind. When a research area is new to you, you can find many sources by doing either a keyword search or a subject search. For a keyword search, choose a word or a phrase that you think is likely to be found in titles or notes in the catalog's records.

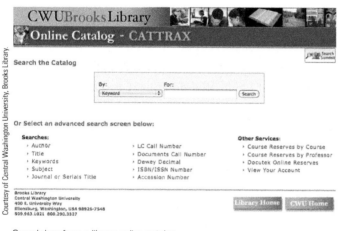

Search box from a library online catalog.

For a subject search, you may be able to find sources by entering words that are familiar to you. However, if your search does not yield promising results, ask a reference librarian (either in person or online) for a subject heading guide or note the subject categories that accompany the search results for sources you have already found. Three types of books are often consulted in the research process: scholarly, trade, and reference books.

- **Scholarly books** are written by scholars for other scholars in order to advance knowledge of a certain subject. Most include original research as well as analysis and interpretation. Before being published, these books are reviewed by experts in the field (in a process referred to as a *peer review*).

- **Trade books** may also be written by scholars, though they may be authored by journalists or freelance writers as well. But the audience and purpose of trade books differ from those of scholarly books. Rather than addressing other scholars, authors of trade books write to inform the general audience, often about the primary research that has been done by others; therefore, trade books are usually secondary sources.
- **Reference books** such as encyclopedias and dictionaries provide factual information. Reference books often contain short articles written and reviewed by experts in the field. The audience for these secondary sources includes both veteran scholars and those new to a field of study.

Encyclopedias and Dictionaries

General encyclopedias and dictionaries such as the *Encyclopaedia Britannica* and the *American Heritage Dictionary* provide basic information on many topics. Specialized encyclopedias and dictionaries cover topics in greater depth. In addition to overviews of topics, they also include definitions of technical terminology, discussions of major issues, and bibliographies of related works. Specialized encyclopedias and dictionaries exist for all major disciplines. Here is just a small sampling:

Art	*Grove Dictionary of Art, Encyclopedia of Visual Art*
Biology	*Concise Encyclopedia of Biology*
Chemistry	*Concise Macmillan Encyclopedia of Chemistry, Encyclopedia of Inorganic Chemistry*
Computers	*Encyclopedia of Computer Science and Technology*
Economics	*Fortune Encyclopedia of Economics*
Education	*Encyclopedia of Higher Education, Encyclopedia of Educational Research*
Environment	*Encyclopedia of the Environment*
History	*Dictionary of American History, New Cambridge Modern History*
Literature	*Encyclopedia of World Literature in the 20th Century*
Music	*New Grove Dictionary of Music and Musicians*

(continued)

Philosophy	*Routledge Encyclopedia of Philosophy, Encyclopedia of Applied Ethics*
Psychology	*Encyclopedia of Psychology, Encyclopedia of Human Behavior*
Religion	*Encyclopedia of Religion*
Social sciences	*International Encyclopedia of the Social Sciences*
Women's studies	*Women's Studies Encyclopedia, Encyclopedia of Women and Gender*

For other specialized encyclopedias, contact a reference librarian or consult *Kister's Best Encyclopedias.*

You may need to do an advanced online search, which allows you to specify a language, a location in the library, a type of book (or a type of material other than a book), and the organization of the results (by publisher, by date of publication, for instance). A keyword search page will provide recommendations for entering specific words. (See the screenshot of an advanced keyword search page from a library online catalog that appears on page 298.)

By using a word or part of a word followed by asterisks, you can find all sources that have that word or word part, even when suffixes have been added. For example, if you entered *environment**, the search would return not only sources with *environment* in the title but also sources whose titles included *environments, environmental,* or *environmentalist.* This shortening technique is called *truncation.* You can enter multiple words by using an operator such as *and* or *or.* You can exclude words by using *and not.* When you enter multiple words, you can require that they be close to each other by using *near;* if you want to specify their proximity, you can use *within,* followed by a number indicating the greatest number of words that may separate them.

Once you locate a source, write down or print out its call number. The call number corresponds to a specific location in the library's shelving system, usually based on the classification system of the Library of Congress. Keys to the shelving system are usually posted on the walls of the library, but staff members will also be able to help you find sources.

In addition to using your library's online catalog, you can access books themselves online, downloading them as PDFs or in other formats for use on a hand-held device such as a Kindle or an iPad. Over two million free books are listed on the University of Pennsylvania's Online Books Page (onlinebooks .library.upenn.edu).

Searching Google Books (books.google.com) or using Amazon.com's "Look Inside!" feature can give you more information about books not available locally. Both sites allow you to search for keywords inside certain virtual texts. If the search locates the keywords, you can then preview the relevant pages of the text to determine if you want to purchase the book or order it from an interlibrary loan service. If the book is in the public domain, you may be able to access the entire text through Google Books.

Periodicals

Periodicals include scholarly journals, magazines, and newspapers. Because these materials are published regularly and more frequently than books, the information they contain is more recent.

- **Scholarly journals**, like scholarly books, contain original research (they are primary sources) and address a narrow, specialized audience. Many scholarly journals have the word *journal* in their names: examples are *Journal of Business Communication* and *Consulting Psychology Journal*.
- **Magazines** and **newspapers** can provide both primary and secondary sources that are usually written by staff writers for the general public. Magazines can be dedicated to a particular topic and carry a combination of news, investigative reporting, researched essays, and opinion pieces. Newspapers—national (such as *The New York Times* and *The Washington Post*), regional, or local—include news coverage, which is intended to be objective, and may also feature ongoing investigative reports, articles, letters, and editorials of interest to researchers.

Your library's online catalog lists the titles of periodicals (journals, magazines, and newspapers); however, it does not provide the titles of individual articles within these periodicals. Although many researchers head straight to an Internet search engine or web browser (Google, Bing, Yahoo!, Internet Explorer), type in the name of the desired article, and locate a copy, many others end up frustrated by such a broad search. You may find that the best strategy for finding reliable articles on your topic is to use an electronic database, available through your library portal. A database (such as ERIC, JSTOR, or PsycINFO) is similar to an online catalog in that it allows you to search for sources by author, title, subject, keyword, and other features. Because so much information is available, databases focus on specific subject areas.

periodicals publications such as magazines and newspapers that are published over a specific period of time (daily, weekly, or monthly)

scholarly journals publications for a specialized audience that contain original research on academic topics

magazines periodical publications for the general public, sometimes focused on a particular subject

newspapers regional, local, or national news publications that also include letters to the editor and editorial opinion pieces

Identifying Sources

You can access your library's databases from a computer in the library or, if you have a password, via an Internet link from a computer located elsewhere. Libraries subscribe to various vendors for these services, but the following are some of the most common databases:

OCLC FirstSearch or EBSCOhost: Contain articles and other types of records (for example, electronic books and DVDs) on a wide range of subjects.

ProQuest: Provides access to major newspapers such as *The New York Times* and *The Wall Street Journal* and to consumer and scholarly periodicals in areas including business, humanities, literature, and science.

LexisNexis: Includes articles on business, legal, and medical topics and on current events.

Advanced keyword search page from a library online catalog.

To find sources through a database, you can use some of the same strategies you use for navigating an online catalog. However, search pages often differ, so there is no substitute for hands-on experimentation. Your library may use a general database, such as OCLC FirstSearch or EBSCOhost.

The first box on the EBSCOhost search page asks you to specify a subject area. Just underneath that box is a drop-down menu that lets you choose among several databases, including ERIC (Educational Resources Information Center), MLA (Modern Language Association), and PsycINFO (American Psychological Association's database of psychological literature). After you choose the specific database you would like to search, you click on the question-mark icon to the right of the search entry box to get directions for searching by keyword, author, title, source, year, or a combination of these attributes. In the Refine Search menu, you can click on a checkbox to limit a search to full texts only. In this case, your search will bring back only sources that include the complete text of an article, which can be downloaded and printed. Otherwise, the database search generally yields the source's bibliographic information and an abstract, which is a short summary of an article's content. (For more on summaries and abstracts, see CHAPTER 3, SUMMARY.) To pages 42–43 find the full text, you note the basic source information—author, title, and publication data—and then look up that book or periodical in the library's online catalog, as described earlier.

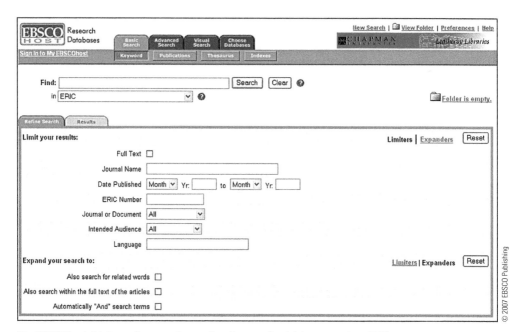

The EBSCOhost database allows you to search various smaller databases, such as ERIC.

Finally, some periodicals are available online. HighWire is a service that lists many scientific and medical journals that offer free articles or issues; you can find this list by going to highwire.stanford.edu/lists/freeart.dtl. The Global Development Network lists journals from a wide range of academic disciplines on its website (gdnet.org). Online articles are not always free, however. Be sure to check for subscription services that are available through your library's website before paying for an archived article on a newspaper's home page. You might save yourself a good deal of money!

Online Sources

.com the domain name used on the Internet for commercial, for-profit entities

.edu the domain name used on the Internet for a U.S. educational institution

.gov the domain name used on the Internet for U.S. governmental branches or agencies

.org the domain name used on the Internet for non-profit organizations

government documents any information printed/published by the local, state, or national government

Books, journals, magazine articles, and newspaper articles can all be found online. But when you read documents on websites, created specifically for access by computer, you need to determine who is responsible for the site, why the site was established, and who the target audience is. To find answers to these questions, you can first check the domain name, which is at the end of the main part of the Internet address. This name will give you clues about the site. An Internet address with the domain name **.com** (for commerce) tells you that the website is associated with a profit-making business. The domain name **.edu** indicates that a site is connected to a U.S. educational institution. Websites maintained by the branches or agencies of the U.S. government have the domain name **.gov**. Nonprofit organizations such as Habitat for Humanity and National Public Radio have **.org** as their domain name.

You can find **government documents** by using library databases such as LexisNexis Academic. In addition, the following websites are helpful:

FedWorld Information Network	fedworld.gov
Government Publishing Office	gpoaccess.gov
U.S. Courts	uscourts.gov

You can also find out about the nature of a website by clicking on navigational buttons such as About Us or Vision. Here is an excerpt from a page entitled "About NPR" on the National Public Radio website:

What is NPR?

NPR is an internationally acclaimed producer and distributor of noncommercial news, talk, and entertainment programming. A privately supported, not-for-profit, membership organization, NPR serves more than 770 independently operated, noncommercial public radio stations. Each member station serves local listeners with a distinctive combination of national and local programming.

TRICKS OF THE TRADE

To stay abreast of new developments on a particular topic, create a Google Alert, which will provide e-mail updates of the latest relevant Google results from news websites and blogs based on your topic.

Metasearch engines are also available. *Meta* means "transcending" or "more comprehensive." Metasearch engines check numerous search engines, including those listed on page 304. Try these for starters:

Dogpile	dogpile.com
Mamma	mamma.com
MetaCrawler	metacrawler.com
WebCrawler	webcrawler.com

Finally, be aware that sometimes when you click on a link, you end up at a totally different website. You can keep track of your location by looking at the Internet address, or URL, at the top of your screen. URLs generally include the following information: server name, domain name, directory and perhaps subdirectory, file name, and file type.

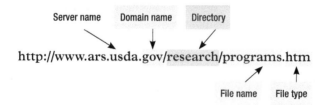

Be sure to check the server and domain names whenever you are unsure of your location. (For more on evaluating websites, see CHAPTER 17, EVALUATING SOURCES.)

✦ TRICKS OF THE TRADE

Before taking notes, jot down essential documentation for your source, in case you need to return to it or cite it. If you expect to have only a few sources, you may want to include complete information on the author, title, and publication data with your notes. If you will be consulting a number of sources, create an entry in your working bibliography, such as the author's name and the page numbers. (See Preparing a Working Bibliography, pages 309–310.)

Audiovisual Sources

The most common audiovisual (multimodal) sources are documentaries, lectures, and interviews, many of which are available on YouTube. In fact, you can search YouTube for topics, people, and places. In addition to multimodal sources, you can search for still images online by using a search engine such as Google Images. Most academic libraries have **special collections** that you might also find useful, such as art collections, including drawings and paintings; audio and video collections, including records, audiotapes, CDs, videotapes, and DVDs; and computer resources, usually consisting of programs that combine text, audio, and video. Pursue such sources only when you can use them purposefully, enriching (not merely decorating) your paper.

special collections library resources on particular topics, people, and places, often including audiovisual and primary sources

- **Documentary films and television programs** are much like trade books and magazines. They are created for a popular audience, with the purpose of providing factual information, usually of a political, social, or historical nature.
- **Lectures** generally take place live at universities and in public auditoriums or are recorded as podcasts or for distribution through iTunes U or university websites. University-sponsored lectures are usually more technical or scholarly than those delivered in a public auditorium. Lecturers can be expected to deliver more objective information on their topic of expertise or to speak their high-profile opinions.
- **Interviews** are a special type of conversation in which a reporter elicits responses from someone recognized for his or her status or accomplishments. Interviews, which are aired for a general audience, aim to provide information about the interviewee's achievements or about his or her views on a specific issue.

interview special type of conversation in which a reporter elicits responses from someone recognized for his or her status or accomplishments

- **Images** can be located by navigating through your library's special collections website or by asking a reference librarian for help. The websites of specific libraries, museums, and government agencies (such as the Library of Congress, the Smithsonian Institution, and the U.S. Census Bureau) often have databases of images.

The last step in using images or audiovisual materials is to give credit to their creators and, if necessary, acquire permission to use them. If you are not publishing your paper in print or online, fair-use laws governing reproduction for educational purposes might allow you to use the image without permission. If you are uploading your paper to a website or publishing it in any other way, determine whether the image is copyrighted; if so, you will have to contact its creator for permission to use it and then include a credit line underneath the image, after the caption.

TRICKS OF THE TRADE

Images such as photographs, drawings, and charts also count as sources meant to be viewed. Although images are not often accessed on their own in the same ways that books, periodicals, or documentaries are, they may constitute an important part of your research, whether or not your final project is meant to be multimedia. For example, you may use photographs to enhance written descriptions or maps and data-rich charts to support claims.

Additional Advice for Finding Sources Online

Most researchers search the Internet first in an attempt to locate text, image, video, and audio sources relevant to their projects. But search engines cover only the portion of the Internet that allows free access. Vast amounts of good materials are available through your school's library; some books and periodicals are available only through the library's database materials and cannot be found using a search engine because library and database services are available only to paid subscribers (and, as a student, you fall into this category). If you do decide to use the Internet, remember that no one search engine covers all of it, and surprisingly little overlap occurs when different search engines are used to find information on the same topic. Thus, using more than one search engine and searching for both free and subscriber-only materials will enrich your search. The following are commonly used search engines:

Ask.com	ask.com
Bing	bing.com
Google	google.com
Yahoo!	yahoo.com

When using a search engine for research, you will probably want to check the Help links to learn about advanced search options. Using these options will allow you to weed out results that are not of interest to you. Advanced searches are performed in much the same way with search engines as they are with online catalogs and databases. You can specify words or phrases, how close words should be to each other, which words should be excluded, and whether the search should return longer versions of truncated words.

FIELDWORK

fieldwork real-world research that commonly includes observation, interviews, and questionnaires

Research in the field helps you develop an understanding of a local situation, an understanding that usually cannot be easily reached through traditional library, online, or laboratory research. Therefore, **fieldwork** usually takes place in a real-world environment. Observation, interviews, and questionnaires are the most common kinds of field research.

Observation

observation watching closely what is happening and trying to figure out why

naturalistic study observation based on direct access to the person or phenomenon being researched

Observation—watching closely what is happening and trying to figure out why—plays a central role in a **naturalistic study**, which is based on observation in a real-world environment. The researcher is right there on the scene, conducting the research, with direct access to the person or phenomenon. In his study of the intellectual processes necessary for conducting ordinary kinds of work, Mike Rose describes how observation works in the field:

> **When at a job site or in a classroom, I observed people at work, writing notes on their activity and, when permissible, taking photographs of the task at hand. Once I got a sense of the rhythms of the work—its moments of less intense focus and its pauses—I would begin asking questions about what people were doing and why, trying to gain an understanding of their behavior and the thinking that directed it. As they got more familiar with me and I with them and their work, I was able to ask increasingly specific questions, probing the reasons for using one implement rather than another, for a**

particular positioning of the body, for the benefits of this procedure over that one. I wondered aloud how they knew what to do, given the materials and constraints of the present task, what they had in mind to do next, how they knew something was wrong. . . . Over time, the exchanges became more conversational, and frequently people on their own began explaining what they were doing and what their thinking was for doing it, a kind of modified think-aloud procedure, long used in studies of problem solving.

—**Mike Rose**, *The Mind at Work* ["On Observation"]

Notice how Rose talks about the material conditions of his observation: he watches, takes notes, sometimes takes photographs, and asks increasingly sophisticated questions as he begins to understand the procedures more and more. Each activity occurs in coordination with the others.

Interviews

All successful questioning involves *background research*—in other words, doing your homework before you begin asking questions. The burden is on the researcher or interviewer to know enough about the person or phenomenon to ask intelligent questions. Good interview questions will help guide your research. Your **interview questions** should serve your research in two ways. First, they should put your subjects at ease so that they willingly talk, amplify their answers, and provide rich examples. Second, your interview questions should progress purposefully from one subject to another. Interview questions that can be answered with *yes* or *no* will not yield much information unless they are followed with a related question. For example, if you follow a question like "Do you like your job?" with a journalist's question ("Why?" "When?" or "How?"), you give your interviewee a chance to elaborate. Effective interviews usually contain a blend of open, or broad, questions and focused, or narrow, questions. Here are a few examples:

> **interview questions** questions designed to put your subject at ease and purposefully progress from one subject to another

OPEN QUESTIONS

What do you think about _____?
What are your views on _____?
Why do you believe _____?

FOCUSED QUESTIONS

How long have you worked as a
_____?
When did you start _____?
What does _____ mean?
Why did you _____?

fredgoldstein/Big Stock Photo

GILLIAN PETRIE, INTERVIEW OF JAN FRESE

The following selections are written transcripts of an interview conducted by Gillian Petrie, a student who decided to interview a long-time nurse, Jan Frese, about the changes she had seen in the profession during her thirty-eight years on the job. Gillian's first question is open-ended and aimed at making her interviewee comfortable.

GILLIAN: Would you like to tell me, how did you get into nursing in the first place, Jan?

JAN: I was a little late getting into nursing, because I was married and I had four children and . . . things were not going well at home and I was going to get a divorce. Well now, how am I going to take care of my children? So, . . . a friend of mine told me about this LPN [Licensed Practical Nurse] school and, um, it was only a year, it only took a year to be a licensed practical nurse, and I thought that—that sounds like a good idea. . . . I ended up doing pretty much everything the RNs did but still getting the LPN pay. . . . [so] I, um, thought I'll go back to school and be an RN . . .; and . . ., do pretty much what I was doing before, but at least I'll get paid for it!

As the interview progresses, Gillian steers her subject to the topic of changes that she has seen over the years in patients' perception of nurses. Gillian now mixes prepared questions with follow-up prompts that encourage her subject to expand on her responses.

JAN: When I worked, um, as an LPN, in fact, we had to wear white dresses, white socks, white shoes, *and* a *cap*. You *absolutely had* to wear a cap. And, um, people respected you. They—they knew you were a nurse. . . . They could tell the difference between, er, um, a nurse's aide [laughs], because you dressed differently . . . They'd say, Well, this is a nurse, she *knows* what she's doing.

GILLIAN: As opposed to . . . ?

JAN: As opposed to now. Well, working in Intensive Care I wear scrubs, which looks like pajamas. You can wear, well—I hate to tell you what I wear on my feet! I've gotten lax in my old age [laughs]. Sloppy old shoes. . . .

GILLIAN: So you think the change in dress has, um—we've sacrificed a little . . .

JAN: I think it has *something* to do with it.

GILLIAN: . . . professional authority?

306 | PART 4 A GUIDE TO RESEARCH

JAN: When I go into a patient's room, *they* don't know *who* I am. I could be the house-keeper, 'cos they have to wear scrubs too. I could be the housekeeper; I could be di-etary, bringing them their tray. They don't know *what* I am and I just, um, . . . I *long* for the old days when I really *looked* like a nurse [laughs]! Because now I—I—I look like somebody who just got out of bed [laughs]!

Toward the end of the interview, Gillian asks if Jan sees any differences in how well people take care of themselves. This question leads into a discussion of nurses' roles as educators. Notice that in the following passage and else-where, Gillian summarizes or rephrases what her subject has said to demon-strate that she understands correctly what she has heard in the interview ("So you feel that now it is a continuous process . . . ").

GILLIAN: An important part of the RN, um, *job* is supposed to be *educating* people. . . .

JAN: Well, I did that, when I was first graduated from RN . . . I had a flip chart . . . and the *people*—they—they *looked* at me with *respect*. Like, *Wow! She* knows what she's *talking* about. . . .

GILLIAN: Do you find it more difficult to educate people now?

JAN: You don't sit down with the *flip* chart like I used to, and educate the whole *family* sittin' there in *front* of you. You just, um, . . . *talk* to 'em when they come out of—of surgery, you just *tell* 'em what's gonna happen. You know, "You've got this breathing tube and when you're a little more awake and your blood gases are good and the tube will come out and then you'll be able to talk. You can't talk now because of the tube." And you just *talk* to 'em. You know, but it isn't like sittin' down, givin' a lesson. But you *teach* all the *time.*

GILLIAN: Mm huh. So you feel that *now* it is a continuous process . . .

JAN: It *is!*

GILLIAN: . . . rather than a sit down, formalized . . .

JAN: Well, that's, you know—it *was* kinda fun [laughs], sitting down and—and being "the teacher." But now it's just like a continuous process; you're right.

Questionnaires

Whereas an interview elicits information from one person whose name you know, questionnaires provide information from a number of anonymous peo-ple. To be effective, questionnaires need to be short and focused; otherwise, people may not be willing to take the time to fill them out. This sharp focus on your research helps guarantee that the results can be integrated into your paper.

The questions on questionnaires take a variety of forms:

- Questions that require a simple yes-or-no answer

  Do you commute to work in a car? (Circle one.)

  Yes   No

- Multiple-choice questions

  How many people do you commute with? (Circle one.)

  0 1 2 3 4

- Questions with answers on a checklist

  How long does it take you to commute to work? (Check one.)

  ___ 0–30 minutes   ___ 30–60 minutes

  ___ 60–90 minutes   ___ 90–120 minutes

- Questions with a ranking scale

  If the car you drive or ride in is not working, which of the following types of transportation do you rely on? (Rank the choices from 1 for most frequently used to 4 for least frequently used.)

  ___ bus   ___ shuttle van   ___ subway   ___ taxi

- Open questions

  What feature of commuting do you find most irritating?

The types of questions you decide to use will depend on the purpose of your project. The first four types of questions are the easiest for respondents to answer and the least complicated for you to process. Open questions should be asked only when other types of questions cannot elicit the information you want.

Be sure to introduce your questionnaire by stating its purpose, explaining how the results will be used, and assuring participants that their answers will be kept confidential. Send out twice as many questionnaires as you think you need because the response rate for such mailings is generally low. To protect participants' privacy, colleges and universities have **institutional review boards (IRBs)** that review questionnaires to make certain you are following the board's guidelines.

institutional review board (IRB) committee set up to protect participants' privacy in field research

Additional Advice on Field Research

When you review the results of a questionnaire or your notes from your observation or an interview, ask yourself questions about what you discovered.

- What information surprised you? Why?
- How does that reaction affect your study?
- What do you now understand better than you did? Which particular results illuminated your understanding?
- What exactly would you like to know more about?

These reflective questions will guide you in determining what else needs to be done, such as to make further observations, go to the library, or conduct another type of field research. The questions will also help with your analysis as you begin the final step of synthesizing or writing up your research. (See also CHAPTER 3, ANALYSIS AND SYNTHESIS.)

pages 45–50

PREPARING A WORKING BIBLIOGRAPHY

Whenever you plan to consult a number of sources in a research project, it is a good idea to keep a record of the core elements of your sources. This source information will comprise your **bibliography**—a list of the sources you have used in your research project. To save yourself work later as you prepare the bibliography for your paper, you may want to dedicate a section of your research log to a **working bibliography**—a preliminary record of the sources you find as you conduct your research. The working bibliography serves as a draft for your final list of references or works cited. (See CHAPTER 19, THE MLA WORKS-CITED PAGE, and CHAPTER 20, THE APA REFERENCES PAGE.)

The following sample templates indicate what source information you should record for books, articles, and websites if you are using MLA style. Even though your citation may not require each piece of information, it will all be useful, should you need to relocate a source.

bibliography a list of sources used in a research project, including author, title, and other publication data

pages 373–375
pages 400–402

working bibliography a preliminary record of source information such as author, title, page numbers, and publication data

CORE ELEMENTS OF MLA STYLE

Author(s): _____

Title of Source (e.g., book, article, online posting, etc.):

_____

Title of Container (a *container* is, for example, the anthology where an essay appears; a magazine where an article appears; or a website where a posting appears): _____

Other Contributors (*other contributors* include, for example, the general editor for a source that appears in an edited collection or a translator for a particular source): _____

Version (include when the source has been published in various versions: for example, The King James Version of the Bible; or the second edition of a textbook): _____

Number (include the number if the source is part of a numbered series, such as a season and episode in a television series [season 4, episode 3] or the volume and number of an issue from a scholarly journal [vol. 217, no. 3]):

_____

Publisher (*note:* magazines, journals, and newspapers do not include the publisher's name): _____

Publication Date (if you are accessing articles online rather than in print, use the date attached to the online publication rather than the date of the print publication): _____

Location (cite page numbers for the location in a book, for example; the location of an online work is commonly indicated by its URL (web address) or DOI (Digital Object Identifier), if the publication supplies a DOI):

_____

Sample Works-Cited Entry in MLA Style

Author   Title of Source   Container

Stein, Joel. "Millennials: The Me, Me, Me Generation." *The New Harbrace Guide: Genres for Composing,* by Cheryl Glenn, 3rd ed., Cengage Learning, 2018, pp. 418–419.

Publisher   Publication Date   Location   Other Contributor   Version

---

ACTIVITY: Using a Working Bibliography in Your Writing

Find three sources related to your research question and list them in your working bibliography with all relevant information.

MindTap®   Reflect on your writing process, practice skills that you have learned in this chapter, and receive automatic feedback.

17 Evaluating Sources

The following is an excerpt from an interview conducted by Sharifa Rhodes-Pitts with Debra Dickerson, author of *The End of Blackness: Returning the Souls of Black Folks to Their Rightful Owners.*

RHODES-PITTS: You've spoken about how *The End of Blackness* grew out of your frustration with the way racial politics get played out in what you call "black liberal" sectors. Can you elaborate a bit on what you mean?

DICKERSON: Part of what brought about the book in the first place was a lifetime spent having to bite my tongue because of the way black liberals wage the battle on race. It doesn't need to be a battle. It ought to be a dialogue—it ought to be a family discussion. Instead you're either with them or you're against them. If you don't think exactly like them you're the enemy or you're insane.

   I think that comes from a couple of things. The moral urgency that there once was—when people were being lynched or were sitting in the back of the bus or being defrauded of their citizenship—is no more. But even though it's 2004 and we don't confront the same problems, people go at it as if it's still 1950 and nothing has changed. A lot of people read about what Fannie Lou Hamer and Martin Luther King went through and slip into an us-against-the-world kind of mode and pretend that things are more dire than they are. There's a temptation to want to feel like you're waging a crusade and the forces of evil are arrayed against you. But I think there's a real sloppiness of thought there.

1. What is your immediate response to the quality of information in this interview? How expert is it? How reliable? How reasonable? What are its strengths and weaknesses?
2. In one paragraph, summarize the interview excerpt as objectively as you can.
3. Because summarizing is a kind of evaluation (you are evaluating as objectively as you can), respond in writing to the following questions with regard to your one-paragraph summary:

   a. How did you decide which of the source's ideas to put into your own words?
   b. How did you indicate the source of any direct quotes you included?
   c. How did you respond to the ideas and opinions expressed in the interview?
   d. How did you credit and cite the source?

4. Now, expand on your responses to these four questions, using parts of your summary paragraph to exemplify each response. What does this new combination of summary and response reveal about the interview itself and your response to the interview?

Readers of academic research papers expect the authors to be critical—not mean-spirited but perceptive, analytical, and objective. They want to know whether facts are accurate or erroneous, whether logic is apt or weak, whether plans are comprehensive or ill conceived, and whether conclusions are valid or invalid. Thus, researchers evaluate their sources in terms of how they can responsibly serve their research project—including how their analysis sets up their own research focus. They try to show that previous research or the current conversation on the topic offers a rhetorical opportunity for their own work. For instance, Dickerson remarks that she wrote her book because she had spent a lifetime "having to bite [her] tongue because of the way black liberals wage the battle on race." Thus the current conversation offered her an opportunity to transform the "battle" into a "dialogue," a "family discussion."

RESPONDING TO YOUR SOURCES

Your research log is a good place to record your initial responses. (See CHAPTER 15, USING A RESEARCH LOG.) You can craft more detailed responses to your sources during the process of writing your paper. For example, in the following entry from his log (page 313), Greg Coles noticed a difference between people's attitudes about spoken slang and written slang, and this distinction

pages 289–291

eventually inspired the thesis of his final draft. (See CHAPTER 19, SAMPLE MLA RESEARCH PAPER.) When you are writing in your log, then, remember that composing your entries carefully may save you time when you write your paper. Notice that Coles wrote down an idea for further research. Like most students, Coles has many obligations besides writing this research paper, so he makes a note about follow-up research he intends to do.

TRICKS OF THE TRADE

Some researchers use different-colored sticky notes, highlighting, underlining, and marginal annotations to indicate different sources. Others keep a computer file of their notes so they can search through that document rather than return to a stack of already read articles.

pages 363–375

Reading with Your Audience and Purpose in Mind

Keeping careful, purposeful notes as you read sources can save you from needless scrambling the night before your paper is due. Not only will you have your citations handy, but the notes themselves will prove useful as you work to support your thesis and confirming reasons. You will also want to use those notes that best align with your purpose and audience. In this chapter, you will learn strategies for evaluating and responding to your sources.

MY PURPOSE AND RESEARCH QUESTION

I've been thinking I'd like to learn more about slang words. Some of my writing teachers have told me that I should never use slang when I write because it's sloppy, but a lot of my favorite books have slang in them. Also, my friends and I use slang all the time when we're talking to each other, and even my teachers occasionally speak with slang too. Why is it that talking and writing should have such different rules about slang? I wonder if some words that start out as slang eventually end up as official words in the dictionary. Also, I know there are communities (like my teachers) that discourage slang, but are there any groups that actively promote slang? These are issues I want to research more.

I think my main purpose will be to explain to other college students why they hear such mixed messages about whether slang is an effective or ineffective form of communication. Depending on what I find out, maybe I will also be trying to persuade my audience that they should be more permissive of slang, or more cautious of it. I might start by asking *What motivates people to use slang?*

Using a Research Log to Evaluate Sources

Researchers make decisions about what to include in their logs by anticipating what kind of information will be most important in helping them answer their research question and document their results. Generally, entries in a research log relate to one of the following activities:

- Establishing the rhetorical opportunity, purpose, and research question
- Identifying the sources
- Summarizing and taking notes
- Analyzing and responding to notes

Now that you have taken notes on the kinds of sources that might be useful to you, you will have a log of which sources you have consulted and be able to evaluate how those sources fit into your research. Your research log also serves as a testing ground for information and thoughts you may include in your paper.

Responding to Your Notes

Most of your entries, regardless of your note-taking system, will consist of detailed notes summarizing and analyzing (or evaluating) the research you are conducting. Often these notes will be based on your reading, but they may also cover observations, interviews, and other types of research. You may have included your responses to what you have recorded from the sources, including whether you agree or disagree, what you question, why you find some item of information particularly interesting, and what connections you draw between one source and another.

In evaluating your sources, your responses should be purposeful. When you find a source with which you agree or disagree, copy down or paraphrase pages 333–335 excerpts you wish to emphasize or dispute (see CHAPTER 18, PARAPHRASING SOURCES). You will want also to note *why* you agree or disagree, so that you can more easily reconstruct your initial response later when you are composing your essay. Taking the time to carefully record your responses to sources will allow you to make a smooth transition from taking notes to composing your essay.

It is crucial to have a system for clarifying which ideas come from the source and which are your own—especially when you are recording source notes and your responses to those notes in the same place. Even professional authors have damaged their research—and their credibility—by assuming that they would remember which ideas came from their sources and which were their own responses to those sources. Guard against this danger by writing your responses in a different-color ink or using a different font, enclosing your responses in brackets, or using some other technique to make the distinction. You might want to use a double-entry notebook. (See CHAPTER 13, THE DOUBLE-ENTRY NOTEBOOK.)

In the following excerpt from Greg Coles's research log, he includes bibliographic information about a news article he is considering using as a source, his summary of the article, and his analysis of or response to it. The red text is Coles's response to and analysis of his summary.

SOURCE 1:

Robson, David. "The Secret 'Anti-Languages' You're Not Supposed to Know." *BBC Future*, 12 Feb. 2016, www.bbc.com/future/story/20160211-the-secret-anti-languages-youre-not-supposed-to-know.

pages 243–244

David Robson explains that slang is sometimes invented specifically to keep certain people from understanding it. Since the fifteenth century, the English language has given birth to a number of "anti-languages," code languages invented by groups of thieves or other social outcasts so that they can communicate with each other without revealing their schemes to other listeners. In order to avoid detection, these slang creators invent a lot of words for a single concept—this practice is called "over-lexicalisation." In Elizabethan England, for instance, the anti-language use by thieves had over twenty words for "thief." Anti-languages are often developed in prisons, but they have also been used as a way of resisting criminal activity. For example, a group of villagers in Mali, Africa, developed an anti-language so that they could fool slave traders. Even though most anti-languages have disappeared over time, some of the words they invented have become part of Standard English, One example of this is the word "butch," which was invented as part of an anti-language used by the gay community in Britain during the early twentieth century, when homosexuality was illegal. After the anti-homosexuality laws were revoked, "butch" became a more common word.

One of the scholars cited in this report, Martin Montgomery from the University of Macau, says that he thinks the internet "will only encourage the creation of slang that share some of the qualities of anti-languages." To prove this, he says, "you just need to look at the rich online vocabulary that has emerged to describe prostitution." This may sound like Montgomery has a negative attitude toward slang, since having more words for prostitution isn't necessarily a good thing—but he's also using the word "rich," which sounds positive. It seems pretty clear, though, that Robson, the author of this report, thinks that slang and anti-languages are good things. The report ends with the sentence "Yet our language may be at its richest and most powerful when it is driven underground." What reasons does each of these writers have for liking slang? It makes the most sense to me to be excited about slang when it's helping people, like in the example with the villagers in Mali. But I guess if slang is making new words for us, then that could be exciting too.

pages 309–310

⚡ TRICKS OF THE TRADE

Instead of keeping a research log, some researchers use the time-tested method of writing information on note cards. Most of these researchers use four-by-six-inch cards, recording one note per card. If a note is particularly long, they staple a second card to it. Keeping separate cards allows a researcher to test different arrangements of information during the drafting stage. If you decide to use note cards, be sure to indicate the source of each note at the bottom of the card so that you will have the information you need to cite or document the source in your paper. (See CHAPTER 16, PREPARING A WORKING BIBLIOGRAPHY, for a list of source information to write down.)

 # QUESTIONING SOURCES

When you read sources critically, you are considering the rhetorical situation from the perspective of a reader, in other words, reading rhetorically. Since you are also thinking about how the sources might be used in your own writing, you are involved in a second rhetorical situation as a writer. Rarely will the rhetorical situation that led to the creation of the source you are consulting be the same as the rhetorical situation you confront in writing for an assignment.

Questions that can help you evaluate your sources fall into five categories: currency, coverage, reliability, reasoning, and author stance. In the following sections, you will learn more about these categories and read brief sample notes that illustrate them.

Currency

Depending on the nature of your research, the currency of sources or of the data they present may be important to consider. Using up-to-date sources is crucial when you are writing about current events or issues that have arisen recently. However, if you are doing historical research, you may want to use primary sources from the period you are focusing on.

QUESTIONS ABOUT CURRENCY

- Do your sources and the data presented in them need to be up to date? If so, are they?
- If you are doing historical research, are your sources from the relevant period?
- Since you began your project, have events occurred that you should take into account? Do you need to find new sources?

Coverage

Coverage refers to the comprehensiveness of research. The more comprehensive a study is, the more convincing are its findings. Similarly, the more examples a writer provides, the more compelling are the writer's conclusions. Claims that are based on only one instance are likely to be criticized for being merely anecdotal.

QUESTIONS ABOUT COVERAGE

- How many examples is the claim based on?
- Is this number of examples convincing, or are more examples needed?
- Are the conclusions based on a sufficient amount of data?

Johnson concludes that middle-school students are expected to complete an inordinate amount of homework given their age, but he bases his conclusion on research conducted in only three schools (90). To be more convincing, Johnson would need to conduct research in more schools, preferably located in different parts of the country.

Reliability

Research, especially research based on experiments or surveys, must be reliable. Experimental results are reliable if they can be replicated in other studies—that is, if other researchers who perform the same experiment or survey get the same results. Any claims based on results supported by only one experiment are extremely tentative.

Reliability also refers to the accuracy of data reported as factual. Researchers are expected to report their findings honestly, not distorting them to support their own beliefs and not claiming ideas of others as their own. Researchers must resist the temptation to exclude information that might weaken their conclusions.

Sometimes, evaluating the publisher can provide a gauge of the reliability of the material. As a rule, reliable source material is published by reputable companies, institutions, and organizations. If you are using a book, check to see whether it was published by a university press or a commercial press. Books published by university presses are normally reviewed by experts before publication to ensure the accuracy of facts. Books published by commercial presses may or may not have received the same scrutiny, so you will have to depend on the reputation of the author and/or post-publication reviews to determine reliability. If you are using an article, remember that articles published in journals, like books published by academic presses, have been reviewed in draft form by two or three experts. Journal articles also include extensive bibliographies so that readers can examine the sources used in the research. Magazine articles, in contrast, seldom undergo expert review and rarely include documentation of sources.

If you decide to use an online source, be sure to consider the nature of its sponsor. Is it a college or university (usually identified by the suffix *.edu*), a government agency (*.gov*), a nonprofit organization (*.org*), a network site (*.net*), or a commercial business (*.com*)? There is no easy way to ascertain the reliability of online sources. If you are unsure about an online source, try to find out as much as you can about it. First click on links that tell you about the mission of the site sponsor and then perform an online search of the sponsor's name to see what other researchers have written about the company, institution, or orga-

pages 300–304 nization. (For more on online sources, see CHAPTER 16, ONLINE SOURCES, AUDIO-VISUAL SOURCES, AND ADDITIONAL ADVICE FOR FINDING SOURCES ONLINE.)

QUESTIONS ABOUT RELIABILITY

- Could the experiment or survey that yielded these data be replicated?
- Are the facts reported indeed facts?
- Is the coverage balanced and the information relevant?
- Are the sources used acknowledged properly?
- Are there any disputes regarding the data? If so, are these disputes discussed sufficiently?
- Was the material published by a reputable company, institution, or organization?

Online Sources and Reliability

Although it was once the case (and not so long ago!) that most sources accessed online were less reliable than those found in print, the difference is becoming less pronounced. Reputable scholarly journals—journals whose content has been reviewed by experts (peer-reviewed)—are found online, and personal web log entries (blogs) are being collected and published in books—even Twitter postings are being archived by the Library of Congress. It is generally still the case, however, that you will locate the scholarly journals you need at your library or through your library's subscription service (such as LexisNexis). Likewise, standards for print publication are still higher than those for the Internet—after all, anyone can put up a website on any topic whatsoever, whereas most print materials have met a minimum set of standards.

Soundness of Reasoning

When writing is logical, the reasoning is sound. Lapses in logic may be the result of using evidence that does not directly support a claim, appealing primarily (or exclusively) to the reader's emotions, or encouraging belief in false authority. Faulty logic often appears with logical fallacies. These fallacies occur often enough that each one has its own name. Some of the most common fallacies are listed below; after each is a question for you to ask yourself as you consider an author's reasoning. (See also CHAPTER 8, LOGICAL FALLACIES.)

QUESTIONS ABOUT REASONING

- *Ad hominem* (Latin for "toward the man himself"). Has the author criticized or attacked the author of another source based solely on his or her character, not taking into account the reasoning or evidence provided in the pages 143–144 source?
- *Appeal to tradition.* Does the author support or encourage some action merely by referring to what has traditionally been done?
- *Bandwagon.* Does the author claim that an action is appropriate because many other people do it?
- *False authority.* When reporting the opinions of experts in one field, does the author incorrectly assume that they have expertise in other fields?
- *False cause* (sometimes referred to as *post hoc, ergo propter hoc,* a Latin phrase that translates as "after this, so because of this"). When reporting two events, does the author incorrectly believe (or suggest) that the first event caused the second event?
- *False dilemma* (also called the *either/or fallacy*). Does the author provide only two options when more than two exist?
- *Hasty generalization.* Are the author's conclusions based on too little evidence?
- *Oversimplification.* Does the author provide unreasonably simple solutions?
- *Slippery slope.* Does the author predict an unreasonable sequence of events?

Stance of the Author

All authors have beliefs and values that influence their work. As you read a work as part of your research, it is your job to decide whether the author is expressing strong views because of deep commitment or because of a desire to deceive. As long as authors represent information truthfully and respectfully, they are acting ethically. If they twist facts or otherwise intentionally misrepresent ideas, they are being dishonest.

QUESTIONS ABOUT THE STANCE OF THE AUTHOR

- Has the author adequately conveyed information, or has the author oversimplified information or ignored relevant information?
- Has the author been faithful to source material, or has the author distorted information and quoted out of context?
- Has the author adequately supported claims, or has the author used unsupported generalizations?

 # PREPARING AN ANNOTATED BIBLIOGRAPHY

annotated bibliography list of sources that includes commentary on each source

An **annotated bibliography** is a list of works cited, or sometimes works consulted, that includes descriptive or critical commentary with each entry. Your response to a source will be based on your evaluation of it. By preparing an annotated bibliography, you show that you have understood your sources and have thought about how to incorporate them into your paper. Even if your instructor does not require an annotated bibliography, you might want to create one if you are working on a research project that will take several weeks to complete, as this type of list can help you keep track of sources. To prepare entries that will help you solidify your knowledge of sources and your plans for using them, follow these guidelines:

pages 342–363 or 380–394

- Begin each entry with bibliographic information. See CHAPTER 19, MLA GUIDELINES FOR DOCUMENTING WORKS CITED or CHAPTER 20, APA GUIDELINES FOR DOCUMENTING REFERENCES if your instructor requires you to use one of these styles.
- Below the bibliographic information, write two or three sentences that summarize the source.
- After summarizing the source, write two or three sentences explaining the usefulness of the source for your specific research project.

Greg Coles included the following source in his annotated bibliography, summarizing it and analyzing its value as a source for his paper:

Bennett, Jessica. "OMG! The Hyperbole of Internet-Speak." *The New York Times*, 28 Nov. 2015, www.nytimes.com/2015/11/29/fashion/death-by-internet-hyperbole-literally-dying-over-this-column.html.

According to Jessica Bennett, one of the features of Internet slang that is currently on the rise is the use of hyperbole—that is, overstatement—to say unremarkable things.

She gives examples of phrases like "Omg literally dying" and "I literally can't even," phrases which seem to imply high emotional intensity but are often texted or posted online by straight-faced young people with little thought. While Bennett argues that the rise of slang hyperbole is relatively recent, she also points out that some of the language trends she identifies have been at work for decades. Citing the work of a linguist named Tyler Schnoebelen, she proposes that one explanation for internet hyperbole is the demands of social media, where people try to make themselves as interesting as possible (and therefore as dramatic as possible) in order to get more "likes."

This source might be useful for two reasons. First, it gives an extensive list of examples of the slang hyperbole that is popular in online social media right now. Second, it explains how the unique demands of social media have created the need for this kind of slang. I've already found other sources that talk about internet slang, but this is the only source that shows even reputable news sources like CNN using slang hyperbole. This evidence will help me argue that the boundaries between "good slang" and "bad slang" are not as easy to determine as many people believe. If I use this source in my paper, I may also need to read Tyler Schnoebelen's work in linguistics, since he can help me make the argument that this slang has arisen to meet a particular kind of need.

ACTIVITY: Creating an Annotated Bibliography

If you have already constructed a working bibliography (see CHAPTER 16, PREPARING A WORKING BIBLIOGRAPHY), add annotations for the sources you think will be most useful. Be sure to include both a summary of the source and an explanation of how the source will be useful to you.

pages 309–310

MindTap® Reflect on your writing process, practice skills that you have learned in this chapter, and receive automatic feedback.

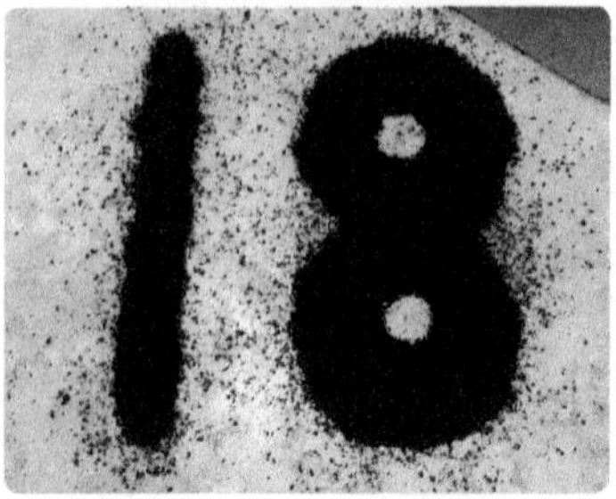

Lisa Moore

18 Synthesizing Sources: Summary, Paraphrase, and Quotation

MindTap® Understand the goals of the chapter and complete a warm-up activity online.

1. The coffee cups pictured here may have been familiar to you, but you may not have thought of them as demonstrating the use of sources. How does Starbucks credit the sources of the quotations? What information is given? What does that information tell you? What information about the sources is left out?
2. Even if you have not seen quotations on coffee cups, you have likely seen them elsewhere; they appear on everything from teabags to tee shirts, bumper stickers to baseball caps. If you wanted to place a quotation on something you own, what item and what quotation would you choose? What source information, if any, would you provide to accompany it?

AVOIDING PLAGIARISM

plagiarism the use of others' words and ideas without adequate acknowledgment

Writers who do not provide adequate acknowledgment of the sources they have used have committed **plagiarism**, the unethical and illegal use of others' words and ideas. By acknowledging your sources, you also give your readers the information they need to find those sources in case they would like to consult them on their own. Such acknowledgment should occur in the body of your paper (in-text citations) and in the bibliography at the end of your

paper (documentation). The Modern Language Association (MLA) and the American Psychological Association (APA) provide guidelines for both formatting papers and acknowledging sources. (See CHAPTER 19, ACKNOWLEDGING SOURCES IN MLA STYLE or CHAPTER 20, ACKNOWLEDGING SOURCES IN APA STYLE.) In pages 338–375 or 376–402 this chapter, you will learn to summarize, paraphrase, and quote from sources. Each of these techniques for recording information can help you achieve your purpose and satisfy your audience.

Which Sources to Cite

If the information you use is considered common knowledge, you do not have to include an in-text citation. Common knowledge is information that most educated people know and many reference books report. For example, you would not have to include an in-text citation if you mentioned that New Orleans was devastated by Hurricane Katrina. However, if you quoted or paraphrased what various politicians said about relief efforts following Katrina, you would need to include such citations.

You should include citations for all facts that are not common knowledge, as well as for statistics (whether from a text, table, graph, or chart), visuals, research findings, and quotations and paraphrases of statements made by other people. Be sure that when you acknowledge sources you include the following:

- The name(s) of the author(s) or, if unknown, the title of the text
- Page number(s)
- A bibliographic entry that corresponds to the in-text citation
- Quotation marks around material quoted exactly

Common Citation Errors

To avoid being accused of plagiarism, be on the lookout for the following errors:

- No author (or title) mentioned
- No page numbers listed
- No quotation marks used
- Paraphrase worded too similarly to the source
- Inaccurate paraphrase
- Images used with no indication of the source
- No bibliographic entry corresponding to the in-text citation

To incorporate sources effectively, you will summarize, paraphrase, or quote and document your sources.

SUMMARIZING SOURCES

Researchers regularly use summaries in their writing to indicate that they have done their homework—that is, that they are familiar with other work done on a topic. In summarizing their sources, researchers restate the information they have read as concisely and objectively as they can, thereby demonstrating their understanding of it and establishing their credibility. Researchers may have additional reasons for using summaries. For instance, they may use the information to support their own view, to deepen an explanation, or to contest other information they have found. In academic research papers, summaries appear most frequently as introductory material. (See pages 42–43 also, CHAPTER 3, SUMMARY.)

Using Function Statements

Depending on your purpose, you may decide to summarize an entire source or just part of it. Summarizing an entire source can help you understand it. To compose such a summary, you may find it useful to first write a function statement for each paragraph. A **function statement** goes beyond restating the content of the paragraph; it captures the intention of the author. For example, an author may introduce a topic, provide background information, present alternative views, refute other writers' positions, or draw conclusions based on evidence provided. It is important to include *attributive tags*—words that attribute information to a source—when using function statements. Words like *believes, describes,* or *emphasizes* or phrases like *according to* or *from the author's perspective* help make the source clear. (See CHAPTER 7, GRAMMAR IN CONTEXT: THINKING RHETORICALLY ABOUT ATTRIBUTIVE TAGS.)

> **function statement** a description of the content of the text and the intention of the author
>
> pages 130–131

Jacob Thomas chose the following article by William Lutz as a possible source for a research paper addressing the question, "How do the media use language to deceive the public?" His function statements follow the article. The paragraphs are numbered for convenience.

Doubts about Doublespeak

WILLIAM LUTZ

During the past year, we learned that we can shop at a "unique retail biosphere" instead of a farmers' market, where we can buy items made of "synthetic glass" instead of plastic, or purchase a "high-velocity, multipurpose air circulator," or electric fan. A "wastewater conveyance facility" may "exceed the odor threshold" from time to time due to the presence of "regulated human nutrients," but that is not to be confused with a sewage plant that stinks up the neighborhood with sewage sludge. Nor should we confuse a "resource development park" with a dump. Thus does doublespeak continue to spread. 1

Doublespeak is language which pretends to communicate but doesn't. It is language which makes the bad seem good, the negative seem positive, the unpleasant seem attractive, or at least tolerable. It is language which avoids, shifts or denies responsibility; language which is at variance with its real or purported meaning. It is language which conceals or prevents thought. 2

Doublespeak is all around us. We are asked to check our packages at the desk "for our convenience" when it's not for our convenience at all but for someone 3

(continued)

Synthesizing Sources

else's convenience. We see advertisements for "preowned," "experienced" or "previously distinguished" cars, not used cars, and for "genuine imitation leather," "virgin vinyl" or "real counterfeit diamonds." Television offers not reruns but "encore telecasts." There are no slums or ghettos, just the "inner city" or "substandard housing" where the "disadvantaged" or "economically nonaffluent" live and where there might be a problem with "substance abuse." Nonprofit organizations don't make a profit, they have "negative deficits" or experience "revenue excesses." With doublespeak it's not dying but "terminal living" or "negative patient care outcome."

4   There are four kinds of doublespeak. The first kind is the euphemism, a word or phrase designed to avoid a harsh or distasteful reality. Used to mislead or deceive, the euphemism becomes doublespeak. In 1984 the U.S. State Department's annual reports on the status of human rights around the world ceased using the word "killing." Instead the State Department used the phrase "unlawful or arbitrary deprivation of life," thus avoiding the embarrassing situation of government-sanctioned killing in countries supported by the United States.

5   A second kind of doublespeak is jargon, the specialized language of a trade, profession or similar group, such as doctors, lawyers, plumbers or car mechanics. Legitimately used, jargon allows members of a group to communicate with each other clearly, efficiently and quickly. Lawyers and tax accountants speak to each other of an "involuntary conversion" of property, a legal term that means the loss or destruction of property through theft, accident or condemnation. But when lawyers or tax accountants use unfamiliar terms to speak to others, then the jargon becomes doublespeak.

6   In 1978 a commercial 727 crashed on takeoff, killing three passengers, injuring 21 others and destroying the airplane. The insured value of the airplane was greater than its book value, so the airline made a profit of $1.7 million, creating two problems: the airline didn't want to talk about one of its airplanes crashing, yet it had to account for that $1.7 million profit in its annual report to its stockholders. The airline solved both problems by inserting a footnote in its annual report which explained that the $1.7 million was due to "the involuntary conversion of a 727."

7   A third kind of doublespeak is gobbledygook or bureaucratese. Such doublespeak is simply a matter of overwhelming the audience with words—the more the better. Alan Greenspan [former Chairman of the Federal Reserve Board for the United States], a polished practitioner of bureaucratese, once testified before a Senate committee that "it is a tricky problem to find the particular calibration in timing that would be appropriate to stem the acceleration in risk premiums created by falling incomes without prematurely aborting the decline in the inflation-generated risk premiums."

The fourth kind of doublespeak is inflated language, which is designed to   8
make the ordinary seem extraordinary, to make everyday things seem impressive, to give an air of importance to people or situations, to make the simple
seem complex. Thus do car mechanics become "automotive internists," eleva-
tor operators become "members of the vertical transportation corps," grocery
store checkout clerks become "career associate scanning professionals," and
smelling something becomes "organoleptic analysis."

Doublespeak is not the product of careless language or sloppy thinking.   9
Quite the opposite. Doublespeak is language carefully designed and constructed
to appear to communicate when in fact it doesn't. It is language designed not to
lead but mislead. Thus, it's not a tax increase but "revenue enhancement" or
"tax-base broadening." So how can you complain about higher taxes? Those
aren't useless, billion dollar pork barrel projects; they're really "congressional
projects of national significance," so don't complain about wasteful government
spending. That isn't the Mafia in Atlantic City; those are just "members of a
career-offender cartel," so don't worry about the influence of organized crime in
the city.

New doublespeak is created every day. The Environmental Protection Agency   10
once called acid rain "poorly buffered precipitation," then dropped that term in
favor of "atmospheric deposition of anthropogenically-derived acidic substances,"
but recently decided that acid rain should be called "wet deposition." The Pentagon, which has in the past given us such classic doublespeak as "hexiform rotatable
surface compression unit" for steel nut, just published a pamphlet warning soldiers
that exposure to nerve gas will lead to "immediate permanent incapacitation."
That's almost as good as the Pentagon's official term "servicing the target," meaning to kill the enemy. Meanwhile, the Department of Energy wants to establish a
"monitored retrievable storage site," a place once known as a dump for spent
nuclear fuel.

Bad economic times give rise to lots of new doublespeak designed to avoid   11
some very unpleasant economic realities. As the "contained depression" continues,
so does the corporate policy of making up even more new terms to avoid the
simple, and easily understandable, term "layoff." So it is that corporations "reposi-
tion," "restructure," "reshape" or "realign" the company and "reduce duplication"
through "release of resources" that involves a "permanent downsizing" or a "pay-
roll adjustment" that results in a number of employees being "involuntarily
terminated."

Other countries regularly contribute to doublespeak. In Japan, where baldness   12
is called "hair disadvantaged," the economy is undergoing a "severe adjustment

(continued)

process," while in Canada there is an "involuntary downward development" of the work force. For some government agencies in Canada, wastepaper baskets have become "user friendly, space effective, flexible, deskside sortation units." Politicians in Canada may engage in "reality augmentation," but they never lie. As part of their new freedom, the people of Moscow can visit "intimacy salons," or sex shops as they're known in other countries. When dealing with the bureaucracy in Russia, people know that they should show officials "normal gratitude," or give them a bribe.

13   The worst doublespeak is the doublespeak of death. It is the language, wrote George Orwell in 1945, that is "largely the defense of the indefensible designed to make lies sound truthful and murder respectable, and to give an appearance of solidity to pure wind." In the doublespeak of death, Orwell continued, "defenseless villages are bombarded from the air, the inhabitants driven out into the country-side, the cattle machine-gunned, the huts set on fire with incendiary bullets. This is called pacification. Millions of peasants are robbed of their farms and sent trudging along the roads with no more than they can carry. This is called transfer of popula-tion or rectification of frontiers." Today, in a country once called Yugoslavia, this is called "ethnic cleansing."

14   It's easy to laugh off doublespeak. After all, we all know what's going on, so what's the harm? But we don't always know what's going on, and when that hap-pens, doublespeak accomplishes its ends. It alters our perception of reality. It deprives us of the tools we need to develop, advance and preserve our society, our culture, our civilization. It breeds suspicion, cynicism, distrust and, ultimately, hos-tility. It delivers us into the hands of those who do not have our interests at heart. As Samuel Johnson noted in 18th century England, even the devils in hell do not lie to one another, since the society of hell could not subsist without the truth, any more than any other society.

SAMPLE FUNCTION STATEMENTS

Paragraph 1: Lutz begins his article on doublespeak by providing some examples: a "unique retail biosphere" is really a farmers' market; "synthetic glass" is really plastic.

Paragraph 2: Lutz defines *doublespeak* as devious language—"language which pre-tends to communicate but doesn't" (22).

Paragraph 3: Lutz describes the wide use of doublespeak. It is used in all media.

Paragraph 4: Lutz defines the first of four types of doublespeak—euphemism, which is a word or phrase that sugarcoats a harsher meaning. He provides an example from the U.S. State Department.

Paragraph 5: Lutz identifies jargon as the second type of doublespeak. It is the specialized language used by trades or professions such as car mechanics or doctors. But Lutz believes the use of jargon is legitimate when it enables efficient communication among group members. Jargon is considered doublespeak when in-group members use it to communicate with nonmembers who cannot understand it.

Paragraph 6: Lutz shows how an airline's annual report includes devious use of jargon to camouflage a disaster.

Paragraph 7: According to Lutz, the third type of doublespeak has two alternative labels: *gobbledygook* or *bureaucratese*. The distinguishing feature of this type of doublespeak is the large number of words used.

Paragraph 8: Lutz states that the final type of doublespeak is inflated language.

Paragraph 9: Lutz is careful to note that doublespeak is not the product of carelessness or "sloppy thinking" (23) but rather an attempt to deceive.

Paragraph 10: Lutz emphasizes that instances of doublespeak are created on a daily basis and provides examples.

Paragraph 11: Lutz attributes increases in the use of doublespeak to a bad economy. Doublespeak serves to gloss over the hardships people experience.

Paragraph 12: Lutz notes that doublespeak is also used in other countries.

Paragraph 13: Lutz singles out the doublespeak surrounding the topic of death as the worst type of doublespeak.

Paragraph 14: Lutz concludes his article by establishing the harmfulness of doublespeak, which can leave us without "the tools we need to develop, advance and preserve our society, our culture, our civilization" (24).

Clustering and Ordering Information in a Summary

After you have written a function statement for each paragraph of an essay, you may find that statements cluster together. For example, the statements Jacob Thomas wrote for paragraphs 4 through 8 of William Lutz's article all deal with the different categories of doublespeak. If an essay includes subheadings, you can use them to understand how the original author grouped ideas. By finding clusters of ideas, you take a major step toward condensing information. Instead of using a sentence or two to summarize each paragraph, you can use a sentence or two to summarize three paragraphs. For example, Jacob might have condensed his function statements for paragraphs 4 through 8 into one sentence: "Lutz claims that euphemism, jargon, gobbledygook (or bureaucratese), and inflated language are four types of doublespeak."

Summaries often present the main points in the same order as in the original source, usually with the thesis statement of the original source first, followed by supporting information. Even if the thesis statement appears at the end of the original source, you should still state it at the beginning of your summary. If there is no explicit thesis statement in the original source, you should state at the beginning of your summary the thesis (or main idea) that you have inferred from reading that source. Including a thesis statement, which captures the essence of the original source, in the first or second sentence of a summary provides a reference point for other information reported in the summary. The introductory sentences of a summary should also include the source author's name and the title of the source.

After you finish your summary, ask yourself the following questions to ensure that it is effective:

- Have I included the author's name and the title of the source?
- Have I mentioned the thesis (or main idea) of the original source?
- Have I used attributive tags to show that I am referring to someone else's ideas?
- Have I remained objective, not evaluating or judging the material I am summarizing?
- Have I remained faithful to the source by accurately representing the material?

Direct quotations can be used in summaries, but they should be used sparingly. Guidelines for quotations are discussed in more detail later in this chapter. All quotations and references to source material require accurate citation and documentation. (For accurate in-text citation and documentation formats, see pages 338–375 or 376–402 CHAPTER 19, ACKNOWLEDGING SOURCES IN MLA STYLE or CHAPTER 20, ACKNOWLEDGING SOURCES IN APA STYLE.)

Sample Student Summary

Jacob Thomas followed the MLA citation and documentation guidelines when writing the following summary. Notice that Jacob chose to include only those details he found most important. The notes he took on paragraphs 3, 6, 9, 11, and 13 were not included.

Jacob Thomas

Professor Brown

English 101, Section 13

22 January 2016

Summary of "Doubts about Doublespeak"

In "Doubts about Doublespeak," William Lutz describes the deviousness of doublespeak, which he defines as "language which pretends to communicate but doesn't" (22). It is language meant to deceive. "Unique retail biosphere" for *farmers' market* and "revenue enhancement" for *taxes* are just a few of the examples Lutz provides. Such use of deceptive language is widespread. According to Lutz, it can be found around the world and is created anew on a daily basis. Lutz defines four types of doublespeak. Euphemisms are words or phrases that sugarcoat harsher meanings. The U.S. State Department's use of "unlawful or arbitrary deprivation of life" for *killing* is an example (22). Jargon is the second type of doublespeak Lutz discusses. It is the specialized language used by trades or professions such as car mechanics or doctors. Although Lutz believes the use of jargon is legitimate when it enables efficient communication among group members, he considers it doublespeak when in-group members use it to communicate with nonmembers who cannot understand it.

Lutz distinguishes the third type of doublespeak, gobbledygook (or bureaucratese), by the large number of words used, which, he says, serve to overwhelm those in an audience. The final type of doublespeak, according to Lutz, is inflated language, which is the use of overelaborate terms to describe something quite ordinary. Lutz concludes his article by establishing the harmfulness of doublespeak. He believes that doublespeak can alter how we perceive the world and thus leave us without "the tools we need to develop, advance and preserve our society, our culture, our civilization" (24).

Work Cited

Lutz, William. "Doubts about Doublespeak." *State Government News*, July 1993, pp. 22–24.

Partial Summaries

Jacob Thomas summarized an entire article. Depending on his purpose and the expectations of his audience, he might have chosen to write a partial summary instead. Partial summaries of varying size are frequently found in research papers. A one-sentence summary may be appropriate when a researcher wants to focus on a specific piece of information. If Jacob had been interested in noting what various writers have said about abuses of language, he could have represented William Lutz's ideas as follows:

In "Doubts about Doublespeak," William Lutz describes abuses of language and explains why they are harmful.

Partial summaries of the same source may vary depending on the research-er's purpose. The following partial summary of Lutz's article focuses on its reference to George Orwell's work, rather than on the uses of doublespeak.

SAMPLE PARTIAL SUMMARY

Authors frequently cite the work of George Orwell when discussing the abuses of language. In "Doubts about Doublespeak," William Lutz describes different types of doublespeak—language used to deceive—and explains why they are harmful. He quotes a passage from Orwell's "Politics and the English Language" in order to emphasize his own belief that the doublespeak surrounding the topic of death is the worst form of language abuse: "defenseless villages are bombarded from the air, the inhabitants driven out into the countryside, the cattle machine-gunned, the huts set on fire with incendiary bullets. This is called pacification. Millions of peasants are robbed of their farms and sent trudging along the roads with no more than they can carry. This is called transfer of population or rectification of frontiers" (qtd. in Lutz 24).

PARAPHRASING SOURCES

A **paraphrase** is like a summary in that it is a restatement of someone else's ideas, but a paraphrase differs from a summary in coverage. A summary condenses information to a greater extent than a paraphrase does. When you paraphrase, you translate the original source into your own words; thus, your paraphrase will be approximately the same length as the original. Researchers usually paraphrase material when they want to clarify it or integrate its content smoothly into their own work.

paraphrase a restatement of someone else's ideas in your own words

A paraphrase, then, should be written in your own words and should cite the original author. A restatement of an author's ideas that maintains the original sentence structure but substitutes a few synonyms is not an adequate paraphrase. In fact, such a restatement is plagiarism—even when the author's name is cited. Your paraphrase should contain different words and a new word order; however, the content of the original source should not be altered. In short, a paraphrase must be accurate. Any intentional misrepresentation of another person's work is unethical.

Below are some examples of problematic and successful paraphrases. The source citations in the examples are formatted according to MLA guidelines.

SOURCE

Wardhaugh, Ronald. *How Conversation Works*. Basil Blackwell, 1985.

ORIGINAL

Conversation, like daily living, requires you to exhibit a considerable trust in others.

PROBLEMATIC PARAPHRASE

Conversation, like everyday life, requires you to show your trust in others (Wardhaugh 5).

SUCCESSFUL PARAPHRASE

Ronald Wardhaugh compares conversation to everyday life because it requires people to trust one another (5).

ORIGINAL

> Without routine ways of doing things and in the absence of norms of behaviour, life would be too difficult, too uncertain for most of us. The routines, patterns, rituals, stereotypes even of everyday existence provide us with many of the means for coping with that existence, for reducing uncertainty and anxiety, and for providing us with the appearance of stability and continuity in the outside world. They let us get on with the actual business of living. However, many are beneath our conscious awareness; what, therefore, is of particular interest is bringing to awareness just those aspects of our lives that make living endurable (and even enjoyable) just because they are so commonly taken for granted.

PROBLEMATIC PARAPHRASE

Without habitual ways of acting and without behavioral norms, life would be too uncertain for us and thus too difficult. Our routines and rituals of everyday life provide us with many of the ways for coping with our lives, for decreasing the amount of uncertainty and anxiety we feel, and for giving us a sense of stability and continuity. They let us live our lives. But many are beneath our awareness, so what is of interest is bringing to consciousness just those parts of our lives that make life livable (and even fun) just because we generally take them for granted (Wardhaugh 21-22).

(continued)

SUCCESSFUL PARAPHRASE

Ronald Wardhaugh believes that without routines and other types of conventional behavior we would find life hard because it would be too unstable and unpredictable. Our habitual ways of going about our everyday lives enable us to cope with the lack of certainty we would experience otherwise. Many of our daily routines and rituals, however, are not in our conscious awareness. Wardhaugh maintains that becoming aware of the ways we make life seem certain and continuous can be quite interesting (21-22).

Attributive tags are used with paraphrases just as they are with function statements. Notice how they help the writer vary sentence structure.

QUOTING SOURCES

Whenever you find a quotation that you would like to use in your paper, you should think about your reasons for including it. Quotations should be used only sparingly; therefore, make sure that when you quote a source, you do so because the language in the quotation is striking and not easily paraphrased. A pithy quotation in just the right place can help you emphasize a point you have mentioned or, alternatively, set up a point of view you wish to refute. If you overuse quotations, though, readers may decide that laziness prevented you from making sufficient effort to express your own thoughts.

TRICKS OF THE TRADE

After completing a developed draft of your paper, identify all the direct quotes used and critically analyze their effectiveness. Try to remember that a paraphrase will work *better* than a quote if all the quote's information is useful but couched in difficult or inexpressive language, and a summary will be preferable if the quote is taking too long to arrive at its crucial point. Only if the exact wording of the quote is what makes it so valuable should it be kept.

Using Attributive Tags with Direct Quotations

The direct quotations in your paper should be exact replicas of the originals. This means replicating not only the words but also punctuation and capitalization. Full sentences require quotation marks and usually commas to set them off from attributive tags. Such a tag can be placed at the beginning, middle, or end of your own sentence.

ATTRIBUTIVE TAG AT THE BEGINNING OF A SENTENCE

André Aciman reminisces, "Life begins somewhere with the scent of lavender" (1).

ATTRIBUTIVE TAG IN THE MIDDLE OF A SENTENCE

"Life," according to André Aciman, "begins somewhere with the scent of lavender" (1).

ATTRIBUTIVE TAG AT THE END OF A SENTENCE

"Life begins somewhere with the scent of lavender," writes André Aciman (1).

Including Question Marks or Exclamation Points

If you choose to quote a sentence that ends with a question mark or an exclamation point, the punctuation should be maintained; no comma is necessary.

"Why are New Yorkers always bumping into Charlie Ravioli and grabbing lunch, instead of sitting down with him and exchanging intimacies, as friends should, as people do in Paris and Rome?" asks Adam Gopnik (106).

"Incompatibility is unacceptable in mathematics! It must be resolved!" claims William Byers (29).

Quoting Memorable Words or Phrases

You may want to quote just a memorable word or phrase. Only the word or phrase you are quoting appears within quotation marks.

Part of what Ken Wilber calls "boomeritis" is attributable to excessive emotional preoccupation with the self (27).

Modifying Quotations with Square Brackets or Ellipsis Points

In order to make a quotation fit your sentence, you may need to modify the capitalization of a word. To indicate such a modification, use square brackets:

Pollan believes that "[t]hough animals are still very much 'things' in the eyes of American law, change is in the air" (191).

You can also use square brackets to insert words needed for clarification:

> Ben Metcalf reports, "She [Sacajawea] seems to have dug up a good deal of the top-soil along the route in an effort to find edible roots with which to impress Lewis and Clark . . ." (164).

For partial quotations, as in the example above, use ellipsis points to indicate that some of the original sentence was omitted.

Using Block Quotations

If you want to quote an extremely long sentence or more than one sentence, you may need to use a block quotation. MLA guidelines call for a block quotation to be set off by being indented one-half inch from the left margin. You should use a block quotation only if the quoted material would take up more than four lines if formatted as part of the regular text of your paper. No quotation marks are used around a block quotation, but double (not single) quotation marks are used within the block quotation, when needed. Notice that the block quotation ends with a period, followed by the page numbers in parentheses.

> Francis Spufford describes his experience reading *The Hobbit* as a young child:
>
>> By the time I reached *The Hobbit*'s last page, though, writing had softened, and lost the outlines of the printed alphabet, and become a transparent liquid, first viscous and sluggish, like a jelly of meaning, then ever thinner and more mobile, flowing faster and faster, until it reached me at the speed of thinking and I could not entirely distinguish the suggestions it was making from my own thoughts. (279)

APA guidelines call for using a block format when quoting forty or more words. The page number for the in-text citation follows *p.* for "page." (For an example of a block quotation in APA style, see CHAPTER 20, SAMPLE APA RESEARCH PAPER.) pages 394–402

MindTap® Reflect on your writing process, practice skills that you have learned in this chapter, and receive automatic feedback.

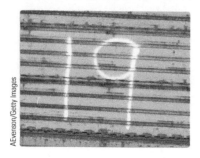

Acknowledging Sources in MLA Style

MindTap® Understand the goals of the chapter and complete a warm-up activity online.

If you are following the style recommended by the Modern Language Association (MLA), you will acknowledge your sources within the text of your paper by referring just to authors and page numbers (a process known as *In-Text Citation*) and include a Works Cited page at the end of your paper. The Works Cited page is sometimes called a *Bibliography*. However, a bibliography is for all works consulted; a Works Cited page only includes those sources you have cited in your paper.

MindTap® Go online to watch a video on using MLA format.

MLA GUIDELINES FOR IN-TEXT CITATIONS

By providing in-text citations and a works-cited list at the end of your paper, you offer your readers the opportunity to consult the sources you used. The name of the author is used in the text when citing sources. If the author's name is unknown, you use the title of the source in the in-text citation.

You will likely consult a variety of sources for any research paper. The following examples are representative of the types of in-text citations you might use.

DIRECTORY OF IN-TEXT CITATIONS ACCORDING TO MLA GUIDELINES

1.   Work by one to two authors

Although the state of New York publishes a booklet of driving rules, **Katha Pollit** has found no books on "the art of driving" **(217).**

No books exist on "the art of driving" **(Pollit 217).**

Other researchers, such as **Steven Reiss and James Wiltz,** rely on tools like surveys to explain why we watch reality television **(734-36).**

Survey results can help us understand why we watch reality television **(Reiss and Wiltz 734-36).**

The authors' last names can be placed in the text or within parentheses with the page number. The parenthetical citation should appear as close as possible to the information documented—usually at the end of the sentence or after any quotation marks. When citing a range of page numbers of three digits, do not repeat the hundreds' digit for the higher number: 201-97.

2.   Work by three or more authors

When citing parenthetically a source by three or more authors, provide just the first author's last name followed by the abbreviation *et al.* (Latin for "and others"): (Stafford et al. 67). The abbreviation *et al.* should not be underlined or italicized in citations.

3. Work by an unknown author

The Tehuelche people left their handprints on the walls of a cave, now called Cave of the Hands
(**"Hands of Time" 124**).

If the author is unknown, use the title of the work in place of the author's name. If the title is long, shorten it, beginning with the first word used in the corresponding works-cited entry ("Wandering" for "Wandering with Cameras in the Himalaya"). If you use the title in the text, however, you do not have to place it in the parenthetical reference.

4. An entire work

Using literary examples, **Alain de Botton** explores the reasons people decide to travel.

Notice that no page numbers are necessary when an entire work is cited.

5. A multivolume work

President Truman asked that all soldiers be treated equally **(Merrill 11: 741)**.

When you cite from more than one volume of a multivolume work, include the volume number and page number(s). The volume and page numbers are separated by a colon.

6. Two or more works by the same author(s)

Online shopping has breached our privacy: "The growth of market psychology to 'cluster' consumers by region, gender, race, education, and age, as well as the use of computer technology, means that our movements and individual tastes are always being tracked as unerringly as though by a bloodhound" **(Williams, *Open* 57)**.

Patricia Williams argues that peace without justice constitutes an illusion (***Intellectual* 91**).

To distinguish one work from another, include a title. If the title is long (such as *On Intellectual Activism*), shorten it, beginning with the first word used in the corresponding works-cited entry. Notice that the first entry includes the author's last name, the first work of the book title, and the page number. A comma separates the author's last name from the book title.

7. When the author's name is not given

The financial market collapse of 2008 was predicted by four so-called outsiders (Lewis, *Big Short*, 1–25).

When the author's name is not given in the sentence, provide the author's name, the title of the work, and the page number in the parenthetical citation.

8. Two or more works by different authors with the same last name

If the military were to use solely conventional weapons, the draft would likely be reinstated
(**E. Scarry 241**).

To distinguish one author from another, use their initials. If the initials are the same, spell out their first names.

9. Work by a corporate or government author

While fifty years ago we wanted to improve the national diet to eliminate dietary diseases like pellagra or rickets, today our dietary concerns focus on chronic life-threatening conditions like heart disease and diabetes **(American Heart Association xiv).**

When the corporation or government agency is listed as the author in the works-cited entry, provide the name of the corporate or government author and a page reference. Sometimes the works-cited entry may include a work by a government or corporate publication first by its title and the government agency or corporation after the title as the publisher. If the work-cited entry begins with a title, treat the in-text citation as you would for an unknown author and cite the title in the in-text citation. (See Item 4, Book by a corporate author, under Books in the Directory of Works-Cited Entries later in the chapter, on page 348.)

10. Indirect source

According to **Sir George Dasent,** a reader "must be satisfied with the soup that is set before him, and not desire to see the bones of the ox out of which it has been boiled" **(qtd. in Shippey 289).**

Use the abbreviation *qtd.* to indicate that you found the quotation in another source.

11. Work in an anthology or book collection

"Good cooking," claims **Jane Kramer,** "is much easier to master than good writing" **(153).**

Either in the text or within parentheses with the page number, use the name of the author of the particular section (chapter, essay, or article) you are citing, not the editor of the entire book, unless they are the same.

12. Poem

The final sentence in **Philip Levine's** "Homecoming" is framed by conditional clauses: "If we're quiet /. . . if the place had a spirit" **(38-43).**

Instead of page numbers, provide line numbers, preceded by *line(s)* for the first citation; use numbers only for subsequent citations.

13. Drama

After some hesitation, the messenger tells Macbeth what he saw: "As I did stand my watch upon the hill / I looked toward Birnam and anon methought / The wood began to move" **(5.5.35-37).**

Instead of page numbers, indicate act, scene, and line numbers.

14. Bible

The image of seeds covering the sidewalk reminded her of the parable in which a seed falls on stony ground **(Matt. 13.18-23).**

Identify the book of the Bible (using the conventional abbreviation) and, instead of page numbers, provide chapter and verse(s).

15. Two or more works in one parenthetical citation

Usage issues are discussed in both academic and popular periodicals **(Bex and Watts 5; Lippi-Green 53).**

Use a semicolon to separate citations.

16. Material from the Internet

Alston describes three types of rubrics that teachers can use to evaluate student writing **(pars. 2-15).**

McGowan finds one possible cause of tensions between science and religion in "our cultural terror of curiosity."

If an online publication numbers pages, paragraphs, or screens, provide those numbers in the citation. Precede paragraph numbers with *par.* or *pars.* and screen numbers with *screen* or *screens.* If the source does not number pages, paragraphs, or screens, refer to the entire work in your text by citing the author.

MLA GUIDELINES FOR DOCUMENTING WORKS CITED

To provide readers with the information they need to find all the sources you have used in your paper, you must prepare a bibliography. According to MLA guidelines, your bibliography should be entitled *Works Cited* (not in italics). It should contain an entry for every source you cite in your text, and, conversely, every bibliographic entry you list should have a corresponding in-text citation. Double-space the entire works-cited list and alphabetize your works-cited list according to the author's last name. The first line of each entry begins flush with the left margin, and subsequent lines are indented one-half inch.

The guidelines in the *MLA Handbook*, 8th edition, have been simplified to focus on nine core elements for your works-cited entries, whatever the medium—print or online. You can find a worksheet to help you record these core elements for your sources in CHAPTER 16, PREPARING A WORKING BIBLIOGRAPHY, pages 309–310 but note that all the core elements are not included for each source in your list. Provide only those elements that apply to the source you are citing.

The core elements include the (1) author(s), (2) title of source, (3) **container**—the source within which an article or posting is found, such as a newspaper or a website, (4) other contributors—such as a translator or an editor, when there is one, (5) version—such as the King James Version of the Bible or the fifth edition of a textbook, (6) number—for example, the volume and/or issue number in a series, (7) publisher, (8) date of publication, and (9) location—page numbers and/or the source's URL (preferably a stable or permalink URL address, if available) or DOI (Digital Object Identifier). A DOI is a unique code of numbers and letters assigned to many scholarly articles (doi: 10.1023/a:1015789513985) and is a permanent link so it will not change once it is assigned.

[margin note: container the term used in MLA style for the source within which an article or posting is found]

When citing a work, begin with the author, followed by a period, and then the title of the source (e.g., book, article, or online posting), also followed by a period.

1. **Author(s).** Alphabetize your works-cited list by author's last name. Use a comma to separate the last name from the first, and place a period at the end of this unit of information (Welty, Eudora.). Other configurations for author entries, and how to alphabetize them, are included later in this chapter.

[margin note: The author's name is followed by a period.]

2. **Title of Source.** The title of a stand-alone work such as a book is italicized (*The World Is Flat*). If there is a subtitle, use a colon to separate the subtitle from the title and italicize every part of the title and subtitle, including any colon (*Visual Explanations: Images and Quantities, Evidence and Narrative*). If the source is part of a larger whole, such as an article, include the title in quotation marks: "Sounding Cajun: The Rhetorical Use of Dialect in Speech and Writing."

[margin note: The title of the source is followed by a period.]

All the elements that follow the title of the source are separated by commas. Provide the appropriate information in the following order. Few source listings will include all nine core elements.

3. **Container,** After the title of the source, include the title of the container in which the source appears (a magazine where an article appears, for example, or a social-networking site where a posting appears). Italicize the full container name—including *A*, *An*, and *The*—for magazines (*The Quarterly*), journals (*Cultural Critique*), and newspapers (*The New York Times*). Also italicize websites (*Google Books*), social-networking sites (*Twitter*), and databases (*ProQuest*). See Online Sources for more on how to include websites, posts on online networks, and databases.

[margin note: A comma follows the name of the container.]

4. **Other Contributors,** When there are other contributors, spell out the relationship of the other contributor to the main source (*edited by, translated by*). You will not always have other contributors in your works-cited entry.

[margin note: A comma follows the names of other contributors.]

[vertical margin tab: MLA]

5. Version, You will also not always have a version for your works-cited entry, but if you are citing a particular edition of a book, you will indicate what version you are citing (for example, *3rd ed.* or *Unabridged version*) to indicate the version of the source you are citing.

A comma follows the version.

6. Number, All journal entries must contain volume and issue numbers, except those journals with issue numbers only. MLA now requires you to abbreviate "volume": *vol.* The issue "number" is abbreviated *no.* Include a period after *vol.* and *no.* and separate with a comma (*vol. 10, no. 3*). A number is also included for a numbered series, such as a season and episode in a television series (*season 4, episode 3*) or a book that is part of a series or is a volume in a multivolume work. As with versions, you will not always have a relevant number for your works-cited entry.

A comma follows the number.

7. Publisher, Use a publisher's full name (*Random House* or *Alfred A. Knopf*), not the parent organization (Random House Penguin Group), and use the abbreviation *UP* for University Press (*Yale UP* for Yale University Press). Do not include business information in the name of the publisher (*Company, Co., Corporation, Corp., Inc.,* or *Ltd.*).

A comma follows the publisher.

Note: Magazines, journals, and newspapers do not include the publisher's name. Websites do not include the publisher's name when it is the same as the name of the website.

Do not include the city where the publisher is located unless it helps clarify who the publisher is. For example, the city where a local newspaper is published might be included in brackets if that city is not included in the name of the newspaper (*The Weekly Gazette* [Colorado Springs]).

8. Date of Publication, The publication date that you provide depends on the type of publication you are citing. The copyright date is included for a book (found on the title page or the page following the title page, called the *copyright page*). For an article in a monthly magazine, include the publication month and year (*Dec. 2015*). Abbreviate the names of all months except May, June, and July. For a weekly or daily publication, indicate the day, the month, and the year (*17 Mar. 2016*). If you are accessing an article, include the date posted online, even if it is different from the date in the print publication.

A comma follows the date of publication.

9. Location. If you are citing a selection within a book or an article within a magazine or online source, you will need to provide the location of your source. MLA now requires that the page numbers be preceded by *p.* or *pp.* or that the online location be included. An online location is indicated with a URL (Internet address—use stable or permalink addresses when they have been assigned) or a DOI (Digital Object Identifier). Note, when including page numbers, larger page numbers should include ranges with two digits, pp. 52-55, pp. 102-09 (include the "0"). Include more digits when needed for clarity, pp. 395–401, pp. 1608–774.

A period concludes the works-cited entry.

CORE ELEMENTS

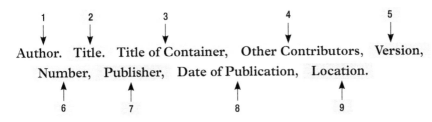

For more details on various types of sources, use the following directory to find relevant sections. For an example of a works-cited list, see the paper at the end of this chapter. If you would like to use a checklist to help ensure that you have followed MLA guidelines, see page 363.

(continued)

Books

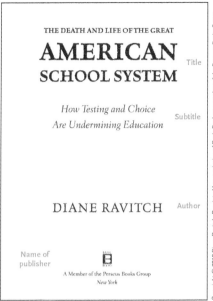

THE DEATH AND LIFE OF THE GREAT

AMERICAN — Title
SCHOOL SYSTEM

How Testing and Choice — Subtitle
Are Undermining Education

DIANE RAVITCH — Author

Name of publisher

A Member of the Perseus Books Group
New York

Copyright © 2010 Diane Ravitch. Reprinted by permission of Basic Books, a member of the Perseus Books Group.

Copyright © 2010 by Diane Ravitch
Published by Basic Books,
A Member of the Perseus Books Group
— Year of publication

All rights reserved. Printed in the United States of America. No part of this book may be reproduced in any manner whatsoever without written permission except in the case of brief quotations embodied in critical articles and reviews. For information, address Basic Books, 387 Park Avenue South, New York, NY 10016-8810.

Books published by Basic Books are available at special discounts for bulk purchases in the United States by corporations, institutions, and other organizations. For more information, please contact the Special Markets Department at the Perseus Books Group, 2300 Chestnut Street, Suite 200, Philadelphia, PA 19103, or call (800) 810-4145, ext. 5000, or e-mail special.markets@perseusbooks.com.

Designed by Pauline Brown

Library of Congress Cataloging-in-Publication Data

Ravitch, Diane.
The death and life of the great American school system : how testing and choice are undermining education / Diane Ravitch.
   p. cm.
Includes bibliographical references and index.
ISBN 978-0-465-01491-0 (alk. paper)
1. Public schools—United States. 2. Educational accountability—United States. 3. Educational tests and measurements—United States. 4. School choice—United States. I. Title.
LA217.2.R38 2009
379.1—dc22

2009050406

10 9 8

Copyright © 2010 Diane Ravitch. Reprinted by permission of Basic Books, a member of the Perseus Books Group.

Title page of The Death and Life of the Great American School System.

Copyright page of The Death and Life of the Great American School System.

SAMPLE WORKS-CITED ENTRY FOR A BOOK

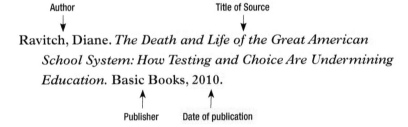

Author — Title of Source

Ravitch, Diane. *The Death and Life of the Great American School System: How Testing and Choice Are Undermining Education.* Basic Books, 2010.

Publisher — Date of publication

Most of the information you need for a works-cited entry can be found on a book's title page. If you cannot find the date of publication on the title page, turn to the copyright page. Works-cited entries for books generally include four core elements.

Author.
Title of Source.
Publisher,
Date of Publication.

1. Book by one author

You, Xiaoye. *Writing in the Devil's Tongue: A History of English Composition in China*. Southern Illinois UP, 2009.

2. Book by two authors

Gies, Joseph, and Frances Gies. *Life in a Medieval City*. Harper and Row, 1981.

When two authors are listed, only the first author's name is inverted. List the authors' names in the order in which they appear on the title page, not in alphabetical order. Include full names for all of the authors, even if they have the same last name.

3. Book by three or more authors

Belenky, Mary, et al. *Women's Ways of Knowing: The Development of Self, Voice, and Mind*. Basic Books, 1986.

For three or more authors, provide the first author's name inverted, followed by the abbreviation *et al.* (not italicized). The first author is the first name as it appears on the title page.

4. Book by a corporate author

American Heart Association. *The New American Heart Association Cookbook*. 6th ed., Clarkson Potter, 2001.

Omit any article (*a, an,* or *the*) that begins the name of a corporate author, and alphabetize the entry in the works-cited list according to the first major word of the corporate author's name. If the corporate author is the same as the publisher, begin with the title of the book and list the corporation as the publisher.

5. Book by an anonymous author

Primary Colors: A Novel of Politics. Warner Books, 1996.

Alphabetize the entry according to the first major word in the title of the work.

6. Book with an author and an editor

Dickens, Charles. *Pickwick Papers*. Edited by Malcolm Andrews, Tuttle, 1997.

Begin the entry with the author's name. Place the editor's name after the title of the book, preceded by *Edited by*.

7. Book with an editor instead of an author

Baxter, Leslie A., and Dawn O. Braithwaite, editors. *Engaging Theories in Interpersonal Communication: Multiple Perspectives.* SAGE, 2008.

Begin the entry with the name(s) of the editor(s), followed by *editors.*

8. Second or subsequent edition

Cameron, Rondo, and Larry Neal. *A Concise Economic History of the World: From Paleolithic Times to the Present.* 4th ed., Oxford UP, 2003.

After the title, include the version of the source. If the source you are citing is a second or subsequent edition, place the number of the edition in its ordinal form, followed by *ed.* for "edition." Note that the letters *th* following the number appear in regular type, not as a superscript.

9. Introduction, preface, foreword, or afterword to a book

Peri, Yoram. Afterword. *The Rabin Memoirs,* by Yitzhak Rabin. U of California P, 1996, pp. 422-32.

Begin the entry with the name of the author of the introduction, preface, foreword, or afterword, followed by the name of the part being cited (e.g., *Afterword*). If the part being cited has a title, include the title in quotation marks between the author's name and the name of the part being cited. Provide the title of the book (see Container, earlier in this chapter), followed by a comma and *by* with the name of the author of the book (see Other Contributors, earlier in this chapter). Complete the entry with the page number(s) of the part being cited after the publication information.

10. Anthology or book collection

Ramazani, Jahan, et al., editors. *The Norton Anthology of Modern and Contemporary Poetry.* 3rd ed., W. W. Norton, 2003.

The entry begins with the anthology's editor(s), with the first (or only) editor's name inverted, followed by a comma and *editor* or *editors.*

11. Single work from an anthology or book collection

Muños, Gabriel Trujillo. "Once Upon a Time on the Border." *How I Learned English,* edited by Tom Miller, National Geographic Society, 2007, pp. 141-48.

Begin the entry with the name of the author of the work you are citing, not the name of the anthology's editor. The title of the work appears in quotation marks between the author's name and the title of the anthology. The editor's name is preceded by *edited by* (not in italics). After the publisher and date of publication, conclude with the numbers of the pages on which the work appears.

12. Two or more works from the same anthology or book collection

Miller, Tom, editor. *How I Learned English.* National Geographic Society, 2007.

Montero, Mayra. "How I Learned English . . . or Did I?" Miller, pp. 221-25.

Padilla, Ignacio. "El Dobbing and My English." Miller, pp. 237-41.

When citing more than one work from the same anthology, include an entry for the entire anthology as well as entries for the individual works. In entries for individual works, list the names of the author(s) and the editor(s) and the title of the work, but not the title of the anthology. Then specify the page or range of pages on which the work appears.

13. Two or more works by the same author

Rodriguez, Richard. *Brown: The Last Discovery of America.* Penguin Books, 2002.

---. *Hunger of Memory: The Education of Richard Rodriguez.* Bantam Books, 1982.

If you have used more than one work by the same author (or team of authors), alphabetize the entries according to title. For the first entry, provide the author's name; for any subsequent entries, substitute three hyphens (---).

14. Two or more works by the same first author

Bailey, Guy, and Natalie Maynor. "The Divergence Controversy." *American Speech,* vol. 64, no. 1, 1989, pp. 12-39.

Bailey, Guy, and Jan Tillery. "Southern American English." *American Language Review,* vol. 4, no. 4, 2000, pp. 27-29.

If two or more entries have the same first author, alphabetize the entries according to the second author's last name.

15. Book with a title within the title

Koon, Helene Wickham. *Twentieth Century Interpretations of* Death of a Salesman: *A Collection of Critical Essays.* Prentice Hall, 1983.

When an italicized title includes the title of another work that would normally be italicized, do not italicize the embedded title. If the embedded title normally requires quotation marks, it should be italicized as well as enclosed in quotation marks.

16. Translated book

Rilke, Rainer Maria. *Duino Elegies*. Translated by David Young, W. W. Norton, 1978.

The translator's name appears after the book title, preceded by *Translated by* (not in italics). However, if the material cited in your paper refers primarily to the translator's comments rather than to the translated text, the entry should appear as follows:

Young, David, translator. *Duino Elegies*. By Rainer Maria Rilke, W. W. Norton, 1978.

17. Multivolume work

Sewall, Richard B. *The Life of Emily Dickinson*. Farrar, Straus, and Giroux, 1974. 2 vols.

Sewall, Richard B. *The Life of Emily Dickinson*. Vol. 1, Farrar, Straus, and Giroux, 1974. 2 vols.

If you cite material from a multivolume work, include the total number of volumes (e.g., *2 vols.*) after the period that follows the date of publication. Provide the specific volume number (e.g., *Vol. 1*) after the title if you cite material from only one volume.

18. Book in a series

Restle David, and Dietmar Zaefferer, editors. *Sounds and Systems*. De Gruyter, 2002. Trends in Linguistics 141.

Provide the name of the series and the series number.

19. Encyclopedia entry

"Heckelphone." *The Encyclopedia Americana*, 2001.

Begin with the title of the entry, unless an author's name is provided. Provide the edition number (if any) and the year of publication after the title of the encyclopedia. Conclude with the medium of publication. Other publication information is unnecessary for familiar reference books.

20. Dictionary entry

"Foolscap." Definition 3. *Merriam-Webster's Collegiate Dictionary*, 11th ed., 2003.

A dictionary entry is documented similarly to an encyclopedia entry. If the definition is one of several listed for the word, provide the definition number or letter, preceded by *Definition*.

Articles

Article in a Journal

You can generally find the name of the journal, the volume and issue numbers, and the year of publication on the cover of the journal. Sometimes this information is also included in the journal's page headers or footers. MLA does not make a distinction between journals that are numbered continuously (for example, vol. 1 ends on page 208, and vol. 2 starts on page 209) and those numbered separately (that is, each volume starts on page 1). To find the title of the article, the author's name, and the page numbers, you will need to locate the article within the journal. See Online Sources, page 355, for information on citing articles from online sources.

Article in a Magazine

To find the name of the magazine and the date of publication, look on the cover of the magazine. Sometimes this information is also included in the magazine's page headers or footers. To find the title of the article, the author's name, and the page numbers, you will have to look at the article itself. If the article is not printed on consecutive pages, as often happens in magazines, give the number of the first page, followed by a plus sign.

ARTICLE IN A JOURNAL

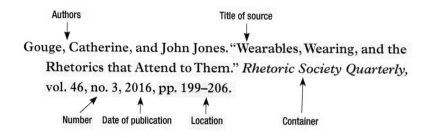

Authors | Title of source

Gouge, Catherine, and John Jones. "Wearables, Wearing, and the Rhetorics that Attend to Them." *Rhetoric Society Quarterly,* vol. 46, no. 3, 2016, pp. 199–206.

Number   Date of publication   Location   Container

ARTICLE IN A MAGAZINE

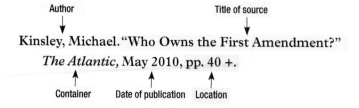

Author | Title of source

Kinsley, Michael. "Who Owns the First Amendment?" *The Atlantic,* May 2010, pp. 40 +.

Container   Date of publication   Location

Works-cited entries for articles generally include the following core elements.

Author.

Title of Source.

Container,

Number,

Date of Publication,

Location.

21. Article in a journal

Burt, Susan Meredith. "Solicitudes in American English." *International Journal of Applied Linguistics,* vol. 13, no. 1, 2003, pp. 78-95.

Place the title of the article in quotation marks after the author's name, separated by periods. The container (the name of the journal) follows, in italics. Provide the volume and issue numbers, the year of publication, and the range of pages.

Cover of an academic journal

The elements that follow the title (container, number, date of publication, and location) are separated by commas.

22. Article in a monthly magazine

Moran, Thomas E. "Just for Kicks Soccer Program." *Exceptional Parent*, Feb. 2004, pp. 36-37.

Include the publication month and year. Abbreviate the names of all months except May, June, and July.

23. Article in a weekly magazine or newspaper

Gonzalez, Jennifer. "Community-College Professor, Visiting Yale, Explores the Ethics of Treating Animals." *The Chronicle of Higher Education,* 23 Apr. 2010, p. A4.

Provide the day, month, and year of publication after the title of the publication.

24. Article in a daily newspaper

Lewin, Tamara. "Teenage Insults, Scrawled on Web, Not on Walls." *The New York Times,* 6 May 2010, pp. A1+.

Provide the day, month, and year of publication. If the article does not appear on consecutive pages, add a plus sign after the first page number.

25. Unsigned article

"Beware the Herd." *Newsweek,* 8 Mar. 2004, p. 61.

Alphabetize the entry according to the first major word in the title, ignoring any article (*a, an,* or *the*).

26. Editorial in a newspaper or magazine

Marcus, Ruth. "In Arizona, Election Reform's Surprising Consequences." Editorial. *The Washington Post,* 5 May 2010, p. A21.

After the title of the editorial, place the word *Editorial,* followed by a period. Then include the name of the newspaper or magazine, the date of publication, and the location.

27. Letter to the editor

Willens, Peggy A. "Re: Government Criticizes BP for Response to Oil Spill." Letter. *The New York Times,* 1 May 2010, p. A30.

Following the author's name, add the subject line enclosed in quotation marks if there is one. Then insert *Letter,* followed by a period. Conclude with the name of the periodical, the date of publication, and the page number.

28. Book or film review

Morgenstern, Joe. "See Spot Sing and Dance: Dog Cartoon 'Teacher's Pet' Has Enough Bite for Adults." Review of *Teacher's Pet,* directed by Timothy Björklund. *The Wall Street Journal,* 16 Jan. 2004, pp. W1+.

Place the reviewer's name first, followed by the title of the review (if any) in quotation marks. Next, provide the title of the work reviewed, preceded by *Review of,* and then mention other contributors important to the review with an indication of their contribution: *directed by* precedes a director's name; *performance by* precedes an actor's name.

Online Sources

When citing online sources, use the list of core elements to guide you just as you would for print. There are a few variations that are specific to online sources. The location for an online source is indicated with a web address—the DOI (Digital Object Identifier) or a stable permalink of the URL, where possible. In addition, online sources frequently have more than one container—for instance, an article might be found in a journal (container 1), which is accessed as part of an online collection (container 2) within a database (container 3). When there is a second and occasionally third container, the names of the second and third containers are placed at the end of the entry and followed by the web address.

Author.

Treat authors as you would for print, with the exception that Internet handles and pseudonyms are acceptable author names for online sources.

Title of Source.

Titles are punctuated as they are in print. When there is no title for a tweet, use the full post included in quotation marks as a title. When citing an e-mail message, use the subject line as the title and enclose the subject line in quotation marks.

Container (Container 1),

Italicize online container names, just as you would for print. Journals, magazines, and newspapers, as well as online collections of works and websites where articles are posted, are all containers. Standardize the name of a website if the punctuation is unusual.

Online sources commonly have more than one container. Often a second and sometimes third container simply hosts the first container—rather than contributes to the content of the source (see Container 2, p. 356). Include the name of the host site (in italics) to help others locate the source. It is placed at the end of the entry, prior to the web address. Host sites include YouTube for videos or ProQuest for online subscription services.

Publisher,

The publisher who sponsors a website is usually at the bottom of the home page (for example, the Oxford English Dictionary's website www.oed.com is published by Oxford University Press). Look at the "About" page to find the publisher who sponsors a website if it is not otherwise clear. A publisher contributes to the content of the site. *Blogspot,* for example, might host a blog but it is not the publisher (see Container 2). The publisher's name is not included when the name of the website would simply be repeated as that of the publisher.

Date of Publication,

Include the date of publication that is posted online when you have accessed your source online, even if the print date of publication is different. If the source includes a time stamp (10:00 a.m.), add the time after the date (day, month, year) and separate the date and time with a comma. If the work was published in a different medium, such as a book, before being published online, use the date that provides the most insight into the source. If the date of publication is the last entry before Container 2, conclude with a period as you would with print.

Location (page numbers or web address).

Sometimes page numbers from the print source are available as part of the database that has been accessed. Include them, and follow with a period if this is the last entry before Container 2. If there is no second container, add a comma and the web address.

Container (Container 2),

When the first container is located within a second or third container, include all the container names. Subsequent containers include databases of works (African Journals Online [AJOL]), social media networks (Twitter), or online library subscriptions (JSTOR); these come after the date of publication (and page numbers, when page numbers are available) and are italicized.

Additional information for the second or third container, such as other contributors, version, number, publisher, and date of publication, is included when it is available, separated by commas.

Location (web address).

Conclude with a web location. MLA prefers a stable or permalink for the URL or a DOI, which is also a permanent link, if either of these is available. Check with your instructor to make sure your instructor does not require different or additional information.

It is important to include information that helps others locate your source online and to avoid extraneous information that might be confusing. MLA no longer requires the date of access or medium. Only include the date of access if the URL is likely to be removed or updated.

Online sources vary significantly; thus, as you prepare your works-cited list, you will need to follow the models shown here closely.

JOURNAL ARTICLE FROM A LIBRARY SUBSCRIPTION SERVICE

Author   Title of source

Mattingly, Carol. "Recovering Forgotten Habits: Anti-Catholic
  Rhetoric and Nineteenth-Century American Women's Container 1
  Literacy." *College Composition and Communication,*
  vol. 58, no. 2, Dec. 2006. *JSTOR, www.jstor.org/stable/2045633.*

Number Date of publication Container 2 (Subscription Service) Location

29. Online book

Austen, Jane. *Emma*. 1815. *Project Gutenberg*, 21
  Jan. 2010, www.gutenberg.org/ebooks/158.

Begin with the information you always provide for an entry for a book (author and title). In this instance, the original publication date is included after the title to provide additional insight into the source. The name of the website (italicized) that houses the book, the date of publication, and the web address conclude the entry. Note that MLA guidelines require concluding each entry with a period, even if the web address does not end in a period.

30. Article in an online publication

Dayen, David. "Snapshot of a Broken System: How
  a Profitable Company Justifies Laying Off 1400
  Workers and Moves Their Jobs to Mexico."
  Salon, 22 Mar. 2016, 2:51 p.m., www.salon.com/

Carol Mattingly

Uncovering Forgotten Habits: Anti-Catholic Rhetoric and Nineteenth-Century American Women's Literacy

This article examines the connection between religion and literacy efforts on behalf of girls and young women in the early nineteenth-century United States by looking at the rapid proliferation of Catholic convent academies and the anti-Catholic sentiment that spurred the growth of proprietary academies, such as those of Mary Lyon and Catharine Beecher. It also examines how religious rhetoric influenced the curriculum in both Catholic and proprietor schools.

*"What training is there compared to that of a Catholic nun? . . .
There is nothing like the training which the Sacred Heart or the
Order of St. Vincent gives to women."*
—Florence Nightingale to Cardinal Manning
June 1852 (qtd. in Callan 149)

Historians have long acknowledged the close relationship between literacy and religion in the American colonies and the early republic, where leaders promoted widespread reading of Scripture. As scholars trace the development of education farther, however, the religious focus diminishes, despite the continued role religion played in literacy efforts, especially those on behalf of girls and women. When examining these early efforts, scholars have focused on such

CCC 58:2 / DECEMBER 2006

160

First page of article in an online journal.

2016/03/22/snapshot_of_a_broken_system_how_a_profitable_company_justifies_laying_off_
1400_people_moved_their_jobs_to_mexico/.

Begin with the information you provide for an entry for a print article. Use the date that is posted on the site you have accessed, including the time stamp when available. Conclude with the location.

31. Article in a print publication accessed online

Cloud, John. "The YouTube Gurus." *Time*, 16 Dec. 2006, content.time.com/time/magazine/
article/0,9171,1570795,00.

Begin with the information you provide for a print citation, but the date of publication will be the date it was posted online (even if it differs from the date on the print publication), and conclude with the online location.

32. Article from a library subscription service

Fenn, Donna. "Generation Why Not." *Inc.*, 2014, pp. 46-54. *ABI/INFORM Complete, ProQuest,*
ezacess.libraries.psu.edu/login?url=http://search.proquest.com.ezaccess.libraries.psu.edu/
docview/1544412697?accountid=13158.

Provide the usual information for the article. A period precedes the listing of subsequent containers. The second container for this article is the *ABI/ INFORM Complete* collection that includes all issues of *Inc.* The collection is housed in the ProQuest library subscription service. The web location within ProQuest follows. If there are no subsequent containers, include a comma after the date of publication (or the page numbers, if page numbers are available) and conclude with the web address.

33. Website

Amon Carter Museum of American Art. 2016, www.amoncartermuseum.org.

Provide the title of the site (italicized), followed by a period. Include the version number (if provided), the name of the publisher if different from the name of the website, and the date of publication or latest update. Conclude with the online location.

34. Article posted on a website

"Blowing Smoke: Chemical Companies Say, 'Trust Us,' but Environmental and Workplace
Safety Violations Belie Their Rhetoric." *Center for Effective Government,* 22 Oct. 2015,
www.foreffectivegov.org/files/regs/blowing-smoke.pdf.

Place the title of the article you are citing in quotation marks before the title of the website. If the name of the website is the same as that of the publisher, only list the website. If the section has an author, list his or her name (inverted) first.

35. Television program accessed online

"AKA Ladies Night." *Jessica Jones,* season 1, episode 1, Marvel Television, 2 Nov. 2015. *Netflix,*
www.netflix.com/watch/_80002312?trackId=200256157&tctx=0%2C0%2C23e03981-3acf-
4974-97f3-83ae3e876383-69793497.

Begin with the title of the episode in quotation marks, followed by a period. Include the title of the program in italics, the season number, and the episode number, followed by the organization that was most responsible for the production or relevant for your research (e.g., the production company or the network where the series aired) and the date the episode aired or the year(s) the series was originally broadcast, followed by the online provider in italics and the web address. See also Items 39 and 40 for Film and Television series.

36. Video posted online

"Jim Holt: 'Why Does the Universe Exist?'" *YouTube,* uploaded by TED, 2 Sept. 2014, www
.youtube.com/watch?v=zOrUUQJd81M.

Provide the title of the video. Then include the container (in italics), who uploaded the video, the date the video was posted online, and the online location.

37. Twitter post

@jkrums. "There's a plane in the Hudson. I'm on the ferry going to pick up the people. Crazy."
Twitter, 15 Jan. 2009, 12:36 p.m., twitter.com/jkrums/statuses/1121915133.

38. E-mail message

Kivett, George. "Hydrogen Fuel Cell Technology." Received by Theodore Ellis, 28 Jan. 2010.

Give the name of the author of the message, the title (taken from the subject line of the message and enclosed in quotation marks), a description of the communication (including the recipient's name), and the date the message was sent.

Other Sources

Film, television, radio, and music

39. Film

Bus Stop. Directed by Joshua Logan, performance by Marilyn Monroe, Twentieth Century Fox, 1956.

Monroe, Marilyn, performer. *Bus Stop.* Directed by Joshua Logan, Twentieth Century Fox, 1956.

Films are created by directors, screenwriters, actors, and many others. If your focus is the film, begin with the title of the film in italics, and then list other contributors (e.g., *directed by, performance by*). If your focus is a contributor to the film, begin with the name of the contributor (last name first), a comma, and a description of the contribution (e.g, *director, performer*), followed by the film title, other contributors, the organization that was most responsible for the production, and the year of release.

40. Television series

Downton Abbey. Created by Julian Fellowes, MASTERPIECE, 2010-2015.

Robbins, Anna Mary Scott, costume designer. *Downton Abbey*. Seasons 5-6, MASTERPIECE, 2014-2015.

Television series, like films, have many contributors. If your focus is the series, begin with the title in italics, and then list key contributors with an indication of their contribution. Unlike film, a television series credits an individual as *created by*. Add the organization that was most responsible for the production or relevant for your research (e.g., the production company or the network where the series aired) and the year(s) the series was originally broadcast.

As with film, highlight the contribution of a particular individual by starting with the individual's name (last name first), followed by a comma and an indication of the nature of the contribution (*performer, director, screenplay writer*).

41. Radio program or television episode

"Back Where It All Began." *A Prairie Home Companion*, narrated by Garrison Keillor, episode 1453, National Public Radio, 2014.

"Confessions." *Breaking Bad*, created by Vince Gilligan, performance by Bryan Cranston, season 5, episode 11, AMC, 2013.

Cranston, Bryan, performer. *Breaking Bad*. AMC, 2008-13.

As with a film or television series, if your focus is the contribution of a specific individual, place the individual's name and the contribution before the title. Otherwise, begin with the title of the segment (in quotation marks), the title of the program (in italics), the season and episode numbers, and other contributors when they are important to the focus of your research (such as the name of an author, performer, director, or narrator). Conclude with the year of the broadcast. If your focus includes the historical context of the episode, you may want to include the exact date that it was aired. For *Breaking Bad*, for example, "Confessions" aired on 5 Aug. 2013.

42. Sound recording

The White Stripes. "Seven Nation Army." *Elephant,* V2 records, 2003.

Begin with the name of the performer, composer, or conductor, depending on which you prefer to emphasize. When referring to an individual song, provide its name in quotation marks after the name of the performer, composer, or conductor. Then provide the title of the album, the manufacturer's name, and the date of the recording. Note that the above entry should be alphabetized as though it begins with *w*, not *t*.

Live performances

43. Play performance

Roulette. By Paul Weitz, directed by Tripp Cullmann, 9 Feb. 2004, John Houseman Theater, New York.

Begin with the title of the play (italicized) followed by a period. Indicate the key contributors and their contribution, such as *by, directed by, performance by,* and the date of the performance, followed by a comma. Then list the location of the performance (the theater and the city). Do not include the city if it is in the name of the venue.

44. Lecture or presentation

Joseph, Peniel. "The 1960's, Black History, and the Role of the NC A&T Four." Gibbs Lecture, 5 Apr. 2010, General Classroom Building, North Carolina A&T State University, Greensboro.

Ryken, Leland. Class lecture, English 216, 4 Feb. 2010, Breyer 103, Wheaton College, Illinois.

Provide the name of the speaker, followed by a period. Then list the title of the lecture (if any) in quotation marks. If the lecture or presentation is untitled, provide a description after the name of the speaker. The sponsoring organization (if applicable) follows, and the date of the lecture or presentation. The location follows, including the city. The city need not be included if it is part of the name of the location.

Images

45. Work of art

Lange, Dorothea. *Migrant Mother.* 1936, Prints and Photographs Division, Library of Congress, Washington.

Provide the artist name and the title of the work (italicized). The date the work was created follows, then the name and location of the institution that houses the work. If the work of art has no title, briefly describe its subject.

46. Graphic novel, comic book, comic strip, or cartoon

Martin, George R.R. *The Hedge Knight II: The Sworn Sword*. Pencils and inks by Mike S. Miller, Jet City Comix, 2014.

Cheney, Tom. "Back Page by Tom Cheney." *The New Yorker*, 12 Jan. 2004, p. 88.

A graphic novel or comic book will begin with the author, then the title (in italics). Other contributors can be included following the title, along with a description of their contribution. Comic books are often published as part of a larger series. Include the title of the comic book (in italics), followed by a period. Then include the name of the series (in italics), when there is one, the issue number (*no. 12*), the publisher, and the date of publication. For a cartoon or comic strip, begin with the name of the artist. Follow with the title of the cartoon or comic strip in quotation marks. Include the name of the publication in italics where the cartoon or comic strip appeared, followed by the date of publication and the page number.

47. Advertisement

McCormick Pure Vanilla Extract. *Cooking Light*, Mar. 2004, p. 177.

Identify the item being advertised before the usual publication information.

48. Map or chart

Scottsdale and Vicinity. Rand, 2000.

Treat the map or chart as you would an anonymous book before including the usual publication information.

Print

49. Pamphlet or bulletin

Ten Ways to Be a Better Dad. National Fatherhood Institute, 2000.

An entry for a pamphlet is similar to one for a book. List the author's name first, if an author is identified.

50. Government publication

United States, Department of Agriculture, Center for Nutrition Policy and Promotion. *Stay Fit on Campus: 10 Tips for College Students to Stay Active*. Government Publishing Office, 2013, purl.fdlp.gov/GPO/gpo65065.

If no author is provided, list the name of the government (e.g., *United States, Montana,* or *New York City*), followed by a comma and the name of the agency issuing the publication, then any part of the agency that is specifically responsible for the publication. The title of the publication follows. Conclude with the usual publication data. If you have accessed the publication online, add the web location after the date of publication.

CHECKING OVER A WORKS-CITED LIST

✓ Is the title, *Works Cited* (not italicized), centered one inch from the top of the page? Is the first letter of each noun, adjective, adverb, and verb capitalized?

✓ Is the entire list double-spaced?

✓ Are initial lines of entries flush with the left margin and subsequent lines indented one-half inch?

✓ Is there a works-cited entry for each in-text citation? Is there an in-text citation for each works-cited entry?

✓ Are the entries alphabetized according to the first author's last name? If the author of an entry is unknown, is the entry alphabetized according to title (ignoring any initial *a, an,* or *the*)?

✓ Are book and periodical titles italicized? Are databases, library subscription sites, social media networks, and websites italicized?

✓ Are quotation marks used to indicate article titles?

SAMPLE MLA RESEARCH PAPER

The MLA recommends omitting a title page (unless your instructor requires one) and instead providing the identification on the first page of the paper. One inch from the top, on the left-hand side of the page, list your name, the name of the instructor, the name of the course, and the date—all double-spaced. Below these lines, center the title of the paper, which is in plain type (no italics, underlining, or boldface). On the right-hand side of each page, one-half inch from the top, use your last name and the page number as a header. Double-space the text throughout the paper, and use one-inch margins on the sides and bottom. Indent every paragraph (including the first one) one-half inch.

The running head includes the author's last name and page number.

The heading and the rest of the paper are double-spaced.

The title of the paper is centered.

The author builds credibility for his argument by analyzing and synthesizing several definitions of "slang."

Since the writer is citing two different sources here, the two citations are divided by a semicolon.

The author clearly states his thesis statement.

Coles 1

Greg Coles

Dr. Cheryl Glenn

ENGL 101

21 April 2016

Slang Rebels

What is slang? Although the word "slang" is used often, research by Bethany K. Dumas and Jonathan Lighter suggests that people have very different opinions about which words and phrases should be classified as slang (10). Robert L. Moore calls slang a "notoriously slippery concept" (61). Summarizing several definitions of slang, he states, "These definitions all have one trait in common: they define slang in terms of an extensive list of traits" (62). Among these traits are the idea that slang is usually spoken instead of written (Hummon 77) and the idea that slang is a response to or rebellion against social norms (Green 103; Moore 61). By combining these two ideas, I argue in this essay that slang is a rebellion against the literate mindset—that is, against the way that writing tries to make us think. Part of the reason slang so easily takes hold of language (Mattiello 7) is that it fulfills our desire to develop language in conversation with human beings instead of following the rules of correctness and incorrectness that usually define written communication.

Most of today's readers would probably consider words like "gleek" (to squirt water between the teeth), "gurgitator" (a competitive eater), and "paleoconservative" (a very conservative person with outdated beliefs) to be "made-up" words. However, writes Mark Peters, "if 'a real word' is one with multiple citations by different authors over a substantial period of time, then they're all real as rain" (110). Though these words do not appear in most dictionaries, they fulfill the requirements of "official words." Perhaps in fifty years they will be so much a part of our language that scientists and anthropologists will use them in formal papers.

Each paragraph begins with an indent of one-half inch (or five spaces).

It is the nature of language to be constantly changing, observes Jean Aitchison (18). This effect is particularly noticeable in the area of slang. Slang words come quickly in and out of usage (Aitchison 21). Yet although slang itself might be called "ephemeral" (Mattiello 9) and "short-lived" (Stenström), its effects on language can be permanent. Most slang disappears with time, but some slang terms transition into general usage and become part of the "established" language (Aitchison 19). Keith R. Herrmann provides a number of examples of now-established English words which began as military slang. Three such examples are the words "boycott," (see Fig. 1) "lynch," "shrapnel," all of which were originally the last names of military officers (319).

The author uses strong topic sentences that help shape the logos of his argument.

The author includes a reference within the paper to the figure and labels the reference Fig. 1.

Since it is clear from the text that Herrmann is the source of this quotation, this citation only needs to include a page number.

Figure 1 *While the term "boycott" was originally a slang term named after Captain C. C. Boycott, the word is now common and is recognized by dictionaries as part of standardized English usage.*

Pacific Press/Getty Images

Though these words are no longer considered slang by most people and are not classified as such by dictionaries (*Shorter Oxford*; *American Heritage*), they all came into being as slang terms. By the same logic, it is possible that "gleek," "gurgitator," and "paleoconservative" could lose their labels as slang and become a part of Standard English, no matter how strange or phony they may sound to people today. In a recent *New York Times* essay, Kory Stamper uses the flexibility of language to defend the validity of slang, writing,

English is fluid and enduring: not a mountain, but an ocean.

A word may drift down through time from one current of English (say, the language of World War II soldiers) to

When a work has no author, use a shortened form of the work's title in your citation.

The block quotation is introduced with a transitional sentence that describes the content of the quotation.

Throughout his essay, the author demonstrates the library research he has conducted, research that enhances not only his ethos but also the logos of the argument.

another (the slang of computer programmers). Slang words are quicksilver flashes of cool in the great stream. (Stamper)

There are two arguments most commonly used to condemn slang, and both rely on a literate, writing-based mindset. The first is that slang is uneducated and improper. Dumas and Lighter, summarizing the broad spectrum of views on slang, quote scholars who call slang an "'epidemic disease'" of language, "'the advertisement of mental poverty,'" "'at once a sign and a cause of mental atrophy'" (6-7). Those who use slang are called "'coarse,'" "'ignorant,'" or "'less educated'" (6, 9). By attacking the education of slang users, these scholars reveal their own bias in favor of literacy instead of spoken language. Education has long been defined in terms of reading and writing (Bellous 9). The very idea of scholarship, after all, implies the existence of writing. In cultures that do not write their language, there is no such thing as study (Ong 8-9). To be "educated" means something entirely different for literate people than it does in cultures that use only spoken words. Education in a non-writing culture involves the passing down of wisdom from one generation to the next through apprenticed, experiential learning, listening, repetition, and assimilation. It has nothing to do with internalizing linguistic rules—and without these rules, there is no reason to look down on slang as "rule-breaking."

MLA

A long quotation includes the last name of the author and the page number unless the source has been accessed from the Internet and has no page number. Note that in a block quotation, the final period appears at the end of the quotation itself—not after the parenthetical citation.

The author introduces two arguments against the use of slang.

The second argument against slang states that slang is inferior to "standard" language. John C. Hodges calls slang "'the sluggard's way of avoiding the search for the exact, meaningful word'" (qtd. in Dumas and Lighter 5). Novelist Tom Robbins writes, "'Slang . . . devalues experience by standardizing and fuzzing it'" (qtd. in Leahy 305). Both of these statements regard slang words as too vague to communicate well. Though they may give a general impression of what is meant, they do not speak precisely. If a thing is called "awesome," for instance, we know only that the speaker thinks it good. If it is called "delicious," we know that it *tastes* good. Formal language demands accuracy. Slang fails to meet the same standards.

Besides being vague, slang can also be ambiguous. "A major general trend among young people at the current time," writes Aitchison, "is the use of 'bad' words to mean 'good, excellent'" (21). Among the words she lists which may mean "good" are "wicked," "bad," "deadly," "filthy," and "savage." Because these words, in a slang context, mean the opposite of their dictionary definitions, they could easily lead to ambiguous communication. "Your shirt is filthy" might mean the shirt is great, or it might mean the wearer should consider a change of clothes. "This cake is deadly" could be a compliment for the cook or a caution for the people about to eat it. The easiest way to avoid this kind of confusion is to use only

This citation shows that your source is quoting from another source. If you can find the original quotation, however, it is always best to do so.

This strong topic sentence also serves as a transition between subtopics.

dictionary definitions. Slang, its detractors say, is too ambiguous to be useful in communication.

These complaints, once again, only make sense within the context of written literacy. In writing, the statement "This cake is deadly" is definitely ambiguous. In speech, however, its meaning could be made clear by the use of non-verbal cues. Accompanied by a smile from the speaker, the statement means that the cake is excellent; a look of horror on the speaker's face or a dead body nearby would suggest a more literal interpretation of the speaker's words. In spoken language, the meanings of words are communicated by context, "which is not, as in a dictionary, simply other words, but includes also gestures, vocal inflections, facial expression, and the entire human existential setting in which the real, spoken word always occurs" (Ong 47). A similar answer may be given in response to complaints of slang's vagueness. A physical context of extreme beauty would make the precise meaning of "awesome" clear.

Even in cases where context or nonverbal clues do not clarify ambiguity, spoken language can resolve this ambiguity by leaving room for listeners to ask clarifying questions whenever necessary. If the new arrival at the party still has not figured out whether the "deadly" cake is delicious or poisonous, she need only ask. Spoken language leaves room for creative or ambiguous speech, because

Throughout his essay, the author skillfully makes assertions that he substantiates with research.

Again, the author uses a topic sentence as a transitional sentence.

words that are spoken do not always need to be understood on the first try. Writing, on other hand, doesn't leave space for question-asking. Walter Ong, reporting Plato's objections to the development of writing, observes that "a written text is basically unresponsive. If you ask a person to explain his or her statement, you can get an explanation; if you ask a text, you get back nothing except the same, often stupid, words which called for your question in the first place" (78). Writing doesn't get a second chance to be understood.

The need for complete clarity in writing may help explain why people tend to oppose the use of slang in writing more than in speech. Leslie N. Carraway, as she cautions against the use of slang in scientific writing, does not argue that slang is altogether unhelpful, just that it is "more appropriate to familiar conversation than to formal speech or science writing" (387). Anna Leahy's objections to slang, specifically regarding its vagueness and inaccuracy, are also set specifically within the written context (305). On the other hand, slang's defenders typically treat it within the context of speech. Elisa Mattiello calls slang "the state-of-the-art vocabulary which people use in familiar relaxed conversations . . . in which educated formal registers would be situationally inappropriate and unconventional language is instead privileged" (35-36). From her perspective, slang and formal language are each appropriate in some contexts and inappropriate in others. For slang, she believes, the appropriate context is spoken conversation. Joseph P. Mazer and Stephen K. Hunt, who study slang in teacher-student communication, also praise slang as a useful tool for spoken communication while ignoring it in writing.

If slang were defended only in terms of speech and condemned only in terms of writing, there would be no need for disagreement. Thus, some of the current disagreement regarding slang could be avoided by specifying what form of slang is under discussion. If phrases like "Slang is good" and "Slang is bad" are modified to state that "Spoken slang is appropriate" and "Written slang is inappropriate," people who have previously disagreed may find unexpected common ground. Conflict still arises, though, when people who typically think about language in terms of writing try to make the rules of literacy apply to spoken language, or when people who primarily view language as a speaking tool try to carry the freedom of their speech into writing.

One of the typically recognized functions of slang is to "oppose established authority" (Moore 61). This function raises the question of precisely which established authority is being opposed. Slang cannot be used as a weapon in opposition to just any authority. It does not, for the most part, oppose governmental authority, because most governments have not legislated the use of slang. Nor could

Instead of citing a specific page from this source, the writer has summarized the entire argument of the source.

MLA

slang be used to oppose an authority which approved of slang. Slang, in itself, is not oppositional. It can oppose an authority only if that authority disapproves of slang. Since slang views language in terms of speech and violates the "rules" of writing, slang opposes authorities who try to enforce a rule-based mindset of written literacy. Most often, these authorities are parental and academic.

The author works to identify with the interests of his peers (his audience), establishing pathos, an authentic emotional connection with the audience.

•Because slang is most often associated with adolescents and young adults (Moore 63), who are already stereotyped as rebellious apart from their linguistic preferences, it is easy to assume that slang is just one more weapon in the arsenal of youths intent on rebellion. However, this is not necessarily the case. Certainly people of this age have a tendency to rebel against authority, and it seems equally certain that slang is a part of this rebellion. Still, a distinction should be made between slang as a part of rebellion and slang as "mere" rebellion with no other rationale. Just because slang fights authority does not mean that it exists for the sole purpose of fighting authority. It is possible that adolescents and young adults who use slang are reacting, at least in part, against the literate mindset being forced onto them. Statements like "Why does it matter how I say it as long as you know what I'm saying?" reveal an innate understanding of language as a spoken, conversational tool defined by social interaction.

•Walt Whitman calls slang "an attempt of common humanity to escape from bald literalism, and express itself illimitably" (573). It is no coincidence that the words "literalism" and "literacy" are so similar in sound: both are derived from the Latin *lit(t)era*, meaning "letter" (*Shorter Oxford*). Slang is an escape from the limits of written letters and the rules that come with them. It is, as William C. Gore writes, "a sign of life in language," a sign that "the structure of language is not liable to stiffen so as to become an inadequate means for the communication of new ideas" (197). In the conflict between spoken language and written language, slang terms are the fighting words of our spoken inheritance.

The author concludes with an appeal to pathos, invoking our "common humanity."

Works Cited •

Aitchison, Jean. "Whassup? Slang and Swearing Among School • Children." *Education Review*, vol. 19, no. 2, 2006, pp. 18–24.

The American Heritage Dictionary of the English Language. 4th ed., 2000.

Bellous, Joyce. "Spiritual and Ethical Orality in Children: Educating an Oral Self." *International Journal of Children's Spirituality,* vol. 5, no. 1, 2000, pp. 9–26.

The works-cited list begins on a new page, with the heading centered.

Every entry on the list begins flush with the left margin and has subsequent lines indented one-half inch (a hanging indent). Entries are listed in alphabetical order.

Carraway, Leslie N. "Improve Scientific Writing and Avoid

Perishing." *American Midland Naturalist,* vol. 155, no. 2, 2006,

pp. 383–94.

Dumas, Bethany K., and Jonathan Lighter. "Is *Slang* a Word for

Linguists?" *American Speech,* vol. 53, no. 1, 1978, pp. 5–17.

*This entry docu-
ments an article
from a professional
journal.*

Gore, William C. "Notes on Slang." *Modern Language Notes,* vol. 11,

no. 7, 1896, pp. 193–98.

Green, Jonathon. "Slang by Dates." *Critical Quarterly,* vol. 48, no. 1,

2006, pp. 99–104.

Herrmann, Keith R. "The War of Words." *War, Literature & the Arts:*

An International Journal of the Humanities, vol. 18, no. 1/2, 2006,

pp. 319–23.

Hummon, David M. "College Slang Revisited: Language, Culture,

and Undergraduate Life." *The Journal of Higher Education,*

vol. 65, no. 1, 1994, pp. 75–98.

Leahy, Anna. "Grammar Matters: A Creative Writer's Argument."

Pedagogy, vol. 5, no. 2, 2005, pp. 304–08.

Mattiello, Elisa. "The Pervasiveness of Slang in Standard and

Non-Standard English." *Mots Palabras Words,* 2005, pp. 7–41,

www.ledonline.it/mpw/allegati/mpw0506Mattiello.pdf.

Mazer, Joseph P., and Stephen K. Hunt. "'Cool' Communication

in the Classroom: A Preliminary Examination of Student

Perceptions of Instructor Use of Positive Slang." *Qualitative Research Reports in Communication*, vol. 9, no. 1, 2008, pp. 20–28.

McGregor, Erik. "The Right to Boycott." Pacific Press / LightRocket, 9 June 2016. *Getty Images*, www.gettyimages.com/photos/539161558.

Moore, Robert L. "We're Cool, Mom and Dad Are Swell: Basic Slang and Generational Shifts in Values." *American Speech*, vol. 79, no. 1, 2004, pp. 59–86.

Ong, Walter J. *Orality and Literacy*. Routledge, 2002.

Peters, Mark. *Bull Shit*. Three Rivers Press, 2015.

Shorter Oxford English Dictionary. 5th ed., 2002.

Stamper, Kory. "Slang for the Ages." *The New York Times*, 3 Oct. 2014, www.nytimes.com/2014/10/04/opinion/slang-for-the-ages.html.

Stenström, Anna-Brita. "From Slang to Slanguage: A Description Based on Teenage Talk." *I Love English Language*, aggslanguage .wordpress.com/slang-to-slanguage. Accessed 27 Nov. 2015.

Whitman, Walt. "Slang in America." *The Collected Writings of Walt Whitman: Prose Works 1892*, edited by Floyd Stovall, vol. 2, New York UP, 1964, pp. 572–76.

MLA

"The Right to Boycott" is the title of the photo, but if it were untitled, the description "Photograph" would be used instead.

This entry is for a source taken from a blog. The access date is included because the article posted on this website did not include a date.

MindTap® Reflect on your writing process, practice skills that you have learned in this chapter, and receive automatic feedback.

istockphoto.com/Ekaterina_Lin

Acknowledging Sources in APA Style

The American Psychological Association (APA) style guide is used by most researchers in the social sciences (anthropology, economics, geography, history, political science, psychology, sociology, and social studies), who regularly acknowledge sources within the text of the paper by referring to the author(s) of the text and the year of its publication (a process known as *In-Text Citation*), and also include a References page at the end. That References page is sometimes called a *Bibliography*. However, a bibliography includes all works consulted; a References page only contains those sources cited in the paper.

APA GUIDELINES FOR IN-TEXT CITATIONS

In addition to the author(s) of the text you consulted and the year of its publication, the APA guidelines require that you specify the page number(s) for any quotations you include; the abbreviation *p.* (for "page") or *pp.* (for "pages") should precede the number(s). For electronic sources that do not include page numbers, specify the paragraph number and precede it with the abbreviation *para.* or the symbol ¶. When no author's name is listed, provide a shortened version of the title of the source. If your readers want to find more information about your source, they will look for the author's name or the title of the material in the bibliography at the end of your paper.

You will likely consult a variety of sources for your research paper. The following examples are representative of the types of in-text citations you might use.

DIRECTORY OF IN-TEXT CITATIONS ACCORDING TO APA GUIDELINES

1.   Work by one or two authors

Wachal (2002) discusses dictionary labels for words considered taboo.

Dictionary labels for taboo words include *offensive* and *derogatory* **(Wachal, 2002).**

Lance and Pulliam (2002) believe that an introductory linguistics text should have "persuasive power" **(p. 223).**

On learning of dialect bias, some students expressed outrage, often making "a 180-degree turnaround" from their original attitudes toward a standard language **(Lance & Pulliam, 2002, p. 223).**

Authors' names may be placed either in the text, followed by the date of publication in parentheses, or in parentheses along with the date. When you mention an author in the text, place the date of publication directly after the author's name. If you include a quotation, provide the page number(s) at the end of the quotation, after the quotation marks but before the period. When citing a work by two authors, use the word *and* between their names; when citing two authors in parentheses, use an ampersand (&) between their names. Always use a comma to separate the last author's name from the date.

2. Work by three, four, or five authors

First Mention

Johnstone, Bhasin, and Wittkofski (2002) describe the speech of Pittsburgh, Pennsylvania, as *Pittsburghese*.

The speech of Pittsburgh, Pennsylvania, is called *Pittsburghese* **(Johnstone, Bhasin, & Wittkofski, 2002)**.

Subsequent Mention

Johnstone et al. (2002) cite *gumband* and *nebby* as words used in *Pittsburghese*.

The words *gumband* and *nebby* are used by speakers of *Pittsburghese* **(Johnstone et al., 2002)**.

When first citing a source by three, four, or five authors, list all the authors' last names. In subsequent parenthetical citations, use just the first author's last name along with the abbreviation *et al.* (Latin for "and others"). The abbreviation *et al.* should not be italicized in citations.

3. Work by six or more authors

Taylor et al. (2001) have stressed the importance of prohibiting the dumping of plastic garbage into the oceans.

In both the first and subsequent mentions of the source, use only the first author's last name and the abbreviation *et al.*

4. Work by an unknown author

A recent survey indicated increased willingness of college students to vote in national elections **("Ending Apathy," 2004)**.

The documents leaked to the press could damage the governor's reputation **(Anonymous, 2010)**.

When no author is mentioned, use a shortened version of the title instead. If the word *Anonymous* is used in the source to designate the author, use that word in place of the author's name.

5. Two or more works by the same author

Smith (2001, 2003, 2005) has consistently argued in support of language immersion.

Bayard (1995a, 1995b) discusses the acquisition of English in New Zealand.

In most cases, the year of publication will distinguish the works. However, if the works were published in the same year, distinguish them with lowercase letters, assigned based on the order of the titles in the bibliography.

6. Two or more works by different authors with the same last name

J. P. Hill and Giles (2001) and **G. S. Hill and Kellner (2002)** confirmed these findings.

When two or more authors have the same last name, always include first initials with that last name.

7. Work by a group

Style refers to publishing guidelines that encourage the clear and coherent presentation of written text **(American Psychological Association [APA], 2009).**

Spell out the name of the group when you first mention it. If the group has a widely recognizable abbreviation, place that abbreviation in square brackets after the first mention. You can then use the abbreviation in subsequent citations: (APA, 2009).

8. Work by a government author

Taxpayers encounter significant problems with two different taxes: the sole proprietor tax and the alternative minimum tax **(Internal Revenue Service [IRS], 2010).**

Spell out the name of the government entity when you first mention it. If the entity has a widely recognizable abbreviation, place that abbreviation in square brackets after the first mention. You can then use the abbreviation in subsequent citations: (IRS, 2010).

9. Indirect source

According to Ronald Butters, the word *go* is frequently used by speakers born after 1955 to introduce a quotation **(as cited in Cukor-Avila, 2002).**

Use *as cited in* to indicate that you found the information in another source.

10. Two or more works in one parenthetical citation

A speaker may use the word *like* to focus the listener's attention **(Eriksson, 1995; Ferrar & Bell, 1995).**

When you include two or more works within the same parentheses, order them alphabetically. Arrange two or more works by the same author by year of publication, mentioning the author's name only once: (Kamil, 2002, 2004).

11. Personal communication

Revisions will be made to the agreement this month **(K. M. Liebenow, personal communication, February 11, 2010).**

Letters, e-mail messages, and interviews are all considered personal communications, which you should cite in the text of a paper. Because personal communications do not represent recoverable data, you should not include entries for them in the references list.

 APA GUIDELINES FOR DOCUMENTING REFERENCES

To provide readers with the information they need to find all the sources you have used in your paper, you must prepare a bibliography. According to APA guidelines, your bibliography should be titled *References* (not italicized). It should contain all the information your readers need to retrieve the sources if they wish to consult them on their own. Except for personal communications, each source you cite in your text should appear in the references list.

Alphabetize your references according to the author's (or the first author's) last name. If the author is unknown, alphabetize according to title (ignoring any initial article—*a, an,* or *the*). When you have more than one source by the same author(s), order them according to the year of publication, with the earliest first.

Frazer, B. (2000).

Frazer, B. (2004).

If two or more works by the same author(s) have the same year of publication, the entries are ordered alphabetically according to the works' titles, and lower-case letters are added to the date to distinguish the entries.

Fairclough, N. (1992a). The appropriacy of "appropriateness."

Fairclough, N. (1992b). *Critical language awareness.*

Fairclough, N. (1992c). *Discourse and social change.*

When an author you have cited is also the first of two or more authors of another entry, list the source with a single author first.

Allen, J. P. (1982).

Allen, J. P., & Turner, E. J. (1988).

When two or more entries have the same first author, alphabetize the list according to the names of subsequent authors.

Fallows, M. R., & Andrews, R. J. (1999).

Fallows, M. R., & Laver, J. T. (2002).

Double-space all of your entries, leaving the first line flush with the left margin and indenting subsequent lines one-half inch. (Your word processor may refer to the indented line as a *hanging indent.*)

For more details on various types of sources, use the following directory to find relevant sections. For an example of a references list, see the paper at the end of this chapter. If you would like to use a checklist to help ensure that you have followed APA guidelines, see page 393.

DIRECTORY OF REFERENCES ENTRIES ACCORDING TO APA GUIDELINES

Books

Articles in Print

(continued)

Books

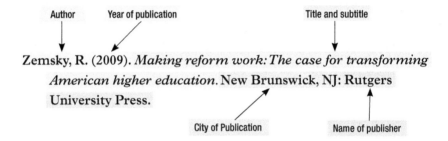

Author   Year of publication   Title and subtitle

Zemsky, R. (2009). *Making reform work: The case for transforming American higher education.* New Brunswick, NJ: Rutgers University Press.

City of Publication   Name of publisher

You can find most of the information you need to write a reference entry on a book's title page. If you cannot find the date of publication on the title page, turn to the copyright page. Reference entries for books generally include four units of information: author, year of publication, title, and publication data.

Author

The author's last name appears first, followed by the first and (if given) second initial. Use a comma to separate the last name from the initials, and place a

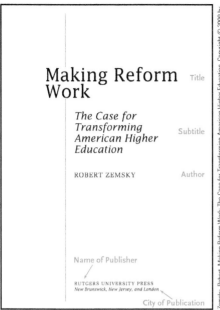

Making Reform Work   *Title*

The Case for Transforming American Higher Education   *Subtitle*

ROBERT ZEMSKY   *Author*

Name of Publisher

RUTGERS UNIVERSITY PRESS
New Brunswick, New Jersey, and London

City of Publication

Library of Congress Cataloging-in-Publication Data

Zemsky, Robert, 1940–
Making reform work: the case for transforming American higher education / Robert Zemsky.
p. cm.
Includes bibliographical references and index.
ISBN 978-0-8135-4591-2 (hardcover : alk. paper)
1. Education, Higher—United States. 2. Educational change—United States. I. Title. II. Title: Case for transforming American higher education.

LA227.4.Z45 2009
378.73—dc22

2008048062

A British Cataloging-in-Publication record for this book is available from the British Library.

Copyright © 2009 by Robert Zemsky   *Year of Publication*

All rights reserved

No part of this book may be reproduced or utilized in any form or by any means, electronic or mechanical, or by any information storage and retrieval system, without written permission from the publisher. Please contact Rutgers University Press, 100 Joyce Kilmer Avenue, Piscataway, NJ 08854-8099. The only exception to this prohibition is "fair use" as defined by U.S. copyright law.

Visit our Web site: http://rutgerspress.rutgers.edu

Manufactured in the United States of America

APA

Title page of Making Reform Work.

Copyright page of Making Reform Work.

period at the end of this unit of information. If there is more than one author, invert all the authors' names, following the pattern described for a single author. Separate the names with commas, adding an ampersand (&) before the name of the last author.

Hooker, R.   Montgomery, M., & Morgan, E.   McCrum, D., Kurath, H., & Middleton, S.

Year of publication

Place the year of publication in parentheses after the author's name. Mark the end of this unit of information with a period.

Title

Include the title and, if there is one, the subtitle of the book. Capitalize *only* the first word of the title and the subtitle, plus any proper nouns. Use a colon to separate the subtitle from the title. Italicize the title and subtitle.

Social cognition: Key readings.

Publication data

For the fourth unit of information, start with the city of publication, followed by the common two-letter state abbreviation. Place a colon between the state abbreviation and the publisher's name. Use a shortened version of the publisher's name if possible. Although the word *Press* or *Books* should be retained, *Publishers, Company* (or *Co.*), or *Incorporated* (or *Inc.*) is omitted.

1. Book by one author

Gladwell, M. (2008). *Outliers: The story of success.* New York, NY: Little, Brown.

2. Book by two or more authors

Alberts, B., Lewis, J., & Johnson, A. (2002). *Molecular biology of the cell.* Philadelphia, PA: Taylor & Francis.

If there are more than seven authors, provide the names of the first six authors, inverted, followed by an ellipsis and the name of the final author.

3. Book with editor(s)

Good , T. L., & Warshauer, L. B. (Eds.). (2002). *In our own voice: Graduate students teach writing.* Needham Heights, MA: Allyn & Bacon.

Include the abbreviation *Ed.* or *Eds.* in parentheses after the name(s) of the editor(s).

4. Book with an author and an editor

Lewis, C. S. (2003). *A year with C. S. Lewis: Daily readings from his classic works* (P. S. Klein, Ed.). Grand Rapids, MI: Zondervan.

Place the editor's name and the abbreviation *Ed.* in parentheses after the title of the book.

5. Book by a corporate author

Modern Language Association of America. (1978). *International bibliography of books and articles on the modern languages and literatures, 1976.* New York, NY: Author.

Alphabetize by the first major word in the corporate author's name. List the publisher as *Author* when the author and the publisher are the same.

6. Book by an anonymous author

Primary colors: A novel of politics. (1996). New York, NY: Warner.

List the title of the book in place of an author. Alphabetize the entry by the first major word of the title.

7. Second or subsequent edition

Cember, H. (1996). *Introduction to health physics* (3rd ed.). New York, NY: McGraw-Hill.

Maples, W. (2002). *Opportunities in aerospace careers* (Rev. ed.). New York, NY: McGraw-Hill.

Provide the edition number in parentheses after the title of the book. If the revision is not numbered, place *Rev. ed.* for "Revised edition" in parentheses after the title.

8. Translated book

de Beauvoir, S. (1987). *The woman destroyed* (P. O'Brien, Trans.). New York, NY: Pantheon. (Original work published 1969)

Insert the name(s) of the translator(s) in parentheses after the title, and conclude with the original publication date. Note the absence of a period at the end of the entry. In the text, provide both publication dates as follows: (De Beauvoir, 1969/1987).

9. Republished book

Freire, P. (1982). *Pedagogy of the oppressed* (2nd ed.). London, England: Penguin. (Original work published 1972)

Conclude the entry with the original publication date. Note the absence of a period at the end of the entry. In the text provide both dates: (Freire, 1972/1982).

10. Multivolume work

Doyle, A. C. (2003). *The complete Sherlock Holmes* (Vols. 1–2). New York, NY: Barnes & Noble.

Maugham, S. W. (1977–1978). *Collected short stories* (Vols. 1–4). New York, NY: Penguin.

Include the number of volumes after the title of the work. If the volumes were published over a period of time, provide the date range after the author's name.

11. Government report

Executive Office of the President. (2003). *Economic report of the President, 2003* (GPO Publication No. 040-000-0760-1). Washington, DC: Government Printing Office.

Provide the publication number in parentheses after the name of the report. If the report is available from the Government Publishing Office (GPO), formerly named the Government Printing Office, that entity is the publisher. If the report is not available from the GPO, use *Author* as the publisher.

12. Selection from an edited book

Muños, G. T. (2007). Once upon a time on the border. In T. Miller (Ed.), *How I learned English* (pp. 141–148). Washington, DC: National Geographic Society.

The title of the selection is not italicized. The editor's name appears before the title of the book. Provide the page or range of pages on which the selection appears.

13. Selection from a reference book

Layering. (2003). In W. Lidwell, K. Holden, & J. Butler (Eds.), *Universal principles of design* (pp. 122–123). Gloucester, MA: Rockport.

Provide the page number or range of pages after the title of the book. If the selection has an author, give that author's name first.

Bruce, F. F. (1991). Hermeneutics. In *New Bible dictionary* (p. 476). Wheaton, IL: Tyndale.

Articles in Print

ARTICLE IN A JOURNAL

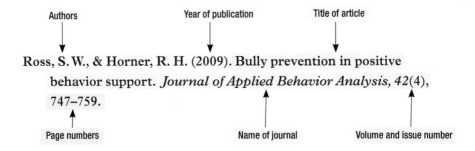

You can generally find the name of the journal, the volume and issue numbers, and the year of publication on the cover of the journal. Sometimes this information is also included in the journal's page headers or footers. To find the title of the article, the author's name, and the page numbers, you'll have to locate the article within the journal.

ARTICLE IN A MAGAZINE

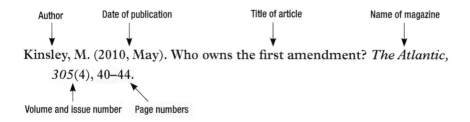

Author Date of publication Title of article Name of magazine

Kinsley, M. (2010, May). Who owns the first amendment? *The Atlantic,*
    305(4), 40–44.

Volume and issue number Page numbers

APA

To find the name of the magazine, the volume and issue numbers, and the date of publication, look on the cover of the magazine. Sometimes this information is also included in the magazine's page headers or footers. For the title of the article, the author's name, and the page numbers, look at the article itself. Reference entries for articles generally include four units of information: author, date of publication, title of article, and publication data.

Author

The author's last name appears first, followed by the first and (if given) the second initial. Use a comma to separate the last name from the initial(s), and place a period at the end of this unit of information. For articles with more than one author, see the information given for book entries earlier in this chapter.

Date of publication

For journals, place just the year of publication in parentheses after the author's name. For magazines, also specify the month and the day (if given). Mark the end of this unit of information with a period.

Cover of an academic journal showing the year of publication, volume and issue numbers (vertically, on left side), and title of the journal.

Title of article

Include the title and, if there is one, the subtitle of the article. (Do not put quotation marks around the title.) Capitalize *only* the first word of the title and the subtitle, plus any proper nouns. Use a colon to separate the subtitle from the title. Place a period at the end of this unit of information.

Publication data

The publication data that you provide depends on the type of periodical in which the article appeared. However, for all entries, include the title of the periodical (italicized), the volume number (also italicized), and the page numbers of the article. If you are using a magazine or a journal that paginates each issue separately, include the issue number as well. Place the issue number (not italicized) in parentheses following the volume number. After the issue number, place a comma and then the article's page numbers.

14. Article in a journal with continuous pagination

McCarthy, M., & Carter, R. (2001). Size isn't everything: Spoken English, corpus, and the classroom. *TESOL Quarterly, 35,* 337–340.

Provide the volume number in italics after the title of the journal. Conclude with the page number or page range.

15. Article in a journal with each issue paginated separately

Smiles, T. (2008). Connecting literacy and learning through collaborative action research. *Voices from the Middle, 15*(4), 32–39.

Provide the issue number (placed in parentheses) directly after the volume number (italicized).

16. Article with three to seven authors

Biber, D., Conrad, S., & Reppen, R. (1996). Corpus-based investigations of language use. *Annual Review of Applied Linguistics, 16,* 115–136.

If there are seven or fewer authors, list all the authors' names.

17. Article with more than seven authors

Stone, G. W., Ellis, S. G., Cox, D. A., Hermiller, J., O'Shaughnessy, C., Mann, J. T., . . . Russell, M. E. (2004). A polymer-based, paclitaxel-eluting stent in patients with coronary artery disease. *The New England Journal of Medicine, 350,* 221–231.

Provide the names of the first six authors, inverted, followed by an ellipsis and the name of the final author.

18. Article in a monthly or weekly magazine

Gross, D. (2010, May 3). The days the Earth stood still. *Newsweek,* 46–48.

Warne, K. (2004, March). Harp seals. *National Geographic, 205,* 50–67.

Provide the month and year of publication for monthly magazines or the day, month, and year for weekly magazines. Names of months are not abbreviated. Include the volume number (italicized), if any, issue number (not italicized), and the page number or page range (not italicized) after the name of the magazine.

19. Anonymous article

Ohio police hunt for highway sniper suspect. (2004, March 16). *The New York Times,* p. A4.

Begin the entry with the title of the article, followed by the date of publication.

20. Article in a newspaper

Lewin, T. (2010, May 6). Teenage insults, scrawled on Web, not on walls. *The New York Times,* pp. A1, A18.

Use *p.* or *pp.* before the page number(s) of newspaper articles. If the article appears on discontinuous pages, provide all of the page numbers, separated by commas: pp. A8, A10–11, A13.

21. Letter to the editor

Richard, J. (2004, March 8). Diabetic children: Every day a challenge [Letter to the editor]. *The Wall Street Journal,* p. A17.

Include the description *Letter to the editor* in square brackets after the title of the letter.

22. Editorial in a newspaper

Marcus, R. (2010, May 5). In Arizona, election reform's surprising consequences. [Editorial]. *The Washington Post,* p. A21.

Include the description *Editorial* in square brackets after the title.

23. Book review

Kakutani, M. (2004, February 13). All aflutter, existentially [Review of the book *Dot in the universe*]. *The New York Times*, p. E31.

In square brackets after the title of the review, indicate that the work cited is a review, provide a description of the medium of the work (e.g., book, film, or play), and include the title of the work.

Sources Produced for Access by Computer

JOURNAL ARTICLE FROM A DATABASE

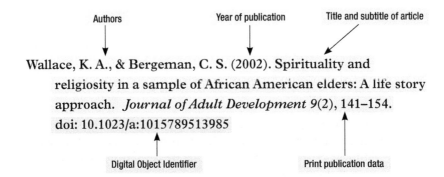

You can usually find much of the information you will need for your reference entry on the first page of the article. Each entry generally includes five units of information: author, year of publication, title and subtitle of the article, print publication data, and Digital Object Identifier (DOI).

Author

The author's last name appears first, followed by the first and (if given) the second initial. Use a comma to separate the last name from the initials, and place a period at the end of this unit of information. For articles with more than one author, see the information given for book entries earlier in this chapter.

Date of publication

For journals, place just the year of publication in parentheses after the author's name. Mark the end of this unit of information with a period.

Title of article

Include the title and, if there is one, the subtitle of the article. Capitalize only the first word of the title and subtitle, plus any proper nouns. Use a colon to separate the subtitle from the main title. Place a period at the end of this unit of information.

Print publication data

The publication data that you provide depends on the type of periodical in which the article appeared. See the information on publication data for periodicals earlier in this chapter.

Digital Object Identifier

Rather than provide a URL for the database or article, include the Digital Object Identifier (DOI), if available. A DOI is assigned to many scholarly articles found online and has the great advantage of being stable. You will usually find the DOI on the first page of the article, near the copyright notice. In cases in which a DOI is unavailable, provide the URL for the source's home page after the words *Retrieved from* (not italicized). Do not place a period at the end of this unit of information.

Electronic sources vary significantly; therefore, as you prepare your list of references, follow the models below closely. On occasion, you may not be able to find all the information presented in a particular model. In such cases, provide as much of the information as you can.

24. Article from a database or from a journal published only online

Moore, A. C., Akhter, S., & Aboud, F. E. (2008). Evaluating an improved quality preschool program in rural Bangladesh. *International Journal of Educational Development, 28*(2), 118–131. doi:10.1016/j.ijedudev.2007.05.003

After the print publication data, include the DOI, if available.

Andersson, G., Carlbring, P., & Cuijpers, P. (2009). Internet interventions: Moving from efficacy to effectiveness. *E-Journal of Applied Psychology, 5*(2), 18–24. Retrieved from http://ojs.lib.swin.edu.au/index.php/ejap

If no DOI is assigned, end the citation with the URL of the journal's home page.

25. Article in an online newspaper

Connelly, J. (2010, May 3). Lessons from the Gulf oil spill. *Seattle Post-Intelligencer.* Retrieved from http://www.seattlepi.com

Provide the full date of the article after the author's name. Conclude with the URL of the newspaper's home page.

26. Message posted to a newsgroup, forum, or discussion group

Skrecky, D. (2004, February 27). Free radical theory of aging falsified [Newsgroup message]. Retrieved from news://ageing/bionet.molbio.ageing

Bradstreet, J. (2010, May 6). The over diagnosis of ADHD and why. [Electronic mailing list message]. Retrieved from http://groups.google.com/group/natural-health/browse_thread /thread/690cbd531a1ea39e

If the author's name is unavailable, the author's screen name may be used. A brief description of the source (such as *Online forum comment*) should be provided in square brackets after the subject line of the message.

27. Document from a website

Robinson, J. (2010). *Grass fed basics*. Retrieved from http://www.eatwild.com/basics.html

Slow Food USA. (2010). *Slow food on campus*. Retrieved from http://www.slowfoodusa.org/index .php/programs/details/slow_food_on_campus

If no author is given, use the name of the organization hosting the website as the author of the document. Provide the date, the name of the document, and the URL for the specific page where the document can be found.

28. E-mail message

Personal communications such as e-mail messages, letters, telephone conversations, and personal interviews do not appear in the references list, but should be cited in the text as follows: (S. L. Johnson, personal communication, September 3, 2009).

29. Podcast

DiMeo, N. (Producer). (2010, March 12). The sisters Fox. *The memory palace*. [Audio podcast]. Retrieved from http://thememorypalace.us

Other Sources

30. Motion picture

Jurow, M. (Producer), & Edwards, B. (Writer/Director). (1963). *The pink panther* [Motion picture]. United States: United Artists.

Begin with the name of the producer or the director, or both. Include the description *Motion picture* in square brackets after the title of the film. Conclude with the country of origin and the name of the movie studio.

31. Television program

Godeanu, R. (Producer). (2004, March 17). *In search of ancient Ireland* [Television broadcast]. Alexandria, VA: Public Broadcasting Service.

Begin with the name of the producer. Italicize the title of the program, and follow the title with the description *Television broadcast* in square brackets.

32. Music recording

Porter, C. (1936). Easy to love [Recorded by H. Connick, Jr.]. On *Come by me* [CD]. New York, NY: Columbia. (1999)

White, J. (2003). Seven nation army [Recorded by The White Stripes]. On *Under great white northern lights* [CD]. Burbank, CA: Warner Bros. Records. (2010)

Start with the name of the songwriter and the date the song was written. If someone other than the songwriter recorded the song, add *Recorded by* and the singer's name in square brackets after the song title. Indicate the medium of the recording in square brackets after the album title. Conclude the entry with the year the song was recorded, in parentheses, if that date is not the same as the date the song was written.

33. Interview

Brock, A. C. (2006). Rediscovering the history of psychology: Interview with Kurt Danziger. *History of Psychology, 9*(1), 1–16.

For a published interview, follow the format for an entry for an article. If you conducted the interview yourself, cite the name of the person you interviewed in the body of your paper and include in parentheses the words *personal communication,* followed by a comma and the interview date. Do not include an entry for a personal interview in the list of references.

CHECKING OVER A REFERENCES LIST

✓ Is the title, *References* (not italicized), centered one inch from the top of the page? Is the first letter capitalized?

✓ Is the entire list double-spaced?

(continued)

- ✓ Are initial lines flush with the left margin and subsequent lines indented one-half inch?
- ✓ Is there an entry in the references list for each in-text citation (except for personal communications)? Is there an in-text citation for each entry in the references list?
- ✓ Are the entries alphabetized according to the first author's last name? If the author of an entry is unknown, is the entry alphabetized according to title (ignoring any initial *a*, *an*, or *the*)?
- ✓ If the list contains two or more entries by the same author, are the entries arranged according to year of publication (earliest one first)?
- ✓ Are book and periodical titles italicized?
- ✓ Is capitalization used for only the first words of book and article titles and subtitles and any proper nouns they contain?

SAMPLE APA RESEARCH PAPER

The APA provides the following general guidelines for formatting a research paper. The title page is page 1 of your paper. In the upper left-hand corner, place a shortened version of your title (no more than fifty characters), all in capital letters; on page 1 only, precede the header with the words *Running head* (not italicized) and a colon. In the upper right-hand corner, put the page number. This manuscript page header should appear on every page, one-half inch from the top of the page and one inch from the left and right edges. Center the full title in the upper half of the title page, using both uppercase and lowercase letters. Below it, put your name and affiliation (double-spaced)—unless your instructor asks you to include such information as the date and the course name and number instead of your affiliation.

If your instructor requires one, include an abstract—a short summary of your research—as the second page of your paper. The abstract should be no longer than 250 words. The word *Abstract* (not italicized) should be centered at the top of the page.

The first page of text is usually page 3 of the paper (following the title page and the abstract). The full title of the paper should be centered one inch from the top of the page. Double-space between the title and the first line of text. Use a one-inch margin on all sides of your paper (left, right, top, and bottom). Do not justify the text; that is, leave the right margin uneven. Indent paragraphs and block quotations one-half inch. Double-space your entire paper, including block quotations.

The page
header has
a running
head (no
more than
50 charac-
ters) on the
left and
page num-
ber on the
right. The
label *Run-
ning head*
appears
only on
page 1. The
header and
page num-
ber should
appear one-
half inch
from the top
of the page
and one
inch from
the left and
right edges.

Perceptions of Peers' Drinking Behavior

Catherine L. Davis

Central Washington University

The title is typed
in uppercase and
lowercase letters
and is centered.
The full title is one
inch from the top
of the page.

An instructor may
require such infor-
mation as the
date and the
course name and
number instead of
an affiliation.

Abstract

This study is an examination of how students' perceptions of their

peers' drinking behavior are related to alcohol consumption and

alcohol-related problems on campus. Four hundred nine randomly

selected college students were interviewed using a modified version of

the Core Survey (Presley, Meilman, & Lyeria, 1995) to assess alcohol

consumption and its related problems.

The abstract
appears on a sep-
arate page, with
the heading cen-
tered. An abstract
generally contains
between 150 and
250 words.

Use one-inch
margins on both
sides of the paper.

Perceptions of Peers' Drinking Behavior

Studies typically report the dangers associated with college

students' use of alcohol (Beck et al., 2008). Nonetheless, drinking is

still highly prevalent on American campuses. Johnston, O'Malley, and

Bachman (1998) found that 87% of the college students surveyed

reported drinking during their lifetime. Most of the students are 21

or 22 years old and report frequent episodes of heavy drinking (i.e.,

binge drinking).

Heavy episodic drinking is particularly problematic. Johnston

et al. (1998) found that 41% of college students engage in heavy

episodic drinking, which they defined as having at least five or more

drinks in a row at least once in the 2 weeks prior to being surveyed.

Heavy episodic drinking is related to impaired academic

performance, interpersonal problems, unsafe sexual activity, and

sexual assault and other criminal violations (Moore, Smith, &

Catford, 1994). The magnitude of such problems has led

Neighbors, Lee, Lewis, Fossos, and Larimer (2007) to conclude

that binge drinking is a widespread problem among college

students.

Massad and Rauhe (1997) report that college students engage in

heavy episodic drinking in response to social pressure or physical

discomfort. Almost half of college students in a survey stated their

Side annotations:

Center the title.

When a work with six or more authors is cited, *et al.* is used in the citation.

The author provides background on the problem of binge drinking.

This is a subsequent mention of a work by three authors.

When authors are named in the text, the year of publication is placed in parentheses after the names.

Researchers have established some reasons for binge drinking among college students.

Margin tab: APA

reason for drinking was to get drunk (Jessor, Costa, Krueger, & Turbin, 2006). Recent research suggests that students' misperceptions of their peers' drinking behavior contribute to increased alcohol consumption (Perkins, 2002).

College students commonly perceive their social peers as drinking more often and in greater quantities than they actually do (Neighbors et al., 2007). When these students see their peers as heavy drinkers, they are more likely to engage in heavy drinking (Neighbors et al., 2007; Perkins & Wechsler, 1996). The goal of this study was to determine whether students' perceptions of their peers' use of alcohol are related to alcohol consumption and alcohol-related problems on campus.

Method

Participants

For the purposes of this study, a randomly selected sample ($N = 409$) of undergraduate students from a university in the Pacific Northwest was drawn. The mean age of participants, 55.8% of whom were female, was 24 years; 54.5% of participants were White, 19% were Hispanic, 14.8% were Asian/Pacific Islander, 5% were African American, 0.5% were American Indian, and 6.3% indicated "Other" as their ethnicity.

This is a subsequent mention of a work by five authors.

Two or more sources in the same parenthetical citation are separated by semicolons and listed alphabetically.

The thesis statement forecasts the content of the paper.

In this section, the writer explains her research methods, including descriptions of her research subjects and the research model she followed.

Instrument

The study used a modified version of the short form of the Core

Survey (Presley, Meilman, & Lyeria, 1995). The Core Survey

measures alcohol and other drug (AOD) use as well as related

problems experienced by college students. For the purposes of this

study, the Core was modified from a self-administered format to an

interview format.

Procedure

Interviews were conducted by telephone. Each interview took an

average of 16 minutes to complete. The refusal rate for this survey

was 12%, and those refusing to participate were replaced randomly.

Alcohol use was defined as the number of days (during the past

30 days) that respondents drank alcohol. *Heavy episodic drinking* was

defined as five or more drinks in a single sitting, with a drink consisting

of one beer, one glass of wine, one shot of hard liquor, or one mixed

drink (Presley et al., 1995). Respondents indicated the number of

occasions in the past 2 weeks that they engaged in heavy episodic

drinking. *Alcohol-related problems* were defined as the number of times in

the past 30 days respondents experienced any of 20 specific incidents.

To determine alcohol-related problems, the interviewer asked

students how many times they (a) had a hangover, (b) damaged

property, (c) got into a physical fight, (d) got into a verbal fight, (e) got

The writer defines her terms.

The writer supplies specific examples of alcohol-related problems.

APA

nauseous or vomited, (f) drove a vehicle while under the influence, (g) were criticized by someone they knew, (h) had memory loss, or (i) did something they later regretted. To determine their perceptions of their peers' drinking, students were asked to respond on a 7-point ordinal scale that ranged from 0 = never to 6 = almost daily.

[The data analysis and statistical report of results have been omitted.]

Discussion

• The relationship found here concerning the normative perception of alcohol use is somewhat consistent with past research (Baer & Carney, 1993; Perkins, 2002) that suggested drinking norms are related to alcohol use. Readers should note, however, that respondents' perceptions of the drinking norm were consistent with the actual norm for 30-day use. This indicates that students are fairly accurate in assessing their peers' drinking frequencies. Unfortunately, the current study did not include a perception question for heavy episodic drinking, making it unclear whether respondents accurately perceive their peers' drinking quantity. Conceptually, misperceptions of drinking quantity might be better predictors of heavy episodic drinking. That is, students might falsely believe that their peers drink heavily when they drink. Such a misperception would be compounded by the fact that most students accurately estimate frequency of their

The writer analyzes her findings and then synthesizes them for discussion.

peers' drinking. The combination of an accurate perception of frequency coupled with an inaccurate perception of quantity might result in an overall perception of most students being heavy, frequent drinkers. As expected, this study also revealed a positive and moderately strong pathway from alcohol use, both heavy episodic drinking and 30-day drinking, to alcohol-related problems.

The author draws reasonable conclusions.

●This study represents an effort to add to the literature concerning college students' alcohol consumption and its related problems. The results of the study suggest that students' perceptions of their peers' drinking habits are important predictors of drinking or drinking-related problems. Future studies along similar lines might help prevention specialists better design media campaigns related to drinking norms and high-risk behaviors.

Alphabetize the entries according to the author's (or first author's) last name. If two or more entries have the same first author, the second author's last name determines the order of the entries.

Indent second and subsequent lines of each entry one-half inch or five spaces. All entries are double-spaced.

● References

Baer, J. S., & Carney, M. M. (1993). Biases in the perceptions of the consequences of alcohol use among college students. *Journal of Studies on Alcohol, 54,* 54–60.

Beck, K. H., Arria, A. M., Caldeira, K. M., Vincent, K. B., O'Grady, K. E., & Wish, E. D. (2008). Social context of drinking and alcohol problems among college students. *American Journal of Health Behavior, 32*(4), 420–430.

Jessor, R., Costa, F. M., Krueger, P. M., & Turbin, M. S. (2006). A developmental study of heavy episodic drinking among college students: The role of psychosocial and behavioral protective and risk factors. *Journal of Studies on Alcohol, 67,* 86–94.

Johnston, L. D., O'Malley, P. M., & Bachman, J. G. (1998). *National survey results on drug use from the Monitoring the Future Study. 1975–1997: Vol. 11* (NIH Publication No. 98-4346). Washington, DC: Government Printing Office.

Massad, S. J., & Rauhe, B. J. (1997). Alcohol consumption patterns in college students: A comparison by various socioeconomic indicators. *Journal for the International Council of Health, Physical Education, Recreation, Sport, and Dance, 23*(4), 60–64.

•Moore, L., Smith, C., & Catford, J. (1994). Binge drinking: Prevalence, patterns and policy. *Health Education Research, 9,* 497–505. doi:10.1093/her /9.4.497

Neighbors, C., Lee, C. M., Lewis, M. A., Fossos, N., & Larimer, M. E. (2007). Are social norms the best predictor of outcomes among heavy-drinking college students? *Journal of Studies on Alcohol and Drugs, 68,* 556–565.

When available for an article accessed through a database, a DOI is included in the entry. No period follows a URL or DOI at the end of an entry.

APA

Perkins, H. W. (2002). Social norms and the prevention of alcohol misuse in collegiate contexts. *Journal of American Studies on Alcohol, 14,* 164–172.

Perkins, H. W., & Wechsler, H. (1996). Variation in perceived college drinking norms and its impact on alcohol abuse: A nationwide study. *Journal of Drug Issues, 26,* 961–974.

Presley, C. A., Meilman, P. W., & Lyeria, R. (1995). Development of the Core Alcohol and Drug Survey: Initial findings and future directions. *Journal of American College Health, 42,* 248–255.

Entries with a single author come before entries with that author and one or more coauthors.

APA

MindTap® Reflect on your writing process, practice skills that you have learned in this chapter, and receive automatic feedback.

istockphoto.com/Peter Booth

Food and the (Cultural) Experience of Taste

MindTap® Understand the goals of the chapter and complete a warm-up activity online.

If you are like most college students, you have participated in lively conversations about cafeteria food. You may be one of those who goes through the cafeteria line, thinking only about how much better a home-cooked meal would be. Yet, years after graduation, many former students long for their school's most memorable foods. When Chowhound.com readers were asked to post stories about their college dining experiences, many contributors to the online discussion wrote about their school's unique delicacies. "Lidi B" of Penn State University opined, "Oh, to have a grilled sticky from the Ye Olde College Diner à la mode with Penn State Creamery ice cream . . . that would just about be heaven. . . ." On a discussion forum for Roadfood's website, "Mosca" reminisced similarly about a food truck just off Cornell's campus: "After 30 years I can still taste the (great) heartburn from the Ithaca hot truck, which was the source of my personal 'freshman 15.'" That hot truck is just one of numerous food trucks serving college campuses today or in the past, such as the Chinese Kitchen at Harvard, the grease trucks at Rutgers, Chuck's at the University of Miami, and the enchilada trucks at the University of Arizona.

This chapter focuses on the experience of food. Fitting responses come in many forms, including food memoirs (see CHAPTER 5, GENRE IN FOCUS: THE FOOD pages 76–77 MEMOIR), position arguments, investigative reports, proposals, and evaluations, as seen in the following selections in this chapter. Your instructor might call on you to consider one of the following opportunities for writing.

Hero Images/Corbis

Food can be a fertile topic for writing. In recent years, reminiscing about the best memories of food in college has begun to include the many food trucks that now appear on or near college campuses.

1. Nearly eighty years ago, anthropologist Margaret Mead identified overnutrition as a particularly American problem and argued for a difficult solution to that problem: an ethical, environmentally aware system of food production in which all Americans are adequately fed, learn and practice moderation, and consider the needs of their fellow Americans. Identify a problem concerning the culture of food in your campus, community, or home life and outline a proposal for solving that problem. (See CHAPTER 9, PROPOSALS.) Determine the rhetorical audience for your proposal (that is, some person or group in a position to act on it), describe the problem, and emphasize the importance of addressing it in what you believe to be the right away. Present your solution in specific detail and include an analysis that shows its appropriateness and feasibility.

pages 156–173

2. In "Out of the Kitchen, Onto the Couch," Michal Pollan investigates a major food trend along with its disturbing consequences in industrialized nations: few people actually cook (even those who watch Food TV). In direct response, Karen Hernandez wrote "Why We Should Ditch the Slow Food Movement," in which she, like Pollan, disparages junk food but touts the advantages of the prepackaged foods (sauces, frozen fruits and vegetables, pasta) for the many working families, single parents, and college students who cannot afford either the money or the time to follow Pollan's slow-food, home-made food movement. In an investigative report, analyze a positive or negative feature of food culture on your campus, in your community, or at home. Be sure to provide concrete evidence and details to support your analysis. (See CHAPTER 7, INVESTIGATIVE REPORTS.)

pages 112–131

3. In "Good-bye, Cryovac" and "Embrace the Food Tech That Makes Us Healthier," authors Corby Kummer and Alberto Mingardi analyze the joys—and luxury—of eating good, high-quality food, whether it is supplied locally or is the result of commerce. Have you recently had a satisfying dining experience that you would like your friends and classmates to enjoy as well? Whether it was a simple snack or a big meal, whether it was

prepared at home or served at a restaurant, whether the food was organic or not, what specific features of your eating experience made it so good? Write an evaluation of that dining experience. (See CHAPTER 10, EVALUATIONS.) Be sure to specify the criteria on which your analysis is based and provide rich, detailed examples that show how the food itself, the company, the service, and/or the atmosphere contributed to the overall dining experience.

pages 174–193

MindTap® Read, highlight, and take notes online.

MARGARET MEAD

Margaret Mead (1901–1978) was an American anthropologist and is best known for her study of adolescence in Coming of Age in Samoa *(1928), a work that influenced the 1960s sexual revolution. Mead also researched the culture of food in the United States, arguing that changes in the American diet could best be understood within the context of cultural shifts. Given the current debates over American diets, eating habits, and agricultural practices, Mead's writing now seems prophetic.*

Waring Abbott/Getty Images

The Changing Significance of Food [Overnourished and Undernourished in America]

In a country pronounced only twenty years before to be one-third ill-fed, we suddenly began to have pronouncements from nutritional specialists that the major nutritional disease of the American people was overnutrition. If this had simply meant overeating, the old puritan ethics might have been more easily invoked, but it was overnutrition that was at stake. And this in a country where our ideas of nutrition had been dominated by a dichotomy which distinguished food that was "good for you, but not good" from food that was "good, but not good for you." This split in man's needs, into our cultural conception of the need for nourishment and the search for pleasure, originally symbolized [by] the rewards for eating spinach or finishing what was on one's plate if one wanted to have dessert, lay back of the movement to produce commercially, non-nourishing foods. Beverages and snacks came in particularly for this demand, as it was the addition of between-meal eating to the three square, nutritionally adequate meals a day that was responsible for much of the trouble.

We began manufacturing, on a terrifying scale, foods and beverages that were guaranteed not to nourish. The resources and the ingenuity of industry were diverted from the preparation of foods necessary for life and growth to foods non-expensive to prepare, expensive to buy. And every label reassuring the buyer that the product was not nourishing increased our sense that the trouble with Americans was that they were too well nourished. The diseases of affluence, represented by new forms of death in middle-age, had appeared before we had . . . conquered the diseases of poverty—the ill-fed pregnant women and lactating women, sometimes resulting in irreversible damage to the ill-weaned children, the school children so poorly fed that they could not learn.

> The diseases of affluence appeared before we had conquered the diseases of poverty.

What we do about food is . . . crucial, both for the quality of the next generation, our own American children, and children everywhere, and also for the quality of our responsible action in every field. It is ultimately concerned with the whole problem of the pollution and exhaustion of our environment, with the danger that man may make this planet uninhabitable within a short century or so. If food is grown in strict relationship to the needs of those who will eat it, if every effort is made to reduce the costs of transportation, to improve storage, to conserve the land, and there, where it is needed, by recycling wastes and water, we will go a long way toward solving many of our environmental problems also. . . .

Divorced from its primary function of feeding people, treated simply as a commercial commodity, food loses this primary significance. . . . Only by treating food, unitarily, as a substance necessary to feed people, subject first to the needs of people and only second to the needs of commercial prosperity—whether they be the needs of private enterprise or of a developing socialist country short of foreign capital—can we hope to meet the ethical demands that our present situation makes on us.

ACTIVITY: Analyzing the Rhetorical Situation

1. What is "overnutrition," and how does Mead argue that it came to be a problem?
2. What specific evidence does Mead provide for her assertion that biological traits as well as social traits lead to the diseases of affluence?
3. Who is the audience for her argument? How are they affected by it?
4. What is her purpose, given that audience? Provide textual evidence for your answer.
5. What rhetorical opportunity does Mead address? What is her thesis statement? What supporting assertions does she make about the roots of this problem? What evidence does she provide to support her assertions about the sources of the problem?
6. How does Mead establish the rhetorical appeals of ethos, logos, and pathos? Provide textual evidence to support your answer. Which of the rhetorical appeals does she rely on most? Be prepared to share your answer with the rest of the class.

Stephen Lovekin/Getty Images

MICHAEL POLLAN

Michael Pollan, a professor of journalism at the University of California, Berkeley, is also a regular contributor to The New York Times, *where he writes about topics at the intersection of nature and culture, including food production, cooking, and gardening. He has also written several books on these issues, including* Cooked, Food Rules, In Defense of Food, *and* The Omnivore's Dilemma. *A longer version of this essay was published by* The New York Times *on July 29, 2009.*

Food and Culture

Out of the Kitchen, Onto the Couch
[The Collapse of Home Cooking]

It's generally assumed that the entrance of women into the work force is responsible for the collapse of home cooking, but that turns out to be only part of the story. Yes, women with jobs outside the home spend less time cooking—but so do women without jobs. The amount of time spent on food preparation in America has fallen at the same precipitous rate among women who don't work outside the home as it has among women who do: in both cases, a decline of about 40 percent since 1965. (Though for married women who don't have jobs, the amount of time spent cooking remains greater: 58 minutes a day, as compared with 36 for married women who do have jobs.) In general, spending on restaurants or takeout food rises with income. Women with jobs have more money to pay corporations to do their cooking, yet all American women now allow corporations to cook for them when they can.

> The more time a nation devotes to food preparation at home, the lower its rate of obesity.

. . .

The fact is that *not* cooking may well be deleterious to our health . . .

. . . A 2003 study by a group of Harvard economists led by David Cutler found that the rise of food preparation outside the home could explain most of the increase in obesity in America. Mass production has driven down the cost of many foods, not only in terms of price but also in the amount of time required to obtain them. The French fry did not become the most popular "vegetable" in America until industry relieved us of the considerable effort needed to prepare French fries ourselves. Similarly, the mass production of cream-filled cakes, fried chicken wings and taquitos, exotically flavored chips or cheesy puffs of refined flour, has transformed all these hard-to-make-at-home foods into the sort of everyday fare you can pick up at the gas station on a whim and for less than a dollar. The fact that we no longer have to plan or even wait to enjoy these items, as we would if we were making them ourselves, makes us that much more likely to indulge impulsively.

. . .

Cutler and his colleagues also surveyed cooking patterns across several cultures and found that obesity rates are inversely correlated with the amount of time spent on food preparation. The more time a nation devotes to food preparation at home, the lower its rate of obesity. In fact, the amount of time spent cooking predicts obesity rates more reliably than female participation in the labor force or income. Other research supports the idea that cooking is a better predictor of a healthful diet than social class: a 1992 study *in The Journal of the American Dietetic Association* found that poor women who routinely cooked were more likely to eat a more healthful diet than well-to-do women who did not. . . .

So cooking matters—a lot. The question is, Can we ever put the genie back into the bottle? . . .

Let us hope so.

ACTIVITY: Analyzing the Rhetorical Situation

1. Pollan opens his piece with a comparison between women in the workplace and women who work in their homes. How does this opening challenge cultural stereotypes? How does this comparison strengthen Pollan's broader argument about American eating habits?

2. What rhetorical opportunity created the need for Pollan to write this essay? Does he specifically name it, or is it simply implied?

3. To whom is Pollan writing? How can you tell?

4. What values does Pollan assume his audience will hold? How does he appeal to these values? What other values could he have used to argue for the importance of home cooking if he had been writing to a different audience?

5. Does reading Pollan's essay persuade you that you should spend more time preparing your own food? If so, what did he say to persuade you? If not, what more would he have needed to say? What more would you need to know?

KAREN HERNANDEZ

Karen Hernandez is a lifelong New Yorker and an undergraduate student at Columbia University, where she studies human rights, especially women's rights. This essay, which was published as a response to "Out of the Kitchen, Onto the Couch" by Michael Pollan, first appeared on The Feminist Wire *on May 12, 2013.*

Karen Hernandez

Why We Should Ditch the Slow Food Movement [A Response to Michael Pollan]

Apparently, pursuing Women's Rights has led to the downfall of the American diet.

At least, this is what Michael Pollan unfairly implies in his 2009 article stating that "[appreciation for cooking was] a bit of wisdom that some American feminists thoughtlessly trampled in their rush to get women out of the kitchen." Pollan has written four books dealing with food and eating; his most recent, *Cooked: A Natural History of Transformation*, is hitting store shelves. Pollan, an advocate for the Slow Food Movement, calls for an appreciation of traditional cooking that involves the use of fresh, local, and organic ingredients, as well as slaving over a stove for hours at a time in order to prepare a meal.

Some of Slow Food's central tenets clash with feminist ideals. Pollan makes this painfully obvious when discussing America's shift from consuming thoughtfully "slow" prepared foods instead of mostly processed foods. He notes that at first glance, this may seem like a blessing, especially for women, but in reality, it is heavily contributing to Americans' unhealthy diets. The industrial foods that Pollan and other Slow Foodies attack *have* indeed been a crucial tool in liberating both women *and* men from the hours spent toiling in their kitchens. While these foods have led to a different way of interacting with food, this doesn't justify villainizing feminism or processed foods for that matter. Especially when the effects of processed foods have not been all negative.

Maybe what we should be scrutinizing is the radical approach that Slow Food demands. Of course, growing your own fruits and vegetables, making your own pasta from scratch, and simmering homemade tomato sauce for hours on end to achieve the perfect consistency can be extremely rewarding. But, how rewarding is this when it's expected of every single meal? This is what Slow Food entails and what Pollan vigorously promotes throughout much of his work.

Unfortunately, not all Americans have the luxury to spend hours upon hours preparing their meals from scratch. Pollan fails in not acknowledging in his writing the working families, the single parent households, and the struggling college students who cannot afford to spend all of their earnings on organically grown local foods and who do not have the time to spare in cooking elaborate meals. Worse, it is irresponsible to condemn processed foods in the way he has. In stating that "processed foods have so thoroughly colonized the American kitchen and diet that they have redefined what passes today for cooking, not to mention food," Pollan offers a negative perception of processed foods without any mention of how completely impossible it would be to feed the 7 billion people on this earth without them.

Of course, I'm not calling for us to roast Pollan on a spit and to set fire to all of our organic local farms. What I am proposing is a middle ground of sorts. To do away with the dichotomy of good food vs. bad food, natural vs. processed; to move away from such a radical standpoint and to understand that good food—and good eating practices—can come from both natural *as well as* processed.

In moving away from the discourse of Slow Food, we must first understand that this movement has reinforced a negative view of the word *processed*. Any time we think of processed foods, what immediately comes to mind is junk food full of sugar and salt: chips, cookies, candies, soda. However, we need to begin considering that healthful foods such as frozen and canned fruits and vegetables, whole grain pastas, cereals, breads, cheese, milk, yogurt, and prepared soups, sauces, and proteins all undergo methods of processing.

> Unfortunately, not all Americans have the luxury to spend hours upon hours preparing their meals from scratch.

Food processing allows for fruits and vegetables that are out of season to be readily available all year round (and to more people), helps to extend the shelf life of our food so that it doesn't spoil so quickly, and makes some foods safer to eat by destroying dangerous bacteria they may contain. Most importantly, processing has freed us from the grueling and time-consuming processes our forbearers endured in order to enjoy tasty nutritious meals.

So I have to ask: What has feminism so thoughtlessly trampled? Because I don't think it was as much a sense of wisdom as it was a narrow and judgmental belief about the roles women "should" take on. This is not to say that we should disregard America's dysfunctional relationship to food. But reinforcing an injurious notion that feminism has harmed society does nothing to resolve the issue of how we relate to food, or how and what we eat. What will help us to further this cause is developing a more inclusive understanding of food, as opposed to the restrictive views Pollan fosters in his books. To feed well all of the people, we need to demand the highest quality food, both natural *and* processed. And we need not demand that women return to the kitchen.

ACTIVITY: Analyzing the Rhetorical Situation

1. Why does Hernandez object to Pollan's argument and to the Slow Food movement? In what ways, if any, does she agree with Pollan?
2. As a relatively unknown voice responding to a well-known writer like Pollan, how does Hernandez establish her own credibility to speak on this issue?
3. What audience do you think is most likely to be persuaded by Hernandez's argument? How does she appeal specifically to this audience? What can her choice of publication venue and the evidence she selects tell us about her intended audience?
4. How would you describe Hernandez's tone in this piece? Why might she have chosen to write using this tone, rather than being more formal or relaxed, harsher or friendlier, funnier or more serious?
5. Imagine that you are a reader who was thoroughly persuaded by Pollan's piece. Has Hernandez changed your stance? If so, what new insights did she offer that challenged your previous view?

CORBY KUMMER

Corby Kummer is a professional food writer and senior editor of The Atlantic. *As a graduate of Yale University, Kummer writes about the Sustainable Food Project beginning at his alma mater. A longer version of this essay was published in* The Atlantic *in October 2004.*

Stephen Voss/Redux

Good-bye Cryovac [Local Foods, College Food Service, and Scraping Your Own Plate]

I recently washed up after a supper consisting of four kinds of vegetables from the farmers' market—all four of them vegetables I usually buy at the local right-minded supermarket. As I considered the vivid, distinctive flavor of every bite, I thought, What is that stuff I've been eating the rest of the year?

One of the twelve residential colleges at Yale University is trying to give students that kind of summertime epiphany at every meal, by serving dishes made from produce raised as close to New Haven as possible. In just two years the Yale Sustainable Food Project has launched two ambitious initiatives to bridge the distance from farm to table: the complete revamping of menus in Berkeley College's dining hall to respect seasonality and simplicity, and the conversion of an overgrown lot near campus to an Edenic organic garden. The garden does not supply the dining hall—it couldn't. Rather, it serves as a kind of Greenwich Mean Time, suggesting what is best to serve, and when, by illustrating what grows in the southern New England climate in any given week. The goal of the project is to sell students on the superior flavor of food raised locally in environmentally responsible (but not always organic) ways, so that they will seek it the rest of their lives.

A few dishes I tasted last summer during a pre-term recipe-testing marathon in Berkeley's kitchen convinced me that this goal is within reach for any college meals program willing to make an initial outlay for staff training and an ongoing investment in fewer but better ingredients. I would be happy to eat pasta with parsnips once a week, for example, the candy-sweet roots sharpened by fresh parsley and Parmesan. In fact, I demanded the recipe. Any restaurant would be pleased to serve fresh asparagus roasted with a subtle seasoning of balsamic vinegar and olive oil alongside, say, filet of beef. Even the chicken breasts, coated with black pepper, grilled, and served with a shallot, garlic, and white-wine sauce, tasted like chicken.

> Not long ago a college would never have thought to mention food in a brochure or on a school tour.

Not long ago a college would never have thought to mention food in a brochure or on a school tour—except, perhaps, in a deprecating aside. Now food is a competitive marketing tool, and by the second or third stop on the college circuit parents and students practically expect to be shown the organic salad bar and told about the vegan options and the menus resulting directly from student surveys. Yale has gone these colleges what I consider to be a giant step further, showing students what they should want and making them want it.

As caring about food has become interwoven with caring about the environment, enjoying good food has lost some of the elitist, hedonistic taint that long barred gourmets from the ranks of the politically correct. The challenge, as with any political movement, is to bring about practical institutional change that incorporates ideals.

It's a very big challenge with college food, almost all of which is provided by enormous catering companies like Sodexho, Chartwells, and Aramark, the company that has run Yale's dining services since 1998. These companies have long offered vegetarian, organic, and vegan choices. But none of those options—not even, sadly, going organic—necessarily supports local farmers and local economies, or shows students how much better food tastes when it's made from scratch with what's fresh. Vegetarian, organic, and vegan foods can all be processed, overseasoned, and generally gunked up, and in the hands of institutional food-service providers they usually are. . . .

Whatever the argument for spending more money on food. . . , the practical successes at Yale should encourage other schools to consider similar changes. [Associate Director of the Yale Sustainable Food Project Josh] Viertel gives the example of granola, a simple seduction tool. At the beginning of this year the Food Project's formula of organic oats, almonds, and raisins, a local honey, and New England maple syrup was so popular that Commons had to take over making it for every college. And the project's recipe is actually cheaper than buying pre-made granola in bulk. Viertel recently began a composting program; the first step is asking students to scrape their own plates, which shows close up the waste involved when they take, say, just one bite of cheese lasagne. Other schools ought to take that same step, even if they stop there. . . .

ACTIVITY: Analyzing the Rhetorical Situation

1. What rhetorical opportunities prompted Kummer's piece on the Sustainable Food Project at Yale University? In what ways is he helping to develop the conversation about the culture of food in the United States?
2. How would you describe Kummer's attitude toward the Sustainable Food Project? Why does he hold this position?
3. What change does Kummer hope to bring about through his writing? Who is the audience with the power to make this change?
4. Kummer's essay includes a narrative element in which he tells the story of his own experience sampling the new food at Yale. Why do you think he includes this story? How effectively does it reach (and move) his audience? How effective might it have been if someone else, not a professional food critic, had written it?
5. What concerns do you think have kept other colleges from making the kinds of dining changes that Yale has made? How does Kummer address, or fail to address, these concerns?

ALBERTO MINGARDI

Alberto Mingardi is an Italian journalist who writes for both American and Italian publications about politics, economics, and the effects of globalization. In this essay, first published in The Wall Street Journal *on May 4, 2015, Mingardi writes about a 2015 Expo in Milan, Italy, an event in which thinkers from around the world were invited to discuss the global food supply.*

Food and Culture

Embrace the Food Tech That Makes Us Healthier— "Locavores" and Other Sustainability Advocates Oppose the Innovations That Extend and Improve Life

World's Fairs used to be an opportunity to examine a better future for society. They were about innovation, progress and development, and brought together inventors and businesses eager to demonstrate technological advancements designed for the greater good of all.

This year's Expo Milano 2015, with the theme "Feeding the Planet, Energy for Life," could have followed the same mold. Since the Industrial Revolution, the West has experienced what economic historian Deirdre McCloskey has called "the great enrichment." With prosperity, nutrition has made huge leaps forward: Better preservation and refrigeration systems, agricultural advancements and antiseptic packaging have made our diet both richer and more varied. There is much to celebrate.

Instead, the Expo has fallen prey to an anti-industrial ideology dressed up as romantic nostalgia. The official charter, a solemn document intended to be "the cultural legacy of Expo Milano 2015," declares "access to sources of clean energy" a "universal right." It calls for the global regulation of "investment in natural resources, particularly in land," and asks for a strategy to better guarantee biodiversity. A veteran campaigner against genetically modified crops, Vandana Shiva of India, is an "ambassador" of the event. The influence of groups like Slow Food, a nongovernmental organization that recently criticized McDonald's sponsorship of the Expo as antithetical to the fair's true spirit, appears to be strong.

The magic word here is "sustainability." When applied to food, the implication is that it would it be better if everybody ate like our grandfathers. Somehow, the less-processed foods of the past are deemed to be tastier and more healthful. Moreover, locavore gurus like Slow Food chairman Carlo Petrini think we should buy most of our vegetables, meat and milk locally, irrespective of prices.

The problem with this picture is that, in reality, our grandfathers didn't eat all that well. When the country was unified under the House of Savoy in 1861, the average Italian could expect to live about 30 years. Some 30% of the population was chronically undernourished. Malnutrition led to diseases such as anemia and rickets.

Historians remind us that better living standards translated into better nutrition. Public sanitation policies, economic growth and the rise of industrialized food production resulted in ever-greater numbers of people being satisfactorily fed. In the West, food scarcity is now a thing of the past. A similar process accompanies economic development even today: South Koreans, for instance, spent one-third of their income on food in 1975; now the figure is just 12%.

Upon arriving at Expo Milano, however, visitors are lectured on the evils of mass food production, as well as on the need to bring agricultural plots into closer proximity with cities—thus favoring local production over food that travels from faraway places. In a pre-Expo event, Italy's Prime Minister Matteo Renzi said

> The magic word here is "sustainability."

that when he was mayor of Florence he requested that 76% of the meals served to the city's 24,000 schoolchildren come from local sources. It's easy to understand that a mayor would prefer to use other people's money to buy from producers who might vote for him. But is local production better by definition?

The food industry has strong economies of scale, made possible by, among other factors, tremendous improvements in conservation techniques. Big restaurant chains optimize their supplies by means of their better bargaining power and superior logistics and thus can often offer meals at modest prices. When it comes to food safety, the sort of reputational mechanisms that are at work in bigger, international industries are likely to be a consumer's best ally. The value of big brands rests, ultimately, on the trust they inspire. Farmers' markets are fun, but you don't know much about how a salad was grown and treated just by looking at a farmer's face. By contrast, big distribution chains have severe standards that are rigorously enforced because they fear a scandal may scare consumers and erode their revenue base.

> We didn't become richer and wealthier by eating locally.

A world of economies of scale and long distribution chains seems to be intolerably far away from the culinary traditions of our grandfathers. But is that really the case? Back when wine was consumed exclusively where it was produced, the quality tended (with few exceptions) to be bad. But as it came to be more extensively traded, wine makers could invest in research and innovation. Now, with a much wider pool of wine drinkers, making wine using environmentally sensible techniques is possible precisely because there are new demands to serve. Had wine remained a local monopoly, it would have been harder for environmentally sensitive and organic producers to find their niche.

We didn't become richer and wealthier by eating locally. One thing that made us richer and wealthier was the ability to trade and better preserve food. We have enjoyed much progress since our grandfathers' time, and progress is precisely what developing countries long for. Why feed them with fairy tales of a romanticized past that never existed?

ACTIVITY: Analyzing the Rhetorical Situation

1. What is Mingardi's attitude toward the Expo Milano? What stance does he take toward the Slow Food Movement? What kind of future does he think the world should be striving for in food production?

2. How does the Expo provide a rhetorical opportunity for Mingardi's response? How effective would Mingardi's essay be without such an Expo?

3. What audience has Mingardi envisioned for this piece? How do his topic choice, his tone, and his use of evidence implicate this audience?

4. Mingardi refers repeatedly to "our grandfathers' time" in this essay. What is the effect of this repetition? How does Mingardi want us to think about the past?
5. Imagine you are an advocate of the Slow Food Movement. What features of Mingardi's essay do you find most persuasive? What counterarguments might you propose?

MindTap® Find additional readings on "Food and the (Cultural) Experience of Taste" online.

COMMUNITY C◌NNECTIONS

1. How do Michael Pollan's reflections and descriptions coincide with or diverge from your experiences with cooking and with food? Take about ten minutes to write your response.
2. Now do the same for the pieces by Mead and Kummer: how do their analyses coincide with or diverge from your experiences or observations about the culture of food in the United States?
3. Do you agree with Mead's argument that "ideas of nutrition [in the United States have] been dominated by a dichotomy which distinguished food that was 'good for you, but not good' from food that was 'good, but not good for you'"? Draw on your experiences in childhood or in college to support your answer.
4. Now that you have considered various arguments made about humans and their relationships with food, how would you describe the culture of food on your campus or in your community? What food options or eating habits seem most significant to you? What economic, political, social, cultural, or biological forces have shaped the culture of food?

MindTap® Reflect on your reading and writing process.

22 The Millennial Generation

The Millennial Generation, or Generation Y, those born between about 1981 and the turn of the century, and Generation Z, or the Internet Generation, who have never known a world without online capabilities, have been described as "digital natives." However, this probably rings true only if the digital world is the sole place you feel at home. Other pronouncements about this generation are also contradictory. The most digitally connected are sometimes also called "socially inept," due to their obsession with online communication and entertainment. At the same time, this generation is described as "better connected" socially (with peers and older folks alike) than any other generation. Millennials, in particular, have been described as narcissistic and characterized as neither hardworking nor selfless. In contrast, the Millennials are also considered to be civic minded (think about all the recent college graduates who have joined Teach for America). Given the widespread and seemingly nonstop discussion of today's Internet Generation, it is no surprise that a variety of opinions about it are in circulation. According to "The Millennial Muddle," by award-winning writer Eric Hoover, "this generation either will save the planet, one soup kitchen at a time, or crash-land on a lonely moon where nobody ever reads."

Each of the pieces of writing in this chapter is a response to the question of what characterizes the Millennial Generation. Thus, these pieces *define* some characteristic of the Millennial Generation, *clarify* how this generation can be distinguished from other generations, and *illustrate* a conception of the Millennials with examples. As you read these selections, think about ways you would define your generation, focusing on its personalities, outlooks, identities, maturation, employment problems and possibilities, education, and social practices and values. Your instructor may ask you to translate your observations into writing with one of the following assignments.

1. Choose a particular feature of the Millennial experience that interests you. For instance, you may be intrigued by the impact of online social media on Millennial thought, or on a particular event like September 11, 2001, that has shaped the world as Millennials know it. Choose an audience you think is unfamiliar with this part of the Millennial experience, or one that might want to learn more about it, and write an investigative report to inform them. (See CHAPTER 7, INVESTIGATIVE REPORTS.) Although the essays in this pages 112–131 chapter may give you a place to start researching, you will also need to do additional library and web research in order to become an expert on your chosen topic.

2. Each of the essays in this chapter offers an answer to the question "What are Millennials like?" Although the authors do not necessarily disagree with one another, each takes a different approach, resulting in five very different visions of what it means to be a Millennial. Putting what you have read in conversation with your own observations and experiences as a Millennial, write a three-page profile of Millennials according to what you think someone from another generation might want to know in order to understand his or her Millennial coworkers or friends or children better. (See CHAPTER 6, PROFILES.) Of course, you will pages 92–111 want to keep in mind as you write that there is no such thing as a "typical" Millennial.

3. Work with another student in your class to make a list of steps you think Millennial college students need to take in order to be successful on the job market after graduation. Using your list, write a brief proposal to the rest of your classmates that turns these steps into a concrete plan of action. (See CHAPTER 9, PROPOSALS.) You will want to focus on what makes your plan pages 156–173 feasible as well as what makes it desirable for your classmates. Be sure to explain why your proposal is better than other types of proposals on this topic they may have heard.

MindTap® Read, highlight, and take notes online.

JOEL STEIN

Joel Stein is a humor columnist for Time Magazine *and a regular contributor to magazines like* Entertainment Weekly *and* The Los Angeles Times. *He is also the author of the book* Man Made: A Stupid Quest for Masculinity. *A longer article of the same name was first published in* Time Magazine *on May 20, 2013.*

Casey Rodgers/AP Images/Algonquin Hotel

Millennials: The Me Me Me Generation

I am about to do what old people have done throughout history: call those younger than me lazy, entitled, selfish and shallow. But . . . [u]nlike my parents, my grandparents and my great-grandparents, I have proof.

Here's the cold, hard data: The incidence of narcissistic personality disorder is nearly three times as high for people in their 20s as for the generation that's now 65 or older, according to the National Institutes of Health; 58% more college students scored higher on a narcissism scale in 2009 than in 1982. Millennials got so many participation trophies growing up that a recent study showed that 40% believe they should be promoted every two years, regardless of performance. . . . They're so convinced of their own greatness that the National Study of Youth and Religion found the guiding morality of 60% of Millennials in any situation is that they'll just be able to feel what's right. . . .

[M]illennials' perceived entitlement isn't a result of overprotection but an adaptation to a world of abundance. . . . In fact, a lot of what counts as typical Millennial behavior is how rich kids have always behaved. The Internet has democratized opportunity for many young people, giving them access and information that once belonged mostly to the wealthy. . . . "Previously if you wanted to be a writer but didn't know anyone who is in publishing, it was just, Well, I won't write. But now it's, Wait, I know someone who knows someone," says Jane Buckingham, who studies workplace changes as founder of Trendera, a consumer-insights firm. "I hear story after story of people high up in an organization saying, 'Well, this person just emailed me and asked me for an hour of my time, and for whatever reason I gave it to them.' So the great thing is that they do feel entitled to all of this, so they'll be more innovative and more willing to try new things and they'll do all this cool stuff."

. . .

Because Millennials don't respect authority, they also don't resent it. That's why they're the first teens who aren't rebelling. They're not even sullen. . . . Here's something even all the psychologists who fret over their narcissism studies agree about: millennials are nice. . . . Millennials are more accepting of differences, not just among gays, women and minorities but in everyone.

. . .

[K]now this: Tom Brokaw, champion of the Greatest Generation, loves Millennials. He calls them the Wary Generation, and he thinks their cautiousness in life decisions is a smart response to their world. "Their great mantra has been: Challenge convention. Find new and better ways of doing things. And so that ethos transcends the wonky people who are inventing new apps and embraces the whole economy," he says. . . .

So here's a more rounded picture of Millennials than the one I started with. . . . They're earnest and optimistic. They embrace the system. They are pragmatic idealists, tinkerers more than dreamers, life hackers. . . .

So . . . whether you think Millennials are the new greatest generation of optimistic entrepreneurs or a group of 80 million people about to implode in a dwarf star of tears when their expectations are unmet depends largely on how you view change. Me, I choose to believe in the children. God knows they do.

ACTIVITY: Analyzing the Rhetorical Situation

1. Stein begins his essay by saying, "I am about to do what old people have done throughout history." How does this statement set the tone for the rest of the essay? Based on this beginning, did you expect the essay to end as it does?
2. What is Stein's attitude toward Millennials? What types of evidence does he use to defend this attitude?
3. How would you describe Stein's ethos (credibility) as a writer? Does he give you a sense of the sort of person he is through the way he writes?
4. Who do you think is Stein's primary audience? How can you tell?
5. How do you respond to this essay as a member of your own generation? Are you persuaded? Pleased? Offended? Would your response be different if you were a member of another generation?

JOEL LANDAU

A reporter for the New York Daily News, *Joel Landau investigates the stories behind online viral videos and their rise to fame. This story first appeared in the* New York Daily News *on December 2, 2013. The video can be seen at* www.youtube.com/watch?v=M4IjTUxZORE.

VIDEO: Filmmaker Apologizes on Behalf of Entire Millennial Generation: "We Suck and We're Sorry"

Stephen Parkhurst, 28, uses sarcasm in a film to challenge the stereotype that people who grew up in the '90s are entitled and lazy.

Stephen Parkhurst had enough of hearing how his generation was lazy. So he did something about it that he hoped wouldn't suck.

Parkhurst created a film entitled "Millennials: We Suck and We're Sorry." The 3:02-minute film is a sarcastic response to criticism facing people who grew up in the 90s, like the 28-year-old filmmaker.

The video is a series of sarcastic statements made by actors among the generation generally defined as people between 18 and 33 years old.

After apologizing for "sucking so much" they admit the problem with fellow Millennials is they just don't want to work hard—unlike the previous generation.

The actors say they should stop waiting tables and living in their parents' basement and instead should go out and get real jobs—who cares if they graduated into a recession, had to deal with the loss of manufacturing jobs and are saddled with debt from ever increasing college tuition.

"If only we could be more like our parents," one actress says.

Members of the generation are feeling the burden. According to a study earlier this year by the American Psychological Association, the average stress level is 5.4 on a scale of 1 to 10—well above the national average of 4.9.

The study found the greatest sources of the generation's angst is finding work, money concerns and job stability.

The New York City resident said he got the idea for the project after reading articles critical of the Millennial generation—specifically that they are entitled and lazy.

"It was getting a little overbearing and I thought a little silly," he said. "I came up with a response video to that."

The film argues Millennials do not bear the responsibility for current problems, such as the collapse of the global economy, two "quagmire" wars, the breakdown of the unions and an environment stripped of its resources—their parents do.

"I do think there's a bit of entitlement in our generation. The '90s is a pretty entitled era, when things were pretty great. I think there's a reason for the entitlement," he said. "I don't see the laziness everyone talks about. At least the people I know, I see people who are driven and successful. I don't see that aspect as much."

New York filmmaker Stephen Parkhurst, 28, says he created *"Millennials: We Suck and We're Sorry"* because he was tired of hearing about how his generation, well, sucks.

Stephen Parkhurst

ACTIVITY: Analyzing the Rhetorical Situation

1. To what rhetorical opportunity is Parkhurst responding? What circumstances created his need to speak?
2. Why might Parkhurst have decided that a video was the appropriate medium to communicate his message? How well does this video provide a fitting response to his rhetorical opportunity?
3. Why have these Millennials chosen to apologize for "sucking so much"? What can this phrasing tell us about the argument they are making?
4. Who do you think is the intended audience for Parkhurst's video? What about the audience for Landau's essay? How can you tell?
5. List the strategies identified by Landau that Parkhurst uses to persuade his audience. Which of the strategies do you think is most effective? Which one seems least effective?

PEW RESEARCH CENTER

The Pew Research Center conducts public opinion polls in the United States to study social and population trends. In this report, first published on September 3, 2015, the researchers summarize the findings of a recent survey about generational identity.

Most Millennials Resist the "Millennial" Label

Survey Report

Millennials will soon become the nation's largest living generation. They already have surpassed Generation X to make up the largest share of the U.S. workforce.

Despite the size and influence of the Millennial generation, however, most of those in this age cohort do not identify with the term "Millennial." Just 40% of adults ages 18 to 34 consider themselves part of the "Millennial generation," while another 33%—mostly older Millennials—consider themselves part of the next older cohort, Generation X.

Millennials Less Likely Than Boomers, Gen X to Embrace Generational Label

% of those in each generation who consider themselves to be part of that generation...

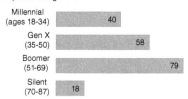

American Trends Panel (wave 10). Survey conducted Mar 10-Apr 6, 2015. Respondents could select more than one generation label.

(continued)

Generational identity is strongest among the Boomers: 79% of those 51 to 69 consider themselves part of the "Baby-Boom generation." Among those 35 to 50 (the age range for Gen X), 58% consider themselves part of "Generation X."

The oldest cohort of Americans is by far the least likely to embrace a generational label. Just 18% of those ages 70 to 87 (the age range of the Silent Generation) actually see themselves as part of the "Silent Generation." Far more Silents consider themselves part of adjoining generations, either Boomers (34%) or the Greatest Generation (also 34%).

The national survey by the Pew Research Center was conducted March 10–April 6 with 3,147 adults who are part of the American Trends Panel, a nationally representative sample of randomly selected U.S. adults surveyed online and by mail. Respondents were given five commonly used terms for generations, including the "Greatest Generation," and asked whether they considered themselves part of these generations.

The survey finds that some generational names—particularly Boomers—are more widely recognized than others. Among all respondents, fully 89% say they have heard of the Baby-Boom generation, while 71% have heard of Gen X. A majority (56%) have heard of the Millennial generation, but just 15% of all respondents (including only 27% of Silents) have heard of the Silent Generation.

The survey also asked if a number of descriptions applied to the people of their generation. Silents are far more likely than people in younger age cohorts to view their own generation in a positive light. Large majorities of Silents say the people of

... differences between old and young in such realms as patriotism, religiosity and political activism have been evident for many years.

their generation are hard-working (83%), responsible (78%), patriotic (73%), self-reliant (65%), moral (64%), willing to sacrifice (61%) and compassionate (60%).

Boomers also tend to have favorable impressions of their generation, though in most cases they are not as positive as Silents.

Generation Gaps: Silents, Boomers See Themselves in a More Positive Light

% of each generation saying each term describes their generation overall

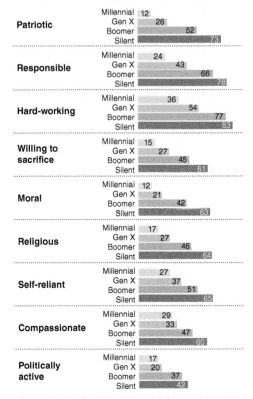

Source: American Trends Panel (wave 10). Survey conducted Mar 10-Apr 6, 2015.

By contrast, Gen Xers and Millennials are far more skeptical in assessing the strengths of their generations. And Millennials, in particular, stand out in their willingness to ascribe negative stereotypes to their own generation: 59% say the term "self-absorbed" describes their generation, compared with 30% among Gen Xers, 20% of Boomers and just 7% of Silents.

To be sure, some of these differences may be related more to age and life stage than to the unique characteristics of today's generations. Responsibilities tend to increase with age. As a result, it is possible that, in any era, older people would be more likely than younger people to view their generation as "responsible." In addition, differences between old and young in such realms as patriotism, religiosity and political activism have been evident for many years.

On several measures—including hard work, responsibility, willingness to sacrifice, and self-reliance—the share in each generation expressing positive views declines step-wise across age cohorts, from the oldest to the youngest.

For example, 83% of Silents describe the people of their generation as hard-working, as do (77%) of Boomers. A narrow majority of Gen Xers (54%) say people of their generation are hard-working, while 36% of Millennials say that phrase describes people in their cohort.

The survey includes 18 descriptions— a mix of positive, negative and neutral terms. On some terms, such as environmentally-conscious, entrepreneurial and rigid, there are no significant differences across cohorts in the shares saying each applies.

There is only one description—"idealistic"— on which a generation other than the Silents views itself most positively: Somewhat more Millennials (39%) than Gen Xers (28%),

Boomers (31%) or Silents (26%) describe their generation as idealistic.

Generational Identity

Generational names are largely the creations of social scientists and market researchers. The age boundaries of these widely used labels are somewhat variable and subjective, so perhaps it is not surprising that many Americans do not identify with "their" generation.

Yet the Boomer label resonates strongly with the members of this generation; the name arose from the fertility spike that began shortly after World War II and continued through the early 1960s. Fully 79% of those born between 1946 and 1964, the widely used age range of this generation, identify as Boomers. That is by far the strongest identification with a generational name of any cohort.

The Millennial generation also encompasses a broad span of adults (currently those born from 1981 to 1997). But just 40% of those in this cohort consider themselves Millennials, while as many as a third (33%) say they belong to Gen X. Among older Millennials (ages 27 to 34), 43% consider themselves Gen Xers, while 35% identify as Millennials. Yet even among younger Millennials (ages 18 to 26), fewer than half (45%) consider themselves part of this generation.

Most adults (58%) born between 1965 and 1980, the birth years of Gen X, identify with "their" generation. Notably, relatively few Gen Xers (just 4%) identify as Millennials, but 15% consider themselves Boomers. Among younger Gen Xers (ages 35 to 42), 68% identify with Gen X; among older Gen Xers, fewer (48%) see themselves as part of this generation, while 24% identify as Boomers.

(continued)

Generational Identity: The Power of 'Boomer'

Share of each generation that identifies as...

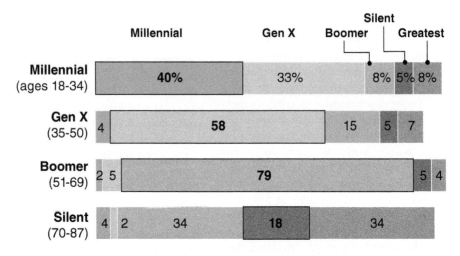

Source: American Trends Panel (wave 10). Survey conducted Mar 10-Apr 6, 2015. 'Other' responses not shown. Respondents could select multiple generation labels.

Large Majority of Boomers Say Their Generational Label Is a Good Fit

% of each who say their generation label applies to themselves...

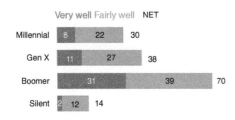

American Trends Panel (wave10). Survey conducted Mar10-Apr 6, 2015. Based on total.

Just 18% of those in the Silent Generation (born 1928 to 1945) consider themselves part of this generation. In part, this reflects the low visibility of the term "Silent Generation," though it has been in use for more than half a century. In coining the name in 1951, *Time* magazine described the Silents as "working fairly hard and saying almost nothing."

Most Silents identify with either the Greatest Generation—people born before 1928—or as Boomers. Older Silents (age 80 to 87) tend to see themselves as part of the Greatest Generation; 51% say they are part of that cohort. Among younger Silents (70 to 79), close to half (45%) identify as Boomers.

Aside from being asked about their generational identity, respondents also were asked how well each generational term applies. In this case, the differences between Boomers and the other three generations are even starker. Seven-in-ten Boomers (70%) say the term "Baby-Boom generation" applies to them very well (31%) or fairly well (39%). Among other generations, no more than about four-in-ten (38% of Gen X) say their generational label is a good fit.

Generational Traits: Negative, Positive, Neutral

As with many positive generational descriptions, there also are wide differences over whether negative terms apply. Millennials are far more likely than older generations to say the terms "self-absorbed," "wasteful," and "greedy" apply to people in their age cohort.

While 59% of Millennials describe the members of their generation as self-absorbed, 49% say they are wasteful and 43% describe them as greedy. On all three dimensions, Millennials are significantly more critical of their generation than older age cohorts are of theirs.

And while Silents are more likely than other generations to say that several positive terms describe their generation, they also are less likely to say some negative terms apply. Only about one-in-ten Silents see the people of their generation as self-absorbed (7%), wasteful (10%) and greedy (8%)—by far the lowest shares of any cohort.

There are smaller differences among generations over whether the term "cynical" describes people in their age cohort: 31% of Millennials say it applies, compared with 24% of Gen X, 16% of Boomers and just 7% of Silents. Relatively few across all

Millennials Most Likely to Attribute Negative Traits to Their Generation

% of each generation saying each term describes their generation overall

Self-absorbed	Millennial	59
	Gen X	30
	Boomer	20
	Silent	7
Wasteful	Millennial	49
	Gen X	29
	Boomer	20
	Silent	10
Greedy	Millennial	43
	Gen X	24
	Boomer	19
	Silent	8
Cynical	Millennial	31
	Gen X	24
	Boomer	16
	Silent	7
Idealistic	Millennial	39
	Gen X	28
	Boomer	31
	Silent	26
Entrepreneurial	Millennial	35
	Gen X	33
	Boomer	35
	Silent	32
Environmentally-conscious	Millennial	40
	Gen X	37
	Boomer	41
	Silent	40
Tolerant	Millennial	33
	Gen X	33
	Boomer	38
	Silent	36
Rigid	Millennial	8
	Gen X	7
	Boomer	7
	Silent	6

Source: American Trends Panel (wave 10). Survey conducted Mar 10-Apr 6, 2015

generations—only about one-in-ten—say the term "rigid" applies.

Millennials are more likely to characterize their generation as "idealistic," but the differences are not large. About four-in-ten Millennials (39%) say the term idealistic

(continued)

applies to people in their cohort, compared with 28% of Gen Xers, 31% of Boomers and 26% of Silents.

On three other descriptions—"environmentally conscious," "entrepreneurial," and "tolerant"—there are no significant differences across generations.

To be sure, young adults are more likely than older people to say there is strong evidence of climate change and to prioritize the development of alternative energy over expanding the production of fossil fuels. Yet Millennials (40%) and Gen Xers (37%) are no more likely than Boomers (41%) or Silents (40%) to describe the people in their generation as environmentally conscious.

And while Millennials are more accepting of homosexuality, interracial marriage and hold more positive views of immigrants, about the same share of Millennials (33%) as those in older age cohorts consider the people in their generation tolerant.

ACTIVITY: Analyzing the Rhetorical Situation

1. Identify an obvious thesis statement for this essay. If you cannot identify one, then write out a sentence that summarizes the authors' stance on the topic.

2. How does the perceived credibility (ethos) of an organization like Pew Research Center affect the way we read this essay? How is credibility established in the essay itself?

3. One of the challenges of writing a piece so full of numerical data is that it can be hard to transition smoothly from one idea to the next. How do these authors handle the challenge of transition? Would you say that the piece reads smoothly? Explain your answer.

4. Which generations are the implied audience of this piece? Does this essay target everyone the same or privilege the interests of some generations over others? Explain your answer.

5. In what ways do these authors expect to change their readers' minds? In what ways was your mind changed by what you read?

DAVID FALLARME

As a digital marketer based in Beijing, China, David Fallarme knows both the importance and the complexity of good communication within the modern international marketplace. This piece originally appeared as a post on his blog, The Marketing Student.

A Look at How Gen Y Communicates

Boomers had it pretty simple back in their youth. Want to connect with your friends? Write them a letter, give them a call or go and see them.

David Fallarme

Postal mail   Phone call   Face to Face

URGENCY

Gen X-ers had a little more fun. They could've e-mailed each other over 28.8 [phone-line dial-up for the Internet] or used their pagers to send 1-sentence messages back and forth.

David Fallarme

Postal mail   Email   Beeper   Phone call   Face to Face

URGENCY

Here's what **Generation Y** uses to stay in touch.

David Fallarme

Wall post   Private message   Email   Instant message   txt   Phone call   Face to Face

URGENCY

(continued)

To an outsider, it can be confusing to understand how Gen Y uses those channels just to talk to each other. After all, Boomers just had three channels and they made friends just fine. To put things in context, here's what my communication habits are like and how I use the above.

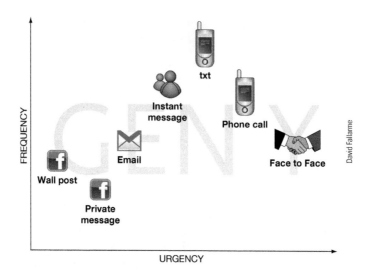

Looking at that chart makes me envy my father's generation. They didn't have to worry about drunk texts. Or having personal information all over the Internet.

ACTIVITY: Analyzing the Rhetorical Situation

1. What changes in communication methods does Fallarme identify in this piece? Why does he argue that these changes are important?
2. Fallarme makes his argument primarily through images rather than through words. How effective is this choice of medium? Explain your answer.
3. How would you describe Fallarme's attitude toward his subject? What does this attitude suggest about his target audience?
4. What do you think was Fallarme's goal in writing this piece? Do you think he succeeded in terms of his target audience?

Since 1998, Beloit College has been releasing the Beloit College Mindset List, a listing of "cultural touchstones" that have shaped the attitudes and experiences of incoming first-year college students. All three authors of the list have extensive experience in higher education, Nief as an administrator and McBride and Westerberg as professors. A reference to the Beloit College Mindset List for the Class of 2014 is found in Chapter 7, Investigative Reports. In the Beloit College Mindset List for the Class of 2014, published in 2010, e-mails were considered "too slow" for effective multitasking.

Beloit Mindset List 2019

Students heading into their first year of college this year are mostly 18 and were born in 1997. Among those who have never been alive in their lifetimes are Princess Diana, Notorious B.I.G., Jacques Cousteau, and Mother Teresa. *Joining them in the world the year they were born were* Dolly the sheep, The McCaughey septuplets, *and* Michael "Prince" Jackson Jr. Since they have been on the planet:

1. Hybrid automobiles have always been mass produced.
2. Google has always been there, in its founding words, "to organize the world's information and make it universally accessible."
3. They have never licked a postage stamp.
4. Email has become the new "formal" communication, while texts and tweets remain enclaves for the casual.
5. Four foul-mouthed kids have always been playing in South Park.
6. Hong Kong has always been under Chinese rule.
7. They have grown up treating Wi-Fi as an entitlement.
8. The NCAA has always had a precise means to determine a national champion in college football.
9. The announcement of someone being the "first woman" to hold a position has only impressed their parents.
10. Charlton Heston is recognized for waving a rifle over his head as much as for waving his staff over the Red Sea.
11. Color photos have always adorned the front page of *The New York Times*.
12. Ellis Island has always been primarily in New Jersey.
13. "No means no" has always been morphing, slowly, into "only yes means yes."
14. Cell phones have become so ubiquitous in class that teachers don't know which students are using them to take notes and which ones are planning a party.
15. The Airport in Washington, D.C., has always been Reagan National Airport.
16. Their parents have gone from encouraging them to use the Internet to begging them to get off it.
17. If you say "around the turn of the century," they may well ask you, "which one?"
18. They have avidly joined Harry Potter, Ron, and Hermione as they built their reading skills through all seven volumes.

(continued)

19. Attempts at human cloning have never been federally funded but do require FDA approval.

20. "Crosstown Classic" and the "Battle of the Bay" have always been among the most popular interleague rivalries in Major League Baseball.

21. *Carry Me Back to Old Virginny* has never been the official song of the Virginia Commonwealth.

22. Phish Food has always been available from Ben and Jerry.

23. Kyoto has always symbolized inactivity about global climate change.

24. When they were born, cell phone usage was so expensive that families only used their large phones, usually in cars, for emergencies.

25. The therapeutic use of marijuana has always been legal in a growing number of American states.

26. The eyes of Texas have never looked upon The Houston Oilers.

27. Teachers have always had to insist that term papers employ sources in addition to those found online.

28. In a world of DNA testing, the Tomb of the Unknowns at Arlington has never included a Vietnam War veteran "known only to God."

29. Playhouse Disney was a place where they could play growing up.

30. Surgeons have always used "super glue" in the operating room.

31. Fifteen nations have always been constructing the International Space Station.

32. *The Lion King* has always been on Broadway.

33. Phoenix Lights is a series of UFO sightings, not a filtered cigarette.

34. Scotland and Wales have always had their own parliaments and assemblies.

35. At least Mom and Dad had their new Nintendo 64 to help them get through long nights sitting up with the baby.

36. First Responders have always been heroes.

37. Sir Paul and Sir Elton have always been knights of the same musical roundtable.

38. CNN has always been available *en Español.*

39. *Heaven's Gate* has always been more a trip to Comet Hale-Bopp and less a film flop.

40. *Splenda* has always been a sweet option in the U.S.

41. The Atlanta Braves have always played at Turner Field.

42. Poland, Hungary, and the Czech Republic have always been members of NATO.

43. Humans have always had the ability to use implanted radio frequency ID chips—slightly larger than a grain of rice.

44. TV has always been in such high definition that they could see the pores of actors and the grimaces of quarterbacks.

45. Mr. Jones and Mr. Smith have always been *Men in Black,* not their next-door neighbors.

46. The proud parents recorded their first steps on camcorders, mounted on their shoulders like bazookas.

47. They had no idea how fortunate they were to enjoy the final four years of Federal budget surpluses.

48. Amoco gas stations have steadily vanished from the American highway.

49. Vote-by-mail has always been the official way to vote in Oregon.

50. . . . and there has always been a Beloit College Mindset List.

ACTIVITY: Analyzing the Rhetorical Situation

1. What features of Millennial culture are most prominent in this list? Do you agree with the list? Are there any significant moments in Millennial culture that you feel have been excluded?

2. What is the purpose of a list like this one, particularly in terms of the intended audience? Who is the intended audience? What explanation can you give for why this list has remained so popular over the years?

3. How does the fact that the list is published by a college affect the way you read it? Would you read it differently if you found it on a friend's blog?

4. Even though there is no traditional thesis in this piece, the list still invites readers to think differently. How does this persuasion happen? Would you say it is effective?

5. Compare the Beloit Mindset List 2019 to the profile by Joel Stein. Describe the rhetorical audience for both pieces. What portrait does each piece create for that audience?

MindTap® Find additional readings on "The Millennial Generation" online.

COMMUNITY C☼NNECTIONS

1. Write for ten minutes in response to one of the pieces you have just read. How do the descriptions of Millennials offered by the author coincide with or diverge from your own experience? As a Millennial, how do you respond to the author's argument?

2. Chart your use of communication technologies in the way that David Fallarme does (in terms of frequency and urgency). How often are you prompted to interpret nonverbal communication when using technology? How often do you rely solely on writing when using communication technology?

3. Show the Beloit Mindset List 2019 to a parent or another representative of an older generation. Ask him or her to tell you more about how these changes in society might be correlated with different ways of thinking. If your conversation partner is willing, work together to imagine five or six items that might be on the Beloit Mindset List 2045.

MindTap® Reflect on your reading and writing process.

Taking Up (Public) Space

MindTap® Understand the goals of the chapter and complete a warm-up activity online.

You have always inhabited public space. Whether you have been waiting in line at the coffee shop, walking on city streets, visiting a museum or memorial site, or strolling across campus, you have known how to use the space, sometimes choosing to do so according to the rules for that space, sometimes not. By now, you are well accustomed to using public space of all kinds.

By definition alone, "public space" invites all people to use it—whether in ways that were planned or in ways that emerge. Urban city streets are designed for automobile traffic, with designated traffic lanes and signals, pedestrian crossings, and parking spots. Yet, on a regular basis, bicycle messengers dart between parked and moving cars, pedestrians jaywalk, and people walk through slow traffic to sell car washes, bouquets, and spices.

This chapter features responses from five writers who used genres such as investigative reports and critical analyses to address an issue surrounding the use of public space, from problems of urban planning and controversial religious monuments to those of imagined privacy and sharing space. (See also, pages 179–181 Alexis Walker's evaluation of downtown development in CHAPTER 10, "DONUTS AT EASTON'S CENTER CIRCLE: SLAM DUNK OR CYCLE OF DETERIORATION?") As these readings illustrate, public spaces by their very nature are of concern to more than just the individuals involved in designing or dominating them. What the spaces allow or prevent and whom they benefit or harm are issues that call for conversation. As you explore this topic, your instructor might call on you to consider one of the following opportunities for writing.

1. In a public space that is familiar to you, what uses emerged from the bottom-up approach, like the one promoted by Jane Jacobs in the graphic novel *Robert Moses: The Master Builder of New York City*, below? Which uses employed the top-down approach to urban planning of Robert Moses? In an investigative report of three to four pages, describe a familiar public space in terms of its use. (See CHAPTER 7, INVESTIGATIVE REPORTS.) pages 112–131

2. Evaluate a public space—on campus or in your community. Explain why it should be evaluated—and for your audience. Provide criteria for your evaluation (function, identity, accessibility, and so on) and evaluate the public space accordingly. As you write, consider your audience (who may or may not share your ideas about criteria), your purpose (which should be relevant for your audience), and the advantages and limitations of using an evaluation to explore your subject. You may find that enhancing your essay with images will strengthen your thesis and support your reasons. (See CHAPTER 10, EVALUATIONS.) pages 174–193

3. Consider a public space that you know well. Analyze how the space brings people together, keeps them apart, or otherwise controls how they interact. Along with this critical analysis, determine whether some groups of people are encouraged to or discouraged from interacting in this space. Draft an essay of three to four pages, making certain to consider your rhetorical situation (opportunity, audience, purpose) to effectively incorporate persuasive strategies in your critical analysis. (See CHAPTER 11, CRITICAL ANALYSES.) pages 194–214

MindTap® Read, highlight, and take notes online.

PIERRE CHRISTIN AND OLIVIER BALEZ

Pierre Christin, a comics writer and professor of French literature at the University of Utah, worked with illustrator Olivier Balez to create the graphic novel Robert Moses: The Master Builder of New York City. *The graphic novel, published in 2014, is a fictionalized account of the historical figure Robert Moses, a controversial urban planner who was highly influential in the mid-twentieth century. Moses tried to clear out New York City slums, usher in automobile-friendly urban designs, and cater to the desires of the city's wealthiest inhabitants. The following selection chronicles Moses's showdown with Greenwich Village activist Jane Jacobs, who used community pressure to defeat his planned Lower Manhattan Expressway, a top-down*

(continued)

approach that would have torn down the abandoned warehouses that had been taken over by beatnik artists and the ethnic community of Little Italy. Jacobs's bottom-up system evolved from the way inhabitants already use the space. She declared Moses's approach to eradicating poverty a "wistful myth" of "civic centers that are avoided" and "low-income projects that become worse centers of delinquency, vandalism."

Robert Moses: The Master Builder of New York City

Pierre Christin and Olivier Balez, ROBERT MOSES: MASTER BUILDER OF NEW YORK CITY

HE SLOWLY BEGINS TO LOSE HIS MANDATE... AS WELL AS HIS PRECIOUS TRIBOROUGH TOLLS IN 1968: IT'S THE END OF A WAR CHEST.

Pierre Christin and Olivier Balez, ROBERT MOSES: MASTER BUILDER OF NEW YORK CITY

THE WHEEL OF FORTUNE TURNS AND NEW YORK RISES UP FROM ITS DERELICTION TO BECOME THE 21ST CENTURY'S UNSURPASSABLE INTERNATIONAL CITY...

Pierre Christin and Olivier Balez, ROBERT MOSES: MASTER BUILDER OF NEW YORK CITY

AT A TIME WHEN TAX EVASION IMPEDES ANY REAL FORM OF PUBLIC INITIATIVE, PEOPLE ARE REDISCOVERING THE GREAT BUILDER, ROBERT MOSES, WHOSE LEGACY HAS ALLOWED THE CITY TO ENDURE...

BUT IT IS JANE JACOBS, VICTORIOUS OVER LOMEX, WHO HAS BECOME THE URBAN HERO, WHO EVERY 28TH OF JUNE HAS A DAY OF COMMEMORATION IN HER HONOUR...

Pierre Christin and Olivier Balez, ROBERT MOSES: MASTER BUILDER OF NEW YORK CITY

CHAPTER 23 TAKING UP (PUBLIC) SPACE | **435**

1. What reasons might Christin and Balez have for choosing a graphic novel as the medium for telling this story? What can this medium do that other media cannot? What are the constraints of the graphic novel?

2. What values lie at the root of Jacobs's conflict with Moses? How do these differences in values lead to differences in the public policies they advocate?

3. Who is the primary audience for Christin and Balez's story? How can you tell? How effective are these collaborators at reaching this audience?

4. How would you describe the tone of the language in these panels? How do the illustrations fit with or contrast with that tone?

5. How does this fictionalized historical account align with present-day issues of urban planning in New York City and elsewhere? Might Christin and Balez be trying to advocate for certain kinds of behavioral change in the present day? If so, what are they advocating, and how can you tell?

ANTHONY FLINT

Anthony Flint is Director of Public Affairs at the Lincoln Institute of Land Policy and the author of several books about urban planning, including Wrestling with Moses: How Jane Jacobs Took on New York's Master Builder and Transformed the American City, *published in 2009. The essay below was first published in* The Atlantic's CityLab *on June 30, 2014.*

© Anthony Flint

Who Really Owns Public Spaces?

A new exhibit at the AIA New York Center for Architecture examines the changing function of parks and other open urban centers.

There's a bit of a house-of-mirrors quality at Open to the Public: Civic Space Now, at the AIA [American Institute of Architects] New York Center for Architecture in New York City's Greenwich Village through September. From the outside, at LaGuardia Place, you peer in and see an umbrella-capped hot dog stand, a Citibike, and a wrap-around mural of Times Square. Step inside, and you'll find the perfect backdrop for a selfie that makes it seem like you're on the crowded steps of the Metropolitan Museum of Art. This is an exhibit about public space, in a public space, with public space outside, all around. This reflection on an essential ingredient of cities requires a moment of orientation.

The very notion of public space, a subject largely reserved for design professionals until about a decade ago, is a hot topic today. The threshold event that pushed it into popular consciousness was probably 2011's Occupy Wall Street encampment in Lower

Manhattan's Zuccotti Park—a privately owned public space, just to add another level of complexity. Worldwide, the protests in Tahrir Square in Cairo that year also underscored the connection between place and public discourse, with all the mobilization power of social media mixed in. In recent years, the practice of guerrilla urbanism—taking over parking spaces or entire streets for mini parklets, spontaneous art displays, and chair bombings [the creation of places to sit where there is no public seating]—has further changed the definition and understanding of public space and its function.

Cities are the story of the century, as *New York Times* architecture critic Michael Kimmelman noted at a Radcliffe Institute lecture earlier this year, and public space is central to civic health. All of this new attention to the design and character of public space is thus quite welcome, but there are all kinds of thorny questions marbled in: rules and regulations, free speech, access and equity. Is the pedestrian zone of Times Square mostly for tourists? Who are the best new public spaces actually being designed for? A park is no longer just a park; as a stage for the theater of public life, it's become more complicated.

The AIA New York exhibit attempts to make sense of its subject by organizing public space into three basic categories: congregation, circulation, and contemplation. The latter is perhaps the easiest to understand: The serene new Four Freedoms Park at the tip of

An Occupy Wall Street gathering at Zuccotti Park. November 15, 2011.

Michael Nagle/Getty Images

Public Space

(continued)

Roosevelt Island on the East River in Manhattan, a completion of a design by Louis Kahn, is open to anyone who can get there.

Anyone who walks the sidewalks of New York realizes how much of the city's life is played out in public. The way that space gets used can seem accidental as much as intentional, from the High Line—the infamous transformation of an elevated railway into a linear park—to the benches at either end of the planted medians along Park Avenue. The steps of the Met were probably not specifically designed to accommodate the hundreds of visitors who hang out there every day, but that lingering has become a signature of the place.

No curator can cover everything in one show, but if this exhibit has one shortcoming, it's the lack of recognition of guerilla or tactical or pop-up urbanism. From San Francisco to

> A park is no longer just a park; as a stage for the theater of public life, it's become more complicated.

Dallas to Portland, Maine, that's really where the action is lately regarding public spaces. It might have also been interesting to delve into the latest cutting-edge thinking on shared space espoused by such thought leaders as urban designer and movement specialist Ben Hamilton-Baillie, who takes former New York transportation commissioner Janette Sadik-Khan's Times Square model a step further by removing all traffic lights and warning signs. The implementation of the Dutch concept of the *woonerf*, which prompts a blending of automobile, bicycle, and pedestrian movement, turns streets into a new kind of public realm based on eye contact and common courtesy. The resulting ballet is seen in such places as Poynton and the Seven Dials intersection in England.

The exhibit looks back as well as forward, and includes the recently rehabilitated McCarren

(David Sundberg/Esto)

McCarren Park Pool.

Pool, a New York City public works project of Robert Moses. And when you walk out of the center, the sometimes tortured history of placemaking is all around. The high-density towers of urban renewal are right across the street; the gardens and ground-floor shops of the Washington Square Southeast development are reasonably active. Then of course there's Washington Square Park to the north—a public space functioning about as well as any urbanist could imagine. The park's fountain is working (thanks to a private benefactor, the Tisch Foundation), people strum guitars, kids run every which way, and the park's famed monumental arch lords over everything.

Nearly a half-century ago, Jane Jacobs fought Moses' proposal to run Fifth Avenue through the greensward. Back then, nobody was openly talking about free speech or democracy movements or whether homeless people should be allowed to congregate there. It was more about mothers and strollers. But it was contested space, as so much of public space in the city was. And remains.

ACTIVITY: Analyzing the Rhetorical Situation

1. For many of us, public space does not seem like a very interesting or controversial thing. For Flint, though, the way we use public space reflects a society's values, conflicts, and distribution of power. What specific evidence does Flint give to support this perspective?

2. Flint teaches his readers about New York City's public spaces by discussing the new exhibit at the AIA (American Institute of Architects) New York Center for Architecture. How does the discussion of the exhibit enhance the case he is making? How might he have made the same argument without talking about the exhibit?

3. To whom is Flint writing? How can you be sure?

4. How is Flint's account of Jane Jacobs and Robert Moses different from Christin and Balez's account in the previous reading? How can you account for the different ways these authors discuss the same historical figures?

5. What is the primary purpose of this piece in terms of Flint's audience? Does Flint simply want to educate his readers? Do his beliefs about public spaces give him a stake in the matter? If so, how does he invite his readers to adopt his point of view?

ABBY PHILLIP

Abby Phillip was White House correspondent at Politico *before joining* The Washington Post *as a national reporter for late breaking news. She most often writes on politics, health, crime, and the Internet, and regularly appears on* ABC *and* MSNBC. *This article appeared in* The Washington Post *on June 30, 2015.*

Ruth Fremson/The New York Times/Redux

(*continued*)

Oklahoma's Ten Commandments Statue Must Be Removed, State Supreme Court Says

Oklahoma's embattled Ten Commandments statue violates the state's constitution and must be removed from the capitol, according to a new ruling from the state's Supreme Court.

The statue—a six-feet-tall and three-feet-wide slab of stone that's shaped vaguely like two tablets—has stood at the statehouse in Oklahoma City since 2012, though it was briefly destroyed and then reinstalled in 2014. It was paid for with private donations and approved by the legislature.

On Tuesday, the state's high court handed down a short but clear ruling saying that the statue must be taken down. According to the court, the Ten Commandments is "obviously" a religious document, and the state constitution prohibits any public property from being used to support a specific religion.

Defenders of the statue have argued that the commandments were placed on the capitol grounds as "historical context," given the influence the Ten Commandments had on the formation of American law. They also argued that it was similar to a Ten Commandments statue in Texas whose legality was upheld by the U.S. Supreme Court.

In the Oklahoma ruling, seven of the court's nine justices noted that their opinion "rests solely on the Oklahoma constitution with no regard for federal jurisprudence."

They continued: "As concerns the 'historic purpose' justification, the Ten Commandments are obviously religious in nature and are an integral part of the Jewish and Christian faiths. Because the monument at issue operates for the use, benefit or support of a sect or system of religion, it violates Article 2,

Section 5 of the Oklahoma Constitution and is enjoined and shall be removed."

Article II, Section V of the state constitution specifies that "no public money or property shall ever be appropriated, applied, donated, or used, directly or indirectly, for the use, benefit, or support of any sect, church, denomination, or system of religion, or for the use, benefit, or support of any priest, preacher, minister, or other religious teacher or dignitary, or sectarian institution as such."

Bruce Prescott, an ordained Baptist minister who was one of the plaintiffs in the case against the statue, said that the statue is "unavoidable" to people walking near the Capitol building, and it gives the impression that the state endorses Christianity as an official religion.

"I'm not opposed to Ten Commandment monuments; I'm opposed to them on government property," he told *The Washington Post* on Tuesday. "How do you take a covenant between God and his people and make it a secular monument?"

Prescott added that Baptists have historically defended the separation of church and state and have insisted that religious texts continue to be interpreted in a religious context.

"If you're saying that it's no longer religious, what have you done to religion?" he said. "They've just completely destroyed the significance and value of the words."

In a statement, Oklahoma's Attorney General Scott Pruitt said the court "got it wrong."

"The court completely ignored the profound historical impact of the Ten Commandments on the foundation of Western law," Pruitt said, according to *KOCO*.

Pruitt said his office will file a petition calling for a stay of the court's order and noted that because of the court's interpretation of the section of the state constitution, it might be "necessary to repeal it."

While it has been in the state capitol, the Oklahoma statue has had other consequences. Religious groups, including the Satanic Temple and a Hindu organization, have proposed their own statues for placement on the capitol grounds. The state Supreme Court's ruling seems to also put a halt to all of those plans as well.

Prescott said that given how politically controversial the Ten Commandment statue is in Oklahoma, he was "pleasantly surprised by the strength of the ruling." He also welcomes talk of revising the constitution to address the issue.

"It's probably good for them to have an open and honest conversation instead of playing games," he added.

ACTIVITY: Analyzing the Rhetorical Situation

1. The American value of "freedom of religion" continues to be applied in multiple ways to civic issues. How do these different interpretations of freedom of religion come into conflict in this case?

2. To what specific rhetorical opportunity is Phillip responding? How is responding with an investigative report (rather than a position argument, for instance) a good rhetorical choice for her?

3. How would you describe Phillip's tone in this essay? Why might she have chosen to adopt this tone to write about an issue like this one?

4. Who appears to be the primary audience for this essay? What clues lead you to that conclusion? How has Phillip shaped her report to appeal to this audience?

5. Even though Phillip's primary purpose is to report on legal proceedings (informing her audience), rather than taking a position on either side of the dispute, her own perspective naturally influences her writing. Where do you find evidence of Phillip's own perspective in this essay? How might she be inviting readers to agree with her?

EMILY BADGER

Emily Badger has worked for The Atlantic *and* The Washington Post *as a reporter. She specializes in urban policy issues, particularly the impact of technology on public space and the relationship between city design and economic mobility. This essay was first published in* The Atlantic's CityLab *on May 16, 2012.*

The Washington Post/Getty Images

(continued)

How Smart Phones Are Turning Our Public Places into Private Ones

Smart phones have miraculously enabled people to stay connected, informed, and entertained, even in transit. We can now text, tweet, Skype, check Facebook updates, email in-boxes, Pandora channels and news feeds from a subway stop or street corner. The distracted walker has become both an urban menace and an April Fool's laugh line.

Tali Hatuka, who heads the Laboratory for Contemporary Urban Design at Tel Aviv University, laments, however, what she sees as the technology's darker side. So many smart phones may now be spoiling the "public" in our public places. Hatuka and colleague Eran Toch, a faculty member in the Department of Industrial Engineering, have been studying smart-phone users relative to their old-school, flip-phone counterparts. And the difference between the two groups is surprisingly stark, with serious implications for the future of public space in cities and the often-uncelebrated role that sociologists say they play.

"It's very interesting to see that some of the basic ideas of public spaces are conceived totally differently by smart-phone users," Hatuka says.

The ubiquitous smart phone may even degrade the way we recognize, memorize and move through cities.

She and Toch have given lengthy surveys to both smart-phone and traditional cell-phone users, quizzing them about their own behavior—where, when and how they use phones—and how they feel about the behavior of others. Smart-phone users, for starters, are much more commonly under the illusion that they have privacy even when walking down a public sidewalk. They're less skittish about having personal conversations in public. They're more detached from their physical surroundings. They're more likely to violate social norms about having disruptive, private phone conversations (and less likely to feel guilty about this).

Smart phones, in short, have given users the impression that they move through communal spaces as if in private bubbles. "They feel that everywhere they are, they have their privacy," Hatuka says. Smart phones have created, the researchers say, "portable private personal territories."

> Smart phones have given users the impression that they move through communal spaces as if in private bubbles.

"The whole idea of public/private as binary is becoming much more complex," Hatuka says. "Instead of thinking about public and private, we have to think about the private sphere becoming more dominant in public. For the smart-phone users, they're totally, constantly engaged with the private sphere, and it's reducing the basic roles of public space."

This is not a good thing. The public sphere plays an important role in our communities: it's where we observe and learn to interact with people who are different from us, or, as academics put it, it's where we come to know "the other."

In their surveys, Hatuka and Toch also asked what sounded like some pretty silly questions about what people remembered of the public spaces they'd visited just 10 minutes earlier: what did those places and the people there look like? Smart-phone users couldn't remember much at all, which is another of way saying that they weren't paying attention in the first place. This suggests, Hatuka says, that the ubiquitous smart phone may even degrade the way we recognize, memorize and move through cities. We will lose many of these benefits when we're one day *all* walking around thumbing our Twitter feeds.

"I think we've already lost many things," Hatuka says. "Five years ago, if you didn't know how to get somewhere in the city, you'd probably stop to ask a stranger." Now, Google Maps can get you there. "So no one is asking anything," Hatuka says. "This kind of stranger communication is a vital thing for a society. The communication of strangers was always one of the key roles of public spaces, observing and exchanging with the other. Because smart phones are supplying so many of these services, this kind of exchange with the stranger is just diminished to almost zero."

So why do smart phones change our behavior so much more radically than their simpler cell-phone predecessors did? Smart phones, Hatuka says, combine numerous spheres: your social network, your email, your news source, your live personal conversations. When you're interacting with each of those spheres while walking through a public park, which social code do you follow? Do you follow the code of the public park (wherein we politely make eye contact with one another), or do you follow the social code of Facebook (wherein you better hurry up and acknowledge all the friends who just "liked" your latest status update)?

As Hatuka and Toch have found, for smart-phone users, the social norms of the physical world are often trumped. They're becoming less important. All of this means we may need a concerted campaign to keep the "public" in the public sphere, to actively encourage people to observe and interact with each other. We may even need to redesign our public places to do this.

"I don't have a solution for that yet," Hatuka says. But she suspects we'll need to tap the very tool that is now harming our public places. "I think we'll need to use technology."

ACTIVITY: Analyzing the Rhetorical Situation

1. Tali Hatuka and Eran Toch, the researchers on whose work Badger is reporting, argue that smartphones are causing people to view public space as private space. According to these researchers, what are the consequences of this shift from public to private? Why do they consider the shift problematic?

2. What tone does Hatuka use when she talks about smartphones? What tone does Badger use? Why do you think their tones are similar or different?

3. Who is the target audience of Badger's report? How can you account for her choice of an investigative report to reach and please this audience?

4. What kind of persuasion do you think Badger wants to accomplish in this piece? Is she simply informing her readers about one point of view, or does she want them to agree with that view? How can you tell?

JAMIE UTT

Jamie Utt is the Founder and Director of Education at an Arizona-based bullying prevention program called Civil Schools. *He is also a contributing writer for the online magazine* Everyday Feminism, *where this essay was first published on September 1, 2015.*

From Manspreading to Mansplaining—6 Ways Men Dominate the Spaces Around Them

A few weeks ago, I was having a meeting with a friend at a coffee shop. It was hot out, I was slouching a bit, and without my really noticing, my legs were sticking out into the aisle. A woman who came by had to walk around them to get inside.

My friend laughed. "Dude, are you manspreading right now?"

"Am I? Maybe. I don't think so. Maybe…"

I totally was.

In truth, at first I was defensive and had assumed that I wasn't mainly because I'm not "that guy"—you know, the super entitled jerk who takes up more space than he deserves. But that's the thing about manspreading. It's not about men actively choosing to be jerks or trying to be sexist and ableist (since the outcome of our manspreading not only takes up space under the guise of our needing more room, but also often makes space less accessible for some people with disabilities).

It's entirely about our socialization—about how we've been taught (in subtle and overt ways) never to consider how entitled to public space we may act or feel.

So when countless women point out (often in hilarious ways) that we're manspreading all over the place, we quickly hear the refrains of "Women do it, too!" and "Stop conflating someone being rude with sexism and toxic masculinity."

But the problem actually *is* toxic masculinity and, by extension, sexism—it's just not as obvious as sexist name-calling or men being physically abusive.

After all, it's our masculine socialization that ingrains in us from the youngest of ages the idea that we are entitled to what's around us.

And this is intensified when we add in other forms of social power (or a lack thereof) to the equation.

When male entitlement compounds with class privilege, White privilege, and other forms of privilege, we see the amplification of this privilege and entitlement. . . .

On the other hand, when White supremacist systems endlessly brutalize and humiliate men of Color while reducing them in the media to strict portrayals of hypermasculinity, then masculinity, the only sense of social power that some men of Color may feel, can show up in hypermasculine expressions or in a sense of entitlement to public space.

We as men have been so inundated with the idea that all space is our space that we, often subconsciously, act as if that's true—both in our body language and in more overt expressions of entitlement like dominating conversations, talking over other people, and harassing women on the street. . . .

> We as men have been so inundated with the idea that all space is our space that we act as if that's true.

Thus, I do think manspreading is a problem—not because it's the ultimate example of misogyny, but because it's a perfect, public representation of the much more concerning issue of sexist male entitlement.

So when we as men experience a lifetime of messages that tie up our identity with entitlement to space and bodies, it makes perfect sense that we would take up more than our fair space on a crowded bus—but we must also understand that this is indicative of something so much bigger.

The point is that, in and of itself, manspreading in public isn't inherently sexist.

But when it's taken in the context of power and oppression and all of the *other* ways that we consciously and subconsciously assert our entitlement into public space, it's suddenly something *entirely* sexist.

With that in mind, here are six spaces in which our entitlement shows up in forms other than manspreading, offered with the hope that we as men will reflect a bit on how we can work toward better ways of being in community.

1. Men Dominate Physical Space

Though I'm not into the whole Crossfit thing, one of the things I have heard many women say is that Crossfit is pretty inclusive and that they're much less likely to experience the "gym dudebro" entitlement at a Crossfit gym.

I can't tell you how many committed female and gender non-conforming gym goers I've talked to about how hard it is to be in gyms with men who *either* constantly hit on and harass them *or* leave little room for them with their grunting, screaming, and throwing weights.

And like manspreading, this might just be a case of individuals being rude if it weren't for all the ways that we as men show entitlement to physical space.

In my own case, it's shown up with my friends on the dance floor. We love to dance, and we love to really get into it. When there's a crowded dance floor, that's not my scene. I want one where we can really move. But when that makes it hard for others to enjoy their time on the dance floor (as we've been accused of in the past), our reaction needs to be less "They're just fun killers" and more "How can we have this awesome time while respecting other people's space?"

From hyper-competitively running over women in mixed gender sports to dudes taking up entire tables in crowded libraries or coffee shops, we could do better to think critically about the physical space we're occupying—and call on other men to do the same.

2. Men Act Entitled to Intellectual Space

Whether we're mansplaining something that people who don't share our gender clearly can understand for themselves or actively contributing to intersectional gender oppression in the academy, men are really good at dominating intellectual space.

This is something I know I'm really good at, and it's something I need to work on.

I show entitlement to intellectual space by talking down to others in online debates or in coffee shop discussions. But it's uniquely problematic when I'm doing this, as I have been known to do, to women about women's issues.

And much like admitting that I, too, am guilty of manspreading, admitting this doesn't mean that I'm a terrible human being, but it does mean that if I really want to be in solidarity, I need to work on it and do better.

(continued)

3. Men Dominate and Control Professional Spaces

We don't need a Harvard study to tell us that the business world is filled with male dominance and entitlement. All we have to do is listen to any woman who works in these environments.

Yet, much like manspreading, we have dudes constantly denying even the possibility that it might be sexism and masculinity that's the problem.

Simply telling women to "lean in" demands nothing of us as men [*Lean In* by Facebook's Chief Operating Officer Sheryl Sandberg on women and leadership]. It frees us from listening and reflecting, rather than dominating and acting entitled in professional environments.

It frees us from working to change male-dominated fields (from kitchens to board rooms) and from following the leadership of women who are demonstrating different ways of leading in the workplace.

If we would claim that our values support women's leadership, we need to call upon our workplaces to reflect less male entitlement and control.

4. Men Regularly Show Entitlement to Social Spaces

I'll be the first to admit it. I've been that guy on countless occasions, the one making a scene and shouting over other people to be the "hilarious" center of attention at a party. And I've been the one who takes off his pants or otherwise acts a fool.

But our entitlement to social space, an entitlement that often gets rewarded by people of all genders, doesn't have to be as obvious as the center of attention at a party.

Many men's voices tend to be on the louder side, but that doesn't mean that we are incapable of regulating our tone of voice so we aren't dominating a room with our booming baritone. Nor do we have to interrupt others to get in that "priceless" joke or to have our point heard.

We can take the time to reflect on how we take up (physical or proverbial) space at parties or dinners, and we can step back. And we can call on other men to listen when we notice that our fellow men are interrupting or talking over.

And it doesn't have to be a cape-wearing, save-the-day sort of moment. It can be as simple as, "What were you saying about _____?" to the person who was interrupted while taking the time to listen.

5. Men Control Political Spaces

We are all well aware of the ways that men are demonstrating feelings of entitlement to women's bodies through the regulation of their healthcare.

But there are far more subtle ways that men demonstrate entitlement in the political sphere

Even among the most "progressive" of men, what are we using our political power and energy for? Are we focusing on electing ourselves or other men? Are we allowing traditional male dominance to shut women out of our various formal and informal political processes?

Because there are all sorts of badass women, genderqueer, and gender non-conforming people we can support who align with our values—but the systems we've created for political process aren't designed to support their election.

It's not enough to say that "more women need to run" if we're not going to actively support changing the culture of politics that values traditional forms of male leadership and that centers "electability" on traditionally masculine ways of being.

6. Men Consistently Demonstrate Entitlement in Intimate Spaces

Let's be clear—none of these other forms of entitlement can be separated from how we as men act as if we're entitled to the bodies of other people, most often women.

There is a direct, demonstrable link between male feelings of entitlement and the incredible rates of sexual violence that we see in the US and elsewhere.

We simply cannot separate manspreading or any other form of male entitlement from sexual violence, intimate partner violence, and male sexual entitlement because they all have the same toxic root: male socialization that tells us we are entitled to take what we want.

> There is a direct, demonstrable link between male feelings of entitlement and sexual violence.

Manspreading, Just Like All Forms of Male Entitlement, Relies on the Silence of Men.

That's why when someone says that we should "focus on more important issues" than how much space men are taking up on the train, I think they're missing the point. We as men should call out manspreading not because it's the worst form of sexism but because it's a symptom of the sickness that is toxic masculinity.

Whether we're talking about manspreading or endemic sexual and intimate partner violence, the harm caused by male entitlement is men's problem to solve.

We make the issue of toxic male entitlement our issue when we as men choose to speak out, to call on men to change, and to, perhaps most importantly, work on ourselves.

And by taking up this challenge, we open the doors to real change.

After all, women can tell men to close their legs on the bus, but public space doesn't get more inclusive until men decide to change.

And women can call on men to stop rape, but it doesn't stop until men choose to change not only ourselves and our attitudes toward sexual entitlement, but also the systems that support and protect rapists.

Because in the end, male entitlement isn't just about the behaviors of individual men. It's about systemic gender violence and control that shows up through the daily entitlement of men, and we need to take responsibility for how we are complicit in those systems.

A simple place to start? Be more aware of how much space we're taking up and call on other men to do the same.

ACTIVITY: Analyzing the Rhetorical Situation

1. According to Utt, what does gender have to do with public space? Why might a seemingly harmless activity like "manspreading" mean something different when performed by a female body?
2. Why might Utt have chosen to write this essay in a list format? Was his choice effective? Why or why not?
3. How does Utt use personal stories in his argument? Do these stories advance the argument or distract from it?

(continued)

4. Why do you think Utt calls attention to his sex and appeals to other men with pro-nouns like "we" and "us"? How does this impact his ethos (credibility) as a writer?

5. Identify the moments where you consider Utt's argument most persuasive. What makes these moments effective? Where, if anywhere, do you think the argument is less likely to persuade?

MindTap® Find more readings on "Taking Up (Public) Space" online.

COMMUNITY C◉NNECTIONS

1. Analyze a public space where you feel completely comfortable: a coffee shop, a campus bar, a grocery store, a museum, a government building, for instance. What are the criteria for your own comfort and ease there? Are there any criteria that the space does not meet in your case? In a three-to four-page essay, describe the place you are analyzing and the reason the analysis is important for you and your audience. State a thesis about the space and then articulate the causes or consequences of your comfort in the space. Be sure to consider the needs and expectations of people who are not comfortable in that same space as you consider alternative viewpoints.

2. Write for ten minutes about the causes or the consequences of being in a specific public space where you do not feel comfortable, following the instructions of the previous prompt (#1), making sure to identify the crite-ria that make others feel very comfortable there. Be prepared to share your response with the rest of the class.

3. Given your experience and observations, consider how smartphones affect the various ways people move through public space. In a brief report, define the problem you are addressing, explaining its significance to you and your audience. Be sure to state a thesis, developing it with good rea-sons that you support with specific examples, details, anecdotes, or data. Your report will include various perspectives and examples of people using their smartphones in public spaces as well as the effects of these uses. Be prepared to share your findings.

4. Write for ten minutes about your response to Moses's planning or Jacobs's objections and opinions. How does one set of these arguments about the use of public space coincide with or diverge from your experiences in a town or city you know well?

MindTap® Reflect on your reading and writing process.

24

Whose Lives Matter?

MindTap® Understand the goals of the chapter and complete a warm-up activity online.

As you already know, people shape different responses to the same rhetorical opportunity for change. Some responses may seem to you more effective than others, but it can be hard to pinpoint where one falls short and others succeed. In what many had hoped was the post-racial world that elected Barack Obama as the 44th president of the United States, protests have arisen in response to the widely publicized deaths of African Americans at the hands of police and others. The 2013 shooting death of Trayvon Martin by a white man on neighborhood watch—and the acquittal of George Zimmerman in his death—sparked what is now an international activist movement called Black Lives Matter (BLM).

The responses in this chapter include an investigative report that compares these recent developments in American civil rights to those that occurred in the mid-twentieth century under the leadership of celebrated figures such as Martin Luther King, Jr. (see CHAPTER 6, GENRE IN FOCUS: THE BIO), as well as pages 93–94 responses in the genres memoir, evaluation, and critical analysis. Some people criticize the movement for contributing to increased racial tension. Still others consider BLM too peaceful, too respectable, and yet too focused on black lives rather than *all* lives. What do you think?

After you have read the essays in this chapter, your instructor might call on you to develop your own ideas through one of the following prompts.

Penn State student Zaniya Joe wears a piece of tape over her mouth that says "Black Lives Matter," as a group of Penn State University students protest in reaction to the events in Ferguson.

Centre Daily Times/Getty Images

1. With the BLM movement organizing demonstrations through social media, many people feel that the protests comprise a visual rhetoric, one immediately available to people all over the globe and serving as perhaps the most fitting response to the opportunity for change. Choose an image or text by a person or a group with a vested interest in the overall effect of the BLM movement. The text can be from this chapter or you can turn to an image or text you find online or in print. In a critical analysis, assess whether the response is a fitting and successful one. (See CHAPTER 11, CRITICAL ANALYSES.) To achieve that goal, consider these questions:

pages 194–214

- Is the intended audience for the text a rhetorical audience, someone who is affected by the issue and has a vested interest in it? Draw on evidence from the text to support your answer.
- If the intended audience is a rhetorical audience, what can it do to resolve the problem?
- Does the response address and fit the rhetorical opportunity for change? How exactly? If not, how might the response be reshaped so that it does fit?
- Is the response delivered in an appropriate medium that reaches its intended audience? If so, describe why the medium is appropriate. If not, explain how it could be adjusted so that it would be appropriate.
- Can you think of other responses to similar rhetorical situations? What genre is commonly used to respond to such situations? Does the creator of this text use that genre? If not, what is the effect of going against an audience's expectations?

Using your responses, craft a formal critical analysis of your chosen text. Begin by choosing a thesis in which you analyze what makes the text rhetorically effective or ineffective. Then, organize your most interesting observations into several major points, using specific examples from the text to elaborate each individual point. Be sure to choose an audience for your critical analysis and write with that audience in mind.

2. Take a stand on the Black Lives Matter movement in the form of a position argument. (See CHAPTER 8, POSITION ARGUMENTS.) After reading the essays in pages 132–155 this chapter, conduct online and library research, tap into your own experiences and observations, and draft a thesis statement that reflects your position toward the movement. Develop your thesis with richly supported reasons and make an authentic, purposeful connection with your audience. Adopt a thoughtful, respectful tone and bring in opposing viewpoints to build your credibility on the subject. Your print essay should be at least five pages long, so you can be sure to acknowledge a wide range of opinions about the movement. You may include images and links to sound and videos if you think doing so will enhance your essay.

MindTap®   Read, highlight, and take notes online.

TODD S. PURDUM

In this piece, which first appeared in Politico *on September 10, 2015, political reporter Todd Purdum examines the civil rights movement of the 1950s and 1960s and the Black Lives Matter movement today. He notes, for example, that fifty year ago, people were infuriated when pro-segregation Alabama politician Bull Connor advocated the use of fire hoses and attack dogs against peaceful civil rights protestors marching in Selma, Alabama. Purdum compares this outrage to the more recent outcry against police brutality in places such as Ferguson, Missouri, after the death of African American teenager Michael Brown in 2014, and in Baltimore, Maryland, after the death of Freddie Gray in 2015.*

Whose Lives Matter?

A landmark year for civil rights shows the path to equality isn't a straight line.

When Presidents Barack Obama and George W. Bush joined a bipartisan, multiracial raft of dignitaries on the Edmund Pettus Bridge in Selma, Alabama, in March, they were officially commemorating the 50th anniversary of a seminal moment in American history: the bloody march that spurred passage of the Voting Rights Act of 1965.

But the gathering in Selma also came amid another landmark year in which the question of civil rights in all its varied guises has once again been at the forefront of the national

(continued)

political and cultural debate, with striking signs of change and progress on so many fronts, tempered by setbacks and stubborn injustices on others.

Perhaps not since 50 years ago, when searing street protests and shining legislative victories riveted the country, has the promise of America's founding creed that all are "created equal," coupled with the enduring difficulty of living up to that pledge, so dominated daily headlines. From Ferguson, Missouri, to the corridors of the Supreme Court, from the streets of Baltimore, to the covers of national magazines and millions of television screens, the latest battles to perfect the union have been on vivid display over the past year.

Just as televised images of Bull Connor's fire hoses and police dogs unleashed on peaceful protesters in Birmingham revealed police misconduct to an outraged America half a century ago, so police body cameras and cellphone videos have now exposed one-on-one police abuses that once would have remained private, sparking comparable calls for change.

In the span of just two weeks this summer, the rainbow banner of gay pride was unfurled in colored lights across the White House to celebrate the Supreme Court's enshrining the right to same-sex marriage nationwide, and the Confederate battle flag's stars and bars were lowered from South Carolina's Capitol grounds at the urging of the Republican governor in the wake of a racist mass shooting in a Charleston church. In similarly short order, a famous male Olympic decathlete re-emerged as Caitlyn Jenner on the cover of *Vanity Fair*, and the Pentagon announced plans to end its ban on transgender troops serving openly in the ranks.

The variety, reach and diversity of movement on civil rights in recent months might boggle the mind of a time traveler from even the early 21st century. In just one not-so-trivial sign of how much has changed in a single lifetime, the picture editor of the *New York Times* lost his job 60 years ago for presuming to publish a photograph of Marilyn Monroe and Joe DiMaggio about to share an open-mouthed smooch on their wedding day; the same newspaper marked the decision on same-sex marriage with a front-page, full-color photo montage of gay couples kissing across the country.

For many Americans, these milestones have been cause for rejoicing. For many others, they have occasioned alarm—and could incite further backlash, whether in the name of social conservatism, religious liberty or claims of color-blindness. But as Obama himself put it at the Selma anniversary celebration, "If Selma taught us anything, it's that our work is never done—the American experiment in self-government gives work and purpose to each generation."

Civil rights has arguably been *the* American story, in a country where the Declaration of Independence proclaims that "all men are created equal," yet the original Constitution counted slaves as three-fifths of a person and denied women the vote. "It is possible to read the history of this country as one long struggle to extend the liberties established in our Constitution to everyone in America," the late writer Molly Ivins once put it.

The fitful redefinition and expansion of civil rights—to include race, sex, sexual orientation, gender identity and physical ability—has been a source of sometimes bloody debate—not least of all in the Civil

> Civil rights has arguably been *the* American story.

War, but continuing to the present day, in which the election of the nation's first black president has prompted both widespread, transracial pride and significant racist backlash.

"I don't think there's ever been a time in American history when civil rights hasn't been a crucial issue," says Erwin Chemerinsky, dean of the law school at the University of California, Irvine. "It's always been front and center in American politics in one way or another. But it's a mistake to think of it as a homogeneous issue."

Or a straight, unbroken line.

Indeed, at any given time, the state of civil rights in America can resemble an M.C. Escher lithograph, with staircases ascending and descending in impossible synchronicity—a movement, or collection of them, driven by pressure from the grass roots, action by the legislature and executive branch, and the mediation of the courts.

"Our work is not done till we all share in progress."

A hundred years after the Civil War, Jim Crow segregation across the Old Confederacy belied the promise of the Union victory and the 13th, 14th and 15th Amendments to the Constitution intended to give blacks full citizenship. The 1964 Civil Rights Act and 1965 Voting Rights Act—the high-water marks of national consensus on race—aspired to rectify that failure.

But it is an unhappy fact that the Watts riots in Los Angeles broke out just five days after President Lyndon B. Johnson signed the Voting Rights Act, sparked by an argument over the arrest of a black motorist on the suspicion of drunk driving. More civil unrest throughout the 1960s, the rise of the Black Power movement, the shattering assassinations of 1968 and Richard Nixon's "Southern strategy" [which appealed to white voter backlash against civil rights

legislation] all combined to splinter public opinion on civil rights in ways that reverberate today.

Most recently, the Supreme Court's 2013 ruling invalidating a crucial section of the Voting Rights Act opened the floodgates for a wave of state measures to limit access to the ballot (through voter I.D. laws, eliminating same-day registration and the like) in ways that disadvantage minorities (and thus Democratic voters) overwhelmingly.

"The current effort to limit voting rights stands in stark contrast to the progress being made on so many other civil rights issues," notes Ari Berman, a political correspondent for the *Nation* and the author of *Give Us the Ballot: The Modern Struggle for Voting Rights in America*. Since the 2010 midterm elections, he adds, half the states in the country have passed laws making it harder to vote.

"In recent years, as the Supreme Court, the Congress and state legislatures across the country have become more rigidly conservative, the counterrevolution against voting rights has reached a fever pitch," Berman says.

It may seem paradoxical that one of the younger branches of the civil rights movement—the crusade for equal treatment of gay Americans—has clocked such major victories even as striking racial and economic inequalities persist and black access to the ballot is under renewed assault.

But veteran civil rights voices insist it is wrong—and invidious—to view the broader civil rights struggle as a zero-sum game, or to try to establish what the scholar Henry Louis Gates once called "a pecking order of oppression." After all, two of the three women leading the #BlackLivesMatter movement, founded in the wake of the fatal shooting of Trayvon Martin, identify as queer, and the Wikipedia page entry of Evan Wolfson, founder and president of the gay rights group Freedom to Marry, shows him seated at his desk in front of a photograph of Martin Luther King Jr.

"The whole idea that you have to pit one against the other, or can only have one victory at a time, is wrong," Wolfson says. "Our work is not done until we all share in progress. It's not that one is moving more quickly than another, it's that we all have a lot of work to do."

ACTIVITY: Analyzing the Rhetorical Situation

1. How does Purdum compare the characteristics of the mid-twentieth-century civil rights movement with the Black Lives Matter movement?

2. Moving from the founding of America hundreds of years ago to events that occurred only a few weeks before this publication, Purdum uses a wide scope for his writing. What advantages does this give him in writing his investigative report? Describe any related limitations in his ability to effectively make his case.

3. What core values lie at the root of Purdum's argument? Does he seem to expect that his readers will share these values? Do you think he is right?

4. How would you describe Purdum's stance toward this subject? Identify specific passages in the text where his tone reveals his attitude toward the subject he is investigating.

5. Do you think Purdum wants to persuade his readers to change their view about present-day civil rights movements? How so? What makes his writing different from the writings of civil rights activists?

ROXANE GAY

Roxane Gay is a professor of English at Purdue University and has written extensively on issues of race, gender, sexuality, and American culture. This essay first appeared as a chapter in her book Bad Feminist, *published by HarperCollins in 2014.*

Frederick M. Brown/ Getty Images

A Tale of Two Profiles

There is no way to truly know whom we need to protect ourselves from. Dangerous people rarely look the way we expect. We were reminded of

this in early 2013 when Dzhokhar ("Jahar") Tsarnaev, who looks like the "boy next door," was identified as one of the two young men suspected in the terrorist bombings near the finish line of the Boston Marathon. Three people were killed and nearly three hundred others injured. This notoriety, I imagine, explains why Tsarnaev was featured on the cover of the August 1, 2013, issue of *Rolling Stone*.

The magazine was accused of exploiting tragedy, glorifying terrorism, and trying to make a martyr or a rock star out of Tsarnaev. But protests aside, the cover is provocative and pointed. It is a stark reminder that we can never truly know where danger lurks. It is also a reminder that we have certain cultural notions about who looks dangerous and who does not. These notions are amply reinforced by the article accompanying the cover, something few people seem to be talking about. The tone of Janet Reitman's reportage and the ongoing conversation about Tsarnaev as a "normal American teenager" are an interesting and troubling contrast to the way we talk about, say, Trayvon Martin, also a "normal American teenager," but not a criminal or terrorist. George Zimmerman killed Martin because Martin fit our cultural idea of what danger looks like. Zimmerman was acquitted for the very same reason.

Most striking in Reitman's extensive and well-reported article is how the people who knew Tsarnaev are still willing to see the man behind the monster. Tsarnaev is described by those who knew him in near reverential terms as "sweet" and "superchill" and "smooth as fuck" and "a golden person, really just a genuine good guy." While Tsarnaev's community acknowledges the terrible things the young man has done and mourns the tragedy of the

bombings, they are unwilling to turn their backs on him.

The article also reveals how shocked Tsarnaev's friends and neighbors were to learn that he and his brother were responsible for such a crime. They were shocked because we have a portrait, in our minds, of what danger looks like and it's not the golden boy on the cover of the *Rolling Stone*. Time and again the word "normal" comes up. He is described as "a beautiful, tousled hair boy with a gentle demeanor, soulful brown eyes." He enjoyed what most teenagers seem to enjoy—popular television shows, sports, music, girls. He smoked "a copious amount of weed." He committed a monstrous act, but he retains his normalcy.

Reitman's article is breathless in its empathy for Tsarnaev. Not only does Reitman meticulously reveal how Tsarnaev went from boy next door to terrorist, she seems desperate to understand why. She is not alone in this. When danger has an unexpected face, we demand answers. Family friend Anna Nikeava discussed the Tsarnaev family's problems and concluded, "Poor Jahar was the silent survivor of all that dysfunction." Poor, poor Jahar. Reitman later notes that "though it seems as if Jahar had found a mission, his embrace of Islam also may have been driven by something more basic: a need to belong." The article seems ultimately to be asking, how can we not have some measure of empathy for a young man with so simple a desire to belong?

The empathy does not end with the reportage. This is also the testimony from Wick Sloane, a community college professor who has taught many young immigrants like Tsarnaev. He says,

> *All of these kids are grateful to be in the United States. But it is the usual thing: Is this the land of opportunity or isn't it? When I look at what they've been through, and how they are screwed by federal policies from the moment they turn around, I don't understand why all of them are not angrier. I'm actually kind of surprised it's taken so long for one of these kids to set off a bomb.*

And there are even more of Tsarnaev's friends, who are still stunned. Friends from college who found a backpack with emptied fireworks fretted about what to do because "no one wanted Jahar to get in trouble." Even after all we know, Tsarnaev benefits from so much doubt from his friends, his community, and those who seek to understand all the terrible things he has done.

This, it would seem, is yet another example of white privilege—to retain humanity in the face of inhumanity. For criminals who defy our understanding of danger, the cultural threshold for forgiveness is incredibly low.

When Trayvon Martin was murdered, certain people worked overtime to uncover his failings, even though he was the victim of the crime. Before his death, Martin had recently been suspended from school because drug residue was found in his backpack. There were other such infractions. This became evidence. He was a normal teenager but he was also a black teenager, so he was put on trial and he was indicted. With Tsarnaev, people continued to look for the good. The bounds of compassion for the "tousle-haired" young man know few limits. Trayvon Martin, meanwhile, should

have walked home without "looking suspicious." He should have meekly submitted himself to Zimmerman's intentions instead of whatever took place on the fateful night of his murder. He should have been above reproach. As Syreeta McFadden noted, "Only in America can a dead black boy go on trial for his own murder."

Reitman's article is a solid piece of journalism. It reveals complex truths about the life of Dzhokhar Tsarnaev. Imagine, though, if *Rolling Stone* had dedicated more than eleven thousand words and the cover to Trayvon Martin to reveal the complex truth of his life and what he was like in the years and months and hours before his death. How did he deal with the burden of being the face of danger from the moment he was born? This is a question fewer people seem to be asking.

> Race profiling is what emboldened an armed George Zimmerman to follow an unarmed young black man walking home.

The way we see danger is, in large part, about racial profiling, a law enforcement practice that has been hotly debated for years because it implicitly connects race to criminality. Racial profiling is what emboldened an armed George Zimmerman to follow an unarmed young black man walking home, even after police told Zimmerman not to pursue Trayvon Martin. Zimmerman saw a young black man and believed he was looking into the face of danger. He hunted the danger down.

The New York City Police Department's "stop and frisk" program allows police to stop, question, and search anyone who raises a "reasonable" suspicion of danger or criminality. The majority of people who are stopped and frisked in New York are black or Latino because these demographics fit our cultural profile of danger. These are the supposed barbarians at the gate, not the boy with the "soulful brown eyes."

Though there are many objections to the "stop and frisk" program and other forms of racial profiling, these practices persist. Former mayor Michael Bloomberg defiantly supported the program. On his radio program he said, "They just keep saying, 'Oh, it's a disproportionate percentage of a particular ethnic group.' That may be, but it's not a disproportionate percentage of those whom witnesses and victims describe as committing the murder. In that case, incidentally, I think we disproportionately stop whites too much and minorities too little."

In her book *The Color of Crime*, Kathryn Russell-Brown says, "Blacks are the repository for the American fear of crime," and also notes that

For most of us, television's overpowering images of Black deviance—its regularity and frequency—are impossible to ignore. These negative images have been seared into our collective consciousness. It is no surprise that most Americans wrongly believe that Blacks are responsible for the majority of crime. No doubt, many of the suspects paraded across the nightly news are guilty criminals. The onslaught of criminal images of Black men, however, causes many of us to incorrectly conclude that most Black men are criminals. . . . This is . . . the myth of the criminalblackman.

Over the past year, countless black men have stepped forward to share their stories of how they have been forced into this myth. But very little has changed.

Racial profiling is nothing more than a delusion born of our belief that we can profile danger. We want to believe we can predict who will do the next terrible thing. We want to believe we can keep ourselves safe. It's good that Dzhokhar Tsarnaev is on the cover of *Rolling Stone*, tousled hair and all. We need a reminder that we must stop projecting our fears onto profiles built from stereotypes. We need a reminder that we will never truly know whom we need to fear.

ACTIVITY: Analyzing the Rhetorical Situation

1. What is the central argument that Gay makes in her critical analysis? What evidence does she use to make her case?
2. To what rhetorical opportunity is Gay responding? How does understanding her context change the way you understand her writing?
3. Is Gay's essay a fitting response to her rhetorical opportunity? How can you tell?
4. Why does Gay spend so much time discussing Jane Reitman's reporting on Dzhokhar Tsarnaev? How does Gay's reading of Reitman help Gay advance her own argument?
5. What are the most persuasive features of this piece? Where does the argument seem less likely to persuade its audience?

MALCOLM-AIME MUSONI

Malcolm-Aime Musoni is an Iowa native, a college undergraduate, and a writer whose work has been published in digital magazines such as Huffington Post *and* Four Pins. *This memoir compares Musoni's own life to the life of 18-year-old African American Michael Brown, who was shot and killed by white police officer Darren Wilson in Ferguson, Missouri, in 2014. The memoir first appeared in* Huffington Post *on August 19, 2015.*

Malcolm Musoni

Being an 18-Year-Old Black Man a Year after Mike Brown

I made my way down the gravel road out of the cemetery as I had done plenty of times before, but to the left of me I saw something that I hadn't seen in all the times I had gone to visit my mom at the cemetery since February: a police car. The cop car had just pulled up, and was parked facing my way. It was a hot day, and I had been running without my shirt on. I put my shirt on, crossed the street, took my phone out of my pocket, and when I was far enough I turned around to make sure the police car wasn't following me. Never before had I ever felt such a wave of anxiety hit me like that due to being in the presence of the police. Long gone are the childlike days when I viewed the police as heroes or the pre-teen days when it seemed like it was the cool thing to flip a policeman off with our middle fingers if they were driving behind us. Those days are gone. I didn't do anything wrong, I didn't commit a crime, I was just minding my own business and going to visit my mom. But the notion that I could mind my own business and not be persecuted in the streets from a policeman was stripped away from me on August 9th 2014 when Mike Brown was unlawfully gunned down by the police.

> When Mike Brown was killed I was immediately scared for my brother . . . A year later I'm scared for myself.

I was 17 when Mike Brown was killed, but now I'm 18; the same age as he was, and never have I ever been more aware of the racism going on in this country. I'm aware of what can happen to me: in the blink of an eye my name can follow a hashtag and have supporters drumming up support for real justice to take place in my honor. It's a scary thing to know that people view you as the enemy and have such hatred for you just because of your skin color and can get away with killing you just because of systematic oppression and racism. Once you realize that, your view of the world changes. When Mike Brown was killed, I was immediately scared for my brother. He's the same build as Mike, and all I could think of was someone trying to kill him. Whenever we would go to stores, I would always try to shush my brother if he was being loud because I didn't want to draw a scene and cause problems. A year later, I'm scared for myself. Now I don't think that just because I'm 3 years younger, taller and skinnier that I have no chance of being gunned down. That's not a reality that lays in my future. My previous naive reality isn't the reality anymore. They're not gonna look at me and say, "Hey just because you don't sag your pants, you're a good black" and then go and kill my brother because he sags his pants. It's not going to happen. The articles of clothing that we wear don't define us to them, and that's something that took time to realize and understand.

When I hit 8th grade, I felt this conflict between myself and my white classmates due to what I would wear and how I talked. There was this constant, "You talk so white", "You're the whitest black kid I know." I would sit and try to ask myself and figure out what did that mean. Their comments turned into "Oh I can say the N word, Malcolm doesn't care; he's the whitest black kid I know." But the reality was I did care, and I did voice my opinion on them saying the N word, but that wasn't listened to. You top that conflict with the internal struggle I dealt with of feeling like I was less of a beauty or a person for being a dark-skinned black person rather than a light-skinned black person, and that can manifest into self-hate. For a year after that, I started to sag my pants and dress a little bit differently. It lasted for a year because my mom and dad weren't putting up with that and because I realized that dressing like that wasn't me. It wasn't who I was. And then Trayvon Martin happened. And a conversation started to take place about black men wearing hoodies. I lived and still live in a neighborhood where we are the only black family living in it. If I was walking through the neighborhood in the rain with a hoodie, I didn't think they would gun me down. I didn't think that was a reality for anyone. But fast forward a couple year later, and the cloth of innocence has been violently ripped from my face and I'm just dangerously trying to exist without my existence being threatened in my own home, my neighborhood, my city, my state and the country my parents decided to call their new home 20 some years ago. It's the struggle of a lifetime that we are having to endure. Nothing is safe anymore.

I see Sandra Bland and I see my 22-year-old sister. It's such a twisted reality that it took that happening to really let it sink in that my sister too could be gunned down as well. It took that for me to know and feel the same fear I feel for my brother for my sister as well. Her taillight needs to be fixed, and that's all it takes for a policeman to pull her over and a routine stop turning wrong. She's never been in contact with the police, so I'm not sure how she would react. But her reaction doesn't even matter because no matter how you treat the police or how much you know your rights, it's not going to change anything. And that's something that I fear when I get my car. I have to hope that my music isn't too loud that it bothers someone at a gas station, or I have to hope that a routine stop is just a routine stop that I can be able to leave and not end up in a jail cell. It's all this fear and baggage that comes with the new responsibilities of being an adult. Not just being an adult but a black man entering adulthood. I live in a smallish town of 48 thousand in Iowa, and everyone is always saying "oh that will never happen to us we live in a good small town." But the town isn't the problem; it's the people in the town and the systems that are put in place to let people get away with abusing their power and using their power as a tool to explore their own personal racism. That's really what it comes down to; it's not the victims.

As time goes on, I'm more and more increasingly aware of my own digital imprint

> Will it take my own killing to get my white friends to use the Black Lives Matter hashtag instead of the All Lives Matter hashtag?

operating under the moniker "fijiwatergod" and what that can mean for me. Just being a teen on social media has ramifications beyond my existence. They can take my tweets and say that I was someone who "had no respect for the law" as a reason to justify what could happen to me. They can take my old tweets from when I was an 11th grader seriously battling depression and say that I killed myself. They can take my pictures of me throwing up the peace sign and say that I was a thug and throwing up a gang sign. They can find marijuana in my system from months prior and say that I was a druggie who was out of his mind and instigated the altercation with the police. Will the media label me as a thug and not an angel and try to humanize my killer? Will the media launch a smear campaign against me? Will it take my own killing to get my white friends to use the Black Lives Matter hashtag instead of the All Lives Matter hashtag? Will my dad be forced to go on TV and say he forgives them? Will there be marches in my honor? Will the mayor of my town encourage peace before the verdict announcing that the policeman will get off unlawfully killing me is read? Will the cop camera and body camera be on, or will that not even matter due to the systems put in place that hold police at an unfair advantage? Will I be the topic of an incredulous Don Lemon panel with Marc Lamont Hill being the voice of reason? Will they find a twisted way to bring my mom's recent death into this and vilify me? These are the questions and thoughts that plague me as an 18 year old black man.

What will they do?

ACTIVITY: Analyzing the Rhetorical Situation

1. How has the death of Michael Brown affected Musoni? For what reasons might Musoni have written this piece even if Brown hadn't been killed?
2. Does Musoni seem like a trustworthy communicator? In what ways does he establish a persona for himself and develop a relationship with his readers?
3. Who is Musoni's audience for this piece? What strategies does he use to appeal specifically to this audience?
4. How does Musoni try to make an emotional connection to the sympathy of his audience in his writing? What connections do you see between his topic and how successful he is in making this connection?
5. How does Musoni want his readers' actions or thoughts to change after reading his writing? How does he try to inspire these changes?

CARIMAH TOWNES

Carimah Townes is a reporter for the online news site ThinkProgress, *where she writes about politics, criminal law, and social justice issues. This essay, a summary of President Barack Obama's statement about the Black Lives Matter movement, was first published at* ThinkProgress *on October 22, 2015.*

Obama Explains the Problem with "All Lives Matter"

Many politicians have taken up the rallying cry of "all lives matter" to criticize the Black Lives Matter movement for focusing on specific injustices done to African Americans. During a criminal justice panel discussion with Police Chief Charlie Beck of the LAPD and Editor-in-Chief Bill Keller of the Marshall Project on Thursday afternoon, President Barack Obama took on that claim and explained why "black lives matter" is an important statement.

"I think the reason that the organizers used the phrase 'black lives matter' was not because they were suggesting nobody else's lives matter," he said. "What they were suggesting was, there is a specific problem that is happening in the African-American community that's not happening in other communities. And that is a legitimate issue that we've got to address."

But the meaning of the phrase has been perverted by media pundits and some members of law enforcement, who argue that it is inflammatory rhetoric. The phrases "all lives matter" and "blue lives matter" sprang up in direct response to activists who have mobilized against police brutality and attacks on black lives.

"It started being lifted up as 'these folks are opposed to police, and they're opposed to cops, and all lives matter.' So the notion was somehow saying black lives matter was reverse racism, or suggesting other people's lives didn't matter or police officers' lives didn't matter," he said.

Obama then pointed out that saying "black lives matter" is not about reducing the importance of other groups.

"I think everybody understands all lives matter. Everybody wants strong, effective law enforcement. Everybody wants their kids to be safe when they're walking to school. Nobody wants to see police officers, who are doing their jobs fairly, hurt," he continued.

Today, black lives matter is not just a rallying cry. Due to activists' efforts to elevate the conversation about police brutality against black communities, the conversation has become a main talking point in the 2015–2016 election cycle. During the first Democratic debate, candidates were asked, "do black lives matter or do all lives matter?"

ACTIVITY: Analyzing the Rhetorical Situation

1. According to President Obama, what is the danger of replacing the phrase "Black Lives Matter" with "All Lives Matter"?
2. What audience do you think is most likely to respond favorably to this piece and to Obama's comments? What audience is most likely to be resistant?
3. What resources does Obama have as a communicator speaking out on this issue? How does he take advantage of these resources in the way he crafts his statements?

(continued)

4. What change of attitude or behavior do you think Townes hoped to accomplish in writing this piece? How does she go about encouraging that change? How might she have reported on Obama differently if she wanted to accomplish a different goal?

WILLIAM J. WILSON

William Julius Wilson is a professor of sociology at Harvard University and a fellow of the Brookings Institution in Washington, D.C., a nonprofit public policy organization that conducts research on social problems. This essay was first published by the Brookings Institution on December 14, 2015.

AP Images/Charles Dharapak

The Other Side of Black Lives Matter

Several decades ago I spoke with a grieving mother living in one of the poorest inner-city neighborhoods on Chicago's South Side. A stray bullet from a gang fight had killed her son, who was not a gang member. She lamented that his death was not reported in any of the Chicago newspapers or in the Chicago electronic media.

I have been thinking about that mother a good deal recently, as the Black Lives Matter movement has dramatically called attention to violent police encounters with blacks, especially young black males. Aided by smart phones and social media, Americans have now become more aware of these incidents, which very likely have occurred at similar levels in previous decades, but were "under the radar."

This is good, of course. But it is not enough. We need to expand the focus of the movement to include groups not usually referenced when we discuss "Black Lives Matter," including that boy in Chicago, who would by now be a grown man, perhaps with children of his own.

Segregation by income amplifies segregation by race, leaving low-income blacks clustered in neighborhoods that feature disadvantages along several dimensions, including exposure to violent crime. As a result, the divide within the black community has widened sharply. In 1978, poor blacks aged twelve and over were only marginally more likely than affluent blacks to be violent crime victims—around forty-five and thirty-eight per 1000 individuals respectively. However, by 2008, poor blacks were far more likely to be violent crime victims—about seventy-five per 1000—while affluent blacks were far less likely to be victims of violent crime—about twenty-three per 1000, according to Hochschild and Weaver.

Violent crime can in fact reach extraordinary levels in the poorest inner-city black neighborhoods. In Milwaukee, Wisconsin, where 46 percent of African Americans live in high poverty neighborhoods—those with poverty rates of at least 40 percent—blacks are nearly 20 times more likely to get shot than whites, and nine times more likely to be murdered.

As Leon Neyfakh points out, some people are reluctant to talk about the high murder rate in cities like Milwaukee because (1) it might distract attention from the vital discussions about police violence against blacks, and (2) it runs the risk of providing ammunition to those who resist criminal justice reform efforts regarding policing and sentencing policy. These are legitimate concerns, of course.

On the other hand, it is vital to draw more attention to the low priority placed on solving the high murder rates in poor inner-city neighborhoods, reflected in the woefully inadequate resources provided to homicide detectives struggling to solve killings in those areas. As Jill Leovy, a writer at Los Angeles Times asserts in her 2014 book *Ghettoside*, this represents one of the great moral failings of our criminal justice system and indeed of our whole society. The thousands of poor grieving African American families whose loved ones have been killed tend to be disregarded or ignored, including by the media.

The nation's consciousness has been raised by the repeated acts of police brutality against blacks. But the problem of public space violence—seen in the extraordinary distress, trauma and pain many poor inner-city families experience following the killing of a family member or close relative—also deserves our special attention. These losses represent another social and political imperative, described to me by sociologist Loïc Wacquant in the following terms: "The Other Side of Black Lives Matter." They do indeed.

ACTIVITY: Analyzing the Rhetorical Situation

1. To what rhetorical opportunity is Wilson responding? How can you tell?
2. Wilson expresses both his admiration for the Black Lives Matter movement and his disagreement with it. What criteria does he use in his evaluation that implies an objection to it? In what sense does he affirm the movement?
3. How does Wilson establish himself as a credible authority on this controversial topic? Does his tone as he responds to other viewpoints affect your reaction to his credibility? What about his status as a university professor? What other factors influence his credibility?
4. Who do you think is Wilson's primary audience? How does he build sympathy for his position with this audience?
5. Imagine that you are a staunch advocate for the Black Lives Matter movement. What parts of Wilson's essay would you find most persuasive? Now imagine you are a staunch opponent of the Black Lives Matter movement. What points persuade you, and where might you challenge his reasoning?

MindTap® Find additional readings on "Whose Lives Matter?" online.

COMMUNITY C❖NNECTIONS

1. Your campus or town undoubtedly has unrest or upheaval of some kind, strong dissatisfaction related to economics, employment, politics, justice, race, athletics, or gender. Look through your local newspaper and identify one such incident of unrest. What rhetorical opportunity for change does this incident present? What is one possible fitting response to that opportunity? Be prepared to share your answer with the rest of the class.

2. Consider a trial being held locally (a case involving irresponsible drinking, murder, embezzlement, theft, assault, or arson, for example). As you keep up with local news (in print or any other medium, even in the form of gossip), try to determine the available means of persuasion used by the prosecution as well as by the defense. Also identify the means of persuasion that remain either unavailable to or untapped by either the defense or the prosecution, given the resources and constraints of the rhetorical situation. List possible reasons why those specific means are not being used. Be prepared to share your findings with the rest of the class.

3. Look for stories in the news and evaluate the ways people of different genders and ethnicities are depicted, using some of the kinds of criteria for evaluating these depictions as you found in Roxane Gay's "A Tale of Two Profiles." Be prepared to share your findings with the rest of the class.

MindTap® Reflect on your reading and writing process.

Whose Lives Matter?

istockphoto.com/jillvhp

STEM vs. STEAM

MindTap® Understand the goals of the chapter and complete a warm-up activity online.

In a purposeful jab at the liberal arts, Florida senator and presidential hopeful Marco Rubio grabbed attention during a presidential debate by calling attention to the need for vocational—not academic—education: "Welders make more money than philosophers; we need more welders and less philosophers."

Although his comment provided fodder for the media, it barely registered in academia itself, where the tensions between the fields of fine, performing, and liberal arts (the "A" in "STEAM") and the sciences, technologies, engineering, and math (STEM) are beginning to spark. Once the centerpiece of an education, the liberal arts comprised essential knowledge for the free person to become an active participant in a democratic society—for a person's ability to vote, plead a case, serve on a jury, serve in the military, travel across social and political borders, and perform socially with intelligence, knowledge, and grace. For the ancient Greeks, grammar (or languages), logic, and rhetoric (successful oral and written communication) were the core liberal arts.

Today's liberal arts usually include the arts, languages, linguistics, literatures, mathematics, the natural sciences, the social sciences, philosophy, psychology, and religious studies—all of them important sources of knowledge, despite the fact that there is not a welder in the list. The twenty-first-century emphasis on success—on professional status, income, and security—has shifted our attention from the kinds of courses that will make us better thinkers, better human beings, and better citizens to courses that will secure our financial future—hence, the emphasis on increasing the number of STEM graduates, those majoring in science, technology, engineering, and math. It is not just a workforce issue, however, as astrophysicist, writer, and science commentator Neil deGrasse Tyson makes clear in his claim that scientific literacy is critical for political decision making and policy. And while some challenge the idea that there is a STEM crisis (see Nora Caplan-Bricker, "New Evidence: There Is No Science Education Crisis"), our nation's goal of increasing the number of STEM graduates by one million by 2022 continues to make national headlines.

In the following series of essays, writers discuss the powers of STEM as well as the necessity of the liberal arts for engendering the problem-solving skills and creative nimbleness needed to create innovative technologies and solutions for twenty-first-century problems. After you read these selections, your professor may call on you to respond to one of the following opportunities for writing.

pages 112–131

1. The following essays all challenge current ways of thinking about education, learning, and knowledge. Which one issue raised in these essays bothers you the most, invites your rhetorical response and an opportunity for change? In an investigative report, begin by describing the issue at hand, offering a tentative thesis. (See CHAPTER 7, INVESTIGATIVE REPORTS.) You will want to conduct research—library, online, and possibly in the field (with interviews and your own observations)—in order to establish the necessary facts, details, and direct quotations that help explain the significance of the issue you are investigating. As you develop your thesis with well-supported reasons, take care to acknowledge various perspectives on the issue.

pages 132–155

2. How do the analyses of Anne Jolly and Nora Caplan-Bricker agree (or not) with yours? Take about ten minutes to respond to their essays, arriving at your own position on the topic. Be prepared to write a position argument on what you believe should be the relationship between STEM and the arts in education. (See CHAPTER 8, POSITION ARGUMENTS.) As you shape your argument, you will need to describe the problem and how it affects your audience, emphasize why addressing the problem now is important, and state a thesis. In your position argument, you will outline the major reasons (assertions that support your thesis) and support them with specific evidence and examples (facts, figures, quotations, narratives). Even as you acknowledge opposing viewpoints, you will want to reinforce to your audience the benefits of supporting your position.

3. Consider Marguerite Del Giudice's essay on why we need more women in the sciences. It is also true that minorities are underrepresented in the science professions. Take ten minutes to define and describe problematic

aspects related to the issue, explain its significance to you and your audience, and then propose a solution for recruiting more women and minorities. If you decide to develop this draft into a formal proposal, take time to discuss the feasibility of your proposal in terms of time, money, effort, and acceptance as well as address possible objections. (See CHAPTER 9, pages 156–173 PROPOSALS.)

MindTap® Read, highlight, and take notes online.

MELISSA DAVEY

Melissa Davey is a journalist for The Guardian, *where this essay was first published on August 3, 2015. The essay features the ideas of prominent American astrophysicist Neil deGrasse Tyson, who argues that nonpartisan scientific research should be the basis of government legislation.*

© Melissa Davey

Neil deGrasse Tyson Calls Scientific Illiteracy a Tragedy of Our Times

Politicians cherry-picking information to suit their own agenda is one of the great tragedies of modern civilization, the astrophysicist Neil deGrasse Tyson said on Monday night's Q&A.

In a panel devoid of politicians, Tyson joined the oncologist and Guardian Australia columnist Ranjana Srivastava, the mathematician and CSIRO marine scientist Beth Fulton, and the mathematics ambassador Adam Spencer to discuss climate change, extraterrestrial life and artificial intelligence.

In response to a question about how scientists prevent scientific ideas becoming politically partisan, Tyson said

Gary Miller/FilmMagic/Getty Images

he did not have a problem with people believing in anything they wanted to. "But if that belief is not based on objective truths, you should not be creating legislation based on it," he said.

"One of the great tragedies of modern society is that we have politicians cherry-picking science in the interests of their own social, cultural, political and religious belief systems, and that's the beginning of the end of an informed democracy."

If politicians and society had strong scientific literacy, Tyson said, there should be no debate within politics as to whether climate change existed.

(continued)

STEM VS. STEAM

"If you're trained to understand how and why science works, then the two opposite factions can have a genuine political discussion about how to react to human-induced climate change," he said. "That's where the debate should happen."

Srivastava said the skepticism of some members of politics about climate science and the repercussions of climate change reminded her of the now discontinued pain relief drug Vioxx, which doctors continued to prescribe in the face of mounting evidence that it was causing strokes, heart attacks and death.

Researchers who tried to highlight these adverse reactions were badmouthed and labelled troublemakers, she said. "If someone had listened to the weight of evidence at the time instead of just saying, 'These people are just trouble,' I think we would have had a different outcome, especially for those families who have lost loved ones."

Unlike Q&As of recent weeks, there was no controversy or fierce disagreement; except when it came to the topic of artificial intelligence. While Spencer worried that advances in technology meant people would be replaced by robots and rendered jobless, Tyson retorted: "That's your weakest argument tonight."

Jobs in new and exciting fields would be created as some professions became automated, Tyson said, creating opportunities and expanding the economy.

Spencer replied: "Suggesting people will just go and retrain, with the greatest respect, I don't think is the strongest argument you've presented tonight either."

To ensure viewers knew there was no animosity between the pair, Spencer tweeted a

> Politicians cherry-picking science in the interests of their own social, cultural, political, and religious belief systems [is] the end of an informed democracy.

photo of himself hugging Tyson after the show, with the caption: "All is forgiven."

Addressing one of several questions about the existence of alien life, Tyson, who is director of the Hayden Planetarium in New York, said it was a mistake to think intelligent life would look like or interact in a similar way as humans.

"We have not successfully shared meaningful thoughts with any other species of life on earth, life with whom we have DNA in common," he said.

"So to presume that some other species of life, which we will have no genetic identity with at all, that somehow we can have a conversation with them and have witty repartee, I think it may be our own hubris to presume that."

He and Spencer agreed it was unlikely such life would be found within our lifetimes, but said it was possible single-cell organisms would be found on other planets.

Panelists were also asked how to get more women into science, technology, engineering and mathematics—STEM subjects—to which Fulton replied that she was lucky to work in a field, ecosystem modelling, that women had helped to shape.

"We just need to encourage more people full stop to get into science and keep it going," she said, while Spencer and Srivastava called for more inspiring female role models in STEM subjects to be promoted to children at school.

The conversation was not restricted to science. The show began with a question about the Adam Goodes saga [Australian soccer star Goodes, of aboriginal descent, was regularly booed when he scored, creating ongoing attention to Australia's racism] which has dominated news headlines for the past couple of weeks.

Srivastava said she and her colleagues had faced numerous racist putdowns during their careers, with some patients linking competency to race.

Some refused to be treated by anyone who was not white, she said, while her senior surgeon colleague wore a suit so he would not be mistaken for a security guard or cleaner.

Fulton said no matter the motivation behind it, booing and bullying was inappropriate, and multiculturalism was a strength in any society. "Diversity makes us stronger, so let's just get past it," she said.

ACTIVITY: Analyzing the Rhetorical Situation

1. What does Tyson mean when he talks about scientific illiteracy? How does he believe that greater scientific awareness will change conversations in the political sphere?
2. Since Davey is summarizing a Q&A event, there is no single thesis that defines her entire article. Why do you think she chooses to emphasize the parts of the Q&A that she does? Why does her article's title reflect a particular moment in the Q&A instead of encompassing the whole event?
3. What are some of the rhetorical challenges Davey faces in writing an article like this one? How does she respond to these challenges? How successful is she?
4. Of the four speakers on the Q&A panel, whose comments do you find most compelling? What is it about their comments that persuades you?

TERENCE MONMANEY

A former staff writer for the Los Angeles Times, *Terence Monmaney is currently the deputy editor of* Smithsonian Magazine, *a publication with a special emphasis on science and technology innovation around the world. The following essay was published by* Smithsonian Magazine *in May 2013.*

How Much Do Americans Know about Science?

The idea that the nation faces a crisis in science education has more than hit home: Many Americans think U.S. teens perform even worse on standardized science tests than they actually do.

That's according to a new national survey by *Smithsonian* and the Pew Research Center that also found unusually strong support for boosting math and science instruction in school.

The survey, done to gauge public scientific literacy and educational priorities, involved a representative sample of 1,006 adults in the continental United States who were reached in March on a landline or cellphone.

(continued)

SPOILER ALERT! Take the Test before Reading Further!

Take our 13-question quiz to test your knowledge of scientific concepts. Then see how you did in comparison with the 1,006 randomly sampled adults asked the same questions in a national poll conducted by the *Pew Research Center* and *Smithsonian* magazine.

SCIENCE AND TECHNOLOGY QUIZ

Question 1 of 13

All radioactivity is man-made. Is this statement . . .

◯ True   ◯ False

Question 2 of 13

Electrons are smaller than atoms. Is this statement . . .

◯ True   ◯ False

Question 3 of 13

Lasers work by focusing sound waves. Is this statement . . .

◯ True   ◯ False

Question 4 of 13

The continents on which we live have been moving their location for millions of years and will continue to move in the future. Is this statement . . .

◯ True   ◯ False

Question 5 of 13

Which one of the following types of solar radiation does sunscreen protect the skin from?

◯ X-rays   ◯ Infrared   ◯ Ultraviolet   ◯ Microwaves

Question 6 of 13

Does nanotechnology deal with things that are extremely . . .

◯ Small   ◯ Large   ◯ Cold   ◯ Hot

Question 7 of 13

Which gas makes up most of the Earth's atmosphere?

◯ Hydrogen   ◯ Nitrogen   ◯ Carbon dioxide   ◯ Oxygen

What is the main function of red blood cells?

◯ Fight disease in the body

◯ Carry oxygen to all parts of the body

◯ Help the blood to clot

Which of these is a major concern about the overuse of antibiotics?

◯ It can lead to antibiotic-resistant bacteria

◯ Antibiotics are very expensive

◯ People will become addicted to antibiotics

Which is an example of a chemical reaction?

◯ Water boiling   ◯ Sugar dissolving   ◯ Nails rusting

Which is the better way to determine whether a new drug is effective in treating a disease? If a scientist has a group of 1,000 volunteers with the disease to study, should she . . .

◯ Give the drug to all of them and see how many get better

◯ Give the drug to half of them but not to the other half, and compare how many in each group get better

What gas do most scientists believe causes temperatures in the atmosphere to rise?

◯ Carbon dioxide   ◯ Hydrogen   ◯ Helium   ◯ Radon

Which natural resource is extracted in a process known as "fracking"?

◯ Coal   ◯ Diamonds   ◯ Natural gas

Quiz answers appear on page 475.

(continued)

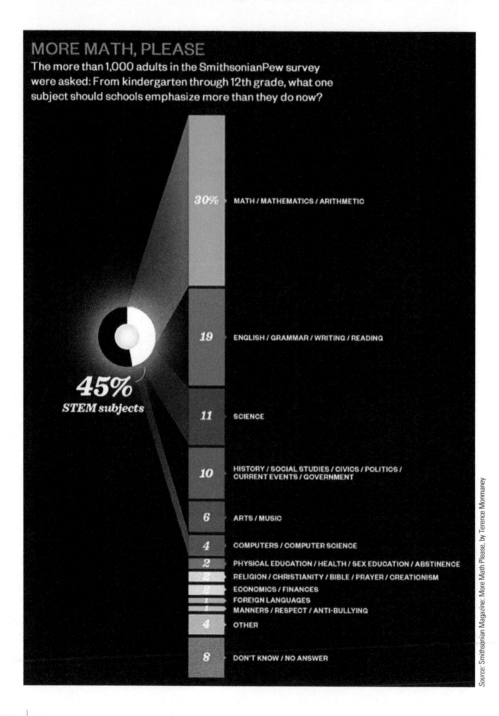

MORE MATH, PLEASE

The more than 1,000 adults in the SmithsonianPew survey were asked: From kindergarten through 12th grade, what one subject should schools emphasize more than they do now?

30% → MATH / MATHEMATICS / ARITHMETIC

19 ENGLISH / GRAMMAR / WRITING / READING

11 SCIENCE

10 HISTORY / SOCIAL STUDIES / CIVICS / POLITICS / CURRENT EVENTS / GOVERNMENT

6 ARTS / MUSIC

4 COMPUTERS / COMPUTER SCIENCE

2 PHYSICAL EDUCATION / HEALTH / SEX EDUCATION / ABSTINENCE

2 RELIGION / CHRISTIANITY / BIBLE / PRAYER / CREATIONISM

2 ECONOMICS / FINANCES

1 FOREIGN LANGUAGES

1 MANNERS / RESPECT / ANTI-BULLYING

4 OTHER

8 DON'T KNOW / NO ANSWER

45%
STEM subjects

Source: Smithsonian Magazine: More Math Please, by Terence Monmaney

Science and technology in the news rang a bell more often than not. A majority correctly noted that nanotechnology involves small things and natural gas is the resource extracted by "fracking," or hydraulic fracturing. The youngest group, 18- to 29-year-olds, matched others on most knowledge questions but flunked the one about fracking. Fifty-eight percent of respondents correctly said the gas most closely associated with global warming is carbon dioxide, compared with 65 percent who got the question right when Pew last posed it in a survey, in 2009. That decline is difficult to explain, given that climate change seems to be a more prominent issue than before.

Supporters of strengthening science, technology, engineering, and math (STEM) education warn that U.S. students are falling behind other nations in technical subjects. This gloomy forecast has sunk in. Asked how 15-year-olds in the United States compare with those in other developed nations on a standardized science test known as PISA, for Program for International Student Assessment, respondents tended to rank American youths at the bottom of the pack. In fact, they place in the middle, scoring 17th out of the 34 developed nations in 2009, the most recent year for which results are available.

Respondents received on average what might be considered a passing grade on the quiz portion

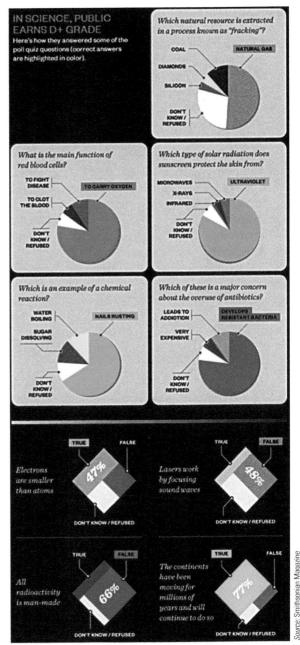

IN SCIENCE, PUBLIC EARNS D+ GRADE
Here's how they answered some of the poll quiz questions (correct answers are highlighted in color).

Which natural resource is extracted in a process known as "fracking"?

What is the main function of red blood cells?

Which type of solar radiation does sunscreen protect the skin from?

Which is an example of a chemical reaction?

Which of these is a major concern about the overuse of antibiotics?

Electrons are smaller than atoms — TRUE / FALSE — 47% — DON'T KNOW / REFUSED

Lasers work by focusing sound waves — TRUE / FALSE — 48% — DON'T KNOW / REFUSED

All radioactivity is man-made — TRUE / FALSE — 66% — DON'T KNOW / REFUSED

The continents have been moving for millions of years and will continue to do so — TRUE / FALSE — 77% — DON'T KNOW / REFUSED

Source: Smithsonian Magazine

(continued)

of the survey, answering 9 out of 13 questions correctly more than half the time. Men scored slightly better than women, though women were better informed about the threat of antibiotic resistance.

The survey included a question that has apparently not been asked in such open-ended fashion in a poll before: What one subject should schools emphasize more? People's answers fell into 12 main categories, with nearly half of respondents offering a STEM subject: 30 percent said mathematics, 11 percent said science, and 4 percent said computers or computer science.

The response, says Scott Keeter, Pew's research director, "reflects a perception that the U.S. is at risk in those areas, that American superiority might be slipping away and needs to be addressed."

After math the subject most often said to need more emphasis in school was reading and writing, favored by 19 percent of those surveyed. Surprisingly few respondents, just 4 percent, called for stronger computer education, perhaps because American youngsters are perceived as having adequate, if not excessive, exposure to computers.

When asked the key reason young people don't pursue degrees in science and math, 22 percent of those surveyed said such degrees weren't useful to their careers and 20 percent said the subjects were "too boring." By far the most common response, though, was that science and math were "too hard," a belief held by 46 percent of respondents.

That might be a problem educators need to study.

ACTIVITY: Analyzing the Rhetorical Situation

1. What stance does Monmaney take toward the common belief that America is facing a crisis in science education? What evidence does he offer to support his perspective?

2. Since Monmaney is reporting on the results of a survey, he faces the challenge of taking sets of numerical data and incorporating them into a readable (and engaging) report. What strategies does he use to bring these survey results to life in his essay? How might you apply these strategies in your own writing?

3. How did the quiz in the middle of the article change the way you read Monmaney's work? Did it draw you in, or was it a distraction? Why do you think he chose to include such a quiz?

4. What particular audience does Monmaney want to persuade with this essay? How does he try to reach that particular audience with his work?

5. Would you call this essay "persuasive"? If so, what makes it persuasive, and what does it seek to persuade you of? How do you think someone who holds a different view from Monmaney would respond to his argument?

CORRECT ANSWERS

1. The correct answer is "False"
2. The correct answer is "True"
3. The correct answer is "False"
4. The correct answer is "True"
5. The correct answer is "Ultraviolet"
6. The correct answer is "Small"
7. The correct answer is "Nitrogen"
8. The correct answer is "Carry oxygen to all parts of the body"
9. The correct answer is "It can lead to antibiotic-resistant bacteria"
10. The correct answer is "Nails rusting"
11. The correct answer is "Give the drug to half of them but not to the other half, and compare how many in each group get better"
12. The correct answer is "Carbon dioxide"
13. The correct answer is "Natural gas"

ANNE JOLLY

A former middle school science teacher, Anne Jolly now develops curricula for STEM students and serves on the Alabama Math, Science, Technology, and Engineering Coalition Board of Directors. This essay first appeared in Education Week on October 16, 2015.

Anne Jolly

STEM vs. STEAM: Do the Arts Belong?

A tug of war is currently looming between proponents of STEM education (science, technology, engineering, and math) and advocates for STEAM lessons, which add art to the mix. Whichever side you come down on, here are some ideas for you to mull over.

STEM

First, consider the why and what of STEM education. Both private and public sectors report that 21st-century workers require skills that many of today's graduates don't have.

Students need more in-depth knowledge of math and science, plus the ability to integrate and apply that knowledge to solve the challenges facing our nation. Children who study STEM also develop a variety of skills that are essential for success: critical thinking and problem solving, creativity and innovation, communication, collaboration, and entrepreneurship, to name a few.

A number of K–12 programs currently fly under the STEM banner. However, a **2014 study** published by the America Society for

(continued)

Engineering Education identified several characteristics of quality STEM programs:

1. The context is motivating, engaging, and real-world.
2. Students integrate and apply meaningful and important mathematics and science content.
3. Teaching methods are inquiry-based and student-centered.
4. Students engage in solving engineering challenges using an engineering design process.
5. Teamwork and communications are a major focus. Throughout the program, students have the freedom to think critically, creatively, and innovatively, as well as opportunities to fail and try again in safe environments.

STEM, then, is a specific program designed for a specific purpose—to integrate and apply knowledge of math and science in order to create technologies and solutions for real-world problems, using an engineering design approach. It's no surprise that STEM programs need to maintain an intense focus.

STEAM

Recently, the idea of adding the arts to STEM programs has been gaining momentum. Surprisingly, I've heard push-back from both camps:

1. **From STEM proponents:** STEM lessons naturally involve art (for example, product design), language arts (communication), and social studies and history (setting the context for engineering challenges). STEM projects do not deliberately exclude the arts or any other subject; rather, these subjects are included incidentally as needed for engineering challenges.

   The focus of STEM is developing rigorous math and science skills through engineering. How can you focus on other subjects (such as art) without losing the mission of STEM or watering down its primary purpose?

2. **From arts proponents:** Engineering and technology can certainly serve the artist and help create art. But if we're talking about how one can use art in engineering . . . as an artist, it seems we're missing the point and devaluing, or not realizing, art's purpose and importance. We have it backwards.

So how exactly can teachers fit the arts into STEM programs and do justice for both STEM and STEAM? What would an ideal STEAM program look like?

That's what artist and educator-turned-STEAM-enthusiast Ruth Catchen is determined to find out. She currently works with a team of STEM writers and program developers who are using crowdfunding to develop and pilot a STEAM program in Colorado.

According to Ruth, the arts are a great learning tool and can serve as an on-ramp to STEM for underrepresented students. Engaging students' strengths using art activities increases motivation and the probability of STEM success. She views art as a way of offering more diverse learning opportunities and greater access to STEM for all types of learners.

> How can you focus on other subjects (such as art) without losing the mission of STEM or watering down its primary purpose?

Art also provides diverse opportunities for communication and expression. Ruth believes that in our technically-focused world, we have a responsibility to educate the whole child to become a global citizen in his or her community. She aims to do just that while staying true to the specific purpose of STEM education.

How Do We Solve the STEM vs. STEAM Conundrum?

Let's circle back to the question of how to include the arts in STEM in an authentic way. We could change the scope of STEM so that it focuses equally on learning in all subject areas—but why do that? We already have effective teaching methods for doing that: problem-based learning.

So let's try another question. Can we combine art with just one of the STEM subjects—perhaps science—and ignore meaningful subjects like math and engineering? We certainly could—but that would be just art and science, not STEAM.

What about having students do individual STEAM projects? Again—that's not faithful to basic STEM principles, which always include teamwork. So would that be STEAM or just a good individual project?

I propose we shape STEAM programs by exploring opportunities where art naturally fits in the STEM arena. Art can be treated as an applied subject—just like math and science. Here are a few ideas for giving STEM projects some STEAM:

- **Design.** Art can serve a practical function. Students might apply design and decoration to products that were created during the course of a design challenge. They could use computer graphics to create logos or stylized designs to include in communications or presentations. Through industrial design, students could improve the appearance, design, and usability of a product created during a STEM project.

- **Performing arts, such as drama and speech.** What about technical or persuasive writing? Those arts fit naturally into the "Communications" stage of the engineering design process. They would work well as part of a STEM project. . . .

- **Creative planning.** As students brainstorm solutions for an engineering problem, encourage them to adopt a playful, inventive, artistic approach. Calling on their artistic right brain can help them to generate more creative and innovative thinking.

Just one word of caution, though. Art is often touted as a method of adding creativity to STEM—but keep in mind that engineers are rarely lacking for creativity and ingenuity. Just look at the world around you for proof.

The purpose of STEAM should not be so much to teach art but to apply art in real situations. Applied knowledge leads to deeper learning.

All of that is to say: I don't yet have a clear picture of what an ideal STEAM project looks like.

In my effort to find some clear examples, I wrote Dr. Howard Gardner to ask him if he had ideas for how to include art in STEM. He responded: "I don't have strong

> The purpose of STEAM should not be so much to teach art but to apply art in real situations. Applied knowledge leads to deeper learning.

(continued)

views about whether arts should become a part of STEM or be self-standing. What is important is that every human being deserves to learn about the arts and humanities, just as each person should be cognizant of the sciences."

I don't think anyone could say it better than that. A STEM program is just one part of a child's education, focusing on math and science. But our children need a well-rounded, quality education that enables them to make informed decisions that will impact the world and the way they live.

We need students who are motivated and competent in bringing forth solutions to tomorrow's problems. When push comes to shove, it's not STEM vs. STEAM—it's about making every student a fully-literate 21st-century citizen.

ACTIVITY: Analyzing the Rhetorical Situation

1. Where does Jolly's position fit into the STEM vs. STEAM debate? Why is she not content to simply pick one side or the other?
2. What strategies does Jolly use to give evidence of her credibility as a communicator? Is she effective in demonstrating her own credibility?
3. Do you think Jolly is writing primarily to teachers? To students? To administrators? To policy makers? Make a list of the strategies you think would be most effective in appealing to each of these audiences; then see which set of strategies most resembles the strategies Jolly uses here.
4. Jolly breaks up her essay into smaller chunks by using visual cues like headings, lists, and bullet points. How do these rhetorical moves change the way you read her work? Do you think she made an effective choice in using them?
5. How might a strong advocate for either STEM or STEAM respond to Jolly's argument? Do you think Jolly is successful in appealing to partisan readers on both sides of the debate?

NORA CAPLAN-BRICKER

Nora Caplan-Bricker is a freelance writer who reports on public policy issues for such venues as New Republic, Slate, *and* National Journal. *This essay was first published by* New Republic *on September 5, 2013.*

New Evidence: There Is No Science-Education Crisis

It's common knowledge that the United States is miles behind other developed countries in STEM (science, technology, engineering, and math) education, and that our economy suffers from, as Bill Gates [founder of Microsoft] has put it, "a severe shortfall of scientists and engineers with expertise to develop the next generation of breakthroughs." And we also know that the humanities are in a downward slide, in part because they've been eclipsed by the dire need to focus on STEM. In the towers of higher education and the annals of our culture, we debate which discipline needs our hand-wringing the most.

If a recent feature in the Institute of Electrical and Electronics Engineers' magazine, *Spectrum*, is to be believed, there's no debate to be had: "The STEM Crisis Is a Myth" advances a convincing case that the U.S. is graduating more than enough scientists and mathematicians to satisfy the demands of its workforce. If this is true, it undermines the arms-race rhetoric pouring out of universities—and, more importantly, out of the federal government—about STEM education. In a speech this April, President Barack Obama said our future depends on "lifting up these subjects for the respect that they deserve," and his proposed 2014 budget pledged another $3.1 billion to STEM schooling. If the sciences are not "in crisis," but are in fact doing just fine, it begs the question: Why are we spending so much to revive them?

The state of affairs *Spectrum* describes is largely summarized by the graph below, which shows there are far more STEM-fluent U.S. residents than available STEM jobs. The article's author, Robert Charette,

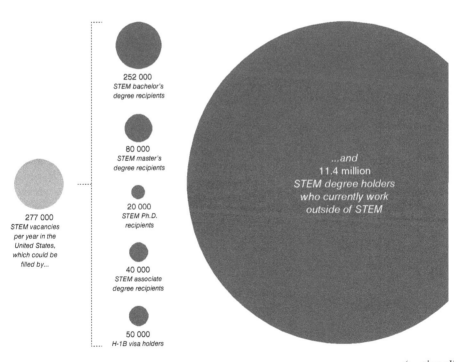

252 000
STEM bachelor's degree recipients

80 000
STEM master's degree recipients

20 000
STEM Ph.D. recipients

277 000
STEM vacancies per year in the United States, which could be filled by...

40 000
STEM associate degree recipients

50 000
H-1B visa holders

...and
11.4 million
STEM degree holders who currently work outside of STEM

(continued)

calculates that there are 11.4 million people with at least a bachelor's degree in a STEM discipline who work outside of STEM, but only 277,000 vacancies in STEM jobs each year. What's more, he says, 392,000 people graduate with STEM degrees annually, and yet the country imports labor to fill shortages (real or imagined) by way of the H-1B visa program. Charette also scoffs at the idea that demand for workers has turned STEM salaries into a gravy train, citing a study from Georgetown that concludes, "At the highest levels of educational attainment, STEM wages are not competitive."

So why is the administration funneling its scant, unsequestered dollars into science education? Charette posits that it's the government's way of fueling the economy—in short, of catering to "the bottom line":

> Companies would rather not pay STEM professionals high salaries with lavish benefits, offer them training on the job, or guarantee them decades of stable employment. So having an oversupply of workers, whether domestically educated or imported, is to their benefit. It gives employers a larger pool from which they can pick the "best and the brightest," and it helps keep wages in check. No less an authority than Alan Greenspan, former chairman of the Federal Reserve, said as much when in 2007 he advocated boosting the number of skilled immigrants entering the United States so as to "suppress" the wages of their U.S. counterparts, which he considered too high.

But that effort to "keep wages in check" is eating up a lot of the federal funding pie—to the detriment of the humanities. Charette reports, "the U.S. government spends more than U.S. $3 billion each year on 209 STEM-related initiatives overseen by 13 federal agencies. That's about $100 for every U.S. student beyond primary school." According to "The Heart of the Matter," a report on the woeful state of the humanities released by the American Academy of Arts & Sciences this summer, the government pays for well over 50 percent of the scientific research done in universities, and close to 75 percent in some disciplines. Meanwhile, the humanities are fronting all but 20 percent of their own costs. The funding Obama apportions for the National Endowments for the Arts and Humanities has been creeping up in recent years, but is microscopic compared to STEM dollars; his proposed 2014 budget raises each endowment's budget by around $200,000, to $145.5 million each.

"The Heart of the Matter" warns that all sources, from private philanthropists to state governments, are "scaling back their investments" in the humanities, "but the federal disinvestment may be the most worrisome indicator": "Federal research funding through the National Endowment for the Humanities, always a small fraction of the federal funding for science and engineering research, has been reduced disproportionately in recent years. The humanities and law were the only research fields in which the federal share of academic research expenditures was appreciably smaller in 2011 than six years earlier."

Of course, it's easy to argue that the humanities don't need as much funding as the sciences. Literary close reading, for instance, doesn't require as many gadgets and gizmos as computer programming, or open-heart surgery; but scholars need money to live on just as much as scientists do. Worse, the imbalance in spending is so heavy that it's creating a skewed perception of value, too. This past winter, Florida Governor Rick Scott proposed charging college

Federally Funded Share of Expenditures for Academic Research and Development in the Humanities and Other Selected Fields, Fiscal Years 2005-2011 (Percent)

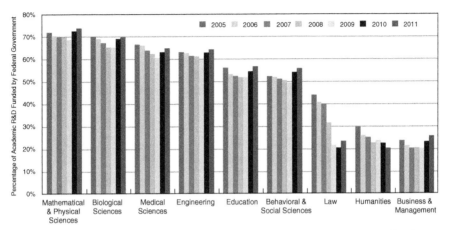

Source National Science Foundation, National Center for Science and Engineering Statistics, Survey of Research and Development Expenditures at Universities and colleges/Higher Education Research and Development Survey (data were accessed and analyzed using the NSF's online data analysis tool, WebCASPAR, at https://webcaspar.nsf.gov/).

Sources of Funding for Academic Research and Development in the Humanities and Other Selected Fields, FY 2011 (Percent)

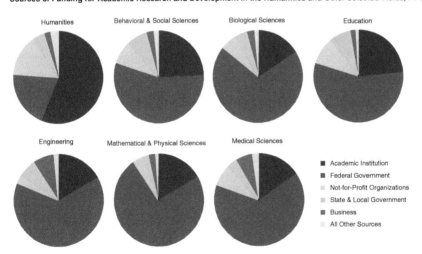

Source: National Science Foundation, National Center for Science and Engineering Statistics, Survey of Research and Development Expenditures at Universities and Colleges/Higher Education Research and Development Survey (data were accessed and analyzed using the NSF's online data analysis tool, WebCASPAR, at https://webcaspar.nsf.gov/).

(continued)

students more for humanities majors while keeping tuition low for quantitative majors that his task force considered "high-skill, high-wage, high-demand." Obama's fiscal policy implies what the task force in Florida was bold enough to say: that STEM fields are a good "return on investment," while arts and letters are not.

This doesn't have to be an either-or proposition. Charette signs off with the somewhat utopian hope that, since "many children born today are likely to live to be 100 and to have not just one distinct career but two or three by the time they retire at 80 . . . we should figure out how to make all children literate in the sciences, technology, and the arts to give them the best foundation to pursue a career and then transition to new ones." It's the kind of generalist entreaty that one usually hears from the humanities camp. It almost sounds like the beginnings of a truce.

ACTIVITY: Analyzing the Rhetorical Situation

1. To what rhetorical opportunity is Caplan-Bricker responding? What situation or situations have created the need for her to write this essay? How fitting is her response to this opportunity?

2. What is the overall effect of the concrete numbers and charts that supplement Caplan-Bricker's argument? What might her use of such data tell you about her rhetorical audience? How do these data affect her credibility?

3. Where does Caplan-Bricker stand on the issue of funding for STEM fields and the humanities? How can you tell what her position is?

4. What strategies does Caplan-Bricker use to invite her readers to adopt her point of view? How effective are these strategies? Has reading this essay influenced your own view at all?

MARGUERITE DEL GIUDICE

Journalist and Pulitzer Prize nominee Marguerite Del Giudice (pronounced JOO-dee-chay) was a staff writer for The Philadelphia Inquirer *and* The Boston Globe *and has written for numerous magazines, including* National Geographic. *This essay from* National Geographic, *which not only addresses the challenges women face in the public sphere but also provides an introduction to various scientific fields, first appeared on November 8, 2014.*

Courtesy of Marguerite Del Giudice

Why It's Crucial to Get More Women into Science

James Gross, a psychology professor at Stanford University, has a 13-year-old daughter who loves math and science. It hasn't occurred to her yet that that's unusual," he says. "But I know in the next couple of years, it will."

She's already being pulled out of class to do advanced things "with a couple of other kids, who are guys," he says. And as someone who studies human emotion for a profession, Gross says, "I know as time goes on, she'll feel increasingly lonely as a girl who's interested in math and science"—and be at risk of narrowing her choices in life before finding out how far she could have gone.

> Why are there still so few women in science, and how might that affect what we learn from research?

Gross's concern speaks volumes about what has been a touchy subject in the world of science for a long time: Why are there still so few women in science, and how might that affect what we learn from research?

Women now make up half the national workforce, earn more college and graduate degrees than men, and by some estimates represent the largest single economic force in the world. Yet the gender gap in science persists, to a greater degree than in other professions, particularly in high-end, math-intensive fields such as computer science and engineering.

According to U.S. Census Bureau statistics, women in fields commonly referred to as STEM (science, technology, engineering, mathematics) made up 7 percent of that workforce in 1970, a figure that had jumped to 23 percent by 1990. But the rise essentially stopped there. Two decades later, in 2011, women made up 26 percent of the science workforce.

It's not that women aren't wanted. "I don't know any institution today that is not trying to hire more women scientists and engineers," says one science historian. But many cultural forces continue to stand in the way—ranging from girls being steered toward other professions from an early age and gender bias and sexual harassment in the workplace to the potentially career-stalling effects on women of having children.

So what difference does it make when there is a lack of women in science? For one, it means women might not get the quality of health care that men receive.

Women in STEM occupations
Share of total STEM workers

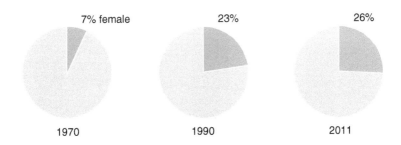

7% female   23%   26%

1970   1990   2011

Emily M. Eng, NG Staff; Edward Benfield. Source: U.S. Census Bureau

(continued)

Women working in STEM occupations

Share of total STEM workers

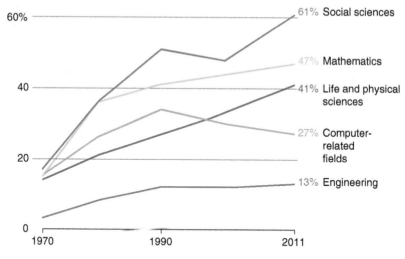

Emily M. Eng, NG Staff; Edward Benfield. Source: U.S. Census Bureau

Selected doctorates awarded, by gender, 2012

Share of academic field

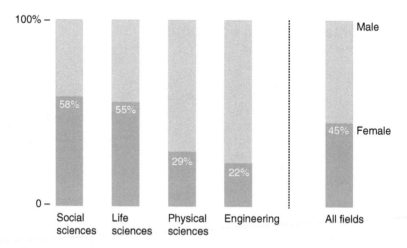

Emily M. Eng, NG Staff; Edward Benfield. Source: National Science Foundation

It's now widely acknowledged that countless women with heart disease have been misdiagnosed in emergency rooms and sent home, possibly to die from heart attacks, because for decades what we know now wasn't known: that they can exhibit different symptoms from men for cardiovascular disease. Women also have suffered disproportionately more side effects from various medications, from statins to sleep aids, because the recommended doses were based on clinical trials that focused largely on average-size men.

Such miscalculated dosages often have not been discovered until the drugs were on the market. Just last year, the U.S. Food and Drug Administration advised women to cut their doses of the sleeping pill Ambien in half, after learning that the active ingredient in the drug remained in women's bodies longer than it did in men's.

Was the oversight in medical research deliberate? No, many scientists say. There was simply a routine procedural bias not to include sex as a variable in scientific research.

For generations, the model used in biomedical research to design drugs and products for everyone has been predicated on the physiology of an average-size male, historically the

MICHAEL NICHOLS/National Geographic Creative

"The blond girl studying apes," was how a National Geographic *editor once referred to primatologist Jane Goodall. That "girl" went on to become world famous for her meticulous field studies of chimpanzees.*

(Photograph by Michael Nichols, National Geographic Creative)

(continued)

standard reference figure in *Gray's Anatomy*, the medical textbook first published in the 1850s.

Even the rats (and other animals) used in scientific experiments have mainly been male. For years, many researchers were concerned that hormone fluctuations in female animals would skew the results of tests, and simply assumed that males could be used to reliably predict effects in both men and women. As a result, "sex, the biggest variable, has not been systematically evaluated and reported in the same way as variables like time, temperature, and dose, even in diseases that are female dominated," says Teresa K. Woodruff, director of the Women's Health Research Institute at Northwestern University.

The National Institutes of Health (NIH), the primary U.S. agency responsible for health-related research, is now correcting this procedural bias. It announced in May that the researchers it funds would be required to start testing theories in female lab animals and female tissues and cells, and to consider sex as a variable in experiment design and analysis.

Woodruff describes the new policy as a "paradigm shift" and "cataclysmic."

"This is categorically the most important thing to happen at NIH, and therefore for the long-term health of America, since 1993, when women were mandated by Congress to be included as participants in clinical research," she says.

The new policy addresses gender bias much earlier in the research pipeline, before testing is done on humans.

A study by McGill University in Montreal last spring generated a lot of hoopla about the role of gender in research, but from a different perspective.

The study found that rats and mice being tested for pain response apparently were afraid of male researchers; it had something to do with how the men smelled. The rodents were so stressed by the male researchers—or even female researchers wearing shirts the men had slept in—that they became desensitized to pain, thus throwing off the test results and raising questions about previous studies in which lab animals were handled by male researchers.

In this case, it wasn't the sex of the lab rats, but of their handlers, that made a difference— another variable that simply hadn't occurred before to anyone.

Gender and the Nature of Discovery

The new NIH stance is what Stanford science historian Londa Schiebinger calls a "gendered innovation," which will make science more relevant to women.

"We can be interested in women and science, and their participation, and how many are here and there," she says. "But the big difference is, what knowledge and technologies do you have? What's the outcome? Who are things designed for?"

Schiebinger is a leader in the Gendered Innovations movement, an international collaborative made up of natural scientists, engineers, and gender experts. Its goal, her project website says, is to "harness the creative power of sex and gender analysis to discover new things."

The website features a couple dozen case studies that, among other things, examine how taking gender into account in research can make a difference in areas such as stem cell work, technologies to assist the elderly, and better diagnosis and treatment of osteoporosis in men, "a huge population" Schiebinger says is being overlooked.

One example involves making public transportation more efficient and responsive.

The gendered innovation would be to have civil engineers, when gathering data to formulate bus and train schedules, consider what Schiebinger calls "the mobility of care"—how people travel in the course of their day to tend to children, the elderly, and households. It's not a typical category of analysis.

Women and men who travel only for employment tend just to go back and forth between home and job. But many also do caring work. "They tend to travel from home to the day care to work," she says. "On the way home they may go food shopping, to the dry cleaners, back to the day care, and home again."

Schiebinger notes that scientists are responding, and that new findings emphasizing the importance of gender in research are continuing to emerge.

One research team testing stem cell therapy on mice had to set aside the study after all the male mice died unexpectedly. The researchers had correctly used male and female mice, Schiebinger says, but "quite unconsciously" only female stem cells. After hearing Schiebinger speak at an event in Norway, a member of the

Marie Curie, the Polish-born French physicist, here seated in her laboratory, was the first woman to win a Nobel Prize and the first person to win twice.

(Photograph by Ann Ronan Pictures/Print Collector/Getty)

research team told her, "Oh! We probably should have used male and female stem cells."

Twenty years ago, "nobody wanted to listen to me," Schiebinger says. They're listening now.

The Power of Collaboration

Including gender in research could attract more women to science as well, Schiebinger says, because careers and avenues of research suddenly can become relevant to women.

(continued)

The LIFE Picture Collection/Getty Images

Rachel Carson, who revealed the unregulated use of DDT and other pesticides by the chemical industry in her book Silent Spring, *would have gotten a Ph.D. in biology from Johns Hopkins University but was overburdened by three jobs and the responsibility of caring for her mother.*

(Photograph by Alfred Eisenstaedt/The LIFE Picture Collection/Getty)

She says that as more women get involved in the sciences—or any field historically dominated by men—the general knowledge in that field tends to expand.

"There are lots of places where you can show the direct link between increase in number of women and outcome in knowledge," she says. "History, primatology, biology, medicine."

It's an idea that dovetails with a major shift that has taken place in how scientific inquiry is being carried out by research teams.

"Collaboration is now the foundation of much of STEM research. . . . this is a huge change," says Beth Mitchneck, who runs the National Science Foundation's ADVANCE program, which supports women in the academic sciences and promotes institutional change.

In science, the stereotypical image of research geniuses making discoveries while working solo has given way to a more collaborative model, in which research is done by teams. Increasingly, these teams are being made up of scientists from different fields.

That's what happened on the Human Genome Project, whose goal was the complete mapping and understanding of all the genes of human beings. It drew researchers from fields that included biology, chemistry, genetics, physics, mathematics, and computer science.

Involving more qualified women, as well as additional "social identities"—gay people, African Americans and Latinos, those with physical disabilities, and others—can enrich the creativity and insight of research projects and increase the chances for true innovation,

says Scott Page, a professor at the University of Michigan who studies diversity in complex systems.

In this sense, the corporate world is evolving more quickly than the science world.

According to the *Atlantic Monthly* magazine's cover story in May, "Half a dozen global studies, conducted by the likes of Goldman Sachs and Columbia University, have found that companies employing women in large numbers outperform their competitors on every measure of profitability."

NASA/Roger Ressmeyer/CORBIS

Mae Jemison, the first African American woman in space, has a background in engineering and medical research. She was the science specialist on a 1992 Spacelab mission.

(Photograph by NASA/Roger Ressmeyer/Corbis)

(continued)

The Internet's "Bro-Coding" Culture

Computer science is one field with very low participation by women. Half or more Internet users are women, and women are known to be early and enthusiastic adopters of most technologies. But the number receiving related bachelor's degrees, for example, actually has been declining; women now make up less than 20 percent of such graduates, based on the latest data analyzed by the National Science Foundation.

As a result, the Internet is being built primarily by white and Asian men. Much of the industry supporting it involves a "bro-coding," Silicon Valley culture in which you're expected to be working even when you're not working.

"You can ask, 'Does that have implications?'" says Page, referring to the homogeneity of the tech workforce: implications for, say, how social media sites such as Twitter and Facebook are organized or for a dating site that's being written largely by straight men. Even if the programmers carefully study the best science they can find, he says, "it's hard to imagine that how they interpret it isn't gendered in some way."

There aren't a lot of women in engineering either (though the numbers vary by subdiscipline, with electrical and mechanical engineering reflecting few women and civil, biological, and chemical engineering showing more). Women received 45 percent of all math- and science-related doctoral degrees in 2012; only 22 percent were in engineering.

What difference does that make?

What we think of as "science problems" affect everyone—children, women, and men. What science decides to solve and for whom things are designed have a lot to do with who's doing the scientific inquiry. Will there be more push to develop drugs for male-pattern baldness

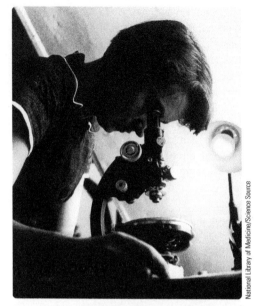

British x-ray crystallographer Rosalind Franklin worked on imaging the structure of DNA. Her data, shared without her knowledge with James Watson and Francis Crick, proved crucial to their discovery of DNA. Watson and Crick won the Nobel Prize in 1962. Franklin had died of cancer by then and was ineligible for the prize.

(Photograph by National Library of Medicine/Science Source)

National Library of Medicine/Science Source

or for a seat belt that won't cause further injury, or death, to pregnant women and their fetuses in car crashes?

Analysts say that more women are needed in research to increase the range of inventions and breakthroughs that come from looking at problems differently than men typically do.

"Look at what's being developed in engineering with 'smart houses,'" says San Francisco State University provost and gender studies professor Susan Rosser. "You get your heat connected and lights turned on and alarm systems set. They're all about control. It's not like what a woman might want"—or be more likely to think of. "Like, can we invent something where the house cleans itself?"

It's certainly not that men couldn't invent a house that cleans itself, she says. They just may be less likely to rank it as high as women might in the hierarchy of possibilities, if they think of it at all.

That women are also raised to be more socially aware than men points to another largely untapped quality in women, particularly in the realm of leadership. What difference might broader emotional intelligence make?

As a rule, says Gross, the Stanford psychologist, women tend to exhibit more "communal"

> Having women's emotional skills in the mix . . . can yield "immensely positive" results in scientific research.

qualities (fostering good relations to build community, creating an inclusive environment), while men tend to exhibit more "agency" qualities (taking leadership, making things happen). Having women's emotional skills in the mix, he says, can yield "immensely positive" results in scientific research.

Women are well-represented in biological sciences, psychology, and medicine (especially the "three *p*'s"—pediatrics, primary care, and psychiatry, branches that typically involve lower pay and more contact with patients than other medical professions). Iranian-born

As a child visiting France with her parents, Mary Leakey—above, as a young unmarried student, with left to right, P. E. Kent and Louis Leakey at Olduvai Gorge in Tanzania—participated in archaeological digs and found ancient stone tools, which set her on the course to become one of the world's most distinguished fossil hunters.

(Photograph by Leakey Family Collection)

(continued)

American mathematician Maryam Mirzakhani of Stanford recently became the first woman to win the world's "Nobel Prize" of mathematics, the Fields Medal, since it was established in 1936.

But even in areas in which the number of women in science is high, they are not proportionally represented among its leaders.

We don't want to just have more talented women, Gross says. We want to make sure that women with well-developed skills don't end up—and it happens all the time—stuck at lower levels working in labs.

"You need them at leadership positions," he says, "directing the field."

A Daughter's Future

James Gross, the Stanford psychology professor, has a vision. It's of a world in which talented girls and boys feel free to pursue lives historically perceived as not appropriate for their gender—"for the simple reason that it's better for them and it's better for society."

In the meantime, he's doing what he can to encourage his 13-year-old daughter to remain open to developing all of her math and science talents—even as she comes to realize how unusual it is for a girl to choose that path, and how lonely it might be.

But he knows there's only so far he can take her on his own.

ACTIVITY: Analyzing the Rhetorical Situation

1. According to Del Giudice, the male-centered attitude in STEM manifests itself in problematic ways. What are those problematic ways? How might women's greater place in STEM improve research and practices?

2. Del Giudice makes many concessions to the opposing point of view—for example, by noting that the exclusion of women from lab trials was not intentional and that women are reasonably well represented in the biological sciences, psychology, and medicine. How do concessions like these change the nature of her argument? Do they make her case less persuasive, or more so?

3. Del Giudice's essay is accompanied by several photographs of women scientists who are never mentioned directly in the text of the essay. How does this use of the visual medium enhance her argument, even when these women's pictures are not discussed in the text itself?

4. Because this piece was published by *National Geographic*, it is likely to be read by science enthusiasts, both male and female. How does Del Giudice show her sensitivity to this audience?

5. Imagine that you are an established scientist who for many years has not believed that there is a problem with gender bias in the sciences. Has Del Giudice persuaded you to reconsider your views? Why or why not?

MindTap® Find additional readings on "STEM vs. STEAM" online.

COMMUNITY C⚙NNECTIONS

1. How do Melissa Davey's and Terence Monmaney's essays coincide with or diverge from your own experiences with scientific literacy in America? Take about ten minutes to write your response. Be prepared to share your response with the rest of the class.
2. Browse your college website and read the promotional materials that the website offers to prospective students in a variety of majors, including both STEM majors and liberal and fine arts majors. How do you see the tension between STEM and STEAM exhibited in the way different programs are described? Based on what you have read, write a letter to a friend who might want to attend your college and predict how your campus's attitudes toward STEM and STEAM will impact your friend's academic experience.
3. Arrange an interview with someone in your community who works in a STEM field. You might ask to meet with a science professor on your campus or an engineer at a nearby firm. Using Del Giudice's essay as a guide, make a list of questions that will help you understand the types of roles that men and women play within this person's field. How does your interviewee perceive these gender dynamics? What, if any, changes does this person wish to see in the way STEM fields are gendered?

MindTap® Reflect on your reading and writing process.

Credits

CHAPTER 1

p. 15: Introduction from LIFE AS WE KNOW IT: A FATHER, A FAMILY, AND AN EXCEPTIONAL CHILD by Michael Bérubé, copyright © 1996 by Michael Bérubé. Used by permission of Pantheon Books, an imprint of the Knopf Doubleday Publishing Group, a division of Penguin Random House LLC. All rights reserved.

CHAPTER 2

p. 20: Produced by urbanest student accommodation; originally posted on http://uk.urbanest.com/blog/index.php/2015/03/17/ultimate-guide-note-taking-class-infographic/.

CHAPTER 3

pp. 40–41: Prizant, Barry M. *Uniquely Human: A Different Way of Seeing Autism*. New York: Simon & Schuster, 2015. 50–52. © Childhood Communication Services, Inc.

pp. 48–49: Jordynn Jack, Autism and Gender: From Refrigerator Mothers to Computer Geeks ["Savants" and "Geniuses"].

CHAPTER 5

p. 76: Clotilde Dusoulier, "Happiness (A Recipe)."

p. 91: Dave Eggers, *A Heartbreaking Work of Staggering Genius.*

CHAPTER 6

p. 93: Reprinted by arrangement with The Heirs to the Estate of Martin Luther King Jr., c/o Writers House as agent for the proprietor New York, NY. Copyright © 1963 Dr. Martin Luther King Jr.; © renewed 1991 Coretta Scott King.

pp. 96–98: Sandra Sobieraj Westfall et al., "Heroes on the Train: 'It Was Either Do Something or Die.'" Published in *People*, Vol. 84, issue 10, Sept. 7, 2015, pp. 54–58.

CHAPTER 7

p. 113: "Why Are Students Coming into College Poorly Prepared to Write?" Article posted on Carnegie Mellon site for Teaching Excellence & Educational Innovation, http://www.cmu.edu/teaching/. Eberly: (412) 268-2896 | Blackboard: (412) 268-9090 Eberly CenterBlackboard @ Carnegie Mellon.

p. 114: Laurie Fendrich, "Bad Student Writing? Not So Fast!"

pp. 116–121: Christine Rosen, "The Myth of Multitasking," *The New Atlantis*, Number 20, Spring 2008, pp. 105–110.

CHAPTER 8

p. 135: Geoffrey Nunberg, *The Official English Movement: Reimagining America.*

p. 154: Michael Ventura, "Taboo: Don't Even Think about It!"

p. 155: John F. Kennedy, inaugural address, Washington, DC, January 1961.

CHAPTER 10

p. 176: Manohla Dargis, "'Star Wars: The Force Awakens' Delivers the Thrills, with a Touch of Humanity."

pp. 176–177: Michael Hiltzik, "Admit It: 'Star Wars: The Force Awakens' Stinks—and Here's Why."

CHAPTER 11

p. 195: Global Village quotation from *Gutenberg Galaxy: The Making of Typographic Man* (1962).

p. 196: Excerpt [Technology Is Shaping Social Patterns] from *The Medium Is the Massage: An Inventory of Effects* by Marshall McLuhan and graphic designer Quentin Fiore, and coordinated by Jerome Agel. It was published by Bantam Books in 1967.

p. 196: From Paul Seaman—21st-century PR issues—May 26, 2011—http://paulseaman.eu/2011/05/marshall-mcluhan-a-media-guru. Retrieved from http://paulseaman.eu/2015/02/marshall-mcluhan-a-media-guru-reconsidered/#more-16726.

p. 196: "McLuhan on McLuhanism," WNET Educational Broadcasting Network, 1966.

p. 213: Susan Gubar, *Rooms of Our Own* (Champaign, IL: University of Illinois Press, 2006).

p. 213: Peter Schjeldahl, "Those Nasty Brits," *The New Yorker*, October 11, 1999, p. 104.

CHAPTER 12

p. 216: Hepworth's quotations are from "Phoenix Poet Myrlin Hepworth: "The Poetics of My Time Are in Hip-Hop," Glenn BurnSilver, Phoenix New Times.com. 8 Jan. 2015. Web. 20 Sept. 2015.

p. 217: *Rattle: Poetry for the 21st Century* magazine. Susan B.A. Somers-Willett. "Can Slam Poetry Matter?" found at www.rattle.com/rattle27/somerswillett.htm.

pp. 221–222: Reprinted with the permission of Scribner, a Division of Simon & Schuster, Inc., from THE COLLECTED POEMS OF MARIANNE MOORE by Marianne Moore. Copyright © 1935 by Marianne Moore, renewed 1963 by Marianne

Moore and T. S. Eliot. All rights reserved. Electronic reproduction with permission of the Estate of Marianne C. Moore. David M. Moore, Esq., Administrator. All rights reserved.

p. 222: Ralph Rees, "The Reality of Imagination in the Poetry of Marianne Moore." Originally published in *Twentieth Century Literature*, vol. 30, nos. 2–3 (Summer–Autumn 1984): pp. 231–41.

CHAPTER 13

p. 239: Student infographic from University of Central Florida, from Professor Pavel Zemliansky.

CHAPTER 14

p. 264: Burciaga, José Antonio, "I Remember Masa" from Weedee Peepo. Published by Pan American University Press, Edinburgh, TX (1988).

p. 265: William Styron, *Darkness Visible* (New York: Random House, 1990), p. 52.

p. 266: Britannica definition of "primates," http://www.britannica.com/eb/article-9105977/primate.

p. 267: Primate Conservation, Inc., http://www.primate.org/about.htm.

p. 267: W. E. Le Gros Clark, *The Antecedents of Man*, 3rd ed. (Chicago: Quadrangle Books, 1971).

pp. 274–275: From Michael McGarrity, *Everyone Dies* (New York: Dutton-Penguin, 2003), pp. 169–71.

CHAPTER 15

p. 285: *Large Still Life Frieze*, Joseph Ablow. Copyright © Joseph Ablow. Reprinted by permission of Pucker Gallery.

CHAPTER 16

pp. 304–305: Mike Rose, *The Mind at Work* (New York: Viking/Penguin, 2004).

p. 310: Stein, Joel. "Millennials: The Me, Me, Me Generation." *The New Harbrace Guide: Genres for Composing* by Cheryl Glenn, 3rd ed., Cengage Learning, 2018.

CHAPTER 17

p. 311: From interview with Debra Dickerson, author of "The End of Blackness: Returning the Souls of Black Folks to Their Rightful Owners" (New York: Pantheon, 2004).

CHAPTER 18

pp. 325–329: William Lutz, "Doubts about Doublespeak." From State Government News (July 1993).

pp. 331–332: Lutz, William. "Doubts about Doublespeak." State Government News July 1993: 22–24. Print.

CHAPTER 21

pp. 405–406: Margaret Mead, from "The Wider Food Situation," Food Habits Research: Problems of the Credits 1960s, National Research Council's Committee for the Study of Food Habits Update.

pp. 407–408: Michael Pollan's *New York Times* article on Slow Food, "Out of the Kitchen, Onto the Couch," July 29, 2009, found at http://www.nytimes.com/2009/08/02/magazine/02cooking-t.html?pagewanted=all&_r=2&.

pp. 408–410: Op-Ed: Why We Should Ditch the Slow Food Movement, May 12, 2013.

pp. 411–412: Used with permission of *The Atlantic Monthly*, from "Good-bye Cryovac," Corby Kummer, volume 294, no. 3, Copyright 2004 The Atlantic Monthly Group, as first published in The Atlantic Monthly. Distributed by Tribune Media Services, permission conveyed through Copyright Clearance Center, Inc.

pp. 412–415: The Wall Street Journal, Opinion/Commentary, May 4, 2015 4:13 p.m. ET, http://www.wsj.com/articles/embrace-the-food-tech-that-makes-us-healthier-1430770426.

CHAPTER 22

pp. 419–421: This story appeared in *New York Daily News*, Monday, December 2, 2013, 11:40 AM. The video can be seen at www.youtube.com/watch?v=M4IjTUxZORE. Joel Landau, "VIDEO: Filmmaker apologizes on behalf of entire Millennial generation: 'We Suck and We're Sorry,'" *New York Daily News*, December 2, 2013.

pp. 421–426: Pew Research Center, "Most Millennials Resist the 'Millennial' Label—Generations in a Mirror: How They See Themselves," Pew Research Center, Sept 3, 2015, http://www.people-press.org/2015/09/03/most-millennials-resist-the-millennial-label/.

p. 421: American Trends Panel (Wave 10). Survey conducted Mar 10–Apr 6, 2015. Respondents could select more than one generation label.

p. 422: American Trends Panel (Wave 10). Survey conducted Mar 10–Apr 6, 2015.

p. 424: American Trends Panel (Wave 10). Survey conducted Mar 10–Apr 6, 2015. "Other" response not shown. Respondents could select multiple generation labels.

p. 424: American Trends Panel (Wave 10). Survey conducted Mar 10–Apr 6, 2015. Based on total.

p. 425: American Trends Panel (Wave 10). Survey conducted Mar 10–Apr 6, 2015.

CHAPTER 23

pp. 433–436: *Robert Moses: The Master Builder of New York City* (Nobrow Books, New York, pub. March 2015).

pp. 441–443: Emily Badger, "How Smart Phones Are Turning Our Public Places into Private Ones," *The Atlantic*, City Lab on May 16, 2012.

pp. 443–447: Jamie Utt, "From Manspreading to Mansplaining—6 Ways Men Dominate the Spaces Around Them," *Everyday Feminism Magazine*, September 1, 2015, http://everydayfeminism.com/2015/09/6-ways-men-dominate-space/.

CHAPTER 24

pp. 454–457: Roxane Gay's *Bad Feminist: Essays*, "A Tale of Two Profiles" on pp. 285–289, Harper-Collins, 2014.

pp. 458–460: Malcolm Musoni, "Being an 18-Year-Old Black Man a Year after Mike Brown," HUFFINGTON POST, Aug 19, 2015, http://www.huffingtonpost.com/malcolm-musoni/being-an-18-year-old-blac_b_8011246.html.

CHAPTER 25

pp. 467–469: Melissa Davey, "Neil deGrasse Tyson Calls Scientific Illiteracy a Tragedy of Our Times," August 3, 2015, *UK Guardian*, http://www.theguardian.com/australia-news/2015/aug/04/neil-degrasse-tyson-on-qa-calls-scientific-illiteracy-a-tragedy-of-our-times.

pp. 475–478: Anne Jolly, "STEM vs. STEAM: Do the Arts Belong?," *Education Week*, Nov 18, 2014, http://www.edweek.org/tm/articles/2014/11/18/ctq-jolly-stem-vs-steam.html.

pp. 482–492: Marguerite Del Giudice, "Why It's Crucial to Get More Women into Science," National Geographic Society, Nov. 8, 2014, http://news.nationalgeographic.com/news/2014/11/141107-gender-studies-women-scientific-research-feminist/.

Glossary of Rhetorical Terms

Chapter 1 Understanding the Rhetorical Situation

rhetoric—communication to achieve a specific purpose with a specific audience

rhetorical opportunity—the issue, problem, or situation that motivates the use of language to stimulate change

writer—someone who uses language to bring about change in an audience

message—the main point of information shaped to influence an audience

audience—those who receive and interpret the message of a communication

rhetorical situation—the context that influences effective communication

purpose—in rhetoric, the reason for a communication

rhetorical purpose—the specific change the writer wants to accomplish through the use of language

rhetorical audience—the specific audience most likely to be changed by a message

stance—the attitude your writing conveys toward your topic, purpose, and audience

genre—a category of writing that has a particular format and features, such as memoir or argument

medium—method of communication: oral, visual, verbal, digital, or print

media (plural of *medium*)—*mass media* is a term used for media like radio, television, and various online forums that can reach a broad audience

Chapter 2 Responding to the Rhetorical Situation

problem—in rhetoric, an issue or situation posed as a question for discussion and exploration

problem-solving approach—in rhetoric, a strategy that uses writing to think through ways of addressing issues or situations

fitting response—a communication whose tone, content, and delivery are carefully constructed to connect to the interests of a specific audience

claim—an assertion that identifies a problem and proposes a solution

thesis statement—a clearly worded statement of your claim that guides the structure of your paper, presentation, or multimedia text

available means of persuasion—rhetorical content and delivery strategies aimed at reaching a particular audience with a message that encourages change, which include the methods of communication as well as the rhetorical appeals

rhetorical appeals—the strategies established by ancient Greeks as the foundation for persuasion: ethos (the ethics of the writer), logos (the logic of the argument), and pathos (the emotional connection with the audience)

ethos—the ethical appeal to the audience's sense of the writer's credibility, good will, and trustworthiness

common ground—a belief or value shared by the writer and audience that provides the basis for agreement

logos—an appeal to the audience's reason through the logical construction of the argument

evidence—support for your claim that includes testimonials and anecdotes, statistics, facts, and expert opinions

pathos—the emotional appeal to the sympathy and empathy of the audience with the purposeful use of language and examples that stir the audience's feelings

Standardized English—a uniform style of grammar, spelling, vocabulary, and pronunciation that is well established as acceptable for educated and professional discourse

resources (advantages**)**—in rhetoric, the means needed to effect change in an audience

constraints (limitations)—the obstacles a writer has to overcome to persuade an audience

Chapter 3 The Writer as Reader

reading process—series of steps, including previewing, skimming, reading, and annotating

Believing and Doubting Game—strategy that includes both reading while believing the writer (and in so doing understanding the writer's message better) and reading while doubting the writer (and in so doing finding the gaps and questions that emerge from the selection)

echolalia—repeating what has just been said as if an echo

summary—a type of writing that condenses a selection to its main points

abstract—a brief objective summary of an article, especially used in writing papers for the social sciences

critical response—a reaction in writing to a text that explains why you agree or disagree with the text

analysis—a breaking of a text down into its constituent parts accompanied by a critical examination of the ways the text responds to the rhetorical situation

synthesis—an examination of how the individual parts of a text or different points of view from different texts fit together and diverge to bring a new perspective to the whole work

synthesis (or critical) question—the question that directs, focuses, and launches your research

Chapter 4 Rhetorical Success in a Digital World

multimedia—images or visuals, text, audio, and video used in combinations in a composition

fonts—styles of print type

serif—fonts with foot-like tips on the ends of letters

sans serif—fonts with no serifs on the ends of the letters

layout—the way words and images are positioned in relation to each other on a page

white space—blank areas around text, graphics, or images

angle of vision—the position of the camera in relation to the image

focal point—the center of activity or attention in the image

cropping—the process of editing an image to draw the viewer's attention to the focal point

infographics—images, tables, charts, pie charts, and figures that condense information into a visual presentation

accessibility—in rhetoric, the extent to which a message is designed to be easy to read by those with disabilities that affect seeing, hearing, and manipulating a particular medium

Chapter 5 Memoirs

memoir—a narrative that reflects on a personal experience or series of experiences

Chapter 6 Profiles

profile—a portrait in words of a person, place, or event

Chapter 7 Investigative Reports

report—a presentation of objective information that investigates current research on a topic

investigative report—an analysis of the "who, what, where, and why" of a topic

attributive tags—phrases that identify the source of your information

Chapter 8 Position Arguments

position argument—the assertion of a point of view about an issue supported by reasons and evidence

parallelism—the repetition of a grammatical structure

Chapter 9 Proposals

proposal—a message that calls for improvement through action

nominalizing—creating a noun from a verb or adjective

Chapter 10 Evaluations

evaluation—a judgment based on relevant criteria and meant to persuade

adjectives—words that modify nouns

adverbs—words that modify verbs

attributive adjectives—words that modify nouns or pronouns directly

predicative adjectives—words that modify nouns or pronouns and always appear after linking verbs (*be, seem, look*)

Chapter 11 Critical Analyses

critical analysis—a careful examination of the causes or consequences of a situation or phenomenon

denotations—the meanings of a word as defined by a dictionary

connotations—the associated meanings of a word

clichés—expressions that have lost their freshness and impact

Chapter 12 Literary Analyses

literary analysis—an argument for reading a text in a certain way

close reading—an examination of the key characteristics (including style and structure) of a text

fiction—prose stories based on the imagination

poetry—a concentrated language relying on sound and image

drama—a performance where a director and actors interpret a script

interpretive question—a question about the meaning, structure, or significance of a text

reading journal—a record of personal thoughts, ideas, and questions about a text

Chapter 13 From Tentative Idea to Finished Project

listing—jotting down tentative ideas to explore a topic

brainstorming—a listing of tentative ideas at one sitting

freewriting—writing to explore ideas on a topic without concern for spelling, grammar, style, or who will read it

questioning—structured speculation used to explore a topic in a new way

journalists' questions—Who? What? Where? When? Why? How?

journal—a private record of your understandings and reactions to reading, assignments, class discussion, and lectures

double-entry notebook—a journal with two distinct columns pairing observation and personal response

clustering—a method using arrows, circles, lines, or other visual cues for connecting ideas

outlining—a structure that lists the main parts and supporting points of an essay

working thesis—a statement that tests a possible framework and controlling idea for your paper

drafting—a process that combines an informal structure with a freewrite

introduction—the opening of your paper, often including your thesis and establishing your credibility on your topic

body—an exploration of your topic that builds a logical structure to support your thesis

conclusion—a final appeal to your audience by making clear how the issue you are exploring affects them

revision—a process of rethinking and rewriting parts of your draft

peer evaluation—a form of collaboration that provides writing advice from fellow students

editing—improving word choice, adding details, and structuring sentences more effectively

proofreading—checking for spelling, typos, grammar, and punctuation errors

Chapter 14 Rhetorical Methods of Development

narration—a detailed account of events as in a story

characters—people in the story

dialogue—direct speech by the characters in a narration

setting—the time and place of a narration

plot—the sequence of events in a narration

anecdote—brief story that illustrates a point

point of view—the perspective of the narrator in telling a story

climax—turning point in a narration

flashback/flash forward—narrative technique that accounts for past or future events

description—a verbal accounting of physical and mental experiences

sensory details—what we see, hear, smell, touch, or taste

sensibility details—having to do with intellectual, emotional, or physical states

exemplification—the use of examples

definition—a classification that distinguishes, describes, and names something

formal (or sentence) definition—a dictionary or encyclopedia reference that classifies, describes, and names something

extended definition—a classification that provides extended information to describe, distinguish, and name something

historical definition—an overview over a period of time of how a concept or term has been used

negative definition—a classification that distinguishes a concept or term by showing what it is not

stipulative definition—a classification that is specific to a particular context

classification and division—the act of creating categories that distinguish information, objects, or other concepts

comparison and contrast—a description of similarities and differences

basis for comparison—shared characteristics that are used to understand objects, people, and ideas

points of comparison—areas that show how two things are the same and how they are different

cause-and-effect analysis—an explanation for how some things have occurred or a prediction that certain events will lead to specific effects

process analysis—breaking down into a series of steps how something occurs

directive process analysis—a series of steps used to teach an audience how to duplicate the occurrence of something

informative process analysis—a series of steps used to explain how something occurs or has occurred

argument—the presentation of a point of view in an effort to persuade an audience that something is true or valid

persuasion—the use of emotions as well as logic to move an audience to change its mind or take action

identifiable issue—specific issue related to a problem that can be argued for or against

Chapter 16 Identifying Sources

primary sources—firsthand accounts or original data

secondary sources—sources that interpret or collect firsthand accounts or original data

periodicals—publications such as magazines and newspapers that are published over a specific period of time (daily, weekly, or monthly)

scholarly journals—publications for a specialized audience that contain original research on academic topics

magazines—periodical publications for the general public, sometimes focused on a particular subject

newspapers—regional, local, or national news publications that also include letters to the editor and editorial opinion pieces

.com—the domain name used on the Internet for commercial, for-profit entities

.edu—the domain name used on the Internet for a U.S. educational institution

.gov—the domain name used on the Internet for U.S. governmental branches or agencies

.org—the domain name used on the Internet for nonprofit organizations

government documents—any information printed/published by the local, state, or national government

special collections—library resources on particular topics, people, and places, often including audiovisual and primary sources

interview—special type of conversation in which a reporter elicits responses from someone recognized for his or her status or accomplishments

fieldwork—real-world research that commonly includes observation, interviews, and questionnaires

observation—watching closely what is happening and trying to figure out why

naturalistic study—observation based on direct access to the person or phenomenon being researched

interview questions—questions designed to put your subject at ease and purposefully progress from one subject to another

institutional review board (IRB)—committee set up to protect participants' privacy in field research

bibliography—a list of sources used in a research project, including author, title, and other publication data

working bibliography—a preliminary record of source information such as author, title, page numbers, and publication data

Chapter 17 Evaluating Sources

annotated bibliography—list of sources that includes commentary on each source

Chapter 18 Synthesizing Sources: Summary, Paraphrase, and Quotation

plagiarism—the use of others' words and ideas without adequate acknowledgment

function statement—a description of the content of the text and the intention of the author

paraphrase—a restatement of someone else's ideas in your own words

Chapter 19 Acknowledging Sources in MLA Style

container—the term used in MLA style for the source within which an article or posting is found

Glossary of Usage

Standardized English is the stylistic option you'll most often choose when working in an academic context. This glossary presents many of those standardized usages and spellings, as well as usages and spellings considered to be conversational (or informal) and even unconventional (or nonstandardized). Using the information in this glossary, you'll be able to make informed decisions about the words you use.

The following labels will help you choose appropriate words for your rhetorical situation.

Conventional Words or phrases listed in dictionaries without special usage labels; generally considered appropriate in academic and professional writing.

Conversational Words or phrases that dictionaries label *informal, slang,* or *colloquial;* although often used in informal speech and writing, not generally appropriate for formal writing assignments.

Unconventional Words or phrases not generally considered appropriate in academic or professional writing and often labeled *nonstandard* in dictionaries; best avoided in formal contexts.

a half a, a half an Unconventional; instead use *half a, half an,* or *a half:* He commutes **a half an** hour to work.

a lot of A conversational expression for *many, much,* or *a great deal of:* ~~A lot of~~ Many people attended the concert. *A lot* is spelled as two words.

a while, awhile *A while* means "a period of time" and most frequently follows the preposition *after, for,* or *in:* They stopped for **a while**. *Awhile* means "a short time." It is not used after a preposition: We rested **awhile**.

accept, except *Accept* is a verb meaning "to receive": He will **accept** the offer. *Except* can be a verb meaning "to exclude": Her criminal record will **except** her from consideration for this job. However, *except* is more commonly used as a preposition meaning "other than": No one knew **except** us. Other forms: *acceptable, acceptance; exception.*

adapt, adopt *Adapt* means "to adjust or change": He will **adapt** to the new climate. *Adopt* means "to take as one's own": The board of directors will **adopt** a new policy. Other forms: *adaptable, adaptation; adoption.*

adverse, averse *Adverse* means "unfavorable": The storm had **adverse** effects on the county's economy. Usually followed by *to, averse* means "reluctant" or "opposed": They are not **averse** to negotiating a compromise. Other forms: *adversity; aversion.*

advice, advise *Advice* is a noun: They asked an expert for **advice**. *Advise* is a verb: He should be able to **advise** us.

affect, effect *Affect* is a verb that means either "to influence" or "to touch the emotions": The threatened strike did not **affect** the company's decision to keep the factory open. The news **affected** us deeply. Psychologists use *affect* as a noun (with the stress on the first syllable) meaning "emotional expression": She noted the patient's lack of **affect**. As a noun, *effect*

505

means "a result": Maren discussed the **effects** of secondhand smoke. When used as a verb, *effect* means "to bring about": They hoped to **effect** real political change. Other forms: *affective; effective.*

agree on, agree to, agree with *Agree on* means "to be in accord with others about something": We **agreed on** the arrangements. *Agree to* means "to accept something" or "to consent to do something": They **agreed to** our terms. They **agreed to** discuss the matter. *Agree with* means "to share an opinion with someone" or "to approve of something": Everyone **agreed with** the chair of the committee. No one **agreed with** my position.

all ready, already *All ready* means "completely prepared": The documents are **all ready** for the meeting. *Already* means "by or before a specified time": We have **already** submitted our final report.

all right Two of the most common meanings of *all right* are "permissible" and "safe": They asked whether it was **all right** to arrive a few minutes late. Everyone in the accident was **all right**. The spelling *alright* is not a generally accepted alternative for *all right*, although it is frequently used in popular writing.

all together, altogether *All together* means "as a group": We sang **all together**. *Altogether* means "wholly, thoroughly": This song is **altogether** too difficult to play.

allude, elude *Allude* means "to refer to indirectly": She **alluded** to the poetry of Elizabeth Bishop. *Elude* means "to evade" or "to escape from": For months, the solution **eluded** the researchers.

allusion, illusion *Allusion* means "a casual or indirect reference": Her **allusion** was to Elizabeth Bishop's poetry. *Illusion* means "a false idea or an unreal image": The magician's trick was based on **illusion**.

among, between According to traditional usage, *among* is used when three or more individuals or entities are discussed: He must choose **among** several good job offers. *Between* is used when referring to only two entities: We studied the differences **between** the two proposals. Current dictionaries also mention the use of *between* to refer to more than two entities when the relationships between these entities are considered distinct: Connections **between** the four coastal communities were restored.

amoral, immoral *Amoral* means "not caring about right or wrong": The prosecutor in the case accused the defendant of **amoral** acts of random violence. *Immoral* means "not moral": Students discussed whether abortion should be considered **immoral**. Other forms: *amorality; immorality.*

amount of, number of Use *amount of* before nouns that cannot be counted: The **amount of** rain that fell last year was insufficient. Use *number of* with nouns that can be counted: The **number of** students attending college has increased. *A number of* means "many" and thus takes a plural verb: **A number of** opportunities **are** listed. *The number of* takes a singular verb: **The number of** opportunities available to students **is** rising.

angry at, angry with *Angry* is commonly followed by either *at* or *with*, although according to traditional usage, *with* should be used when the cause of the anger is a person: She was **angry at** the school for denying her admission. He was **angry with** me because I corrected him in public.

anxious, eager *Anxious*, related to *anxiety*, means "worried" or "nervous": They are **anxious** about the test results. *Eager* means "keenly interested" or "desirous": We were **eager** to find a compromise. Current dictionaries report that *anxious* is often used as a synonym for *eager,* but such usage is still considered conversational.

anymore, any more *Anymore* means "any longer" or "now" and most frequently occurs in questions or negative sentences: We do not carry that product **anymore**. Its use in positive sentences is considered conversational; *now* is generally used instead: All they do ~~anymore~~ now is fight. *Any more* means "additional": Do you need **any more** help?

anyone, any one *Anyone* means "anybody": I did not see **anyone** familiar. *Any one* means "one from a group": **Any one** of them will suffice.

anyplace, everyplace, someplace As synonyms for *anywhere, everywhere,* and *somewhere,* these words are considered informal.

as, like According to traditional usage, *as,* not *like,* should begin a clause: Her son talked **like** ~~as~~ she did. When used as a preposition, *like* can introduce a phrase: He looks **like** his father. That scarf feels **like** silk.

as regards Unconventional. See **regard, regarding, regards.**

assure, ensure, insure *Assure* means "to state with confidence": He **assured** us that the neighborhood was safe. *Ensure* and *insure* can often be interchanged to mean "to make certain," but only *insure* means "to protect against loss": The researcher **ensured** [OR **insured**] the accuracy of the test results. Homeowners **insure** their houses and furnishings.

averse See **adverse, averse.**

awhile See **a while, awhile.**

bad Unconventional as an adverb; use *badly* instead: Some fans behaved ~~bad~~ badly during the game. However, as an adjective,

bad can be used after sensory or linking verbs (*feel, look, sound, smell,* and *taste*): I felt **bad** that I could not attend her recital.

being as, being that Unconventional; use *because* instead: ~~Being as~~ Because it was Sunday, many of the stores were closed.

better, had better *Better* is conversational. Use *had better* instead: They **better** had better buy their tickets tomorrow.

between See **among, between.**

breath, breathe *Breath* is a noun: I was out of **breath**. *Breathe* is a verb: It was hard to **breathe**.

bunch Conversational to refer to a group: A ~~bunch~~ group of students gathered in front of the student union.

busted Unconventional. Use *broken* instead: The printer was ~~busted~~ broken, so none of us had our papers ready on time.

can, may According to traditional definitions, *can* refers to ability, and *may* refers to permission: He **can** read music. You **may** not read the newspaper during class. According to current dictionaries, *can* and *may* are sometimes used interchangeably to denote permission, though *may* is generally preferred in formal contexts.

can't hardly, can't scarcely Both are examples of a double negative, used in some regions of the United States but unconventional. Use *can hardly* or *can scarcely* instead: I **can't** hardly believe it happened.

capital, capitol, Capitol A *capital* is a governing city; it also means "funds": The **capital** of California is Sacramento. They invested a large amount of **capital** in the organization. As an adjective, *capital* means "chief" or "principal": This year's election is of **capital** importance. It may also refer to the death penalty: In some countries, espionage is a **capital** offence. A *capitol* is a statehouse; the *Capitol* is the U.S. congressional building in Washington, DC.

censor, censure, sensor As a verb, *censor* means "to remove or suppress material that is deemed objectionable or classified": In some countries, the government **censors** the news. As a noun, *censor* refers to a person authorized to remove material considered objectionable or classified: The **censor** cleared the report. The verb *censure* means "to blame or criticize": The committee **censured** her. The noun *censure* is an expression of disapproval or blame: She received a **censure** from the committee. A *sensor* is a device that responds to a stimulus: The motion **sensor** detected an approaching car.

center on, center around *Center around* is conversational. Use *center on* or *revolve around* to mean "focus on" for formal occasions. The critic's comments **centered ~~around~~** on health care.

cite, sight, site *Cite* means "to mention": She could easily **cite** several examples of altruism. *Sight*, as a verb, means "to see": The crew **sighted** land. As a noun, *sight* refers to the ability to see or to a view: Her **sight** worsened as she aged. We had never seen such a **sight!** *Site*, as a verb, means "to situate": They **sited** their new house near the river. As a noun, *site* means "a location": The **site** for the new library was approved. Other forms: *citation, citing; sighting.*

climactic, climatic *Climactic* refers to a high point (a climax): The film's **climactic** scene riveted the viewers to their seats. *Climatic* refers to the climate: Global warming is creating **climatic** changes.

coarse, course *Coarse* means "rough" or "ill-mannered": Several people objected to his **coarse** language. A *course* is "a route" or "a plan of study": Because of the bad

weather, we had to alter our **course**. She must take a **course** in anatomy. *Course* is used in the expression *of course.*

compare to, compare with *Compare to* means "to consider as similar": The film critic **compared** the actor **to** Humphrey Bogart. *Compare with* means "to examine to discover similarities or differences": He **compared** early morning traffic patterns **with** late afternoon ones.

complement, compliment *Complement* means "to balance" or "to complete": Their voices **complement** each other. *Compliment* means "to express praise": After the reading, several people **complimented** the author. Other forms: *complementary* (they have **complementary** personalities); *complimentary* (her remarks were **complimentary**). *Complimentary* may also mean "provided free of charge": I received two **complimentary** books.

compose, comprise *Compose* means "to form by putting together": The panel is **composed** of several experts. *Comprise* means "to consist of": The course package **comprises** a textbook, a workbook, and a CD-ROM.

conscience, conscientious, conscious, consciousness *Conscience* means "a sense of right and wrong": His questionable actions weighed on his **conscience**. *Conscientious* means "careful": She appreciated her **conscientious** research assistant. A *conscientious objector* is a person who refuses to join the military for moral reasons. *Conscious* means "awake": For a few minutes, I wasn't **conscious**. I lost **consciousness** for a few minutes. *Conscious* may also mean "aware": I was **conscious** of the risks involved in starting a new business.

consequently, subsequently *Consequently* means "as a result": They exceeded their budget and **consequently** had little to spend during the holidays. *Subsequently* means "then" or "later": He was arrested and **subsequently** convicted of fraud.

continual, continuous *Continual* means "recurring": **Continual** work stoppages delayed progress. *Continuous* means "uninterrupted": The high-pitched **continuous** noise distracted everyone. Other forms: *continually; continuously.*

convince, persuade *Convince* means "to make someone believe something": She **convinced** us that she was the best candidate for the office. *Persuade* means "to motivate someone to act or change": They **persuaded** me to write a letter to the editor. According to current dictionaries, many speakers and writers now use *convince* as a synonym for *persuade.*

could of See **of.**

council, counsel A *council* is a committee that advises or makes decisions: The library **council** proposed a special program for children. A *counsel* is a legal adviser: The **counsel** said he would appeal the case. *Counsel* also means "advice": They sought her out for her wise **counsel**. As a verb, *counsel* means "to give advice": The adviser **counsels** people considering career changes.

course See **coarse, course.**

criteria, criterion A *criterion* is "a standard": The most important **criterion** for judging the competition was originality. *Criteria* is the plural form of *criterion:* To pass, the students had to satisfy three **criteria** for the assignment.

data, datum *Datum* means "fact"; *data,* the plural form, is used more often: The **data were** difficult to interpret. Some current dictionaries note that *data* is frequently used as a mass entity (like the word *furniture*), appearing with a singular verb.

desert, dessert *Desert,* with the stress on the first syllable, is a noun meaning "a barren land": Cacti grow in the **deserts** of Arizona. As a verb, with the second syllable stressed, *desert* means "to leave": Because of his behavior, his research partners **deserted** him. *Dessert* means "something sweet eaten at the end of a meal": I ordered chocolate ice cream for **dessert**.

device, devise *Device* means "mechanism": The **device** indicates whether a runner has made a false start. *Devise* means "to create": They **devised** a new way of packaging juice.

differ from, differ with *Differ from* means "to be different": His management style **differs from** mine. *Differ with* means "to disagree": We **differed with** each other on just one point.

different from, different than *Different from* is normally used before a noun, a pronoun, a noun phrase, or a noun clause: His technique is **different from** yours. The results were **different from** what we had predicted. *Different than* is used to introduce an adverbial clause, with *than* serving as the conjunction: The style is **different than** it was ten years ago.

discreet, discrete, discretion *Discreet* means "tactful": Because most people are sensitive to this issue, you must be **discreet**. Related to *discreet, discretion* means "caution or self-restraint": Concerned about their privacy, the donors appreciated the fundraiser's **discretion**. *Discrete* means "distinct": The course was presented as three **discrete** units.

disinterested, uninterested *Disinterested* means "neutral": Scientists are expected to be **disinterested**. *Uninterested* means "lacking interest": Knowing nothing about the sport, I was **uninterested** in the score.

distinct, distinctive *Distinct* means "well-defined" or "easily perceived": We noticed a **distinct** change in the weather. *Distinctive* means "characteristic": The **distinctive** odor of chlorine met us in the entryway to the pool.

dyeing, dying *Dyeing,* from *dye,* means "coloring something, usually by soaking it": They are **dyeing** the wool today. *Dying,* from *die,* means "losing life" or "fading": We finished our hike just as the light was **dying**.

eager See **anxious, eager**.

effect See **affect, effect**.

elicit, illicit *Elicit* means "to draw out": Her joke **elicited** an unexpected response from the audience. *Illicit* means "illegal": The police searched for **illicit** drugs.

elude See **allude, elude**.

emigrate from, immigrate to *Emigrate* means "to move from one's own country": His ancestors **emigrated from** Norway. *Immigrate* means "to move to a different country": They **immigrated to** Australia. Other forms: *emigrant; immigrant.*

eminent, imminent *Eminent* means "well-known and respected": An **eminent** scientist from the University of Montana received the award. *Imminent* means "about to happen": As conditions worsened, a strike was **imminent**.

ensure See **assure, ensure, insure**.

especially, specially *Especially* means "remarkably": The summer was **especially** warm. *Especially* also means "particularly": Tourists flock to the island, **especially** during the spring and summer months. *Specially* means "for a particular purpose": The seeds were **specially** selected for this climate.

etc. Abbreviation of *et cetera,* meaning "and others of the same kind" or "and so forth." In academic writing, it is generally used only within parentheses. Avoid using *and etc.:* A noise forecast is based on several factors (time of day noise occurs, frequency of noise, duration of noise, ~~and etc.~~).

everyday, every day *Everyday* means "routine": They took advantage of **everyday** opportunities. *Every day* means "each day": He practiced **every day**.

everyplace See **anyplace, everyplace, someplace**.

except See **accept, except**.

explicit, implicit *Explicit* means "expressed directly": The **explicit** statement of her expectations left little room for misinterpretation. *Implicit* means "expressed indirectly": Our **implicit** agreement was to remain silent.

farther, further *Farther* usually refers to geographic distance: They drove **farther** than they had planned. *Further* indicates additional effort or time: Tomorrow they will discuss the issue **further**.

fewer, less *Fewer* is used before nouns referring to people or objects that can be counted: **fewer** students, **fewer** printers. *Less* is used before noncount or abstract nouns: **less** water, **less** interest. *Less than* may be used with measurements of distance or time: **less than** ten miles, **less than** two years.

first, firstly, second, secondly Although *first* and *second* are generally preferred, current dictionaries state that *firstly* and *secondly* are well-established forms.

foreword, forward A *foreword* is a preface or introduction to a book: In the **foreword**, the author discussed his reasons for writing the book. *Forward* means "in a frontward direction": The crowd lunged **forward**.

former, latter *Former* refers to the first and *latter* refers to the second of two people or items mentioned in the previous sentence: Employees could choose between a state pension plan or a private pension plan. The majority chose the **former**, but a few believed the **latter** would provide them with more retirement income.

further See **farther, further.**

good, well Use *well* instead of *good* to modify a verb. You played ~~good~~ well today. *Good* and *well* can be used interchangeably to mean "in good health": I did not feel **well** [OR **good**] when I woke up.

had better See **better, had better.**

hanged, hung *Hanged* means "executed by hanging": They were **hanged** at dusk. *Hung* means "suspended" or "draped": She **hung** a family photo in her office.

herself, himself, myself, yourself Unconventional when not used as reflexive or intensive pronouns. Jean and ~~myself~~ I prepared the presentation. I **myself** led the discussion.

hopefully Conversational for "I hope": ~~Hopefully,~~ I hope the weather will improve.

hung See **hanged, hung.**

i.e. Abbreviation of *id est,* meaning "that is." In academic writing, it is generally used only within parentheses and is followed by a comma: Everyone donated the same amount (**i.e.,** fifty dollars). Outside of parentheses, use *that is* rather than *i.e.:* The office will be closed for the autumn holidays, **that is,** Labor Day, Columbus Day, Veterans' Day, and Thanksgiving.

illicit See **elicit, illicit.**

illusion See **allusion, illusion.**

immigrate to See **emigrate from, immigrate to.**

imminent See **eminent, imminent.**

immoral See **amoral, immoral.**

impact Considered unconventional in academic writing when used as a verb to mean "to affect": The hurricane will ~~impact~~ affect coastal residents. However, according to current dictionaries, this usage is common in business writing.

implicit See **explicit, implicit.**

imply, infer *Imply* means "to suggest indirectly": I did not mean to **imply** that you were at fault. *Infer* means "to conclude or deduce": Given his participation at the meeting, I **inferred** that he would support the proposal.

in regards to Unconventional. See **regard, regarding, regards.**

ingenious, ingenuous *Ingenious* means "creative": This **ingenious** plan will satisfy everyone. *Ingenuous* means "innocent or naive": No one knew for sure whether she was truly **ingenuous** or just shrewd.

inside of, outside of Delete *of* when unnecessary: They met **outside** ~~of~~ the fortress.

insure See **assure, ensure, insure.**

irregardless A double negative (*ir-* means "not" and *-less* means "not having") that is used in some regions of the United States for *regardless* but is unconventional.

its, it's *Its* indicates possession: The Republican Party concludes **its** convention today. *It's* is a contraction of *it is*: **It's** difficult to predict the outcome. Confusion over *its* and *it's* is responsible for many usage errors.

kind, sort, type Use *this* or *that* to refer to one *kind, sort,* or *type;* avoid using the word *a:* **This kind** [OR **sort** OR **type**] of **a** leader is most effective. Use *these* or *those* to refer to more than one: **These kinds** [OR **sorts** OR **types**] of leaders are most effective.

kind of, sort of Conversational to mean "somewhat": The rock-climbing course was ~~kind of~~ somewhat difficult.

later, latter *Later* means "afterward": The concert ended **later** than we had expected. *Latter* refers to the second of two people or items mentioned in the previous sentence. See also **former, latter**.

lay, lie *Lay* (*laid, laying*) means "to put" or "to place": I will **lay** the book on your desk. *Lie* (*lay, lain, lying*) means "to rest" or "to recline": She **lay** perfectly still, trying to hear what they were saying. *Lay* takes an object (to **lay** something), but *lie* does not. The present tense of *lay* and the past tense of *lie* (which is *lay*) are often confused because they are spelled the same way.

lead, led The noun *lead* is a kind of metal: The gas had **lead** added to it. The verb *lead* means "to show the way" or "to go in front": The director will **lead** the campaign. The past tense of the verb *lead* is *led*: He **led** a discussion on the origins of abstract art.

less, less than See **fewer, less.**

liable *Liable* generally means "likely" but with a negative connotation: If they do not wear the appropriate gear, they are **liable** to harm themselves. Because of her experience, she is ~~liable~~ likely to win easily.

lie See **lay, lie.**

like See **as, like.**

literally Used in conversation for emphasis. In academic writing, *literally* indicates that an expression is not being used figuratively: My friend **literally** took the cake—at least the few pieces that were left after the party.

lose, loose *Lose* means "to misplace" or "to fail to succeed": She hates to **lose** an argument. *Loose* means "unfastened" or "movable": One of the boards had come **loose**.

lots, lots of Conversational for *many* or *much:* ~~Lots of~~ Many fans traveled to see the championship game. You will have ~~lots much~~ to do this year. See also **a lot of**.

may See **can, may.**

may of, might of See **of.**

maybe, may be *Maybe* means "possibly": **Maybe** we will have better luck next year. *May* and *be* are both verbs: I **may be** late.

media, medium *Media*, the plural form of *medium*, should be followed by a plural verb. The **media** ~~is~~ are covering the event. However, current dictionaries note the frequent use of *media* as a collective noun taking a singular verb.

morale, moral *Morale* means "confidence" or "spirits": **Morale** was always high. *Moral* means "ethical": She confronted a **moral** dilemma. *Moral* may also mean "the lesson of a story": The **moral** of the story is live and let live.

myself See **herself, himself, myself, yourself.**

number of See **amount of, number of.**

of Often mistakenly used for the unstressed auxiliary verb *have:* They must **of** have [OR could **have**, might **have**, may **have**, should **have**, would **have**] left early.

OK, O.K., okay All three spellings are acceptable, but usage of any of the forms is considered conversational: The teacher gave her ~~O.K.~~ permission to the students. Did the manager ~~okay~~ agree to the expense?

outside of See **inside of, outside of.**

passed, past *Passed* is the past tense of the verb *pass:* I **passed** city hall on my way to work. *Past* means "beyond": The band marched **past** the bleachers.

persecute, prosecute *Persecute* means "to harass" or "to oppress": The group had been **persecuted** because of its religious beliefs. *Prosecute* means "to take legal action against": They decided not to **prosecute** because of insufficient evidence. Other forms: *persecution; prosecution.*

perspective, prospective *Perspective* means "point of view": Our **perspectives** on the issue differ. *Prospective* means "potential": **Prospective** graduate students must take an entrance exam.

persuade See **convince, persuade.**

plus *Plus* joins nouns or noun phrases to make a sentence seem like an equation: Supreme talent **plus** rigorous training **makes** this runner hard to beat. Note that a singular form of the verb is required. Avoid using *plus* to join clauses: She takes classes Monday through Friday, **plus** and she works on weekends.

precede, proceed To *precede* is to "go before": A determiner **precedes** a noun. To *proceed* is to "go on": After a layover in Chicago, we will **proceed** to New York. Other forms: *precedence, precedent; procedure, proceedings.*

prejudice, prejudiced *Prejudice* can be a noun or a verb: Because of his **prejudice**, he was unable to make a fair decision. Be aware of your own bias so that you do not **prejudice** others. *Prejudiced* is an adjective: The authorities were racially **prejudiced**.

principal, principle *Principal* is a noun meaning "head" or an adjective meaning "main": The **principal** met the students at the door. The state's **principal** crop is wheat. *Principle* is a noun meaning "standard or belief": The doctrine was derived from three moral **principles**.

proceed See **precede, proceed.**

prosecute See **persecute, prosecute.**

prospective See **perspective, prospective.**

quotation, quote In academic writing, use *quotation*, rather than *quote*, to refer to a copied sentence or passage: Her introduction included a **quote** quotation from *Rebecca*. *Quote* expresses an action: My friend likes to **quote** lines from recent movies.

raise, rise *Raise* (*raised, raising*) means "to cause to increase or move upward": The Federal Reserve Board **raised** interest rates. *Rise* (*rose, risen, rising*) means "to get up" or "to increase": Prices **rose** sharply. *Raise* takes an object (to **raise** something); *rise* does not.

regard, regarding, regards These words are used appropriately in the expressions *with regard to, as regards, in regard to,* and *regarding:* I am writing **with regard to** your purchasing my computer. (*As regarding, in regards to,* and *with regards to* are unconventional.)

respectfully, respectively *Respectfully* means "considerately": The scholars **respectfully** disagreed with each other. *Respectively* means "in that order": The diplomat introduced her to the representative, the senator, and the governor, **respectively**.

rise See **raise, rise.**

second, secondly See **first, firstly, second, secondly.**

sensor See **censor, censure, sensor.**

sensual, sensuous *Sensual* refers to physical pleasure, especially sexual pleasure or indulgence of an appetite: The band's lead singer was renowned for his **sensual** movements. *Sensuous* refers to aesthetic pleasure, for example, in response to art: She found the **sensuous** colors of the painting very soothing. Other forms: *sensuality; sensuousness.*

set, sit *Set* means "to place" or "to establish": We **set** the date for the meeting: May 4. *Sit* means "to take a seat": The judges of the competition **sat** on the left side of the stage. *Set* takes an object (to **set** something), but *sit* does not.

should of See **of.**

sight See **cite, sight, site.**

sit See **set, sit.**

site See **cite, sight, site.**

so *So* emphasizes another word that is followed by a *that* clause: We arrived **so** late **that** we could not find a place to stay. Avoid using *so* without a *that* clause; find a more precise modifier instead: She was **so** spectacularly successful.

someplace See **anyplace, everyplace, someplace.**

sometime, sometimes, some time *Sometime* means "at an unspecified time": We will move **sometime** in June. *Sometimes* means "every so often": **Sometimes** the weather changes abruptly. *Some time* means "a short period": After **some time** had passed, they were able to reach a compromise.

sort See **kind, sort, type.**

sort of See **kind of, sort of.**

specially See **especially, specially.**

stationary, stationery *Stationary* means "at a standstill": The planes on the runway were **stationary** for two hours. *Stationery* means "writing paper and envelopes": He objected to the new logo on the **stationery**.

subsequently See **consequently, subsequently.**

than, then *Than* links both parts of a comparison: The game lasted longer **than** we had expected. *Then* means "after that": Read the contract closely; **then** sign it.

that, which *Which* introduces nonessential (nonrestrictive) clauses and is preceded by a comma: The world's tiniest fish, **which** is *Hippocampus denise,* was found in Indonesia. *That* generally introduces essential (restrictive) clauses: He wants to develop a bar code **that** can be used to identify animals. *Which* can be used in an essential clause introduced by a preposition: The legal battle **in which** we find ourselves seems endless.

that, who In essential (restrictive) clauses, *who* is generally used to refer to people: They did not know the protestors **who** [OR **that**] organized the rally.

their, there, they're *Their* is a possessive form: **Their** donation was made anonymously. *There* refers to location: We worked **there** together. *There* can also be used as an expletive: **There** are some unanswered questions. *They're* is a contraction of *they are:* **They're** performing on Wednesday.

theirself, theirselves Unconventional for *themselves.* They discussed the topic among ~~theirselves~~ themselves.

then See **than, then.**

there See **their, there, they're.**

they're See **their, there, they're.**

thru Use *through* in academic writing: He lived ~~thru~~ through two world wars.

to, too, two *To* is a preposition, usually signaling a direction: They sent the petition **to** everyone in the neighborhood. *To* is also an infinitive marker: They planned **to** finish their work by Friday. *Too* means "also": She goes to school and works **too**. *Too* also means "excessively": We have made **too** many commitments. *Two* is a number: She moved here **two** months ago.

toward, towards *Toward* is preferred in American English.

type See **kind, sort, type.**

uninterested See **disinterested, uninterested.**

unique *Unique* means "one of a kind" and thus is not preceded by a word such as *most* or *very:* San Francisco is ~~very~~ ~~unique~~. However, according to current dictionaries, *unique* is frequently used to mean "extraordinary."

weather, whether *Weather* refers to the condition of the atmosphere: The **weather** report is usually accurate. *Whether* introduces alternatives: He must decide **whether** to sell now or wait for the market to improve.

well See **good, well.**

whether See **weather, whether.**

which See **that, which.**

who, whom *Who* is the subject or subject complement of a clause: Leon Bates, ~~whom~~ *who* I believe has great potential, will soon be competing in international events. (*Who* is the subject of *who has great*

potential.) *Whom* is used as an object: Anna Holmes, ~~who~~ *whom* I met at a convention three years ago, has agreed to speak to our study group. (*Whom* is the object of *I met.*) According to current dictionaries, *who* is frequently used in the object position when it does not follow a preposition. See also **that, who.**

whose, who's *Whose* is a possessive form: The procedure was developed by a researcher **whose** mother will benefit from the innovation. *Who's* is the contraction of *who is:* **Who's** responsible for writing the report?

with regards to Unconventional. See **regard, regarding, regards.**

would of See **of.**

your, you're *Your* is a possessive form: **Your** review was chosen for publication. *You're* is the contraction of *you are:* **You're** almost finished.

yourself See **herself, himself, myself, yourself.**

Index

517

coverage, of sources, 317
Cowley, Geoffrey, 236, 237
credibility, establishing, 247–248.
	See also ethos, as rhetorical
	appeal
	in critical analyses, 208
	in evaluations, 188
	in literary analyses, 231, 233
	in oral presentations, 68
	in position arguments, 149–150
	in profiles, 105
credit, assigning to audiovisual
	material, 303
criteria, for evaluation, 188
critical analyses, 194–211
	analysis and synthesis in,
		201–202
	characteristics of, example
		demonstrating, 199–201
	cultural analysis as, 195–197
	as fitting response, 194,
		202–206
	guide to writing, 207–210
	key features of, 198
	medium of delivery for, 194,
		206
	opportunity for change in,
		identifying, 194, 203–204
	revision and peer review in,
		210–211
critical question, 46
critical reading, in rhetorical situa-
	tion, 35–36
critical response, in reading pro-
	cess, 43–44
cropping, 59
cultural analysis, 195–197. *See also*
	critical analyses
cultural signs, 59
currency, of sources, 316
curriculum, thematic readings on,
	465–493

Dargis, Manohla, 175–176
Darkness Visible (Styron), 265
databases. *See* online databases
date of publication
	in References list (APA style),
		383, 387, 390
	in Works Cited list (MLA style),
		310, 344, 356
Davey, Melissa, 467–469
Davis, Catherine L., 395–402
definition
	clear, 213–214
	as rhetorical method, 266–268
Del Giudice, Marguerite, 482–492
delivery
	Demosthenes on, 68
	medium of. *See* medium of de-
		livery; *specific forms, e.g.,* social
		networking/networks
	vocal and visual quality of,
		67–68

demo, as presentation element,
	71–72
Demosthenes, 68
denotations, 212
dénouement, 219
description
	in critical analysis, 208
	in evaluation, 188
	in investigative report, 125–126
	in literary analysis, 232
	in memoir, 87, 88
	in position argument, 150
	in profile, 104, 106
	in proposal, 166
	as rhetorical method, 264
details, in descriptive writing, 264
determiners, for coherence, 154
development. *See* rhetorical meth-
	ods of development
dialect, 32
dialogue, 12, 55, 227
	attributive tags and, 131
	in literary analysis, 219
	in memoirs, 77, 78, 86, 87
	in narration, 262, 263
	in profiles, 100
Dickerson, Debra (interview
	subject), 311
dictionaries
	as research source, 295–296
	use of, 110
	in Works Cited list (MLA style),
		351
dictionary definition, 214
digital composing environment. *See*
	multimedia texts
"digital natives," 51, 416
Digital Object Identifier (DOI),
	343, 344, 356, 391
direct quotations
	attributive tags for, 335–336
	paraphrasing vs., 335
	in summaries, 330
directive process analysis, 273–274
disability, referring to, 111
discussion group or forum
	in References list (APA style),
		392
	in Works Cited list (MLA style),
		358
documentary films, 302
documenting sources. *See* Refer-
	ences list (APA style); Works
	Cited list (MLA style)
Dogpile (metasearch engine), 301
DOI (Digital Object Identifier),
	343, 355, 356
domain name, 300
"Donuts at Easton's Center Circle:
	Slam Dunk or Cycle of
	Deterioration?" (Walker),
	179–181, 432
double-entry notebook, 243–244,
	314

"Doubts about Doublespeak"
	(Lutz), 325–328
downloading online documents,
	296
drafting, in writing process,
	247–249
	final draft example (MLA
		style), 253–261
	first draft example, 249
drama, 227
	in-text citation for (MLA style),
		341
	in Works Cited list (MLA style),
		361
dramatic soliloquy, 219
Dusoulier, Clotilde, 76

e-mail messages, 75
	APA References list and, 380,
		392
	in Works Cited list (MLA style),
		359
EBSCOhost, 298, 299
editing. *See also* revision
	Facebook page, 64
	of images, 59
	in writing process, 253
edition
	in References list (APA style),
		385
	in Works Cited list (MLA style),
		310, 344
editor
	in References list (APA style),
		384, 386
	in Works Cited list (MLA style),
		348–349
editorial
	in References list (APA style),
		389
	in Works Cited list (MLA style),
		354
.edu (URL suffix), 300, 318
education, thematic readings on,
	465–493
Eggers, Dave, 91
either/or (logical fallacy), 144, 319
Elbow, Peter, 38
elements, rhetorical. *See* rhetorical
	elements
ellipsis points, in quotations,
	235–237, 336–337
"Embrace the Food Tech That
	Makes Us Healthier—
	'Locavores' and Other
	Sustainability Advocates
	Oppose the Innovations That
	Extend and Improve Life"
	(Mingardi), 404, 412–414
emotional connection, using design
	for, 56–59. *See also* pathos, as
	rhetorical appeal
"emotionally charged event," as
	presentation element, 71

in-text citations for: APA style, 379; MLA style, 341
infographics, 61–62
in References list (APA style), 385–386
in Works Cited list (MLA style), 362–363
grammar, rhetorical context and adjectives and adverbs, 192–193
attributive tags, 130–131
coherence, 154–155
ellipses points, 235–237
inclusive language, 109–111
linking ideas, 172–173
precise language, 212–214
verb tense, 91
graphic novels, 60–61, 433–435
in Works Cited list (MLA style), 362
Great Gatsby, The (Fitzgerald), 230
group, in-text citation for (APA style), 379
Gubar, Susan, 213
guilt by association (logical fallacy), 144
Gutenberg Galaxy: The Making of Typographic Man (McLuhan), 195

hanging indent, 373, 381
"Happiness (A Recipe)" (Dusoulier), 76
hasty generalization (logical fallacy), 144, 319
headline, as presentation element, 71
Heartbreaking Work of Staggering Genius, A (Eggers), 91
Help links, for advanced searches, 304
Helvetica font, 54
Hepworth, Myrlin, 216
"Herb's Chicken" (Seitz), 79–81
Hernandez, Karen, 404, 408–410
"Heroes on the Train: 'It Was Either Do Something or Die'" (Westfall et al.), 96–98
HighWire, 300
Hiltzik, Michael, 176–177
Historian, The (Kostova), 230
historical definition, 267
"holy smokes" moment, as presentation element, 71
Hoover, Eric, 416
How Conversation Works (Wardhaugh), 333–335
"How Much Do Americans Know about Science?" (Monmaney), 469–474
"How Smart Phones Are Turning Our Public Places into Private Ones" (Badger), 441–443

"I Have a Dream" (King), 93
"I Remember Masa" (Burciaga), 264
ideas
clarification of, 314–315
exploring and organizing. *See* rhetorical methods of development; *specific strategies, e.g.,* narration
linking techniques, 172–173
synthesis of, reading for, 46–49
identifiable issue, 276–277
support for, 277
illness, referring to, 111
imagery, 219
images
in multimedia design, 55, 59–61
as research source, 303
rhetorical audience and, 9, 10–11, 13
rhetorical opportunity and, 6–9
storytelling through, 59–61
in Works Cited list (MLA style), 361–362, 375
in-text (parenthetical) citations
APA style for, 376–380
MLA style for, 338–342
inclusive language, 109–111
indirect sources, in-text citations for
APA style, 379
MLA style, 341
infographics, 20, 61–62, 239
information
clustering and ordering, in a summary, 329–330
medium of delivery for, 275
positioning in sentences, 172
providing, as rhetorical purpose, 288
informative process analysis, 273, 274–275
Instagram, 195
institutional review board (IRB), 308
Internet, 195
addresses. *See* URLs (Uniform Resource Locators)
citing material from (MLA style), 342
search limitations, 303–304
Internet Generation, 416
interpretive question, 228
interview questions, 305
interviews, 302, 305
personal, APA References list and, 380, 392
in References list (APA style), 393
transcript excerpts, 306–307, 311
in Works Cited list (MLA style), 359
introduction to book, in Works Cited list (MLA style), 349

introductions, writing, 247–248
in critical analysis, 208
in evaluation, 187–188
in investigative report, 125–126
in literary analysis, 232
in persuasive memoir, 86–87
in position argument, 149–150
in profile, 104–105
in proposal, 166–167
for questionnaire, 308
introductory elements, attributive tags and, 131
invention strategies, 239–244
investigative reports, 112–128
analysis and synthesis in, 121
characteristics of, example demonstrating, 116–121
as fitting response, 112, 122–124
guide to writing, 125–127
key features of, 115–116
medium of delivery for, 112, 124
opportunity for change in, identifying, 112, 123
questions asked in, 114
revision and peer review in, 128
issue number, in Works Cited list (MLA style), 310, 344
issue (topic), identifiable, 276–277
"It's Time to Rethink the Drinking Age" (Amethyst Initiative), 29–30

J (online reviewer), 230
Jack, Jordynn, 48–49
Jobs, Steve, 71–72
Jolly, Anne, 475–478
journal articles
in References list (APA style), 386, 388, 390–391
in Works Cited list (MLA style), 352–353, 357, 358
journalists' questions, 114, 242, 305
journals
articles in. *See* journal articles
reading journal, 228
scholarly, 297
on social media, 64–65
writing journal, 242–243
JSTOR, 297, 356

Kennedy, John F., 155
keyword search, 296
King, Martin Luther, Jr., 93
Kostova, Elizabeth, 230
Kummer, Corby, 404, 410–412

Landau, Joel, 419–420
language
conventions of, 109–111
figurative, 219
inclusive, 109–111
precise, 212–214

rhetorical opportunity, 2, 4–6
  for change, identifying. *See*
    opportunity for change,
    identifying
  creating, 9–10
  engaging in, 5–9
  images as responses to, 14
  message and, 6–9
  and research question, 282–284
  response to, 77
  visual response to, 53
  writer and, 5–9
rhetorical purpose
  audience and, 10–12
  critical analyses and, 205–206
  evaluations and, 185–186
  forms of, 288
  investigative reports and, 123
  literary analyses and, 229–230
  memoirs and, 84–85
  multimedia text and, 62–72
  position arguments and,
    147–148
  profiles and, 102–103
  proposals and, 165
  research response and, 287–289
rhetorical situation
  active (critical) reading in, 35–36
  advantages of. *See* resources, of
    rhetorical situation
  analyzing, 9–10
  constraints of. *See* constraints,
    of rhetorical situation
  elements of, 2. *See also* rhetori-
    cal elements
  language conventions and,
    109–111
  in multimedia texts, 51–52
  problem-solving approach in, 19
  in research response, 280–281
  responding to. *See* fitting response
Rhodes-Pitts, Sharifa (interviewer),
  311
rhyme, 219
rhythm, 219
Roadfood.com, 403
*Robert Moses: The Master Builder of
  New York City* (Christin and
  Balez), 433–435
Rooms of Our Own (Gubar), 213
Rose, Mike, 304–305
Rosen, Christine, 116–121
running head, in sample research
  paper
  in APA style, 394
  in MLA style, 363

Samy, Mohammad, 239
sans serif fonts, 55
Schjeldahl, Peter, 213
scholarly books/journals, 294,
  297, 318
Seaman, Paul, 196
search engines, 297, 301, 303–304

second/subsequent edition, in Works
  Cited list (MLA style), 349
secondary sources, 293–294, 295,
  297
Seitz, Anna, 198–201
sensibility details, in descriptive
  writing, 264
sensory details
  in descriptive writing, 264
  in evaluation, 188
  genre and, 12
  in memoirs, 78, 84, 87
sentence definition, 266–267
sentences
  attributive tags in, positioning
    of, 335–336
  old-new patterns in, linking
    ideas through, 172
  quoted, ellipsis use in, 236
  structure of, coherence and, 155
serif fonts, 55
setting, 59, 219, 262
sexual orientation, referring to, 111
Shawn, Allen, 48
simile, 219
Simkanin, Stacy, work examples by,
  240–245, 247–249, 252, 253
  research paper in MLA style,
    254–261
single work, in-text citation for
  (MLA style), 340
skimming, in reading process, 36
Slate Audio Book Club, 230
slide, as presentation element, 71
slippery slope (logical fallacy),
  144, 319
"Smokers Never Win" (advertisement), 132–133
social networking/networks. *See also*
  Facebook; Twitter
  McLuhan and, 195
  as medium of delivery, 64–65
Sojourner Truth, 24–26, 27, 31–32
Somers-Willett, Susan B. A., 217
sound/sound recording
  in multimedia design, 55
  in References list (APA style),
    393
  via video, 66–68
  in Works Cited list (MLA style),
    361
source information, for bibliography, 309–310
sources, in research, 293–304
  acknowledging, 323–324. *See
    also* in-text (parenthetical)
    citations
  audiovisual, 302–303
  books, 294–297
  coverage of, 317
  currency of, 316
  documenting. *See* References
    list (APA style); Works Cited
    list (MLA style)

evaluating and responding to,
  311–315
  keeping track of. *See* research
    logs; working bibliography
  online. *See* online sources
  paraphrasing of, 333–335
  periodicals, 297–300
  primary vs. secondary, 293–294
  quoting, 335–337
  reliability of, 317–318
  summarizing, 324–333
  synthesizing, 322–337
speaker, 219
special collections, 302
square brackets, modifying quotations with, 336–337
stance. *See* author's stance
Standardized English, 25
"'Star Wars: The Force Awakens'
  Delivers the Thrills, with
  a Touch of Humanity"
  (Dargis), 175–176
statements
  function, 325, 328–329
  thesis. *See* thesis/thesis statement
statistics, 24, 27. *See also* infographics
  in critical analysis, 209
  in investigative report, 126
  in position arguments, 136,
    137, 150
Stein, Joel, 418–419
"STEM vs. STEAM: Do the Arts
  Belong?" (Jolly), 475–478
sticky notes, 313
stipulative definition, 214, 267–268
Storybooth, CMA, 56
storytelling
  images for, 59–61
  narration as, 262–264
structured questioning, 241–242
Styron, William, 265
summaries/summarizing
  clustering and ordering infor-
    mation, 329–330
  function statements, 325, 328–329
  one-sentence example, 43
  partial, 332–333
  in reading process, 42–43
  of sources, 324–332
  student sample, 330–332
symbols, 59, 219
synonym, definition and, 214
synthesis
  in critical analysis, 201–202
  in evaluation, 182
  in investigative report, 121
  in literary analysis, 226
  in memoir, 82
  in position argument, 142
  procedural steps for, 47
  in proposal, 162
  reading for, 45–49
  as rhetorical purpose, 288
  of sources, 322–337